2

AF621993

Peace, Justice, and Security Studies

SEVENTH EDITION

Peace, Justice, and Security Studies

A CURRICULUM GUIDE

EDITED BY
Timothy A. McElwee
B. Welling Hall
Joseph Liechty
Julie Garber

Viva Books

New Delhi | Mumbai | Chennai | Kolkata | Bangalore | Hyderabad | Kochi | Guwahati

Copyright © Lynne Rienner Publishers, Inc.

First Indian Edition 2011

VIVA BOOKS PRIVATE LIMITED

- 4737/23 Ansari Road, Daryaganj, New Delhi 110 002
  E-mail: vivadelhi@vivagroupindia.net, Tel. 42242200
- 76, Service Industries, Shirvane, Sector 1, Nerul, Navi Mumbai 400 706
  E-mail: vivamumbai@vivagroupindia.net, Tel. 27721273, 27721274
- Jamals Fazal Chambers, 26 Greams Road, Chennai 600 006
  E-mail: vivachennai@vivagroupindia.net, Tel. 28290304, 28294241
- B-103, Jindal Towers, 21/1A/3 Darga Road, Kolkata 700 017
  E-mail: vivakolkata@vivagroupindia.net, Tel. 22836381, 22816713
- 7, Sovereign Park Apartments, 56-58, K. R. Road, Basavanagudi, Bengaluru 560 004
  E-mail: vivabangalore@vivagroupindia.net, Tel. 26607409, 26607410
- 101-102 Mughal Marc Apartments, 3-4-637 to 641, Narayanguda, Hyderabad 500 029
  E-mail: vivahyderabad@vivagroupindia.net, Tel. 27564481, 27564482
- Beevi Towers, First Floor, SRM Road, Kaloor, Kochi 682 018, Kerala
  E-mail: vivakochi@vivagroupindia.net, Tel: 0484-2403055, 2403056
- 232, GNB Road, Beside UCO Bank, Silpukhuri, Guwahati 781 003
  E-mail: vivaguwahati@vivagroupindia.net, Tel: 0361-2666386

www.vivagroupindia.com

Published by arrangement with

Lynne Rienner Publishers, Inc.
1800 30th Street, Suite 314
Boulder, Colorado 80301
USA

All rights reserved. No part of this book may be reproduced or utilized in any form or by any means, electronic or mechanical, including photocopying, recording or by any information storage or retrieval systems, without permission in writing from the publisher.

This edition is for sale in the Indian subcontinent only. Not for export elsewhere.

ISBN : 978-81-309-1532-6

Published by Vinod Vasishtha for Viva Books Private Limited, 4737/23, Ansari Road, Daryaganj, New Delhi - 110 002. Printed and bound by Raj Press, R-3, Inderpuri, New Delhi - 110 012.

S0000 / S0810

Contents

Preface

A GAP OF NEARLY FIFTEEN YEARS SEPARATES THE SIXTH AND SEVenth editions of this curriculum guide. In the very middle of that period are the events of September 11, 2001, events that many claim changed the world in profound ways. The difficulty in preparing a curriculum guide is anticipating these sorts of cataclysmic events and divining the important issues for the next five, ten, or fifteen years. But the field of peace studies, which is at least sixty years old in its current form, now has a reasonably long view that can place periodic dramatic events in historical perspective. In the long run, the issues do not change as much as people's reaction to them. The sixth edition of the curriculum guide was published at the end of the Cold War. War remains. The fifth edition came just as the Soviet Union was disconnecting its heavy-handed union. Repression remains. The seventh edition comes on the heels of the "war on terror." Terrorism remains. In some respects, nothing is new under the sun.

But in peacebuilding, a great deal has transpired in fifteen years. Even though conflicts roil around the world, much progress has been made in nurturing the institutions of international organization. While superpowers may act predictably and unilaterally, multilateral organizations are gaining traction in establishing institutions for the rule of law. While multinational corporations are, in some cases, larger than the economies of whole countries and operate outside the law, other forces of globalization have yielded greater concern for human rights, arms control, and environmental responsibility. And while culture has been a major source of conflict in the world, it is increasingly a rich resource for resolving conflict.

This collection of essays and syllabuses is designed to further these gains in peacebuilding by supporting the work of faculty who teach undergraduate peace, justice, and security studies. Seven writers point the direction for the field on six fronts: terrorism and security; international organization and the rule of law; globalization; conflict transformation; peace theory; and the social and cultural influences on justice, peace, and security. These chapters are directed at faculty and leaders in peace education, but are apt reading for students as well, grounding them in the major themes of the discipline.

The seven chapters that open the book are the foundation for the syllabuses in Part 2. This edition contains seventy syllabuses that instructors may use and adapt for their classes. These course descriptions are from some of the premier thinkers in the field.

The seven editions in this series of curriculum guides are markers in the history of the discipline. The evolution of the title itself tells something of the progression of peace studies. First called *Peace and World Order Studies,* more recent editions have adopted the term "security" in the title to reflect all threats to human security and well-being, including environmental degradation, cultural conflict, poverty, and cultural repression. In this edition, we add "justice" to the title, acknowledging the difference between a negative peace that is imposed forcefully and a positive, enduring peace that necessarily requires justice. Even the professional association of peace studies faculty has, in the last ten years, added the word "justice" to its name when it merged the Consortium on Peace Research, Education, and Development with the Peace Studies Association to become the Peace and Justice Studies Association. Words matter.

Peace, justice, and security studies are shifting in other ways. One of the fastest-growing edges in the field is conflict transformation. A boom in thinking about the uses of negotiation, mediation, and reconciliation to transform conflict into social change is manifest in the scores of academic centers, think tanks, institutes, and programs. In this edition of the guide, significant space is devoted to the concept of conflict transformation—internationally and interpersonally—as well as to the important skills of conflict resolution.

Michael Klare, who has been associated with this series of guides across the years, notes that the conflicts of the last century over ideology and territory are quickly becoming wars over scarce resources—energy, water, food. Also, religion plays a greater role in regional and international wars than it did in the past. And nonstate actors, such as corporations and militias, are jostling for power and competing for influence in the political realm. In yet another shift, the field of peace studies is expanding to include the resources of other disciplines in the work of resolving conflict and restoring justice. Originally the domain of international relations, history, political science, security studies, and occasionally religion and philosophy, peace studies is rapidly closing ranks with sociology, anthropology, psychology, economics, gender studies, communication, the arts, journalism, and environmental studies. Nearly every sector of higher education has an interest in human security, evidenced by the growth in peace studies programs of many types to some 350 programs in the United States alone and 450 globally.

In 1994, when the sixth edition was published, the Internet was not yet so large and resource rich. There is, of course, a great danger in this new opportunity. Many of the resources that are available on the Internet today may disappear tomorrow, change URLs, or lack the credibility of peer-reviewed print materials. When relying on Internet resources, the guide offers the names of websites where texts can be found, but does not always provide entire addresses precisely because of their changeability. With enough bibliography and a minimal amount of searching, most of these resources can be easily found. In a very few cases, Internet resources must be purchased. The US Institute of Peace (USIP) provides two resources that are not included in this volume. One is an up-to-date list of films and documentaries. The other is *Building Global Peace, Conflict, and Security Curricula at Undergraduate Institutions: A Curriculum Development Guide for Colleges and Universities*. Faculty who wish to develop majors, minors, or programs in peace studies, conflict studies, or security studies at their institutions may wish to consult the USIP guide for helpful approaches.

* * *

We want to thank the various people and institutions who helped re-energize the curriculum guide after a period of dormancy. An advisory group met early in the process to consult with the editors about the large movements, universal ideas, and developing trends in peace studies in order to shape the most relevant resource possible and support the work of teachers and students. Members of the advisory committee include Patrick Coy (Kent State University), Caroline Higgins (Earlham College), Howard Richards (Earlham College, emeritus), Clint Fink (Purdue University), Berenice Carroll (Purdue University), and Michael Klare (Hampshire College). They pushed mightily for resources that would reach out to new communities, such as the arts and education. They pressed for a volume that would include more international voices than we were able to collect, though we succeeded in including a diversity of ethnic and gender representation. And they would like to have had a volume available in languages other than English. The shortcomings of this volume in those respects are the fault of the editors and the limited resources of staff and finances.

Lynne Rienner Publishers has been a faithful publisher of the curriculum guide through several editions. Our own amateur efforts could never replace the professional assistance we have received from Rienner's editorial, production, and marketing departments. This is only one of Rienner's publications about peace. The company's support of peace publishing represents a faith in the "marketability" of peace studies and the notion that peace is possible, preferable, and perhaps inevitable.

This project would not have been possible without the financial support of the Lilly Endowment Inc., which supports the Plowshares peace studies collaborative of Earlham, Goshen, and Manchester Colleges. Seeing some critical mass for peace education and peace research in Indiana, the Lilly

Endowment has helped these three colleges strengthen their peace studies programs and promote peace research. The grant from the Lilly Endowment, dubbed Plowshares, has supported the contributors, editors, and production of this book. The Institute for World Order (now the Institute for Policy Studies) and Hampshire College have taken their turns at this important task. Now the Plowshares schools are happy to carry on the work for these times.

—the Editors

Peace, Justice, and Security Studies

1

Introduction

BARBARA J. WIEN

EDUCATORS IN THE UNITED STATES HAVE GIVEN BIRTH TO FOUR waves of peace studies in the last sixty years. Each generation of academic study has looked and felt very different but has moved us to a deeper, richer, clearer, more relevant understanding of militarism and the war system.[1] Educators have worked hard with their students to envision a new global civil society based on nonviolence, ethical considerations, multicultural respect, tolerance, social justice, economic well-being, ecological balance, and democratic participation. Yet a great unfinished agenda still beckons, and we must employ highly effective responses to the most pressing challenges facing humanity today. To best serve our young people, we must stretch the limitations of our teaching to go far beyond the current state of peace studies.

It is important to bear in mind that peace studies derives its research, teaching base, data, and insights from a systematic body of knowledge known as peace research, now over fifty years in development, and from social movements for human transformation spanning centuries, which call into question the inevitability of war and oppression. Although movements for social change have raised profound questions for educators, peace studies cannot be as easily dismissed by critics as an outgrowth of current political activism. The best scholarship and academics have not been polemical or ideological. There are over 800 peace research institutes around the world, employing some 15,000 researchers at last count in the United Nations directory. Peace education, although informed by and helping to inform social movements, draws on empirical findings and inquiry from history, anthropology, archaeology, psychology, education, biology, economics, international relations, women's studies, literature, and philosophy, to name several. What follows are my own impressions from twenty-five years of working inside social protest movements, as an organizer with low-income communities in US inner cities and a curriculum development specialist with hundreds of college campuses to establish peace studies programs.

The First Wave: A Legal Blueprint for World Disarmament

The first wave of peace studies came in the early 1950s in the wake of World War II. Most US courses and programs were rooted in Western perspectives on using international law, world federalism, and transnational organizations such as the United Nations to address military conflicts. At its core was the notion that the whole system of competing nation-states fighting over scarce resources could be replaced with an orderly world system based on respect for the rule of law. This is an enduring and worthy cause. The World Federalists Association had a large following at the time. Harvard University and select law schools offered courses on "World Peace Through World Law," based on the famous tome by Grenville Clark and Louis Sohn. Talk of disarmament was in the air, and actual policy proposals were being advanced, such as the McCloy-Zorin Agreement (UN Document A/4879). The possibility of a world disarmed held great promise, if only war as an instrument of foreign policy could be controlled by a benign world authority. But the greed and power of the arms industries proved too great, the ambitions, insecurities, and reach of the superpowers too immense, and the minds of the politicians too small. The dream went unfulfilled.

Even though a small number of pacifist colleges, such as Manchester College (Church of the Brethren) and Quaker schools, included perspectives on racial equality, nonviolence, and social justice, peace studies in the 1950s was in large measure a top-down, elitist, Western, white blueprint for world order. Absent were voices from the global South, feminist scholars, or mass nonviolent movements for revolutionary change. This was destined to change in subsequent decades.

The Second Wave: US Imperialism and the Radicalization of American Youth

The second wave of peace studies was born with the civil rights movement and the onset of the Vietnam War and took the form of nonviolence trainings through black colleges and churches, activists' workshops, and teach-ins on campuses. The African American struggle for freedom and equality inspired many student organizers and helped set the stage for the antiwar movement. The first civil rights trainings were conducted in the early 1950s. The first antiwar teach-ins were held in New York's Union Square in 1964 and at the University of Michigan in 1965. Soldiers returning to colleges and universities from Vietnam bore witness to the war and testified at the Winter Soldier hearings, questioning the morality of the war, politicians, and military commanders. Many nonviolent strategies and training methods born in the civil rights movement were tried in the student antiwar movement. The hypocrisy of what the United States claimed to represent and what our race relations and foreign policies were in reality became increasingly apparent, fueling a radical awakening of youth in the United States.

Pentagon and State Department officials Richard Barnet and Marcus Raskin broke with the Kennedy administration on US policy in the Vietnam War and wrote "The Vietnam White Papers," revealing the actual numbers of Vietnamese and US fatalities. The White Papers sparked more teach-ins across the country. Students went on strike and walked out of classes in droves to protest the war and US imperialism. Their campus-based protests and rallies were frequently met with force and widespread police abuse. Students were savagely beaten, arrested, jailed, and fatally shot at Jackson State College in Mississippi and Kent State University in Ohio. Two students died and nine were wounded at Jackson State. The Center for Peaceful Change at Kent State University was erected on the site where four students were killed by the Ohio National Guard. The program endures today.

A fundamental questioning of American society began to take root. Class struggle, racial divides, and the war were being addressed directly in peace studies courses. Capitalist values, culture, and domination were called into question. Course records from the University of Wisconsin, the University of California, Columbia University, American University, and many others list books such as *The Fire Next Time* by James Baldwin, *Soul on Ice* by Eldridge Cleaver, *Up Against the Ivy Wall* by Jerry Avorn, and *The Strawberry Statement: Notes of a College Revolutionary* by James Simon Kunen in the syllabuses. Many of the classes were student-led. Complementing the antiwar movement, a new environmental consciousness also began to take root, spawning the first Earth Day in 1970. Soon the works of Norman Cousins, Avery Lovins, and Francis Moore Lappé critiquing lifestyle and values found their way into peace studies classes and programs. A fundamental rethinking of the conventional wisdom and logic of our society was being supplanted gradually by a new planetary consciousness. Students and faculty examined what we grew, ate, wore, bought, drove, built, and traded and proposed alternatives to energy policy, consumption, and care of mind, body, and health. This critical thinking would manifest itself years later as baby boomers took leadership positions in our society and insinuated these new ideas into our mainstream institutions and culture.[2]

The Third Wave: Ronald Reagan Gives Peace Studies a Big Boost

The third wave of peace studies came at the height of the Reagan administration in the 1980s. Unlike the US peace movements of the 1960s, the antinuclear protests of the 1980s were not campus-based, and yet surprisingly the campus benefited greatly. Literally thousands of courses on the nuclear threat were taught on college campuses and in high schools across the country. The impetus for this far-reaching curricular movement came ironically and unwittingly from right-wing, conservative commentators and key intellectual architects of the Reagan administration, who were publishing and speaking openly about fighting and winning a nuclear war. In the fall of 1982, in town meetings and local referenda, 73 percent of the US public surveyed voted to freeze the arms race. Concerned citizens and pillars of the US establishment, such as bishops, doctors, lawyers, and four-star generals, became alarmed at the US military buildup, the escalation of the nuclear arms race, and the corresponding rhetoric about the Soviet Union. Taking the lead from such groups as Physicians for Social Responsibility, which asked what doctors could do to prevent nuclear war, educators felt compelled to ask what they might contribute to ending war. The response was to establish groups such as Educators for Social Responsibility, Teachers for Justice and Peace, Concerned Philosophers for Peace, and United Campuses to Prevent Nuclear War.

This broader support from the mainstream—religious leaders, lawyers, and other professionals—meant that the response to peace education on campuses met with much less resistance than had the teach-ins of the Vietnam War. Momentum grew in 1982, when 400 social scientists gathered in New York City to discuss "The Role of the Academy in Addressing the Threat of Nuclear War," with high-level sponsorship from the Rockefeller Foundation and other establishment organizations.

However, surveys in 1979 and 1989 by the Consortium on Peace Research, Education, and Development (COPRED), under contract with the United Nations Educational, Scientific, and Cultural Organization (UNESCO), indicated that peace studies in the United States was limited at best, its definition was watered down, and it suffered from poor content and conceptualization.

With few exceptions, curricula basically fell into two extreme categories. The first category included those courses slanted toward strategic studies and military policy. These courses were more concerned with understanding the evolution of nuclear strategies and deterrence theory than with the underlying conditions for a disarmed world. They emphasized technical solutions over building political relationships. The basic conceptualization in these courses was dangerously misleading. The COPRED report pointed out that unless corrected, teachers might be training and preparing "arms control" experts who are versed in weapons technology but who would fail to advance one iota the goal of disarmament.

The second category of courses was somewhat better. However, they were long on advocacy and short on providing students with concrete skills and a critical political framework for exploring questions of human security and disarmament. Students were not challenged to develop their analytical and research capabilities. Absent were both substantive criteria by which students might assess security policies and practical negotiation and conflict resolution skills.

A Critique of the Fourth Wave

Despite the deteriorating financial conditions facing many colleges and universities today, peace studies enrollments are on the rise all over the United States. Course offerings have increased. Interest among students is greater now than ever, even after they have been urged to study something more "marketable." Content and conceptualization are more rigorous. Research methods are more sophisticated. The political climate has completely shifted. Degree programs in the study of peace and nonviolence meet with none of the resistance from university administrations they met in the past. In the wake of the nation's most disastrous college shooting at Virginia Polytechnic Institute and State University on April 16, 2007, a Peace Studies Center has been established to commemorate the thirty-two students killed. Local residents, students, and faculty made the decision to transform the scene of the shooting into a community and campus resource for conflict resolution, academic study, reflection, meditation, and research. Only twenty-nine US undergraduate programs existed in 1981. Today, there are over 320 peace studies programs in the United States out of a total of 450 worldwide, including dozens of master's and Ph.D. programs at schools such as the University of Notre Dame, the University of Cincinnati, George Mason University, and the American University.

Conflict resolution, mediation, and negotiation studies, which developed as a separate field, are today included in most peace studies programs. As former syndicated newspaper columnist and peace educator Colman McCarthy is fond of saying, peace and nonviolence are the grand road map of where we want to go, while conflict resolution and mediation are the skills to drive the car to get there.

The fourth wave of peace studies offers a better and more balanced blend of strategic issues, normative considerations, and policy alternatives. There is greater sophistication among the faculty in using data and arguments that were formerly the sole preserve of Pentagon officials and strategic experts. I see a critical mass of professors and graduates who recognize and can effectively counter the conventional wisdom and arguments of the foreign policy elites in any debate.

However, peace studies programs are failing to challenge the frightening, creeping new nature of warfare. We barely stand up to the status quo and are not considered a force with which to be reckoned. We are too caught up in our daily grind; we seem to be giving one great big collective yawn about Abu Ghraib, torture and prisoner abuse, Guantanamo, and the private mercenaries running the war in Iraq and Afghanistan in our name. Greater attention must be focused on the privatization of war; the new mercenaries; the role, nature, and dynamics of the military-industrial complex; and the reinforcing "iron quadrangle" of private military contractors, Congress, the White House, and the Pentagon. The system of checks and balances as the cornerstone of our republic has been gravely compromised. A glaring case of this kind of abuse of power is the Iraq War and the no-bid defense contracts awarded to Vice President Dick Cheney's business partners.[3]

Instructors must put greater stress on understanding the basic assumptions and dynamics fueling militarism and the war system, such as: What are armaments? What do they represent? Who makes armaments and for what purposes? Who buys them and for what purposes? What is deterrence? Where has it led us? At what cost? Using world military expenditures or the federal budget as illustration, the economic argument should be much more prominent.[4] There is insufficient attention to conventional arms and their role in the dynamic international political environment where conflicts are waged. Few faculty appreciate the role that conventional arms sales play in the conduct of our foreign policy and the resulting leverage we yield with regimes. Too often weapons sales are made without regard to the geopolitical and strategic conditions that can lead to war, as in the case of the Central Asian republics, Israel, the Gulf states, and many others.

Peace studies scholars are weak at integrating feminist scholarship into peace studies. Feminist critiques of the war system and military institutions, including rape, patriarchy, political violence, spirituality, economics, and alternative futures, are significant but too often underrepresented.[5] Fostering a culture of peace is at the heart of women's studies. Feminist scholars explore *power with* rather than *power over* others. Here I am speaking of the presence of cooperative social relationships and institutions in what is known as "positive peace." Such a notion flies in the face of our competitive, male-dominated institutions, values, and power relationships, yet it is what is most gravely and desperately needed. There is an enormous difference between preventing war and creating a peaceful society. Television violence, early childhood socialization, war toys, violent technologies, ecological balance, and spiritual alienation are just a few aspects of our corporate, male culture that must be critically examined. When shaping the curriculum, more attempts should be made to draw in women's studies, the arts, humanities, ecology, early childhood education, and political psychology.

Further, the contributions of black studies are notably absent from most courses. A content analysis of the leading peace studies textbooks by a team of doctoral students at the University of Cincinnati in the late 1990s revealed a total absence of black scholars or African American perspectives, despite the clear pedagogical value of hearing primary sources. A survey and catalog of existing literature and course offerings at historically black colleges and universities is completely missing in our work. Funding should be sought and partnerships developed. Too often we lack any insight into the legitimate viewpoints of minority populations and people of color. Race is still an explosive issue in this country, despite what conservative pundits would have us think, and we have so many unresolved questions in race relations in the United States that peace studies programs should be modeling a true dialogue on race with our counterpart in black studies programs. Peace studies courses and sister-college relationships were started at one time at Spelman College, Morehouse College, the College of Atlanta, Grambling State University, and Fisk University in the 1980s with funding from the MacArthur Foundation. What became of those programs and relationships?

One reason for the drop-off in interest by scholars in sister disciplines may be that we show an insufficient understanding of the deeper, underlying causes of conflict rooted in world political and economic structures. For many reasons, faculties in other countries cover these concepts much better than their US counterparts. There is almost an aversion on the part of US faculty to dealing fundamentally with North-South questions, international debt, declining terms of trade for the global South, and a new international economic order. The World Social Forum (WSF) sums it up with the slogan "Another World Is Possible." Each year the WSF draws enormous crowds—80,000 activists in Nairobi and thousands in Atlanta, Georgia, in summer 2007 during the first US Social Forum. How can we ignore such vast social movements and what they represent? There must be a growing realization among US academics that without systemic changes in the present world political economy, we will never be able to establish or achieve a disarmed world.

The subject of internal militarization is absent in most courses, and yet it is a phenomena in Colombia, Israel, China, the United States, Russia, and Pakistan, among many other countries. An example of how militarization is used on domestic populations is the US "war on drugs." Substantial research and materials exist on the relationship between militarism and repression, enough to warrant a concentration in the curriculum, but I seldom find courses linking disarmament to human rights.

Programs should explore a new concept of human security over national security. Our students have little appreciation for what a massive shift of federal spending would mean in terms of industrial policy, increased trade, jobs, environmental protection, renewable energy, and a better quality of life for our nation's poor. The subject of "economic conversion" has been dismissed or taken off the table since the 1980s. It is our job to place it squarely back as the centerpiece. Within two years after World War II, the United States retooled and shifted 90 percent of its military industries back to civilian use (the outbreak of the Korean War derailed the effort). So economic conversion can be done. It has been done. That being said, economic conversion should not be viewed as a central strategy to achieve disarmament. It is misleading to think that if we just dismantle war industries we could create a peaceful foreign policy. Conversion should be tied to deep reductions in military spending, new alternative energy policies, multilateral peacekeeping, alternative security arrangements, nonprovocative defense policies, and much more.

Finally, instead of reinventing the conventional options of negotiations and arms control or immediately adopting a nonviolent strategy, peace studies programs should explore a continuum of alternative defense policies. Nations can take many confidence-building initiatives and trust-enhancing steps. The literature in this area is weak at best.

A Call to Greater Militancy and Direct Action

At this monumental and tragic political moment in our history, the paradox is that our efforts to improve the status of peace education in the United States have succeeded to a large extent. Against the agony of yet another US imperial war, this time in Iraq, and the very real prospect of global, planetary ecological collapse, peace studies is on the rise and is a highly respected academic discipline. Although it is true that we are graduating thousands of young people with a different mind-set, worldview, and set of skills to improve the human condition, is it enough? Now that we have greater numbers and respectability and are no longer fighting a rearguard action just to keep our programs alive, what will we do with our newfound place in the academy? Is teaching these subjects enough? Can we be a prophetic voice for young people, a positive nonviolent force on campuses and in our communities? Is it enough simply to model just and right relationships? Is it within our power and control to help lead the United States in new and humane directions? Should we? Is that the role of an educator?

My fear is that we have become complacent, when what is needed is a much greater sense of militancy, urgency, and nonviolent direct action on our part. We have a role to play, and we are not conducting ourselves effectively. I have no doubt if we tested the limits of political respectability and truly challenged the status quo, we would meet with resistance in certain parts of the country and perhaps jeopardize our programs and tenure, but perhaps not. Perhaps our colleagues and students are waiting for us to do something much more ambitious and daunting. We won't know until we try.

We must put forward a bold and hopeful vision of the future for our students. We cannot create a world that we cannot first envision. We must offer hope. Young people are starving for hope and a positive vision from what I have witnessed while teaching at Georgetown (2001), Columbia (2002), and Catholic Universities (2007). I saw it in their eyes. We owe them that much.

Then we must find the courage to stir up trouble for those who are benefiting from the war system. This will come at a price, but don't forget we stand on the shoulders of a lot of courageous educators who came before us in the abolitionist, civil rights, and antiwar movements.

At this stage in human evolution, much will depend on the efforts of dedicated teachers to bring forth a new generation of people who do not believe in the use of force to get their way in the world. Politicians currently have the power to make policy, but teachers are those who forge the foundation on which the future of the world will be built. This is also power, a great power that teachers must use now. We cannot leave it to the next generation of educators. Let us act not in fear, but in our deep abiding commitment to education.

Notes

1. Richard A. Falk and Samuel S. Kim, eds., *The War System: An Interdisciplinary Approach* (Boulder: Westview, 1980), xvi, 659.

2. Leonard Steinhorn, *The Greater Generation: In Defense of the Baby Boom Legacy* (Macmillan Publisher, 2006).

3. See William Hartung's important works on this topic to enrich any course, including *And Weapons for All* and *How Much Are You Making on the War Today, Daddy? A Guide to War Profiteering in the Bush Administration.*

4. See "Cost of War" data from the National Priorities Project, www.nationalpriorities.org.

5. See some of the earliest works, such as *Reweaving the Web of Life* by Pam McAllister, *Star Wars and the State of Our Souls* by Patricia Mische, *Sexism and the War System* by Betty Reardon, or *Educating for Peace from a Feminist Perspective* by Brigit Brock-Utne.

PART 1

Current Themes in Peace, Justice, and Security Studies

2

Terrorism and Security in a Post-9/11 World

STEPHEN ZUNES

THE SEPTEMBER 11, 2001, ATTACKS AGAINST THE UNITED STATES BY Al-Qaida—and subsequent major attacks by affiliated groups in Spain, Great Britain, and elsewhere—have focused attention on the phenomenon of international terrorism as a fundamental security issue. Terrorism as a means of advancing a political agenda has existed for centuries, but technological advances have brought the potential damage irregular groups are able to inflict to an unprecedented scale, requiring those concerned with international security to look beyond just state actors, classical deterrence, and other conventional ways of thinking in order to address this very real threat. A concomitant concern is the way in which this threat has been abused by governments to justify political repression and engage in acts of war, most notably the 2003 US invasion of Iraq, which have actually increased the threat from terrorism.

Just what constitutes "terrorism"? The noted linguist and social critic Noam Chomsky likes to quote the famous story told by St. Augustine regarding a notorious pirate who was placed before the emperor following his capture. When the emperor asked him why he engaged in such theft and pillage, the pirate replied that, except for the fact that his actions were on a smaller scale, they were no different from the crimes committed by the empire; they merely went by another name. The clear analogy, Chomsky observes, is in regard to the policies of the United States and other great powers toward terrorism in the Middle East and elsewhere. It is true that so many people have rarely been killed at once in an act of political violence as were killed on 9/11, but what was unprecedented about those attacks was not the scale, but the target—the United States. The United States has bombed twenty-six different countries since the end of World War II, resulting in millions of casualties, but Americans are unaccustomed to being bombed themselves. Indeed, even though the United States has been responsible for the large-scale killings of civilians in the past, no Vietnamese or Nicaraguan or any other victim of US policy had ever flown planes into US buildings.

The term "terrorism" originated in reference to state violence, specifically the "terror" practiced by the French government following the revolution in the late 1700s. To this day, the vast majority of political killings targeting unarmed civilians are carried out by governments, many of which are backed by the United States and other Western democracies that claim to be leading the war on terrorism. However, terrorism in most political and academic discourse refers to nonstate actors. The US State Department, for example, defines terrorism as "premeditated, politically motivated violence perpetrated against non-combatant targets by subnational groups or clandestine agents, usually intended to influence an audience."[1]

The Geography of Terrorism

Even with this more restrictive term, it is important to note that the most widespread incidents of terrorism in recent decades have come not from Islamic groups and have not targeted Western nations. The majority of terrorist attacks and most casualties from terrorism have taken place in Africa, with only minimal attention from the media, most governments, and academia. During the 1980s, the Mozambican National Resistance (RENAMO) terrorists backed by the apartheid regime in South Africa were responsible for the deaths of hundreds of thousands of civilians in Mozambique. During that same period, the United States joined South Africa in supporting the National Union for the Total Independence of Angola (UNITA), which was responsible for many tens of thousands of civilian deaths in that country. Millions have died since the early 1990s as a result of actions by terrorist groups in Liberia, Sierra Leone, Uganda, and Democratic Republic of Congo, and in 1994 alone, in just a six-week period, militias backed by the Rwandan government massacred over 800,000 Tutsis and Hutu moderates in a campaign of genocide.

Also in recent decades, terrorist attacks by the Tamil Tigers—who pioneered the use of suicide bombers—killed thousands on the Indian Ocean island state of Sri Lanka, and during the 1980s, US-backed contra terrorists in Nicaragua killed many thousands of civilians in that Central American country.

Despite the fact that the worst terrorist groups in recent decades are not Islamic in orientation, nor have they tended to target advanced industrialized countries or Middle Eastern allies of Western states, most curricula addressing terrorism in Western academic institutions focus upon extremist groups that do. Any peace studies curriculum addressing terrorism, therefore, should place proportional attention on the countries in which terrorism actually takes place rather than on the countries where Western media coverage tends to concentrate.

Similarly, coverage of the topic of "state sponsorship of terrorism" has generally focused upon governments such as Iran and Libya, which have been opposed by Western nations, but not the United States, which has backed terrorist groups in recent decades in such countries as Cuba, Nicaragua, Angola, and Afghanistan; indeed, many of the most notorious terrorists in the world today originally received their training from the Central Intelligence Agency (CIA) as part of US efforts to undermine leftist governments in those countries. Curricula dealing with governmental support for terrorism should address such phenomenon regardless of the ideological orientation or strategic alliances of the countries in question. In addition, a distinction must be made between terrorist groups that receive direct state support through funding and training, those that receive sanctuary without direct state support, and those that operate independently underground within a given country.

Despite a tendency by Western governments to lump together all groups that engage in acts of terrorism, any serious study of the topic—while not minimizing the moral and legal problems with any form of terrorism under any circumstances—should make clear distinctions regarding groups that engage in terrorism, which is particularly relevant regarding the question of prevention. For example, small bands of armed militants whose primary purpose has been to wage terrorist campaigns—such as the Red Army Faction, the Symbionese Liberation Army, and Red Brigades—have arisen periodically in Western nations. Their extremist ideology and violent attacks have so alienated the population within their countries, however, that existing law enforcement mechanisms have usually been sufficient to control them.

A very different phenomenon is popular, multifaceted political movements—often nationalist in orientation—that include an armed wing containing a terrorist component, such as Palestine's Hamas, Lebanon's Hizbullah, or Northern Ireland's Sinn Fein. In these cases, strategies that focus on the use of force alone without addressing the underlying political grievances are likely to fail.

There is also the new phenomenon of Al-Qaida and related groups that transcend national identities and embrace an apocalyptic ideology and genocidal tactics. The very real threat from such megaterrorism has led even some in the peace studies field to acknowledge that some use of force may be necessary. However, the use of small commando units, special forces operations, and related tactics would be more effective in dealing with such decentralized networks of underground terrorist cells than air strikes and other more blunt instruments.

Underlying Causes

There is a dangerous assumption at the highest levels of many governments that terrorism is simply a military or law enforcement problem and that the threat can be addressed through a "war on" what is essentially a tactic. Even in cases in which a well-targeted use of force might be necessary, the underlying conditions that lead to terrorism must be addressed as well. A 2001 United Nations report on terrorism emphasized the need to focus on the underlying causes of terrorism, declaring that "were all states to do this in an unbiased way . . . the incidence of terrorist acts would dramatically decline."[2] Indeed, the embrace of reprehensible tactics and ideologies by some armed irregular does not negate the validity of some of the popular concerns that have given rise to such movements. One need not justify the reasons that motivate some to engage in acts of terrorism to understand them, yet a failure to recognize them puts people in peril.

A recent United Nations report noted

> when governance is bad, resistance against corrupt rule gains followers and support; when unpopular rulers cannot be voted away in democratic procedures, advocates of political violence find a wide audience; when rulers stand above the law and use the law as a political instrument against their opponents, the law loses its credibility; when long-standing injustices in society are not resolved but allowed to continue for years without any light in sight at the end of the tunnel, we should not be amazed that desperate people—and others championing their cause—are willing to die and to kill for what they perceive to be a just cause.[3]

It has long been recognized that governments that fail to respect internationally recognized human rights, including the right of self-determination, often create conditions that spawn terrorism. The inability of the oppressed to have their legitimate grievances addressed by legal means can lead some to attempt to advance their cause through illegitimate tactics. Only rarely have terrorist movements emerged within democratic societies or where a people's national identity has been respected. Some democratic countries have been successful at ending terrorist threats emerging from national minorities by improving their conditions.[4]

In recent years, from Afghanistan to Algeria and beyond, radical Islamic movements that engaged in terrorism have grown to prominence as a direct consequence of massive social dislocation caused by war and misguided economic policies. Policies designed to minimize such traumatic dislocation will be far more successful than military threats if the goal is to encourage political moderation in Islamic countries. To effectively challenge the threat from radical Islamic movements, the United States must shift its focus from simply trying to crush such movements to pursuing policies that discourage their emergence.

Such a new focus would include not only dislocation through war and dictatorship but also economic dislocation, such as that resulting from the current neoliberal economic orthodoxy pushed by the United States and international financial institutions. For example, policies pursued through the International Monetary Fund and World Trade Organization tend to exacerbate social divisions, resulting in great resentment among the poor at the perceived injustice of economic changes. A recent United Nations report noted that although democracy is one of the most effective tools in preventing terrorism, the widening gap between the world's rich and poor will continue to erode efforts to contain the threat.[5] Instead, there must be greater emphasis on supporting sustainable economic development so that the benefits of foreign investment, the market, and globalization can be more fairly distributed with minimal social disruption. Stability requires economic policies that are more broad-based and sustainable, both in terms of the environment as well as in creating greater social equality from which the largest number can benefit from economic growth. Nongovernmental organizations can play a particularly important role in challenging the structural and psychological environment within which terrorism is produced.[6] Well-targeted development projects can also help gain sufficient allies to reach those most vulnerable to terrorist recruitment, those who cannot be reached by governments themselves.

Simply addressing the security aspects of terrorism, then, confronts the symptoms rather than the underlying causes. The struggle against terrorism cannot be won until the world's more powerful nations cease their pursuit of policies that have alienated such large segments of the international community. George Semaan, editor of the London-based Arabic publication *Al Hayatt,* observed not long after 9/11 that the United States cannot root out terrorism "unless it changes its attitude as to how to develop and defend its interests by building a network of relations based on respect of the interests of others, particularly the weak and those whose rights have been denied."[7]

Although the tactics of terrorists can never be justified, whatever their grievances, it is crucial to recognize that the most effective weapon in combating terrorism would be for governments to take measures that lessen the likelihood that their citizens would become targets. This would include changing foreign policies that result in the suffering of civilians overseas, which then lead some to justify killing civilians in Western countries in retaliation. For example, Osama bin Laden's key grievances in 2001—US support for the Israeli occupation, the ongoing US military presence in the heart of the Islamic world, the humanitarian consequences of US policy in Iraq, and support for corrupt Arab dictatorships—resonate among the majority of the world's Muslims. Very few Muslims support terrorism of any kind, particularly on the scale practiced by Al-Qaida, yet as long as there is such widespread hostility to US Middle East policy, it will not be difficult for such terrorists to find willing recruits.

Changing US policy will not satisfy bin Laden and other extremists, nor should any country be expected to change any policy simply for the sake of appeasing terrorists. However, changing policies that are already questionable on moral or legal grounds becomes all the more crucial when doing so could also reduce the threat from terrorism, since it will substantially reduce their potential following and, by extension, their ability to do damage.

During World War II, President Franklin D. Roosevelt told the American public that any attempt by the United States to impose a peace "would bring no security for us or for our neighbors. Those who would give up essential liberty to purchase a little temporary safety deserve neither liberty nor safety."[8] The current idea that the United States must show its enemies who is more powerful will simply not work, since the enemies know this already and have planned their attacks accordingly. As Michael Klare observed, terrorists rationalize their actions because they see themselves as "strong and resolute in spirit but weak in military power against those who are weak or corrupt in spirit but strong in military power."[9] Instead of demonstrating that the United States is militarily stronger—which they already know—a more effective policy would be to show that US values are better.

■ Nonviolent Alternatives

Given that the primary sources of political impetus to terrorists are authoritarian regimes, foreign occupation, or other means that restrict the right of self-determination, a key means of reducing the risk that people will resort to terrorism is to advance the understanding of alternative means of addressing these grievances, such as the application of strategic nonviolent action.

The Bush administration, backed by a bipartisan majority in Congress, justified the US invasion of Iraq on the grounds that in order to remove the dictatorship in Iraq, which it alleged was backing international terrorism, it was necessary for the United States to invade Iraq, overthrow its government, and occupy the country for an indefinite period. However, even putting aside the fact that most of the claims put forth regarding Iraqi support for international terrorism were false or exaggerated, the invasion of Iraq has instead transformed Iraq into the country with the most serious problem of terrorism in the world. Clearly, then, invasions and occupations are not the most effective means of overthrowing dictatorships if the goal is to reduce the threat of terrorism.

Since about 1980, a number of terrorist groups have arisen around the world to fight autocratic regimes, such as those in Egypt, Algeria, Saudi

Arabia, Uzbekistan, and elsewhere. Despite rhetoric supporting democracy, the United States and other Western governments have propped up these regimes with military aid, arms sales, and military training in the name of "antiterrorism." Yet it is repression by these regimes that has led to the rise of terrorist groups in the first place.

However, this same period has witnessed the emergence of a series of broadly based nonviolent social movements that have succeeded in toppling dictatorships and forcing democratic reforms in scores of countries. Even the relatively conservative Washington-based Freedom House, after examining the sixty-seven countries that have moved from authoritarianism to varying degrees of democratic governance over the past few decades, published a study concluding that these transitions did not come as a result of foreign intervention and only rarely through armed revolt or voluntary elite-driven reforms.[10] In the overwhelming majority of cases, change came through democratic civil society organizations engaging in massive nonviolent demonstrations and other forms of civil resistance, such as strikes, boycotts, tax refusal, occupations of public space, and other forms of noncooperation. Similar tactics can and have been used to resist foreign military occupations as well. If the oppressed peoples living under autocratic regimes more fully recognized that strategic nonviolent action is actually more effective than the use of terror in challenging their oppression, the tendency to engage in terrorism would wane substantially. Nonviolent action can also be an effective means of challenging foreign occupation and other forms of foreign domination, as illustrated by the role of nonviolent campaigns in East Timor, Lebanon, and parts of Eastern Europe.

In both cases—dictatorships and foreign occupation—pressure through the application of strategic nonviolent action by citizens in Western democracies against their governments' support for dictatorships and occupation forces can also play an important role in challenging the kinds of repression that can potentially provoke the emergence of terrorist groups. For example, nonviolent action campaigns in North America, Europe, and Australia played a significant role in ending Western backing of Indonesia's occupation of East Timor and Western investment in apartheid South Africa.

In addition, there have been a number of cases in which those broadly sympathetic to the goals of terrorist groups have engaged in nonviolent action to protest the use of terrorism in the name of the cause, such as in the region of Spain where the Basque Homeland and Freedom (ETA) has, during several periods, felt obliged to modify its strategy in light of intense nonviolent protest against the ETA's terrorism. Many in the Catholic community in Northern Ireland supported Women for Peace in the late 1970s and their challenge to the leadership of the Provisional Irish Republican Army (PIRA; known also as the IRA but signifying the resurgence of the IRA of 1919–1920) to stop violence.

Sometimes the victims of terrorism have been able to garner support and challenge repression through nonviolent action, such as African Americans standing up against the terrorism of the Ku Klux Klan. In addition, the application of third-party nonviolent intervention, such as US citizens volunteering for Witness for Peace in Nicaragua, led to a demonstrable reduction in attacks by contra terrorists. More recent interventions by Peace Brigades International in such countries as Colombia and Sri Lanka have helped reduce terrorist violence in those countries as well.

International Cooperation

Given that terrorism is an international problem, it needs international solutions. In the aftermath of 9/11, the United Nations stressed the application of legal concepts and just values through a three-pronged system: dissuading groups from embracing terrorism, denying groups access to the resources and means necessary to act, and cooperating at the international level ("dissuasion-denial-cooperation").[11]

Unfortunately, the use of diplomatic, investigative, and international police channels to identify, track down, arrest, and bring to justice members of terrorist cells is made less effective by the tendency of the United States and some other countries to use the threat of international terrorism as an excuse for interventions to advance unrelated economic or strategic agendas. Such policies of unilateral military interventionism are likely to result in even greater terrorism. Combating terrorism would be even more effective if done in cooperation with the United Nations and other international organizations, such as Interpol. The use of a truly multinational force governed by international law would come across to those in countries where terrorists are based as a just international protection effort in the global fight against terrorism. By contrast, invasions, air strikes, and other unilateral military actions by the United States, Israel, and other countries that sacrifice civilian lives have been portrayed by the extremists as a manifestation of US imperialism, have tended to actually strengthen terrorist groups, and at the very least have resulted in making many nations—particularly in the Middle East—more reluctant to provide much-needed support in tracking down terrorists hiding within their borders and to more fully cooperate in antiterrorism efforts.

The most effective means of countering terrorism have traditionally been nonmilitary, such as good intelligence, interdiction, and the disruption of the financial networks that support terrorists. All of them require cooperation with other nations. Some countries, however, including the United States and Israel, have long preferred unilateral initiatives for combating terrorism and have often opposed efforts by the United Nations and other international agencies to address the problem. For example, in December 1987, the United Nations General Assembly passed a strongly worded resolution that "unequivocally condemns, as criminal, all acts, methods and practices of terrorism wherever and by whomever committed," and spelled out specific ways states had to assist each other in preventing terrorism. Concerned at the way some governments have labeled legitimate national liberation struggles as "terrorist" even when their actions were directed solely at armed forces, the resolution also stated that

> nothing in the present resolution could in any way prejudice the right to self-determination, freedom and independence, as derived from the Charter of the United Nations, of peoples forcibly deprived of that right referred to in the Declaration on Principles of International Law concerning Friendly Relations and Co-operation among States in accordance with the Charter of the United Nations, particularly peoples under colonial and racist regimes and foreign occupation or other forms of colonial domination.[12]

Angered at the clause regarding the right to self-determination, Israel and the United States voted against the resolution, the sole negative votes.

If there is evidence that terrorists are receiving support from any foreign government, the United Nations Security Council has usually been willing to cooperate with sanctions and other measures. Resolutions sponsored by the United States during the 1990s targeting Libya, Sudan, and Afghanistan in response to these countries' role in harboring terrorists have passed overwhelmingly and were, in the Libyan and Sudanese cases, successful at bringing terrorist suspects to justice.

Other effective tools include support of international conventions and institutions that can track down and punish terrorists and prevent future terrorism, including the International Criminal Court, tighter controls on money laundering, and curbing the small arms trade. In addition, the fight against terrorism requires greater international cooperation in support of treaties to curb chemical, biological, and nuclear weapons and materials, especially to prevent them from falling into the hands of terrorist networks or states that harbor these networks.

■ The Politicization of the Debate

Despite these important questions regarding the appropriateness of unilateral military action to address the threat from Al-Qaida and other terrorist groups, the US position has remained, in President George W. Bush's words immediately following 9/11, "You are either with us or with the terrorists."[13] This has made even the most thoughtful and nuanced critiques of US policy appear to some supporters of US policy as tantamount to defending mass murderers. As a result, at the very time thoughtful questioning of US counterterrorism policy has been most important, it has been difficult to address these issues in mainstream political and scholarly discourse.

Another implication of this Manichean view of the world is that a country's willingness to support the US war on terrorism has taken priority over concerns about human rights abuses, corruption, environmental destruction, violations of international law, or even nuclear proliferation, all of which contribute to the threat from terrorism. Even prior to the Bush administration and 9/11, Thomas Donilon, chief of staff to former secretary of state Warren Christopher, insisted that "the central organizing principle" of US foreign policy would not be in regard to any of these other important concerns but instead would be "the effort against terrorism."[14] Human Rights Watch, in a open letter to Secretary of State Colin Powell, warned how governments could "cynically take advantage of this cause to justify their own internal crackdowns on perceived political opponents, 'separatists' or religious activists, in the expectation that the United States will now be silent." Human Rights Watch also noted how "there already is a sense that the United States may condone action committed in the name of fighting terrorism that would have been condemned just a short time ago."[15] Since September 2001, the United States has largely silenced its previous opposition to Russian repression in Chechnya and Chinese repression against what the Communist government calls "separatists and terrorists" in Tibet and Xinjiang. The United States has also renewed military support—previously suspended on human rights grounds—to Indonesian forces engaged in serious human rights violations in West Papua. The widespread violations of international humanitarian law by Israeli forces in the West Bank, Gaza Strip, and Lebanon have been defended as part of the war against terrorism, not just by the Bush administration but by leading congressional Democrats, including those who had formerly been outspoken defenders of human rights elsewhere. A subsequent Human Rights Watch report emphasized that the US antiterrorist campaign "risks reinforcing the logic of terrorism unless human rights are given a far more central role." The report also noted the increased use of double standards by the US government, where "rebel or insurgent attacks on civilians are condemned, but government attacks on civilians . . . are ignored." Of particular concern was how US support for repressive allies like Egypt and Saudi Arabia leaves their people "with the desperate choice of tolerating the status quo, exile or violence." The result, says Human Rights Watch, is that the failure of the United States to use its leverage against its allies has contributed to the radicalization of the Middle East.[16]

Related to this are US efforts to repoliticize the lending practices of the World Bank, International Monetary Fund, and other international financial institutions that, since the end of the Cold War, had been increasingly basing their decisions more on exclusively economic criteria.

These steps by the United States come on the heels of US abrogation of the Kyoto Protocols on global warming and the 1972 treaty on strategic arms limitation, as well as the rejection of the International Criminal Court and other international treaties, such as those banning land mines or the use of child soldiers. With the United States now formally rejecting the requirement under the Geneva Convention that all member states must abide by international treaties they have signed and ratified, the United States is appearing to increasing numbers of peoples around the globe as a kind of rogue superpower. The goal of US policy in the Middle East, acknowledges top Bush administration officials, is to "shape" the world "to preclude the rise of another global rival for the indefinite future." The only way to reach that goal is through war, since, according to one top Bush adviser, "in that part of the world, nothing matters more than resolute force and will."[17] It is an attitude that more closely resembles Cecil Rhodes and Rudyard Kipling than Woodrow Wilson or John F. Kennedy, a fact not lost on many Muslims, whose most paranoid fears of a United States determined to run the world appear to be coming true. It is perhaps not surprising, therefore, that the Middle East has become such a hotbed of terrorism.

■ A Holistic Approach

Sociologist, activist, and peace studies scholar George Lakey outlines a holistic approach to defense against terrorism that relies primarily on eight nonmilitary techniques.[18] Most of these techniques have been applied with varying degrees of success in a number of countries, though no country has systematically applied all eight techniques to date, therefore failing to realize the full potential of nonmilitary methods for countering terror. Four of these approaches—ending repression, encouraging sustainable economic development, ending military occupation and related forms of foreign intervention, and engaging in strategic nonviolent action—have already been addressed in this chapter.

In addition, Lakey emphasizes the following:

• *Reducing marginalization through respecting culture.* As Great Britain has seen from the emerging internal terrorist threats from Muslim minorities, cultural marginalization is neither safe nor sensible. A cultural policy that honors rather than marginalizes minority cultures can substantially reduce the threat of terrorism, which was one of the methods Canada used to overcome the terrorist threat in Quebec during the 1970s.

• *Educating and training for nonviolent conflict.* Terror is more likely to happen when a population tries to suppress conflicts instead of waging them. Populations can be taught a pro-conflict rather than a conflict-averse orientation, asserting rights through nonviolence, as many feminist women in Western countries taught themselves during the 1970s through assertiveness workshops. Such training presents a special opportunity (and challenge) for peace studies teachers.

• *Negotiating.* Though governments often claim that they "don't negotiate with terrorists," the reality is that such negotiations often do take place in one way or another. More can be learned to negotiate effectively in ways that recognize the legitimacy of certain grievances espoused by those who engage in terrorism without providing legitimacy for the tactics.

• *Establishing post-terror recovery programs.* Not all acts of terrorism can be prevented, no more than can all crimes or natural disasters. Systematic efforts can help encourage a degree of resilience in societies so they avoid becoming rigid with fear and blindly reactive in their responses. A more nuanced response to terror helps prevent the phenomenon of self-fulfilling prophecies, in which a cycle of violence ends up killing innocents on both sides and hardening political positions, thus making an end to the violence so difficult.

Conclusion

As with fields such as international relations and strategic studies, the events of 9/11 and its aftermath have posed unprecedented challenges for the field of peace studies. At the same time, peace studies can provide some important and unique analyses and recommendations to address this global threat and thereby provide an important service to scholars, students, activists, and policymakers.

A peace studies curriculum addressing terrorism and international security should balance an appreciation of the very real threat posed by megaterrorism in the post-9/11 era, a thoughtful critique of current counterterrorism policies, and an understanding of alternative policies to address the challenges posed by terrorism, such as the holistic nonviolent approaches put forward by George Lakey and others. In addition, a balanced analysis of the geographic range of terrorism, the different kinds of groups that engage in terrorism, the role of governments in supporting terrorism, and the underlying causes of terrorism should be addressed, along with the importance of international cooperation in addressing challenges to international security. Moreover, a better understanding of the underlying causes of terrorism and nonviolent means of addressing these causes are critical to balance the overemphasis in mainstream policy discourse on military solutions.

Notes

1. US Department of State, *Patterns of Global Terrorism 1994,* April 1995, vi.

2. "Terrorism and Human Rights," Commission on Human Rights, United Nations Economic and Social Council, June 27, 2001.

3. Alex P. Schmid, "Terrorism and Human Rights: A Perspective from the United Nations," *Terrorism and Political Violence* 17, no. 1 (2005): 25–35.

4. Gregory D. Miller, "Confronting Terrorisms: Group Motivation and Successful State Policies," *Terrorism and Political Violence* 19, no. 3 (2007): 331–350.

5. United Nations News Centre, "Democracy Vital in Fight Against Terrorism, Says Secretary-General," December 17, 2007.

6. Dipak K. Gupta, "A Review of *Globalization and the Future of Terrorism: Patterns and Predictions,* by Brynjar Lia," *Terrorism and Political Violence* 18, no. 4 (2006): 603–604.

7. Cited in Joel Campagna, "The Arab Press Sends Mixed Message," *World Press Review* 48, no. 11 (November 2001).

8. Barbara Kingsolver, "Reflections on Wartime," *Washington Post,* November 23, 2001.

9. Michael Klare, "Asking 'Why': Global Affairs Commentary," *Foreign Policy in Focus Project* (September 2001), www.fpif.org/commentary/0109why.html.

10. Adrian Karatnycky, *How Freedom Is Won: From Civic Resistance to Durable Democracy* (Washington: Freedom House, 2005).

11. Jayantha Dhanapala, "The United Nations' Response to 9/11," *Terrorism and Political Violence* 17, no. 1 (2005): 17–23.

12. United Nations General Assembly, A/RES/42/159, 94th plenary meeting, December 7, 1987.

13. George W. Bush, presidential address, September 20, 2002.

14. Jim Lobe and Abid Aslam, "Foreign Policy Shift: The Terrible Trade-Offs: Global Affairs Commentary," *Foreign Policy in Focus Project* (September 25, 2001), www.fpif.org/commentary/0109tradeoff.html.

15. Human Rights Watch, Letter to Secretary of State Colin Powell, September 24, 2001.

16. Cited in Jim Lobe, "Human Rights Watch Scores US 'Hypocrisy' on 'War on Terrorism,'" Inter Press Service, January 17, 2002.

17. Conn Hallinan, citing US special envoy Zalmay Khalizad (first quote) and Princeton University professor and Bush administration adviser Bernard Lewis (second quote), in "A US Cabal Pulling America to War," *Foreign Policy in Focus Project,* May 3, 2002, www.fpif.org/commentary/2002/0205cabal.html.

18. This section is derived from Lakey's syllabus, which can be found in Chapter 10.

3

Effective International Law and Institutions

ROBERT C. JOHANSEN

IN HIS CLASSIC TYPOLOGY OF THE CAUSES OF WAR, THE REALIST Kenneth Waltz draws upon Jean-Jacques Rousseau's parable of the stag and the hare to illustrate how life-threatening conflicts arise even among people who have good intentions, act rationally, and set out to cooperate.[1] Rousseau imagines five men, living in a state of nature, who are hungry. Their choice: cooperate or die of starvation. They agree to cooperate and form a hunting party to capture a stag, because each could satisfy his hunger with one-fifth of the venison from a successful hunt. But the cooperative venture fails when, before the stag is captured, one of the hunters sees a hare nearby. Since his hunger could be satisfied by capturing the hare, he deserts the cooperative hunt, catches the hare, and eats, but the stag escapes because the hunter left his post. The defector pursued his singular interest over the group's common interest and the agreement he made with the others. As Waltz notes, "The story is simple; the implications are tremendous. . . . in cooperative action, even where all agree on the goal and have an equal interest in the project, one cannot rely on others."[2] I could restate the moral this way: In the absence of any overarching authority to make human conduct predictable, even efforts at cooperative, rational conduct may lead to division and eventual destruction. Because the defector could not be sure that others would remain in the stag hunt, he defected. If he did not go after the hare, someone else might have, leaving him with only death-threatening hunger to reward his group solidarity.

Four decades ago Garrett Hardin made a similar point, still largely ignored.[3] He asked us to imagine that we are separate owners of sheep and goats. Our herds graze in pastures held in common surrounding a rural medieval village. To maximize our harvest of meat, wool, and milk, we each gradually expand the size of our separate herds until eventually the pastures are grazed down to the ground and the grass begins to die. Topsoil erodes. Despite our common interest in lush grass, it disappears, and each of us has less to eat than we had before overgrazing began. We have sacrificed long-term self-interest and common interests by pursuing short-term self-interest and expanding our herds. Yet for any one of us not to expand *our* herd would not be rational or self-protective, especially if others would expand while you or I did not. The pastures would die anyway. Again, the moral of the story is that even rational conduct can lead to self-destruction in the absence of an agreement reliably enforced by an overseeing authority encompassing all relevant people in order to ensure cooperative action.

People are likely to destroy the commons if it is not protected by an inclusive political umbrella that brings enough predictability to human conduct to align it with and provide incentives for the protection of common interests. All would be well if the herd owners simply would have organized themselves to implement an agreement to limit each person's herd to the size that, when added to others' herds, would enable them to enjoy but not destroy the common pastures. A village council able to set a limit on the size of each herd and all herds together could have maximized the harvest from the pastures without destroying them. Similarly, a simple agreement among the hunters that anyone who leaves his assigned post while trapping a stag in order to catch a hare instead will be required to share the hare with the rest, if reliably implemented, would enable the hunting party to succeed.

In these two parables exists the wisdom essential for understanding the utility of international laws and representative international organizations for peacebuilding and the reason they hold central importance in the field of peace studies.[4] Yet the parables do not answer the question, Why do we not have more effective international laws and organizations to maintain peace and advance fundamental human rights? Answering that question is one of the purposes of peace studies. In this chapter I discuss how peace scholars might, in their teaching and research, open minds to the need for establishing sufficient global governance to enable "all to be well" within global society. The main focus is on the potential role of international norms and institutions in preventing war, as well as nonwar forms of political, ethnic, and religious violence, and in reducing structural violence.

I begin by discussing the need, revealed both in the parabolic logic of Rousseau and Hardin and in the current practice of world affairs, for changing the existing international system from one that privileges the threat and use of military force to one that privileges making peace through peaceful means. I then examine two different approaches to changing the international system and its operational rules: the first emphasizes military dominance and the second multilateral law enforcement. I then explore several arguments made by critics of the more peaceful, rule-of-law approach and suggests how students of peace studies might respond to these criticisms. I conclude by envisioning global governance initiatives on which political realists and students of peace research might agree.

The Security Needed to Strengthen International Law and Intergovernmental Organizations

In order to maximize peace for all people on earth, students of peace studies should, through their research, teaching, and public policy advocacy, encourage national governments and the international community to take practical steps toward transforming the existing balance-of-power system into a more democratic, peace-capable system that can increase human security while decreasing the role that military power plays in today's world. These steps rely on international norms and institutions as the linchpin in strategic peacebuilding at the global level. Success in this strategy over time would, in effect, "domesticate" the international system to the extent that serious conflicts among groups could be resolved, as they are domestically, with legal (nonwar) processes and instruments.[5] Gradual domestication of an international system would also increase the prospects for justice, human rights, and environmental sustainability. Making progress in implementing these values would reinforce efforts to achieve a dependable peace.

Both political realists and their peace studies critics acknowledge that the relative anarchy of the balance-of-power system makes the occasional threat and use of military force likely.[6] One difference between these two schools is that realists tend to accept anarchy, in the form of the present international system, as a given. Peace researchers are more likely to acknowledge that human beings may change the structure of the international system.

The aforementioned logical conclusion—that in anarchic contexts even rational conduct may lead to destruction—is true *only as long as* one operates within the state of anarchy portrayed in the two parables. Significantly, we need not assume that the system in which we live is inescapable. It is possible to rise above the dilemma between short-term self-protection and long-term collective destruction if rational thought would lead the hunters and owners of sheep and goats to address the need for an association that would change the system in which they lived just enough to create an overarching authority able to ensure sufficient cooperative conduct, including self-restraint in hunting and animal husbandry, to protect common interests.

If the balance-of-power system no longer protects the security commons, if it no longer provides a tolerable means of war prevention because it does not deter governments from imperial ambitions or nongovernmental actors from megaterrorism, and if it does not prevent the spread and use of weapons of mass destruction, then no one on earth can be safe. It becomes desirable to replace the balance-of-power system with something better, a system that could increase cooperation, reliably, among *all* actors. As the parables suggest, it would need to be an all-inclusive form of global governance.

Skeptics of the need for international system change may argue that we do not live in a system of international anarchy. To be sure, the international system as a whole, and regional parts of it, are constituted with an ever-increasing web of international norms and institutions, such as the United Nations and its affiliated agencies, the European Union, the World Trade Organization, the Universal Declaration of Human Rights, the African Charter of Human and Peoples' Rights, and the International Criminal Court (ICC). But this web of constraints and opportunities for transnational cooperation is not sufficiently effective to provide dependable security and peace. Equally important, the growing web of international influences, norms, and institutions, which are a significant part of what we mean by "globalization," are not democratic in form or consequence. Globalization without democratization of global institutions becomes tyranny, so the human species faces huge governance problems, even if we could have permanent "peace" imposed by the powerful. An imposed global apartheid system, separating the fortunes of the rich from the destinies of the seemingly superfluous poor, would deny both peace and justice in the long run.

Still, the very existence of this web of cross-border connections and interpenetrations demonstrates the current weaving of a global social fabric. It suggests a means by which international law and organization are capable of changing the international system, leading it away from anarchy and, with proper direction, toward a reduction in the role of military power in world affairs.

The stag hunt and the tragedy of the commons show us clearly why we need governance on the local level. By logical extension, they also show why we need governance on *every* level, including the global, where human groups are frequently in contact with each other and need dependable forms of cooperation. When the commons is threatened on the global level, when elements essential for life, such as water, energy, food, and security, are threatened by defectors and even by actors who, in a limited sense, may be well-intentioned and rational, a reliable organization of shepherds and its global functional equivalent are absolutely necessary. If people are interested in saving the security commons from threats of terrorism, imperial ambitions, and readily available weapons of mass destruction, there is no escaping the need for more effective international law and organization. Rationality can prompt us to change the system, establish the minimal essential overarching authority, and protect everyone's security.

Many people do not understand the extent to which their separate, competitive conduct violates their own long-term self interest. They do not understand that their own interests pervasively connect them to the interests of the entire human species, other species, and the planet's well-being. Most people also do not understand how to move, without cataclysm, from one international system to another. Students of peace studies are called to shed light on these points and to examine the difference between two policy approaches for managing conflict evidenced in recent international relations.

■ Responses to Insecurity: Military Dominance or the Rule of Law?

Faced with insecurities, whether arising from strategic rivals, fear of terrorists, the spread of weapons of mass destruction, dependence on oil, or economic desperation, national governments are forced to make a fundamental choice. They may choose to dissociate themselves from others while relying on their own military power for their security, or they may seek to engage others in a network of relationships and rules to enhance security through mutual accommodations and agreements. A powerful country such as the United States seems tempted to employ the former approach, relying less on goodwill or help from others and more on self-help exerted through a strategy of military dominance. The Bush administration embarked on this approach even before the tragic events of September 11, 2001, but the most explicit, written articulation of this policy came after those events, which generated enough public fear that most people simply accepted the Bush policies expressed in the National Security Strategy report of September 2002. In this official statement, the president proclaimed that the United States aimed to be militarily dominant throughout the world. Officials have claimed and exercised a "right" to intervene militarily in any other country that appears to threaten the United States, as determined by the United States, even before the threat is imminent. The United States has warned that it will use military force unilaterally if others do not support US policymakers.[7]

The United States in practice abandoned half a century of policies based on multilateral diplomatic means. Fear and self-centeredness, encouraged by the anarchic international system, have led to the US dominance strategy. This strategy in turn caused the already unreliable balance-of-power system to become more war-prone. Built into a balance-of-power system is the tendency for states to seek military power either to dominate others or to prevent others from dominating them.

A contrasting diplomatic approach, which could be informed by half a century of experience in building international norms and institutions to make international relations more predictable but which should also move beyond those twentieth-century experiences, would enhance the rule of law in international affairs. In this approach, conduct would be guided by mutually agreeable principles or rules, ideally informed by humanitarian values and based on mutual respect. In this approach, national governments adjust conflictual relationships by following norms or laws that determine how conflicts should be resolved. In a marriage, this strategy of negotiation is informed by a mutual desire to use fair principles to transform conflicts into a better, often more equitable, relationship. In societies governed by a reasonably humane rule of law, legislation and adjudication specify how to manage conflicts that people are unable to manage through informal means (that is, out of court). Using legal instruments to ensure a person's compliance with the law may be coercive, of course, but this rule-of-law approach does not normally include collective violence, even in enforcement procedures.

A key value in the rule-of-law approach is reciprocity. "Reciprocity" means that one party does not insist on rights for itself that it does not grant to others, and one party does not impose duties on others without willingly accepting them itself. People who honor reciprocity avoid double standards. Reciprocity is well understood by people of every culture and religion. It is the basis for fair play and for keeping agreements. It is expressed in Immanuel Kant's categorical imperative, which specifies that people should live in a way that would enable them to be happy if their conduct were universally practiced by everyone else. Reciprocity is present in the Golden Rule's call to do unto others as we would have them do unto us. This norm, or one closely resembling it, exists in every major religious tradition.[8] International laws and intergovernmental organizations can and often do build on this foundation.

The Promise in More Effective International Laws and Institutions

As the United States expanded westward across North America in the 1800s, in some parts of the Wild West where local government had not yet been established to enforce the law, vigilantes employed by one or several landowners might occasionally do battle with other settlers with opposing interests. Before a sheriff and a judge were established, people took the law into their own hands, often bending it and sometimes breaking it. After the sheriff and other public officials were asked to enforce the law on behalf of an entire community, violence usually declined, even though the laws and the officials were always imperfect. The basis for establishing more peaceful social relationships was that people gave up their freedom to be violent toward others or to make war on others. They agreed to be nonviolent in return for being recognized as equal subjects in a society governed by laws that were made by representatives of the community acting on behalf of the members of the community.

Changing from a system of vigilantes, where the code of conduct was "every-man-for-himself," to a more inclusive political system with a sheriff and a judicial process, is analogous to moving from a war system to a peace system internationally. The utility of a more inclusive political dynamic is demonstrated in the European Union, which has, for example, ended French-German wars that were commonplace before the overarching European system was established to protect Europeans from ever-more-destructive military technologies and to govern how they might wage conflicts nonviolently.

Eventually the scope of the political unit and legal system necessary to protect us from destructive technologies with worldwide reach and worldwide consequences, such as nuclear fallout or disruption of climate, must be worldwide. The great powers are the slowest to learn the need for security-enhancing international law because they believe they can protect their interests without it. In addition, those who have most recently been victimized by imperialism or global inequities are also slow to accept more effective international institutions, unless they are clearly democraticized, because the international mechanisms they have known have not been fair. Moreover, the spread of technologies of mass destruction appears to enable them to threaten (and thereby to hope they can deter) those who would assert power against them.

Nonetheless, many forces point toward a global system of governance. Today, even the militarily unchallengeable single superpower cannot secure itself satisfactorily through military means alone. Interdependence has advanced to the point where people with box cutters on civilian airliners can frighten a powerful country. Almost any determined country armed with crude nuclear weapons could destroy large parts of the United States or any other country. I see no way to reverse the interdependence of nations and to make them invulnerable to each other. For that reason, conflict management strategies that privilege the independence and dominance of states in an anarchic international system will not work.

To be sure, some people, especially the neoconservatives and the religious right in the United States, believe that a strategy of dominance and self-help will succeed. But in the long run their faith is surely misplaced, because dominance usually generates fierce opposition and hostility, as illustrated in research showing a clear correlation between an increase in suicide bombing against the United States and the forward deployment of US military power.[9] The vulnerabilities of even a huge superpower are pervasive and unavoidable. Although the United States has the capacity to destroy any other country's military capability, its military power cannot make the United States secure. Nor can it bring other people together to address the growing list of common problems that simply must be addressed if the United States and the human species are to survive with dignity. Of course, the dominance approach also violates the principles of reciprocity and democracy, as well as the compassionate ethical principles of all religious traditions and the values of human dignity, so it is unacceptable for these reasons also.

In contrast, the rule-of-law approach, despite its complexities and difficult setbacks, turns out to be the most promising strategy in practice because it is the only strategy that can provide the basis for bringing all security stakeholders, including the most adversarial, together to talk about developing rules to govern conduct. When policymakers prefer strategies of dominance, peace research suggests, these strategies are frequently based on policymakers' tendency to engage in the psychological mechanisms of denial, of avoidance of underlying reasons for conflict, and of projection of repressed impulses on an adversary.[10] In today's world, instead of a dissociative conflict strategy or foreign policy, we need an associative or cooperative strategy that brings all stakeholders in the world together to iron out acceptable rules that will govern how to wage conflicts without war. This approach is also morally preferable because it aims to govern conduct by implementing principles of fairness and respect. Using this approach, peace researchers need to develop peacebuilding strategies employing international norms and institutions.

Quincy Wright, often considered the founder of the discipline of international relations, was a professor of international law at the University of Chicago when he wrote a small book entitled *The Role of International Law in the Elimination of War,* in which he said that international law's "first task is to establish rules of order to prevent war." Moreover, he said, "peoples should demand that governments identify the national interest with the progress and maintenance of international law." He concluded that "peace, adjudication, and law are each dependent on the others, and their reciprocal development is the way to a more satisfactory world."[11] Peace and multilateral cooperation to uphold international law tend to reinforce each other. You cannot have one for long without the other. The United States and many other political cultures still have not learned the lesson that was plainly visible half a century ago, so peace studies programs still have much work to do.

Today we face an enormous contest between the rule-of-law approach and the military dominance approach. Despite the appeal of the dominance approach to powerful elites, especially in the United States, China, and Russia, proponents of the rule-of-law approach hold some strong cards of legitimacy. The power in the principles of reciprocity and international human rights appears to be surprisingly strong, as does the attraction of democratic ideas, backed by civil societies in Europe and many other democratic states. Equally noteworthy is the low utility of military power for purposes other than destruction. After violating the UN Charter and Security Council preferences by initiating a war against Iraq, the United States soon returned to the United Nations to ask this international institution to help it make the peace. In addition, after attacking the International Criminal Court and saying it would not refer cases to it because to do so would legitimize the ICC, the United States later decided it would be politically too costly for it to veto a UN resolution, as it had threatened to do, calling for investigation and prosecution of Darfur atrocities by the ICC.

These and other examples illustrate the inutility of war in constructing peace and the potential utility of law and legitimate international institutions in managing conflict. The United States, with armies no other country or combination of countries could stand against, has failed for several years to establish peace and tranquility in a small, weak country that it quickly conquered. It has also failed to stop genocide in Sudan. In both cases it has reluctantly, belatedly acknowledged a useful role for international law and institutional legitimacy. The dominance strategy and the neoconservative moment in the United States are doomed to failure in the long run.

■ Applying the Rule-of-Law Strategy

Because the rule-of-law strategy is a promising and ethically desirable strategy for managing conflicts, it deserves more attention from both policymakers and peace researchers. Researchers need to document the conditions under which the rule-of-law approach works best in order to guard against bad laws enforced by ruthless, violent means. When laws are constituted through democratic processes and reinforced by democratic values that include minority rights and other human rights, they both enhance the values of human dignity and contribute to peacebuilding. Of course, the democratic principle cannot be instantly implemented in global political processes, but peace researchers can identify the first measured steps, which could be taken immediately, toward more proportional representation for those who are underrepresented in international councils. We can focus on the implementation of democratic values and demilitarization in global society as the destination toward which we persistently move.

With this in mind, peace researchers can spell out how the rule-of-law approach would be likely to work in practice in addressing difficult security issues. To illustrate, no problem is more troubling for the future of US and world security than the proliferation of nuclear weapons. The rule-of-law strategy would begin by noting that there are *two* kinds of proliferation, both problematic and both interrelated. The most frequently noticed problem in the United States is the threat of "horizontal" proliferation, in which weapons may spread to those who have never possessed them, such as North Korea or Iran or Al-Qaida. The other kind is "vertical" proliferation, in which those countries that already have nuclear arsenals obtain additional weapons or develop more advanced warheads for more sophisticated means of delivering them. Moreover, even the continued *possession* of nuclear weapons by nuclear weapons states encourages some non-nuclear states to want to obtain them.

The Bush administration's goal of preventing Iran, North Korea, and Al-Qaida from obtaining nuclear weapons is desirable. But peace research suggests that the administration's means are doomed to failure to the extent that they are rooted in a strategy of dominance. For some states to insist on possessing nuclear weapons while denying that others may obtain them is not an effective or intelligent antiproliferation policy. Instead of halting vertical proliferation, the United States pursues it while insisting that horizontal proliferation must stop. The rule-of-law approach suggests that reciprocity could be a basis for bridging differences between adversaries. It suggests that the most effective policy to stop *horizontal* proliferation would aim to stop *vertical* proliferation as well.

Instead of practicing reciprocity, the United States and most nuclear weapons states insist on double standards—one for themselves and their allies and another for their adversaries. Washington has told Iran that it must dismantle its uranium enrichment facilities while the United States keeps its facilities running.[12] The United States insists that the International Atomic Energy Agency (IAEA) inspect North Korean and Iranian nuclear facilities even though it has never allowed the IAEA to inspect US nuclear weapon facilities. While asking others not to test or develop nuclear weapons, the United States lays plans to develop new nuclear weapons, even though it has conducted more nuclear tests than the rest of the world combined and even though it has more extensive non-nuclear means of protecting its security than any other country on earth.

The United States has also shirked rule-of-law obligations that it voluntarily agreed to and that the Senate ratified, making these obligations part of the supreme law of the land. The United States withdrew from the Anti-Ballistic Missile treaty, for example, but when North Korea withdrew from the Nuclear Non-Proliferation Treaty, Washington accused it of flouting its legal obligations. Meanwhile, the United States has not honored its obligations under that treaty. In Article VI, the United States committed itself "to pursue negotiations in good faith" to end the nuclear arms competition and to achieve "nuclear disarmament." Moreover, when the other nuclear weapons countries agreed to the Comprehensive Test Ban Treaty (entered into force in 1996), which called for a ban on tests that every US president from Harry S. Truman through Bill Clinton had endorsed, the Bush administration opposed it. The US Senate refused to ratify it. Even though the United States has refused this test ban, it has attempted to force other countries, outside a reciprocal legal framework, to refrain from testing.

As this illustration suggests, the rule-of-law approach could identify weapons constraints that do not jeopardize anyone's security in the short run while opening the door to more far-reaching constraints and more intrusive and effective international inspection and enforcement later on.

■ Responding to Critics of the Rule-of-Law Strategy

Some critics of the rule-of-law approach doubt that changes in the existing balance-of-power system are possible or desirable. Students of peace studies and active peacebuilders need to understand these critics and respond to their criticisms with creativity, additional dialogue, and an expanded research and writing agenda that is inspired by what John Paul Lederach has aptly called "the moral imagination."[13] If peacebuilding is to be effective and sustained, it cannot escape being a creative act. It has many dimensions that this chapter cannot begin to explore. Yet one might begin dialogue with critics by an initiative as modest as identifying and collating the insights of thoughtful realists who have acknowledged the inadequacies of the present international system. Hans Morgenthau, for example, a seminal figure for realists, toward the end of his life wrote that the "technological revolutions of our age have rendered the Nation-State's principle of political organization as obsolete as the first modern industrial revolution of the steam engine did feudalism." These changes, already visible to him in the 1980s, meant that "the governments of Nation-States are no longer able to perform the functions for the sake of which civilized governments have been instituted in the first place: to defend and promote the life, liberty, and pursuit of happiness of its citizenry."[14]

Students of peace studies could establish a large database of reputable authorities and historical examples shedding light directly on the need for and possibilities of more democratic regional and global governance. Further research could examine the extent to which a phased strategy for replacing the rule of force with the rule of law in world affairs can be disaggregated into safe steps, each of which is intrinsically valuable and able to appeal even to those skeptical about long-term visions of change. It is not necessary for a person to believe that the balance-of-power system can be replaced in order to believe that it might be possible to make that system somewhat more peaceful, more just, and even more democratic. Further research might show that many first-phase recommendations for establishing an *alternative* international system can also improve the peaceful functioning of the *existing* system. Teachers and researchers could also collect case studies and analyze the conditions in which nonviolent means may help to dismantle oppressive rule and hold officials accountable to international laws of peace and human rights.

A second way to counter critics is to address the widely held belief that it is utopianism of the worst sort to think that we can replace the rule of military force with the rule of law because the world is simply too diverse and lacks a sense of community. Peace researchers might examine and explain how rule-of-law societies already exist in large, extremely diverse contexts. Some of them span an entire continent or subcontinent and contain enormous diversity and social conflicts not unlike those that humanity faces globally. If the enormous religious, racial, class, and linguistic diversity in a country such as India, for example, can come under a rule-of-law governance structure, the global system may also be able to come under a much more limited form of global governance designed to protect the species from destruction. People can communicate and physically travel around the entire planet in less time today than was necessary for people to travel or send a message from Philadelphia to Boston at the time that the United States came under one inclusive security umbrella. In any case, the rule of law in large, diverse societies is analogous to establishing a global peace system.

Third, we can also learn much more about the possibilities for building a global peace system by further study of incipient supranationality in the European Union, where diverse national sovereignties have established supranational forms of adjudication that hold societies and their state officials accountable to high human rights standards. Of course, these structures took a long time to establish, so we must be prepared for a long struggle, but we also have some reason to believe that matters can move rapidly when the time is right. The possibility of war among European countries remained high for centuries, yet today there is no expectation of war among members of the European Union. How did this change come about so soon after the horrors of Nazism and the total ravaging of Europe?

Moreover, some degree of global governance—although democratically deficient—already exists in the security system of the UN Security Council, the International Monetary Fund, and the World Trade Organization. What can these bodies teach us about nurturing democratic global governance?

Fourth, peace researchers might conduct longitudinal opinion surveys asking respondents (and candidates for political office) if they can imagine a future time when every government and every person on earth must obey at least a few rules, such as rules governing the possession and use of extremely hazardous materials, whether these threaten physical security, such as weapons of mass destruction, or environmental security, such as greenhouse gas emissions. If so, are we nearing that time now? If we are, who should make the rules, monitor them carefully, enforce them, and adjudicate conflicts over their implementation?

Fifth, more widespread teaching and learning of inclusive beliefs and values would be useful. Many Europeans believe that benefits flow from effective international laws, transnational governance, and multilateral cooperation, an understanding not abundantly present in current US leadership or citizenry. How might mutually cooperative beliefs emphasizing human solidarity and the security commons be nurtured? This understanding is one reason European public opinion opposed the US attack on Iraq and wanted to give UN inspectors, already in Iraq, more time to see if there was any place in Iraq where weapons of mass destruction might be hidden. Further study is needed on the debate leading up to the US-initiated war, because it was a classic clash between a rule-of-law strategy, articulated by continental European governments and by public opinion on the Continent and in the United Kingdom, and a dominance strategy, advanced by the Bush administration in the United States and the governing elites in the UK and elsewhere who chose to jump on the US bandwagon. Because UN inspectors were in Iraq confirming day-by-day that there was no imminent threat from Iraq, neither a claim of self-defense nor of preemptive self-defense had much credibility. International law has not justified initiating a war to bring about regime change since before World War II. Indeed, German officials were prosecuted by US officials and subsequently convicted in the international war crimes trial at Nuremberg of crimes against the peace for initiating war. How could US officials later succeed in justifying starting a war? Students of peace studies need to study these realities and educate others about them to lay the groundwork for moving beyond the present system.

A sixth illustration of how peace researchers could employ the tools of their trade more deftly to establish a more democratic and peaceful international system would be to address the dysfunctional consequences of the global democratic deficit in today's balance-of-power system. Unless this deficit and the relative deprivation that accompanies it are overcome, we will not enjoy peace for long. In an interdependent yet politically fragmented and economically segregated world—a global equivalent of an apartheid house divided against itself, half slave, half free—can anyone be secure from threats beyond their national borders when technologies of destruction are readily available and there are no globally effective laws governing them? How many of the rich and powerful really believe it is possible to reduce political polarization and extremism by denying others equitable participation in global governance processes that make the rules affecting them? What evidence can be gathered to show the likely consequences of refusing to replace a strategy of military dominance with a rule-of-law strategy for conflict management?

Peace researchers can demonstrate that constitutionalizing the obligations of dominant societies to poor societies, and the latter's obligations to the former, can secure a sustainable peace. If we fail to specify mutual obligations in a global understanding, Alexander Wendt points out, dire consequences are likely. He notes that if decisionmakers adhere to the belief that state sovereignty means that "power and violence can be exercised against non-members [of one's own state] without any accountability," then those satisfied with an anarchic system of sovereign states will keep us in a structure of overlapping despotisms and probable violence, given the extranational reach of today's military technologies. There is probably less accountability and more despotism in today's anarchic balance-of-power system, encompassing the latest military technologies and environmental predations, than would be likely in a crudely representative system of global governance.[15]

Given more accurate information, which peace researchers continually need to provide, people across a wide ideological spectrum could agree on many short-term measures and some long-term changes to encourage democratic global governance and the rule of law in world affairs. Many on the political right as well as on the left prefer enforcing law through legal political means rather than resorting to war to stop an abuse of power. Of course, many people will remain skeptical about both the feasibility and the desirability of what I propose here. But the line separating those who agree with my proposal from those who disagree is not a line separating pacifists from nonpacifists. It is more often a line separating those people with an inclusive identity expressing human solidarity and internationalism, on the one hand, from those with a more exclusive in-group identity expressing a narrow national or tribal identity, on the other. It is a line between those committed to cooperative multilateralism based on the rule of law and those with faith in the utility of the unilateral use of military force on the other. It is a line between those who want to include all humanity in their sense of moral obligation, following the categorical imperative or an ethic like the Golden Rule, and those who are more exclusive, thinking that they have moral responsibilities mainly to their own tribe or nation rather than to all people.[16] These divisions are real and deep. Those favoring nationalist dominance strategies now hold the upper hand in the United States. But the tides of history are clearly running against statist solutions, especially those in which one state claims sovereignty for itself but the right to violate the sovereignty of others. An urgent focus for peace researchers should be on how to help a militarily dominant, wealthy state resist the temptation to turn further to the political right and thereby compound its problems, particularly when it genuinely fears threats posed against it and when the forces of history make it impossible to retain its predominance. What can be done to help people of relative goodwill avoid the tendency to grasp more tightly the instruments of unilateral military predominance and instead to become open to cooperative measures? It is not easy to give up the immediate satisfaction of catching the hare or of having the largest, most well-fed herd on the commons. But it is possible. If the wild beast of anarchy can be bridled and the international system domesticated, then a publicly maintained peace over the global security commons could flourish.

Those pursuing a rule-of-law strategy of conflict management seek to create a system of global governance in which people would no longer feel forced to choose between the two unacceptable alternatives of either war or surrender in the face of conflict. They would create a third alternative, a global analogue to the use in domestic society of law and legal enforcement.

Even as individuals, those supporting a global rule-of-law society can expand the modest degree of human solidarity and global community that already exists. Those people who are uncomfortable when obligations to care for others are not honored beyond national boundaries can reject foreign policies that privilege their own tribe or nation at the expense of others. When their values are not adequately expressed in the foreign policies of their own nation, and where there appears to be little immediate prospect of implementing more compassionate policies, they may give primary political loyalty to a global polity that they envisage, even though it is not yet a reality.[17] They can imagine a polity in which all people are recognized to be of equal moral worth and of great value, where they are treated not as disposable objects but as ends in themselves.

Notes

1. Kenneth Waltz, *Man, the State and War* (New York: Columbia University Press, 1959), 167–171.

2. Ibid., 168.

3. Garrett Hardin, "The Tragedy of the Commons," *Science* 162 (December 13, 1968): 1243–1248.

4. I use "peacebuilding" in this chapter in a very broad sense to mean "social integration." The term encompasses both policy and structural changes, both post- and preconflict situations, and intrastate, interstate, and global contexts.

5. Nearly four decades ago, Inis Claude described the "domestication of international relations" as a process that would encourage "the introduction of features more characteristic of intrastate than of traditional interstate relationships." *Swords into Plowshares: The Problems and Progress of International Organization* (New York: Random House, 1971), 17. Domestication aims to make international law enforcement more reliable without relying more heavily on military power. See Robert C. Johansen, "The Future of United Nations Peacekeeping and Enforcement: A Framework for Policymaking," *Global Governance* 2, no. 3 (1996): 299–333.

6. In practice, the present balance-of-power system impedes lasting peace, the growth of democracy nationally and globally, and international protection of human rights.

7. White House, *The National Security Strategy of the United States of America,* http://www.whitehouse.gov/nsc/nss.pdf.

8. See, for example, Brian D. Lepard, *Rethinking Humanitarian Intervention* (University Park: Pennsylvania State University Press, 2002), 39–146.

9. Robert Pape, *Dying to Win: The Strategic Logic of Suicide Terrorism* (New York: Random House, 2005).

10. See Alice Miller, *For Your Own Good: Hidden Cruelty in Child-Rearing and the Roots of Violence* (New York: Farrar, Straus and Giroux, 1983), xiii–xvii; 3–102; Alice Miller, "The Political Consequences of Child Abuse," *Journal of Psychohistory* 26 (1998): 574–585; Ralph K. White, "Psychology and Alternative

Security: Needs, Perceptions, and Misperceptions," in *Alternative Security*, edited by Burns Weston (Boulder: Westview, 1990), 176–205; Ralph K. White, *Fearful Warriors: A Psychological Profile of US-Soviet Relations* (New York: Free Press, 1984).

11. Quincy Wright, *The Role of International Law in the Elimination of War* (Manchester: Manchester University Press; New York: Oceana Publications, 1961), 86–87.

12. Assistant Secretary of State Stephen Rademaker, speaking at the review conference of the Nuclear Nonproliferation Treaty, insisted that the only acceptable solution, which it previously also demanded of North Korea, "must include permanent cessation of Iran's enrichment and reprocessing efforts, as well as dismantlement of equipment facilities related to such activity." David E. Sanger, "US Demand Deepens Gulf with Iran over Nuclear Facilities," *New York Times*, May 3, 2005, http://www.nytimes.com/2005/05/03/international/middleeast/03npt.html#, accessed December 7, 2007.

13. John Paul Lederach, *The Moral Imagination: The Art and Soul of Building Peace* (New York: Oxford University Press, 2005).

14. See Hans J. Morgenthau, "The New Diplomacy of Movement," *Encounter* 43 (August 1974): 57, reprinted in *Waiting for the Millennium*, edited by J. Martin Rochester (Columbia: University of South Carolina Press, 1993), 233–247.

15. For discussion of the points in this paragraph, see Alexander Wendt, "Why a World State Is Inevitable," *European Journal of International Relations* 9 (2003): 491–542, accessed at http://ejt.sagepub.com/cgi/content/abstract/9/4/491. Wendt asks, "whether justified or not, to whom is the United States accountable for its recent killing of thousands of civilians in Kosovo, Afghanistan, and Iraq? Whatever the accountability problems in a world state might be, they seem far less than those in anarchy" (526).

16. This idea is well expressed by Charles Beitz in *Political Theory and International Relations* (Princeton, NJ: Princeton University Press, 1979), 157: "We should not view national boundaries as having fundamental moral significance." Moreover, because "boundaries are not coextensive with the scope of social cooperation, they do not mark the limits of social obligation."

17. Many peace researchers might appreciate Richard Falk's sense of "an affiliation to a polity that exists only in my political imagination as a preferred future, and a commitment to honor its present claims by accepting the obligations to work toward its creation, becoming in the process a citizen-pilgrim (shaped by an as yet uncreated future)." Richard Falk, "Manifesting World Order: A Scholarly Manifesto," in *Journeys Through World Politics: Autobiographical Reflections of Thirty-Four Academic Travelers*, edited by Joseph Kruzel and James N. Rosenau (Lexington, MA: D. C. Heath, 1989), 153–164.

4

Globalization: Economy, Environment, and Culture

JOANNA SWANGER

THIS CHAPTER TAKES AS ITS POINT OF DEPARTURE TWO DISTINCT but related questions: First, what can peace studies contribute to the understanding of the relationship between globalization of the economy, globalization of the environment, and globalization of culture? Second, why does globalization matter to peace studies?

The answers to these questions depend on the operative definition of "globalization." Discerning the most apt definition of globalization for the educational project of peace studies can be daunting, for one of the most striking features of the word "globalization" is that it is now used with the utmost of nonchalance even though, by virtue of the intensity of contestation of its meaning, the word has earned a place as a contested concept alongside such nominal markers of modernity as "democracy" and "freedom." It is a term whose precise shades of meaning differ among individuals, and it is also a term that conveys polar opposites. For the purposes of this chapter, globalization is characterized as a process of cultural change set within a particular historical context. Here cultural change does not mean the trappings of quotidian life typically imagined when "culture" is taken to be a classification within the social sciences, the particular realm delegated to the anthropologists (as "the economic" is the delegated purview of economists, "the social" of sociologists, and "the political" of political scientists). Instead, the reference is to the basic cultural structure of modernity itself: production for exchange—that is, the cultural structure providing the rules by which we utilize monetized exchange for the purposes of distribution and profit incentives for the purposes of production.[1]

The brief period that corresponds roughly to the span from the Great Depression to the oil shocks of the 1970s marked the height of social consensus regarding the value of social democracy. In that period many nation-states around the world sought to temper the conditions arising from this basic cultural structure and succeeded temporarily, to varying extents, in creating social safety nets by introducing such measures as antidiscrimination laws, minimum wages and collective bargaining, unemployment insurance, pension plans, state-sector provision of utilities, systems of public education and public health, and environmental regulations. This attempt to guarantee a modicum of social justice within the boundaries of nation-states was built on a foundation that accepted the premises of Keynesian macroeconomics, but, bearing out the predictions of many economists, it proved unworkable and unsustainable over the long term, ushering in the current phase of capitalism.[2] Globalization—a return to free market economics (i.e., neoliberalism) on a world scale, rejecting any measures resembling socialism or even social democracy—happened, therefore, because social democracy did not work. This definition of the term has been chosen in part because it is a leitmotif that appears in one form or another in nearly all the competing definitions of globalization and in part because the term demands a definition that is at once sufficiently overarching and analytically precise.[3]

The history of the term "globalization" sheds light on the particular historical context that this definition highlights. Although the first documented use of the term was in the 1960s, it was not until the early 1990s, following the collapse of the Soviet Union, that globalization gained wide currency.[4] In its first usages of the 1990s, the term carried an element of triumphalism and was being used to indicate that following the Soviet Union's demise, capitalism no longer faced any large-scale barriers to its expansion or the potential of any immediately viable alternatives being erected at the level of the nation-state (through alliance with the Soviet Union).[5] As it was used in the immediate wake of gaining wider acceptance in the 1990s, but before "antiglobalization" organizations began to use it as well, the term also carried the connotation of an enticing intermingling of products (e.g., the year-round availability of relatively exotic produce in US groceries), technological wizardry, and the expansion of markets on an unprecedented scale, all of which meant an ever-broadening aperture for the expression of consumer choice, which, according to the tenets of liberal economics, implied as a corollary expanding levels of generalized prosperity.[6]

Yet despite the sense of triumphalism that such uses of the word carry, globalization also connotes a certain level of anxiety, as if its utterance served as an incantation of a desire not fully backed by belief: that there could be a new form of capitalism that would bring to all only prosperity and no dislocations and that would thus provoke no resistance.[7] A related use of the term, set explicitly within a discourse of anxiety, is documented by Jonathan Diskin and Tim Koechlin, who demonstrate that the construct of globalization was used in the early 1990s to make the case for a state that was, in effect, coterminous with the corporation.[8] Also in Diskin and Koechlin's analysis, the term implied the hope that resistance would not make an appearance. The social arrangement of capitalism, however, has long been challenged, and the challenges are not going away, even though the main forms these challenges took in the twentieth century—social democracy and socialism—have failed. In fact, because a diverse protest movement has coalesced around the very phrase "antiglobalization," the use of the word "globalization" now carries with it the disturbing imagery of deforestation; desertification; the demise of small producers in both agricultural and commercial sectors; the primacy of foreign direct investment and the transformation of economies to create "good investment climates" (by, for instance, sidelining unions or making them illegal); rising rates of unemployment in the formal sector; falling real wage rates in the formal sector; increased participation in the informal sector; an increase in child labor; and a return to human trafficking, especially for the purpose of sexual slavery.[9] It is the inexorable elicitation of this chiaroscuro that makes globalization so fascinating and gives rise to debates within many disciplines concerning whether globalization can actually transform the world—whether at local levels or in "higher" or "wider" realms—for the better. Giving due consideration to the spatial dimension is critical; indeed, the disciplinary debates typically turn on discernment of the relationship between "the local" and "the global," that is, whether and to what extent the flow of influence is effectively bidirectional or predominantly unidirectional; whether and to what extent the characteristics of each and the relationship between the two are overdetermined; whether the local and the global can even be counterposed axially; or whether globalization means the dissolution of boundaries both real and metaphorical so that the two are effectively collapsed together and lose the meanings they once had.[10]

In economics, the lines of debate are fairly clear, although not, one must emphasize, as starkly drawn as the loudest voices within the antiglobalization movement might have us believe. It is true that one group among the proponents of globalization comprises economists who advocate neoliberalism on principle and appear not to be overly concerned either with the immediate human consequences of globalization or with immediate or long-term ecological implications (this argument might be characterized as globalization-as-shibboleth), but since the turn of the twenty-first century, it is exceedingly difficult to find representative published works that do not frame their authors' arguments in terms of an ethical good (e.g., the *eventual* reduction of poverty; the *eventual* environmental benefits that will obtain when rising incomes translate to demand for higher environmental standards).[11] Whether these policies are, in fact, the best way to achieve these ethical outcomes is an issue separate from a key underlying premise sometimes taken for granted. The key underlying premise is that globalization is the only generator of wealth. It is a premise that should be examined. It should also be noted that there are economists who are well known for recanting earlier stances advocating globalization as a solution to poverty and others who have softened but not recanted earlier stances.[12]

Even among the staunchest advocates of globalization within the field of economics, pains are often taken to insist that at least some of the concerns of antiglobalization scholars and activists are legitimate, as well as to call for the creation of institutions to make globalization function better in ways that leave the most vulnerable members of society less plainly exposed to the vagaries of the international market. Jagdish Bhagwati, for example, concedes that a farming family making the shift from staple to cash crops, set within the context of increased interconnectedness and therefore increased competition, faces a much higher chance of "sudden misery" than Adam Smith might have been able to imagine in his time, and that institutions to mitigate this increased economic insecurity must accordingly develop alongside globalization.[13] Joseph Stiglitz goes even further in acknowledging the legitimacy of several common criticisms of globalization. He calls for greater transparency in international financial transactions, greater inclusion of nongovernmental organizations in policy decisions, debt forgiveness in some instances, and the greater assumption of the obligations adhering to risk by creditors who have been foolhardy. Stiglitz even claims, in contrast to the doctrine of the Washington consensus, that the right kinds of regulation are preferable to an unfettered market.[14] It must be noted that this open concession to ethical considerations is quite a recent shift and a radical departure from some prominent traditions in economics that explicitly eschewed questions of ethics. For peace studies, a field that does not shy away from normative discourse, this offers a welcome opening in the debate over globalization.

Rarely do economists speak openly of questions of peace, but their words often make clear that the perception of the potential of violence lurks behind their prescriptions. Both economists who advocate extending globalization in its current form and those who are critical of this stance and call for reforms to "make globalization work" imply that theirs is the path to a more peaceful world.[15] Still other economists argue that current economic structures must be substantially transformed in order to usher in the possibilities for sustainable peace.[16] Among the latter, the field of peace studies should highlight the work of feminist and ecologically minded economists—a point to which this chapter shall return.

Nevertheless, among works by economists advocating globalization, we also find a particular seam of arguments in which phenomena commonly raised as specters by the antiglobalization movement are not only accepted but also embraced for their emancipatory potential. Examples include the linked phenomena of the growth of the informal sector, increased transnational migration flows, and increased participation by women as part of the "economically active population" (i.e., those whose labor is remunerated and therefore counted toward gross domestic product).[17] Scholars may attest to the emancipatory potential of such phenomena. Whether they are experienced as such by the groups and individuals they are said to emancipate is the critical question and one that scholars wedded to particular traditions of academic rigor in the social sciences will likely never be able to answer, although champions of agency do valiantly continue the effort. Some key questions for peace studies to consider with regard to the debate over globalization in the economic realm are whether the processes referenced in the term "globalization" are mitigating poverty or exacerbating it and why, and whether—and why—our economic structures contribute to a greater likelihood of war or of peace.

The cultural aspect of globalization that has received the greatest emphasis is the technological (Kellner's "technocapitalism"), which has made possible a kind of "sustained cultural interaction" that, prior to the twentieth century, only warfare and campaigns of religious conversion had come close to matching in scale.[18] These interactions have given rise to a heated debate over whether globalization means an increasing homogenization of culture, whether the economic processes of globalization might allow for effective cultural penetration of the North Atlantic by the South/East, and whether the human ability for cultural creation is so strong as to defy, ultimately, all economic pressure, whether it be tending toward homogenization or heterogenization/hybridization.[19] The debate was particularly heated in the mid- to late 1990s and appears at the beginning of the twenty-first century to have at least momentarily settled into an appropriately agitated acceptance of the complexity of contingency well summarized by Arjun Appadurai when he states: "If *a* global cultural system is emerging, it is filled with ironies and resistances."[20] Arguing the nature and efficacy of these "ironies and resistances" has now taken center stage in the debates over the cultural ramifications of globalization, supplanting the globalization-as-centripetal-or-centrifugal-force question. Appadurai points out that the arguments that posit globalization as a cultural homogenizer fail to consider that "at least as rapidly as forces from various metropolises are brought into new societies they tend to become indigenized in one or another way."[21] This process of indigenization can be seen as a kind of resistance, but resistance to what, and to what end?

Appadurai writes that the critiques warning of globalization as cultural homogenizer, which tend to come from the left, often speak of globalization when the more precise words "Americanization" or "commoditization" could as easily suffice. If, then, "indigenization" is happening in the realm of the production and circulation of culture (e.g., food, music, the visual arts) as commodity, so that expressions of resistance can be purchased in lieu of one's having to consume a dominant product straight from the metropole, then one might legitimately ask, How much resistance is in this resistance?[22] By the end of the twentieth century, many voices—especially in fields such as anthropology, philosophy, and political science—appeared to be joining voices from "the dismal science" in the expressions of optimism that globalization had truly marked a rupture with the past, opening up the potential for a kind of micro-agency in which individuals were freed from the constraints of the nation-state as never before in the post-Westphalian era.[23] Hailing the inception of a world that engendered possibilities heretofore unimaginable, Appadurai wrote the following words, published in 1996: "The world we live in today is characterized by a new role for the imagination in social life."[24] The terrorist attacks on the United States in 2001 and the ensuing "War on Terror[ism]" sadly make these words ring as hollow as if they had been uttered in 1871, but peace studies must still consider relatively optimistic views like Appadurai's—another point to which this chapter shall return.

When it comes to the relationship between globalization and the environment, the debates are no less complex. Certainly the wide array of both actually and potentially harmful environmental consequences attributed directly or indirectly to globalization has been well documented.[25] These consequences include the increasing commercialization of agriculture (with attendant reliance upon commercial seeds, fertilizer, and massive irrigation); the loss of small-scale sustainable agricultural techniques; the loss (through restructuring, systematization, patenting, or migration) of indigenous knowledge supportive of ecological balance; the spread of monoculture; the proliferation of genetically modified organisms; the loss of biodiversity; rural-to-urban migration (with the attendant growth of peripheral communities without access to environmentally sound systems of water delivery or sewage removal); increasing industrialization; urban sprawl; pollution of water, air, and soil; toxic wastes; soil erosion; deforestation; desertification; loss of habitat; species extinction; global climate change; and, in a select segment of the global population, rising living standards giving way to dramatically increased consumption and thus increased waste streams. It must also be emphasized that among humans, the effects of these phenomena are felt most profoundly by historically marginalized groups: those living in poverty, people of color (indigenous peoples in particular), and women the world over.[26] All these issues are of critical importance to peace studies, as the connection between environmental devastation, resource scarcity, and war and other forms of cultural collapse is well established.[27]

Critics see globalization as binding all of life together in a single (ultimately detrimental) fate. Proponents of globalization offer several lines of counterargument. One is that the institutions of globalization can help to bind all life together for a common good, and an example might be the "globalization of environmental values through the Kyoto Protocol."[28] Another is the so-called Kuznets Curve effect: the data set said to illustrate that although economic growth might initially harm the environment, the effect tends to reverse itself in nation-states with rising gross domestic products (GDPs).[29] Objections to each one of these counterarguments, taken on its own terms, might be raised, but the field of peace studies loses an opportunity if its practitioners do not seek to shift the kinds of questions being asked. Indeed, in the realm of environmental issues, it becomes most starkly clear that very often the nature of discourse surrounding globalization is such that questions that should be asked are instead buried. The case of the Mexican-US border cities of Ciudad Juárez and El Paso, as a location of the maquiladora industry, itself often taken as emblematic of globalization, is illustrative. Foreign corporations shifting production to the Mexican border zone gain the advantage, simultaneously, of lax environmental regulations on one side of the line and the close proximity of a major consumer market on the other. The location of the maquiladora industry is thus entirely dependent upon both the existence and the location of a specific international boundary, which, in this instance, happens to traverse the Chihuahuan Desert. While much attention has been focused on the harmful health and environmental effects of toxic products utilized and discharged by the maquiladora industry, rarely, if ever, are the deeper ecological questions asked: How long can this desert sustain a human population of 3 million and growing, and is it ethical to locate a major industrial base in this particular ecosystem? Unless and until the sole reliance upon the profit motive as the basic organizing principle of the global economy is also questioned, these are questions that in an important sense we cannot afford to ask; they do not fit the criteria now mainly used to determine plant location. Similarly, as long as the cultural structures undergirding the global economy remain disembedded from ecological dictates, nation-states that claim that following the Kyoto Protocol jeopardizes "economic growth" and the protocol must therefore wait will always, unfortunately, have a legitimate argument. Some key points of insertion for peace studies in the debate on the relationship between globalization and the environment lie in examining structures of governance and in seeking symbiosis between economic structures and ecological mandates.

This brief tour through the central debates on globalization reveals how fraught with contested issues the word is and demonstrates that educators in the field of peace studies should certainly seek to develop among students an appreciation for the political implications of the use of the term. Within peace studies, globalization is quite useful as shorthand for many of the dynamics that bear directly upon the potential for peace. Indeed, anyone familiar with the field of peace studies who reads the list of "disturbing images" above will notice a similarity: globalization sometimes seems to function as a synonym for a handful of phenomena that would be considered manifestations of "structural violence."[30] Part of the reason that globalization has been adopted by practitioners within peace studies stems from the interdisciplinary nature of the field: the word is set in the midst of a great, lived debate in which all the disciplines have something to contribute and in which the rationale for interdisciplinary studies is particularly compelling. This is why globalization matters to peace studies: the debate over the very *meaning* of globalization is inseparable from the question of how to achieve peace and stability in today's world.

As such, we can consider it round two of the debate between Johan Galtung and Kenneth Boulding being carried on in a new era, this time (thanks in part to the new technologies attributed to globalization itself) by many millions around the world. The proponents of globalization consider it a stabilizing force that will make the world more peaceful once the benefits of these processes reach all areas of the globe, much as Boulding argued that achieving peace would depend on bolstering the institutions of liberty and property.[31] The detractors, however, consider globalization a further exacerbation of extant injustices and as such a barrier to sustainable peace. It is therefore apropos to revisit one of Boulding's criticisms of Galtung's use of the term "structural violence," since globalization certainly can and often does function as stand-in for the concept of structural violence. Boulding considers Galtung's structural violence to be a metaphor: "The metaphor is that poverty, deprivation, ill health, low expectations of life, a condition in which more than half the human race lives, is 'like' a thug beating up the victim and taking his money away from him in the street."[32] Boulding is critical of this metaphor not only because he considers it inaccurate as a metaphor, but also because he considers metaphor more "dangerous" than models because the former holds more persuasive power.[33] Does globalization merit the warning against hypostasizing? Perhaps, yet the processes to which this term alludes have undeniably material (even deeply somatic) consequences. Nevertheless, if we choose an inaccurate metaphor as an organizing principle, it can cloud our judgment, engendering an inability to discern the nature of causes and therefore blinding us to solutions as well.

Globalization as a theoretical device, then, has come under similar criticism. Even though it has provided a basis for organizing to resist such measures as those taken to increase the ease with which transnational capital flows are accomplished (e.g., the liberalization of capital controls, which facilitates bear raids), or those taken to enhance the power of bodies and systems of transnational governance (such as the World Trade Organization and its successors), it has been argued that globalization is far too totalizing. It emphasizes structure and does not sufficiently allow agency.[34] If the very opposition of structure and agency can cause our attention to stray from crucial considerations—because of the obvious urgency of the necessity of a recognition of both—it does lead to an important point: the processes indicated by the word "globalization" are not in fact omnipotent nor, indeed, omnipresent, and speaking and acting as though they are can be disempowering.[35]

This is a critical point. As Paulo Freire wrote in a work that was published posthumously: "As great as the conditioning power of the economy may be over our individual and social behavior, I cannot accept being completely passive before it. To the extent that we accept that the economy, or technology, or science, it doesn't matter what, exerts inescapable power over us, there is nothing left for us to do other than renounce our ability to think, to conjecture, to compare, to choose, to decide, to envision, to dream."[36] And this is precisely something peace studies has to contribute to the understanding of globalization and its relationship to the economy, the environment, and culture. The task of presenting alternatives (i.e., demonstrating, very concretely, that globalization is not in fact totalizing) is a major contribution to be made by those within the field of peace studies, for it is a field that proceeds—indeed, must proceed—from an acknowledgment of the importance of historicizing, separating what is indeed natural from what has only been presumed to be "natural" and is instead the cultural reified.

Peace studies has an abiding interest in proving that peace is in fact possible, and the field has therefore drawn upon work demonstrating, for example, that some cultures are more peaceful than others (and in some cultures, many, if not most, forms of violence are virtually unknown, or had been before the arrival of colonialism).[37] It has also highlighted work in the fields of psychology and education that demonstrates that individuals—even in highly individualistic and even atomized cultures like that of the United States—are capable of overcoming self-centeredness and aggressive and antisocial behavior to live according to norms and ethics of care.[38] In a similar fashion, it currently falls to peace studies to take on the specific task of highlighting ways of organizing the economy so as to facilitate sustainable peace.

The triumphalism that accompanied the early uses of the term globalization—best epitomized in Margaret Thatcher's oft-quoted claim: "There is no alternative"—is reinscribed, usually quite unintentionally, every time we take as a given certain cultural structures while simultaneously trying to discern the causes of war and devoting our attentions to conflict resolution.[39] If we accept the premise that poverty and related forms of exclusion give rise to violence in all its forms, either through misguided attempts to challenge these injustices or, more commonly, through attempts to preserve the status quo—a premise on which there is growing consensus across the political spectrum—then peace studies must examine and address the causes of poverty.[40] The question that perhaps sheds the most light on the prospects for peace is also the most basic: why are fundamental needs going unmet? Peace studies must go further, however, and also seek to answer why efforts to eradicate poverty are continually thwarted. The reason that social democracy—the greatest concerted attempt by humanity thus far to ameliorate poverty—was supplanted by globalization is that it was undermined by the basic cultural structure of modernity.

Generalized prosperity within this cultural structure depends upon and thus mandates sustaining and continually increasing levels of consumption and investment, which is precisely what globalization's advocates both promise and assume. Leaving aside the ecological implications of such a mandate, there are other implications that bear directly on the possibility of addressing poverty and therefore also on the possibility for sustainable peace. The social democracies of the mid-twentieth century were a classic example of the attempt to pursue distributive justice at the nation-state level as a path toward peace. As such, they might be considered a test case of Kenneth Boulding's proposition that the freedom granted by the institution of property rights is the ultimate guarantor of peace because within the boundaries of property lies the otherwise elusive autonomy (which many, Boulding included, consider the key to creating peace-engendering institutions), a proposition that globalization's proponents echo today.[41] The freedom granted by the institution of property rights, however, also includes consumers' rights not to consume and, even more importantly, investors' rights not to invest, and this carries direct implications for nation-states pursuing forms of distributive justice premised on the acceptance of this particular cultural structure. If a given community operating within this structure, expressing its highest ethical and democratic ideals, chooses to raise wages or environmental standards beyond the level that "the market will allow," they will most likely face a capital strike or capital flight or both, followed by rising unemployment and rising rates of poverty.[42] It is not the profit motive per se but rather the *addiction* to the profit motive that makes a society so dependent upon meeting the needs of capital that it lacks capacity for autonomy, integrity, and ethical judgment. As long as we accept the premise of capital accumulation as the *sole* or *principal* motor that starts and drives the entire production process, it will always be in the interest of wage earners that capitalists appropriate profits, for upon this premise all else is founded; if the needs of capital are not first met, other needs, if met at all, will wait indeterminately. The reason that needs are going unmet has nothing to do with lack of effort or even a shortage of good intentions. It is because the very purpose of human effort in this cultural structure is not meeting needs, but rather accumulating money (the logic of exchange).[43] As long as this premise is not challenged but accepted as a given, the violence that accompanies unmet needs will persist, and an inordinate amount of resources will have to be given over to the projects of peacekeeping (i.e., truce enforcements) and peacemaking (i.e., high-level diplomatic negotiations) rather than peacebuilding.[44]

A central question for peace studies then becomes, How do we mobilize resources to meet needs in a sustainable way? Certainly the answer is not to try again, without serious alteration and supplementation, methods that have already failed; nor is it to seek to forgo the use of the profit motive, which has proven an adept method for mobilizing resources on a large scale (even though matching resources to needs is not among its design strengths). We must instead open a new imaginary altogether and create, in theory and practice, the very thing that Appadurai had hoped that globalization would signify: "a new role for the imagination in social life." If the fact of unmet needs consistently gives rise to violence, and if the capacity for peoples around the world to act with autonomy, integrity, and ethical judgment is a necessary condition for sustainable peace, then economic structures must be designed to reward rather than punish the enactment of ethics in forms such as cooperation, sharing, and all the best attributes of the human character that quietly coexist alongside the better known self-interest. As Corinne Kumar writes, "We must seek new understandings of democracy; that will include a concept of freedom that is different from that which is enshrined in the Enlightenment and its Market. There is an urgent need to reinvent the political; to *infuse the political with the ethical: the new political imaginary speaks to an ethic of care*."[45]

Examples of the emergence of a new imaginary are already far too numerous to be contained in even a series of volumes, so a few summaries will have to suffice for the present purpose. Just as globalization was beginning to enter the popular vocabulary, India was hoping to leverage a comparative advantage in eucalyptus and promote it as a key export. Confronted with the incursion of the eucalyptus monoculture, rural residents in Karnataka, knowing that this fast-growing pulpwood would destroy the wider ecological balance upon which they depended for their livelihoods, undertook what they called a "pluck-and-plant *satyagraha*." Intentionally building upon Mohandas Gandhi's campaign of *swadeshi* (national self-reliance) but carrying the concept of self-reliance all the way to the local level, 2,000 people took an oath of nonviolence and then uprooted young eucalyptus saplings, planted native species in their place, and pledged to care for the new plants. Ramachandra Guha emphasizes that the participants in this movement were both trying to defend their interests "and passing judgment on . . . prevailing social arrangements" in which the property rights of a private corporation trumped the local needs of both people and the ecosystem in its entirety. Guha writes that the aim of this satyagraha was "not merely to insist, 'This land is ours,' but also (and equally significantly) to ask, 'What are trees for?'"[46] The question is actually far more significant than the statement because it poses a wider challenge. Holding up indigenous knowledge systems as more holistic and ecologically sound, it challenges not only the eucalyptus monoculture but also represents a cultural challenge to the encroaching logic of exchange as itself a kind of monoculture. This movement represented not merely resistance but the enactment of better ways of organizing the structures that guide everyday life, which sometimes are new, sometimes are resurrections of practices that have historical roots much deeper than those basic cultural structures currently undergirding the global economy, and most often are amalgamations of the very long tried (but forgotten or suppressed) and the barely imagined. The growing movement for recognition of the gift economy in practice is another cause for hope. The gift economy includes all labor that is done not for profit but instead as a kind of gift, such as parenting and many basic tasks in the realms of kinship and friendship; thus it is widely known throughout nearly all human cultures but is rarely acknowledged as a proven method of matching resources to needs. Peggy Antrobus writes, "By making visible the gift paradigm, and valuing it for itself, we can foster economic and social relations based on an other-orientation that aims to satisfy needs, creates bonding and cooperation rather than egoism, isolation, and competition."[47]

The phenomena of rising oil prices, resource scarcity and continued resource wars, an increased sense of insecurity, continuing political violence, short- and long-term economic crises, and severe environmental and climate catastrophes are converging and beginning to affect groups who have historically been relatively shielded from these crises' effects (including large segments of the middle class and even the leisure class in the global North), a testament to the new degree of interconnectedness engendered by globalization. This convergence seems to be giving way to a shift in which the emerging consensus on the necessity for major transformation is allowing people to see that change is not only necessary, it is also possible. "In this sense," writes Paola Melchiori, "the situation of Argentina, where the economic system collapsed in 2001 as a result of an expropriation process which combined forced privatizations, export of capital, and massive corruption, was . . . [an] exemplar." She continues: "The crisis was terrible, people were starving, but another economy was being discovered and used, awakening an enormous energy among people, developing . . . a 'healthy crisis' of the social imaginary. Other ways to survive, other social fabrics, became visible and imaginable."[48]

If humanity is to respond to the processes associated with globalization and transform them in order to engender a more peaceful world, peace studies will have to play a critical role in the transformation. Michael Featherstone argues that if globalization truly marks a rupture giving rise to an integration not seen before, then it should also give rise to "emergent dimensions of social life" that challenge modes of conceptualization within the academy and herald the dissolution of boundaries between disciplines.[49] As of this writing, there is nothing that indicates that anything remotely resembling such a dissolution is occurring, even as the academy's claims of the value of "interdisciplinarity" grow louder with each passing generation, and even as the problems of the world seem to cry out with increasing urgency for answers that cannot even be enunciated without crossing the boundaries of disciplines. Peace studies must not only navigate the crossing and breaking of these boundaries but must also lead the way in the dissolution of the barriers between the academy and the world "outside," so that the former might also have the opportunity to learn what much of the latter already knows.[50]

Notes

1. Cultural structures (which are sometimes known by approximate synonyms such as symbolic structures, social formations, ideologies, mythologies, worldviews, mentalities, language games, social texts, and discourses) are meanings that guide human behavior. See Howard Richards, *Letters from Quebec* (Toronto: Elliott Chapin, 1992), 101–117; and Howard Richards and Joanna Swanger, *The Dilemmas of Social Democracies: Overcoming Obstacles to a More Just World* (Lanham, MD: Lexington Books, 2006), 31, 43–58. The concept of the cultural structure builds on the work of Pierre Bourdieu and of linguist John Searle. Bourdieu, *The Logic of Practice,* translated by R. Nice (Stanford, CA: Stanford University Press, 1990); John Searle, *Speech Acts* (Cambridge: Cambridge University Press, 1969).

2. See David Harvey, *The Condition of Postmodernity* (Oxford: Basil Blackwell, 1990); and Richards and Swanger, *The Dilemmas of Social Democracies.* Accompanying these economic transformations were technological innovations that gave rise to the spread of telecommunications and specifically to electronic financial markets, which allowed financial capital the speed and mobility necessary to realize operations on a global scale.

3. Students in peace studies should by all means be invited to sort through these competing definitions, parse their meanings, and seek to understand precisely what is at stake with the different uses of the term. Two of the most concise and thorough treatments of the different definitions of globalization are Douglas Kellner, "Theorizing Globalization," *Sociological Theory* 20, no. 3 (November 2002): 285–305; and Michael Featherstone, "Genealogies of the Global," *Theory, Culture, and Society* 23, nos. 2–3 (2006): 387–392. Those two sources should be the starting points for those interested in a survey of the literature on globalization across the disciplines. Robertson's genealogy is also a helpful introduction. See Roland Robertson, *Globalization: Social Theory and Global Culture* (London: Sage, 1992). Analytical precision must be matched with synthetic potential; as Josiah Heyman writes: "Strong generalizations are absolutely required if we are to confront strong problems and engage in strong debates." See Heyman, "Conclusion: Understandings Matter," in *Confronting Environments: Local Understanding in a Globalizing World,* edited by James G. Carrier (Walnut Creek, CA: AltaMira, 2004), 184. It should be noted that it is precisely the sentiment that Heyman expresses here that has caused many within peace studies to embrace the term "globalization," for this term might also signify a new and profound acknowledgment of interdependence, which would in turn support the kinds of multilateral and collective approaches to

shared problems that theorists and practitioners contributing to peace studies have long advocated. See, e.g., Mary Kaldor, *Global Civil Society: An Answer to War* (Cambridge: Polity, 2003). I return to more hopeful leveragings of globalization below.

4. Marshall McLuhan referred to the mass-mediated "global village" in his 1962 work, *The Gutenberg Galaxy.* The sense in which McLuhan used the term "global" in that work echoes throughout the current debates on globalization.

5. See, e.g., Francis Fukuyama, *The End of History and the Last Man* (New York: Free Press, 1992); and Thomas Friedman, *The Lexus and the Olive Tree* (New York: Farrar, Straus and Giroux, 1999).

6. Some use the term "globalization" to refer solely to the technological innovations that facilitate transnational flows of capital. Kellner advocates that this particular process be designated "technocapitalism": this word "points to a new configuration of capitalist society in which technical and scientific knowledge, computerization and automation of labor, and information technology and multimedia play a role in the process of production analogous to the function of human labor-power, mechanization of the labor process, and machines in an earlier era of capitalism" (Kellner, "Theorizing Globalization," 289–290). Zygmunt Bauman uses the phrase "liquid modernity" to designate the world engendered in the new era of ever-quickening transnational capital flows. See Bauman, *Liquid Modernity* (Cambridge: Polity Press, 2000). As for those who use "globalization" to indicate, solely or primarily, the fact that a greater array of consumer products is now available in select markets, Featherstone believes it could be characterized, more basically, as "the banal cosmopolitanism of consumer culture," a phenomenon with historical roots nearly as old as trade itself (Featherstone, "Genealogies of the Global," 390). Formal expressions of the "antiglobalization movement" include the anti–World Trade Organization (WTO) protests in Seattle in 1999, protests against World Bank and International Monetary Fund policy in Washington, D.C., in 2000, protests at the Free Trade of the Americas Summit in Quebec in the spring of 2001, protests in Genoa in the summer of 2001, and the entire World Social Forum movement, which started in Porto Alegre, Brazil, in 2001 and has been growing and spreading throughout the world since. Anthropologist David Graeber states that it was the corporate media that coined the phrase "antiglobalization movement." Indeed, many, if not most, participants in this movement would rather emphasize what they advocate rather than what they oppose. The deliberate choice of "Another World Is Possible" as the motto of the World Social Forum illustrates the point. See David Graeber, "The Globalization Movement: Some Points of Clarification," *Items and Issues* 2, nos. 3–4 (2001): 12–14.

7. Yet indeed there did arise, for a brief period during the "dot-com boom" in the United States, a strange corollary to the correct proposition that holds that profit arising from the production process (as opposed to the realm of circulation) does not hold position of primacy as a driving force within capitalism: the corollary that profit itself had lost primacy, which was the underlying argument when people were encouraged to invest in unprofitable companies. The spread of this discourse is documented in Thomas Frank, *One Market Under God: Extreme Capitalism, Market Populism, and the End of Economic Democracy* (New York: Anchor Books, 2000). See also Hazel Henderson, *Beyond Globalization: Shaping a Sustainable Global Economy* (West Hartford, CT: Kumarian Press, 1999), on the rise of the "casino economy."

8. Jonathan Diskin and Tim Koechlin, "Liberal Political Economy and Global Capitalism," *Review of Radical Political Economics,* Vol. 26 (1994): 86–94.

9. The imagery that springs to mind depends nearly entirely on one's geographic location. In the global South, the word often connotes such phenomena as rural-to-urban migration, the growth of the informal sector, and the increasing participation of the very young and very old in income-generating labor. In the global North, the images include those associated primarily with deindustrialization and outsourcing/offshoring. The two themes shared in common are those of increasing disparities in wealth and increasing economic insecurity, which, according to globalization's proponents, are acknowledged as part of a temporary albeit painful phase, as the market makes the necessary "corrections." See Jeremy Brecher, Tim Costello, and Brendan Smith, *Globalization from Below* (Boston: South End Press, 2000); and Zillah Eisenstein, *Global Obscenities: Patriarchy, Capitalism, and the Lure of Cyberfantasy* (New York: New York University Press, 1998). Of course, Brecher, Costello, and Smith, in advocating "globalization from below," are among those who see in the transformations wrought by globalization the potential for more authentic forms of democracy than have formerly existed, as nonstate actors in particular (e.g., Doctors Without Borders, the Rainforest Action Network, Amnesty International) forge alliances that might also become truly global in scope and press demands both upon nation-states and upon global institutions. Others advocating optimism vis-à-vis the potential leveraging of global alliances include Arjun Appadurai, *Fear of Small Numbers: An Essay on the Geography of Anger* (Durham, NC: Duke University Press, 2006), 131–137; Kaldor, *Global Civil Society;* and Michael Hardt and Antonio Negri, *Multitude: War and Democracy in the Age of Empire* (Harmondsworth: Penguin, 2005).

10. For a thorough and excellent treatment that illustrates the complexity of these questions, see Arjun Appadurai on the global production of locality in *Modernity at Large: Cultural Dimensions of Globalization* (Minneapolis: University of Minnesota Press, 1996), 178–199. For a treatment that speaks directly to the relationship of globalization to the economy, the environment, and culture, with direct implications for peace studies, see Carrier, *Confronting Environments.*

11. Douglas Irwin, *Free Trade Under Fire* (Princeton, NJ: Princeton University Press, 2002); Philippe LeGrain, *Open World: The Truth About Globalization* (London: Abacus, 2002); Martin Wolf, *Why Globalization Works* (New Haven, CT: Yale University Press, 2004). Examples of the globalization-as-shibboleth line of reasoning, which purposely excludes ethical considerations, are more common in documents not intended for publication, such as the infamous "Toxic Memo" written by World Bank economist Lawrence Summers for six World Bank colleagues and then leaked. Summers offers a sample of this reasoning: "The measurement of the costs of health impairing pollution depends on the foregone earnings from increased morbidity and mortality. From this point of view a given amount of health impairing pollution should be done in the country with the lowest cost, which will be the country with the lowest wages. I think the economic logic behind dumping a load of toxic waste in the lowest wage country is impeccable and we should face up to that." Summers is quoted in Susan George and Fabrizio Sabelli, *Faith and Credit: The World Bank's Secular Empire* (Boulder, CO: Westview, 1994), 98–99.

12. The best example of the former is Joseph Stiglitz, *Making Globalization Work: The New Steps to Global Justice* (New York: W. W. Norton, 2007); of the latter, Jeffrey D. Sachs, *The End of Poverty: Economic Possibilities for Our Time* (New York: Penguin Press, 2005).

13. Jagdish Bhagwati, *In Defense of Globalization* (Oxford: Oxford University Press, 2004), 12–13. It is interesting that many economists who advocate globalization are now openly challenging the neoliberal orthodoxy that held as anathema

state interventions in the market. Michael J. Trebilcock, for example, states that globalization can only generate wealth, not distribute it properly; this latter task belongs to institutions other than the market. He writes: "To the extent that a correlation between globalization and inequality exist[s], it is unclear whether it should be attributed to the causal effects of globalization, or more simply the lack of appropriate redistribution mechanisms at the state level." See Trebilcock, "Critiquing the Critics of Economic Globalization," *Journal of Law and International Relations* 1, nos. 1–2 (December 2005): 225–226.

14. Stiglitz, *Making Globalization Work.*

15. Trebilcock, for example, writes: "More homogeneity of values, especially liberal values, would . . . seem a small price to pay for avoiding the huge human costs of ethnic and religious conflicts." Trebilock, "Critiquing the Critics," 216–217. Trebilcock's argument in the field of economics has resonance as well within the liberal cosmopolitan school of thought within political science, which has made generous contributions to debates in the field of peace studies. In addition to the work of Kaldor, see, for example, David Held, *Democracy and the Global Order: From the Modern State to Cosmopolitan Governance* (Stanford: Stanford University Press, 1995); Richard Falk, *Predatory Globalization* (Oxford: Blackwell, 1999), a work that argues for a global civil society; and Ulrich Beck, *What Is Globalization?* (Oxford: Blackwell, 2000), a work that argues for a "transnational state." Authors responding to this particular line of debate include Fernando Coronil, "Towards a Critique of Globalcentrism," *Public Culture* 12, no. 2 (Spring 2000): 351–374; Arif Dirlik, *Postmodernity's Histories* (Lanham, MD: Rowman and Littlefield, 2000); and scholars in the Subaltern Studies Group and in the field of postcolonial studies more broadly.

16. For just a small sampling of a fortunately quickly growing field, see Marilyn Waring, *If Women Counted: A New Feminist Economics* (San Francisco: HarperCollins, 1988); Herman E. Daly, *Beyond Growth: The Economics of Sustainable Development* (Boston: Beacon Press, 1996); Henderson, *Beyond Globalization;* and Brian Milani, *Designing the Green Economy: The Postindustrial Alternative to Corporate Globalization* (Lanham, MD: Rowman and Littlefield, 2000).

17. Hernando de Soto offers the best concise version of these arguments in *The Other Path: The Invisible Revolution in the Third World* (New York: Harper and Row, 1989); and *The Mystery of Capital: Why Capitalism Triumphs in the West* (New York: Basic Books, 2000).

18. Arjun Appadurai, *Modernity at Large: Cultural Dimensions of Globalization* (Minneapolis: University of Minnesota Press, 1996), 27.

19. Works emphasizing homogenization include Cees J. Hamelink, *Cultural Autonomy in Global Communications* (New York: Longman, 1983); Pico Iyer, *Video Night in Kathmandu* (New York: Knopf, 1988); and Benjamin R. Barber, *Jihad vs. McWorld* (New York: Ballantine, 1996). Works emphasizing heterogenization (or hybridization) include James L. Watson, ed., *Golden Arches East: McDonald's in East Asia* (Cambridge: Stanford University Press, 1998); Nestor Garcia Canclini, *Hybrid Cultures: Strategies for Entering and Leaving Modernity,* translated by Christopher L. Chiappari (Minneapolis: University of Minnesota Press, 1993); and Appadurai, *Modernity at Large.* In between are works that emphasize the potential for cultural penetration of the North Atlantic by the South/East; see, e.g., K. Iwabuchi, *Recentering Globalization* (Durham, NC: Duke University Press, 2002). Arjun Appadurai has proffered works that offer both good summaries and treatments of these debates. See also Arjun Appadurai, ed., *Globalization* (Durham, NC: Duke University Press, 2002).

20. Appadurai, *Modernity at Large*, 29. There is also a growing consensus in the academy that globalization and postmodernism appropriately correspond. Appadurai writes: "The new global cultural economy has to be seen as a complex, overlapping, disjunctive order that cannot any longer be understood in terms of existing center-periphery models. . . . Nor is it susceptible to simple models of push and pull . . . or of surplus and deficits . . . or of consumers and producers. . . ." Ibid., 32.

21. Ibid.

22. If we are informed that McDonald's in Paris sells baguettes, should we respond with "Vive le résistance"?

23. As these debates on the emancipatory potential of the processes associated with globalization are playing out in the social sciences and humanities, activists and their advocates are also weighing in on what the new and seemingly ever-shifting terrain of interconnectedness and disjuncture might hold and whether globalization promises anything of use for the cause of resistance. Of the most important works to take into consideration in this matter are Gilles Deleuze and Félix Guattari's *A Thousand Plateaus*, and Michael Hardt and Antonio Negri's *Empire* and *Multitude*. Deleuze and Guattari write of the processes of deterritorialization and reterritorialization in late capitalism and address the possibilities for agency by endlessly mutating "desiring machines." Hardt and Negri are even more explicitly optimistic concerning agency in the cause of resistance to "Empire"; in fact, for Hardt and Negri, resistance is ubiquitous. Students in peace studies, who have an interest in emancipation in all its forms, should delve into these important questions on the nature and possibilities of agency and what constitutes emancipation. Good starting points are to read these works in conjunction with succinct and powerful critiques, such as those put forth by N. Katherine Hayles on Deleuze and Guattari and by Caroline Higgins on Hardt and Negri. See Deleuze and Félix Guattari, *A Thousand Plateaus: Capitalism and Schizophrenia*, translated by Brian Massumi (Minneapolis: University of Minnesota Press, 1987); Michael Hardt and Antonio Negri, *Empire* (Cambridge, MA: Harvard University Press, 2000); Hardt and Negri, *Multitude;* N. Katherine Hayles, "Desiring Agency: Limiting Metaphors and Enabling Constraints in Dawkins and Deleuze/Guattari," *SubStance* 94–95 (2001): 144–159; Caroline Higgins, "History and Subjectivity in the Age of Globalization: The Multitude in Hardt and Negri's *Empire*," unpublished paper, available at http://www.earlham.edu/pags/content/faculty_publications.html.

24. Appadurai, *Modernity at Large*, 31. To be sure, Appadurai's interpretation of globalization in the post-2001 world has altered substantially, as his 2006 *Fear of Small Numbers* indicates; nevertheless, his arguments are put forth here as representative of a significant line of interpretation prior to 2001. In calling our attention to the importance of the political imaginary, Appadurai is drawing upon a school of thought that includes, among others, Benedict Anderson, *Imagined Communities: Reflections on the Origin and Spread of Nationalism* (London: Verso, 1983); Cornelius Castoriadis, *The Imaginary Construction of Society* (London: Polity Press, 1990); Fredric Jameson, *The Political Unconscious: Narrative as a Socially Symbolic Act* (Ithaca, NY: Cornell University Press, 1981); Ernesto Laclau and Chantal Mouffe, *Hegemony and Socialist Strategy: Toward a Radical Democratic Politics* (London: Verso, 1985); Raymond Williams, *Marxism and Literature* (Oxford: Oxford University Press, 1977); and Antonio Gramsci, *Selections from the Prison Notebooks*, translated by Quintin Hoare and Geoffrey Nowell Smith (New York: International Publishers, 1989).

25. See, e.g., Hilary F. French, *Vanishing Borders: Protecting the Planet in the Age of Globalization* (London: Earthscan, 2000); Alf Hornborg, *The Power of the*

Machine: Global Inequalities of Economy, Technology, and Environment (Walnut Creek, CA: AltaMira, 2001); and Jordi Díez and O. P. Dwivedi, eds., *Global Environmental Challenges: Perspectives from the South* (Toronto: Broadview Press, 2007).

26. On the ecological consequences of the subjugation of indigenous knowledges to the dominant economic paradigm, see Vandana Shiva, *Monocultures of the Mind: Perspectives on Biodiversity and Biotechnology* (London: Zed Books, 2000). For a brief overview of the relationships between environmental issues and both the lives of women and the construct of gender, from an ecofeminist perspective, see Mary Mellor, "Gender and the Environment," in *Ecofeminism and Globalization: Exploring Culture, Context, and Religion,* edited by Heather Eaton and Lois Ann Lorentzen (Lanham, MD: Rowman and Littlefield, 2003).

27. See, e.g., Michael T. Klare, *Resource Wars: The New Landscape of Global Conflict* (New York: Henry Holt, 2001); and Jared Diamond, *Collapse: How Societies Choose to Fail or Succeed* (New York and London: Penguin Books, 2005).

28. Trebilcock, "Critiquing the Critics," 213.

29. Ibid. On these arguments, see also Gilberto C. Gallopín and Paul Raskin, *Global Sustainability: Bending the Curve* (London: Routledge, 2002).

30. Galtung defines "structural violence" as the "avoidable denial of what is needed to satisfy the fundamental needs." Johan Galtung, *The True Worlds: A Transnational Perspective* (New York: Free Press, 1980), 67.

31. Kenneth Boulding, "Twelve Friendly Quarrels with Johan Galtung," *Journal of Peace Research* 14, no. 1 (1977): 80–83; Thomas P. M. Barnett, *The Pentagon's New Map: War and Peace in the Twenty-first Century* (New York: G. P. Putnam's Sons, 2004); Friedman, *The Lexus and the Olive Tree;* Jennifer Morrison Taw and Bruce Hoffman, *The Urbanization of Insurgency: The Potential Challenge to US Army Operations* (Santa Monica: RAND, 1994); Fukuyama, *The End of History.*

32. Boulding, "Twelve Friendly Quarrels," 83.

33. He writes: "Violence, whether of the streets and the home, or of the guerilla, of the police, or of the armed forces, is a very different phenomenon from poverty. The processes which create and sustain poverty are not at all like the processes which create and sustain violence, although like everything else in the world, everything is somewhat related to everything else." Ibid.

34. In her critique of the function of desire in Deleuze and Guattari and of the relationship between structure and agency in Dawkins's *The Selfish Gene,* N. Katherine Hayles offers this apt understanding, appropriate for locating ourselves within globalization: "Neither completely constrained nor entirely free, we act within these systems with partial agency amid local specificities that help to determine our behavior, even as our behavior also helps to configure the system." Hayles, "Desiring Agency," 158.

35. Diskin and Koechlin make this point brilliantly in their critique of the use of the construct of globalization by Robert Reich and Lester Thurow. Diskin and Koechlin, "Liberal Political Economy."

36. Paulo Freire, *Pedagogy of Indignation* (Boulder, CO: Paradigm, 2004), 33.

37. See, e.g., Shanshan Du, *"Chopsticks Only Work in Pairs": Gender Unity and Gender Equality Among the Lahu of Southwest China* (New York: Columbia University Press, 2002); Graham Kemp and Douglas Fry, *Keeping the Peace: Conflict Resolution and Peaceful Societies Around the World* (New York: Routledge, 2004); Douglas Fry, *The Human Potential for Peace: An Anthropological Challenge to Assumptions About War and Violence* (New York: Oxford University Press, 2006).

38. Jean Piaget, *The Moral Judgment of the Child* (London: Trench, Trubner, 1932); Lawrence Kohlberg, "Continuities and Discontinuities in Childhood and Adult Moral Development Revisited," in *Collected Papers on Moral Development*

and Moral Education (Cambridge, MA: Moral Education Research Foundation, Harvard University, 1973); Carol Gilligan, *In a Different Voice: Psychological Theory and Women's Development* (Cambridge, MA: Harvard University Press, 1982).

39. Carolyn Nordstrom writes that when high-level peace talks proceed without taking into consideration the wider voices of civil society that speak from intimate knowledge of the root causes of violence, "conflict resolution lives up to its name: resolving the same conflicts that surface again and again over time and space because the core issues were never adequately addressed." See Carolyn Nordstrom, "The Eye of the Storm: From War to Peace—Examples from Sri Lanka and Mozambique," in *Cultural Variation in Conflict Resolution: Alternatives to Violence,* edited by Douglas P. Fry and Kaj Björkqvist (Mahwah, NJ: Lawrence Erlbaum Associates, 1997), 92.

40. Advisers to the US military have acknowledged poverty as destabilizing, a fundamental obstacle to peace. See Barnett, *The Pentagon's New Map;* and Taw and Hoffman, *The Urbanization of Insurgency.* See also Nikki R. Keddie, "The New Religious Politics: Where, When, and Why Do 'Fundamentalisms' Appear?" *Comparative Studies in Society and History* 40, no. 4 (October 1998): 696–723.

41. Boulding, "Twelve Friendly Quarrels," 83.

42. Charles Lindblom, "The Market as Prison," *Journal of Politics* 44 (1982): 325–336; Richards and Swanger, *The Dilemmas of Social Democracies.*

43. Richards and Swanger, *The Dilemmas of Social Democracies.* Economics reflects this structure in not being designed to take "need" per se into account, as one economist attests: "In economics, 'need' is a non-word. Economics can say much which is useful about desires, preferences, and demands. But 'need' is presumably a moral, psychological, or physical imperative which brooks no compromise or adjustment—or analysis. If we 'need' something, we must have it: there is literally no alternative of either substitution or abstinence. But the assertion of absolute economic 'need'—in contrast to desire, preference, and demand—is nonsense." See William R. Allen, *Midnight Economist: Broadcast Essays III* (Los Angeles: International Institute for Economic Research, 1982), 23.

44. On the common neglect of the crucial process of peacebuilding, Nordstrom writes: "Global politics has handed down a legacy relegating conflict resolution to the realm of politico-military leaders and to the offices of specialists: in a word, to elites far removed from the epicenters and impact of bloodletting. The fact that implementing peace is a long and complex process is largely lost in this orientation, as is the fact that peace is ultimately forged on the ground." Nordstrom, "The Eye of the Storm," 92. Gray Cox argues that peacebuilding can never be a process imposed from "above" or from "without" but instead must start from an understanding of people's social world as they conceive it. See Cox, *The Ways of Peace: A Philosophy of Peace as Action* (New York: Paulist Press, 1986), 72. He writes that peace "employs *critical participatory research* and *maieutic reasoning* to pursue shared commitments to *expressions, projects* and *practices*" (ibid., 129–130, italics in original). That people—and women in particular—who have been marginalized in colonial and postcolonial periods have unique contributions to make to peacebuilding is thoroughly explicated in Sanam Naraghi Anderlini, *Women Building Peace: What They Do, Why It Matters* (Boulder, CO: Lynne Rienner, 2007).

45. Corinne Kumar, "Supryia and the Reviving of a Dream: Toward a New Political Imaginary," in *Women and the Gift Economy: A Radically Different Worldview Is Possible,* edited by Genevieve Vaughan (Toronto: Inanna Publications, 2007), 305, italics in original.

46. Ramachandra Guha, "The Environmentalism of the Poor," in *Between Resistance and Revolution: Cultural Politics and Social Protest,* edited by Richard G.

Fox and Orin Starn (New Brunswick, NJ: Rutgers, 1997), 28–29. See also Shiva, *Monocultures of the Mind,* 29–38.

47. Peggy Antrobus, "The Gift Economy in the Caribbean: The Gift and the Wind," in *Women and the Gift Economy: A Radically Different Worldview Is Possible,* edited by Genevieve Vaughan (Toronto: Inanna Publications, 2007), 233. These are the kinds of values underpinning cultures of solidarity, and the lack of successful construction of these kinds of cultures was the key reason that social democracies fell prey to the structural constraints imposed by the current design of the global economy. See Richards and Swanger, *The Dilemmas of Social Democracies.*

48. Paola Melchiori, "From Forced Gifts to Free Gifts," in *Women and the Gift Economy: A Radically Different Worldview Is Possible,* edited by Genevieve Vaughan (Toronto: Inanna Publications, 2007), 319. The importance of viewing both older and extant practices with new optics cannot be overstated, for this is how transformative potential can be unlocked. José Luis Coraggio makes the case, for example, that the work of many people who might be considered entrepreneurs or small business owners should actually be viewed more as part of the use-value economy (which he terms the "people's economy") and not as contributions to the logic of exchange. See Coraggio, *La gente o el capital* (Buenos Aires: Espacio Editores, 2004). On the positive transformations of the Argentine economy, see also Howard Richards, *Solidaridad, Participación, Transparencia: Conversaciones sobre el socialismo en Rosario, Argentina* (Rosario: Tinta Roja, 2007).

49. Featherstone, "Genealogies of the Global," 389.

50. Corinne Kumar writes, "We need 'new universalisms,' not ones that 'deny the many and affirm the one,' not universalisms that are born of 'eurocentricities or patriarchalities,' but ones that will give rise to an authentic cultural pluralism by being 'rooted in the particular.'" Kumar, "Supryia and the Reviving of a Dream," 304. On the importance of indigenous epistemes and their relation to the academy, see Rauna Kuokkanen, "The Gift Logic of Indigenous Philosophies in the Academy," in *Women and the Gift Economy: A Radically Different Worldview Is Possible,* edited by Genevieve Vaughan (Toronto: Inanna Publications, 2007), 71–83.

5

Conflict Resolution, Conflict Transformation, and Peacebuilding

PATRICK G. COY

GIVEN THE EXPLOSIVE GROWTH IN THE FIELD OF PEACE AND CONflict studies over the past two decades, addressing the triple topics of conflict resolution, conflict transformation, and peacebuilding in a single chapter is rather difficult. Thus I begin by treating only selected, yet prominent and influential, dimensions of the conflict resolution arena: principled negotiation, problem-solving mediation, and transformative mediation. Contrasting "transformative mediation" with "conflict transformation" in terms of their different understandings of empowerment and change will serve as a segue into a discussion of the broad arena of conflict transformation and the many approaches to peacebuilding it contains. The peacebuilding models of the United Nations will be contrasted with those of nongovernmental organizations (NGOs) and civil society, especially with regard to their differences in scope and goals for change. The twin concepts of change and empowerment will be referenced in various places to help map the intersections and to suggest some of the key differences between conflict resolution, conflict transformation, and peacebuilding.

Scholars and students of peace and conflict studies recognize that to create the conditions for sustainable peace, conflict must be seen as a potentially positive mechanism for social and political change. The early, major theoretical works by two of the field's pioneers—Morton Deutsch and Louis Kriesberg—extended Lewis Coser's argument that social conflicts have some mixture of destructive and constructive dimensions. They showed that understanding any particular social conflict as primarily destructive or primarily constructive depends on a host of variables, only one of which has to do with the ways the conflict is actually waged by the disputing parties.[1] Early attempts to develop an ethics of conflict intervention were in turn built on this understanding that social conflicts and community disputes could be positive forces for change in communities by nurturing what James Laue called "proportional empowerment," redressing power disparities among parties, affecting public policies, and even modifying social and political structures.[2] Our field rests on the premise that conflict is not the problem that needs to be addressed. Instead, linked together and manifested in and through social conflicts are multiple problems going by the names "violence," "injustice," "disrespect," "oppression," and "inequality." Constructive conflict engagement is facilitated by nonviolent struggles, conflict resolution skills, and peacebuilding measures that work together to overcome these destructive forces, thereby revealing the creative potentialities of social conflicts.

Conflict Resolution

At the heart of conflict engagement and its potential resolution is negotiation. Taking place as they do in a range of settings between all sorts of parties and conducted in a plethora of different ways, negotiations may actually be the foundational practice of conflict resolution. When one sets aside the poles of the conflict continuum—acquiescence through avoidance or overt submission on the one end, and victory through competitive or violent engagement on the other—it is difficult to imagine the resolution of a conflict without negotiations playing a noteworthy role. Certainly no model for teaching and practicing negotiation has been more influential than "principled negotiation," or interest-based bargaining.

Negotiation

This problem-solving approach—predicated upon win-win philosophies—is closely associated with the Program on Negotiation at Harvard University. Roger Fisher and William Ury first published this approach in a slim volume entitled *Getting to Yes* in 1981. Packaged and written in an accessible manner, this practical primer has become the field's first and, to date, only national bestseller; it has been translated into thirty-one languages, selling upward of 5 million copies worldwide. Nearly thirty years later, this approach continues to be widely taught (albeit in modified forms, thanks in part to critiques from various quarters) in undergraduate and even graduate peace studies and conflict resolution programs as well as in alternative dispute resolution programs in law schools. Variants of an interest-based approach to negotiations are common in collective bargaining in the public sector.[3] They are also widely practiced in diplomatic circles and form the foundational skill set upon which many facilitators and mediators rely and build. Interest-based bargaining has made a significant impact in the broad arena of public policy disputes generally and also in its intersections with environmental conflicts.[4] This area of practice and its numerous subfields go by many different names, including environmental conflict resolution, public sector dispute resolution, consensus building, collaborative conservation, deliberative democracy, collaborative policymaking, and still others. Consequently, training in public sector dispute resolution tactics is increasingly present in both undergraduate and graduate curricula in peace and conflict studies.

Mediation

Insofar as mediation often provides the medium in which negotiations occur, perhaps the shortest and sweetest definition of mediation is simply "facilitated negotiation." And if negotiation is the foundational practice of conflict resolution, then mediation is its chief assistant. Mediation is increasingly used in interpersonal quarrels between neighbors when they find their way to a community mediation center or when the courts refer them there. It is also often the tactic of choice in environmental policy disputes that have multiple stakeholders, including government agencies that understand that if stakeholders are given a say in policies that affect them, they are more likely to adhere to those policies willingly and to ensure their implementation.[5] Of course, mediation also has a long and storied history in ethnic conflicts on the national level, as it does in international conflicts involving states and nations.[6] There are as many ways to practice mediation as there are contexts within which it has been applied.

Mediation can also be categorized in multiple ways, including by the social position of the mediator vis-à-vis the disputing parties, by the stage of the conflict at which mediation occurs, by the activities of the mediator, and by the mediation model used. Distinctions along these dimensions have led to a number of mediation typologies or categorization schemas, some more useful than others in teaching and training.[7] To provide but one example, the "contingency model" of third-party intervention ties analysis of the particular stage that a conflict is in with what is thought to be the corresponding, appropriate type of mediation attempted.[8]

We can also think of mediation as an important arena in which conflict *resolution* and conflict *transformation* intersect and bleed into each other, thanks in part to the various models of mediation. At one end of the mediation spectrum is the facilitative, or problem-solving, approach to conflict intervention. At the opposite end is transformative mediation. I will treat them in that order.

Problem-solving approaches. Marked by the use of interest-based negotiations, what is known as problem-solving mediation is often driven by the goal of settling the conflict. The dominant approach in the reformist stream of alternative dispute resolution (ADR) in the United States, problem-solving mediation is part of efforts to modify the court system so that it offers a broader spectrum of services.

These reformers speak figuratively of creating "multidoor courthouses." Instead of funneling all disputes through one door leading only to courtrooms with a judge or jury waiting to issue a pronouncement, they envision a legal system in which some disputants might still be assigned to the judge or the jury, whereas others are sent to a hearing room, or to mediation, arbitration, or some hybrid approach. Many lawyers, paralegals, and former judges who mediate within the ADR movement practice and promote the problem-solving approach to mediation.[9] These mediators rely heavily upon caucuses and shuttle diplomacy, work under time constraints imposed by the courts, and are not always shy about pressuring parties to settle. Mediators operating on the far edge of the problem-solving model will also offer evaluative comments and opinions with regard to disputant positions and even interests.

Transformative mediation. At the other end of the continuum is transformative mediation. According to its main proponents, this approach is strongly values-based, concerned as it is with the "growth" and even the "moral" development of the disputants. Transformative mediators are only secondarily interested in attaining formal resolution to the conflict. Here the third party is primarily concerned with disputants experiencing recognition and achieving empowerment. Recognition refers to "the evocation in individuals of acknowledgement and empathy for the situation and problems of others." Empowerment means "the restoration to individuals of a sense of their own value and strength and their own capacity to handle life's problems."[10] Like the peacebuilding aspects of conflict transformation that we will examine later, transformative mediation also embraces change as a key goal. But here the change is focused on internal changes in the disputants and on transformations in their relationships.

The most widespread application and institutionalization of the transformative approach to mediation has occurred within the US Postal Service's REDRESS program (resolve employment disputes, reach equitable solutions swiftly) over the past fourteen years. That experiment is old enough now to have produced empirical data about the effects of transformative mediation on a varied workplace with diverse employee and supervisor pools. To cite but one example, the research by Lisa Bingham and her colleagues is based on over 180,000 exit surveys collected over the first ten years of the program, 1994–2004. They found support for the notion that the systematic application of the transformative mediation model to a wide variety of workplace conflicts in the postal service's REDRESS program has resulted in important shifts in the organizational culture of the postal service.[11] Most agencies and their mediators privilege to varying degrees one or another model in practice, many hybrid approaches exist that combine transformative principles with problem-solving tactics. In fact, hybrid models are probably dominant in the field at this point.

For example, even though community, neighborhood, and individual empowerment approaches have long been integral to community mediation centers in the United States, many centers nonetheless teach and practice a hybrid model of mediation that incorporates aspects of the problem-solving approach with transformative principles.[12] This more community-based stream of the ADR movement is motivated by a desire to help individual citizens take back control of their conflicts from an inequitable court system. The approximately 500 community mediation centers in the United States are driven by the notion that most citizens can usually fashion constructive solutions to their own disputes, independent of the legal system, if they are provided supportive conflict resources. This less reformist and more grassroots wing of the ADR movement grew out of the many social movements of the 1960s–1970s. It administers mediation and other conflict resolution services through neighborhood and community-based institutions that, although parallel to the courts and taking referrals from the courts, strive nonetheless for independence from the legal system.[13] Ongoing training of volunteer community mediators who reflect the diversity of the communities served, modeling constructive conflict behaviors, and neighborhood organizing work are all understood to have additive, "trickle-out" empowerment effects in communities, neighborhoods, workplaces, and families, as indigenous community leadership is empowered and conflict patterns change over time. Equally important, these community-based agencies aim to be exercises in citizen participation and democratic governance.

This approach to mediation is apparently succeeding in building community capacities in some areas and doing less well in others. For example, a recent qualitative and quantitative study of 174 community mediation centers affiliated with the National Association for Community Mediation found that they have created moderate to strong linkages across organizations, established diverse funding sources and referral streams, and created boards of directors that are broadly representative of their respective communities. Community-based mediation agencies have, however, been somewhat less successful with participatory decisionmaking and other means of citizen involvement.[14] In addition, they face strong pressures of co-optation, the mixed "blessing" of many social movements that experience success in achieving some of their goals.[15] Clearly, the goals for conflicts in this approach go beyond relationship changes and internal changes in the disputants.

With regard to the intersection of mediation skills training and curriculum concerns in peace and conflict studies programs, it seems best that we introduce students to the particular philosophies that undergird the various mediation models as well as to the specific tactics and unique techniques used in the respective approaches. Indeed, after teaching and training on the various mediation approaches in my university course and also in community seminars, I frequently use an exercise in which all students/trainees situate themselves and the model of mediation they aspire to practice on a continuum with problem-solving mediation on one end and transformative mediation on the other. When this is complemented by small-group discussions based on questions designed to elicit each student's reasons, hopes, and fears about where they placed themselves on the mediation continuum, the more likely outcome is critically, self-reflective practitioners. And critically self-reflective practitioners—who are also skilled in the full range of conflict resolution tools—are much more likely to select the tool or approach that is most appropriate to a particular conflict and that best resonates with the needs of individual disputants.

Conflict Transformation

Although empowerment and recognition are at the heart of transformative mediation within conflict resolution, the focus there remains primarily short term and is directed at the individual disputants. When we move out of the realm of conflict resolution and transformative mediation into the broader arena of conflict transformation, we focus less on mediation and more on a much wider set of skills and tactics associated with peacebuilding. Here mediation is only one of a host of skills and tactics.[16] In peacebuilding, so closely associated with conflict transformation, empowerment and change are equally prized as conflict outcomes, but the field of view is much wider, theoretically encompassing structural changes beyond the individual disputants. Like the feminist worldview that has influenced it, conflict transformation's field of view is also intended to be far deeper, addressing the root causes of social conflicts as much as possible while recognizing that some conflicts are not resolvable until and unless fundamental arrangements are changed. Over time, the goal is to assist countries, societies, and groups to move from violent and destructive conflicts to peaceful, constructive conflicts through building up local capacities and indigenous conflict skill sets. Thus coordination among different kinds of actors from various levels of society is vital. In addition, conflict transformation's temporal dimension extends further into the future, thereby accommodating the long-term developments that are generally necessary to accomplish broad-based social and structural changes. Many of the principles and insights that lie at the heart of conflict transformation are linked to and in some cases owe their influence to the important work of feminists long active in the field of peace and conflict studies.[17]

Peacebuilding

Johan Galtung originally popularized the term "peacebuilding," distinguishing it from peacekeeping and peacemaking. As he uses it, peacebuilding is geared toward moving a society recently experiencing violent conflict in the direction of "positive peace." Positive peace is contrasted with negative peace, with the latter referring simply to ending violent conflict. The peace sought after via peacebuilding, meanwhile, is much broader and more inclusive. It encompasses ending direct violence, structural violence, and cultural violence, the last of which makes the first two forms of violence feel acceptable, even normal, and allows them to go largely unchallenged. Finally, positive peace refers to putting in place, through creative approaches to conflict transformation, those structures and cultural practices that will assist all members of a society in reaching their full human potential.[18]

Many others have further developed the theory and practice of peacebuilding within a conflict transformation framework, so much so that it has become an immense field, multifaceted and somewhat unwieldy. On the one hand, it is a welcome development, evidence of the robust nature of peacebuilding ventures across the globe. On the other hand, it may easily occasion conceptual confusion about how to treat the field analytically or even how to describe its historical development.[19] For purposes of brevity, I will divide the peacebuilding landscape into two: (1) operations mounted by the United Nations, (2) followed by work based primarily in domestic and or international nongovernmental organizations, even while recognizing there is considerable overlap. Nonetheless, it remains true that UN peacebuilding efforts are increasingly focused on state building and concomitant strengthening of state-based institutions. This is a function, in part, of the dawning recognition that for even a fragile and truncated version of peace to endure for very long following the withdrawal of international peacekeepers, there must be a "threshold of nationally recognized, sufficiently effective and broadly legitimate institutions" in place.[20] Of course, in conflict and postconflict scenarios, the issue of institutional legitimacy remains problematic and is often highly contested by grassroots groups and movements working for systemic changes in political and economic systems. In contrast, NGO and civil society endeavors have focused less on state building or on establishing and strengthening institutions per se and more on creating what John Paul Lederach calls "smart flexible social platforms" from which local people may engage in cultural practices that will facilitate the desired long-term changes in society.[21] In short, NGO-based peacebuilding concentrates on deepening productive relations among ethnic groups and on improving civil society capacities across a fuller spectrum of social sectors than is typical of UN-based ventures.

The dissolution of the Soviet Union and the end of the Cold War in the late 1980s resulted in an increase in ethnic conflicts and civil wars associated with a host of political transitions. These developments moved the United Nations into the peacebuilding field in a major way.

In his 1992 report "An Agenda for Peace," delivered to the UN Security Council, then Secretary-General Boutros Boutros-Ghali identified creating, strengthening, and maintaining social and political structures to support sustainable approaches to peace as defining dimensions of the United Nations' "post-conflict peacebuilding." In the intervening years—and partly in response to certain shortcomings of UN missions—some UN operations have paid increasing attention to the complex of mechanisms associated with transitional justice themes (healing, reconciliation, accountability) and strengthening political, legal, and educational systems that support human rights awareness and nurture cultures of peace. Equally important in the development of UN peacebuilding is the effort to seek greater integration with civil society and the companion peacebuilding efforts of NGOs.

As part of a broad-based reform effort at the United Nations in 2005, former Secretary-General Kofi Annan proposed the establishment of a United Nations Peace Building Commission. It was set up in December 2005, commencing its work in the summer of 2006.[22] There are some empirical data to suggest that UN peacebuilding operations have been particularly effective on selected (relatively narrow, short-term) measures associated with such issues as preventing a return to large-scale violence and establishing minimal levels of political participation. Non-UN operations, however, often have more robust social and cultural goals with longer time frames.[23] I provide an overview of major trends within the NGO community in what follows.

The goals of most civil society peacebuilding efforts include the long-range aspects of conflict transformation, which often require that conflicts become worse before they get better. In the early 1970s—when the field of peace and conflict studies was still quite young—British Quaker and mediator Adam Curle emphasized that moving to negotiation and mediation too early in a social conflict disadvantages lower-power groups whose challenges to the status quo are driven in part by structural violence and embedded injustices. If these social conflicts are "resolved" prematurely, power disparities and injustices are frozen in place, and the peace achieved is partial, uneasy, and unsustainable. Consequently, the broader goals of conflict transformation also remain beyond reach. Curle developed an extremely useful peacemaking matrix (now liberally adapted and improved upon by many others) that charts the dynamic relationships between consciousness raising and training, which lead to nonviolent confrontation. Resulting power shifts among the parties subsequently lead to negotiation and mediation, and eventually create various degrees of sustainable peace.[24]

Waging and even escalating social conflicts through coercive nonviolent action—to expose injustices, raise costs for oppressors, mobilize oppressed constituencies, and appeal to institutional allies—is an important dimension of conflict transformation that contributes to a just and sustainable peace. Martin Luther King Jr. equated nonviolent action with what he called "creative tension." Here the activist intentionally escalates the conflict and even provokes violent responses as a temporary step on the long and winding path to what we now call conflict transformation.[25] Thus comprehensive curricula in peace and conflict studies programs must include not only training in the conflict resolution skills of negotiation, mediation, facilitation, strategic planning, and consultation, but in organizing strategies and in nonviolent action tactics as well. Diana Francis has argued usefully that conflict transformation includes all the tactics, skills, and roles associated with conflict resolution, aided by well-timed, strategic nonviolent actions (i.e., actions based on sound comparative-power analyses and appropriately geared to the stages of a social conflict).[26]

Thanks in part to the complexities inherent in contemporary conflicts occurring within globalized economies, the intervention of "neutral" or "objective" outsiders as prominent third parties has been markedly deemphasized within the peacebuilding work of civil society groups. In its place the training and building up of local capacities for conflict resolution and transformation are privileged. These approaches are often marked by a commitment to understanding and empowering indigenous approaches to conflict resolution, as opposed to delivering prepackaged models that are unlikely to be sensitive to context, culture, timing, and the diversity of local conflict actors. Lederach's contrast between prescriptive and "elicitive" pedagogies crystallizes these differences and has been particularly influential in international peacebuilding scenarios, even if the peace and conflict studies community has not always been as successful in applying this approach in our own classrooms.[27]

In the elicitive model of peacebuilding, the intervener is more of an animator and less of a classic resource provider. Since uncovering and empowering domestic capacities for conflict transformation is the norm, local peacebuilding efforts may ripple across and up and down the social spectrum, transforming relationships in the short term and even social structures and cultural practices in the long run. These approaches include drawing on the practical and symbolic resources and skills of women and local minorities and the cultures of constructive conflict resolution and peacemaking with which they are associated and have long nurtured, even if in obscure and unrecognized ways.[28] With empowerment and animation the guiding rule, the intervener endeavors to develop cooperative, collegial working partnerships in those social sectors where the work is most likely to have broad impact. These working relations are modified, in turn, by the third party being honest and clear about what her or his "value-added" is, in other words, what she or he brings to the peacebuilding toolbox that is distinct from yet complementary to what is already present and available within the local community.[29] In this regard, Lederach's peacebuilding pyramid has been particularly influential, much reproduced in a wide range of publications and frequently applied in various settings.

Using various levels of leadership within the local population as the frame through which to view peacebuilding efforts, he placed the affected population on a pyramid. The pyramid is divided into three primary levels: "top leadership" (i.e., military, political, and religious leaders with particularly high visibility) sits in the upper third of the pyramid; "middle-range leadership" that is respected across an entire social sector (i.e., academics, intellectuals, NGO officers, and religious and ethnic leaders) occupies the middle section of the pyramid; and "grassroots leadership" (i.e., local leaders, indigenous NGO officers, local health officials, refugee camp leaders, etc.) occupies the broad bottom or base of the pyramid. In this model, particular peacebuilding tactics are tied to the types of local actors or leaders who would be undertaking the activities. The peacebuilding work of upper-level leaders is characterized as a "top-down" model, that of lower-level leaders is termed "bottom-up peacebuilding," and the peacebuilding work carried on by the middle-level leaders was originally labeled, somewhat clumsily, "middle-out."

The model emphasizes peacebuilding work that is attuned to issues of "vertical capacity," in other words, enhancing the ability of local leaders from various sectors of the triangle to create social and political spaces where they can link up in their work. It also focuses on peacebuilding's "horizontal capacity," that is, nurturing personal relationships and collegial networks that take advantage of cross-cutting identities, whether ethnic, religious, geographic, or linguistic. This focus on vertical and horizontal capacities has the effect of emphasizing social spaces, or occurrences of integration, where the horizontal and vertical connections intersect. This, in turn, privileges the peacebuilding efforts of middle-level leaders, given their social positions at multiple "intersections." Thus, Lederach has more recently emphasized that the activities of those in the middle third of the triangle are better thought of as "web-based" peacebuilding, where strands intersect to provide overall strength to the web of peaceful relations.[30]

There are a variety of other useful peacebuilding models on the conflict transformation landscape. Lisa Schirch's "map of peacebuilding" consists of four categories, each of which highlights specific tasks.[31] The first category, "waging conflict nonviolently," includes a variety of nonviolent direct action tactics to escalate conflicts constructively, whereas the "reducing direct violence" category includes creating more safe political spaces and protecting local activists through nonviolent protective accompaniment, humanitarian programs, cease-fires, early warning measures, stronger legal systems, and zones of peace.[32] The third category, "building capacity," includes training, reconstruction efforts that incorporate a host of economic and political development projects, and ongoing research and evaluation regarding community needs. The fourth category, "transforming relationships," includes rituals to heal trauma, restorative justice measures, and a host of transitional justice mechanisms. When the four categories are considered together and put into a larger framework tied to the stages of the conflict and tempered by both the short-term and the long-range goals of the local communities, a holistic model of peacebuilding linked to the transformation of social conflicts emerges.

Cases of international peacebuilding have accumulated since the mid-1990s. As this chapter suggests, scholars in peace studies are gradually learning more about what works in some situations and what does not work in others. The dominant civil society approach from the margins or from the bottom up is far from a cure-all; it comes with its own set of considerable dangers. Some of them include losing sight of the long-range nature of sustainable peacebuilding and attempting to do too much too soon with too many parties. Conflict transformation comes neither quickly nor easily; it is a long hard slog that must be led by those most affected by the conditions giving rise to the conflicts. A related danger in civil society peacebuilding is a lack of cooperation and integration with other actors, international and domestic, already on the scene. When cooperative and knowledge-sharing practices are missing, capacity is reduced, and local needs may be sacrificed.[33]

In addition, the possibility of further reinforcing local inequalities that run along gender, class, or ethnic lines is ever present and usually magnified as an outcome of the violent conflict that societies have just experienced. International workers have spending habits that may radically tip the local economic scales, altering housing patterns and local economies in deleterious ways. Equally problematic are the ways in which peacebuilding efforts done in partnership with civil society groups can be co-opted by the locally powerful so that the work ends up unwittingly blunting conflict escalations that might otherwise challenge an inequitable status quo. Co-optation dangers are the bugaboo of social movements worldwide.[34] To put all of this just a bit more plainly, we are learning that good intentions—and sometimes even good practices—frequently are not enough to guarantee that we live up to the always honorable "do no harm" maxim, which is at the heart of humanitarian aid ventures and ought to be heeded by peacebuilding programs as well.[35] Finally, novel and robust challenges from below, like the World

Social Forum process and associated movements that aim to change political and economic systems, are already redefining how politics get done and how conflicts can be waged constructively within a globalized economy and an integrated state system. Following the lead of these movements and organizing challenges to structured injustices from within our own neighborhoods, communities, and regions is also a constitutive dimension of conflict transformation, properly understood.[36]

Cautious Optimism

It has always seemed to me that most approaches to conflict resolution and transformation that have defined our field (only some of which have been profiled here) share in common a certain clear-eyed yet warm-hearted optimism about humankind. I say that our optimism is clear-eyed because those of us who teach, train, and work in the conflict field know as well as anyone the many destructive costs associated with making poor conflict choices. We know that people have and will continue to wage conflicts destructively when they perceive that they have few other viable options. We have seen as much not just through game theory but in the living laboratories that comprise our work in a variety of field settings with real-life disputants. People in conflict desire change, and they often need empowerment—broadly conceived—to recognize viable options to bring about those changes. In a certain way, the peace and conflict studies field is defined by the work of helping disputants discover other conflict options—more constructive and less destructive ones. Similarly, our warm-hearted optimism is also born of both theory and experience in the field. We know if people recognize that more constructive conflict tactics may meet their needs, they will often choose those routes, provided they have the means and the skills to use those tactics. And so our work of constructive conflict engagement, rooted in empowerment to bring about change, continues—in the classroom, in the training seminar, at the community meeting, around the mediation table, and in innumerable other settings. As we learn how best to walk alongside people engaged in conflict and change efforts, we must also learn to follow as well.

Notes

1. Morton Deutsch, *The Resolution of Conflict: Constructive and Destructive Processes* (New Haven, CT: Yale University Press, 1973); Louis Kriesberg, *The Sociology of Social Conflicts* (Englewood Cliffs, NJ: Prentice Hall, 1973); Lewis Coser, *The Functions of Social Conflict* (New York: Free Press, 1956).

2. James Laue and Gerald Cormick, "The Ethics of Intervention in Community Disputes," in *The Ethics of Social Intervention,* edited by Gorden Bermant, Herbert Kelman, and Donald Warwick (New York: Halsted Press, 1978), 205–232.

3. Renaud Paquet, Isabelle Gaétan, and Jean-Guy Bergeron, "Does Interest-Based Bargaining (IBB) Really Make a Difference in Collective Bargaining Outcomes?" *Negotiation Journal* 16, no. 3 (2000): 281–296.

4. Kirk Emerson, Tina Nabatchi, Rosemary O'Leary, and John Stephens, "The Challenges of Environmental Conflict Resolution," in *The Promise and Performance of Environmental Conflict Resolution*, edited by Rosemary O'Leary and Lisa B. Bingham (Washington, DC: Resources for the Future, 2003), 3–26.

5. For a profile of community mediation in the United States, see the many useful articles in the special issue of *Mediation Quarterly* devoted to evaluating community mediation's progress after twenty-five years: *Mediation Quarterly* 17, no. 4 (2000). Also see the website for the National Association for Community Mediation, http://www.nafcm.org/. On the practice of mediation in environmental conflict resolution, see Rosemary O'Leary and Lisa Bingham, *The Promise and Performance of Environmental Conflict Resolution* (Washington, DC: Resources for the Future, 2003); and Lawrence Susskind, Sarah McKearnan, and Jennifer Thomas-Larmer, *The Consensus Building Handbook: A Comprehensive Guide to Reaching Agreement* (Thousand Oaks, CA: Sage, 1999).

6. Multiple case studies of mediation in ethnic conflicts can be found in the following three collections: John Paul Lederach and Janice Moomaw Jenner, eds., *A Handbook of International Peacebuilding: Into the Eye of the Storm*, 1st ed. (San Francisco: Jossey-Bass, 2002); Luc Reychler and Thania Paffenholz, eds., *Peacebuilding: A Guide* (Boulder, CO: Lynne Rienner, 2001); Chester A. Crocker, Fen Osler Hampson, and Pamela R. Aall, *Herding Cats: Multiparty Mediation in a Complex World* (Washington, DC: United States Institute of Peace Press, 1999). Many ethnic conflicts become internationalized. An analysis of mediation in 869 of these instances found that a directive style of mediation increased the probability of successful conflict management than did less directive approaches. See Jacob Bercovitch and Karl Derouen Jr., "Mediation in Internationalized Ethnic Conflicts: Assessing the Determinants of a Successful Process," *Armed Forces and Society* 30, no. 2 (2004): 147–170. And for an overview of the practices of mediation in international conflicts more generally, see Saadia Touval and I. William Zartman, "International Mediation in the Post–Cold War Era," in *Turbulent Peace: The Challenges of Managing International Conflict*, edited by Chester Crocker, Fen Osler Hampson, and Pamela Aall (Washington, DC: US Institute of Peace, 2001), 427–444.

7. Useful categorization schemas covering the horizon of mediation-related third party roles include these three: Louis Kriesberg, "Varieties of Mediating Activities and Mediators in International Relations," in *Resolving International Conflicts: The Theory and Practice of Mediation*, edited by Jacob Bercovitch (Boulder, CO: Lynne Rienner, 1996), 219–233; Christopher Mitchell, "The Process and Stages of Mediation: The Sudanese Cases," in *Making War and Waging Peace*, edited by David R. Smock (Washington, DC: US Institute of Peace Press, 1993), 139–159; and William Ury, *The Third Side: Why We Fight and How We Can Stop*, updated and expanded, revised edition (New York: Penguin Books, 2000), 251.

8. For the original articulation of the contingency approach, see Ronald Fisher and L. Keashly, "The Potential Complementarity of Mediation and Consultation Within a Contingency of Third Party Consultation," *Journal of Peace Research* 28, no. 1 (1991): 29–42. A recent assessment of its utility as applied in the field is included in Ronald J. Fisher, "Assessing the Contingency Model of Third-Party Intervention in Successful Cases of Prenegotiation," *Journal of Peace Research* 44, no. 3 (2007): 311.

9. For an example of a popular training manual based on the problem-solving model of mediation, see Mark D. Bennett and Scott H. Hughes, *The Art of Mediation*, 2nd ed. (Notre Dame, IN: National Institute for Trial Advocacy, 2005).

10. Certainly the single most influential publication on transformative mediation is Robert A. Baruch Bush and Joseph P. Folger, *The Promise of Mediation: Responding to Conflict Through Empowerment and Recognition* (San Francisco: Jossey-Bass, 1994). The quotations on recognition and empowerment are from p. 2.

11. For a helpful review of the outcomes of transformative mediation in the United States Postal Service, see Lisa B. Bingham, "Employment Dispute Resolution: The Case for Mediation," *Conflict Resolution Quarterly* 22, nos. 1–2 (2004): 145–174.

12. An excellent mediation training manual that falls between the two poles of the continuum (but still sits closer to the problem-solving end) is Jennifer E. Beer and Eileen Stief, *The Mediator's Handbook,* 3rd ed. (Gabriola Island, BC: New Society Publishers, 1997).

13. For a critical analysis of how the complicated relationship between the court system and community mediation in the United States has evolved, see Timothy Hedeen and Patrick G. Coy, "Community Mediation and the Court System: The Ties That Bind," *Mediation Quarterly* 17, no. 4 (2000): 351–367.

14. Beth Gazley, Won Kyung Chang, and Lisa Blomgren Bingham, "Collaboration and Citizen Participation in Community Mediation Centers," *Review of Policy Research* 23, no. 4 (2006): 843–863. For two other useful evaluations of the community mediation approach, see Timothy Hedeen, "The Evolution and Evaluation of Community Mediation: Limited Research Suggests Unlimited Progress," *Conflict Resolution Quarterly* 22, no. 1 (2004): 101–133; and Daniel McGillis, *Community Mediation Programs: Developments and Challenges* (Washington, DC: National Institute of Justice, 1997).

15. For an overall model of the co-optation pressures facing social movements that includes multiple stages and steps, using community mediation's relationship with the legal system as an example, see Patrick G. Coy and Timothy Hedeen, "A Stage Model of Social Movement Cooptation: Community Mediation in the United States," *Sociological Quarterly* 46, no. 2 (2005).

16. Lisa Schirch's model of strategic peacebuilding is perhaps an extreme example insofar as she subsumes nearly the whole arena of conflict work (from early warning to education, from environmental protection to military intervention, and about a dozen more areas of practice) under the nexus of peacebuilding. See Schirch, "Linking Human Rights and Conflict Information: A Peacebuilding Framework," in *Human Rights and Conflict: Exploring the Links Between Rights, Law, and Peacebuilding,* edited by Julie Mertus and Jeffrey W. Helsing (Washington, DC: US Institute of Peace Press, 2006), 63–95. Also see Schirch, *The Little Book of Strategic Peacebuilding* (Intercourse, PA: Good Books, 2004).

17. For a useful distilling of seven main feminist contributions to peace and conflict studies, see Moolakkattu Stephen John, "Feminism and Peace Studies: Taking Stock of a Quarter Century of Efforts," *Indian Journal of Gender Studies* 13, no. 2 (2006): 137–162. For a summary of feminist contributions to nonviolent action theory, see Lynne M. Woehrle, "Feminist Debates About Nonviolence," in *Nonviolence: Social and Psychological Issues,* edited by V. K. Kool (Lanham, MD: University Press of America, 1993), 207–220.

18. Johan Galtung, "Three Approaches to Peace: Peacekeeping, Peacemaking, and Peacebuilding," in *Peace, War, and Defence: Essays in Peace Research* (Copenhagen: Christian Ejlers, 1975), 282–304. Also see two later books among Galtung's voluminous writings that build upon and expand this early typology: Galtung, *Peace by Peaceful Means: Peace and Conflict, Development and Civilization* (London: Sage, 1996); and Galtung, *Transcend and Transform: An Introduction to Conflict Work* (London and Sterling, VA: Pluto Press in association with Transcend, 2004).

19. For a useful analysis of the current peacebuilding work of twenty-four selected governmental and intergovernmental bodies and an attempt to chart what the authors see as an ill-defined range of activities and nomenclatures, see Michael Barnett, Hunjoon Kim, Madalene O'Donnell, and Laura Sitea, "Peacebuilding: What Is in a Name?" *Global Governance* 13, no. 1 (2007): 35–58.

20. Charles T. Call and Elizabeth M. Cousens, "Ending Wars and Building Peace: International Responses to War-Torn Societies," *International Studies Perspectives* 9, no. 1 (2008): 9.

21. John Paul Lederach, *The Moral Imagination: The Art and Soul of Building Peace* (New York: Oxford University Press, 2005), 126–129.

22. For a basic introduction to the UN Peacebuilding Commission, see this article: United Nations, "The UN Peacebuilding Commission: Questions and Answers," *UN Chronicle* 43, no. 1 (2006): 12–13.

23. Michael W. Doyle and Nicholas Sambanis, *Making War and Building Peace: United Nations Peace Operations* (Princeton, NJ: Princeton University Press, 2006). This and other recent publications evaluating peacekeeping operations are reviewed in Call and Cousens, "Ending Wars and Building Peace," 1–21.

24. Adam Curle, *Making Peace* (London: Tavistock Publications, 1971). Curle recognizes, of course, that the relationships between the various tactics is not purely linear insofar as backtracking and skips occur in the "progression" of a particular social conflict. I continue to find the Curle matrix helpful in teaching students how to do conflict analysis in my Introduction to Conflict Management and my Nonviolence: Theory and Practice courses at Kent State. Among the many useful adaptations of the Curle matrix are those in the following works: Paui Wehr, *Conflict Regulation* (Boulder, CO: Westview Press, 1979); John Paul Lederach, *Building Peace: Sustainable Reconciliation in Divided Societies* (Washington, DC: US Institute of Peace Press, 1997); Simon Fisher, ed., *Working with Conflict: Skills and Strategies for Action* (London: Zed Books, 2000); Diana Francis, *People, Peace, and Power: Conflict Transformation in Action* (London: Pluto Press, 2002); Schirch, *The Little Book of Strategic Peacebuilding;* and Oliver Ramsbotham, Tom Woodhouse, and Hugh Miall, *Contemporary Conflict Resolution: The Prevention, Management, and Transformation of Deadly Conflicts,* 2nd ed. (Cambridge: Polity, 2005).

25. See especially the letter King wrote from the Birmingham jail to white clergymen in response to their entreaties to him to be more patient and to engage in less provocative forms of protest: Martin Luther King Jr., "Letter from Birmingham City Jail," in *Nonviolence in America: A Documentary History,* edited by Staughton Lynd and Alice Lynd (Maryknoll, NY: Orbis, 1995), 254–267.

26. Francis, *People, Peace, and Power,* 264. See especially Chapter 2, "Theory for Conflict Transformation."

27. John Paul Lederach, *Preparing for Peace: Conflict Transformation Across Cultures* (Syracuse, NY: Syracuse University Press, 1995). Two examples of efforts to apply an elicitive pedagogy to conflict resolution education in the context of a US peace and conflict studies degree program include Timothy Hedeen, "Dialogue and Democracy, Community and Capacity: Lessons for Conflict Resolution Education from Dewey, Montessori, and Freire," *Conflict Resolution Quarterly* 23, no. 2 (2005): 185–202; and Hedeen, "The Reverse Jigsaw: A Process of Cooperative Learning and Discussion," *Teaching Sociology* 31, no. 3 (2003): 325–332.

28. For contrasts between peacebuilding efforts based in the United Nations, other international governmental organizations, or major powers, and civil society–based "peacebuilding from below" approaches, see the excellent comparative analyses in chaps. 8 and 9, respectively, in Ramsbotham, Woodhouse, and Miall, *Contemporary Conflict Resolution.*

29. John Paul Lederach, "Where Do I Fit In?" in *A Handbook of International Peacebuilding: Into the Eye of the Storm*, edited by John Paul Lederach and Janice Moomaw Jenner (San Francisco: Jossey-Bass, 2002), 37–48.

30. Lederach, *Preparing for Peace*, 37–55; and Lederach, *Moral Imagination*, 78–86.

31. Schirch, *The Little Book of Strategic Peacebuilding*.

32. On accompaniment, see Patrick G. Coy, "Protective Accompaniment: How Peace Brigades International Secures Political Space and Human Rights Nonviolently," in *Nonviolence: Social and Psychological Issues*, edited by V. K. Kool (Lanham, MD: University Press of America, 1993), 235–244; Coy, "Negotiating Danger and Safety Under the Gun: Consensus Decision Making on Peace Brigades International Teams," in *Consensus Decision Making, Northern Ireland, and Indigenous Movements*, Research in Social Movements, Conflicts and Change, Vol. 24 (Oxford: Elsevier Science and JAI Press, 2003), 85–122; and Liam Mahony and Luis E. Eguren, *Unarmed Bodyguards: International Accompaniment for the Protection of Human Rights* (Bloomfield, CT: Kumarian Press, 1997). On zones of peace, see Landon E. Hancock and Christopher R. Mitchell, *Zones of Peace* (Bloomfield, CT: Kumarian Press, 2007).

33. For both positive and negative examples of these peacebuilding problems on the ground with Peace Brigades International in the context of Sri Lanka's ethnic conflict, see Patrick G. Coy, "Cooperative Accompaniment by Peace Brigades International in Sri Lanka," in *Transnational Social Movements and Global Politics: Solidarity Beyond the State*, edited by Jackie Smith, Charles Chatfield, and Ron Pagnucco (Syracuse, NY: Syracuse University Press, 1997), 81–100; and Patrick G. Coy, "Shared Risks and Research Dilemmas on a Peace Brigades International Team in Sri Lanka," *Journal of Contemporary Ethnography* 30, no. 5 (2001): 575–606.

34. Coy and Hedeen, *A Stage Model of Social Movement Cooptation*.

35. Mary B. Anderson, *Do No Harm: How Aid Can Support Peace—or War* (Boulder, CO: Lynne Rienner, 1999).

36. For an excellent interpretation of the significance of grassroots movements for social, political, and economic change, including the World Social Forum process and associated movements, see Jackie Smith, *Social Movements for Global Democracy* (Baltimore: Johns Hopkins University Press, 2008). Also see Joe Bandy and Jackie Smith, *Coalitions Across Borders: Transnational Protest and the Neoliberal Order* (Lanham, MD: Rowman and Littlefield, 2005).

6
The Relation of Peace Studies to Nonviolence

BARRY GAN

PEACE STUDIES AND NONVIOLENCE EDUCATION EMERGED IN ACADEMIA during the latter half of the twentieth century, at a time when political realism dominated national and international landscapes. The twenty-first century has seen the rise of neoconservatism, what Charles Krauthammer has called "democratic realism" and what others see as a rebirth of Wilsonianism—making the world safe for democracy. Robert M. Gates, US secretary of defense, acknowledged these different strains of current US policy in a speech at the World Forum on the Future of Democracy, saying that "once again [people are] talking about the competing impulses in US foreign policy: realism versus idealism, freedom versus security, values versus interests."[1] These competing concerns—but especially fear about terrorism coupled with a sense of retributive justice—have divided not only much of the Western world but also peace educators and nonviolent activists. Nonetheless, it is clear that no matter what terms one gives to domestic and foreign policies, no matter which of these impulses is championed by academics or activists, politicians or pundits, whether people pursue idealism or realism, national security or worldwide democracy, they are all in one way or another mired in the attitude that the end justifies the means, an attitude that will remain both morally and politically bankrupt until such time as people, policies, and programs embrace the concept of principled nonviolence, if not principled nonviolence itself.

Political Realism, Idealism, and Neoconservatism

Political realism is the view that the chief role of the state is to secure its own power and interests and that, consequently, either (1) morality cannot meaningfully be applied to domestic or foreign policy formulation, or (2) morality should not be a consideration in domestic or foreign policy formulation, or (3) if it is a consideration, it is never an overriding consideration.[2] In short, it is, among other things, the view that national security or interest trumps morality in foreign and domestic policy. Political realism finds its clearest expression in Niccolò Machiavelli's *The Prince,* but it found new life in the twentieth century as a reaction against Woodrow Wilson's alleged efforts to inject morality into international relations, as a response to his alleged failures in this arena. Political realism maintains that nations that concern themselves with advancing moral causes are ineffective and sometimes even foolhardy in the international and domestic arenas, which are, political realists maintain, Hobbesian states of nature. The proper concern of nation-states is, simply, to ensure the security of the state for the well-being of its citizens, preferably peacefully but, if necessary, by military force.

Political idealism, however, is the view that a nation should be concerned both with securing its own values for its citizens and also with promoting those values around the world. "Making the world safe for democracy" was the slogan that captured Woodrow Wilson's foreign policy, and that concern brought a reluctant US citizenry into World War I. Although Wilson's program called for bringing about such changes worldwide through diplomacy and peaceful means, he became one of the most militarily interventionist presidents in US history.

Neoconservatism, as expressed in the *Project for the New American Century,* is "dedicated to a few fundamental propositions: that American leadership is good both for America and for the world; and that such leadership requires military strength, diplomatic energy and commitment to moral principle."[3] It amounts to a blueprint for US world dominance in the twenty-first century. The architects of this project are some of the major advisers to George W. Bush's administration: Elliot Abrams, Jeb Bush, Dick Cheney, Norman Podhoretz, Donald Rumsfeld, and Paul Wolfowitz, to name a few.

Nonetheless, many reasons exist to doubt that George W. Bush's foreign policy is genuinely neoconservative. Indeed, one current debate among contemporary political scientists is whether Bush is a realist, an idealist, or a neoconservative. Certainly many of those who have peopled his administration are neoconservatives, people who, like Wilson, believe that the United States has values worthy of promotion abroad, either because they are better values than others or because the promotion of those values will provide more security for the United States itself.

But one of the reasons that political scientists disagree about the nature of Bush's foreign policy is that his policy seems to rest on multiple justifications. The war in Iraq was initially a war that looked like it was being waged by realists, those who would secure the world from Iraq's weapons of mass destruction when, supposedly arguably, diplomacy had failed. But when it was "discovered" that there were no weapons of mass destruction, as if weapons inspectors hadn't been saying so previously, then the weight of the justification shifted to the need to depose Saddam Hussein and undertake "nation building," an activity that George W. Bush had ridiculed in his first campaign for the presidency. Nation building by deposing dictators and urging the creation of a constitution sounds a lot like "making the world safe for democracy," and so Bush's foreign policy took on a Wilsonian tone. Indeed, the neoconservatives in the Bush administration, and those on the fringes of his administration do appear very much to be a cross between political realists and Wilsonian idealists.

Many would argue, and have argued, that the neoconservative agenda is not about democracy at all, that it is a smokescreen for making the world safe for multinational corporations, or a smokescreen for a few powerful individuals to make money and create conditions under which they can continue to do so. Many would argue that neoconservatives toss about the terms "democracy" and "capitalism" as if they were synonymous.

Regardless of how one classifies the Bush administration, however, history already makes it abundantly clear that both Wilsonianism *and* neoconservatism have led to numerous military interventions. These interventions have negatively affected far more noncombatants than combatants, and they are a direct consequence of the implicit (and sometimes explicit) view, common not only to Wilsonianism and neoconservatism but also to political realism, that the end justifies the means, whatever means are necessary for whatever ends these political philosophies put forward.

This view is quite apparent in recent US and British doctrines. The March 2006 White House National Security Strategy report claims: "If necessary, however, under long-standing principles of self defense, we do not rule out the use of force before attacks occur, even if uncertainty remains as to the time and place of the enemy's attack."[4] Britain has joined with the United States in such use of force, most notably in Iraq. Israel, too, has seen fit to attack other nations without having been attacked, ostensibly in the name of self-defense. This was Israel's rationale, for example, when it attacked and destroyed the Osiraq nuclear reactor, under construction in Iraq in 1981.

In fact, there is nothing "long-standing" about such a principle of self-defense. No consensus exists in international law about applying the principle in such a manner. The United States and Israel both have been condemned by international bodies for their use of preemptive force as clear violations of the UN Charter. Article 51 of the UN Charter explicitly states: "Nothing in the present Charter shall impair the inherent right of individual or collective self-defense if an armed attack occurs against a Member of the United Nations."[5] Nonetheless, the United States, regarding itself as the world's only superpower, has pursued its interests at the point of a sword regularly since World War II whenever it has seen fit—even though no nation has initiated hostilities against the United States since December 7, 1941. This has been true whether the dominant philosophy has been political realism or, more recently, neoconservatism. Furthermore, neoconservatives regard the readiness and willingness to use military force in preemptive strikes as a right, not as a violation of international law.

The view that the end justifies the means, common to realism, Wilsonianism, and neoconservatism, also has frightening domestic consequences. Because these philosophies assert the primacy of national security or interests, even the rights of individual citizens in democratic nations can be denied or ignored if they are deemed to be secondary to national interest. The infamous Patriot Act, still very much in force in the United States, allows wiretaps without court orders, secretly breaking and entering homes without warrants, indefinite detention of US citizens with no right of habeas corpus, all in the name of national security. Democrats and Republicans, realists and neoconservatives alike, perhaps even a few who would think of themselves as modern-day Wilsonians, have approved and reauthorized this act.

In Britain, the recently passed Civil Contingencies Act adopts a similar posture. Statewatch is an organization that monitors state and civil liberties in Europe. Before the Civil Contingencies Act became law, Tony Bunyan, the editor of Statewatch's journal, said:

> The limited concessions made by the government in no way change the fundamental objections to this bill. . . . The powers available to the government and state agencies would be truly draconian. Cities could be sealed off, travel bans introduced, all phones cut off, and websites shut down. Demonstrations could be banned and the news media be made subject to censorship. New offences against the state could be "created" by government decree. . . . This is Britain's Patriot Act. At a stroke democracy could be replaced by totalitarianism.[6]

In short, the view that the end justifies the means is alive and well in the twenty-first century. Not only is it applied in international relations in violation of international law, but more significantly, it is being used to justify suppression of civil liberties in the very countries that enshrine these liberties in their laws. For such reasons the political philosophies that justify means on the basis of their ends—political realism, Wilsonianism, and neoconservatism—are dangerous political doctrines because in the final analysis they place the power and interest of the state above the rights of those citizens who have entrusted it with their well-being.

Nonviolence of the Weak

The nonviolence of the weak is nonviolence that is practiced by those who do not have the means to practice violence effectively but would do so if they could and if they thought it would be effective. This attitude is present in political behavior everywhere. One finds it in dictators like Ferdinand Marcos, who ascended to the presidency of the Philippines by the power of the ballot and then maintained his position through the power of the bullet. One finds it in the behavior of US president George Bush, who campaigned for his first term in office on a promise of working together with Congress and then proceeded to trample on the minority party Democrats. Mohandas Gandhi called this sort of nonviolence the "nonviolence of the weak." He believed it akin to cowardice.[7]

Gene Sharp, the major contemporary theorist of nonviolent political action, is critical of Gandhi's use of the term "nonviolence of the weak." He would like to distinguish cowardice from expedient nonviolence. Sharp says: "If people in a difficult situation have felt helpless, and then attempt to act by resorting to nonviolent action, is not the earlier condition of helplessness changed?"[8] Sharp continues by pointing out Gandhi's own admission that the militarily weak and the helpless become stronger through the use of nonviolence as a technique.[9] A few pages later Sharp clinches his argument:

> Since Gandhi affirmed the possibility of practitioners of expedient nonviolent action maintaining the recommended attitudes and emotions toward members of the opponent group, and also on another occasion identified the "nonviolence of the weak" as "non-violence of the mere body without the cooperation of the mind," even the view that all expedient nonviolent action falls within his classification of the "nonviolence of the weak" is cast into doubt.[10]

Pragmatic or Expedient Nonviolence

It thus makes sense to distinguish cowardice from what Sharp has called expedient nonviolence and others have called pragmatic nonviolence, from nonviolence as an active technique or policy, from nonviolence practiced because it is believed to be, in general, more effective and less destructive than violence. As a political philosophy this position has been articulated best by Gene Sharp, notably in his 1973 magnum opus, *The Politics of Nonviolent Action.* Although Sharp doesn't object to injecting moral concerns into nonviolent political action—that is, he doesn't object to those who pursue nonviolent political action out of moral considerations—he also doesn't believe that effective nonviolent political action requires a creed or moral commitment.[11]

Sharp has been followed in this approach by Peter Ackerman and Jack DuVall, who in recent years have marketed exceptionally well the strategy, tactics, and efficacy of nonviolent political action, most especially in its use to promote democracy around the world and bring down dictators. The recent increase in interest in the study of nonviolent action around the world is in no small part due to the efforts of Ackerman and DuVall and their focus on the value of nonviolence in spreading democracy. The PBS special called *A Force More Powerful,* a volume by the same title written by Ackerman and DuVall on which the special was based, and a follow-up documentary, *Bringing Down a Dictator,* have all enjoyed wide distribution and glowing recognition. Like Sharp, Ackerman and DuVall both insist that nonviolent action (they eschew use of the noun "nonviolence") can be practiced effectively as a policy without a moral commitment to nonviolence, without having to adopt a creed, moral or otherwise.[12] The education that they promote through the International Center on Nonviolent Conflict is utilized primarily by those seeking to spread democracy via nonviolent methods, a variant on making the world safe for democracy.

Principled Nonviolence

Principled nonviolence is the nonviolence of those who practice nonviolence because they are committed to it as a creed or moral principle, perhaps even *the* moral principle. Gandhi and Martin Luther King Jr. both understood nonviolence in this way. Unlike the nonviolence of the weak, they would not abandon nonviolent tactics in favor of violent tactics simply because they thought that certain political goals could be achieved more decisively, quickly, or effectively through the use of violence. And unlike practitioners of nonviolence of the weak or advocates of pragmatic nonviolent action, they would not resort to violence even if they believed that violence was *necessary* to achieve a desired goal. Gandhi split with the Indian government for this reason over the issue of a standing army for defense. The Student Nonviolent Coordinating Committee (SNCC) split with King, too, at least in part, because some of SNCC's members were impatient with the slow pace of nonviolence. It is probably accurate to say that both Gandhi and King believed that no gains brought by violence would be effective in the long run. And it is also probably accurate to say that they believed that intentional and sustained use of violence precludes obtaining any morally legitimate goal. Gandhi spoke of such nonviolence as the "nonviolence of the strong," but it seems more accurate to call this approach "principled nonviolence."

Two features about principled nonviolence should be noted. First, principled nonviolentists work with a very expanded notion of what constitutes violence and what constitutes nonviolence. Everything from a negative thought to the sarcasm on sitcoms counts as violence. Oppression counts as violence. Insensitivity could count as violence. Nonviolence includes the pursuit of justice, the elimination of oppression, the development of inner peace, and constant sensitivity to others. For principled nonviolentists, these concepts of violence and nonviolence are wide and full of implications.

Second, for principled nonviolentists, the means *are* the ends. If one is pursuing justice and is insensitive to the needs and interests of others in doing so, then one is not pursuing justice. If one is seeking an end to violence but doing so by becoming oppressive or violent oneself, even if it is to a lesser degree than the violence one is seeking to eliminate, then one is not seeking an end to violence. As Gandhi said in *Hind Swaraj,* "The means may be likened to a seed, the end to a tree; and there is just the same inviolable connection between the means and the end as there is between the seed and the tree."[13]

Implications of Expedient Nonviolence

These observations should make it clear that political realism, Wilsonianism, neoconservatism, *and* pragmatic nonviolence are all prescriptions for realizing some goal or other. Unlike principled nonviolence, they all seek some goal that often differs from the means themselves. When one set of means is insufficient for achieving that goal, another set of means is adopted. And if the goal is attained, the means are discarded. Tom Hastings once described the principle as the Kleenex principle. "Use nonviolence if it will work. And when you're done with it, throw it away." This is why India, which used nonviolence in its pursuit of independence from Britain, sought standing armies and nuclear weapons once that independence was obtained. Its nonviolence, as Gandhi often complained, was merely pragmatic, not principled.

Pragmatic nonviolence, political realism, Wilsonianism, and neoconservatism all share a goals-oriented approach to politics. Realism aims at security through power; Wilsonianism aims at the spread of democracy, ideally through diplomacy but also through the barrel of a gun if necessary; neoconservatism charts a middle course—securing nations through the spread of democracy by any effective means. And pragmatic nonviolence? Well, it aims at whatever it wishes. Gene Sharp, on at least one occasion, was asked whether or not nonviolent action could be used for malicious as well as benevolent ends, and he said that he didn't see why not.[14] That is not a possibility for principled nonviolence. The line between violence and nonviolence can blur dangerously when one's nonviolence is merely expedient, merely pragmatic.

A former activist with the Green Party in Germany recently said of principled nonviolence, "Your nonviolence is passive. You are unwilling to be aggressive, to take the initiative." She described a nonviolent protest in Germany in the 1980s during which Greens distributed flowers to the police standing with weapons around the demonstrators. She described this action as the equivalent of "flipping a finger" to the police.[15] However, from the perspective of a principled nonviolentist, she was mistaken. Principled nonviolentists have no difficulty with being assertive, with taking initiative, and even with distributing flowers to the police. But they have difficulty with an attitude that sees that initiative as "flipping the finger."

Here's another example: in September 2007, MoveOn ran an ad in the *New York Times* that referred to the commanding general in Iraq, General David Petraeus, as "General Betray Us." This ridicule was offered because of suspect testimony that Petraeus had provided days earlier to Congress. Although many nonviolentists would reject this woman's characterization of the flower incidents and many have repudiated the tone of the MoveOn .org ad, still many others are invigorated by these sorts of displays and characterizations. They are examples of taunting public officials, one of 198 nonviolent tactics offered by Gene Sharp in *The Politics of Nonviolent Action*.[16] However, they are not genuinely nonviolent actions. They are instances of violence operating on a less brutal level than the power politics of governments. The list of 198 "nonviolent tactics" includes other tactics such as "rude gestures" and "nonviolent harassment," tactics that show that lesser forms of violence are alive and well, even encouraged by some who practice pragmatic nonviolence.

Conclusion

For the most part, scholars in the fields of peace studies come from backgrounds in the social sciences—sociology, political science, international relations, economics, and psychology. Sometimes they are in the fields of philosophy or education. What they share is an interest in finding means other than violence for settling conflicts. However, in this respect peace educators are no different from almost everyone else, even from experienced military professionals, who are themselves often reluctant to resort to violence.

And there's the rub. Gene Sharp, Johan Galtung, and others have shown that within the political arena there is a vast and untapped area suitable for study and practice. The area includes peace education, conflict resolution, nonviolent political action; much work remains in mapping out this area and applying results of this research to human practices. To the extent that peace studies and pragmatic nonviolence simply offer a wider smorgasbord of tactics for settling disputes without physical violence, they are doing good work. But if that is all that peace studies and pragmatic nonviolence offer, then they are not offering anything substantially different in *kind* than political realism, Wilsonianism, or neoconservatism. Because when push comes to shove, when goals cannot be achieved nonviolently, they will acknowledge the use of violence as legitimate.

Scholars may shrug and will likely object: "It is not our job to promote particular values. It is our job to study, impartially, the laws that govern the universe, including those that govern human behavior. It is not our job to espouse nonviolence as a creed; it is our job to identify those nonviolent tactics and strategies that can be successful. Of course, we hope that in identifying such tactics and strategies, we can contribute greatly to peace and justice in the world."

This point of view fails to carry peace and nonviolence studies forward far enough. In the first place, accepting the status quo is to accept a political principle that the ends justify the means: any failure to critique that major principle underpinning the dominant political philosophies of the last 100 years tacitly accepts that principle. To pursue democracy, security, and justice through gunboat diplomacy wins few converts. To install "democratic" leaders in Iraq, to perceive the strength and security of the United States in terms of its ability to inflict harm and ward off attack, to promote justice in Iran through the nonviolent overthrow of its constitutional government: these behaviors belie what they allegedly seek.[17] Precisely *because* people have pursued security, democracy, and justice as ends that justify all other means, those goals have not been forthcoming. In the long run the populations who suffer these practices learn that politics is about outcome, not about process.

But if peace and justice studies have to teach anything, it is that politics must be about process, not outcome. And in the final analysis, only principled nonviolence teaches that lesson. To teach by example, to live the life that one espouses, is not only morally admirable, it is strategically more powerful. Principled nonviolentists see the end *in* the means, in the process. For principled nonviolentists, the goal is being reached *as* it is being sought. Some of these goals are empowerment, self-realization, respect toward others, noncoercion, just treatment of others, and due process.

Gandhi acknowledged that nothing in principle or practice precludes principled nonviolentists from working alongside pragmatic nonviolentists in seeking particular goals. Their means and goals are often congruent. Large numbers of people are often more decisive than the purity of a few participants in achieving particular goals. And oftentimes in this process, some of those large numbers are won over to nonviolence as a creed.

Gandhi allowed those committed to pragmatic nonviolence in his campaigns, but he would not allow them to lead his campaigns. He felt that campaigns would be stronger if the participants were committed to nonviolence as a creed. He worried that nonviolence that is merely expedient could be shaken, especially under trying conditions. So, for example, if the participants at the Dharasana Salt Works had returned violence for violence, the force of the action would have been lost. The object was not to overpower those who guarded the works; it was either to win them over or to win over many others not present, those who were not yet committed to the independence struggle one way or the other. Few people would have been won over to the independence struggle simply because a few hundred people violently occupied the salt works.

In the second place, purity of heart in the long run is not only more moral than pragmatic nonviolence, which is merely expedient; it is also more strategic. And that particular aspect adds to its moral weight. Here's why: if a person's opponents sense that he or she will resort to violence when push comes to shove, opponents have every reason to believe that they are nothing more than a means to his or her ends, that they might be oppressed if they lose. And the opponents have every reason to attempt to provoke a violent response. The opponents will resist more vehemently and be less likely to be won over by pragmatic than by principled nonviolence. More important, however, is the attitude of those people who sit on the fence, who have no particular stake in the struggle. A nonviolentist's goal is to involve that silent majority that has not yet chosen sides in a conflict. And if that silent majority, largely unconcerned with the issue at hand, perceives that nonviolent means are merely expedient, they will be less likely to believe that one victor or the other makes a difference. They will be viewed the way many view Democrats and Republicans these days: they talk a good game, but when push comes to shove they'll act the same way. So what's the difference? For strategic *and* moral reasons, the difference needs to *be* there, not merely appear to be there.

For these reasons, principled nonviolence needs to underpin peace studies. This imperative should be seen neither as a precondition for the study and practice of nonviolence and peace studies nor as a precondition for the establishment of such programs. But it is an ideal to be pursued and, hopefully, realized.

Notes

1. Robert Gates, speech at the World Forum on the Future of Democracy, September 17, 2007, Williamsburg, Virginia, http://www.defenselink.mil/speeches/speech.aspx?speechid=1175.

2. Robert Holmes, *On War and Morality* (Princeton, NJ: Princeton University Press, 1989), 50–59.

3. Thomas Donnelly, *Rebuilding America's Defenses* (Washington, DC: Project for the New American Century, 2000), http://www.newamericancentury.org/RebuildingAmericasDefenses.pdf.

4. White House, *The National Security Strategy* (Washington, DC: Government Printing Office, 2006), http://www.whitehouse.gov/nsc/nss/2006/.

5. United Nations, *The Charter of the United Nations,* chapter 7, http://www.un.org/aboutun/charter/chapter7.htm.

6. Matthew Tempest and David Batty, "Q&A: The Civil Contingencies Bill," *Guardian Unlimited,* January 7, 2004.

7. Mohandas Gandhi, *The Collected Works of Mahatma Gandhi,* vol. 74 (Warwickshire, UK: Obscure Press, 2006), 158.

8. Gene Sharp, *Gandhi as a Political Strategist* (Boston: Porter Sargent, 1979), 284.

9. Ibid., 285.

10. Ibid., 298.

11. Gene Sharp, unpublished lecture delivered at the Gandhi-King Society/Concerned Philosophers for Peace meetings at the American Philosophical Association meeting in Boston, December 1991.

12. Peter Ackerman and Jack DuVall, *A Force More Powerful: A Century of Non-violent Conflict* (Hampshire, UK: Palgrave Macmillan, 2001).

13. Mohandas Gandhi, *Hind Swaraj* (Columbia, MO: South Asia Books, 1998), chap. 16.

14. Gene Sharp, lecture at Rochester Zen Center conference, 1986.

15. Anne Foerst, class lecture at St. Bonaventure University, September 2007.

16. Gene Sharp, *The Politics of Nonviolent Action* (Boston: Porter Sargent, 1973).

17. W. Michael Reisman, "The Raid on Baghdad: Some Reflections on Its Lawfulness and Implications," *European Journal of International Law* (1994): 7–8.

7

Dynamics Affecting Conflict, Justice, and Peace

George A. Lopez

I BEGIN THIS CHAPTER WITH THREE VIGNETTES ILLUSTRATIVE OF THE controversies surrounding peace studies in US colleges and universities. The first occurred two decades ago when I was asked by the editor of the *Annals of the American Academy of Political and Social Sciences* to assemble a special issue of articles on "Peace Studies: Past and Future." The request came in light of substantial increase in the creation of peace programs in the 1980s. This trend was perceived by many as sparked by the "liberal academy's" reaction to the renewed Cold War and Ronald Reagan's saber rattling about nuclear weapons. In that volume, Chad Alger's chapter was entitled "Peace Studies at the Crossroads: Where Else?" Alger's central thesis held that peace studies in the academy must always be at the crossroads of controversies in the field, whether that lie in the creative tensions among research, education, and activism, or in the contested definitions of peace and its component parts as articulated differently by local and global peace movements.[1]

A second story involves my conversations with a university colleague on January 17, 1991, the day after the beginning of US bombing of Iraq in what would be called the Gulf War. I had just held the first day of class for the spring semester for my "Intro to Peace Studies" class. The on-paper class registration of forty-eight that had been recorded for most of December and early January had ballooned to 126 students "wanting in" to the course. When I labeled this as a "teachable moment" about which I admitted some excitement, one of my colleagues asserted that I should not let any new enrollees in the course. His claim was that those who would only consider taking the course when they had to face the uncertainty of war—and potentially their own vulnerability to it—had revealed themselves to be driven by narrow self-interest and not any real interest in peace. He further went on to point out that people generally only claim that they were conscientious objectors to war when a war breaks out, not in times of peace when they actually have the reflective leisure time to formulate the logic of such claims at their objective best.

The last encounter occurred in the earlier part of the twenty-first century as I was serving as a consultant to the development of a peace studies program at a US university. In a one-on-one meeting with a campus dean, this administrator expressed concern that to add peace studies as a structured minor or major to their curriculum was giving in to the fads and fears of the time, that is, life in a world after September 11, 2001. Worse yet, claimed the dean, there already existed in the curriculum a series of multidisciplinary programs that were the product of "special interests": African American studies, environmental studies, gender studies, and so on. The administrator asserted emphatically that with the addition of peace studies, their institution might well become known as a "studies studies" university!

When woven together, these stories illustrate an important set of questions that has dominated campus discussions, and especially dissension, regarding the scope and development of peace studies. First, how can we fairly and fully assess the developments in the transdisciplinary field of peace studies, the central concept of which is both cherished yet elusive and subject to a wide array of social, political, and cultural influences that occur in real time? Second, how are scholars and citizens to assess the observed reality that "boom times" in peace studies correlate strongly with the emergence of war, rumors of war, and more recently terrorism? And finally, how much growth and change at the core of our field is a product of a current "threat to peace," rather than developments consonant with the actual changing contours of violence, or knowledge about violence, or both?

The Changing Definition of Peace—and Thus Peace Studies

Since its appearance in US academic circles with the creation of the first full program at Manchester College in 1948, peace studies has been subject to the critique that it suffers from *not* being a credible area of substantive inquiry and *for* being a theme motivated by political, cultural, and social events of the day and current prevailing ideologies. The former challenge most often originates in a paradigmatic view of the world that blends Thomas Hobbes and Carl von Clausewitz and forms the heart of political realism. It claims that war and related organized violence is so consistent a state of affairs that to study peace is to engage in the art of wishful thinking. The committed realist contends that in a tough, nasty, and cruel world, if you want peace, you must prepare for war. Thus, proceeds the argument, if you want to learn peace within the confines of the university, then you should study war. The notion that peace should be taught by those who have never experienced or fought in war makes little sense to them.[2]

Many scholars in the peace research field would assert that peace studies has always maintained a reasonable balance between the study of causes of war and war prevention. But the difference between war studies—or, more generally, strategic studies—and peace studies is that the latter regards the former's focus on war prevention as the study of only one type of peace. Thus, a number of us in mainstream peace studies consider the realist position a matter of taste or preference (and thus valid in its own terms) and not the kind of paradigmatic disagreement that would denigrate the academic rigor or integrity of peace studies' place in the academy. Moreover, with so much of the social science and international relations perspective being devoted to the systematic (some would claim "scientific") study of war and violence, we are not surprised by the realist claim. Since the 1960s, scholars in peace studies have maintained that the dominance of war studies is precisely what necessitated an explicit focus on the causes of and sustaining factors for peace.

The critique of being a fad demands serious scrutiny. To have a university field of research and teaching driven by concerns of the present free of critical analysis would constitute little more than current affairs discussion. But to provide the concepts, theoretical frameworks, and policy relevant findings by which very current trends in violence can be understood more clearly *does* comprise the business of the university and its curriculum. The tensions often emerge when peace researchers teach courses dealing with contemporary violence, such as on terrorism or the wars in Iraq and Afghanistan, as these events unfold. If done comprehensively, such courses can most certainly assess these current crises through the lens of the critical scholarship available on how such wars have proceeded in the past and how they relate to peace.

In this context, peace studies may well express frustration about or comment critically on the themes and methods—that is, the concern for strategy, power, arms, and force—that realists have brought to the study of war, violence, and peace. Conversely, realists have had little patience with the inclusion of what they consider tangential or "soft" factors involved in the peace researcher's study of violence, such as the dynamics of local culture, the relevance of religion, issues of justice, and the dynamics of peace processes.[3] Moreover, because peace studies does not assume war to be the natural or normal state of human affairs, its skepticism about contemporary military ventures separates it drastically from the realist in kind. And by methodological disposition, realism would withhold critique about war until more distance has emerged between the assessment made by the scholar and the violence that is unfolding. The result is that peace studies is critiqued as too "present minded," as if faculty teaching such classes rely on scant evidence save the daily headlines for their core text and are also injecting their own skepticism about war into the classroom in inappropriate ways. Any good college or university should have both perspectives reflected in its curriculum, but the pattern in the United States has been the dominance of the realists and the relative few with a peace studies perspective.

But if peace studies is neither a curricular fad nor defined by the problems or violence of the daily headline, then what is the justification for the explosion of themes and topics that are offered under the peace studies label? With introductory courses in the field that range from considerations of gang violence and human rights to war, one would easily come to the conclusion that all good things and most horrible things can be taught under the peace studies rubric *and* that no two peace studies programs look very much alike. However anarchic—or worse—this may appear from outside the field or to those beyond the university walls, there indeed exists a core—and maybe even a "canon" in the classical sense—to peace studies. But as a field that studies the diversity and changing contours of violence and the challenges of building sustainable peace that occur in the real world, peace studies has rightly expanded, rather than narrowed and refined, its focus since the 1980s.[4]

From its inception as a multidisciplinary field, peace studies has included the concepts, methods, and findings of diverse disciplines while focusing on three general areas of study: the causes and conditions that generate and sustain violent conflict; the mechanisms and models for the resolution of violent conflict; and the norms, practices, and institutions for building peace. Within these three major themes of investigation—or subfields—peace researchers pursue scholarly inquiry, teaching, and occasionally advocacy across different levels of social analysis—that of individuals, of social groups, within nations, about nations, and in the international system. This approach yields the rather broad matrix of diverse topics and themes as areas of legitimate inquiry displayed in Table 1 of the aforementioned volume of twenty years ago.[5]

Looking at Table 7.1, it is not difficult to ascertain why peace studies has retained its claim to be a *multi*disciplinary venture. The first column illustrates the work of a range of the social science disciplines; the last column includes to a broader range of disciplines from comparative religion to international law. Even twenty years ago, as the middle column demonstrates, there would be a mixture of "traditional" areas of inquiry, such as law and diplomacy, but enhanced by the introduction of "newer" fields such as mediation and negotiation. In fact, the middle column was rather thin in the 1960s when compared to the others. The dramatic increase in the conflict resolution literature and practice of the next two decades explains its breadth and depth as a pillar of the field. Moreover, the rise in prominence

Table 7.1 Subfields of Peace Studies

	Areas of Substantive Focus		
Level of human interactions	Causes and consequences of violent conflict	Mechanics of managing, reducing, or resolving violent conflict	Development of values, norms, and insitutions for building peace
Individual	Individual, social, and political violence	Communication skills; negotiation and mediation	Personal nonviolence: ethical and religious approaches to individual action
Social group (intranational)	Riots and revolutions; ethnic, factional, or violent conflicts	Social-conflict analysis; arbitration, negotiation, and mediation	Nonviolent direct action; religious, ethnic, or social-group approaches to peace
National and international	War; terrorism; low-intensity violence; arms races and arms trade	Diplomacy: international negotiation, arbitration, and mediation; international law, international organizations, and multilateral peacekeeping forces	International law, international organizations, and multilateral peacekeeping forces; world-order modeling; nonviolent national defense

Source: Michael S. Lund, *Preventing Violent Conflict: A Strategy for Preventive Diplomacy* (Washington, DC: US Institute of Peace Press, 1996). Used by permission of the United States Institute of Peace.

of the conflict resolution subfield within universities explains the dramatic increase in peace programs in the United States during the 1980s, *not* the actions or disposition of Ronald Reagan.

Even as this template—or others like it—could serve as an intellectually defensible schema for specifying the substance of peace studies, the bloody internal wars, genocidal violence, the end of the Cold War, and a plethora of peace agreements of the 1990s pushed the contours of the field far beyond the teaching and research terrain described in Table 7.1. Specifically, as detailed succinctly in Figure 7.1, via Michael Lund's portrayal of the cycles of violent conflict and its management, the blending of the old with the new research and praxis established the scholar-practitioner territory for peace studies that prevails today.[6]

On the one hand, the left-hand side and apex of the Lund curve represents much of the traditional research and teaching agenda of peace studies (and its allied fields, international relations and security studies). But Figure 7.1 also captures well the areas of changing global realities faced at the policy, intellectual, and praxis levels in coping with the period after violence. Since the mid-1990s, the peace studies field has reflected these multiple meanings and layers of "peace." From the more generic and historically labeled peacemaking level, events and cases have forced a necessary

Figure 7.1 The Life Cycle of International Conflict Management

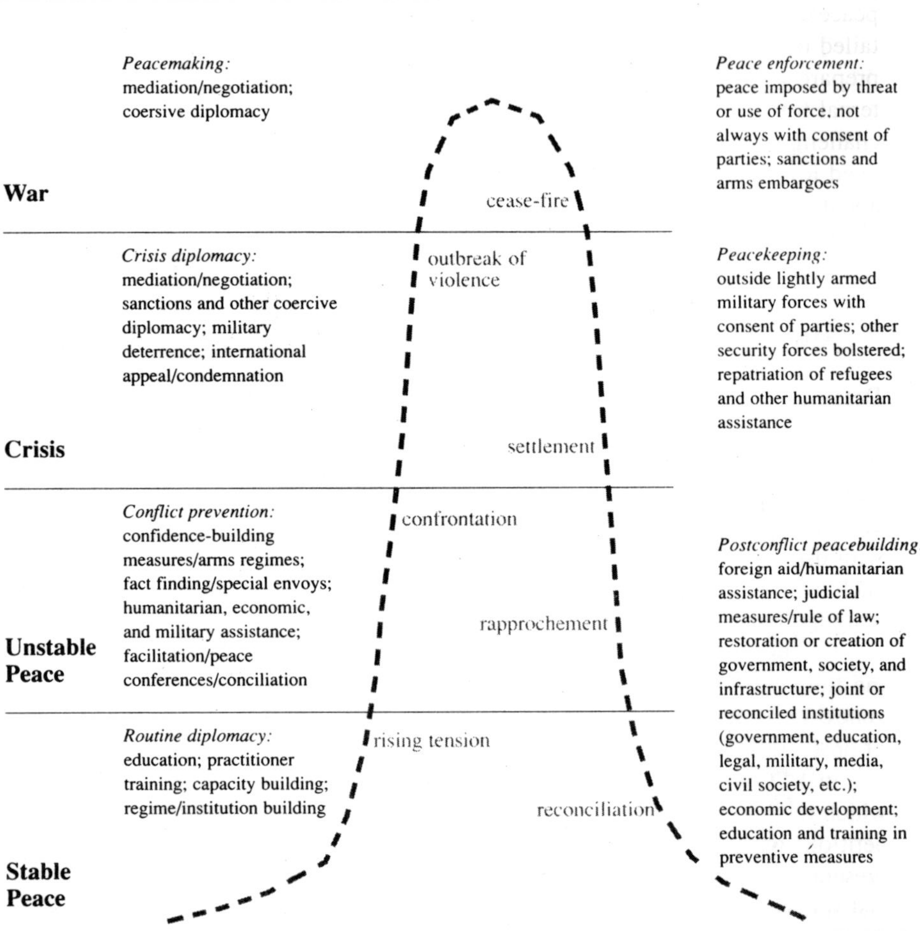

Source: Michael S. Lund, *Preventing Violent Conflict: A Strategy for Preventive Diplomacy* (Washington, DC: US Institute of Peace Press, 1996). Used by permission of the United States Institute of Peace.

distinction to be made among peace enforcement, peacekeeping, and peacebuilding. The first encompasses the arrangements and actors needed to hold, and sometimes impose, a tentative or disagreeable peace among parties, as well as the resort to coercive sanctions to stimulate peace. Peacekeeping has moved far beyond the study of how the United Nations forces serve as interpositionary troops while diplomatic peace is achieved at the bargaining table. It involves a series of humanitarian, organizational, and legal dynamics that set the framework for more stable peace.

Of greatest significance for peace studies has been the sharpened delineation and interpretation of the quite varied tasks encompassed in postconflict peacebuilding. Learning from the harsh and difficult postwar experiences detailed by practitioners, university peace studies has a broadened mandate to prepare global citizens who know how the combination of internal and external forces for peace can be mobilized across a wide array of civil society challenges to restore a functioning, governable collectivity. At its most developed level in 2008, peace studies is thus engaged in research and teaching about strategic peacebuilding—the art and science of how communities can emerge to a functioning sociopolitical order after a long cycle of violence.[7]

■ The "Studies-Studies" Challenge

Detailing these expanding boundaries of violence and peace that university peace studies expects to address with intellectual rigor explains only a portion of the changes in the field. As an endeavor that derives some of its core concepts and research questions from the fundamental disciplines of the academy, peace studies has refined and redefined itself over time in accord with disciplinary innovations, discoveries, and reformulations. To discuss each of these lies beyond the scope of this chapter, but some particular new insights deserve note.

Of significant influence on the development of teaching and research in the field has been such groundbreaking work as the anthropology of war zones. This genre has burst some of the mythology and certainly the mystique of how wars unfold in the lives of people subject to them and loosened the dominance of a political science perspective as the exclusive lens through which we examine war.[8] Through the articulation of models of resource competition and crime (thus bridging to the anthropologists), economists have presented a strong argument regarding "greed" as a counterhypothesis to social science explanations for violence that have traditionally been based on the "grievance" of one party versus another.[9] And sociologists and political scientists have brought increased sophistication to the study of global social movements. The result has been a significant cluster of findings and insights that challenge the conceptualization of peace and raise wider questions of globalization and peace.[10]

Even more far-reaching—both in the exploration of the depth of the human experience of violence and in its stimulation of new ideas and approaches to studying peace within the academy—has been the influence of other interdisciplinary fields on peace studies. This "studies-studies" challenge promotes skepticism in some, as in the dean mentioned at the opening of this chapter. But the cross-fertilization of conceptualization, causation, and methods of inquiry has enriched the field in many ways. Two particular interdisciplinary areas of study in their own right, gender (or women's) studies and environmental studies, each deserve more thorough analysis for their interface with peace studies than they receive here. But illustrating some of the connections and impact will serve to make the point that such multi-multi-disciplinary approaches do not dilute the intellectual content of research or teaching about peace.

Having emerged from a new consciousness generated by the success of the women's movement in the 1970s, and aided by new perspectives in research and teaching brought to the social sciences and humanities, women's studies has had an enduring conceptual and methodological impact on peace studies. Women's suffrage comprised its own case of nonviolent direct action for social change but was also linked to wider global concerns regarding transnational coalitions of citizens who would stand against war, as in the Women's International League for Peace and Freedom.

The intellectual paradigm of the women's movement generated themes and areas of inquiry in various disciplinary areas, which in turn helped to challenge and ultimately change peace studies. Some of these occurred in the fields of cognitive psychology, moral education, and sociobiology, as researchers explored whether women's ways of doing and knowing are directly in contrast with those of males. The work of Carol Gilligan complemented others like Elise Boulding, author of *The Underside of History,* and Linda Rennie Forcey to legitimize the analysis of women and peace on its own terms. The wider social critique that Carol Cohn would make of militarism and nuclearism, and that Cynthia Enloe detailed playing out in a myriad of ways within American consciousness and in programs in other nations, stimulated a widened agenda of research and education on such defense matters.[11]

As with other areas of inquiry in peace studies, the interaction with women's studies also had to keep pace with challenges and changes dictated by "the real world." In this context the wars in the former Yugoslavia were marked by a turning point in what has been a gender issue of war since such organized violence began. As part of a campaign of various mass atrocities perpetrated primarily by Serbs on Bosnian Muslims, the Serbian forces moved from the practice of spontaneous and individualized rape as a spoil of war to a strategic policy of forced abduction and systematic gang rape of Bosnian women for reasons of humiliation, ethnic impregnation, and destruction of Muslim family structures. The outrage that followed led to the successful campaign to register rape as a war crime. Further, in the adoption of UN Security Council Resolution 1325 (2000) the international community specifically addressed the impact of war on women and women's contributions to conflict resolution and sustainable peace. These themes are now are fully part of peace studies generally and strategic peacebuilding in particular.

The escalatory cycle portrayed in Lund's diagram above examines—as has been the tradition in the field—those social, economic, and political forces that give rise to violence (see Figure 7.1). But recent cases of protracted violence have taught us that the hatred, factionalism, and other social factors that serve as the more direct and observable causes of violence may also have structural and environmental factors preceding and predetermining them. Thus, environmental studies, a multidisciplinary field that had to pay its own dues in battles over academic legitimacy and curricular credibility since the 1970s, moved to the forefront of discussion about peace studies in autumn of 2007, when former US vice president Al Gore was awarded the Nobel Peace Prize.

For a vocal segment of US society, tying Gore's warnings about climate change to peace illustrates both the dominance of the "liberal agenda" at work in academic and international circles and the irrelevance of both environmental studies and peace studies to serious, ever-present security threats in this age of terrorism. Those sharing this view have missed some important new realities regarding security and peace. For example, various intelligence agencies have been debating for some time the metrics for tracking how climate change and other environmental factors have now become a "threat multiplier" aligned with various other factors in nations susceptible to other threats, most especially state failure, internal war, and terrorism.

For more than two decades, social and physical scientists like those at the Trudeau Center for Peace and Conflict Studies in Toronto have specified with increasing precision the direct links between environmental changes and political violence. These are neither idle theories nor ideologically driven claims, but assertions grounded in evidence on how ecological degradation affects peace and security concerns in diverse locales. In fact, the case evidence that links environmental issues to different facets of peace research is diverse and substantial. Before the genocides in Rwanda and Darfur, these regions experienced drought and loss of farming and grazing land that, in turn, prompted rural population movements and a demand for government response to the devastation. These environmentally driven changes were then used by brutal leaders to mobilize latent ethnic hatred and the mass killings of one group by another.

Just weeks before Gore was awarded the Nobel Peace Prize, the world community struggled to reach some kind of consensus on what to do with dictatorial Burmese military rulers who refused to permit international aid and relief experts into their country to administer disaster relief after a devastating storm. Even though the deaths and refugee crisis caused by this recent event are rightly prominent, few know that for twenty years the ruling junta financed a large portion of its repressive military hardware purchases through rapid depletion of Burma's forests and black market timber sales.

Similarly, we know there are environmental dimensions to peace agreements. For example, whatever political arrangements Israel and the Palestinian Authority leaders may forge in creating a viable two-state solution, all experts also know that, since nearly half of Israeli water supplies come from aquifers that exist under West Bank territory, there will be no final peace without an effective, fair plan for sharing water rights. Thus varied events and trends have pushed environmental crises to the forefront of those economic, social, and political forces that prompt the violence that destroys the governance capacity of weak states and thwarts efforts for peace with justice and stability.

Conclusion

As a hybrid of the more traditional academic disciplines, the peace studies field has undergone considerable conceptual and methodological expansion and redefinition since the end of the Cold War. This has been due to the changing nature of global violence and its causes, the diversity of themes and techniques relevant to peace (making, -keeping, -enforcing, and -building), and the inevitable new focuses that have developed in the many disciplines from which peace studies has always drawn some of its central research questions and teaching themes. It has involved, as well, cross-referencing and cross-fertilization with other transdisciplinary academic fields of study, such as environmental studies and gender studies. These changes are hardly the result of fad or political bias but are an attempt—within serious critical inquiry about large-scale violence and its potential reduction and resolution—to keep pace with the complexities of engaging in that task in the real world.

Those who cast suspicions toward peace studies should not be dismissed lightly. Critiques regarding lack of focus, including that peace studies seems to appear to treat *all* good—and only some terrible—things under its wide intellectual umbrella, should be debated openly and with the intellectual passion such important issues deserve. This chapter provides one illustration of how quite varied thematic and policy concerns can be forged into a constellation of ideas and approaches that have sophistication, academic credibility, and the very central grounding in the real world that the field demands.

Assertions that peace studies teaches anti-Americanism or inherently advocates an anti-Western way of life have arisen anew and intensely since 9/11.[12] They take aim at certain peace studies curricular offerings and especially at the praxis dimension of the field, claiming that internships and experiential learning opportunities generate unpatriotic student activism. These claims have become a cottage industry and, when found to be groundless or a selective cheap shot, they should be exposed for the base ideological and near-libelous claims they often are. When they are made on the basis of verifiable evidence, they must be engaged directly and honestly. So too should the argument that peace studies violates the academy norm that faculty must be "above the fray" or "value neutral" in their teaching of social issues. This latter concern has been a topic of civil discussion regarding "the relevance of the curriculum" and "service learning" questions in US higher education for decades. Peace studies has much to add to this debate.

This chapter recognizes the wide array of topics that encompass peace studies as being both essential and essentially contested. Such a scrutiny occurs at a time when war and terrorism abound, and thus some feel the stress on the parameters and practice of our field of peace studies. But this places peace studies exactly where, two decades ago, Chad Alger argued we must be—at the crossroads—and nowhere else!

Notes

1. Chadwick F. Alger, "Peace Studies at the Crossroads: Where Else?" in *Peace Studies: Past and Future,* The Annals of the American Academy of Political and Social Science, vol. 504, edited by George A. Lopez (Thousand Oaks, CA: Sage Publications, 1989), 117–127.

2. One of the best examples of this approach can be found in Michael Howard, *The Invention of Peace* (New Haven, CT: Yale University Press, 2001).

3. The curious irony of the post–9/11 period and the US war in Iraq is the pronounced recognition of the relevance of peace research categories now advocated by rather "realist" generals and politicians, who have come to realize that it is precisely the oft-labeled "soft" factors of local culture, the role of religion, and local understandings of justice that are the key elements in ending the Iraq War and the war on terror.

4. The three best recent books that present a synthetic blending of the more well-established peace studies themes with the newer dimensions of the field are Peter Wallensteen, *Understanding Conflict Resolution: War, Peace and the Global System,* 2nd rev. ed (London: Sage, 2007); Oliver Ramsbotham et al., *Contemporary Conflict Resolution,* 2nd rev. ed. (Cambridge: Polity, 2007); and David Cortright, *Peace: A History of Movements and Ideas* (Cambridge: Cambridge University Press, 2008).

5. Table reproduced from George A. Lopez, "Preface," in *Peace Studies: Past and Future,* The Annals of the American Academy of Political and Social Science, vol. 504 (July 1989), edited by George A. Lopez (Thousand Oaks, CA: Sage Publications, 1989), 11.

6. As adapted and displayed as Figure 7.1, "The Life Cycle of International Conflict Management," from "Introduction," *Turbulent Peace,* edited by Chester A. Crocker et al. (Washington, DC: US Institute of Peace Press, 2001), xxviii.

7. The fullest articulation of this comprehensive approach will be published as Daniel Philpott, ed., *Strategies for Peacebuilding* (Oxford: Oxford University Press, forthcoming, 2009).

8. For the best example, see Carolyn Nordstrom, *Shadows of War* (Berkeley: University of California Press, 2004).

9. Karen Ballentine and Heiko Nitzschke, eds., *Profiting from Peace: Managing the Resource Dimensions of Civil War* (Boulder, CO: Lynne Rienner, 2005); and

Karen Ballentine and Jake Sherman, eds., *The Political Economy of Armed Conflict: Beyond Greed and Grievance* (Boulder, CO: Lynne Rienner, 2004).

10. See, for example, Jackie Smith, *Social Movements for Global Democracy* (Baltimore: Johns Hopkins University Press, 2007).

11. See Elise Boulding, *The Underside of History* (Boulder, CO: Westview, 1976); Linda Rennie Forcey, "Women as Peacemakers," *Peace and Change* 16, no. 4 (October, 1991): 331–354; "Slick 'ems, Glick 'ems, Christmas Trees, and Cookie Cutters: Nuclear Language and How We Learned to Pat the Bomb," *Bulletin of the Atomic Scientists* (June 1987); Cynthia Enloe, *Bananas, Beaches, and Bases: Making Feminist Sense of International Politics* (Berkeley: University of California Press, 2000).

12. The most widely circulated essay in this regard in the past few years has been Bruce Bawer, "The Peace Racket," *City Journal* (Summer 2007).

PART 2
Course Syllabuses

8

Introduction to Peace and Justice Studies

FROM ITS INCEPTION IN 1948, PEACE STUDIES HAS BEEN BROAD AND interdisciplinary in nature, which is why it has appeared in many places in university curricula. Religion, history, philosophy, sociology, political science, security studies, environmental studies, communications, psychology, economics, literature, the arts, and even business administration lay claim to the principles of peace through peaceful means, whether they seek peace between individuals, groups, or states. An overview of peace studies is therefore also broad in nature, though introductory courses may be organized by major themes, such as interpersonal conflict, philosophical bases of peace, or social and political analyses of conflict and peace.

The courses in this section represent an array of approaches to the basic concepts of peace studies. Nathan C. Funk asks the large, philosophical questions, such as, What is peace? What is violence? Thomas E. Boudreau approaches from the field of political science and international relations, thinking of peace studies as a concern for nation-state actors. Abbie Jenks draws from various disciplines to expose students to the common terminology of the field, and Katy Gray Brown introduces students to a basic language of peace studies that includes terms such as positive peace, negative peace, and structural violence. Finally, Gloria Rhodes takes an interpersonal approach to peace studies, helping students master principles of open, productive communication.

8.1 Roots of Conflict, Violence, and Peace

Nathan C. Funk
Conrad Grebel University College

COURSE DESCRIPTION

Introductory undergraduate course for general education students or peace studies or related majors.

This course introduces a range of issues addressed by the field of peace and conflict studies and provides students with conceptual tools for exploring causes of destructive conflict and conditions for peaceful human relations. By exposing students to multiple paradigms for understanding the roots of conflict and the nature of peace, the course encourages critical reflection on influential theories about violence and peacemaking as well as intellectual engagement with the challenges facing humanity in the present era. Through readings, lectures, class discussions, writing assignments, and tests, each student is encouraged to conceptualize the underlying sources of major contemporary conflicts and to identify approaches to the promotion of peaceful change.

By the end of the term, students should be able to provide thoughtful answers to the following questions:

• What do we mean when we speak of "peace," "conflict," and "violence"? Are there different kinds of violence? Is peace simply an absence of direct violence, or is it something more than that? What is the relationship between peace and justice?

• What are some of the different schools of thought to consider when analyzing sources of conflict between individuals, groups, and states? Why do analysts often disagree about sources of conflict and violence? What are the implications of these disagreements for policymaking and peace advocacy?

• How do our understandings of conflict, violence, and peace relate to our understanding of power? Does power necessarily presuppose coercion and the threat of violence? What forms of power and influence are available to those who seek to refrain from or prevent violence?

REQUIRED TEXTS

Larry J. Fisk and John L. Schellenberg, eds. *Patterns of Conflict, Paths to Peace*. Peterborough, ON: Broadview Press, 2000.

Readings assigned in the course schedule.

RECOMMENDED TEXTS

These two texts are good resources for students who desire additional commentary on concepts discussed in Fisk and Schellenberg.

David P. Barash and Charles P. Webel. *Peace and Conflict Studies*. Thousand Oaks, CA: Sage, 2002.

Ho-Won Jeong. *Peace and Conflict Studies: An Introduction*. Burlington, VT: Ashgate, 2000.

COURSE SCHEDULE

Part 1: Introduction

Week 1: Conflict, Violence, and Peace

What issues does the field of peace and conflict studies seek to address? How shall we define terms like "conflict," "violence," and "peace"? What are some of the major schools of thought within peace and conflict studies?

Fisk and Schellenberg, preface and chapter 1 ("Shaping a Vision: The Nature of Peace Studies").

Week 2: Debates About Aggression

To what extent is aggressive behavior innate in human beings, and to what extent is it learned? What is at stake in debates about human nature?

Barash and Webel, "The Individual Level," in *Peace and Conflict Studies*.

Week 3: Power Politics: Peace Through Coercive Power

What have classical political theorists—particularly representatives of the "power politics" or "realist" school of thought—said about conflict, violence, and peace? What are some of the strengths and weaknesses of their explanations?

Barash and Webel, "The State Level," in *Peace and Conflict Studies*.

Ralph K. White. "Nobody Wanted War." In *War and Peace in an Age of Terrorism: A Reader,* edited by William M. Evan. Montreal: Pearson Education, 2006, 195–201.

Part 2: World Order: Peace Through Humane Global Governance

Week 4: World Order Perspectives on Conflict and Violence

What impact do environmental and economic issues have on prospects for conflict and violence? Can a strengthening of human rights norms play a role in preventing political violence? What can be done to reduce the incidence of armed conflict?

David P. Barash. "International Law." In *Approaches to Peace: A Reader in Peace Studies,* edited by David P. Barash. New York: Oxford University Press, 2000, 106–113.

Michael T. Klare. "The Era of Multiplying Schisms: World Security in the Twenty-First Century." In *World Security: Challenges for a New Century,* edited by Michael T. Klare and Yogesh Chandrani. New York: St. Martin's Press, 2000, 59–77.

Week 5: Proposals for Reforming Global Governance

Should a comprehensive understanding of peace include the absence of structural violence, ecological balance, and provision of other "global public goods"? What kinds of global governance arrangements are most appropriate for today's world?

Fisk and Schellenberg, chapter 3 ("Disentangling Disputes: Conflict in the International Arena").

Abdul Aziz Said. "Is the UN Ready for the World? Is the World Ready for the UN?" *UN Vision* (November–December 1994): 3–6.

Week 6: Midterm Exam

Part 3: Conflict Resolution: Peace Through Communication

Week 7: Sources of Conflict and Conflict Escalation

How has the field of conflict resolution sought to enhance our understanding of contemporary interstate and intrastate conflicts? What role do psychological and cultural factors (e.g., perceptions, attitudes, identities, historical narratives) play in the conflict escalation process?

Fisk and Schellenberg, chapter 2 ("Working It Out: Conflict in Interpersonal Contexts").

John Paul Lederach. "Understanding Conflict" and "Social Transformation of Conflict." In *Mediation and Facilitation Training Manual: Foundations and Skills for Constructive Conflict Transformation,* 3rd ed. Akron, PA: MCS, 1996, 44–47.

Week 8: Options for Transforming Conflictual Relationships

What must happen within and between groups involved in violent conflict if they are to move toward an improved relationship? What are the options for third-party intervention?

Paul B. Pedersen. "The Cultural Context of Peacemaking." In *Peace, Conflict, and Violence,* edited by Daniel J. Christie, Richard V. Wagner, and Deborah DuNann Winter. Upper Saddle River, NJ: Prentice Hall, 2001, 183–192.

Sarah Rosenberg. "Humiliation." Beyond Intractability Knowledge Base (website), July 2003, www.beyondintractability.org/m/Humiliation.jsp.

Luc Reychler. "Listening." In *Peacebuilding: A Field Guide,* edited by Luc Reychler and Thania Paffenholz. Boulder, CO: Lynne Rienner, 2001.
John Paul Lederach. "The Moral Imagination: The Art and Soul of Building Peace," September 30, 2004 (1 page), http://www.beyondintractability.org/audio/john_paul_lederach_at_acr/?nid=6728.

Part 4: Nonviolence:
Peace Through Collective Action and Advocacy

Week 9: Nonviolent Perspectives on Power and Social Change
How can parties to conflict confront power asymmetries and opportunistic, unprincipled adversaries without resorting to violence? How have some individuals and movements sought to promote peace and change amid inhospitable circumstances?

Fisk and Schellenberg, chapter 4 ("Nonviolence: A Road Less Travelled").
Aung San Suu Kyi. "Freedom from Fear." In *Freedom from Fear and Other Writings,* edited by Michael Aris. New York: Viking, 1991.

Week 10: Approaches to Nonviolent Action
How does nonviolence work? What can nonviolent social movements achieve, and on what basis should we evaluate them?

Fisk and Schellenberg, chapter 5 ("From Protest to Cultural Creativity: Peace Movements Identified and Revisited").
Elise Boulding. "Cultures of Peace and Communities of Faith." In *Transforming Violence: Linking Local and Global Peacemaking,* edited by Judy Zimmerman Herr and Robert Herr. Waterloo, ON: Herald Press, 1998.

Part 5: Transformation:
Peace Through Learning and Moral Development

Week 11: Peaceful Behavior as Learned Behavior
What are the implications of viewing violence and war as cultural institutions? Can peace be learned?

Fisk and Schellenberg, chapter 6 ("Shaping Visionaries: Nurturing Peace Through Education").
Lana L. Hostetler. "Preparing Children for Peace." In *Rethinking Peace,* edited by Robert Elias and Jennifer Turpin. Boulder, CO: Lynne Rienner, 1994.

Week 12: Conclusion
What is the role of "vision" in shaping the human future? Where do we go from here?

Václav Havel. "The End of the Modern Era." In *Social Theory: The Multicultural and Classic Readings,* edited by Charles Lemert. Boulder, CO: Westview, 1993.

Jim Wallis. "Faith Works." In *The Impossible Will Take a Little While: A Citizen's Guide to Hope in a Time of Fear,* edited by Paul Rogat Loeb. New York: Basic Books, 2004.

Fisk and Schellenberg, epilogue, 195–210.

Week 13: Final Exam

TEACHING NOTES

As an introductory peace studies course, "Roots of Conflict, Violence, and Peace" is likely to provide many students with their first opportunity for sustained reflection on matters pertaining to war, peace, and the problem of aggressive human behavior. Although some students are likely to have a reasonably (or perhaps even impressively) well-informed understanding of local and global conflicts, many will be hoping for an approach to instruction that makes concepts "come alive" and demonstrates the subject matter's personal relevance. For maximum effectiveness, pedagogy should (1) clearly define and illustrate core concepts during carefully structured but dynamic lectures, (2) reinforce abstract ideas about conflict and peace with weekly video clips, and (3) provide scope for discussion about how course content relates to current events and debates. Completing short essays and reporting on an "enrichment activity" (i.e., a topical public lecture or community event) during the term can also enhance student capacity to integrate, evaluate, and apply course material.

At the beginning of each term, it is useful to remind students that the subject matter covered by peace and conflict studies courses is inevitably open to multiple interpretations. Students will not always agree with ideas presented in course readings, lectures, and discussions. This is a good thing because disagreements provide opportunities to test, clarify, and evaluate ideas. What matters is not whether everyone in the classroom can agree, but whether people who hold differing views can engage one another with respect and integrity. The first class session provides an excellent opportunity to introduce the notion of collaborative learning (each person in the classroom is potentially a "resource" for every other person) and the practice of active listening, through which one listens not only for words, opinions, and ideas but also for the experiences, emotions, and commitments that inform them. Each of the five major paradigms explored during the term is likely to have at least one advocate in the classroom—a fact that affords opportunities for deeper learning about the subject matter and about the world.

8.2 Peace Paradigms

Thomas E. Boudreau
Syracuse University

COURSE DESCRIPTION

Upper level undergraduate or graduate course.

This course provides an overview of the history, development, and current expression of contending theoretical and practical approaches to preserving international peace, their basic assumptions and methods, and specific applications to current conflicts. Special attention is given throughout the semester to alternatives to war or terrorism. For the purpose of analysis and discussion, these contending approaches will be grouped into the following four paradigms:

1. Peace through power. The focus will be on the threat or use of governmental power, including military force and bilateral or regional alliances to secure the peace. We will read theories of realism, neorealism, and the multiple critics of these schools in this section.

2. Peace through law—world order and institutions. Contending paradigms of international order will be examined, including human rights regimes and the rule of law. We will use the book *Bounding Power: Republican Security Theory from the Polis to the Global Village* (Princeton University Press, 2006) by Daniel Deudney. This book presents the theory of "Republican Security Theory" as an alternative to realism, neorealism, or traditional liberalism.

3. Peace through communication—conflict resolution. We will examine the possible resolution of prolonged conflict through enhanced communications, third-party intervention, problem solving, identity affirmation, and relationship transformation. We will read the works of Mohammed Abu-Nimer and Roger Fisher, among others, in this section.

4. Peace through nonviolence—contemporary nonviolent social and spiritual movements. Here we will study the nonviolent strategies and tactics of Mohandas Gandhi and Dr. Martin Luther King Jr., their philosophies of nonviolence, and other spiritually based nonviolent social movements. We will read the works of Charles Tilly, Eric Hoffer, Hannah Arendt, Margaret Mead, and Newton Garver, among others. The goals of such movements are often to obtain political, economic, or ecological justice through the "mobilization of the masses" on a national and/or international level.

REQUIRED TEXTS

Robert J. Art and Robert Jervis, eds. *International Politics: Enduring Concepts and Contemporary Issues,* 8th ed. New York: Pearsons/Longman, 2007.

Daniel Deudney. *Bounding Power: Republican Security Theory from the Polis to the Global Village.* Princeton, NJ: Princeton University Press, 2006.

Mohammed Abu-Nimer. *Reconciliation, Justice, and Coexistence: Theory and Practice.* Lanham, MD: Lexington Books, 2001.

Gene Sharp. *The Politics of Nonviolent Action: Power and Struggle.* Boston: Porter Sargent, 1973.

Paul Wallace. *White Roots of Peace: The Iroquois Book of Life,* 2nd rev. ed. Santa Fe, NM: Clear Light Books, 1994.

Albert Camus. *Neither Victims Nor Executioners.* Translated by Dwight McDonald. Originally published in *Combat* (1946. http://www.ppu.org.uk/e_publications/camus1.html.

Roger Fisher, Bruce M. Patton, and William L. Ury. *Getting to Yes: Negotiating Agreement Without Giving In.* New York: Houghton Mifflin, 1992.

RECOMMENDED TEXTS

Graham Allison. *Essence of Decision.* Boston: Little Brown, 1971.

Johan Galtung. *Peace by Peaceful Means.* Boulder, CO: Sage, 1996.

Abdul Aziz Said, Charles O. Lerche Jr., and Charles O. Lerche III. *Concepts of International Politics in Global Perspective,* 4th ed. Upper Saddle River, NJ: Prentice Hall, 1995.

COURSE SCHEDULE

Week 1: Paradigms as Maps

The Contested Concept of "Paradigm Shift" (Kuhn).

Camus, *Neither Victims Nor Executioners,* introduction.

Week 2: Peace Through Power? Political Realism and Neorealism

Art and Jervis, *International Politics,* "Six Principles of Political Realism" by Hans Morgenthau.

Art and Jervis, *International Politics,* "A Critique of Morgenthau's Principles of Political Realism" by J. Ann Tickner.

Art and Jervis, *International Politics,* "The Anarchic Structure of World Politics" by Kenneth N. Waltz.

Art and Jervis, *International Politics*, "Anarchy and the Struggle for Power" by John J. Mearsheimer.

Alexander Wendt. "Anarchy Is What States Make of It." *International Organization* 46, no. 2 (Spring 1992): 391–425.

Week 3: Peace Through Power?
The Use of Force in International Affairs

Thucydides, "The Melian Dialogue."

Art and Jervis, *International Politics*, "The Four Functions of Force" by Robert Art.

Art and Jervis, *International Politics*, "The Diplomacy of Violence" by Thomas C. Schelling.

Art and Jervis, *International Politics*, "Coercive Diplomacy" by Robert Art.

Art and Jervis, *International Politics*, "Offense, Defense and the Security Dilemma" by Robert Jervis.

Art and Jervis, *International Politics*, "What Is Terrorism?" by Bruce Hoffman.

Week 4: Peace Through Power? Just War Theory—
a Critical Framework or Critical Failure?

David Smock. *Religious Perspectives on War.* Washington, DC: US Institute of Peace, 2002.

Week 5: Peace Through World Order? Realism or Reform?

Daniel Deudney, *Bounding Power*, Part 1: Traditions and Theory. Princeton, NJ: Princeton University Press, 2008.

Week 6: Peace Through World Order?
A New Law of Nations

Deudney, *Bounding Power*, Part 2: From the Polis to Federal Union. Princeton, NJ: Princeton University Press, 2008, 91–192.

Week 7: Peace Through World Order?

Deudney, *Bounding Power*, Part 3, 193–278.

Week 8: Peace Through World Order?

Art and Jervis, *International Politics*, chapter 3: "The Mitigation of Anarchy," 69–127.

Week 9: Peace Through Conflict Resolution?

Abu-Nimer, *Reconciliation, Justice, and Coexistence*, introduction, chapters 1–8, 10, 13, and conclusion.

Week 10: Peace Through Conflict Resolution?
The Great Law of Peace
Wallace, *White Roots of Peace.*

Week 11: Peace Through Nonviolence: What Is Violence?
Galtung, part IV, chapter 1, "Cultural Violence," 196–210.

Week 12: Peace Through Nonviolence:
Thoreau, Gandhi, Dr. King, and Dorothy Day
Sharp, *The Politics of Nonviolent Action: Power and Struggle.*

View before class *Gandhi,* produced by Richard Attenborough, DVD, 1982.

Martin Luther King Jr. "Letter from a Birmingham Jail," originally published 1964, available online at Martin Luther King Jr. Papers Project, Stanford University.

Week 13: Peace Through Transformation: Individual and Community Transformation
Henry David Thoreau, "On the Duty of Civil Disobedience."
Boudreau, "Building Human Cooperation Through Peace Studies." *Gandhi Marg* 11, no. 4 (January–March 1990): 389–402.
Paul Smoker and Linda Groff. "Creating Global-Local Cultures of Peace." *Peace and Conflict Studies* 3, no. 1 (June 1996), http://www.gmu.edu/academic/pcs/smoker.htm.

Week 14: Peace Through Reconciliation
and Identity Affirmation
President John F. Kennedy's American University Speech, June 1963.
Thomas E. Boudreau. "Conflict Reduction Through Identity Affirmation." *Peace and Conflict Studies* (Spring 2003).
Amitai Etzioni. "The Kennedy Experiment." *Western Political Quarterly* 20, no. 2, part 1 (June 1967): 361–380.

Week 15: Class Summary and Review
Albert Camus, *Neither Victims Nor Executioners.*

TEACHING NOTES

The course challenges students to think creatively and critically about the possible relationships among various theories and strategies developed in international relations theory for realizing peace. Some of the key assumptions of peace strategies to be examined include the use of military force, the evolution of global order values, the effectiveness of nonviolent activism, the role of improved communications, the transformative potential of mass movements, and moral beliefs or behavior.

Combining theory with policy applications, this course fosters the development of analytical skills for addressing peace and conflict resolution problems. Ultimately, it encourages students to envision their own creative, multidisciplinary approaches to the resolution of conflict and to the building of peaceful and just societies.

8.3 Introduction to Peace Studies

Abbie Jenks
Greenfield Community College

COURSE DESCRIPTION

Undergraduate (community college) course for liberal arts students and majors in peace and justice studies and psychology.

An interdisciplinary study of the concepts of peace and the interplay of economic, sociological, psychological, historical, political, technological, cultural, ideological, and environmental factors since the end of the Cold War, this course familiarizes students with the salient concepts of positive and negative peace, peacemaking, and the principles of a culture of peace.

This class will function primarily through active discussion, small group activities, independent discovery and research, readings, dialogue, video, speakers, social actions, and role-play/classroom activities. In other words, it will be less about lecture and more about active participation. A reading by one of you followed by a minute of silence for reflection will begin each class.

REQUIRED TEXTS

David Barash, ed. *Approaches to Peace: A Reader in Peace Studies*. Oxford University Press, 2000.

SUGGESTED TEXTS

Joseph Fahey and Richard Armstrong, eds. *A Peace Reader: Essential Readings on War, Justice, Nonviolence, and World Order*. Paulist Press, 1992.

David P. Barash and Charles P. Webel. *Peace and Conflict Studies*. Sage, 2002.

COURSE SCHEDULE

Week 1: Introduction

What is peace studies? Why study peace? What is a culture of peace? Learn about the United Nations Educational, Scientific, and Cultural Organization (UNESCO). Review the course. Daily moment of silence.

Barash, *Approaches to Peace*, introduction.

Week 2: Why War?
Study individual psychological and sociological factors leading to war. Question why we fight and whether it is a biological imperative.

Barash, *Approaches to Peace,* 9–35 (Freud, Lorenz, Mead, Sumner, Tuchman, Janis) and 36–59 (Howard, Galtung, Boulding, poetry, Klare). The focus is on the role of nationalism and new types of conflicts.

Week 3: Negative Peace
Contact the Veterans Education Project (http://www.vetsed.org/#resource) to locate a veteran in your area who can speak to the class.

Define "negative peace" and talk about means of preventing war.

Barash, *Approaches to Peace,* 65–69; 80–90 (James, O'Brien, Myrdal).

Week 4: Reducing Conflict
Focus on ways to reduce conflict and shift understanding of how we are taught to solve conflicts.

Barash, *Approaches to Peace,* 90–106 (Fischer and Ury, Osgood).

Week 5: Positive Peace
Explore the role of international law and the United Nations in building positive peace.

Barash, *Approaches to Peace,* 106–126 (Barash, Goulding, Kant).

Week 6: Positive Peace (cont.)
Learn to prevent structural violence and define how positive peace is different from negative peace.

Barash, *Approaches to Peace,* 131–149 (Leopold, Friere, King).

Week 7: Human Rights
Consider inviting a local speaker who is working for economic sustainability on the local level.

Barash, *Approaches to Peace,* 149–164 (Barash, Oxfam).

Week 8: Nonviolence
Barash, *Approaches to Peace,* 171–180 (Thoreau, Tolstoy, Millay).

Week 9: Gandhian Nonviolence
Consider inviting a local peace activist to speak to the class. This session focuses on one's personal transformation into an advocate and practitioner of nonviolence.

Barash, *Approaches to Peace,* 184–197 (Gandhi, Sharp).

Week 10: Religious Inspiration
View in class segments of *A Force More Powerful,* DVD.

Barash, *Approaches to Peace,* 203–211 (Hindu, Buddhist, Taoist).

Week 11: Religious Inspiration (cont.)
Barash, *Approaches to Peace,* 211–221 (Jewish, Christian, Muste, Merton, Kennan).

Week 12: Peace Movements, Transformation, and the Future
Barash, *Approaches to Peace,* 228–242 (Young, Boulding).

Week 13: The Future
Envisioning the future: a culture of peace. What does it look like?

Barash, *Approaches to Peace,* 242–263 (Falk, Reardon, Havel, poetry).

Week 14: Final Project Presentations
"If we have no peace, it is because we have forgotten that we belong to each other."—Mother Teresa

8.4 Introduction to Peace Studies

Katy Gray Brown
Manchester College

COURSE DESCRIPTION

Undergraduate introductory course for general education students or peace studies majors.

This course provides an introduction to peace studies—an interdisciplinary field that considers questions such as, How can human conflicts be resolved in ways that promote justice and peace? We will explore the definitions, conditions, and causes of violence, nonviolence, war, and peace, be they between nations, groups, or individuals. In this work, we will study distinctions between the concepts of *negative peace,* or the absence of war, and *positive peace,* understood as the presence of values and practices that promote justice and well-being within a society, such as economic and social justice and environmental stewardship. The class will also distinguish between overt forms of violence (collective or individual) and what Johan Galtung has termed *structural violence:* those practices that disadvantage people through unjust political or economic systems and/or cultural traditions. Participants in the class will explore a broad range of historical examples of people responding creatively to situations of violence and injustice and, from this study, construct their own understandings of creative response to conflict.

REQUIRED TEXTS

See reading assignments in the course plan.

COURSE PLAN

Week 1

"Seville Statement on Violence." United Nations Educational, Scientific, and Cultural Organization (UNESCO). 1986. http://www.unesco.org/cpp/uk/declarations/seville.pdf.

Natalie Angier. "Is War Our Biological Destiny?" *New York Times,* November 11, 2003.

Bowling for Columbine, produced and directed by Michael Moore, MGM, DVD, 2003, 119 minutes. View before class.

Week 2

Howard Zinn. "Violence and Human Nature." In *Passionate Declarations.* New York: HarperCollins, 2003.

Chris Hedges. "Introduction." In *War Is a Force That Gives Us Meaning.* New York: Anchor Books, 2002.

David P. Barash and Charles P. Webel. "The Meanings of War." In *Peace and Conflict Studies.* London: Sage, 2002.

Week 3

Jeff Nygaard. "Propaganda, Part I." *Nygaard Notes,* November 18, 2005, www.nygaardnotes.org, read sections from issues 311, 313, 314, 315.

Faces of the Enemy, produced by Sam Keen, Quest Productions, DVD, 1987, 58 minutes. View in class.

Week 4

Dan Hollack. "Bloody Century." In *Hell, Healing, and Resistance,* by Daniel Hollack. Plough Publishing, 1999.

The Ground Truth, produced by Patricia Foulkrod, Universal Studios Home Entertainment, DVD, 2006, 78 minutes. View segments in class.

Week 5

Barash and Webel, "Peace Through Strength?" In *Peace and Conflict Studies.*

Tim O'Brien. "On the Rainy River." In *The Things They Carried.* Boston: Houghton Mifflin, 1998.

Hearts and Minds, produced by Peter Davis, 1974, Criterion Collection, DVD, 2002, 112 minutes. View segments in class.

Weeks 6 and 7

Bill Galvin et al. *Draft Counselor's Manual.* Washington, DC: National Interreligious Service Board for Conscientious Objectors/Center on Conscience and War, 2002.

The Conscientious Objector, produced by Terry Benedict, Cinequest Films, DVD, 2007, 101 minutes. View segments in class.

Week 8

Robert L. Holmes and Barry L. Gan. "General Introduction." In *Nonviolence in Theory and Practice.* Long Grove, IL: Waveland Press, 2005.

Michael Nagler. "'Work' vs. Work." In *The Search for a Nonviolent Future.* Maui, HI: Inner Ocean Publishing, 2004.

Gene Sharp. "198 Methods of Nonviolent Direct Action." Albert Einstein Institution, 1973, http://www.aeinstein.org/organizations103a.html.

Week 9

Martin Luther King Jr., "Letter from a Birmingham Jail." Martin Luther King Jr. Papers Project, Stanford University, 1964, http://www.stanford.edu/group/King/popular_requests/frequentdocs/birmingham.pdf.

A Force More Powerful, produced by Steve York, Santa Monica Pictures, DVD, 1999. View the segment on Nashville sit-ins in class.

Martin Luther King Jr. "Declaration of Independence from the War in Vietnam" (1967). In *The Power of Nonviolence,* edited by Howard Zinn Boston: Beacon Press, 2002.

Week 10

Howard Zinn. "A War to Save the Jews?" In *Strength Through Peace,* edited by Colman McCarthy. Center for Teaching Peace, 2002.

Ken Brown. "Was the 'Good War' a Just War?" In *Nonviolent America: History Through the Eyes of Peace,* edited by Louise Hawkley. Newton, KS: Mennonite Press, 1993.

Philip Hallie. "From Cruelty to Goodness." In *Vice and Virtue in Everyday Life,* edited by Christina Hoff Sommers and Fred Sommers. New York: Harcourt College, 2001.

Howard Zinn. "Just and Unjust War." In *Passionate Declarations: Essays on War and Justice,* edited by Howard Zinn. New York: HarperCollins, 2003, 67–105.

Howard Zinn. "A Warrior Turns Pacifist." In *Strength Through Peace,* edited by Colman McCarthy. Center for Teaching Peace, 2002.

A Force More Powerful, DVD. Watch the segment on Danish resistance in class.

Week 11

Joan Bondurant. *Conquest of Violence: The Gandhian Philosophy of Conflict.* Princeton, NJ: Princeton University Press, 1988, v–35.

Weeks 12 and 13

This class focuses on student-generated issues and case studies. Students will facilitate class discussion on the social justice issues they have explored in small groups. They will frame the issues for the rest of the class and structure our discussion for the day they've selected.

Week 14

Thich Nhat Hanh. "Compassionate Listening," and other selections from *Anger,* by Thich Nhat Hanh. Riverhead Trade, 2002.

Colman McCarthy. "Do Small Things in a Great Way." In *Strength Through Peace,* edited by Colman McCarthy. Center for Teaching Peace, 2002.

8.5 Exploring Conflict and Peace

Gloria Rhodes (with thanks to Vernon Jantzi)
Eastern Mennonite University

COURSE DESCRIPTION

Introductory elective course for all undergraduates and a requirement for peace and conflict studies majors.

An overview of the field of peace and conflict studies, this course is designed to introduce students to issues of conflict and peacebuilding at personal, local, national, and global levels. The course lays out basic theories, key terms, and concepts associated with conflict, war, violence, justice, and peace and introduces students to peacebuilding frameworks and skills. An overview of current global issues is central to the course, along with an exploration of our rights, roles, and responsibilities as individuals and as a nation. Students will discover and attend to their own conflict styles and learn skills for dealing with conflict on an interpersonal level. They will participate in a peacebuilding project on campus or in the local community, and they will learn to analyze a conflict and explore peacebuilding by focusing on a current conflict or justice situation in the world.

Students satisfactorily completing the course will:

- Articulate issues of justice and peace at personal, local, and global levels.
- Distinguish the concepts of conflict, violence, justice, peace, and peacebuilding.
- Reflect on how their personalities, biographies, and identity relate to who they are and how they handle conflict situations.
- Analyze a personal conflict and develop and apply an approach for moving from destructive to constructive responses.
- Investigate a local conflict or situation of injustice (including campus and/or local issues) and participate in a small group peacebuilding project.
- Identify global issues of justice, peace, and conflict (e.g., poverty, population, globalization, militarization, gender, religion, and many more) and consider our responses and responsibilities.
- Research an ongoing conflict/justice situation in the world, analyze it, and offer strategies that could be pursued to produce a sustainable peace.
- Learn about peacebuilding and conflict transformation through stories/cases of peacebuilders in our community, our nation, and around the world.

REQUIRED TEXTS

Susan Gilmore and Patrick Fraleigh. *Communication Style Profile for Students*. Eugene, OR: Friendly Press. For additional personal conflict styles tools, use the Enneagram, Kraybill, or Myers-Briggs tools.

Marshall Rosenberg. *Nonviolent Communication: A Language of Life*, 2nd ed. Encinitas, CA: PuddleDancer Press, 2003. Articles and resources at www.nonviolentcommunication.com

Robert M. Jackson, ed. 2007. *Annual Editions: Global Issues, 2007–2008*. Dubuque, IA: McGraw-Hill, 2007.

Lisa Schirch. *Little Book of Strategic Peacebuilding*. Intercourse, PA: Good Books, 2004.

RECOMMENDED TEXTS

David P. Barash and Charles P. Webel. *Peace and Conflict Studies*. Thousand Oaks, CA: Sage Publications, 2002.

Robert Herr and Judy Zimmerman Herr, eds. *Transforming Violence: Linking Local and Global Peacemaking*. Scottdale, PA: Herald Press, 1999.

Peter Dula and Alain Epp-Weaver, eds. *Borders and Bridges: Mennonite Witness in a Religiously Diverse World*. Telford, PA: Cascadia Press, 2007.

Donald E. Miller et al. *Seeking Peace in Africa: Stories from African Peacemakers*. Telford, PA: Cascadia Press, 2007.

RECOMMENDED WEBSITES

Facing the Future, http://www.global-issues.net/. This organization provides resources for global issues education. They have a list of references that could also be used as texts for this section.

United Nations, http://www.un.org/issues/. Covers global issues on the UN agenda.

Christian Science Monitor, http://www.csmonitor.com/world/globalIssues.html.

US Department of State, http://usinfo.state.gov/pub/ejournalusa/global_issues.html.

Compare websites of the following: Human Rights Watch, Amnesty International, Jubilee, the World Bank, the International Monetary Fund, and the Office of the UN High Commissioner for Human Rights (http://www.unhchr.ch/index.htm).

RECOMMENDED VIDEO SOURCES

Wide Angle (Seasons 1–4), News and Public Affairs, Thirteen/WNET, New York. www.thirteen.org and www.pbs.org, wideangle@thirteen.org.

Journey to Planet Earth, Season 1 (1999) and Season 2 (2003), The State of the Earth (2005), and *Future Conditional (2005).* Documentaries produced by Marilyn Weiner and aired on public television.

COURSE SCHEDULE

Week 1: Overview of Justice, Peace, and Conflict Studies

Overview of course assignments.

Sorting out conflict and violence: What causes conflict? What causes violence?

Conflict dynamics, levels, and structures: Constructive and destructive forms.

Sources of knowledge about conflict: Why are sources important?

Bring a current news story about conflict or violence.

Resources for faculty:

Mennonite Conciliation Service. *Mediation and Facilitation Training Manual: Foundations and Skills for Constructive Conflict Transformation.* Akron, PA: MCS, 2000.

Hugh Miall, Oliver Ramsbotham, and Tom Woodhouse. *Contemporary Conflict Resolution.* Cambridge: Polity Press, 1999.

Week 2: What Is Peace? What Is Justice? Introduction to Peacebuilding and Conflict Transformation

Who am I in a conflict? (Understanding our conflict styles, unpacking our conflict biography, our identities as a source of conflict and resource for peace.)

Read Gilmore and Fraleigh.

Analyzing interpersonal conflict: What leads to peace? How can we transform destructive conflict into constructive conflict?

Bring a current news story about peace or justice.

Week 3: Strategies for Reducing Interpersonal Destructive Conflict

Read Rosenberg, *Nonviolent Communication* (NVC), chapters 1–3 and 4–6.

Skills practice, using NVC to talk about difficult issues.

Week 4: Nonviolent Communication

Read Rosenberg, *Nonviolent Communication,* chapters 7–9, 10–12, 13, and Epilogue.

Skills practice.

Week 5: Local Issues of Conflict and Justice: Immigration, Employment, Housing

Guest speakers from local justice or peace organizations.

Analyzing conflict (local and global context):

- Identity (gender, ethnicity, religion, sexual orientation).
- Basic human needs.
- Conflict analysis tools (e.g., conflict mapping, the onion, pyramid, ABC analysis).

Exam 1.

Resources for faculty:

John W. Burton. *Conflict: Resolution and Prevention.* London: Macmillan Press, 1990, chapters 1–3 (for basic human needs and conflict).

Simon Fisher, ed. *Working with Conflict: Skills and Strategies for Action.* New York: Zed Books, 2000 (for basic conflict analysis tools).

Jay Rothman. *Resolving Identity-Based Conflict in Nations, Organizations, and Communities.* San Francisco: Jossey-Bass, 1997 (for identity issues and conflict).

Week 6: Global Issues Introduction

Unit 1: Global Issues in the Twenty-First Century

Read Jackson, *Annual Editions: Global Issues, 2007–2008,* chapter 1.

Unit 2: Population and Food

Read Jackson, *Annual Editions: Global Issues, 2007–2008,* chapter 2.

Group project planning (interviews assignment).

Week 7: Global Issues

Unit 3: Global Environment and Natural Resources

Read Jackson, *Annual Editions: Global Issues, 2007–2008,* chapter 3.

Group project interviews due.

Video: your choice from *Journey to Planet Earth* series.

Week 8: Global Issues

Unit 4: Political Economy—Globalization

Read Jackson, *Annual Editions: Global Issues, 2007–2008,* chapter 4, articles 13–17.

Group project implementation and documentation.

Prepare characters for role playing.

Week 9: Global Issues

Unit 4: Political Economy—Globalization (cont.)
(global economy role play)
Group project implementation and documentation.

Role-play instructions: Divide the class into two groups (if more than twelve to fifteen students per group, create four equal groups). One group represents pro-globalization/pro–free trade interests. Subdivide the group into pairs of students to represent the World Trade Organization, the International Monetary Fund, the World Bank, and other related organizations or interests (I have included the US State Department, and other US private and public organizations that support free trade). The second group includes the antiglobalization and fair trade/trade justice movements. Subdivide into pairs of students to represent their choice of nongovernmental organizations, including consumer groups, trade unions, faith groups, aid agencies, and environmental groups such as the American Federation of Labor–Congress of Industrial Organizations (AFL-CIO) or other labor organizations, Human Rights Watch and/or Amnesty International, the Women's International Coalition for Economic Justice, American Friends Service Committee Jubilee (http://www.jubilee research.org/), the Presbyterian Church USA, Global Exchange, or Public Citizen. In the role play, groups 1 and 2 come together for mutual understanding. Each group must work together to prepare a ten- to twelve-minute presentation for the class, representing its position. All students must be prepared to role-play their positions. After the formal group presentations, students may respond in character. The instructor serves as the moderator.

Resources for faculty:
The following websites offer examples of role plays related to trade and globalization (accessed February 20, 2008):

- http://www.hull.ac.uk/pal/teaching_activities/Examples/example_10/index.html.
- http://www.hull.ac.uk/pal/teaching_activities/Examples/example_2/index.html.
- http://www.imf.org/external/np/exr/center/students/hs/think/lesson4.pdf.
- http://www.nya.org.uk/Global-Youth/Template.asp?NodeID=91276.

Week 10: Global Issues

Unit 4: Political Economy—Globalization (cont.)
Case: Latin America. Read Jackson, *Annual Editions: Global Issues, 2007–2008,* chapter 4, articles 18, 19.

Case: China, Central Africa. Read Jackson, *Annual Editions: Global Issues, 2007–2008,* chapter 4, articles 22, 23.

Video from *Wide Angle* series: *To Have and Have Not.*

Exam 2.

Week 11: Global Issues

Unit 5: Conflict: Nuclear Energy and Weapons
Read Jackson, chapter 4, articles 24, 25, 27, 32, 33.

Unit 5: Security and Terrorism
Read Jackson, *Annual Editions: Global Issues, 2007–2008,* Unit 5, articles 28–30.

Video suggestions: *On the Brink,* PBS *Journey to Planet Earth* series (conflict and environmental issues); *Scared Sacred,* National Film Board of Canada, or a clip from *Terrorism, a World in Shadows,* Ambrose Video (conflict and terrorism).

Week 12: Global Issues

Unit 5: Conflict
Case: Darfur. Read Jackson, *Annual Editions: Global Issues, 2007–2008,* chapter 5, articles 31, 34.

Conflict analysis example.

Unit 5: Prospects for Peace
Read Jackson, *Annual Editions: Global Issues, 2007–2008,* chapter 5, articles 35, 36.

Week 13: Global Issues: Peacebuilding

Unit 6: Cooperation
Read Jackson, *Annual Editions: Global Issues, 2007–2008,* chapter 6, articles 37–40.

Strategic peacebuilding case: Wajir district of Kenya, for example. Read Schirch.

Guest speaker: India or Northern Ireland, for example.

Resources for faculty:
Hizkias Assefa. "The Meaning of Reconciliation." In *People Building Peace: 35 Inspiring Stories from Around the World,* edited by Paul van Tongeren et al. Utrecht: European Centre for Conflict Prevention, 1999.
Paul van Tongeren et al., eds. *People Building Peace II: Successful Stories of Civil Society.* Boulder, CO: Lynne Rienner, 2005.

Week 14: Potential for Wholeness and Healing

Unit 7: Values and Visions

Read Jackson, *Annual Editions: Global Issues, 2007–2008,* chapter 7, articles 41–43.

Unit 7: Restorative Justice

Trauma healing.

Exam 3.

Resources for faculty:

Harold Coward and Gordon S. Smith. *Religion and Peacebuilding*. http://www.google.com/books?id=AlfrHagjAA8C&dq=religion+and+peacebuilding&pg=PP1&OTS=FG. Albany: State University of New York Press, 2004.

Pat Howley. *Breaking Spears and Mending Hearts: Peacemakers and Restorative Justice in Bougainville*. London: Zed Books/Federation Press, 2002.

Carolyn Yoder. *The Little Book of Trauma Healing: When Violence Strikes and Community Security Is Threatened*. Intercourse, PA: Good Books, 2005.

Week 15: Reconciliation

Case: South Africa (for example).

Group project presentations.

Resources for faculty:

Harold Coward and Gordon S. Smith. *Religion and Peacebuilding*. http://www.google.com/books?id=AlfrHagjAA8C&dq=religion+and+peacebuilding&pg=PP1&OTS=FG. Albany: State University of New York Press, 2004.

Mennonite Conciliation Service. *Mediation and Facilitation Training Manual: Foundations and Skills for Constructive Conflict Transformation*. Akron, PA: MCS, 2000.

TEACHING NOTES

One of the strategies I use at least once per week, often more, is to begin class by asking, "What's happening in the world (or on campus, or locally)?" We talk about how current events that students share are related to conflict and social justice. The students are encouraged to pay attention to local, national, international, and independent media. Students regularly report these discussions to be one of the highlights of the class.

I use many video or audio clips (recent movies, NPR or PBS offerings, etc.) as discussion starters and as practice for analyzing conflict and injustice. For peacebuilding cases, I bring in visiting peacebuilders or other students or faculty working for peace. There are also many cases to draw from (see Peter Dula and Alain Epp-Weaver, eds., *Borders and Bridges: Mennonite Witness in a Religiously Diverse World;* Paul van Tongeren et al., eds. *People Building Peace II: Successful Stories of Civil Society.* Boulder, CO: Lynne Rienner, 2005.

Students in this course are required to write personal reflective essays, undertake a group project on a local issue, and practice conflict analysis on an issue of global conflict in order to examine conflict at three levels.

9
Violence and Nonviolence

IN CONTRAST TO THE USUAL ASSUMPTION THAT SOCIOPOLITICAL power must be attained and sustained through force, even deadly force, nonviolence rejects the use of violence and asserts that power is based on the consent of the people. Power is understood as pluralistic, given that all governments depend on the cooperation of the governed. A government or any other form of social organization that seeks to maintain power through the use or threatened use of violence has already lost the very power it seeks. This distinction is captured concisely in Hannah Arendt's often-cited adage: "Power and violence are opposites; where the one rules absolutely, the other is absent."

Regarding the important distinction between passive nonresistance and active nonviolence, Gandhi's concept of satyagraha is key. The term is literally translated as "clinging to truth" but is often abbreviated as "soul force," which speaks more directly to this distinction. While rejecting violence, nonviolence is nonetheless active rather than passive and employs nonviolent force. Jonathan Schell captures this distinction most concisely in his observation, "Violence is a method by which the ruthless few can subdue the passive many. Nonviolence is a means by which the active many can overcome the ruthless few." Another distinction must be made between adherents to principled nonviolence and those who believe that nonviolence is a practical method of social change. Pacifists represent the former well, whereas the writings of Gene Sharp illustrate the latter.

Each of the four syllabuses in this chapter include primary source readings from major theorists of nonviolent social change such as Leo Tolstoy, Mohandas Gandhi, and Martin Luther King Jr., as well as resources that describe the application of nonviolent methods. Kenneth L. Brown integrates a rich array of primary readings and applies theory through case studies. His approach encourages students to wrestle with the moral and practical implications of nonviolence in such historical cases as Nazi Germany and the Israeli-Palestinian conflict today. Like Brown, Maria J. Stephan begins with the theoretical bases of nonviolence, considers the strategic dimensions of nonviolence in protracted and complex conflict, and concludes with an exploration of the role of nonviolence in the promotion of democracy. Nathan C. Funk's syllabus provides an opportunity to evaluate the efficacies of violent and nonviolent change, including the impact of political realism. He also explores classical Christian approaches to war, such as pacifism and just war theories. Richard Johnson's course is devoted entirely to Gandhi's life and philosophy of nonviolence.

9.1 Nonviolence: Theory and Practice

Kenneth L. Brown
Manchester College

COURSE DESCRIPTION

Upper-level undergraduate or master's-level course in peace studies or philosophy.

This course briefly surveys the theory of nonviolence as exemplified by practitioners such as Mahatma Gandhi and Martin Luther King Jr., and the categories of alternative responses to violence as developed by Gene Sharp in his three-volume *Politics of Nonviolent Action.* Classic case studies, such as Gandhi's Salt March of 1930, Danish resistance to German occupation from 1940 to 1945, student civil rights tactics in the US South in the 1960s, Solidarity strikes in Poland in 1980, nonviolent revolution in the Philippines in 1986, and the intifada in Palestine are examined through documentaries and texts. During the final week, students will share paper topics on applying nonviolent alternatives to a historical, present, or possible conflict from the context of their own cultural and political backgrounds.

REQUIRED TEXTS

Robert L. Holmes and Barry L. Gan. *Nonviolence in Theory and Practice,* 2nd ed. Long Grove, IL: Waveland Press, 2001.

Manfred B. Steger and Nancy S. Lind. "Violence: Definitions and Concepts." In *Violence and Its Alternatives: An Interdisciplinary Reader,* by Manfred B. Steger and Nancy S. Lind. New York: St. Martin's, 1999.

Michael Nagler. *Is There No Other Way?* Makawao, HI: Inner Ocean Publishing, 2003.

Robert J. Lifton. "Doubling: The Faustian Bargain." In *Web of Violence: From Interpersonal to Global,* edited by Jennifer Turpin and Lester Kurtz. Urbana: University of Illinois Press, 1997.

David McReynolds. "Philosophy of Nonviolence." Essay series no. 15. New York: A. J. Muste Memorial Institute.

Gene Sharp. *The Politics of Nonviolent Action.* 3 vols. Boston: Porter Sargent, 1973.

Joe Fahey and Richard Armstrong. *Peace Reader.* Mahwah, NJ: Paulist Press, 1992.

William James. "The Moral Equivalent of War." 1907. http://www.barnard.edu/amstud/resources/nationalism/james.htm.

David Barash. *Approaches to Peace.* New York: Oxford University Press, 2000.

Henry David Thoreau. *"Civil Disobedience" and Other Essays.* BN Publishing, 2006. http://www.transcendentalists.com/civil_disobedience.htm.

David Daube. "The Women of the Bible and Greece." In *Civil Disobedience in Antiquity,* edited by David Daube. Edinburgh: Edinburgh University Press, 1972.

Joan Bondurant. *Conquest of Violence: The Gandhian Philosophy of Conflict.* Princeton, NJ: Princeton University Press, 1988.

Gandhi, produced by Richard Attenborough, DVD, 1982.

Peter Ackerman and Jack DuVall. *A Force More Powerful: A Century of Nonviolent Conflict.* New York: Palgrave Macmillan, 2001.

The Meeting, directed by Bill Duke, written by Jeff Stetson, Monterey Media, DVD, 1989, 73 minutes.

Kenneth Smith and Ira Zepp: "King: Nonviolence and Agape." In *Search for the Beloved Community,* Kenneth Smith and Ira Zepp. Valley Forge, PA: Judson Press, 1974.

Colman McCarthy, ed. *Strength Through Peace.* Washington, DC: Valley Forge Press, 2001.

CLASS SESSIONS AND READINGS

1. Definitions of Violence and Nonviolence

Holmes.

Steger and Lind, "Violence: Defnitions and Concepts," xv–xxvi.

2. Analyses and Prospects

Nagler, chapter 2.

Turpin and Kurtz, "Doubling the Faustian Bargain," by Robert J. Lifton, 30–44.

3. Theoretical Bases for Nonviolent Alternatives

McReynolds, part 1.

Sharp, part 1, chapter 1.

4. Techniques of Nonviolent Action

Fahey and Armstrong, "Techniques of Nonviolent Action," by Gene Sharp.

Sharp, part 1, chapter 2.

James, "The Moral Equivalent of War," in Barash, or online at http://www.barnard.edu/amstud/resources/nationalism/james.htm.

5. Issues

Thoreau, "Civil Disobedience" in Barash, or online at http://www.transcendentalists.com/civil_disobedience.htm.

Holmes and Gan, "The Women of the Bible and Greece," by Daube.

6. Gandhi

Bondurant, 3–35.

Watch before class *Gandhi,* DVD.

7. Gene Sharp

Sharp, 82–87.
Nagler, "Constructive Program" and "Fighting Fire with Water."
McReynolds, part 2.

Watch in class "India: Movement for Self-Rule," in *A Force More Powerful,* DVD.

8. Martin Luther King Jr.

Holmes, "How Transforming Power Was Used . . . Against Race Prejudice in America," by Apsey.
Holmes, "Letter from a Birmingham Jail," by King.

Watch in class Episode 1, *A Force More Powerful,* DVD.

9. The Challenge of Remedial Violence

Browse Internet biographical resources on Malcolm X.

Watch in class *The Meeting,* video.

Smith and Zepp, "King: Nonviolence and Agape," 54–69, 132–140.

10. World War II: What About Hitler?

McReynolds, part 4.

Watch in class "Denmark," in *A Force More Powerful,* DVD.

McCarthy, "A War to Save the Jews?" by Zinn.
McCarthy, "Warrior Turns Pacifist" by Zinn.
McCarthy, "Nonviolent Weapons of the Spirit."

11. Parameters of Nonviolent Action

McReynolds, parts 3–7.

Students begin presenting paper topics.

12. Poland and Solidarity

Ackerman and DuVall, "Poland: Power from Solidarity," in *A Force More Powerful.*

Students present paper topics.

13. The Philippines

Ackerman and DuVall, "Philippines: Restoring Democracy," in *A Force More Powerful.*

Students present paper topics.

14. Palestine

Ackerman and DuVall, "Intifada: Campaign for a Homeland," in *A Force More Powerful.*

Students present paper topics.

15. Reflections

Ackerman and DuVall, "Victory Without Violence," in *A Force More Powerful.*

Nagler, "Toward a Metaphysics of Compassion."

9.2 Nonviolent Conflict: Between "Soft" and "Hard" Power

Maria J. Stephan
International Center on Nonviolent Conflict

COURSE DESCRIPTION

Graduate seminar, adaptable for upper-level undergraduates in political science, sociology, and peace and conflict studies.

In the past decade, three undemocratic regimes were removed from power by organized, civilian-led nonviolent movements. In Serbia (2000), Georgia (2003), and Ukraine (2004–2005), opposition movements challenged governmental tyranny and electoral fraud—and won—using demonstrations, strikes, boycotts, civil disobedience, and noncooperation *in a premeditated and strategic fashion.* In Lebanon, nearly a million Christians, Muslims, and Druze took to the streets in a remarkable display of nonviolent civic power to demand government accountability and to force the withdrawal of Syrian troops in 2005. Opposition groups and movements in Zimbabwe, Belarus, Egypt, Iran, Burma, West Papua (Indonesia), Western Sahara, and the occupied Palestinian territories are currently engaged in nonviolent struggles for basic rights and freedoms.

Nonviolent conflict is a method that occurs outside traditional political channels and involves civilians wielding nonviolent sanctions in an attempt to deny legitimacy and practical support to a ruler or other power holder. Historically, the impact of nonviolent struggles on interstate and intrastate relations has been great. The Gandhi-led Indian independence movement, the "people power" movement in the Philippines that toppled the Marcos dictatorship, the nonviolent ouster of Augusto Pinochet in Chile, the Polish Solidarity movement that dismantled communist authoritarian rule, and the antiapartheid struggle that brought democracy to South Africa are only a few examples in which broad-based, nonviolent, civic resistance has been used to delegitimize authoritarian or unjust rulers and dissolve their pillars of support. In all these cases, power shifted hands when masses of people stopped obeying and used nonviolent sanctions to separate the rulers from their sources of power. Yet, as brutally suppressed nonviolent movements in China, Tibet, and Burma demonstrate, this form of struggle is never guaranteed to succeed.

This seminar will begin with a discussion of the main theories underlying nonviolent conflict, including theories of power, contention, and strategy.

We will employ analytical insights from various academic disciplines—notably sociology, political science, and strategic studies—to analyze the dynamics underlying this phenomenon.

The seminar will address the following questions: Why do certain civilian-led struggles succeed while others fail? What are key strategic considerations for groups that choose nonviolent struggle? What roles have media and communications technology played in past and current struggles? How have external actors influenced local movements—positively and negatively? We will analyze historical and contemporary cases of civilian-led struggles, including movements for civil and political rights, struggles against dictatorships and authoritarian regimes, and movements for self-determination and against foreign occupations.

REQUIRED TEXTS

Peter Ackerman and Christopher Kruegler. *Strategic Nonviolent Conflict: The Dynamics of People Power in the Twentieth Century.* Westport, CT: Praeger, 1994.

Mark Palmer. *Breaking the Real Axis of Evil.* Lanham, MD: Rowman and Littlefield, 2005.

Kurt Schock. *Unarmed Insurrections: People Power Movements in Nondemocracies.* Minneapolis: University of Minnesota Press, 2005.

Anders Boserup and Andrew Mack. *War Without Weapons.* London: Frances Pinter, 1974.

RECOMMENDED TEXTS

Peter Ackerman and Jack DuVall. *A Force More Powerful: A Century of Nonviolent Conflict.* New York: Palgrave Macmillan, 2001.

Gene Sharp. *Waging Nonviolent Struggle: Twentieth-Century Practice and Twenty-First Century Potential.* Boston: Porter Sargent, 2005.

Robert Helvey (US Army, Ret.). *On Strategic Nonviolent Conflict: Thinking About the Fundamentals.* Boston: Albert Einstein Institution, 2004.

COURSE SCHEDULE

Unit 1: Nonviolent Conflict: Theories and Critiques

Class 1: Introductions and Course Overview

Class 2: What Is Nonviolent Conflict?

Gene Sharp. *There Are Realistic Alternatives.* Boston: Albert Einstein Institution, 2003, 1–16, http://www.aeinstein.org/organizations/org/TARA.pdf.

Schock, *Unarmed Insurrections,* intro and chapter 1.

Peter Ackerman and Jack DuVall. "People Power Primed." *Harvard International Review* (Summer 2005): 42–47.

Doug McAdam and Sidney Tarrow. "Nonviolence as Contentious Interaction." *PS: Political Science and Politics* 33, no. 2 (June 2000): 149–154.

Kurt Schock. "Nonviolent Action and Its Misconceptions: Insights for Social Scientists." *PS: Political Science and Politics* 36, no. 4 (October 2003): 705–712.

Class 3: Power, Violence, and Collective Defiance

Hannah Arendt. "On Violence" (Part II). In *Crises of the Republic,* by Hannah Arendt. New York: Harcourt Brace, 1972, 134–155.

Doug Bond. "Nonviolent Direct Action and Power." In *Justice Without Violence,* edited by Paul Wehr, Heidi Burgess, and Guy Burgess. Boulder, CO: Lynne Rienner, 1994, 59–81.

Martin Luther King Jr. "Letter from a Birmingham Jail." In *Nonviolence in Theory and Practice,* edited by Robert Holmes and Barry Gan. Longrove, IL: Waveland Press, 2005, 101–113.

Recommended reading:

Henry David Thoreau. "On the Duty of Civil Disobedience." In *Walden and On the Duty of Civil Disobedience,* by Henry David Thoreau. New York: Knopf, 2006.

Class 4: Structure and Agency:
Can Good Skills Overcome Bad Conditions?

Ackerman and Kruegler, *Strategic Nonviolent Conflict,* foreword, introduction, chapters 1–2.

Helvey, *On Strategic Nonviolent Conflict,* chapters 6 and 9, http://www.aeinstein.org/organizations/org/OSNC.pdf.

Palmer, *Breaking the Real Axis of Evil,* chapter 7 ("The Use of Nonviolent Force").

Schock, *Unarmed Insurrections,* chapter 2 and conclusions.

Recommended reading:

Boserup and Mack, chapter 3, "The Ability to Withstand Repression."

Brian Martin and Wendy Varney. "Nonviolence and Communication." *Journal of Peace Research* 40, no. 2 (March 2003): 213–232.

Class 5: Strategic Dimensions of
Nonviolent Conflict and Major Challenges

Ralph Summy. "Nonviolence and the Case of the Extremely Ruthless Opponent." *Pacifica Review* 6, no. 1 (1994).

Brian Martin. "Gene Sharp's Theory of Power." *Journal of Peace Research* 26, no. 2 (1989): 213–222.

David Hess and Brian Martin. "Repression, Backfire, and the Theory of Transformative Events." *Mobilization* 11, no. 1 (June 2006): 249–267.

Boserup and Mack, chapter 2, "The Analogy with Guerilla Warfare," 68–82.

Recommended reading:

Brian Martin. *Justice Ignited: The Dynamics of Backfire*. Lanham, MD: Rowman and Littlefield, 2007, introduction, chapters 2–4.

Class 6: The Role of External Actors (Part I)

Palmer, *Breaking the Real Axis of Evil,* introduction, chapters 1–6.

Adrian Karatnycky and Peter Ackerman. "How Freedom Is Won: From Civic Resistance to Durable Democracy." Freedom House Report, 2005, summary, http://www.freedomhouse.org/uploads/special_report/29.pdf.

John Crist, Harriet Hentges, and Daniel Serwer. *Strategic Nonviolent Conflict: Lessons from the Past, Ideas for the Future*. Special Report 87, May 1, 2002, US Institute of Peace, http://www.usip.org/pubs/special reports/sr87.html.

Jennifer Windsor. "Breaking the Poverty-Insecurity Nexus: Is Democracy the Answer?" In *Too Poor for Peace? Global Poverty, Conflict, and Security in the Twenty-First Century,* edited by Lael Brainard and Derek Chollet. Washington, DC: Brookings Institution Press, 2007, chapter 10.

Recommended reading:

Jessica Tuchman Matthews. "Power Shift." *Foreign Affairs* 76 (January–February 1997).

Unit 2: Case Studies: Successes and Failures

Class 7: Asia

Schock, *Unarmed Insurrections,* chapters 3–5 (Philippines, Burma, China, Nepal, Thailand).

Joshua Paulson. "Uprising and Repression in China." In *Waging Nonviolent Struggle,* edited by Gene Sharp. Boston: Porter Sargent, 2005, chapter 22.

Recommended reading:

Ackerman and DuVall, *A Force More Powerful,* chapter 10 ("The Philippines: Restoring Democracy").

Sharp, *Waging Nonviolent Struggle,* chapter 8 ("The Muslim Pashtun Movement for the North-West Frontier of India, 1930–1934" by Mohammad Raqib).

Class 7: Europe

Ackerman and Kruegler, *Strategic Nonviolent Conflict,* chapter 8 ("Solidarity vs. the Polish Communist Party, 1980–81").

Sharp, *Waging Nonviolent Struggle,* chapter 27 ("Removing the Dictator in Serbia, 1996–2000," by Joshua Paulson).

Anika Binnendijk and Ivan Marovic. "Power and Persuasion: Nonviolent Strategies to Influence State Security Forces in Serbia (2000) and Ukraine (2004)." *Communist and Post-Communist Studies* (September 2006): 1–19.

Georgi Kandelaki. "Rose Revolution: A Participant's Story." Special Report 167 (July 2006), US Institute of Peace.

Recommended reading:

Pavol Demes and Joerg Forbrig. "Pora—'It's Time' for Democracy in Ukraine." In *Revolution in Orange,* edited by Anders Aslund and Michael McFaul. Washington, DC: Carnegie Endowment for International Peace, 2006, chapter 5.

Ackerman and DuVall, *A Force More Powerful,* chapter 3.

Class 8: Latin America

Ackerman and DuVall, *A Force More Powerful,* chapter 7.

Palmer, *Breaking the Real Axis of Evil,* 110–125.

Recommended reading:

Ackerman and Kruegler, *Strategic Nonviolent Conflict,* chapter 7 ("El Salvador: The Civic Strike of 1944").

Class 9: Africa

Schock, *Unarmed Insurrections,* chapter 3 ("People Power Unleashed: S. Africa and the Philippines").

Ackerman and DuVall, *A Force More Powerful,* chapter 9.

Mark Palmer, *Breaking the Real Axis of Evil,* 125–138.

Maria J. Stephan and Jacob Mundy. "Transforming the Battlefield: The Unarmed Intifada in the Occupied Western Sahara." *Journal of Military and Strategic Studies* (Spring 2006).

Recommended reading:

Maggie Makanza. "The Anatomy of the Zimbabwean Problem." Paper presented at the Public Discussion Forum hosted by the Zimbabwe Social Forum and the Institute for Justice and Reconciliation, Cape Town, South Africa, August 10, 2006, http://kubatana.net/html/archive/opin/060810mm.asp?sector=OPIN.

Class 10: Middle East/North Africa

Ralph Crow, Philip Grant, and Saad Ibrahim. *Arab Nonviolent Political Struggle in the Middle East.* Boulder, CO: Lynne Rienner, 1990, chapters 2, 4, 6.

Maria J. Stephan. "Fighting for Statehood: The Role of Civilian-Based Resistance in the East Timorese, Palestinian, and Kosovo Albanian Self-Determination Movements." *Fletcher Forum of World Affairs* 30, no. 2 (Summer 2006): 57–81.

Stephen Zunes. "Unarmed Resistance in the Middle East and North Africa." In *Nonviolent Social Movements,* edited by Stephen Zunes, Lester Kurtz, and Sarah Beth Asher. Boston: Blackwell, 1999.

Souad Dajani. "Nonviolent Resistance in the Occupied Territories: A Critical Reevaluation." In *Nonviolent Social Movements: A Geographical Perspective,* edited by Stephen Zunes, Lester R. Kurtz, and Sarah Beth Asher. Boston: Blackwell, 1999.

Recommended reading:

Ackerman and DuVall, *A Force More Powerful,* chapter 11 ("The Intifada: Campaign for a Homeland").

Unit 3: Local Struggles and External Actors

Class 11: Civil Society and Democracy Promotion

Thomas Carothers. "The Backlash Against Democracy Promotion." *Foreign Affairs* (March–April 2006).

"The Backlash Against Democracy Assistance." National Endowment for Democracy, June 8, 2006.

Peter Ackerman and Michael Glennon. "The Right Side of the Law." *American Interest* (September–October 2007): 41–48.

Recommended reading:

Thomas Carothers. "From the Bottom Up: Civil Society." In *Aiding Democracy Abroad: The Learning Curve,* by Thomas Carothers. Washington, DC: Carnegie Endowment for International Peace, 1999, 207–251.

"Report of the Independent Task Force on Threats to Democracy." In *Protecting Democracy: International Responses,* edited by Morton Halperin and Mirna Galic. Oxford: Lexington Books, 2005.

Class 12: Terrorism and Transnational Activism

Hardy Merriman and Jack DuVall. "Dissolving Terrorism at Its Roots." In *Nonviolence: An Alternative for Defeating Global Terror(ism),* edited by Senthil Ram and Ralph Summy. Hauppauge, NY: NOVA Publishers, 2007, 221–234.

Clifford Bob. "Merchants of Morality." *Foreign Policy* (March–April 2002).

Sidney Tarrow. *The New Transnational Activism.* Cambridge: Cambridge University Press: 2005, chapters 3 and 11.

Ackerman and DuVall, *A Force More Powerful,* chapter 13.

TEACHING NOTES

This course is designed to be interactive, and teachers should consider employing a variety of media, including documentary films, the videogame of strategic nonviolent conflict called *A Force More Powerful: The Game of Nonviolent Strategy* (www.afmpgame.com), and newspaper reports of nonviolent campaigns taking place around the world. Inquiries about purchasing the films *A Force More Powerful: A Century of Nonviolent Conflict; Bringing Down a Dictator;* and a film on the 2005 Orange Revolution in Ukraine, *Orange,* should be directed to York Zimmerman (www.yorkzim.com).

The thirty- to thirty-five-minute film segments from the Emmy-nominated *A Force More Powerful* are perfect for classroom use. Teachers may choose to use the *A Force More Powerful* companion book (Ackerman and DuVall) more extensively, particularly when the cases overlap with those depicted in the film. Also, the fifty-five-minute film, *Bringing Down a Dictator,* about the Serbian Otpor movement, tends to be wildly popular with students. Assignments might include one or more papers with a thematic or regional focus, journal entries on playing the videogame, and a final paper that asks students to place themselves in the shoes of a strategist leading a contemporary nonviolent struggle. Alternatively, students could be asked to focus on the positive and negative roles played by external actors (government, nongovernmental organizations, international organizations, business, the media, solidarity groups) in assisting local nonviolent movements. In order to receive daily news items about various nonviolent struggles taking place around the world (news items are organized by region), teachers should write to ICNC@nonviolent-conflict.org and request that they and/or their students be added to the ICNC "Daily Digest" mailing list. These news items, taken from mainstream and nonmainstream sources, prompt great blackboard and in-class discussions about various themes related to nonviolent conflict. Using those items is a great way to supplement the core readings and films.

9.3 Violence, Nonviolence, and War

Nathan C. Funk
Conrad Grebel University College

COURSE DESCRIPTION

Intermediate undergraduate-level course for general education students or peace studies and related majors.

This course explores debates concerning the relative merits of violent and nonviolent strategies for pursuing high-value social and political goals, with particular emphasis on the need to engage and evaluate claims pertaining to the efficacy of nonviolent action. Students will critically examine a range of views, from political realism and just war theory to pacifism and various forms of nonviolent resistance. The following questions will guide the inquiry:

- Why have war and organized violence often been regarded as necessary evils or even as social goods?
- What interests and functions has war served? What are the moral, human, environmental, and financial costs of war?
- Under what circumstances can nonviolent methods of defending or advancing social and ethical values succeed in the face of determined opposition? To what extent can nonviolent strategies of social change or defense be substituted for violent strategies? Is social learning possible?

By the end of the term, students in this course should be able to

- Identify functions and dysfunctions of violence in contemporary societies and in world politics.
- Explain various moral and ethical positions pertaining to the use of violent sanctions by states and nonstate political movements.
- Demonstrate mastery of key concepts linked to nonviolence.
- Evaluate strategies for replacing organized violence with nonviolent action in instances of acute social and political conflict.
- Articulate a personal political philosophy or ethic concerning matters of war, violence, and peaceful change.

REQUIRED TEXTS

Robert L. Holmes and Barry L. Gan. *Nonviolence in Theory and Practice*, 2nd ed. Long Grove, IL: Waveland Press, 2001.

Readings listed in the course schedule.

COURSE SCHEDULE

Part 1: Introduction

Session 1: Meeting One Another and Defining Our Purpose

Session 2: Confronting the Problem of Violence

Jonathan Schell. *The Unconquerable World: Power, Nonviolence, and the Will of the People*. New York: Metropolitan Books, 2003. Read the introduction.

Gene Sharp. *Social Power and Political Freedom*. Boston: Porter Sargent, 1980. Read chapter 10 ("Seeking a Solution to the Problem of War").

Douglas P. Fry. *The Human Potential for Peace: An Anthropological Challenge to Assumptions About War and Violence*. New York: Oxford University Press, 2006. Read chapter 5 ("The Cross-Cultural Peacefulness-Aggressiveness Continuum").

Further reading:

Earl Conteh-Morgan. *Collective Political Violence: An Introduction to the Theories and Cases of Violent Conflicts*. New York: Routledge, 2004.

Veena Das et al., eds. *Remaking a World: Violence, Social Suffering, and Recovery*. Berkeley: University of California Press, 2001.

Elizabeth Kandel Englander. *Understanding Violence*. Mahwah, NJ: Lawrence Erlbaum Associates, 1997.

Ronald J. Glossop. *Confronting War*, 4th ed. Jefferson, NC: McFarland, 2001.

Chris Hedges. *War Is a Force That Gives Us Meaning*. New York: Public Affairs, 2002.

Samuel Peleg. "Who Participates in Protracted Conflicts and Why? Rediscovering the Group and Its Needs." In *The Understanding and Management of Global Violence*, edited by Harvey Starr. New York: St. Martin's Press, 1999.

Charles Tilly. *The Politics of Collective Violence*. New York: Cambridge University Press, 2003.

Jennifer Turpin and Lester R. Kurtz, eds. *The Web of Violence: From Interpersonal to Global*. Chicago: University of Illinois Press, 1997.

Part 2: Traditional Arguments About Violence and War

Session 3: War in Political Realism

Steve Forde. "Classical Realism." In *Traditions of International Ethics*, edited by Terry Nardin. New York: Cambridge University Press, 1992.

Phil Williams, Donald M. Goldstein, and Jay M. Shafritz, eds. *Classic Readings of International Relations*. Belmont, CA: Wadsworth Publishing,

1994). Read "Relations Among Sovereigns," by Hobbes (28–30) and "Six Principles of Political Realism," by Morgenthau (34–38).
J. E. Hare and Carey B. Joynt. *Ethics and International Affairs*. London: Macmillan, 1982. Read chapter 2 ("The Political Realists").

Further reading:
Roger Boesche. *The First Great Political Realist: Kautilya and His Arthashastra*. Oxford: Lexington Books, 2002.
Thomas Hobbes. *The Leviathan*. Baltimore: Penguin Books, 1968.
Michael E. Howard. *Clausewitz*. Oxford: Oxford University Press, 1983.
Niccolò Machiavelli. *The Prince and the Discourses*. New York: Modern Library, 1950.
Sunzi. *The Art of War*. Toronto: Oxford University Press, 1971.
Max Weber. *Politics as a Vocation*. Philadelphia: Fortress Press, 1965.

Session 4: Just War Theory
Paul Christopher. *The Ethics of War and Peace: An Introduction to Legal and Moral Issues*, 2nd ed. Prentice-Hall, 1999. Read chapter 3 ("Saint Augustine and the Tradition of Just War").
Brian Orend. *The Morality of War*. Peterborough, ON: Broadview Press, 2006. Read chapter 1 ("A Sweeping History of Just War Theory").

Further reading:
Michael Cranna and Nils Bhinda. *The True Cost of Conflict*. New York: New Press, 1995.
Neta C. Crawford. "Just War Theory and the US Counterterror War." *Perspectives on Politics* 1, no. 1 (March 2003): 5–25.
Terry Nardin. *The Ethics of War and Peace: Religious and Secular Perspectives*. Princeton, NJ: Princeton University Press, 1996.
Carolyn Nordstrom. *A Different Kind of War Story*. Philadelphia: University of Pennsylvania Press, 1997.
Michael Walzer. *Just and Unjust Wars: A Moral Argument with Historical Illustrations*. New York: Basic Books, 1977.

Session 5: Religious and Ethical Objections
Holmes and Gan, introduction, xvii–xxii.
Holmes and Gan, Part I ("Preview," "Nonviolence in Eastern Philosophy and Religion," "Judaism, Christianity, and Islam," "From *Apology* and *Crito*," "Plato").
Holmes and Gan, Part IV ("Preview," and "James").

Further reading:
Hagen Berndt. *Non-Violence in the World Religions: Vision and Reality*. London: SCM Press, 2000.

Robert L. Holmes. *On War and Morality*. Princeton, NJ: Princeton University Press, 1989.

Glenn D. Paige. "Political Science: To Kill or Not to Kill." *Social Alternatives* 19, no. 2 (May 2000).

Daniel L. Smith-Christopher, ed. *Subverting Hatred: The Challenge of Nonviolence in Religious Traditions*. Cambridge, MA: Boston Research Center for the Twenty-First Century, 1998.

David R. Smock. *Perspectives on Pacifism: Christian, Jewish, and Muslim Views on Nonviolence and International Conflict*. Washington, DC: US Institute of Peace, 1995.

Part 3: Nonviolent Responses to Conflict

Session 6: Philosophical Bases of Nonviolence

Holmes and Gan, Part I ("Thoreau").

Holmes and Gan, Part II ("Preview," "Tolstoy," "Gandhi," "King").

Holmes and Gan, Part III ("Preview," "Women" by Bacon).

Further reading:

Joan V. Bondurant. *Conquest of Violence: The Gandhian Philosophy of Conflict*. Berkeley, CA: University of California Press, 1965.

Mohandas K. Gandhi. *An Autobiography: The Story of My Experiments with Truth*. Boston: Beacon Press, 1957.

Gandhi. *Non-Violent Resistance*. New York: Schocken Books, 1951.

Richard Gregg. *The Power of Nonviolence*. Canton, ME: Greenleaf Books, 1959.

Martin Luther King Jr. *Why We Can't Wait*. New York: New American Library, 1963.

Thomas Merton, ed. *Gandhi on Non-Violence: A Selection of Writings from Mahatma Gandhi*. New York: New Directions, 1964.

Krishnalal Shridharani. *War Without Violence*. Bombay: Bharatiya Vidya Bhavan, 1962.

Session 7: Principles and Methods of Nonviolent Action

Holmes and Gan, Part IV ("Peace Through Strength" by Norman).

Holmes and Gan, Part V ("Preview," "Nonviolent Action," "The Technique," "Liberation Without War," "Personal Perfection"). Also choose one of the following: C. Chong or R. Taylor.

Further reading:

Nicholas F. Gier. *The Virtue of Nonviolence: From Gautama to Gandhi*. Albany: State University of New York Press, 2004.

Václav Havel. *Open Letters: Selected Writings 1965–1990*, edited by Paul Wilson. New York: Random House, 1991.

Gene Sharp. *Gandhi as a Political Strategist, with Essays on Ethics and Politics*. Boston: Porter Sargent, 1979.

Sharp. *The Politics of Nonviolent Action: Part One: Power and Struggle*. Boston: Porter Sargent, 1973.

Sharp. *The Politics of Nonviolent Action: Part Two, The Methods of Nonviolent Action*. Boston: Porter Sargent, 1973.

Sharp. *There Are Realistic Alternatives*. Boston: Albert Einstein Institution, 2003. www.aeinstein.org.

Thomas Weber. "Nonviolence Is Who? Gene Sharp and Gandhi." *Peace and Change* 28, no. 2 (April 2003): 250–270.

Session 8: Dynamics of Nonviolent Action

Holmes and Gan, Part VI ("Preview," "The Philippines," "South Africa," "Cesar Chavez").

James Satterwhite. "Christian Peacemaker Teams as an Alternative to 'Redemptive Violence.'" *Peace and Change* 31, no. 2 (April 2006): 222–243.

Further reading:

Peter Ackerman and Jack DuVall. *A Force More Powerful: A Century of Nonviolent Conflict*. New York: Palgrave, 2000.

Peter Ackerman and Christopher Kruegler. *Strategic Nonviolent Conflict: The Dynamics of People Power in the Twentieth Century*. Westport, CT: Praeger, 1994.

Aung San Suu Kyi. *Freedom from Fear and Other Writings*, edited by Michael Aris. New York: Penguin, 1995.

Mark Juergensmeyer. *Gandhi's Way: A Handbook of Conflict Resolution*. Berkeley: University of California Press, 1984.

Gene Sharp. *The Politics of Nonviolent Action: Part Three, The Dynamics of Nonviolent Action*. Boston: Porter Sargent, 1973.

Part 4: The Challenge of Transforming Violent Conflict

Session 9: Criteria for Evaluating Nonviolent Action

Brian Orend. "Evaluating the Pacifist Alternative." In *The Morality of War*, by Brian Orend. Peterborough, ON: Broadview Press, 2006.

Michael N. Nagler. "'Work' Versus Work." In *Is There No Other Way? The Search for a Nonviolent Future*, by Michael N. Nagler. Berkeley, CA: Berkeley Hills Books, 2001.

Further reading:

Peter Ackerman and Christopher Kruegler. *Strategic Nonviolent Conflict*. Westport, CT: Praeger, 1994.

Ronald M. McCarthy and Gene Sharp. *Nonviolent Action: A Research Guide*. New York: Garland, 1997.

Kurt Schock. "Nonviolent Action and Its Misconceptions: Insights for Social Scientists." *PS: Political Science and Politics* 36, no. 4 (October 2003): 705–712.

Ralph Summy. "Nonviolence and the Case of the Extremely Ruthless Opponent." *Pacifica Review* 6, no. 1 (1994).

Session 10: Nonviolence and International Relations

Robert J. Burrowes. "Cross-Border Nonviolent Intervention: A Typology." In *Nonviolent Intervention Across Borders,* edited by Yeshua Moser-Puangsuwan and Thomas Weber. Honolulu: University of Hawai'i Press, 2000.

Holmes and Gan, Part IV ("Pacifism and Invasion").

Holmes and Gan, Part VI ("World War II," and "Lithuania's Nonviolent Struggle").

"In Depth: Romeo Dallaire." CBC News Online, March 9, 2005, http://www.cbc.ca/news/background/dallaire/.

Further reading:

Robert Burrowes. *The Strategy of Nonviolent Defense: A Gandhian Approach.* New York: State University of New York Press, 1996.

Ronald J. Glossop. *Confronting War,* 4th ed. Jefferson, NC: McFarland, 2001.

Thomas Hastings. *Nonviolent Response to Terrorism.* Jefferson, NC: McFarland, 2004.

Mahendra Kumar. *Violence and Nonviolence in International Relations.* Delhi: Thomson Press, 1975.

Jonathan Schell. *The Unconquerable World.* New York: Metropolitan Books, 2003.

Session 11: Nonviolence and Identity Conflict

Holmes and Gan, Part V ("The Practice of Nonviolence" and "Satyagraha").

Holmes and Gan, Part VI ("Examples of Nonviolence," "Nonviolent Soldier of Islam," "Living Truth," and "Nonviolence").

Roger Powers et al., eds. *Protest, Power, and Change.* New York: Garland, 1997.

Read "Identity Theory" by Terrell A. Northrup, 239–241.

Further reading:

Mohammed Abu-Nimer. *Nonviolence and Peace Building in Islam.* Gainesville: University Press of Florida, 2003.

Robert C. Johansen. "Radical Islam and Nonviolence: A Case Study of Religious Empowerment and Constraint Among Pashtuns." *Journal of Peace Research* 34, no. 1 (February 1997): 53–71.

Alberto L'Abate. "Nonviolent Interposition in Armed Conflicts." www.gmu.edu/academic/pcs/labate.htm.

Marc Gopin. "Religion, Violence, and Conflict Transformation." *Peace and Change* 22, no. 1 (January 1997): 1–31.

Yehezkel Landau. *Healing the Holy Land: Interreligious Peacebuilding in Israel/Palestine*. Washington, DC: US Institute of Peace, 2003, www.usip.org/pubs/peaceworks/pwks51.html.

James Satterwhite. "Forestalling War in Kosovo: Opportunities Missed." www.nonviolentpeaceforce.org/research/forestalling_war_in_kosovo.htm.

Daniel L. Smith-Christopher, ed. *Subverting Hatred: The Challenge of Nonviolence in Religious Traditions*. Boston: Boston Research Center for the Twenty-First Century, 1998.

Rebecca Spence and Jason McLeod. "Building the Road as We Walk It: Peacebuilding as Principled and Revolutionary Nonviolent Praxis." *Social Alternatives* 21 (Autumn 2002): 61–64.

Paul Wehr. *Justice Without Violence*. Boulder, CO: Lynne Rienner, 1996.

Session 12: Visions for the Future

Elise Boulding. "Demilitarization." *Cultures of Peace: The Hidden Side of History*. Syracuse, NY: Syracuse University Press, 2000.

Jennifer Turpin and Lester R. Kurtz, eds. "Untangling the Web of Violence." In *The Web of Violence: From Interpersonal to Global*, edited by Jennifer Turpin and Lester R. Kurtz. Chicago: University of Illinois Press, 1997.

Further reading:

Adam Curle. *Another Way: Positive Response to Contemporary Violence*. Oxford: John Carpenter, 1995.

Martin Luther King Jr. *Where Do We Go from Here: Chaos or Community?* Boston: Beacon Press, 1967.

Mary King. *Mahatma Gandhi and Martin Luther King, Jr.: The Power of Nonviolent Action*. Paris: UNESCO, 1999.

Michael N. Nagler. *Is There No Other Way? The Search for a Nonviolent Future*. Berkeley, CA: Berkeley Hills Books, 2001.

William H. Shannon. *Seeds of Peace: Contemplation and Nonviolence*. New York: Crossroad, 1996.

Tod Schneider. *Transcending Violence*. Victoria, BC: Trafford, 2002.

Stephen Zunes, Lester R. Kurtz, and Sarah Beth Asher, eds. *Nonviolent Social Movements: A Geographical Perspective*. Malden, MA: Blackwell, 1999.

Session 13: Integrative Final Exam

TEACHING NOTES

This class encourages students to engage arguments about war and nonviolence through personal reflection and collective deliberation. Key tasks for the instructor include (1) designing a framework of assignments that encourages and rewards active and timely engagement with course readings (for example, a series of eight short "reading responses" submitted at the beginning of class); and (2) maintaining an "open space" in which students are free to express diverse opinions. Because many students have strong opinions about matters such as just war theory and the ethics of nonviolence, the real challenges are elevating the level of class deliberations and broadening participation, not simply generating discussion. Providing incentives to complete reading assignments can increase the number of students who come to class prepared for collaborative learning through small-group dialogue and structured debates. Balancing full-class discussions with small-group activities helps create a "safe" space for less vocal students to express their opinions. Instructors can encourage lively classroom exchanges by modeling active listening and by underscoring that what matters most is not whether or not everyone can agree, but whether or not all members of the classroom community are willing to engage one another with respect and integrity.

In addition to reading responses and an integrative final examination (predominantly in essay format), the instructor may wish to provide students with multiple options for a major course project such as (1) a research paper, (2) a two-part essay, or (3) a service learning project. Students opting for a more traditional research paper or an essay assignment could write about ways in which ideas explored in class have been (or might be) used in real-life conflict situations. Students who choose service learning could become involved with a local civil society organization that addresses issues related to violence and nonviolence in the community or in the world; this type of project could include a reflective journal or an investigation of the ethical and philosophical foundations of their organization's practice.

9.4 Gandhi

Richard Johnson
Indiana University–Purdue University, Fort Wayne

COURSE DESCRIPTION

Intermediate-level course for majors in peace studies, political science, sociology, and philosophy; also appropriate for general education.

This course provides students with a deeper understanding and experience of Mohandas K. Gandhi by offering readings, photos, and film from a wide variety of perspectives. It offers a historical context for Gandhi's life and affords students an opportunity to examine their own lives as they examine Gandhi's. A major goal of the course is to help students improve their ability to read, write, and discuss critically; to form and deepen a sense of community within the class; and to bring greater awareness of nonviolence, peace, and justice in Gandhi's time and in ours.

REQUIRED TEXTS

Eknath Easwaran. *Gandhi the Man: The Story of His Transformation.* Tomales, CA: Nilgiri Press, 1997.

Bart Gruzalski. *On Gandhi.* Belmont, CA: Wadsworth, 2001.

Richard L. Johnson, ed. *Gandhi's Experiments with Truth: Essential Writings by and About Mahatma Gandhi.* Lanham, MD: Lexington Books, 2005.

Peter Rühe. *Gandhi.* New York: Phaidon Press, 2001.

COURSE SCHEDULE

Session 1: Introduction

Johnson, *Gandhi's Experiments with Truth,* introduction and chapter 1.
Rühe, *Gandhi,* "Early Years," "Awakening in South Africa."

Gandhi's Experiments with Truth, introduction and chapter 1:

- Gandhi: "My life consists of nothing but . . . experiments with truth."
- Gandhi: "God is Truth . . . Truth is God."
- Gandhi's view of the connection of religion, spirituality, and morality with politics.
- Satyagraha.

Constructive Programme.
Gandhi's family and his marriage at age thirteen.
Gandhi's years in London (vegetarianism and religion).
Gandhi's experience on the train from Durban to Pretoria.
Leo Tolstoy, John Ruskin, and Shri Rajchandra.
Brahmacharya.
Mass meeting in Johannesburg, September 11, 1906, as foundation of satyagraha.
Hind Swaraj.

Session 2

Gandhi's Experiments with Truth, chapters 2 and 3.

Chapter 2:
"What shall I do with myself?"
Gandhi's four essential elements of political power.
Untouchables in the Sabarmati Ashram, 1915.
Satyagraha campaigns in Champaran, Ahmedabad; the Rowlatt satyagraha in 1919 and the Non-Cooperation Campaign of 1920–1922.
Gandhi's break with Britain.
Gandhi's justification of the Constructive Programme.
The salt satyagraha.
Gandhi, "The most powerful individual in India."
Fasting.
"Whole village work."
The British government and the Indian National Congress during World War II.
"Quit India" campaign.
The partition of India and Pakistan.
Gandhi's assassination and Gandhi's contributions.

Chapter 3:
Eating meat.
"Double shame" and "religious ferment."
Ruskin's *Unto the Last.*
"The Champaran inquiry was a bold experiment in Truth and Ahimsa."
Hartal.
"A Himalayan Miscalculation."
Gandhi's "Farewell."

Session 3

Gandhi's Experiments with Truth, chapters 4 and 8; *Gandhi the Man* ("The Transformation"); *On Gandhi,* chapter 8.

Gandhi's Experiments with Truth, chapter 4:
- Sheth Haji Habib's "solemn declaration."
- "The struggle itself was victory."
- Tolstoy Farm.
- Women in the satyagraha campaign of 1913.
- "Who would not love to die for one's motherland?"
- Great March of 1913.
- Was the satyagraha campaign in South Africa a success?

Gandhi's Experiments with Truth, chapter 8:
- "Truth force," "love force," and "soul force."
- Coercion and noncoercion.
- The influence of Salter and Henry David Thoreau on Gandhi.
- Gandhi's near-death experience and fearlessness.

Gandhi the Man, "The Transformation":
- The secret of success: "Every difficulty . . . an opportunity for service."
- *Bhagavad Gita.*

On Gandhi, chapter 8:
- Relationship between action and inner work.

Session 4

Ghandi's Experiments with Truth, chapters 5 and 9; *Gandhi the Man* ("The Way of Love").

Gandhi's Experiments with Truth, chapter 5:
- Gandhi on modern civilization.
- Gandhi: Indians gave dominion to British.
- Gandhi on religion.
- Outer and inner components of swaraj.
- Terrorist action against the British.
- Relationship of soul force (satyagraha) and history.
- Spiritual disciplines of swaraj.
- Gandhi on dangers of technology.
- Gandhi's letter to Millie Polak.
- Nonviolent revolution.
- Gandhi on nationalism.

Gandhi's Experiments with Truth, chapter 9:
- Gandhi's reliance on Eastern and Western ideas.
- Four elements of swaraj: national independence, political freedom of the individual, economic freedom of the individual, and spiritual freedom of the individual, or self-rule.

Gandhi the Man ("The Way of Love"):
- Krishna Kripalani and Gandhi on the effectiveness of nonviolence.

Satyagraha as "love in action."
Loving people, hating evil.
Gandhi on satyagraha as a service to both India and England.

Session 5

Gandhi's Experiments with Truth, chapters 7 and 15; *Gandhi* ("The Dawn of Nonviolent Resistance in India").

Gandhi's Experiments with Truth, chapter 7:
"True Education in the Ashrams."
Gandhi: "Religion to me is a living faith in the Supreme Unseen Force."
Gandhi: "The best propaganda is not pamphleteering, but for each one of us to try to live the life we would have the world to live."
Gandhi on Christianity.
The danger of relying on conscience.
Gandhi's famous cable to H. G. Wells.
Economics and spirituality.
Trusteeship of the wealthy and the cooperation of the poor.
Gandhi on education.
Gandhi links fasting with "LOVE" and the "heart."
Gandhi's conception of Hinduism.
Gandhi on labor and capital.
Means and ends.
Nonpossession and nonstealing.
The "science of non-violence."

Gandhi's Experiments with Truth, chapter 15:
Gandhian, neo-Gandhian, Gandhi-like.
Christian or Christlike?
Rebelling against class interests.
"Minimum agenda for being neo-Gandhian."

Session 6

Gandhi's Experiments with Truth, chapter 7; *Gandhi the Man* (Appendix: "How Nonviolence Works," by Timothy Flinders).

Gandhi's Experiments with Truth, chapter 7:
Comment on Gandhi's writings on peace.
Separation of "religion and State."
"Oceanic circle" of village republics.
Comment on Gandhi's writings on principles.
Gandhi's writings on religion.
Sarvodaya (the well-being of all).
What is satyagraha?
Gandhi on "boundless selfless service."

Gandhi on socialism and communism.
"Purification and Progress through Self-Suffering."
Swadeshi.
Gandhi's writings on truth.
Gandhi's writings on vows.
Gandhi: "Economic war is no better than armed conflict."
Gandhi's writings on women and men.
Gandhi's last months.

Gandhi the Man (Appendix: "How Nonviolence Works"):
Flinders's explanation of satyagraha.

Session 7

Gandhi's Experiments with Truth, chapter 10; *On Gandhi,* chapters 2–3.

Gandhi's Experiments with Truth, chapter 10:
Ronald J. Terchek on "Gandhi's sense of Indian independence."
Gandhi on power; St. Augustine on state power.
The state as "The New Idol."
Gandhi's view of democracy for India.
Majorities and minorities in a democracy.
Political pluralism and cultural pluralism.
Gandhi on bureaucracy.
"Gandhi's Ideal Democracy."

On Gandhi, chapter 2:
Nonviolence as a method of transformation.

On Gandhi, chapter 3:
"Challenge to the paradigm of justifiable violence."

Session 8

Gandhi's Experiments with Truth, chapters 11 and 12; *On Gandhi,* chapters 4 and 7; *Gandhi* ("Salt March and Its Consequences, 1930–1939").

Gandhi's Experiments with Truth, chapter 11:
Gandhi on talking to terrorists.
Origins of imperialist and anti-imperialist violence.
Failure of Non-Cooperation Campaign of 1920–1922.
Success of the Salt Campaign.
Gandhi on the failure of winning by violence.

Gandhi's Experiments with Truth, chapter 12:
East versus West on human rights.
Relationship of rights and duties.
"Gandhi's Vision of Authentic Humanity."
"Theory and Practice of Moral Growth."

Putting ideals into action.
Is there a role for compromise?
Practical nonviolence.
Human interdependence.

On Gandhi, chapter 4:
Gandhi on humans and animals.

On Gandhi, chapter 7:
Living in community.
Gandhi's critique of urban living.

Session 9

Gandhi's Experiments with Truth, chapters 6 and 13; *Gandhi the Man* ("Mother and Child," Part 1); *Gandhi* ("Quit India, 1939–1944").

Gandhi's Experiments with Truth, chapter 6:
"The constructive programme may otherwise and more fittingly be called construction of *poorna swaraj* or complete independence by truthful and non-violent means."
Communal unity "means an unbreakable heart unity."
The importance of *khadi* to Gandhi.
The status of women in India.
Fundamental laws of health and hygiene.
Gandhi on the importance of provincial languages and Hindi as a national language.
The importance of economic equality to nonviolent independence.
The place of civil disobedience in a nationwide nonviolence effort.
Nonviolence and "conscious body-labour."

Gandhi's Experiments with Truth, chapter 13:
Obstructive Programme and the Constructive Programme.
Conflicts between caste Hindus and Untouchables, Muslims and Hindus, women and men, peasants and city dwellers, labor and capital.
The purpose of spinning cloth.
Nagler on the possibilities for a Constructive Programme today.

Gandhi the Man ("Mother and Child," Part I):
Khan Abdul Ghaffar Khan, the "Frontier Gandhi."
Ghaffer Khan's shared roots with the Taliban.
Nonviolence as a collective and an individual discipline.
Gandhi ("Quit India, 1939–1944").

Session 10

Gandhi's Experiments with Truth, chapter 14; *Gandhi the Man* ("Mother and Child," Part II); *Gandhi* ("A Tragic Freedom, 1944–1948").

Gandhi's Experiments with Truth, chapter 14:
Gandhi as "The Anti-Imperialist Leader."
Gandhi as "The Guru."
Gandhi: *Mahatma,* saint, and *homo religious.*
Gandhi as "The Fraud."

Gandhi the Man ("Mother and Child," Part II):
Service without expectation of reward.
Meditation and other spiritual disciplines.
Gandhi ("A Tragic Freedom, 1944–1948").

Session 11

Gandhi's Experiments with Truth, chapter 16; *On Gandhi,* chapters 5 and 6; *Gandhi* ("Farewell").

Gandhi's Experiments with Truth, chapter 16:
The relationship between Gandhi and contemporary political thinking.
Doug Allen on interpreting Gandhi.
Relinquishing attachments to self.
Essential unity of all existence.
The self as understood through self-other relations.
Gandhi's metaphysical foundation.

On Gandhi, chapter 5:
Gandhi on achieving "equitable distribution."
Appropriate technology.

On Gandhi, chapter 6:
Self-reliance and independence versus globalization (i.e., mass production and industrialism).
Gandhi ("Farewell").

Session 12

Gandhi's Experiments with Truth, chapters 17 and 18; *On Gandhi,* chapter 9.

Gandhi's Experiments with Truth, chapter 17:
Gandhi's critics and admirers.
Gandhi's religious universalism.
On religious fundamentalism.
"Unity of man, the indivisibility of means and ends, and a non-Manichean view of the world."
Satyagraha: a redefinition of revolution.
Redefinitions of liberty (swaraj), equality (*samata*), citizenship (*nagarikata*), rights (*adhikar*), obligation (dharma), and tolerance (*sahishnuta*).
Gandhi's ability to "live his thought."

Gandhi's Experiments with Truth, chapter 18:
Gandhi's "five great calls for problem-solving action."
Glenn Paige's five current problems to be solved.
Five elements of Gandhi's legacy: "*spiritual*" nonviolence, "respect for *science,*" *individual and mass action,*" "*compassionate constructiveness,*" and "*creative courage.*"
Will nonviolent transformative action eventually prevail? What will the transformation look like? How long will it take?

On Gandhi, chapter 9:
What is Gandhi's legacy according to Gruzalski? According to you?

Session 13
Gandhi's Experiments with Truth, chapter 19; *Gandhi the Man* ("Gandhi the Man").

Gandhi's Experiments with Truth, chapter 19:
A "Gandhian Moment."
"Revived Gandhism of the 1990s."
"The Uncertain September 11 Effect."

Gandhi the Man ("Gandhi the Man"):
Meister Eckhart.
Gandhi: "The art of dying follows as a corollary from the art of living."

TEACHING NOTES

The Gandhi course relies heavily on student preparation. To help them in the discipline of reading and discussion, I administer a quiz each week by converting most topics in the syllabus into essay questions, typing one question to a sheet. I duplicate questions so that I have enough single questions for everyone in the class. Then I distribute one sheet (one question) to each student and give them the first part of the session to respond. After collecting the quizzes, I arrange students in small groups to discuss their responses to the different essay questions. The small group picks the question that intrigues them most and prepares several discussion points for the whole class. When their turn comes to report, I choose the reporter from the group so all must be prepared. I ask him or her to present the small group's work to the class for discussion. After thorough reporting and discussion, we move on to the next small group.

Writing assignments. Each week students write a 500-word critical response to one or more of the reflection topics listed in the course schedule and based on the readings and Rühe photos. I ask them to email written responses to me by 7:00 p.m. the day before class meets. They also write a more extensive analysis (1,500 words) of a topic they choose in the second half of the course.

In a more reflective assignment, students try their hands at their own "experiments with truth." They must come up with a project intended to help them bridge the "inner" and the "outer" in their own lives. A one-paragraph proposal is due in the first month of the course. A three-page written description of the project and an oral report in class are due in class in the last week of the course.

Exams. The final exam is an essay test. In addition, each student schedules a brief oral examination with the instructor at the end of the course.

10

Terrorism

FOR DECADES, POLITICAL REALISM, WITH ITS EMPHASIS ON THE PROtection of national sovereignty through the control of external threats, has dominated the field of international politics and influenced global perspectives in peace studies. However, the end of the Cold War and concomitant shifts in the international distribution of power prompted major reformulations of these assumptions at the end of the twentieth century. Then the events of September 11, 2001, forced the world to reconsider these and related questions yet again. Major issues at hand range from the effects of terrorism by nonstate actors to the presence of internal terrorist threats and to the cost and consequences of state terrorism. More inclusive inquiries include questions pertaining to new dimensions of human security, such as those associated with environmental and cultural degradation, and the relationship between the expansion of terrorism and global economic injustice.

Modern technology in an era of globalization and eroded sovereignty has reduced the distance between assumed security and internal or external threats. In response to perceived new security threats, the world has turned abruptly from global cooperation, the rule of law, and the role of the United Nations and now faces national security states, aggressive nationalism, military interventionism, and risks to world order associated with US imperial ambitions. The US-led wars in Iraq and Afghanistan and Washington's global campaign against terrorism serve as signal illustrations of such security policies.

The syllabuses in this section provide a wealth of perspectives from which one may address these concerns. Danielle Taana Smith and Uli Linke focus on the manner in which war, terrorism, and societal persecution have expanded the number of refugees and displaced persons around the world. Their course encourages students to engage in conversations within their local communities on these concerns and concludes with an evaluation of programs designed to restore the rights and dignity of refugees. George

Lakey has structured an excellent course around eight nonmilitary techniques for defending against terrorism, including, for example, the role of nonrepressive police work and the infrastructure of norms and laws. Beginning with a review of security concepts in the abstract, B. Welling Hall proceeds with the question, "What does it mean to say that the world changed forever on September 11, 2001?" Following a review of Samuel Huntington's thesis of the "clash of civilizations," her course examines whether terrorism represents a new form of warfare that supersedes previous conceptions of war. Michael Smith's syllabus provides a foundation for a sociological survey of terrorism and genocide. His approach assesses whether conflicts of ideology, race, ethnicity, religion, and class are associated with the contemporary expansion of terrorism and genocide."

10.1 War and Terror: The Global Displacement of Populations

Danielle Taana Smith and Uli Linke
Rochester Institute of Technology

COURSE DESCRIPTION

Upper-level elective in sociology, anthropology, political science, and peace and justice studies.

Daily we watch, seemingly helplessly, as people are displaced from their communities, homelands, and countries and subsequently seek asylum around the world, sometimes in our own local communities. Causes of displacement include war, violence, persecution, and modes of terror that increasingly affect the lives of women and children. In addition to the loss of human life and potential, the ensuing consequences of violent displacement include poverty, disease, physical and psychological trauma, hopelessness, and vulnerability to human rights abuses.

In this course, we explore how the rights and dignity of refugees can be protected. We also examine processes of community organization that emerge as refugees attempt to integrate into their host societies. For refugees who eventually return to their homelands, we address how they can resume normal lives in societies that are still struggling with the aftermath of war, violence, and the absence of vital infrastructures. Most importantly, we inquire how the trauma of displacement can be minimized.

REQUIRED READINGS

The readings include articles and documents concerning the global refugee crisis.

COURSE SCHEDULE

Part 1: Introduction and Overview

Week 1: Who Are the Displaced?

Walter Kälin. "Questions and Answers About Internally Displaced Persons." Office of the United Nations High Commissioner for Human Rights (UNHCHR), 2007, http://www.ohchr.org/english/issues/idp/issues.htm.

UNHCHR. "Handbook on Procedures and Criteria for Determining Refugee Status Under the 1951 Convention and the 1967 Protocol Relating to the

Status of Refugees, Part One." 1992, orig. pub. UNHCHR 1979, http://www.unhcr.org/publ/PUBL/3d58e13b4.pdf.

Exercise: Reflect on and write about people who are displaced within the United States and around the world. Who are these displaced people? What are the reasons for displacing people from their homes and countries?

Week 2: Causes and Consequences of Population Displacements

United Nations. "The State of the World's Refugees: Human Displacement in the New Millennium." New York: Oxford University Press, 2006, http://www.unhcr.org/static/publ/sowr2006/toceng.htm.

US Committee for Refugees and Immigrants. *Refugee Reports* 22 (2001), http://www.refugees.org/article.aspx?id=1237&rid=1178.

In-class exercise: View the film *Lord of War* (2005), written and directed by Andrew Niccol. "In the 80s in Little Odessa, the Ukrainian immigrant Yuri Orlov (Nicolas Cage) decides to change his economical [*sic*] life and becomes an arm [*sic*] dealer with his brother Vitaly Orlov (Jared Leto). His business of gunrunner supplying illegal weapons in disturbed areas of the planet increases with the end of the Cold War, and Yuri bribes a Russian general to sell most of his arsenal. Meanwhile, he becomes a millionaire and uses his money to seduce the beautiful Ava Fontaine (Bridget Moynahan), and they get married, having a son. The detective Jack Valentine (Ethan Hawke) chases Yuri trying to put him in jail, but in the end he understands that Yuri is a necessary evil for the interest of his nation" (written by Claudio Carvalho, Rio de Janeiro, Brazil, Internet Movie Database).

Part 2: Global Human Rights and National Policies

Week 3: Refugees and International Human Rights

UNHCHR. "Universal Declaration of Human Rights." 1948, 1989, http://www.unhchr.ch/udhr/lang/eng.pdf.

Amnesty International. *Reasonable Fear: Human Rights and United States Refugee Policy.* New York: Amnesty International USA, 1990.

Exercise: Identify people in your community who, in the course of their jobs, affect the lives of immigrants and refugees.

Week 4: US Refugee and Immigration Policies

US Citizenship and Immigration Services. "Immigration and Nationality Act (INA)." 2006. http://www.uscis.gov/propub/ProPubVAP.jsp?dockey=baeb6daf5705c4f8629f8b6ea9f7c64d.

US Department of Health and Human Services, Office of Refugee Resettlement. "The Refugee Act." http://www.acf.hhs.gov/programs/orr/policy/refact1.htm.

Exercise: Review and respond to US and international legislation relating to immigration and refugee and asylum status.

Part 3: Reshaping Communities

Week 5: Refugee Communities: Displacement and Integration

Erik Stenström. "Resettlement as a Multi-faceted Protection Tool and Its Relationship to Migration." Paper presented at the Global Consultations on International Protection Regional Resettlement Meeting, Oslo, Norway, November 6–7, 2001, http://www.unhcr.org/protect/PROTECTION/3c55256b5.pdf.

V. Robinson and C. Coleman. 2000. "Lessons Learned? A Critical Review of the Government Programme to Resettle Bosnian Quota Refugees in the United Kingdom." *International Migration Review* 34, no. 4 (2000): 1217–1244.

Exercise: Identify and contact an immigrant or refugee group in your community.

Week 6: Local Communities of Refugees and Others Who Are Displaced

Andrey Ivanov et al. "At Risk: Roma and the Displaced in Southeast Europe." United Nations Development Programme Regional Bureau for Europe and the Commonwealth of Independent States, Bratislava, 2006. http://www.europeandcis.undp.org/uploads/public/File/rbec_web/vgr/Fast Facts_At_Risk_report.pdf. Read the introduction, Part I (Roma), Part II (Displaced persons), and Policy Recommendations.

Exercise: Identify and contact an immigrant or refugee group in your community.

Week 7: Community Partnerships for Successful Resettlement

Office of Refugee Resettlement. "Annual Report to Congress." 2002. http://www.acf.hhs.gov/programs/orr/data/arc_02.htm.

A. Ramaliu and W. E. Thurston. "Identifying Best Practices of Community Participation in Providing Services to Refugee Survivors of Torture: A Case Description." *Journal of Immigrant Health* 5, no. 4 (2003): 165–172.

Exercise: Identify and contact a community, religious, or professional group in your community that provides services for refugees.

Part 4: Life in the Aftermath

Week 8: Economic Self-Sufficiency and Poverty

Office of Refugee Resettlement. Annual Report to Congress, 2000, http://www.acf.hhs.gov/programs/orr/data/00arc2.htm#_Ref532872905.

Tom Giossi et al. "Breaking Through Barriers of Refugee Self-Sufficiency." *Refugee Works, The National Center for Refugee Employment and Self-Sufficiency* 5, no. 3 (2004). Read entire issue.

Exercise: Conduct a community visit. Develop a relationship with the contacted group by attending or arranging a local meeting to learn more about the group's mission and objectives.

Week 9: Physical and Mental Health

M. S. Macksoud and J. L. Aber. "The War Experiences and Psychosocial Development of Children in Lebanon." *Child Development* 67, no. 1 (1996): 70–88.

B. D. Stein et al. "A Mental Health Intervention for Schoolchildren Exposed to Violence: A Randomized Controlled Trial." *Journal of the American Medical Association* 290, no. 5 (2003): 603–611.

Exercise: Watch the film *Well-Founded Fear,* directed by Michael Camerini and Shari Robertson, 2000. "This documentary film takes us to an in-depth look at the asylum process of the federal US Immigration and Naturalization Service (INS). Foreigners that are already in the United States, having fled their home countries, have the opportunity to apply for asylum through the INS. If a person's case establishes a 'well-founded fear' of his/her home country, the adjudicating immigration officer approves his/her asylum application. If a person's case does not quite meet up to the officer's expectation of a 'well-founded fear,' it is referred to an immigration judge for a decision" (Oliver Chu, Internet Movie Database).

Week 10: The Differential Impact of Refugee Status on Women and Children

Jeanne Ward and Mendy Marsh. "Sexual Violence Against Women and Girls in War and Its Aftermath: Realities, Responses, and Required Resources." Briefing paper prepared for the United Nations Symposium on Sexual Violence in Conflict and Beyond, Brussels, June 21–23, 2006. http://www.unfpa.org/emergencies/symposium06/docs/finalbrusselsbriefingpaper.pdf.

UNHCHR. "Convention on the Rights of the Child." 1989. http://www.ohchr.org/english/law/pdf/crc.pdf.

Exercise: Conduct a community visit. Work with the community group to develop a plan as to how best students can be engaged in collaboration in order for the group to achieve its established objectives. Collaboration depends on the group's needs and objectives, but could entail hosting one-time events such as awareness fairs or more long-term events such as tutoring programs and adult literacy programs.

Week 11: Family Dynamics and Cultural Integration

A. Portes and M. Zhou. "Should Immigrants Assimilate?" *Public Interest* 116 (1994): 18–33.

A. J. Umana-Taylor, R. Bhanot, and N. Shin. "Ethnic Identity Formation During Adolescence: The Critical Role of Families." *Journal of Family Issues* 27, no. 3 (2006): 390–414.

Exercise: Conduct a community visit. Implement a small-scale socializing activity that builds on the collaboration with community group, such as movie night or potluck dinner. The intent is to facilitate interactions between students and members of the community.

Week 12: Educational Attainment

Richard Neugebauer. "School-Based Interventions for Children Exposed to Violence." *Journal of the American Medical Association* 290, no. 19 (2003): 2541–2542.

Janet Chang and Thao N. Le. "The Influence of Parents, Peer Delinquency, and School Attitudes on Academic Achievement in Chinese, Cambodian, Laotian or Mien, and Vietnamese Youth." *Crime and Delinquency* 51, no. 2 (2005): 238–265.

Raymond Buriel et al. "The Relationship of Language Brokering to Academic Performance, Biculturalism, and Self-Efficacy Among Latino Adolescents." *Hispanic Journal of Behavioral Sciences* 20, no. 3 (1998): 283–297.

Exercise: Complete your assessment of the refugee community.

Week 13: Return and Reintegration of Refugees into Their Countries of Origin

Ron Redmond. "Iraq: UNHCR's Preliminary Repatriation and Reintegration Plan for Iraq." 2003. http://www.unhcr.org/news/NEWS/3ea938204.html.

Inter-Parliamentary Union. "The Prevention of Conflicts and the Restoration of Peace and Trust in Countries Emerging from War: The Return of Refugees to Their Countries of Origin, the Strengthening of Democratic Processes and the Hastening of Reconstruction." Resolution of the 99th Inter-Parliamentary Conference, Windhoek, South Africa, April 10, 1998. http://www.ipu.org/conf-e/99-1.htm.

Atle Grahl-Madsen et al., eds. *The Living Law of Nations: Essays on Refugees, Minorities, Indigenous Peoples, and the Human Rights of Other Vulnerable Groups*. Arlington, VA: N.P. Engel, 1996.

Exercise: Work on organization of a refugee forum.

Part 5: Student and Community Engagement in Developing Effective Refugee Policies

Week 14: Student Presentations

Exercise: Students will discuss issues refugees experience as they struggle to integrate into their host society and present policy measures to aid in their successful resettlement.

Week 15: Refugee Forum

Exercise: Provide a forum for an immigrant, refugee, or someone who works with these groups to share their stories publicly.

TEACHING NOTES

This course is designed to engage students in forming their own ideas about global refugee issues and the impact of refugees on local communities. Students will be encouraged to make their own observations and reach their own conclusions. Students are expected to complete the assigned readings before class and to participate in class discussions of the readings. Participation includes reflecting on the readings and commenting on them in class. The course is also based on experiential learning and is intended to be hands-on. To this end, we send students out into the local community to spend a significant proportion of class time speaking to people and agencies about refugees. Students will be graded on their written responses to the weekly assigned readings and assignments. The final assignment is to make a presentation about a salient issue facing diverse refugee groups and to devise policy suggestions to meet the resettlement needs of refugees in local US communities.

The course exercises were adapted from activities listed in *Well-Founded Fear: Facilitators' Guide,* a film by Shari Robertson and Michael Camerini.

10.2 Nonviolent Responses to Terrorism

George Lakey
Swarthmore College

COURSE DESCRIPTION

Intermediate- or upper-level undergraduate course for peace and justice studies majors and related majors.

This course explores eight nonmilitary techniques for combating terrorism, most of which have been used successfully in various contexts, but few of which have been used by the US government after September 11, 2001. Twenty-four sessions are divided into four units:

1. Nonviolent Struggles: Resources for Creating Responses.
2. Who Are Those Who Use Terror, and What Do They Want?
3. Eight Nonmilitary Techniques for Defending Against Terror.
4. Application to a Concrete Situation.

The course emphasizes the historical and contemporary resource of nonviolent struggle; such struggle provides the least understood source of power for defending against violence. Documentary films are used to supplement the readings.

Biases: Even though the terror used directly by governments is a major problem in the world, this course does not focus on state-sponsored terrorism; the primary attention of this course is on nonstate actors. And we will spend little time analyzing the flaws of military defense against terrorism; the focus here is on creative alternatives.

You will need tools for your work in this course. Following are eight nonmilitary techniques for defending against terror. Keep this list handy and refer to it as you read case studies and as you plan for your term paper.

Eight Nonmilitary Techniques for Defending Against Terror

1. *Nonrepressive police work and the infrastructure of norms and laws.* Police work can be less or more effective. Things that would make it more effective include more coordination with other police forces, more community policing, more of a pro-law/justice orientation on the part of states, and more global agreements, such as the International Criminal Court, the Kyoto Treaty, and the Ottowa Convention on land mines.

2. *Ally building and the infrastructure of economic development.* Although there is rarely a direct link between poverty and terrorism, there are indirect links of great importance. Case studies show that economic development may be an effective tool against terrorism (or may not). How could

economic development make a difference? Could it help a group gain allies in the search for nonviolent alternatives?

3. *Policy changes and the concept of reckless behavior.* It is now clear that states sometimes make choices that invite—almost beg for—a terrorist response, as when, for instance, one group occupies someone else's land or seizes their resources. How can states learn not to be reckless in this way, endangering the lives of their people?

4. *Negotiation.* Governments often say, "We don't negotiate with terrorists," but history shows that they do, in one form or another. How can this technique be used most effectively?

5. *Reducing marginalization through paying attention to culture.* As Britain has learned, marginalizing a group within your population is not safe or sensible; terrorists grow under those conditions. This is also true on a global level. Much marginalizing behavior is unconscious, but it can be reduced.

6. *Nonviolent protest/campaigns among defenders.* Terrorism happens in a political context and is therefore influenced by that context. Some terror campaigns have lapsed because they lost popular support. The rise and fall of support for terrorism is in turn influenced by social movements using people power (nonviolent struggle). How can this technique be enhanced?

7. *Education/training for conflict.* Terror happens when a population tries to suppress conflicts instead of waging them. A technique for reducing terror is to teach pro-conflict attitudes and skills.

8. *Post-terror recovery programs.* Not all terror can be prevented, any more than all crime or natural disasters. But populations can build resilience through, for example, trauma work, so the society doesn't become rigid with fear and create more terrorism through retaliation.

REQUIRED TEXTS

Arnold Mindell. *Sitting in the Fire.* Portland, OR: Lao Tse Press, 1995.

Robert A. Pape. *Dying to Win: The Strategic Logic of Suicide Terrorism.* New York: Random House, 2005.

Gene Sharp. *Waging Nonviolent Struggle: Twentieth-Century Practice and Twenty-First-Century Potential.* Boston: Porter Sargent, 2005.

A Force More Powerful, produced by Steve York, A Source More Powerful Films, DVD, 1999.

Bringing Down a Dictator, starring Ivan Marovic, Srdja Popovic, and Slobodan Milosevic, directed by Steve York, produced by Miriam Zimmerman, A Source More Powerful Films, DVD, 2002.

Occasional readings as assigned in the course schedule.

RECOMMENDED TEXTS

Martin Luther King Jr. *Why We Can't Wait*. New York: Penguin Signet, 2000. Describes the dynamics of countering racist violence in the Birmingham, Alabama, campaign.

George Lakey. *Powerful Peacemaking*. Gabriola Island, BC: New Society Publishers, 1987. Explains some conditions under which social movements can use their opponents' violence against them.

Martin Oppenheimer. *The Hate Handbook: Oppressors, Victims, and Fighters*. Lanham, MD: Rowman and Littlefield, 2005. A sociological description of contemporary hate groups.

Kathryn Watterson. *Not by the Sword*. New York: Simon and Schuster, 1995. A case study of successful intervention that turned around a Ku Klux Klan terrorist.

COURSE SCHEDULE

Session 1: The Nature of This Course

We will focus on the Norwegian example of adaptation of their previous nonviolent struggles of the 1920s and 1930s to the different challenge of World War II Nazi occupation. Can we adapt successfully to today's threats?

Unit 1: Nonviolent Struggles: Resources for Creating Responses (14 case studies)

Session 2: Nazi Violence as Iconic in the Discourse About Struggle

Sharp, *Waging Nonviolent Struggle*, chapters 9 (Norway), 10 (Berlin), and 30 (theory about repression).

View before class *A Force More Powerful* (segment on Danish resistance to Nazi occupation).

Response paper (300–600 words): Imagine yourself in one of the situations we're studying where people are confronting Nazi violence—Norwegian teacher, Danish resister, German wife—and consider: What are actions I might personally be willing to take? What actions would be hardest for me? Where might I draw support to do what I otherwise might not do?

Session 3: Racism and Dehumanization as Ingredients of Terrorist Violence

Sharp, *Waging Nonviolent Struggle*, chapters 16 (Namibia), 19 (South Africa), and then 3 (nature of nonviolent struggle).

View *A Force More Powerful* (segment on the South African struggle against apartheid).

Sessions 4 and 5: Relation of Fear and Terrorism
View *A Force More Powerful* (segment on Chileans deposing Pinochet dictatorship).

Sharp, *Waging Nonviolent Struggle,* chapters 11 (Guatemala), 17 (Argentina), and then 2 (theory of power).

Response paper (300–600 words): Describe at least ten ways in which nonviolent social movements have handled the problem of fear of repression among their participants. Be specific. It's useful also to show how the specific tactic or method works. Draw from the readings and the video documentaries for your examples. For example, Norwegians wore small potatoes on their lapels as a symbol of solidarity. When they saw others wearing the potatoes, they were reminded that they were not alone and felt more brave. If time and space allow, identify a method you have used at a scary time in your life to assist yourself to be brave.

Sessions 6 and 7: Power, Organizing, and Leadership in Dealing with Violence
View *Bringing Down a Dictator.*

Sharp, *Waging Nonviolent Struggle,* chapters 21 (Burma), 26 (Thailand), and then 34 (theory about redistribution of power).

Session 8: Cultural Resources in Facing Violence
View *A Force More Powerful* (Nashville sit-ins).

Sharp, *Waging Nonviolent Struggle,* chapters 12 and chapter 8.

Response paper (300–600 words): From the chapters of *Waging Nonviolent Struggle* assigned in Unit 1, identify at least four concepts that illuminate the nature of nonviolent struggle and look promising for application to defense against terrorism by nonstate actors. An example might be learning to control our fear and become braver, which is strategically important and can be promoted through low-risk collective actions that don't invite vicious reprisals, as in banging pots in Chile or wearing potatoes in Norway.

Describe these concepts to show you understand them and brainstorm some possible uses for an antiterror strategy. An outlandish example might be Westerners flying into Saudi Arabia as tourists and then doing highly public but low-key vigils, dressed in some particular way or carrying something symbolic that shows the humanity of Western people.

Unit 2: Who Are Those Who Use Terror, and What Do They Want?

Session 9: Forms of Terrorism
Pape, *Dying to Win,* chapters 1–3.

Session 10: The Strategic Logic of Suicide Terrorism

Pape, *Dying to Win,* chapters 4–8.

Michael Scheuer and Nicholas Lemann, presiders. "Winning or Losing? An Inside Look at the War on Terror," symposium at the Council on Foreign Relations, February 3, 2005. www.cfr.org.

Session 11: The Individual Logic of Suicide Terrorism

Pape, *Dying to Win,* chapters 9–11.

Raphael F. Perl. *International Terrorism: Threat, Policy, and Response.* Congressional Research Service, 1/3/07. www.opencrs.com/document/RL33600.

Written assignment: Turn in your choice of country/region for your term paper (2–3 paragraphs describing who's threatening whom and how).

Unit 3: Eight Nonmilitary Techniques for Defending Against Terror

Session 12: Policy Changes and the Concept of Reckless Behavior

States sometimes make choices that invite a terrorist response, for example, occupying someone else's land. When does reevaluation make sense?

Pape, *Dying to Win,* chapter 12.

Geoff Pingree and Lisa Abend. "In Spain, Bitter Rift over Fighting Terror." *Christian Science Monitor,* January 16, 2007 (about policy response to ETA).

Response paper (300–600 words): Consider some implications of the probable Al-Qaida terrorist attack on Spain, Spain's withdrawal from Iraq, Italy's withdrawal, and now the United Kingdom's withdrawal from Iraq. Is it all right for governments to give in to pressure exerted by terrorist violence? If a government decides it is wise to change a policy (like occupying Iraq or the Arabian Peninsula), what are possible ways of doing so that do not reward terrorism?

Session 13: Negotiation

Governments often say, "We don't negotiate with terrorists," but history shows that they do, in one form or another. How can this technique be used most effectively?

Jon B. Alterman. "How Terrorism Ends." Report of the US Institute of Peace, May 25, 1999. www.usip.org/pubs/specialreports/sr990525.html.

Roger Fisher. "A Policy Towards Terrorism," unpublished article (1986) available from Harvard Negotiation Project website, www.pon.harvard.edu/hnp/writing/articles/author.shtml.

Mark Brzezinski and Ray Takeyh. "Getting to Yes on Iran." *Boston Globe,* February 6, 2007. A report to Congress about the Indonesian separatist movement in Aceh can be found at the website of the MIPT Terrorism Knowledge Base, http://www.terrorisminfo.mipt.org/pdf/CRS_RS20572.pdf.

Session 14: Nonrepressive Police Work and the Infrastructure of Norms and Laws

How can police work become more effective: international coordination, community policing, more global law/agreements, more checks on repression by police?

"French Police in 'Terror' Swoop." BBC, February 14, 2007, BBC website. For an example of results of positive police/community relations, see news.bbc.co.uk/2/hi/europe/6360453.stm.

Brian Michael Jenkins. "Building an Army of Believers: Jihadist Radicalization and Recruitment." Testimony by a senior adviser to Rand Corporation. www.rand.org/pubs/testimonies/2007/RAND_CT278-1.pdf.

Tom Regan. "British Police Identify Terror Suspects: Original Tip Came from a Member of Britain's Muslim Community." *Christian Science Monitor,* August 11, 2006. www.csmonitor.com/2006/0811/dailyUpdate.html.

Diana Marcum. "Police 'Anti-Terror Unit' Infiltrates Fresno Anti-War Group." *Fresno Bee,* October 4, 2003.

Kenneth Ballen. "The Myth of Muslim Support for Terror." *Christian Science Monitor,* February 23, 2007. www.csmonitor.com/2007/0223/p09s01-coop.html.

Sessions 15 and 16: Ally Building and the Infrastructure of Economic Development

Although there is rarely a direct link between poverty and terrorism, there are indirect links of great importance. How can economic development make a bigger difference, such as in gaining allies?

Kim Cragin and Peter Chalk. "Terrorism and Development: Using Social and Economic Development to Inhibit a Resurgence of Terrorism." Rand Corporation, 2003. www.rand.org/pubs/monograph_reports/MR1630. Study of Northern Ireland, Philippines, West Bank/Gaza.

Susan E. Rice. "The National Security Implications of Global Poverty." Speech at the University of Michigan Law School, January 30, 2006. www.brookings.edu/speeches/ 2006/0130globaleconomics_rice.aspx.

David Ludden. "Good Cops, Bad Cops, and the World Bank." *HIMAL* (June 2002).

Sessions 17 and 18: Reducing Marginalization by Paying Attention to Culture

As Britain has learned, marginalizing a group within your population is not safe; terrorists grow under those conditions. This is also true on a global level. Much marginalizing behavior is unconscious; how can it be reduced?

Mindell, *Sitting in the Fire,* chapters 1–10.

Response paper (300–600 words):

1. How do you relate personally to the idea of unconsciously holding rank? Briefly share an example of a time when you were angered or depressed by the cluelessness of someone of higher rank.
2. How do you imagine this dynamic could play out in the case you're exploring for your term paper? What might members of the marginalized group run into that could rub their sores raw? How might resentment and anger under the surface be fueled by continued unconsciousness on the part of higher-ranking people?
3. Although your personal ethical standards may prevent you from justifying violence, in what ways does Mindell assist you to understand the etiology of violent behaviors in oppressive situations, such as your paper is examining?

Session 19: Nonviolent Protest/Campaigns Among Defenders

Terrorism happens in a political context and is therefore influenced by that context. Some terror campaigns have lapsed because they lost popular support. The rise and fall of support for terrorism is in turn influenced by social movements using people power (nonviolent struggle). How can this technique be enhanced?

Hardy Merriman and Jack DuVall. "Dissolving Terrorism at Its Roots." In *Nonviolence: An Alternative for Countering Global Terror(ism),* edited by Ralph Summy and Senthil Ram. Hauppauge, NY: Nova Science, 2007.

Sessions 20 and 21: Classroom Exercise: Strategy Game

Find the instructions for a strategy game at the website for Training for Change (www.TrainingforChange.org). You will need six teams representing active groups in Eslandia, where a terrorist movement is growing. Groups defending against terrorism apply tools learned in the course so far. Debrief after the game.

Session 22: Education/Training for Conflict

Terror happens when a population tries to suppress conflicts instead of waging them. Terror is a nightmare occurring to a people afraid to dream.

A technique for reducing terror, therefore, is to teach a pro-conflict attitude and the skills that go with it.

Assignment: Bring a draft outline of your term paper to class. During class, collect and redistribute outline drafts among students for a peer review process in class and over the next five days. In that time period, peer reviewers should return drafts to authors, and authors will revise drafts and hand them in to the professor.

Session 23: Post-terror Recovery Programs

Not all terror can be prevented, any more than all crime or natural disasters. This technique emphasizes resilience in a population so it doesn't become rigid with fear and create self-fulfilling prophecies. Politically, the goal of this technique is to prevent a cycle of hawks on one side "arming" the hawks on the other side.

Mindell, *Sitting in the Fire,* chapter 14.

Also search the Internet for material on "trauma healing."

Unit 4: Application to Concrete Situations

Session 24: Strategy Clinic

Divide the session into two time periods of thirty minutes each, Session A and Session B. In Session A, post the first four of the nonmilitary techniques at the top of the syllabus in the four corners of the room. A single student whose work in the term paper outline shows competency in one of the four techniques goes to the appropriately labeled corner. Students who need help in developing these four techniques in their papers, go to the appropriate corner to consult with the competent peer. In Session B, the process is repeated for the last four nonmilitary techniques.

Session 25: Strategy Clinic

Use the same procedure as in the previous class but do not designate a student as a resource person for each technique. Allow students to consult with each other about how they've used the techniques in their drafts. Use only twenty minutes for each session. Ask for volunteers to make oral presentations in session 26.

Session 26: Presentations Begin

Each student presenter has five minutes to present one or two techniques from his or her paper that have worked especially well in the case study. Save fifteen minutes at the end of the session to talk together about the concept of "strategic synergy": how do some of the techniques/tools interact in such a way that a stronger nonviolent defense becomes possible?

Sessions 27 and 28: Presentations Continue

Sessions 29: Review and Evaluation of the Course

TEACHING NOTES

This is challenging subject matter, both intellectually and emotionally: intellectually because the reigning paradigm is that defense against terror is mainly a question of military strategy; emotionally because fear is embedded in the discourse (which, indeed, is the intention of the terrorists!). Students therefore need (1) a very clear structure of ideas (the "toolbox"); (2) a vivid and emotionally sensitive introduction to the power of nonviolent action to gain any distance at all from the reigning paradigm and the paralyzing impact of fear; (3) a very clear framework in which to apply their tools (a specific country where terror is a threat); (4) coaching during the application of the tools; and (5) a sense of teamwork to support them to dare to use their imaginations. Applying tools mechanically is better than not at all, but strategizing is an art. The sensibility of a strategist grows through engagement with narrative rather than with abstract principles.

Students will benefit from not looking at the problem from the point of view of ethics. They will become freer intellectually and emotionally more able to exercise their imaginations if they don't tie themselves up with the rights and wrongs of violent responses to terror, but instead join a curriculum-based "common ground" of pragmatism. As they seek to apply their tools, the key question will be, How does Country X need to make its police work more effective, to use economic development more strategically, and to bring alienated minority youth into dialogue with mainstream culture?

Pretending that one is without emotion invites emotion to push us around. Students need, therefore, opportunities to personalize, to see themselves living, for example, in occupied Denmark or under tyranny in Chile, and at the same time to have the opportunity not to leap into self-judgment. The response sheet assignments support that work. As a teacher I give permission in as many ways as I can (for example, through humor) to students to be real; to acknowledge fears, hopes, fatigue, anger, sadness, and joy; and to acknowledge how overly self-critical they can be.

10.3 The International Relations of September 11

B. Welling Hall
Earlham College

COURSE DESCRIPTION

Upper-level undergraduate seminar course in political science, international relations, and peace studies.

What does it mean to say that "the world changed forever on September 11, 2001"? Our goal in this course will be to investigate this question among others, such as:

- Were thousands of persons brutally murdered because of an inevitable clash of civilizations?
- Is terrorism a new form of warfare that overrides all previous expectations and "rules" about war?
- Is Islamic militancy a legacy of the proxy wars fought by the United States and the Soviet Union during the latter half of the twentieth century?
- Who were the Taliban? Were Afghan women rescued from gender apartheid by Operation Enduring Freedom?
- What does terror mean for the future of global order?

Our discussion of these and related questions will be guided by reading and writing about books, essays, and interviews, including a variety of disciplinary perspectives that inform the causes, consequences, and debates immediately surrounding the events of 9/11.

REQUIRED TEXTS

Samuel P. Huntington. *The Clash of Civilizations and the Remaking of World Order.* New York: Simon and Schuster, 1996. Huntington is a noted US political scientist whose essays on the inevitability of a clash between the Islamic world and Western democracies have been powerfully influential among the decisionmaking elite in the United States. This book was initially published five years before 9/11.

Mary Kaldor. *New and Old Wars: Organized Violence in a Global Era,* 2nd ed. Stanford, CA: Stanford University Press, 2007. Kaldor is a British peace studies scholar. Her work is very highly regarded, both in peace studies and international studies circles, as a pathbreaking work that establishes important new approaches for thinking about violence by nonstate actors. This book was originally published about nine months prior to 9/11. Its second edition includes an appraisal of the war in Iraq.

John K. Cooley. *Unholy Wars: Afghanistan, America, and International Terrorism.* Pluto Press, 2000. Cooley is an ABC news correspondent who started writing about the relationship between US foreign policy and its support of international terrorists in Afghanistan during the Soviet war in Afghanistan in the 1980s. The first edition of this book was published almost two years before 9/11.

Anne E. Brodsky. *With All Our Strength: The Revolutionary Association of the Women of Afghanistan.* Routledge, 2002. Brodsky is a US social psychologist who has spent many months living with Afghan women in exile. Her work is important as the first (and to date only) book-length study of the lives and community aspirations of the Revolutionary Association of the Women of Afghanistan, which was established more than a decade before the Taliban came to power. Brodsky's book was published after 9/11.

Ken Booth and Tim Dunne. *Worlds in Collision: Terror and the Future of Global Order.* Palgrave: 2002. This collection of essays is edited by Welsh professors of international politics. More importantly, this collection includes essays by both Western and non-Western scholars across political, economic, and social strata on the meaning of "terror," "order," and "worlds." The collection was published after 9/11.

Sharon Hoover, ed. *Answering Terror: Responses to War and Peace After 9/11/01.* Friends Publishing Corporation, 2006. An anthology of essays edited by a Quaker peace activist, including exchanges generated by an impassioned plea by Scott Simon of National Public Radio.

RECOMMENDED TEXT

Phillipe Sands. *Lawless World: America and the Making and Breaking of Global Rules.* Viking, 2005.

COURSE SCHEDULE

Week 1: Introduction: Overview, Ground Rules, Expectations

Week 2: The Concept of a Clash of Civilizations and Its Dissenters

Booth and Dunne, *Worlds in Collision,* chapter 1.
Huntington, *The Clash of Civilizations,* Part I.

Week 3: The Concept of a Clash of Civilizations (cont.)

Huntington, *Clash,* remainder.

Week 4: New Wars Prior to 9/11

Kaldor, *New and Old Wars,* chapters 1–3.

Week 5: New Wars Prior to 9/11 (cont.)
Kaldor, *New and Old Wars,* chapters 4–7.

Week 6: Prehistory of Al-Qaida:
New Wars as a Legacy of the Cold War?
Cooley, *Unholy Wars,* chapters 1–8.

Week 7: New Wars as a Legacy of the Cold War (cont.)
Cooley, *Unholy Wars,* remainder.

Week 8: Remembering September 11, 2001
Smithsonian Institute. "The September 11 Digital Archive." http://911digitalarchive.org/. CNN. "Day of Terror Video Archive." http://edition.cnn.com/SPECIALS/2001/trade.center/day.video.10.html.

Week 9: Remembering September 11, 2001 (cont.)
The Avalon Project at Yale Law School. "September 11, 2001: Attack on America." http://www.yale.edu/lawweb/avalon/sept_11/sept_11.htm.

Week 10: The Immediate Aftermath of 9/11
in the United States
Booth and Dunne, *Worlds in Collision,* chapters 1–4.

Week 11: The Impact of the Taliban and 9/11 on Afghanistan
Brodsky, *With All Our Strength,* all.

Week 12: A Just War on Afghanistan
Booth and Dunne, *Worlds in Collision,* chapters 5–11, and 23.

Week 13: The Immediate Policy Consequences of 9/11:
The Search for Order
Booth and Dunne, *Worlds in Collision,* part 2 (Order).

Week 14: The Road Not Taken:
Peaceful Responses to Terrorism
Hoover, *Answering Terror: Responses to War and Peace After 9/11/01.*

Week 15: The Global War on Terror
White House. *National Security Strategy of the United States of America.* 2006. http://www.whitehouse.gov/nsc/nss.html.
Sands, *Lawless World,* chapters 7, 8, and 9.

Week 16: Conclusion
Presentations of student work.

TEACHING NOTES

I teach this course as a writing-intensive course and give three different kinds of writing assignments: (1) weekly responses to the reading, due approximately twenty-four hours before the scheduled reading is discussed in class; (2) two short papers that will involve comparing class texts with each other and with texts "external" to the course, such as websites and newspaper articles; and (3) a research project that will produce an annotated bibliography and a chronology.

The weekly responses to reading should address each of the following questions in a concise but engaging manner: (1) What seem(s) to be the author's/authors' main idea(s)? (2) Identify two passages that were not self-explanatory. What remains to be explained? (3) Identify two passages that are thought-provoking. What do you want to discuss? (4) Synthesis: What connections can you make between the assigned reading and other texts you have read recently?

The first short paper is 1,200–1,500 words long. The purpose of this essay is to address a question posed by the instructor, comparing some texts read in class with a new text selected by the professor. In constructing this essay, students are expected to draw upon ideas initially drafted in their weekly responses.

The second short paper is 1,500–1,800 words long. This essay should answer the question, "What does it mean to say that 'the world changed forever on September 11, 2001'?" As a starting point you may choose to agree or disagree with the assertion. As with paper 1, in constructing this essay you are expected to draw upon ideas initially drafted in your weekly responses.

The annotated bibliography, in combination with the chronology, is a research assignment that is conducted in conjunction with bibliographic instruction. The annotated bibliography pulls together a variety of resources in print and online that can help student researchers answer a subset of questions about September 11, its causes and consequences.

The chronology goes with the annotated bibliography, although they are not due at the same time. It would be impossible to list every significant date and event that accounts for some significant aspect of September 11 and its consequences. Therefore, this chronology will pertain to a subset of dates and events that are pertinent to answering a specific question addressed by the annotated bibliography.

For teachers who are not historians, a chronology may be an unusual tool. The following rubric can be useful for students in understanding the assignment and for faculty members in evaluating it.

* * *

The International Relations of September 11
Rubric for Evaluating Chronology

	1	2	3	4	Total
Introduction	Introduction makes no connection to other readings or events.	Introduction makes generic, unelaborated connection to unspecified readings or events.	Introduction makes unelaborated connection to specific readings or events.	Introduction makes original, insightful links to other readings or events.	
Organization of Chronology	Chronology can not be understood because there is no clear sequence of thought.	Chronology is difficult to follow because themes and topics jump around.	Material is presented in a logical sequence that reader can follow.	Material is presented in a logical, engaging sequence that reader can follow easily.	
Mastery of Material	Student does not demonstrate a grasp of primary concepts.	Student identifies main points in the reading.	Student is at ease with several concepts and provides some context.	Student demonstrates familiarity with conceptual scheme, including some nuances.	
Synthetic Thinking	Chronology makes no connection to other course readings or events.	Chronology makes generic, unelaborated connection to unspecified course readings or events.	Chronology makes unelaborated connection to specific course readings or events.	Chronology makes original, insightful links from this reading to other course readings or events.	
Mechanics	Chronology has four or more spelling, grammatical, or citation errors.	Chronology has three or more spelling, grammatical, or citation errors.	Chronology has no more than two spelling, grammatical, or citation errors.	Chronology has no more than one spelling, grammatical, or citation error.	
Length	Number of entries seems seriously out of alignment with assignment.		Number of entries seems mildly out of alignment with assignment.	Approximately 25 entries.	
Total points					

10.4 Sociology and Terrorism of Genocide

Michael W. Smith
Saint Anselm College

COURSE DESCRIPTION

Intermediate- or upper-level undergraduate course for majors in sociology, political science, peace studies, or criminal justice.

Sociologists' study of terrorism and genocide is grounded in the theoretical study of historical circumstances and their influence on (1) social forces and social structure; (2) individual and collective memories and behavior leading to social movements; (3) social groups, group dynamics, and group identity; (4) conflicts of ideology, race, ethnicity, religion and social class; and (5) the motivations for and sources of terrorism and genocide.

Assuming that political crimes are committed for ideological reasons and that terrorism and genocide are political crimes, we can say that the activity of terrorism and genocide are committed for ideological purposes. Such crimes may take one of two forms: crimes by government and crimes against government. Crimes by government include violations of human rights, violations of civil liberties, illegal enforcement of laws, and genocide. Crimes against government range from different forms of protests to espionage, assassination, and terrorism.

The focus of this course will be a comparative, historical, and sociological analysis of the political crimes of genocide and terrorism. Through course readings, assignments, and films, students will examine the ideological justifications proffered by the perpetrators of terrorism and genocide, as well as the response by victims, governments, and international forums (e.g., the United Nations, the Hague International War Crimes Tribunal) to these political crimes.

This course uses multimedia technologies, including the Internet, an electronic course management system, and films. The use of these different teaching approaches will personalize these incomprehensible events in ways that are difficult to convey through a traditional texts and lecture format.

REQUIRED TEXTS

Gus Martin. *The New Era of Terrorism.* Thousand Oaks, CA: Sage, 2004.
William Hewett. *Defining the Horrific.* Lawrence: University of Kansas Press, 2004.
Peter Maas. *Love Thy Neighbor.* New York: Random House, 1996.

Selected readings assigned in the course schedule.

COURSE SCHEDULE

Week 1: Rethinking Terrorism in the New Era

Martin, *The New Era of Terrorism,* 1–28.

Frank Hagan. "Crimes by Government: Secret Police, Human Rights, and Genocide." In *Political Crimes: Ideology and Criminality,* by Frank Hagan. Boston: Allyn and Bacon, 1997, 25–53.

Frank Hagan. "Crimes Against Government: International Terrorism." In *Political Crimes,* 132–156.

9/11, directed by James Hanlon, Gedeon Naudet, and Jules Naudet, Columbia Broadcasting System, DVD, 2002. View in class.

Week 2: Defining/Conceptualizing the Threat of Terrorism in the New Era

Martin, *The New Era of Terrorism,* 29–88.

Karen Armstrong. "Was It Inevitable? Islam Through History." In *How Did This Happen?* edited by J. Hage and G. Rose. Council on Foreign Affairs, 2001, 53–70.

Mark S. Hamm. "Conceptualizing Hate Crime in a Global Context." *Criminology: Cross-Cultural Perspectives,* 91–108.

Robert Perdue. "The Ideology of Terrorism." In *Criminology: Cross-Cultural Perspectives,* edited by Robert Heiner. Belmont, CA: Wadsworth, 1995, 79–90.

9/11 Through Saudi Eyes, produced by Bassem Abdallah, directed by Bader Ben Hirsi, with English and Arabic subtitles, DVD, 2002. View in class.

Week 3: The Causes of Terrorism and the Behavior of Terrorists

Martin, *The New Era of Terrorism,* 89–122; 48–174.

Walter Laqueur. "Terrorist Motives: Marx, Muhammed, and Armageddon." In *The New Terrorism,* edited by Walter Laqueur. New York: Oxford University Press, 1999, 79–99.

Walter Laqueur. "Religion and Terrorism." In *The New Terrorism,* 127–153.

Ahmed Rashid. "A Vanished Gender: Women, Children and Taliban Culture." In *Taliban,* by Ahmed Rashid. New Haven, CT: Yale University Press, 2000, 105–116.

America at a Crossroads: Europe's 9/11, produced and directed by David Alter, PBS.com, 2007. View in class.

Week 4: The Rise of Terrorism in the New Era

Martin, *The New Era of Terrorism,* 123–149; 175–202.

Robin Morgan. "Official Terrorism: The State of Man." In *The Demon Lover: The Roots of Terrorism,* by Robin Morgan. New York: Pocket Books, 2001, 85–123.

Robin Morgan. "The Love-Death: Religion, Philosophy and Aesthetics." In *The Demon Lover,* 124–153.

Robin Morgan, "What Do Men Know About Life? The Middle East." In *The Demon Lover,* 243–287.

Week 5: Issues and Options for Counterterrorism in the New Era

Martin, *The New Era of Terrorism,* 203–256.

George W. Bush. "Military Order: Detention, Treatment, and Trial of Certain Non-Citizens in the War Against Terrorism." *Federal Register,* November 13, 2001.

Laura Donahue and Juliette Kayem. "Federalism and the Battle over Counter-Terrorist Law: State Sovereignty, Criminal Law Enforcement, and National Security." *Studies in Conflict and Terrorism* 25 (2002): 1–18.

Week 6: Who Shall Lead? Forging Alliances, Going Solo, or Isolationism

Martin, *The New Era of Terrorism,* 256–278.

Wesley Clark. "Waging the New War: What's Next for the US Armed Forces." In *How Did This Happen?* edited by J. Hage and G. Rose. Council on Foreign Affairs, 2001, 242–253.

Raphael F. Perl. "Terrorism, the Future, and US Foreign Policy." *CRS Issue Brief for Congress.* Congressional Research Service–Library of Congress, 2001, 1–17.

Ahmed Rashid. *Challenging Islam: The New-Style Fundamentalism of the Taliban.* New Haven, CT: Yale University Press, 2000, 83–94.

Week 7: Defining Genocide and Democide

Hewett, *Defining the Horrific,* introduction, chapters 1–2.

Browse the website of R. J. Rummel at www.hawaii.edu/powerkills.

Week 8: The Armenian and Ukrainian Genocides

Hewett, *Defining the Horrific,* chapters 3–4.

Browse the website of the Armenian National Institute at www.armenian genocide.org/.

Week 9: The Holocaust

Hewett, *Defining the Horrific,* chapter 5.

Browse the websites of the Center for Holocaust and Genocide Studies at the University of Minnesota (www.chgs.umn.edu) and the United States Holocaust Memorial Museum (ushmm.org).

Week 10: The Rape of Nanking and the Cambodian Genocide
Hewett, *Defining the Horrific,* chapters 6–8, 11–12.

Browse the website of the Cambodian Genocide Project at Yale University (www.yale.edu/cgp).

Week 11: The Balkans and Ethnic Cleansing
Hewett, *Defining the Horrific,* chapter 13.
Maas, *Love Thy Neighbor.* Read entire book.
The Prosecution of the Tribunal against Sloban Milosevic, Milam Milutinovic, Nikola Sainovic, Dragoljub Ojdanic, and Vlajko Stoljiljkovic, Second Amendment Indictment, Case No: IT-99-37-PT. The Hague: The International Tribunal for the Former Yugoslavia, 2001.
Pretty Village, Pretty Flame, directed by Srdegan Dragojevic, with English subtitles, DVD, 1996. View in class.

Browse the website of the United Human Rights Council at www.united humanrights.org.

Weeks 12–13: The Rwandan and Sudanese Genocides
Hewett, *Defining the Horrific,* chapter 9.
Sometimes in April, directed by Raoul Peck, 2005. View in class.
A Good Man in Hell: General Romeo Dallaire and the Rwanda Genocide, interview by Ted Koppel, DVD, 2002. View in class.

Browse websites about Rwanda and Sudan at www.hrw.org/reports/1999/rwanda, www.yale.edu/gsp/sudan, www.gendercide.org.

TEACHING NOTES

The course uses online discussion groups to interact between classes and in preparation for class. During the course of the semester, I post a question after class on Thursday night. Each student is required to post a response by a set time on Monday. Students are then required to read their classmates' responses and send comments to at least two of those responses by a set time on Tuesday. On Wednesday, each student is required to reply to all classmates who sent comments on his or her initial answer to the instructor's question.

I also require a group research project and class presentation of twenty to thirty minutes that uses multimedia technology. Groups should consist of three people, one of whom is designated a leader. The group chooses three possible topics and then meets with me to finalize a single topic. The topics I suggest are (1) Homeland Security versus Civil Liberties; (2) The Effectiveness of the Wars in Afghanistan and Iraq Against International Terrorism; (3)

Should Those Who Commit Genocide Be Prosecuted by the International Criminal Court or by Aggrieved Countries? (4) Denial of the Armenian Genocide; (5) Genocide Through Government Edict (the Holocaust); (6) The Rape of Nanking: Genocide or the Consequences of War? (7) Cambodia's "Killing Fields"; (8) Ethic Cleansing in Bosnia-Herzegovina; (9) The Rwandan Genocide and International Response; or (10) Ethnicity, Religion, and Race in the Sudanese Genocide.

After the Holocaust, the international community said "Never Again!" Yet genocides and other crimes by governments against civilian populations continue. I ask students, based upon their viewing of *Sometimes in April* and their understanding of the Rwandan genocide, to address the following question: What role should or can the United Nations play in reducing the likelihood of future genocides, or should this role be assumed by the United States or by those neighboring countries where the genocides may emerge?

11
War

ALTHOUGH PEACE STUDIES EMERGED AS A DISCIPLINE IN RESPONSE to the direct violence and atrocity of war, this curriculum guide demonstrates that the field has moved in many directions since, inspired in part by the notion that studying war distracts from the ultimate goal of achieving a just and sustainable peace. Eschewing that particular characterization of the field, this group of syllabuses takes on war, weapons, and the *para bellum* hypothesis ("If you wish for peace, prepare for war") as the problem that is to be tested and understood, if not solved. Although some posit a tension between war as rational policy and war as obscenity (Richard K. Betts), others focus on the specific conduct of war (R. Charli Carpenter) and how, for example, gender identity is manipulated to create warriors (Daniel Lieberfeld). All the courses described in this chapter recommend the use of film in order to discuss the proposition that war is hell; *The Battle of Algiers* is recommended by several of the professors. Three of the courses (those by Morton Ender, Lieberfeld, and B. Welling Hall) use film extensively in order to grasp the co-evolution of the viewing machine and the killing machine, and understand the political, sociological, and cultural consequences of war. Raising and addressing the question of whether the world is safer or more dangerous after the Cold War (Betts) and the significance of the global war on terror (Carpenter) for the future of war, as a group these syllabuses also call upon instructors to process the emotional impact of this material on their students, including some suggestions as to how to do so (Hall).

11.1 War, Peace, and Strategy

Richard K. Betts
Columbia University

COURSE DESCRIPTION

For upper-level undergraduates and graduate students.

The course emphasizes problems in the relationship between political ends and military means. Students must grapple with the terms of reference in both dimensions. The course is organized thematically, not by cases, but illustrative examples are drawn from conflicts in Europe, Asia, the Middle East, and Africa. The course emphasizes issues in the twentieth century and in US national security policy.

Questions animating this course include: Why is force often used in international politics? What causes peace? How do wars, or competitions shaped by the lurking possibility of war, affect international relations and individual societies? How can governments best prepare to prevent wars or to win them if they occur? By what standards should resort to force, or strategic and tactical choices in combat, be judged legitimate or immoral? How are the prevention, outbreaks, processes, and outcomes of mass violence (or crises resolved short of combat) determined by politics, ideology, diplomacy, technology, economics, geography, military plans and tactics, intelligence, or arms control? What are the similarities and differences among conflicts between states, within states, and between states and transnational groups (such as terrorists)? How important is terrorism? How do weapons of mass destruction coerce or deter? Is the world safer or more dangerous after the Cold War? Can war be made obsolete?

COURSE SCHEDULE

Unit 1: Introduction: The Nature and Functions of War

1. Three visions of conflict: Does war have a future?
2. Concepts of national security and philosophy of war.
3. Political ends and military means: rationality.
4. War is hell: Insanity and obscenity.
5. The perspective between pacifism and militarism.

Richard K. Betts, ed. *Conflict After the Cold War,* updated 2nd ed. New York: Longman, 2005:

Francis Fukuyama, "The End of History."

John Mueller, "The Obsolescence of Major War."
John J. Mearsheimer, "Why We Will Soon Miss the Cold War."

Samuel P. Huntington. *The Clash of Civilizations and the Remaking of World Order.* New York: Simon and Schuster, 1996, chapter 1.

Carl von Clausewitz. *On War,* edited and translated by Michael Howard and Peter Paret. Princeton, NJ: Princeton University Press, 1976, book I, chapters 1 and 2. (Only an unabridged German-language edition is an acceptable alternative to this translation. Do not read a different translation.)

Sun-Tzu. *The Art of Warfare,* translated by Roger T. Ames. New York: Ballantine, 1993, chapters 3–4, 6–7, 10–11. (The Sawyer, Griffith, or Huang translations are also acceptable.)

Paul Fussell. *Wartime.* New York: Oxford University Press, 1989, chapter 18.

Unit 2: The Causes of War and Peace

1. Psychology and anthropology: Instinct, ritual, or continuation of sport by other means.
2. Religion: Fighting for God.
3. Main paradigms: Realism and liberalism.
4. Autarky or interdependence.
5. Ideology and fraternity.
6. Feudalism, capitalism, Marxism, militarism.

Kenneth Waltz. *Man, the State, and War.* New York: Columbia University Press, 1959, chapters 2–4, 6–8.

Betts, *Conflict After the Cold War:*
Thucydides, "The Melian Dialogue."
E. H. Carr, "Realism and Idealism."
Geoffrey Blainey, "Power, Culprits, and Arms."
Margaret Mead, "War Is Only an Invention—Not a Biological Necessity."
Immanuel Kant, "Perpetual Peace."
Norman Angell, "The Great Illusion."
Geoffrey Blainey, "Paradise Is a Bazaar."
V. I. Lenin, "Imperialism, the Highest Stage of Capitalism."
Joseph Schumpeter, "Imperialism and Capitalism."
Kenneth N. Waltz, "Structural Causes and Economic Effects."
Richard Rosecrance, "Trade and Power."
Michael Doyle, "Liberalism and World Politics."

Unit 3: Securing Peace:
The Balance of Power and Institutions for Cooperation

1. What is stability? Equilibrium or peace.
2. The meanings of the balance of power.
3. The effects of unipolarity, bipolarity, and multipolarity.

4. International organization, "regimes," and collective security.

Inis L. Claude. *Power and International Relations.* New York: Random House, 1962, chapters 2–3.
G. F. Hudson. "Collective Security and Military Alliances." In *Diplomatic Investigations,* edited by Herbert Butterfield and Martin Wight. Cambridge, MA: Harvard University Press, 1968.

Betts, *Conflict After the Cold War:*
Robert Gilpin, "Hegemonic War and International Change."
Robert Keohane and Joseph Nye, "Power and Interdependence."

Kimberly Zisk Marten. *Enforcing the Peace.* New York: Columbia University Press, 2004, chapters 2–3.

Unit 4: The Choice of War or Peace: Conquest, Coercion, Crisis Management

1. The spectrum of choice: Concession, compromise, combat.
2. Setting the price of peace: Political stakes vs. military costs.
3. Setting the price of war: Blood, treasure, and risk.
4. Deterrence, reassurance, crisis management, and "accidental" war.
5. Cases: 1914, 1938, 1962.
6. The theory of coercive force.
7. The practice of coercive force: Bombing.

Thomas Schelling. *Arms and Influence.* New Haven, CT: Yale University Press, 1966, chapters 2–4.
Robert A. Pape. *Bombing to Win.* Ithaca, NY: Cornell University Press, 1996, chapters 2–3, 7, 9. (Ph.D. students: For criticism, see Barry D. Watts, "Ignoring Reality," and Pape's rebuttal, "The Air Force Strikes Back: A Reply to Barry Watts and John Warden," *Security Studies* 7, no. 2 [Winter 1997–1998].)
General Wesley K. Clark. *Waging Modern War.* PublicAffairs, 2001, chapters 8–12.

Unit 5: Modern War: Constraints, Conditions, Conduct

1. Geography: Natural security and vulnerability.
2. Economy: Resources, power, and strategy.
3. Combined arms: Armies, navies, air forces.
4. Campaigns and logistics.

Betts, *Conflict After the Cold War:*
Niccolò Machiavelli, "Money Is Not the Sinews of War, Although It Is Generally So Considered."
Alan S. Milward, "War as Policy."

Michael Howard. *War in European History.* New York: Oxford University Press, 1974, chapters 4–6.

John Keegan. *The Face of Battle*. New York: Viking, 1976, chapter 4, 210–237, 242–279.

Unit 6: Policy, Strategy, and Operations: Integrating Political Ends and Military Means

1. Three levels of analysis.
2. Technology: Innovations and interactions.
3. Plans: Organization, doctrine, tactics, obstacles.
4. Military effectiveness: What produces success in combat?
5. Attack and defense: Aggressive, preventive, preemptive, and defensive war.
6. How ends determine means; how means determine ends.

Clausewitz, *On War*, book I, chapter 7; book II, chapter 3; book III, chapter 1; book VI, chapters 1, 3, 5; book VII, chapters 1–5.

Stephen Biddle. *Military Power*. Princeton, NJ: Princeton University Press, 2004, chapters 2–3. (Ph.D. students: See criticisms by five scholars and Biddle's response in "*Military Power:* A Roundtable Review," *Journal of Strategic Studies* 28, no. 3 [June 2005].)

Betts, *Conflict After the Cold War:*
Robert Jervis, "Cooperation Under the Security Dilemma."
Jack S. Levy, "The Offensive/Defensive Balance of Military Technology."
Michael Shaara. *The Killer Angels*. New York: Ballantine, 1975.

Unit 7: Ends and Means in Total War and Limited War

1. Estimating costs, benefits, and feasibility.
2. Estimating the culminating point of victory.
3. Total war: World Wars I and II.
4. Limited war: Korea and Kuwait.

Clausewitz, *On War*, book VII, chapter 22; book VIII, chapters 1–3, 6.

Michael Geyer. "German Strategy in the Age of Machine Warfare, 1914–1945." In *Makers of Modern Strategy: From Machiavelli to the Nuclear Age*, edited by Peter Pret. Princeton, NJ: Princeton University Press, 1986.

Samuel Eliot Morison. *Strategy and Compromise*. Boston: Little, Brown, 1958.

Michael R. Gordon and General Bernard E. Trainor. *The Generals' War*. Boston: Little, Brown, 1995, chapters 18–20.

Michael R. Gordon and General Bernard E. Trainor. *Cobra II*. London: Atlantic Books, 2006, chapter 8 and epilogue.

Unit 8: Unconventional Warfare and Terrorism

1. People's war, counterinsurgency, and incentives for "asymmetric" strategies.

2. Linkages between conventional and unconventional war.
3. Stealth, strength, and the advantages of attack over defense.
4. Secular and sacred motivations.

Clausewitz, *On War,* book VI, chapter 26; book VIII, chapter 5.
Col. C. E. Callwell. *Small Wars,* 3rd ed. London: His Majesty's Stationery Office, 1906, chapters 3, 7.
Harry G. Summers Jr. *On Strategy.* Novato, CA: Presidio Press, 1982, chapters 1, 7–11, 15.
Andrew F. Krepinevich Jr. *The Army and Vietnam.* Baltimore: Johns Hopkins University Press, 1986, chapters 1, 6–8, 10.

Betts, *Conflict After the Cold War:*
T. E. Lawrence, "Science of Guerrilla Warfare."
Mao Tse-tung, "On Guerrilla Warfare."
Samuel P. Huntington, "Patterns of Violence in World Politics."
Martha Crenshaw, "The Strategic Logic of Terrorism."
Mark Juergensmeyer, "Religious Radicalism and Political Violence."

Marc Sageman. "Jihadi Networks of Terror." In *Countering Modern Terrorism,* edited by Katharina von Knop, Heinrich Neisser, and Martin van Creveld. Bielefeld: W. Bertelsmann Verlag, 2005.
Robert A. Pape. *Dying to Win.* New York: Random House, 2005, chapters 4, 7, and 10.
Osama bin Ladin et al. "Jihad Against Jews and Crusaders: World Islamic Front Statement," February 23, 1998. http://www.fas.org/irp/world/para/docs/980223-fatwa.htm.
"Full Transcript of Bin Ladin's Speech." October 30, 2004. http://english.aljazeera.net/NR/exeres/79C6AF22-98FB-4A1C-B21F-2BC36E87F61F.htm.

View *The Battle of Algiers* before the end of Unit 8. Refer to these questions as you view the film:

• Were the tactics used on either or both sides illegitimate? Does the legitimacy or illegitimacy of terror or torture depend on the nature of the tactics or the justice of the cause they serve?

• By what criteria were the tactics employed effective or counterproductive?

• Could either side have hoped to win without using those tactics?

• In what respects are the issues posed by Al-Qaida today similar to and different from those in this case?

• Is Colonel Mathieu's character evil, admirable, tragic, or something else?

• How do the French and FLN strategies reflect Huntington's points about the "tripartite" nature of revolutionary war or Mao's points about guerrillas and population being "fish" and "sea"?

• Have US intelligence services learned the wrong lessons from this film?

Unit 9: Society, Polity, Culture, and Capability

1. Nationalism, state expansion, and social mobilization.
2. Civil-military relations.
3. Recruitment, conscription, organization.
4. Culture and combat effectiveness.
5. Combat motivation: When fighting can get one killed, what makes one fight?

Betts, *Conflict After the Cold War:*

Edward Mansfield and Jack Snyder, "Democratization and War."
Chaim Kaufmann, "Possible and Impossible Solutions to Ethnic Civil Wars."
Radha Kumar, "The Troubled History of Partition."

Edward Shils and Morris Janowitz. "Cohesion and Disintegration in the Wehrmacht in World War II." *Public Opinion Quarterly* 12, no. 2 (Summer 1948).

Omer Bartov. *Hitler's Army.* New York: Oxford University Press, 1991, chapters 3–4.

Kenneth Pollack. *Arabs at War.* Lincoln: University of Nebraska Press, 2002, "Conclusions and Lessons." (Ph.D. students see Risa A. Brooks, "Making Military Might: Why Do States Fail and Succeed? A Review Essay," *International Security* 28, no. 2 [Fall 2003].)

Unit 10: When Is War Murder? The Moral Calculus of Killing

1. Absolute versus utilitarian criteria.
2. Atrocities: Cold blood and passion.
3. Are some lives worth more than others?
4. Is terrorism ever legitimate?

Michael Walzer. *Just and Unjust Wars.* 3rd ed. New York: Basic Books, 2000, chapters 4, 6, 9, 16, 19.

View *Saving Private Ryan* before lectures for Unit 10. Refer to questions in Walzer, *Just and Unjust Wars,* p. 19.

Unit 11: The Nuclear Revolution: Theory and Practice

1. Nuclear weapon effects.
2. Deterrence and "compellence."
3. Rationality, uncertainty, and credibility.
4. Limited war and escalation.
5. Nuclear war plans and operational doctrine.
6. Cold War crises.

Lawrence Freedman. *The Evolution of Nuclear Strategy,* 3rd ed. New York: Palgrave, 2003, chapters 6–9, 12, 14–16, 19.

Paul Fussell. "Thank God for the Atom Bomb." In *Thank God for the Atom Bomb and Other Essays,* by Paul Fussell. New York: Summit Books, 1988.

Unit 12: Threat Assessment and Defense Planning

1. Aggression or security dilemma?
2. Intentions and capabilities.
3. Deterrence and provocation.
4. Intelligence and uncertainty.
5. Strategic assumptions and US force planning.

Eyre Crowe, "Memorandum on the Present State of British Relations with France and Germany," January 1, 1907, and Thomas Sanderson, "Observations on Printed Memorandum on Relations with France and Germany, January 1907." In *British Documents on the Origins of the War, 1898–1914,* vol. 3: *The Testing of the Entente, 1904–6,* edited by G. P. Gooch and Harold Temperley. London: HMSO, 1928. Read pp. 399–405 and 414–419 carefully; skim the rest.

Documents 551, 553, and 650 on the Munich crisis in *Documents on British Foreign Policy, 1919–1939,* Third Series, vol. 2: *1938,* edited by E. L. Woodward and Rohan Butler, assisted by Margaret Lambert. London: HMSO, 1949.

Richard K. Betts and Thomas Christensen. "China: Getting the Questions Right." *National Interest* 62 (Winter 2000–2001).

Barry R. Posen and Andrew L. Ross. "Competing Visions for US Grand Strategy." *International Security* 21, no. 3 (Winter 1996–1997).

Unit 13: Arms Control

1. Political, economic, and military rationales for arms regulation.
2. Weapons of mass destruction (WMD): Cold War negotiations.
3. Conventional forces: "Defense dominance"?
4. The arms trade.
5. The costs and benefits of regulation.
6. Regional conflicts and incentives for proliferation.
7. WMD after the Cold War: Biological, chemical, nuclear.

Betts, *Conflict After the Cold War:*

Samuel P. Huntington, "Arms Races: Prerequisites and Results."

Charles H. Fairbanks Jr. and Abram N. Shulsky, "Arms Control: The Historical Experience."

Kenneth N. Waltz, "The Spread of Nuclear Weapons: More May Be Better." (For elaboration of this argument and rebuttals by Scott Sagan, see Scott D. Sagan and Kenneth N. Waltz, *The Spread of Nuclear Weapons: A Debate Renewed.* New York: W.W. Norton, 2003.)

Unit 14: Conclusion: Evolving Bases of Conflict and Cooperation

1. Environmental sources of conflict.
2. Religion.
3. Power without force?
4. A "revolution in military affairs"?
5. Information warfare.
6. Nonlethal weaponry.
7. Theories, experience, and prediction.
8. Culture and conflict.

Betts, *Conflict After the Cold War:*
Thomas Homer-Dixon, "Environmental Changes as Causes of Acute Conflict."
Richard K. Betts, "The Delusion of Impartial Intervention."
Eliot A. Cohen, "A Revolution in Warfare."

Biddle, *Military Power,* chapter 10.
Huntington, *The Clash of Civilizations and the Remaking of World Order,* chapters 10, 12.

FILMS

The Battle of Algiers (1967), directed by Gilo Pontecorvo, screenplay by Franco Solinas, 2 hours, 5 minutes. For Unit 8 of the course. To understand the film, you must know the essential story of the Algerian war of independence. Remember that the French did not consider Algeria a colony but a part of metropolitan France (it had about a million European settlers). Although the movie is fiction, several characters are composites of real historical figures (one of the FLN leaders plays himself in the movie). The realism of this film is demonstrated by the fact that after early showings, the producers had to insert a notice at the beginning that it was not a documentary. Although obviously pro-FLN, the film is also unusual in the extent to which it does not demonize the French but empathizes with them. (Interestingly, the actor who played Colonel Mathieu was a French communist!)

Saving Private Ryan (1998), directed by Stephen Spielberg, screenplay by Robert Rodat, 2 hours, 49 minutes. For Unit 10. Look at the first twenty-five minutes (the assault on Omaha Beach) as one of the least unrealistic of Hollywood portrayals of combat. (Paul Fussell, of all people, approved heartily of this sequence.) Look at the rest of the film as an evocation of dilemmas about risking, deliberately spending, or wrongfully taking lives in wartime.

Zulu (1964), directed by Cy Endfield, screenplay by John Prebble and Cy Endfield, 2 hours, 19 minutes. Relevant to Units 6 and 9. The cinematic version of the famous defense of Rorke's Drift in 1879. Ignore the subplot about the missionary and his daughter, inserted to help market the movie.

Also, distinguish questions about military effectiveness from questions about political legitimacy (the British soldiers are portrayed as heroes in the film but were in the service of an imperial land grab). Focus on the linkages among organization, doctrine, tactics, technology, professionalism, and combat effectiveness on both sides of the engagement.

All Quiet on the Western Front (1930), directed by Lewis Milestone, adapted by Maxwell Anderson, screenplay by George Abbott, from the novel by Erich Maria Remarque, 2 hours, 12 minutes, including restored footage. Relevant to Units 1 and 9. This is *the* classic antiwar novel and film of the interwar period, banned in several countries. Star Lew Ayres famously became a conscientious objector in World War II.

Paths of Glory (1959), directed by Stanley Kubrick, screenplay by Stanley Kubrick, Calder Willingham, and Jim Thompson, from the novel by Humphrey Cobb, 1 hour, 27 minutes. Relevant to Units 1, 9, and 10. Note the vast distance between high command and battlefield and the contrast between collective mission and individual justice.

Twelve O'Clock High (1949), directed by Henry King, screenplay by Sy Bartlett and Beirne Lay Jr., 2 hours, 12 minutes. Relevant to Units 4, 7, and 9. The problem of achieving military effectiveness at the price of driving men to their limits in the development of the US "precision" bombing campaign in 1943–1944.

A Gathering of Eagles (1963), directed by Delbert Mann, screenplay by Robert Pirosh, 1 hour, 56 minutes. Relevant to Units 4 and 11. Before watching, get over the fact that this film is more saccharine than the other films mentioned here. In its glitzy Hollywood way, it presents social and organizational issues in elite unit command, personnel management, and operational combat readiness and provides insight into the most important US military organization of the Cold War era: SAC. The film is in many respects a nuclear-age echo of *Twelve O'Clock High.*

TEACHING NOTES

This is a graduate lecture course open to advanced undergraduates. It is designed to be challenging. Any student who cannot or does not wish to read and ponder a heavy load of material should not take this course. All students must (1) complete assigned readings; (2) attend all lectures, arriving on time; (3) view two of the films listed above; and (4) take the final examination on the scheduled date. Undergraduates must also (5) take the midterm examination and (6) attend discussion sections (optional for graduate students). Required readings other than the ones in the Betts book are on reserve in the library. This is a survey course. In order to allow maximum time for reading, there is no writing assignment. The reading load averages 214 pages per week but is concentrated disproportionately in sections 4 and 6–8. The total number of pages of reading required for the course is 2,996.

11.2 Rules of War: The Ethics of Destruction in International Politics

R. Charli Carpenter
University of Pittsburgh

COURSE DESCRIPTION

Upper-level undergraduate course.

Why has the international community outlawed flamethrowers and land mines, but not nuclear weapons? Why would soldiers ever follow the rules of war in conflict situations, and when are they most likely to break them? How are international security norms evolving in an age of failed states, civil war, and global terrorism? This course evaluates the role of international ethical norms in regulating the practice of organized political violence. We will begin by considering different approaches for systematically studying the effects of ethical norms on international policymaking. Next we consider the origins and evolving dynamics of the laws of war, explore why political actors so often violate these rules and the conditions under which they follow them, and examine the political and ethical dilemmas involved in enforcing them. Specific topics covered include weapons bans, terrorism, humanitarian intervention, the protection of noncombatants, and sexual violence as a tool of war. The course will conclude with an assessment of continuity and change in global security norms after September 11, 2001.

REQUIRED TEXTS

The reading load for this course is heavy. You are not required to read every word. Use your time strategically but try to understand the main points of all the readings as well as the similarities and contrasts between the arguments made by different authors.

Readings *Required for All Students* constitute the minimum amount of work essential to do well in the class and will form the basis of class discussions and exercises. You are expected to come to class having absorbed the basic substance of, and being prepared to raise questions about, all the required readings. I recommend reading both with a highlighter (to make visible the basic points of the articles and books for later re-skimming) and with a pen (for writing comments and questions to yourself in the margins).

The course readings come from a variety of sources. Articles available on the Internet are indicated in the assignments that follow. Books and texts can be purchased or used on reserve in the library. Short readings culled from the media on specific current events will be handed out in class, posted online, or emailed to you several days before class and will provide the context for in-class debates and exercises. Be sure to print them and bring them with you to class.

REQUIRED FOR ALL STUDENTS

Michael Byers. *War Law: Understanding International Law and Armed Conflict*. New York: Grove, 2005.
Roy Gutman and David Reiff, eds. *Crimes of War: What the Public Should Know*. New York: W. W. Norton, 1999.
Johnson, James Turner. *Morality and Contemporary Warfare*. New Haven, CT: Yale University Press, 2001.
Julie Mertus. *Bait and Switch: Human Rights and US Foreign Policy*. New York: Routledge, 2004.

COURSE SCHEDULE

Module 1: Introduction

Unit 1: Introduction

Gutman and Reiff, *Crimes of War*, preface.
Johnson, *Morality and Contemporary Warfare*, introduction.
Mertus, *Bait and Switch*, chapter 1.
Byers, *War Law*, introduction.

Unit 2: Three Kings Film Screening

Three Kings, directed by David O. Russell, Warner Bros., 1999, 114 minutes. Starring George Clooney and Nora Dunn.

Unit 3: Rules of War: An Overview

Johnson, *Morality and Contemporary Warfare*, chapter 1.
Byers, *War Law*, chapters 1, 4, 5, 6, 10, and 12.
Gutman and Reiff, *Crimes of War*, "International Humanitarian Law: An Overview," by Weschler.
"International Humanitarian Law: Answers to Your Questions" (online).
"Charter of the United Nations" (online).

Unit 4: The Geneva Regime in World Politics

Martha Finnemore, "Rules of War and Wars of Rules." In *Constructing World Cultures*, edited by John Boli and George M. Thomas. Stanford, CA: Stanford University Press, 1999, 149–168.

Mary Anderson. "Norms of Humanitarian Conduct." In *Do No Harm,* by Mary Anderson. Boulder, CO: Lynne Rienner, 1999.

Mertus, *Bait and Switch,* chapter 2.

International Committee of the Red Cross. "The ICRC's Mandate and Mission." www.icrc.org.

Module 2: Thematic Issues

Unit 5: Means and Methods of Warfare

Gutman and Reiff, *Crimes of War,* sections on "Biological Weapons," "Chemical Weapons," "Nuclear Weapons," and "Weapons."

Eric Adams. "Shoot to Not Kill." *Information Warfare Monitor.* Advanced Research Network Group, May 2003, http://www.infowar-monitor.net.

Review ICRC webpage on "Weapons and IHL." www.icrc.org.

Review ICRC webpage on "Means and Methods of Warfare."

Unit 6: Protecting Civilians

Johnson, *Morality and Contemporary Warfare,* chapter 4.

Byers, *War Law,* chapter 10.

Gutman and Reiff, *Crimes of War,* 84–87.

Review ICRC webpage on "Civilians in the Power of the Enemy."

Unit 7: Protecting Detainees

Gutman and Reiff, *Crimes of War,* 102–106.

Byers, *War Law,* chapter 11.

Review ICRC webpage on "Prisoners of War and IHL."

Unit 8: Women and International Humanitarian Law

Judith Gardam and Michelle Jarvis. "A Gender View of the Shaping of IHL." In *Women, Armed Conflict, and International Law,* by Judith Gardam and Michelle Jarvis. New York: Springer, 2001.

Charlotte Lindsey. "Women and War: An Overview." *International Review of the Red Cross,* no. 839 (September 30, 2000): 561–579. http://www.icrc.org.

Gutman and Reiff, *Crimes of War,* 323–329.

Review ICRC webpage on "Women and IHL."

Module 3: Evaluating the Rules of War

Unit 9: Implementing the Rules in Foreign Policy Circles: Influencing States

Mertus, *Bait and Switch,* chapter 3.

Mark Danner. *Torture and Truth*. New York: Review Books, 2004.
Ward Thomas. "Norms and Security: The Case of International Assassination." *International Security* 25, no. 1 (Summer 2000): 105–133.

Unit 10: Implementing the Rules in the Field: Influencing Weapons-Bearers

Mertus, *Bait and Switch,* chapter 3.
Franke Wilmer. "The Social Construction of Conflict and Reconciliation in the Former Yugoslavia." *Social Justice* 25, no. 4 (1998).
Joanna Bourke. "War Crimes." In *An Intimate History of Killing,* by Joanna Bourke. New York: Basic Books, 2000.

Review ICRC website on "The Roots of Behavior in War."

Unit 11: Enforcing the Rules of War: Humanitarian Intervention

Gutman and Reiff, *Crimes of War,* "Humanitarian Intervention," by Reiff.
Johnson, *Morality and Contemporary Warfare,* chapter 3.
Michael Ignatieff. *Virtual War: Kosovo and Beyond.* New York: Henry Holt, 2000.

Unit 12: Punishing Rule Breakers: The Politics of War Crimes Tribunals

Johnson, *Morality and Contemporary Warfare,* chapter 6.
Gutman and Reiff, *Crimes of War,* "War Crimes, Categories of."
Davida Kellogg. "Jus Post Bellum." *Parameter,* September 22, 2002, http://www.encyclopedia.com/doc/1G1-91564617.html.

Unit 13: Changing the Rules: The Role of Advocacy Networks

Margaret Keck and Kathryn Sikkink. *Activists Beyond Borders: Advocacy Networks in International Politics*. Ithaca, NY: Cornell University Press, 1998, selections.
Mertus, *Bait and Switch,* chapter 4.

Unit 14: Final Discussion: Rules of War and Their Limits

Johnson, *Morality and Contemporary Warfare,* chapter 7.
Mertus, *Bait and Switch,* chapter 5.
Byers, *War Law,* epilogue.

TEACHING NOTES

I typically alternate lectures about basic language, concepts, organizations, and modes of action within the Geneva regime with small group work or simulations that enable students to imagine themselves facing hard choices in applying these rules, either as combatants in conflict situations, humanitarian organizations negotiating access to civilians, or leaders and Pentagon officials considering rules of engagement. Most students come to class with a sense of idealism about just war theory; I want them to leave feeling more pragmatic about the realities of the Geneva regime, which includes its limited enforcement power and ambiguity. However, the risk is always that students may become cynical and jaded. It's important to temper that with cases in which the rules of war have been followed, as well as those in which atrocities have occurred, and a sense that the existence of the rules themselves has made the world a better place, if only marginally. It is also important to leave time in class to help students process how the material is affecting them emotionally.

11.3 War in Film and Literature

Daniel Lieberfeld
Duquesne University

COURSE DESCRIPTION

Intermediate or advanced undergraduate course in general education, peace studies, political science, comparative literature, and film.

The course uses films and literature to gain insights into core questions about war and peace: What accounts for the glamour and attraction that war holds for many people? How do normal men become able to kill enemy soldiers or even noncombatants? How is becoming a warrior linked to gender identity? How is killing sanctioned as a moral act? How does another group become "the enemy"? What psychological price do soldiers pay for killing? What sort of obstacles do veterans face in reintegrating into civilian life? To what extent can combat experience be conveyed through words and images? What myths do societies create about war? How can literature and film perpetuate or contest such myths?

Specific topics include nationalism and World War I (*All Quiet on the Western Front, Paths of Glory*), insurgency and counterinsurgency (*The Battle of Algiers, Generation Kill*), war trauma and its aftermath (*Maus, Survival in Auschwitz*), nuclear weapons and the Cold War (*The Fog of War, Dr. Strangelove*), domestic politics and the mythologization of the Vietnam war (*Winter Soldier, Full Metal Jacket, Rambo, If I Die in a Combat Zone*), American triumphalism and mythmaking (*Saving Private Ryan*), antiwar satire (*Duck Soup*), the media and censorship of images and ideas about war (*Control Room*), and how computer and video games can desensitize players to violence and inscribe gender and racial hierarchies (*Game Over*). Most of the perspectives explored are American, but the course also includes works by several non-US artists. An article with more detail about the course is "Teaching About War Through Film and Literature" in *PS: Political Science and Politics* 40, no. 3 (July 2007): 571–574. The complete syllabus and sample handouts can be accessed at www.policycenter.duq.edu/facLieberfeld.htm.

REQUIRED TEXTS

Erich M. Remarque. *All Quiet on the Western Front.* New York: Vintage, 2005.

Primo Levi. *Survival in Auschwitz* (originally *If This Be a Man*). New York: Simon and Schuster, 1996.

Tim O'Brien. *If I Die in a Combat Zone: Box Me Up and Ship Me Home.* New York: Broadway, 1999.

Art Spiegelman. *Maus II: And Here My Troubles Began.* New York: Pantheon, 1992.

Evan Wright. *Generation Kill: Devil Dogs, Iceman, Captain America, and the New Face of American War.* New York: Berkley, 2008.

REQUIRED FILMS

The following films are to be viewed outside of class time.

Paths of Glory, directed by Stanley Kubrick, 1957, 87 minutes.
Dr. Strangelove, directed by Stanley Kubrick, 1964, 95 minutes.
The Battle of Algiers, directed by Gillo Pontecorvo, 1966, 125 minutes. (Note: this film is subtitled—watch a recent print.)
Winter Soldier, Winterfilm Collective, 1972, re-released 2005, 95 minutes.
Full Metal Jacket, directed by Stanley Kubrick, 1987, 116 minutes.
Saving Private Ryan, directed by Steven Spielberg, 1998, 169 minutes.
Three Kings, directed by David O. Russell, 1999.
The Fog of War: Eleven Lessons from the Life of Robert S. McNamara, directed by Errol Morris, 2003.
Control Room, directed by Jehane Noujaim, 2004, 86 minutes.
Hotel Rwanda, directed by Terry George, 2004.

In-class excerpts from:
The Sands of Iwo Jima, directed by Allan Dwan, 1949, 109 minutes.
Rambo: First Blood, Part II, directed by George P. Cosmatos, 1985, 96 minutes.
Duck Soup, directed by Leo McCarey (with the Marx Brothers), 1935, 70 minutes.
Fahrenheit 911, directed by Michael Moore, 2004, 122 minutes.
Game Over: Gender, Race, and Violence in Video Games, directed by Nina Huntemann, 2000, 60 minutes.

COURSE SCHEDULE

Unit 1: Soldiers' Camaraderie; Grieving and the Dead; Nationalist Mythmaking; Foot Soldiers' and Officers' Divergent Perspectives

Rupert Brooke, "The Soldier," 1915.
Wilfred Owen, "Dulce et Decorum Est."

View *Paths of Glory.*

Unit 2: The Psychological Costs of Killing;
Obstacles for Veterans in Reintegrating into Civilian Life
Remarque, *All Quiet on the Western Front.*

Unit 3: Training and Indoctrination for Combat;
War and Gender Identity
O'Brien, *If I Die in a Combat Zone.*

View *Full Metal Jacket.*

Unit 4: The Conscript's Relation to the Community;
Truth Telling and Fiction in War
View *Winter Soldier.*

Tim O'Brien. "On the Rainy River" and "How to Tell a True War Story." In *The Things They Carried,* by Tim O'Brien. Franklin Center, PA: Franklin Library, 1990.

Jeffrey Smith. *War and Press Freedom: The Problem of Prerogative Power.* New York: Oxford University Press, 1999, pp. 215–219.

Unit 5: Nationalist Interpretations of Lost Wars
and the Myth of the "Stab in the Back"
View *Rambo: First Blood, Part II* (excerpts).

Jerry Lembcke. *The Spitting Image: Myth, Memory, and the Legacy of Vietnam.* New York: New York University Press, 1998, excerpt. See also Lembcke, "Debunking a Spitting Image," *Boston Globe,* April 30, 2005, http://www.boston.com/news/globe/editorial_opinion/oped/articles/2005/04/30/debunking_a_spitting_image/.

Unit 6: War as Adventure;
Innocence and Moral Responsibility in War
View *Three Kings.*

Unit 7: Traumatic Experience in War;
Civilian Deaths in US Invasion of Iraq
Wright, *Generation Kill.*

Unit 8: War Films and Mythmaking;
World War II in Contemporary Culture and Politics
View *Saving Private Ryan* (before class).

View excerpt from *Sands of Iwo Jima* (in class).

Also consider viewing Eastwood's *Flags of Our Fathers.*

Unit 9: Video Games and War, Race, and Gender
View *Game Over: Gender, Race, and Violence in Video Games* (in class).

Unit 10: War and Genocide; Heroism in War
View *Hotel Rwanda.*

Unit 11: Satiric Perspectives; Nuclear Weapons and the Cold War
View *Dr. Strangelove.*

View *Duck Soup* (excerpt).

Unit 12: War and the Understanding of What Is Human and What Is Lost in Dehumanization
Levi, *Survival in Auschwitz.*

Donald Niewyk. "Holocaust: The Genocide of the Jews." In *Century of Genocide: Critical Essays and Eyewitness Accounts,* edited by Sam Toten, William S. Parsons, and Israel W. Charney. New York: Routledge, 2004, pp. 127–129, 140–159 (used as background for Levi and Spiegelman).

Unit 13: Intergenerational Transmission of War-Related Trauma; Genocide's Costs to Survivors
Spiegelman, *Maus II.*

Unit 14: Insurgency and Counterinsurgency; Politics of Torture
View *The Battle of Algiers.*

Unit 15: Political Responsibility in War; Mass Media and War
View *The Fog of War.*

View *Fahrenheit 911* (excerpt).

View *Control Room* (excerpt).

TEACHING NOTES

The meta-theme of the course is the contrast between the mythology typical of nationalist and propagandist conceptions of war and the lived experiences of actual soldiers. Throughout, the course juxtaposes narratives that report soldiers' experiences and their skepticism toward nationalist and militarist culture, alongside cultural products that romanticize war and that try to raise popular support for war and militarism. At the outset, I ask students to contrast the religious-nationalist images of war in the poem "The Soldier," written by Rupert Brooke before his death early in World War I, with the poem

"Dulce et Decorum Est," written by fellow soldier Wilfred Owen. Owen describes a scene of death, blinding, and asphyxiation wrought by mustard gas and advises readers not to repeat the "old Lie" about the sweetness of dying for one's country. Brooke and Owen's divergent perspectives can serve as reference points for juxtaposition and analyses of other works. Contrasting perspectives can help students see how cultural products may convey political messages and that the "lessons" of a war, particularly a lost one, are heavily political. Students can recognize that a film like *Rambo: First Blood, Part II* draws more on the plot conventions of the action comic than on the actual history of the Vietnam War, but focused analysis can help them understand the film's political messages and their significance.

Artificial images of heroism and glory can be usefully contrasted with blatantly satirical perspectives on war. For example, Kubrick's *Dr. Strangelove* memorably lampoons the fallibility of political and military leaders, as well as the culture that links war and masculine identity.

The media's reporting of war is a theme in several works, particularly *Control Room* (a documentary about Al-Jazeera television and the Iraq War), *Three Kings,* and parts of *Fahrenheit 9/11*. *The Battle of Algiers* and *Generation Kill* also comment indirectly on the political significance of the media in counterinsurgency warfare, and *Hotel Rwanda* illustrates how media can propagate genocidal ideology or help mobilize international opinion in favor of humanitarian intervention.

I identify several of the main course themes in early works and keep referencing them as we encounter them in subsequent works, while also layering in additional themes rather than treating each theme discretely.

Students should view the films outside regular class time. The class can decide on a regular time for screenings in an on-campus auditorium. I also make a copy available for viewing in the library, or students can rent (or possibly download) films to view at home. After they have watched a film outside class, I select some scenes for in-class screening and discussion. Most students do the reading and viewing voluntarily, but I find it useful to give weekly, extremely short quizzes, consisting of two factual, not interpretive questions that should be obvious to anyone who did the assignment. Students can, for any reason, opt out of no more than two of these "ridiculously easy quizzes" during the semester. I also vary the emotional difficulty of the works: Due to the at-times intense and disturbing nature of the subject matter, I try to pace course materials so that students encounter a comic/satirical perspective every few weeks.

Some students may be unclear about generic terminology, such as "documentary," "memoir," "fiction," and "fiction based on fact." It may be helpful to ask them to identify each work's genre while noting that some works deliberately blur these categories, particularly O'Brien's (although not *If I Die in a Combat Zone*). Some students may find this element of ambiguity in O'Brien's work, and the overt unreliability of some of his narrators, discomfiting. It may be helpful to discuss the difference between authors' deliberately misleading readers and their using a fictional version of real experience to express an underlying truth or reveal the complexities and ambiguities that often characterize soldiers' experiences of war. Beyond merely describing what happens in a book or film or merely responding on the level of "I liked it," students should learn to see the works, especially the films, not as fully formed products whose origins are unquestioned, but as carefully crafted fabrications reflecting deliberate choices by individuals and teams of people who have elected to tell a particular story in a particular way and containing a political perspective that can and should be interrogated. Beyond written assignments, I provide questions for in-class discussion that encourage students to develop this capacity.

In teaching a course about the cultural politics and the politics of war, particularly regarding controversial current or recent events such as the Iraq War, one may well be faced with the question of how much of one's own political outlook to reveal. It may be helpful to explain to students that the guiding principle is distinguishing reality from myth. Rather than criticizing the adherents of particular political views or parties, the course tries to promote students' willingness to think critically, as opposed to unthinking acceptance of government propaganda. A concise overview of the extensive history of US governments' use of Hollywood films as pro-war propaganda can be found in Jeffrey Smith's *War and Press Freedom: The Problem of Prerogative Power* (Oxford University Press, 1999), 215–219.

One can also discuss with students how democracy makes citizens responsible for their government's decisions on war and peace and for how the country's military is used—and how, particularly during war, officials often deny citizens' rights and obligations to question official decisions. In this regard, the class should give sufficient consideration to examples of propagandist works, so that students understand what the more critical work is reacting to and why.

11.4 Cinematic Images of War and the Military

Morten G. Ender
US Military Academy at West Point

COURSE DESCRIPTION

Upper-level seminar for majors in peace studies, sociology, political science, film, and literature.

This course promotes a greater understanding of the inextricable link between war, the military, and films from a social and cultural perspective. Twentieth-century films, such as J. Stuart Blackton's *Tearing Down the Spanish Flag,* D. W. Griffith's *Birth of a Nation, Triumph of the Will, Private Benjamin, Saving Private Ryan, The Thin Red Line,* and the recent *Jarhead* demonstrate that the cinema, the viewing machine, has evolved with the armed forces, the war machine. This course provides in-depth study of some of the many films, both in the United States and abroad, depicting wars and militaries.

War and military films can be compared to their civilian counterparts in their treatments of the present social and cultural climate. Yet although war and the military are clearly influenced by the larger society in which they are embedded, they do not completely reflect the larger sociocultural climate. Moreover, what makes this course both novel and valuable is the concern for the massive yet often neglected social institution of the military and the war periods that are treated as anomalies in our history. They are often treated as moments of extremity in our sociocultural history and as periods overlooked until organization, indeed social life, return to normal. This course lifts the veil from a vibrant social institution and historic moments such as the Civil War, World War I, World War II, the Korean Conflict, Vietnam, the invasion of Grenada, the Gulf War, and more recent, so-called global war on terror. It examines them as momentous cinematic periods in our collective social life during the twentieth century, clearly a dark century with respect to war, and the beginning of the twenty-first century.

The specific course goal we seek to accomplish is this: Given a film from any country, in the genres of war or the military, involving social interaction among people and the social context of war or the military organization, use a sociological orientation to (1) provide an explanation for the social and cultural context of the film; (2) analyze and evaluate how war and the military as an institution are depicted in the film; (3) assess how a film's depiction of war and the military influences the relationship between society and the military; and (4) understand cinema in general to determine the social, psychological, and cultural significance of war and the military as they are depicted in film. This represents what students should be able to do upon successful completion of this course.

REQUIRED TEXTS

Thomas Doherty. *Projections of War: Hollywood, American Culture, and World War II*. New York: Columbia University Press, 1999.

Norman K. Denzin. *Images of the Postmodern Society: Social Theory and Contemporary Cinema*. Newbury Park, CA: Sage, 1998.

Robert Eberwein, ed. *The War Film*. New Brunswick, NJ: Rutgers University Press, 2005.

Ryan Gilbey. *Groundhog Day*. BFI Modern Classics, 2004.

Lawrence Suid. *Guts and Glory: The Making of the American Military Image in Film*. Lexington: University of Kentucky Press, 2002.

Michael Anderegg. "Home Front America and the Denial of Death in MGM's *The Human Comedy*." *Cinema Journal* 34, no. 1 (1994): 3–15.

Morten G. Ender. "Military Brats: Film Representations of Children from Military Families." *Armed Forces and Society*, 32, no. 1 (2005): 24–43.

Morten G. Ender, Paul T. Bartone, and Thomas A. Kolditz. "The Fallen Soldier: Death and the US Military." In *Handbook of Death and Dying: The Responses to Death*, vol. 2, edited by Clifton D. Bryant. Thousands Oaks, CA: Sage, 2003, 544–555.

George A. Huaco. *The Sociology of Film Art*. New York: Basic Books, 1965.

COURSE SCHEDULE

Week 1: Course Introduction

Doherty, *Projections of War,* chapter 1 (pages 1–15).

Suid, *Guts and Glory,* chapters 1–4.

Eberwein, *The War Film,* introduction.

Week 2: Sociological Perspective

Michael C. Kearl, "A Sociological Tour of Cyberspace," http://www.trinity.edu/~mkearl/index.html. Browse the website for sociological insights.

Huaco, *The Sociology of Film Art,* 1–50.

Week 3: Postmodern Theory

Denzin, *Images of the Postmodern,* chapters 1–4 (pp. 1–64) and 11 (pp. 149–157).

Suid, *Guts and Glory,* chapters 14–15.

Week 4: Socialization

Kearl, "A Sociological Tour of Cyberspace," http://www.trinity.edu/mkearl/socpsy.html. Read the page on sociological social psychology and theories.

Films (view any two): *Annapolis, Basic, Full Metal Jacket, Heartbreak Ridge, Major Payne, An Officer and a Gentleman, Private Benjamin, A Soldier's Story, Stripes, TAPS.*

Week 5: Sex, Gender, and Masculinity

Yvonne Tasker, "Soldiers' Stories: Women and Military Masculinities in *Courage Under Fire*," found in *The War Film*, edited by Eberwein.

Jake Willens. "Women in the Military: Combat Roles Considered." http://www.cdi.org/issues/women/combat.html.

Thomas Doherty, "The New War Movies as Moral Rearmament," found in *The War Film*, edited by Eberwein.

Suid, *Guts and Glory*, chapters 8, 9, 13, and 19.

Films (view any two): *Aliens* (*Alien 2*), *G. I. Jane, Basic, Hanna's War, Private Benjamin, Rambo, Tank Girl.*

Week 6: Families

Suid, *Guts and Glory*, chapter 16.

Ender, "Military Brats," http://afs.sagepub.com/content/vol32/issue1/.

Films (view any two): *Antwone Fisher, The Best Years of Our Lives, Blue Sky, Brats: Our Journey Home, The Great Santini, Heaven and Earth, The Marriage of Marie Braun, Pink Floyd: The Wall, Swing Shift, The White Rose.*

Week 7: Race and Ethnicity

Doherty, *Projections of War*, chapter 9.

Robert Burgoyne, "Race and Nation in *Glory*," in *The War Film*, edited by Eberwein.

Woodman, "Represented at the Margins: Images of African American Soldiers in Vietnam War Combat Films," in *The War Film*, edited by Eberwein.

Kearl, "A Sociological Tour of Cyberspace," http://www.trinity.edu/~mkearl/index.html.

Films (view *Glory* and one other): *A Soldier's Story, Birth of a Nation, Glory, Tuskegee Airmen.*

Week 8: Death

Kearl, "A Sociological Tour of Cyberspace," http://www.trinity.edu/~mkearl/race.html.

Anderegg, "Denial of Death in MGM's *The Human Comedy*" (handout available on reserve).

Films (view *The Human Comedy* and any other): *The Human Comedy, All Quiet on the Western Front, Courage Under Fire, The Deer Hunter, Gardens of Stone, Saving Private Ryan, The Sullivans.*

Week 9: Humor

Doherty, *Projections of War,* chapter 8.

Films (view any two): *M*A*S*H*, Buck Privates, Dr. Strangelove, Duck Soup, The General, The Great Dictator, Major Payne, Renaissance Man, Russkies, Stripes.*

Week 10: Military Academies

Films (view any two): *Annapolis, The Three Rooms of Melancholia, The West Point Story, The General's Daughter.*

Week 11: International Films

Films (view any two): *The White Rose; Das Boot; Colonel Redl; Europa, Europa; For a Lost Soldier; Life Is Beautiful; Mephisto; Open City; The Seventh Seal; The Triumph of the Will.*

Week 12: Global War on Terrorism Documentaries

Films (view any two): *A Company of Soldiers, Gunnar Palace, The War Tapes, Baghdad ER.*

Week 13: Groundhog Day

Gilbey, *Groundhog Day,* entire book.

Film: *Groundhog Day.*

Week 14: Futuristic Films

Students take the lead in class to discuss futuristic treatments in films such as *Star Wars* and *Starship Troopers.*

TEACHING NOTES

This course is primarily a three-credit seminar structured around a weekly social theme and how it plays out in film. I meet with the class two hours each week and ask them to use the third hour for watching films outside class. We watch some films collectively outside class and some individually. We do not watch all the films each week; rather, we choose one, two, or three films to watch and discuss. Sometimes students will select films not on the list.

Further, I have structured the course around a forum for analysis. The goal is to be able to analyze a film for a specific set of ideas that contribute to our understanding of the military and war and cinema from primarily a sociological perspective, but also from historical, political, religious, cultural, and feminist perspectives. This course also cross-fertilizes and focuses on issues of peace and social justice. The specific course goal is described in the course description and represents what I would expect students to be able to do upon successful completion of this course. Given an existing film related to the armed forces, war, civil-military relations, diversity, values, morality, culture, or social justice, students will use a sociological orientation to evaluate how these topics are being depicted in the film, account for why these topics are depicted as they are, and assess the influence of these depictions on the conduct of war and on the military as an institution.

11.5 The Bomb

B. Welling Hall
Earlham College

COURSE DESCRIPTION

Upper-level undergraduate elective for political science and peace and security studies.

In this course we will examine the twentieth- and twenty-first-century culture and proliferation of the bomb as a weapon that has the capacity to end life on earth. This is neither a course in guns and boats nor a course in physics; we will spend as little time as possible discussing the configurations of arsenals and weapons characteristics. We will look at materials in multiple genres, including history, political science, social psychology, military strategy, political activism, and legal studies. We will also include fiction and documentary film as texts. The reading load for the course is heavy; expect to devote at least three hours a week in preparation for each class hour.

Many students are familiar with Albert Einstein's famous statement: "In the nuclear age everything has changed except our ways of thinking, and thus we drift toward unparalleled catastrophe." The primary goal of this course is to critically improve our skills in "ways of thinking," or what political scientists sometimes call "modes of analysis." At the end of the course, students should be able to describe in some detail, with accuracy and insight, several of the multiple aspects of the nuclear predicament in its various stages and manifestations.

Given their developing skills in description and explanation and our review of the history of the nuclear age(s), they will also be encouraged to prescribe actions that address issues discovered in the prior modes of analysis. Although this is most difficult to do, it is what needs to be done to have any hope of finding a resolution to the predicament.

REQUIRED TEXTS

Graham Allison and Philip Zelikow. *Essence of Decision: Explaining the Cuban Missile Crisis*, 2nd ed. New York: Longman, 1999.

Helen Caldicott. *The New Nuclear Danger: George W. Bush's Military-Industrial Complex*. New York: New Press, 2004.

Tom Clancy. *The Hunt for Red October* (any edition).

Lawrence Freedman. *Deterrence*. London: Polity Press, 2004.

Charles Osgood. *An Alternative to War or Surrender.* Urbana: University of Illinois Press, 1962.

Scott D. Sagan and Kenneth Waltz. 2003. *The Spread of Nuclear Weapons: A Debate Renewed: With New Sections on India and Pakistan, Terrorism, and Missile Defense,* 2nd ed. New York: W.W. Norton, 2003.

Martin J. Sherwin. *A World Destroyed: Hiroshima and Its Legacies,* 3rd ed. Stanford, CA: Stanford University Press, 2003.

COURSE SCHEDULE

Week 1: Course Introduction

Sherwin, *A World Destroyed,* introduction and part 1.

View before class *Hiroshima,* directed by Koreyoshi Kurahara and Roger Spottiswoode, 2005, 178 minutes.

Week 2

Sherwin, *A World Destroyed,* chapters 3–6.

View before class *War and Peace in the Nuclear Age: Dawn,* produced by Peter Raymont and Chana Gazit, Public Broadcasting System, 1989, http://openvault.wgbh.org/wapina/barcode49036nitze1_3/index.html.

Week 3

Sherwin, *A World Destroyed,* chapters 7–9.

View before class *War and Peace in the Nuclear Age: A Bigger Bang for the Buck,* Public Broadcasting System, 1989, http://openvault.wgbh.org/wapina/barcode49549cline1_3/index.html.

Week 4

View before class "In the Shadow of Sakharov." *Frontline,* produced by Sherry Jones, Public Broadcasting Corporation, 1991, 90 minutes, http://www.pbs.org/wgbh/pages/frontline/programs/info/1001.html.

"Sakharov: Soviet Physics, Nuclear Weapons, and Human Rights." Website of the Center for the History of Physics, American Institute of Physics, 2008, http://www.aip.org/history/sakharov/index.htm.

View before class *Fail-Safe,* directed by Sidney Lumet, 1964, 112 minutes.

Week 5

Allison and Zelikow, *Essence of Decision,* chapter 1–2.

View before class *War and Peace in the Nuclear Age: At the Brink,* produced by Peter Raymont and Chana Gazit, Public Broadcasting System, 1989, http://openvault.wgbh.org/wapina/barcode48984bundy_2/index.html.

Week 6

Allison and Zelikow, *Essence of Decision,* chapters 3–5.

View before class *Thirteen Days,* directed by Roger Donaldson, 2001, 147 minutes.

Week 7

Allison and Zelikow, *Essence of Decision,* chapters 6–7.
Osgood, *An Alternative to War or Surrender,* chapters 1–3.

View before class *War and Peace in the Nuclear Age: The Education of Robert McNamara,* produced by Austin Hoyt, Public Broadcasting System, 1989, http://openvault.wgbh.org/wapina/barcode50060healy_2/index.html.

Week 8

Osgood, *An Alternative to War or Surrender,* chapters 4–6.
John F. Kennedy. "Radio and Television Address to the American People by President Kennedy on the Nuclear Test Ban Treaty, July 26, 1963." http://www.ratical.org/co-globalize/jfk072663.html.

Week 9

Begin reading either Freedman, *Deterrence,* or Clancy, *The Hunt for Red October.*

View before class *The Russians Are Coming, the Russians Are Coming*, directed by Norman Jewison, 1966, 126 minutes.

Week 10

Clancy, *The Hunt for Red October.*

View before class *The Hunt for Red October,* directed by John McTiernan, 1998, 135 minutes.

Freedman, *Deterrence,* chapters 1–4.

View before class *War and Peace in the Nuclear Age: One Step Forward,* produced by David Espar and Carol Lynn Dornbrand, Public Broadcasting System, 1989, http://openvault.wgbh.org/wapina/barcode49748nitze2_2/index.html.

Week 11

Freedman, *Deterrence,* chapters 5–8.
Sagan and Waltz, *The Spread of Nuclear Weapons,* chapters 1–2.

View before class *War and Peace in the Nuclear Age: Have and Have-Nots,* produced by Sue Crowther, Public Broadcasting System, 1989, http://openvault.wgbh.org/wapina/barcode48888menon_3/index.html.

Week 12

Sagan and Waltz, *The Spread of Nuclear Weapons,* chapters 3–5.

View before class *Nuclear War Between India and Pakistan?* script by Jon Lottman, 1998, 29 minutes.

View before class *War and Peace in the Nuclear Age: Reagan's Shield,* produced by Graham Chedd, Public Broadcasting System, 1989, http://openvault.wgbh.org/wapina/barcode49900weinberger_4/index.html.

Week 13

Caldicott, *The New Nuclear Danger,* preface, introduction, chapters 1–4.

View before class *If You Love This Planet,* directed by Terri Nash, produced by Edward Le Lorrain, 1982.

Week 14

Caldicott, *The New Nuclear Danger,* chapters 5–9.

View before class *Helen's War,* directed by Anna Broinowski, 2004, 84 minutes.

View before class *Blast from the Past,* directed by Hugh Wilson, 1999, 112 minutes.

TEACHING NOTES

A term project is an important element in this course; its bits and pieces add up to 35 percent of the course grade. I work closely with students to find topics that they love. They will find ideas for questions by browsing through the required readings for this course, recent newspaper headlines, back issues of the *Bulletin of the Atomic Scientists* and other journals of opinion, and websites of organizations such as the Coalition to Reduce Nuclear Dangers (www.clw.org) and the Friends Committee on National Legislation (www.fcnl.org).

I also assign students a documentary and film journal. They will write approximately 350 words for each film. Each entry should include images or words that created a strong impression, a discussion about the relationship between ideas presented in the given documentary and in course texts, and questions and concerns the film raises for them.

12
International Organization and the Rule of Law

THE NOTION THAT SOME FORM OF INTERNATIONAL ORGANIZATION might both promote the well-being of the individual and secure peace for the international community by clearly articulating legal norms is an ancient idea in peace studies, most famously linked to the work of Kant in his eighteenth-century essay *Perpetual Peace*. The syllabuses collected in this section of the curriculum guide pull this liberal premise into the twenty-first century by introducing students to the proliferating range of international organizations (beyond the United Nations and the International Criminal Court) and conceptions of international norms (with a heavy emphasis on human rights). Each of the instructors presenting a syllabus below indicates, in some fashion, that a key learning outcome for students is to "understand and promote social responsibility" (Robert Elias) or think about "reducing human suffering" (Daniel Chong). These goals are to be achieved by studying the evolution of norms, legal standards, and enforcement mechanisms in international organizations and, in almost all the courses described below, trying on a multiplicity of roles: attempting to think as a human rights advocate in a simulation (Maria J. Stephan and Richard Robyn), responding to policy memos (R. Charli Carpenter), or considering a query (Robert C. Johansen). It is noteworthy that each of the instructors deliberately introduces ethical dilemmas into the syllabus. For example, can the provision of humanitarian assistance sometimes do harm? If so, then how should the international community respond both lawfully and legitimately to crises? Students are thus exposed to the skills of critical debate and argument so intrinsic to the promotion of rule of law.

12.1 International Organization and Law

Richard Robyn
Kent State University

COURSE DESCRIPTION

Upper-level undergraduate course for general education students and majors in political science, peace studies, and international relations.

In the latter half of the twentieth century, international organizations (IOs) proliferated and became more prominent actors on the world stage. Despite their tremendous growth in that amount of time and into the twenty-first century, especially in the era after September 11, 2001, IOs have shared power and influence uneasily with nation-states, arguably still the most powerful actors in world affairs. Who would doubt now the importance of the United States as a powerful nation-state making self-interested decisions, or the difficulties that might cause with the United Nations, for example? And yet, daily headlines from places such as Iraq and Afghanistan attest to the importance IOs have in peoples' lives.

The overall objective of this course is to provide a solid grounding for both a theoretical and practical understanding of international organizations: their relationship to international law, raison d'être, formation, growth, place in the contemporary world, and impact on world politics. To that end, we will first examine IOs in the broad context of international relations theory and then look more closely at several IOs in particular: the United Nations (and especially its International Court of Justice, international war crimes tribunals, and International Criminal Court), European Union (EU), North Atlantic Treaty Organization (NATO), and others, although we will not necessarily limit ourselves to those organizations.

Students who take this course should have a grounding in world politics or public policy.

REQUIRED TEXTS

Margaret P. Karns and Karen Mingst. *International Organizations*. Boulder, CO: Lynne Rienner, 2004.

Readings assigned in the course schedule.

RECOMMENDED NEWS SOURCES

New York Times (online or in print).

CNN News (on television and online).
News Hour (on television), Public Broadcasting System.
UN Wire, online publication of the United Nations Foundation, www.unwire.org.
Security Council Report, online newsletter of the *Security Council Report* in affiliation with Columbia University's Center on International Organization, www.securitycouncilreport.org.

COURSE SCHEDULE

Unit 1: Orientation and Megatrends

Session 1: Orientation to the Course
Megatrends: The Context for International Organizations.

Unit 2: IO Theory and Historical Development

Session 2: The Pieces of Global Governance
Karns and Mingst, *International Organizations*, chapter 1.

Session 3: Theoretical Foundations of International Organization and International Law
Karns and Mingst, *International Organizations*, chapters 2 and 3.

Unit 3: The United Nations

Session 4: Origins, Principles, Evolution, and Structure
Discuss "What has the UN done?" September 11 discussion.

Karns and Mingst, *International Organizations*, chapter 4.

Browse the UN website, www.un.org.

Browse *Security Council Report* website, www.securitycouncilreport.org.

Session 5: People of Note: Ban Ki-Moon and Kofi Annan
Read a biographical article about Ban at the UN website, www.un.org.

Session 6: Major Functions 1: International Peace and Security
Karns and Mingst, *International Organizations*, chapter 8.

Session 7: Major Functions 2: Economic Development (People of Note: Bono and Mohammad Yunus)
Karns and Mingst, *International Organizations*, chapter 9.

Read the website for Debt AIDS Trade Africa (DATA), www.data.org. The website includes a short biographical note about founder Bono.

Read Grameen Foundation website, www.grameenfoundation.org.

Session 8: Other Functions, Current Issues, and the UN and Its Critics
Discussion and review.

Session 9: International Organizations on the Web
Search and browse websites for information about the United Nations, International Criminal Court, International Court of Justice, and European Union, for example. Links available at http://www.personal.kent.edu/~rrobyn/.

Unit 4: International Law: Theory and Practice

Session 10: International Law:
Overview, and the International Court of Justice
Karns and Mingst, *International Organizations,* all index entries listed under "International Law."

Session 11: International Law and Human Rights:
International War Crimes Tribunals
Karns and Mingst, *International Organizations,* chapter 10 (413–419).
Tina Rosenberg, "Tipping the Scales of Justice," *World Policy Journal* (1995): 55–64.

Read and debate "Should the United States Support a Strong and Independent International Criminal Court?" *Foreign Affairs Great Debate Series,* May 6, 1998.

Session 12: New Developments in International Law:
The International Criminal Court and Nation Building

Unit 5: A New World Order?

Session 13: What is the New World Order?
Globalization, the United States, and the World
Karns and Mingst, *International Organizations,* chapter 7.
Jessica Mathews, "Power Shift," *Foreign Affairs* 76, no. 1 (January–February 1997): 50–66.
Anne-Marie Slaughter, "The Real New World Order," *Foreign Affairs* 76 no. 5 (September–October 1997): 183–197.

Unit 6: UN Security Council Simulation

Session 14: UN Security Council Simulation: The Iraq Situation
Study the Iraq situation or another international conflict at the UN Security Council website (www.securitycouncilreport.org) and recreate the Security

Council in class. Assign roles to students and background materials from the website to prepare them for a Security Council debate.

Session 15: Security Council Simulation (cont.)

Session 16: Conclude Simulation and Debrief

Unit 6: Regional International Organizations

Session 17: Regional IOs: The European Union—Historical Development and Structure

Karns and Mingst, *International Organizations,* chapter 5.

Session 18: The EU: Integration Theory and the EU and Its Critics

Geoffrey Garrett et al., "The European Court of Justice, National Governments, and Legal Integration in the European Union," *International Organization* 52, no. 1 (Winter 1998): 149–176.

Session 19: The EU: Current Status and Future Prospects

No additional readings. Update students on current issues facing the European Union and provide analysis.

Session 20: The EU: European Identity

Read Richard Robyn. *The Changing Face of European Identity.* New York: Routledge, 2005, introduction.

Session 21: The EU: European Identity (cont.)

Continue discussion of Robyn, *The Changing Face of European Identity,* introduction.

Session 22: Current Issues in the Future of European Security—NATO or the Common Foreign and Security Policy? IO Profiles—Security

Read Richard Holbrooke, "America, a European Power," *Foreign Affairs* 74, no. 2 (March–April 1995): 38–51.

Unit 7: IO Issue Areas

Session 23: Nonstate Actors: Nongovernmental Organizations (NGOs); Human Rights and Environmental IOs

Karns and Mingst, *International Organizations,* chapter 6.

Session 24: Nonstate Actors: NGOs (cont.); Working in International Organizations; Human Rights and Environmental IOs (Person of Note: Ken Saro-Wiwa)
Read "Life in Romania," blog by Adrianne Brakefield, Peace Corps volunteer in Romania, http://www.xanga.com/adrianne_22.

Session 25: Global Concerns: Environment; Environmental IOs.
Karns and Mingst, *International Organizations,* chapters 10 and 11, 419–457.

Unit 8: Wrap-Up

Session 26: Building a Global Community (Person of Note: Aung San Suu Kyi)
Karns and Mingst, *International Organizations,* chapter 12.

TEACHING NOTES

"Megatrends" in the first unit refers to eight global trends I highlight that I feel provide a context for the work of IOs in a variety of fields (perhaps any and all IOs, in fact). These trends relate to global demographics, energy, destructive potential, social mobilization, and others.

I highly recommend the UN Security Council simulation to provide a needed break in the semester and some more direct engagement and fun. A few years ago, I started discussing "Persons of Note in IOs" to personalize what can seem to be institutional biases in a typical political science course. Students seem to appreciate it.

For writing assignments, I ask for a reaction paper and an IO profile. For the reaction paper, students pick one issue or controversy from *UN Wire* that interests them and write 500–600 words in reaction to it. They must give a brief rundown of the topic (basic facts, current situation, and why it is an important issue). They then bring the topic forward, providing their own personal analysis: How should the issue be treated or solved? Should the UN deal with it? Or is it better handled by another IO, a state, or no institution? Why or why not? If they believe another IO or state should handle it, they should clearly name which one(s). Finally, they give their own assessment of the future direction of this issue.

The IO profile offers students the opportunity to integrate in a more formal way the information learned in the course about international organizations. The paper should be approximately 1,500–2,000 words and will be (1) a substantive analysis of one IO other than the UN, including its evolution, current structure, and functions; and (2) a critical analysis of the IO's past behavior and current role in world politics, culminating in the student's own independent assessment of its conduct.

12.2 The United Nations and Global Security

Robert C. Johansen
University of Notre Dame

COURSE DESCRIPTION

Upper-level undergraduate course for students of peace and conflict studies, security studies, and international relations.

The purpose of this course is (1) to increase understanding of how to achieve national security, global security, and human security; (2) to explore the United Nation's role in enhancing security and fundamental human rights for all people; and (3) to develop critical thinking skills useful for making morally responsible decisions on major security questions facing all people in the world. Students will explore questions such as: What are today's most serious security problems? How do we decide what are the most prudent and ethically desirable ways to address them? What role does the United Nations play? What role might it play? Does the United States need the United Nations? What obligations do we have to our fellow citizens in the United States and to people in other countries? Under what conditions can these obligations best be met through unilateral action or multilateral action? Under what conditions are war, humanitarian intervention, and United Nations peace operations practical and desirable? When and how should government officials and individuals be held accountable to international legal standards for acceptable conduct?

COURSE SCHEDULE

Session 1: Class Introduction
How are human security and national security related? Which do you value most highly?

Session 2
How do assumptions about conflict and its resolution shape our approach to security and the role of the United Nations?

John Paul Lederach. *The Little Book of Conflict Transformation.* Intercourse, PA: Good Books, 2003, 3–39.

Session 3

How does "conflict transformation" prepare us to address war as "a force that gives us meaning"?

Lederach, *The Little Book of Conflict Transformation,* 40–71.

Chris Hedges. *War Is a Force That Gives Us Meaning.* New York: Anchor Books, 2002, 1–17.

Session 4

How do evolving ideas about sovereignty, the balance-of-power system, and the United Nations system shape security problems?

Karen A. Mingst and Margaret P. Karns. *The United Nations in the Twenty-First Century.* Boulder, CO: Westview, 2007, 1–16.

Session 5

To what extent have efforts to employ collective security been successful in war prevention? Why has the UN system not evolved into a more effective instrument for preventing war and genocide?

Mingst and Karns, *The United Nations in the Twenty-First Century,* 17–52.

Hedges, *War Is a Force That Gives Us Meaning,* 19–41.

Session 6

To what extent is the United Nations an independent actor? What international political and legal dynamics, especially with the permanent members, enable the UN to succeed?

Mingst and Karns, *The United Nations in the Twenty-First Century,* 53–82.

Nicole Deller, Arjun Makhijani, and John Burroughs. *Rule of Power or Rule of Law?* New York: Apex, 2003, 1–18.

Session 7

How does current US security policy fit traditional ideas of sovereignty and the balance of power system, the evolving UN system, and new global realities? To what extent does US security policy serve US security needs?

White House. *The National Security Strategy of the United States of America.* 2006, 1–35.

G. John Ikenberry. "America's Imperial Ambition." *Foreign Affairs* 81 (September–October 2002): 44–60.

Session 8

What is the nature of the UN role in the maintenance of peace and security? How should we evaluate its success?

Mingst and Karns, *The United Nations in the Twenty-First Century*, 83–132.

Session 9

How does the nature of war influence what the international community can do to curtail it?

Hedges, *War Is a Force That Gives Us Meaning*, 43–82.

Ian Buruma. "Theater of War." *New York Times Book Review* (September 17, 2006): 1ff.

Mary Kaldor. *New and Old Wars*. Stanford: Stanford University Press, 2007, introduction and chapter 6 (optional).

Session 10

How does the nature of war influence what the international community can do to curtail it? (cont.). To what extent are unilateral and multilateral policies useful in US foreign policy? In UN peace operations?

Hedges, *War Is a Force That Gives Us Meaning*, 83–121.

David Armstrong. "Dick Cheney's Song of America." *Harper's Magazine* 305 (October 2002): 76ff.

Thomas Donnelly. "The Underpinnings of the Bush Doctrine." *National Security Outlook: AEI Online*, February 1, 2003, American Enterprise Institute for Public Policy Research, www.aei.org/publications.

Charles Krauthammer. "The Unipolar Moment Revisited." *National Interest* 70 (Winter 2003): 517.

Session 11

Under what conditions are UN peace operations likely to succeed?

Michael Doyle. "War Making and Peace Making: The United Nations' Post–Cold War Record." In *Turbulent Peace: The Challenges of Managing International Conflict*, edited by Chester A. Crocker, Fen Osler Hampson, and Pamela Aall. Washington, DC: US Institute of Peace Press, 2001, 529–560.

Stephen John Stedman. "International Implementation of Peace Agreements in Civil Wars: Findings from a Study of Sixteen Cases." In *Turbulent Peace: The Challenges of Managing International Conflict*, edited by Chester A. Crocker, Fen Osler Hampson, and Pamela Aall. Washington, DC: US Institute of Peace Press, 2001, 737–52.

Robert C. Johansen, ed. *A United Nations Emergency Peace Service: To Prevent Genocide and Crimes Against Humanity*. New York: World Federalist Movement Institute for Global Policy, 2006, 21–41.

Robert C. Johansen. "Enforcing Norms and Normalizing Enforcement for Humane Governance." In *Principled World Politics: The Challenge of*

Normative International Relations, edited by Paul Wapner and Edwin J. Ruiz. Lanham, MD: Rowman and Littlefield, 2000, 209–230 (optional).

Session 12

Debate 1: Does the United States Need the United Nations?

Shashi Tharoor. "Why America Still Needs the United Nations." *Foreign Affairs* 82 (September–October 2003): 67–80.

G. John Ikenberry. "The End of the Neo-Conservative Moment." In *Liberal Order and Imperial Ambition*, by G. John Ikenberry. London: Polity, 2006, 229–243.

Paul Berman. "Neo No More." *New York Times Book Review*, March 26, 2006, 1ff.

Browse the Carnegie Council on Ethics and International Affairs website on this issue, http://www.cceia.org/.

Session 13

What is the importance of the Universal Declaration of Human Rights?

Paul Gordon Lauren. *The Evolution of International Human Rights: Visions Seen*. Philadelphia: University of Pennsylvania Press, 2003, 199–270.

Session 14

How do UN institutions enhance respect for human rights? To what extent do human rights and humanitarian affairs contribute to human security and provide an antidote to war?

Mingst and Karns, *The United Nations in the Twenty-First Century*, 167–210.

Universal Declaration of Human Rights, http://www.un.org/overview/rights.html.

Convention on the Rights of the Child, www.unhchr.ch/html/menu3/b/k2crc.htm (optional).

Session 15

Is the International Criminal Court likely to improve enforcement of international human rights and enhance human security?

Deller, Makhijani, and Burroughs. "The Rome Statute of the International Criminal Court," in *Rule of Power or Rule of Law*, 113–128.

Robert C. Johansen. "The Impact of US Policy toward the International Criminal Court on the Prevention of Genocide, War Crimes, and Crimes Against Humanity," *Human Rights Quarterly* 28, no. 2 (2006): 301–331.

United Nations Convention on the Prevention and Punishment of the Crime of Genocide, www.unhchr.ch/Huridocda/Huridocda.nsf/(symbol)/E.CN.4.RES.2003.66.En?Opendocument.

Session 16
Debate 2: Should the United States join the International Criminal Court?

John R. Bolton. "The United States and the International Criminal Court." US Department of State, 2002, http://www.state.gov/t/us/rm/13538pf.htm.
John R. Bolton. "American Justice and the International Criminal Court." US Department of State, November 3, 2003, http://www.state.gov/t/us/rm/25818.htm.
Robert C. Johansen. "U.S. Opposition to the International Criminal Court: Unfounded Fears." Policy Brief No. 7, June 2001, http://www.nd.edu/~krocinst/polbriefs/pbrief7.html.
Sarah B. Sewall, Carl Kaysen, and Michael P. Scharf. "The United States and the International Criminal Court: An Overview." In *The United States and the International Criminal Court*. Lanham, MD: Rowman and Littlefield, 2000, 1–27 (optional).

Session 17
To what extent does UN work for economic development and humanitarian assistance contribute to peacebuilding?

Mingst and Karns, *The United Nations in the Twenty-First Century,* 133–166.

Session 18
What role can the United Nations play in addressing an expanded view of security?

Mingst and Karns, *The United Nations in the Twenty-First Century,* 211–238.
Deller, Makhijani, and Burroughs, *Rule of Power or Rule of Law?* 101–112.

Session 19
Debate 3: To what extent and in what ways does the war in Iraq, and the extent to which it is largely executed by the United States, increase or decrease security?

James Baker, et al. "The Iraq Study Group Report." US Institute for Peace website, http://www.usip.org/isg/iraq_study_group_report/report/1206/index.html. Read the "Executive Summary," 6–8.
George W. Bush. "Transcript of President Bush's Address to Nation on US Policy in Iraq." *New York Times,* January 11, 2007.
David E. Sanger. "Bush Adds Troops in Bid to Secure Iraq." *New York Times,* January 11, 2007.
Editors. "Time to Leave." *The Nation* 283, no. 21 (2006): 3–6.

Session 20
Under what conditions does unilateralism or multilateralism contribute to maintenance of peace and security?

John J. Mearsheimer and Stephen M. Walt. "An Unnecessary War." *Foreign Policy* 134 (January–February 2003): 51–61.
Kofi Annan. *Adoption of Policy of Pre-Emption Could Result in Proliferation of Unilateral, Lawless Use of Force*. United Nations press release, September 23, 2003, www.un.org/News/Press/docs/2003/sgsm8891.doc.htm.
George W. Bush. 2003. *President Bush Addresses United Nations General Assembly*. White House news release, September 23, 2003, www.whitehouse.gov/news/releases/2003/09/ print/20030923-4.html.
Michael Dobbs. "US Had Key Role in Iraq Buildup." *Washington Post*, December 30, 2002, A1.

Session 21
What roles should the United Nations and the United States play in reducing terrorism?

Richard Falk. *The Great Terror War*. New York: Olive Branch Press, 2003, xi–xviii; 1–37.

Session 22
Debate 4: Should the United Nations play a central role in counterterrorism? If so, what should that role be?

Jeffrey Laurenti. "A Transformed Landscape: Terrorism and the UN After the Fall of the World Trade Center." In *Combating Terrorism: Does the U.N. Matter . . . and How?* edited by Jeffrey Laurenti. New York: United Nations Association of the United States of America, 2002, 19–31.
Thomas E. McNamara. "Targeting Terrorism." In *A Global Agenda: Issues Before the 60th General Assembly of the United Nations*, edited by Angela Drakulich. New York: United Nations Association of the United States of America, 2005, 183–188.
Neal Higgins. "Terrorism, Iraq and the Laws of War." In *A Global Agenda 2005–2006: Issues Before the 60th General Assembly of the United Nations*, edited by Angela Drakulich. New York: United Nations Association of the United States of America, 2005, 230.
UN resolutions on terrorism, in Laurenti, *Combating Terrorism*, 41–45 (optional).

Session 23
How can the United Nations establish a more effective regime to stop the proliferation of nuclear weapons?

Deller, Makhijani, and Burroughs, *Rule of Power or Rule of Law?* 19–40.
Warren Hoge and Sheryl Gay Stolberg. "Bush Rebukes North Korea; US Seeks New UN Sanctions." *New York Times*, October 10, 2006, A1, A6.

David E. Sanger. "For US, a Strategic Jolt." *New York Times,* October 10, 2006, A1, A6.

Norimitsu Onishi. "North Korea Warns of More Nuclear Tests." *New York Times,* October 12, 2006, A8.

Session 24

Debate 5: To address the proliferation of weapons of mass destruction effectively, should the United Nations attempt to stop Iran, North Korea, and all other states from the further development of nuclear weapons by instituting universal norms of constraint, perhaps through international regulation of the processing of weapons-grade nuclear material, in all countries of the world?

Deller, Makhijani, and Burroughs, *Rule of Power or Rule of Law?* 41–57.

Session 25

What role should the international community play in the regulation of intercontinental missiles and the full range of weapons of mass destruction?

Deller, Makhijani, and Burroughs, *Rule of Power or Rule of Law?* 58–91.

Session 26

If war is a force that gives life meaning, what is the most effective antidote or ethically desirable substitute for it? What role should the international community play in encouraging the antidote or substitute?

Hedges, *War Is a Force That Gives Us Meaning,* 122–185.

Session 27

What is the likely future of the United Nations in the maintenance of peace and security? What is your preferred future for it?

Mingst and Karns, *The United Nations in the Twenty-First Century,* 239–260.

Deller, Makhijani, and Burroughs, *Rule of Power or Rule of Law?* 129–140.

Joseph A. Camilleri. "Major Structural Reform." In *Democratizing Global Governance,* edited by Esref Aksu and Joseph A. Camilleri. Hampshire, UK: Palgrave Macmillan, 2002, 255–270.

Session 28

How can the need for global cooperation and the pull of national interests best be managed to enhance national and global security? Who speaks for humanity and the human interest?

Browse the world's first interparliamentary forum, www.e-parl.net.

Gregory D. Foster. "A New Security Paradigm." *World Watch* 18, no. 1 (2005): 36–46.

TEACHING NOTES

The primary emphasis of this course is on careful analysis of required readings, thoughtful participation in class discussions, and role playing in debates. Students will acquire (1) substantive knowledge about major security issues and how the United Nations can help address them; (2) skills in research, analysis, and formulation of recommendations for global peacebuilding; and (3) skills in active listening and constructive discussion and criticism.

Each student works with one or more students to prepare for role playing in a substantive debate and class discussion on a key issue. Each small group must provide and post an annotated bibliography of approximately half a dozen sources before the debate and identify one reading from the bibliography for classmates to read before the date of the debate and discussion.

Every participant should read a daily newspaper with substantial coverage of international affairs, such as the *New York Times,* creatively applying theory to current political decisions. Students may also browse journals such as *Foreign Affairs, Ethics and International Affairs, Journal of Peace Research,* and *World Politics,* and websites listed in textbooks or mentioned in class. Insofar as possible, each student is encouraged to develop his or her own theoretical framework, identifying and explaining the utility of the UN system for achieving security.

12.3 Human Rights and Global Change

Robert Elias
University of San Francisco

COURSE DESCRIPTION

Upper-level undergraduate course for politics and international studies departments.

Human Rights and Global Change explores domestic and global human rights and their role in a changing world order. It focuses on the level of repression in the world and the impact of governments, multinationals, churches, universities, and human rights advocates on political and economic development. Strategies for global justice and change are examined, with a focus on human rights activists and movements. More specifically, the course assesses the interdisciplinary literature on international law, human rights, and global politics and studies the meaning and origins of international human rights norms and standards. It examines the nature and sources of repression, victimization, and human rights violations and how they can be explained as forms of human interaction and organization. It explores the structure of the international human rights legal system, including governmental and nongovernmental institutions at the global, national, and local levels. It describes the political economy and organizational structure of human rights decisionmaking. It distinguishes between relative and universal human rights standards and articulates a critical perspective for evaluating the international human rights system, including its legal, political, and economic foundations. Students use tools of legal analysis and argumentation to address human rights controversies, such as terrorism, humanitarian intervention, cultural imperialism, and the impact of US foreign policy. Finally, the course examines case studies of human rights violations and activism, focusing on activists and movements.

REQUIRED TEXTS

Reza Baraheni. *God's Shadow: Prison Poems.* Indiana University Press, 1976.

David Forsythe. *Human Rights in International Relations.* Cambridge University Press, 2006.

William Felice. *The Global New Deal: Economic and Social Human Rights.* Rowman and Littlefield, 2003.

Jonathan Power. *Like Water on Stone: The Story of Amnesty International.* Northeastern University Press, 2001.
William Blum. *Rogue State: A Guide to the World's Only Superpower.* Common Courage Press, 2005.
Nikki van der Gaag. *The No-Nonsense Guide to Women's Rights.* Rawat Publications, 2005.
Noam Chomsky. *Hegemony or Survival.* Holt, 2004.
Jonathan Barker. *No-Nonsense Guide to Terrorism.* W.W. Norton, 2003.

COURSE OUTLINE

Units 1–2: Introduction: What Are Human Rights?

Main topics: Origins, evolution, and content; differences—political, economic, cultural, and religious; and universalism versus relativism.

1. Bringing Repression to Life
   Read excerpts from Baraheni, *God's Shadow.*
2. Historical and Ideological Perspectives: Common Ground?
   Read Forsythe, *Human Rights in International Relations,* chapter 1.
3. Causes of Repression: Human Nature, Institutions, Systems?
4. Looking Ahead: Case Study Proposals Due in Two Weeks

Units 3–4: International Relations: Victimizers or Guardians?

Main topics: Nongovernmental human rights organizations; multinational corporations; universities; religious institutions; mass media.

1. Order Versus Justice: States Versus Peoples
   Read Forsythe, *Human Rights in International Relations,* chapter 2.
2. Rights Covenants: National, Regional, and International Law
   Read Forsythe, *Human Rights in International Relations,* chapter 3.
   Read Felice, *The Global New Deal,* chapters 1 and 3.
   Read Walter Laqueur and Barry Rubin, *Human Rights Reader,* Temple University Press, 1979, pages 197–203, 215–233 (and skim 203–306).
3. Supranationals: Governments, Law and Enforcement
   Read Forsythe, *Human Rights in International Relations,* chapters 4 and 5.
4. Transnationals: A Clash of Interests?
   Read Forsythe, *Human Rights in International Relations,* chapters 7 and 8.
   Read Power, *Like Water on Stone,* chapters 6 and 7.
5. Due Dates: Case Study Due

Units 5–6: Rights Violations: A World of Suffering

1. The Political Economy of Repression
   Read Felice, *The Global New Deal,* chapter 2.
2. Political Repression: Tyranny, Torture, Killings, and Detention

Read Power, *Like Water on Stone,* introduction, prologue, chapters, 1, 5, 8, and 9.

3. Economic Repression: War, Poverty, Underdevelopment, Ecocide
   Read Felice, *The Global New Deal,* chapters 4 and 7.
4. Global Apartheid: Sex, Race, and Ethnicity
   Read van der Gaag, *The No-Nonsense Guide to Women's Rights* (complete).
   Read Felice, *The Global New Deal,* chapters 5 and 6.

Units 7–8: Exporting Repression

1. The Rhetoric of Humanitarianism
   Read Forsythe, *Human Rights in International Relations,* chapter 6.
2. Imperial Reality: Varieties of Intervention
   Read Blum, *Rogue State,* introduction and chapters 3–27.
3. Humanitarian Intervention? From Kosovo to Kabul to Baghdad
   Read Chomsky, *Hegemony or Survival,* chapters 1–3, 6, and 7.

Units 9–10: Terrorism

1. What Causes Terrorism?
2. Group, State, and Market Terrorism
   Read Barker, *No-Nonsense Guide to Terrorism,* introduction and chapters 1–4.
   Read Power, *Like Water on Stone,* chapter 6.
3. Fighting Terrorism
   Read Chomsky, *Hegemony or Survival,* chapters 4, 5, 8, 9, and afterword.
   Read Blum, *Rogue State,* chapters 1 and 2.
   Read Barker, *No-Nonsense Guide to Terrorism,* chapter 5.

Units 11–12: Case Study Presentations

1. Hear reports on nongovernmental organizations, activists, rights problems, nations.
2. Looking ahead: Continue your own research, reading articles and watching videos. Case study papers due in one week.

Unit 13: Political Action for Human Rights and Global Change

1. The Politics of Human Rights
   Read Forsythe, *Human Rights in International Relations,* chapter 9.
   Read Power, *Like Water on Stone,* chapter 10.
2. What Is to Be Done?
   Read Felice, *The Global New Deal,* chapter 8.

CASE STUDY PRESENTATION/PAPER

We'll be examining various nongovernmental human rights organizations, activists, and movements, which will involve library or field investigations. Since the prior course materials will have adequately examined human rights problems and tragedies, we'll use these case studies instead to focus on human rights success stories.

You will prepare an oral presentation and written paper on a successful human rights effort. You will work in a team of two people to investigate an NGO, activist, or movement (chosen from a list in the syllabus). You'll be asked to jointly give your report to the class in a short, informal presentation of ten minutes (five minutes for each team member). You'll be evaluated on your group research and investigation and oral presentations and on your individual, written paper (eight pages). Even though you should collaborate with your teammate on your oral report, you must write your paper independently from your teammate. See the lists in the syllabus of groups or nations to investigate. (*Note:* In an exceptional case, with approval, you may investigate a specific rights problem or a troubling national human rights record, as long as the problem or record has not been significantly examined already in the course, the readings, or the videos.)

POSSIBLE CASE STUDY TOPICS

Human rights activists: Salvador Allende (Chile), Petra Kelly (Germany), Elvia Alvarado (Honduras), Martin Luther King Jr. (United States), Oscar Arias Sanchez (Costa Rica), William Kunstler (United States), Jean-Bertrande Aristide (Haiti), Dalai Lama (Tibet), Aung San Suu Kyi (Myanmar/Burma), David Lange (New Zealand), Roger Baldwin (United States), Li Lu (China), Peter Benenson (Britain), Wangari Maathai (Kenya), Daniel and Philip Berrigan (United States), Malcolm X (United States), Stephen Biko (South Africa), Nelson Mandela (South Africa), Juan Bosch (Dominican Republic), Sean McBride (Ireland), Helen Caldicott (Australia), Rigoberta Menchu (Guatemala), Helder Camara (Brazil), Chico Mendes (Brazil), René Cassin (France), A. J. Muste (United States), Cesar Chavez (United States), Alva Myrdal (Sweden), Jim Corbett (United States), Julius Nyerere (Tanzania), Miread Corrigan and Betty Williams (N. Ireland), George Orwell (Britain), Olaf Palme (Sweden), Dorothy Day (United States), Linus Pauling (United States), Simone de Beauvoir (France), Alfredo Garcia Robles (Mexico), David Dellinger (United States), Oscar Romero (El Salvador), Bernadette Devlin (Ireland), Bertrand Russell (Britain), Alexander Dubček (Czech Republic), Andrei Sakharov (Russia), Henri Dunant (Switzerland), Ken Saro-Wiwa (Nigeria), Astrid Einarsson (Sweden), Eisaku Sato (Japan), Albert Einstein (Germany), Oscar Schindler (Germany), Adolfo Perez Esquivel (Argentina), Mother Teresa (India), Franz Fanon (Algeria), E. P. Thompson (Britain), Ita Ford, Maura Clarke, Jean Donovan, and Dorothy Kazel (United States), Desmond Tutu (South Africa), Mohandas Gandhi (India), Theo van Boven (Netherlands), Che Guevara (Argentina), Mordechai Vánunu (Israel), Dag Hammarskjöld (Sweden), Koigi Wa Wamwere (Kenya), Michael Harrington (United States), Elie

Wiesel (United States), Václav Havel (Czech Republic), Emiliano Zapata (Mexico), Victor Jara (Chile), Roy Bourgeois (United States), Maha Ghosananda (Cambodia), Thich Quang Do (Vietnam).

Human rights groups and movements: American Friends Service Committee/Quaker UN Office (United States/Switzerland), anti-apartheid movement (South Africa), Anti-Slaver Society (Britain), Bangladesh Rural Advancement Committee (Bangladesh), Catholic Worker Movement (United States), Charter 77/Velvet Revolution (Czechoslovakia), Chinese Democracy Movement (China), Chipko Movement (India), Cultural Survival (United States), European Nuclear Disarmament (Britain), Feminist Center for Information and Action (CEFEMINA, Costa Rica), Friends of the Earth (Britain), Grassroots International (United States), Green Movement (Germany, etc.), Greenbelt Movement (Kenya), Greenham Common Women (Britain), Greenpeace (Canada), Helsinki Citizen's Assembly (Austria), Human Rights Watch (United States), Institute for Food and Development Policy (Food First, United States), International Commission of Jurists (Switzerland), International Labour Organization (Switzerland), International League for Human Rights (United States), International Physicians for the Prevention of Nuclear War (United States), International Red Cross (Switzerland), International Rehabilitation and Resource Centre for Torture Victims (Denmark), intifada movement (Palestine), Irish Republican movement (Ireland), liberation theology movement (Latin America), Lokayan (India), Minority Rights Group (Britain), Mondregon Industrial Cooperatives (Spain), Mothers of the Plaza de Mayo (Argentina), Oxfam (Britain), Peace Brigades (United States), PEN Center (United States), Sanctuary movement (United States), Sarvodaya Shramadana Movement (Sri Lanka), Six S Association/NAAM Movement (Burkina Faso), Survival International (Britain), United Nations Educational, Scientific, and Cultural Organization (UNESCO) (France), UN High Commissioner for Human Rights (Switzerland), UN Human Rights Committee (Switzerland), Women Living Under Muslim Laws (France), Working Women's Forum (India), World Council of Churches (Switzerland), Worldwatch Institute (United States), Yesh Gvul (Israel), Zapatista Movement (Mexico).

Possible country reports: Afghanistan, Argentina, Bosnia, Burma (Myanmar), China, Colombia, Democratic Republic of Congo, Cuba, Egypt, El Salvador, Guatemala, Haiti, India, Indonesia (including East Timor), Iran, Iraq, Korea, Liberia, Mexico, Nigeria, Northern Ireland, Pakistan, Palestine, Peru, Philippines, Russia, Rwanda, Saudi Arabia, Somalia, South Korea, Sri Lanka, Turkey, United States.

Alternative media resources: New Internationalist, Peace Review, Z Magazine, The Nation, Utne Reader, The Progressive, Mother Jones, Radical America, Socialist Review, World Press Review, Village Voice, In These Times, Tikkun, Alternatives, Against the Current, Sojourners, Ms. Magazine, On the Issues, New Political Science, Multinational Monitor, and *Catholic*

Worker. Many of these print sources have good websites. For examples of alternative Internet and television media, see Free Speech TV, Democracy Now, Alternet.org, and CommonDreams.org.

FILM RESOURCES

In the Name of the Father (133 minutes), starring Daniel Day-Lewis and Emma Thompson. The film is set in Northern Ireland, amid the conflict between the Irish and British. It portrays the true story of the false arrest and imprisonment of innocent men.

Of Love and Shadows (104 minutes), starring Antonio Banderas and Jennifer Connelly. Set in Chile, the film portrays the political awakening of a Chilean amid the repression of the military dictatorship; based on actual events and the novel by Isabel Allende.

Nuremberg (179 minutes), starring Alec Baldwin and Jill Hennessy. Set in Germany, this is a courtroom drama about the post–World War II "trial of the century" of Nazi war criminals.

Closet Land (95 minutes), starring Madeleine Stowe and Alan Rickman. A citizen is arrested without charges and faces the fine line between psychological and physical torture.

Manufacturing Consent (120 minutes), featuring Noam Chomsky. This documentary demonstrates US media bias and the false consciousness of American public opinion.

Burning Season (123 minutes), starring Raoul Julia and Sonia Braga. A true story of Chico Mendes and his struggle to preserve the rainforest and indigenous rights in Brazil.

Fourth World War (74 minutes), a film about globalization, violence, and economic injustice in Argentina, Mexico, Korea, and South Africa.

Killing Fields (142 minutes), featuring Sam Waterston and John Malkovich. The film tells the story of Khmer Rouge repression and genocide in Cambodia in the 1970s.

What I Learned About US Foreign Policy (120 minutes). A compilation about US foreign policy from World War II through the Gulf War and sanctions on Iraq during the Clinton administration. Watch to the end.

Hijacking Catastrophe (64 minutes). The political campaign to convert the war on terrorism into the war on Iraq.

Plan Colombia (54 minutes). Addresses the war on drugs, terrorism, and repression in Colombia.

Palestinian Diaries (60 minutes). Features the struggles of daily life and repression under Israeli occupation.

Rwandan Nightmare (40 minutes). On the genocide in Rwanda between Hutus and Tutsis.

Death and the Maiden (103), starring Sigourney Weaver and Ben Kingsley. Based on the true story of women's oppression under the dictators in Latin America.

China After Tianenmen (88 minutes). Shows threats to political freedom following the suppression of the Chinese democracy movement.

Bringing Down a Dictator (56 minutes). Features the student movement that overthrew the repressive Yugoslavian dictator, Slobodan Milosevic.

Long Night into Day (95 minutes), on the South Africa Truth and Reconciliation Commission, showing a restorative justice approach rather than a punishment approach to human rights violations.

TEACHING NOTES

The course is taught through a combination of presentations and class discussions. Rather than dwelling on one case of repression after another, I embed cases in broader human rights themes. The course challenges students to stretch their conception of human rights from the narrower US perspective, emphasizing political and civil rights, to broader international standards, including economic, social, and cultural rights. The course includes considerable coverage of the impact of US foreign policy—according to Amnesty International and other human rights organizations, the United States has a greater impact on human rights than any other nation. At the same time, it's important to examine the human rights questions from a multinational perspective.

Besides the reading materials, I require that students attend a human rights film series, composed of a combination of conventional and documentary videos. The films are discussed in class each week, and students are expected to integrate the films into their written assignments. Finally, examining human rights abuses can make students jaded and cynical. Thus, it's important to devote a portion of the course (at the end) to positive case studies. This is not done to sanitize the situation but to give credit to the progress and accomplishments of various human rights activists and organizations. I assign students the task of developing and delivering case study presentations on human rights "success" stories. This helps them leave the course with some optimism about a difficult situation.

12.4 Humanitarianism in World Politics

R. Charli Carpenter
University of Pittsburgh

COURSE DESCRIPTION

Upper-level undergraduate or graduate course for students in peace and conflict studies, political science, and policy studies.

This course examines the politics of humanitarianism in international society. We consider what humanitarianism means to different actors, how humanitarianism should work in principle, and how the "humanitarian sector" in world politics actually functions. The course covers state-centered humanitarianism (such as military intervention) as well as transnational efforts (e.g., nongovernmental organizations, or NGOs, and international organizations, or IOs). Because of time constraints, we focus on assistance rather than development organizations and on man-made rather than natural disasters. Throughout the course, we will consider whether current policy trends (humanitarian intervention, the war on terrorism) support or undermine humanitarian norms in international society. At the end of this course, students should be able to

1. Describe key moral principles underlying the humanitarian regime, including contradictions between and organizational variation among these principles.
2. Describe and explain the existing humanitarian architecture, as well as how it influences the nature of humanitarian action.
3. Recognize the complexity of the political environment in which humanitarian players operate and identify specific organizational responses to this complexity.
4. Develop and assess policy solutions to resolve specific ethical and political dilemmas in humanitarian practice.
5. Engage in the basic steps of academic research and policy analysis and writing.

REQUIRED TEXTS

Thomas Weiss and Cindy Collins. *Humanitarian Challenges and Intervention: World Politics and the Dilemmas of Help*, 2nd ed. Boulder, CO: Westview, 2000.

Mary Anderson. *Do No Harm: How Aid Can Support Peace—or War.* Boulder, CO: Lynne Rienner, 1999.

Ian Smillie and Larry Minear. *The Charity of Nations.* Bloomfield, CT: Kumarian, 2005.

David Rieff. *A Bed for the Night: Humanitarianism in Crisis.* New York: Simon and Schuster, 2003.

Julie Mertus. *War's Offensive on Women: The Humanitarian Challenge in Bosnia, Kosovo, and Afghanistan.* Bloomfield, CT: Kumarian, 2000.

Humanitarian Studies Unit. *Reflections on Humanitarian Action: Principles, Ethics, and Contradictions.* London: Pluto, 2001.

Additional readings as assigned in the course schedule.

COURSE SCHEDULE

Module 1: Humanitarian Principles and Politics

Unit 1: Introduction to the Concept of Humanitarianism

What do we understand by "humanitarianism"? What do we understand by "politics"? What do we bring to the course and what do we hope to get out of it?

Smillie and Minear, *The Charity of Nations,* introduction.
Weiss and Collins, *Humanitarian Challenges and Intervention,* introduction.
Rieff, *A Bed for the Night,* introduction.
Mertus, *War's Offensive on Women,* introduction.

Recommended reading:
Humanitarian Studies Unit, introduction, in *Reflections.*

Unit 2: The Humanitarian Sector in World Politics

Who are the key players and terms of reference in the humanitarian policy domain? How are resources channeled through the system? What relationships of power are implicit in the system?

Weiss and Collins, *Humanitarian Challenges and Intervention,* chapter 2.
Rieff, *A Bed for the Night,* chapter 3.
Smillie and Minear, *The Charity of Nations,* chapter 1.
Jonathan Benthall. "Humanitarianism, Islam, and September 11." Humanitarian Policy Group, July 11, 2003, http://www.odi.org.uk/HPG/papers/hpgbrief11.pdf.

Recommended reading:
David Sogge, "Subalterns on the Aid Chain," in Humanitarian Studies Unit, *Reflections,* 120–141.

Unit 3: Humanitarian "Principles" Versus "Politics"

What are the key ethical principles underlying "humanitarian" practice? How do these ethical principles interrelate? Do they contradict one another? How should trade-offs between them be resolved?

Weiss and Collins, *Humanitarian Challenges and Intervention,* chapter 1.
Weiss, "Principles, Politics, and Humanitarian Action." *Ethics and International Affairs* 13 (1999).
Rieff, *A Bed for the Night,* chapter 2.

Recommended reading:
Xabier Etxeberria, "The Ethical Framework of Humanitarian Action," in Humanitarian Studies Unit, *Reflections,* 78–99.
Adam Roberts, "Humanitarian Principles in International Politics," in Humanitarian Studies Unit, *Reflections,* 23–55.
Joanna MacRae and Adele Harmer, eds. "Humanitarian Action and the 'Global War on Terror.'" Humanitarian Policy Group, July 14, 2003, http://www.odi.org.uk/HPG/papers/hpgreport14.pdf.

Module 2: Humanitarian Policy and Players

Unit 4: Explaining Humanitarianism in State Foreign Policy

Why would self-interested states engage in costly foreign policy initiatives for purely moral reasons? Which variables affect the likelihood of state humanitarianism, particularly military intervention? Why do some emergencies get more attention than others?

Weiss and Collins, *Humanitarian Challenges and Intervention,* chapters 3 and 7.
Smillie and Minear, *The Charity of Nations,* chapter 6.
Gorm Rye Olsen, "Humanitarian Crises: What Determines the Level of Emergency Assistance?" *Disasters* 27, no. 2 (2003): 109–126.
David S. Gibbs. "Realpolitik and Humanitarian Intervention." *International Politics* 37, no. 1 (March 2000): 41–55.

Unit 5: The Global Media in Humanitarian Politics

How do journalists interface with humanitarian aid agencies, and how does this relationship drive media portrayals of humanitarian crises? To what extent are journalists and documentarians participants in humanitarian affairs? What ethical obligations exist between journalists and recipient populations?

Rieff, *A Bed for the Night,* chapter 1.
Smillie and Minear, *The Charity of Nations,* chapter 7.

Recommended reading:

Mariano Aguirre, "The Media and the Humanitarian Spectacle," in Humanitarian Studies Unit, *Reflections,* 157–176.

Steven S. Ross. "Towards New Understandings: Journalists/Humanitarian Relief Coverage." http://www.fritzinstitute.org/PDFs/InTheNews/2004/NGLS_0304.pdf.

Unit 6: Modes of Action Within the "Humanitarian Transnational"

What is the relationship among donors, UN agencies, northern NGOs, southern NGOs, and beneficiaries? How do specific organizations differ in their modes of action in the field? What coordination problems or opportunities does this create? How does the political economy of humanitarian aid affect outcomes on the ground? Should humanitarian actors be held accountable to donors or to beneficiaries?

Weiss and Collins, *Humanitarian Challenges and Intervention,* chapter 5.
Smillie and Minear, *The Charity of Nations,* chapter 9.
Mertus, *War's Offensive on Women,* chapter 4.

Recommended reading:
Paul Bonard. "Modes of Action Used by Humanitarian Players." Geneva: ICRC, 1999. http://www.cicr.org/WEB/ENG/siteeng0.nsf/htmlall/p0722?OpenDocument&style=Custo_Final.4&View=defaultBody2.

Module 3: Humanitarian Operations

Unit 7: In-Class Field Simulation

Given an organizational mandate, a set of political constraints, and only certain resources, how would your specific organization react to specific developments in a field-based simulation?

Weiss and Collins, *Humanitarian Challenges and Intervention,* chapter 4.

Recommended reading:
Francisco Rey, "The Complex Nature of Actors in Humanitarian Action," in Humanitarian Studies Unit, *Reflections,* 99–119.

Unit 8: Emergency Assistance—Case Study: Rwanda

What are the benefits and pitfalls of introducing humanitarian aid into a conflict zone? How can aid best support peace, and in what ways can it prolong violent conflict? What lessons can be learned from the experience of relief to refugees after the Rwandan genocide?

Anderson, *Do No Harm,* 1–76.
Rieff, *A Bed for the Night,* chapter 5.
Smillie and Minear, *The Charity of Nations,* chapter 8.

Recommended reading:

Joanne Raisin and Alexander Ramsbotham, "Relief, Development and . . . ," in Humanitarian Studies Unit, *Reflections,* 142–156.

MacRae and Harmer, eds., "Humanitarian Action and the 'Global War on Terror.'"

Unit 9: Practical Protection—Case Studies: Bosnia and Darfur

What does "protection" mean in conflict zones? Who should be protected? By whom? From whom? Can humanitarian protection be meaningful in the absence of military intervention? To what extent do outsiders themselves pose threats to civilian populations?

Rieff, *A Bed for the Night,* chapters 4 and 5.

Julie Mertus. "Bosnia-Herzegovina: Uprooted Women." In *War's Offensive on Women,* by Julie Mertus. Sterling, VA: Stylus, 2000.

Diane Paul. "Protection in Practice." Relief and Rehabilitation Network. July 1999, 17–23.

Recommended reading:

Asmita Naik. "Protecting Children from the Protectors." *Forced Migration Review* 15 (October 2002). www.fmreview.org/FMRpdfs/FMR15/FMR 15.7.pdf.

Victoria Wheeler. "Politics and Practice: The Limits of Humanitarian Protection in Darfur." *Humanitarian Exchange Magazine* 30 (June 2005). www.odihpn.org/report.asp?id=2568.

Unit 10: Identifying, Assisting, and Protecting Vulnerable Groups

View and discuss *Turtles Can Fly,* directed by Bahman Ghobadi, DVD, 2004, 95 minutes.

What forms of protection or assistance would have changed the outcome for the displaced persons in this film? If you were to design a humanitarian operation for this internally displaced persons (IDP) camp, what types of programs would you set up? In what ways are humanitarian practitioners themselves vulnerable in conflict zones?

Module 4: Conclusion

Unit 11: The Future of Humanitarianism?

Smillie and Minear, *The Charity of Nations,* "The Way Ahead?"

Rieff, *A Bed for the Night,* conclusion.

TEACHING NOTES

I typically alternate lectures on basic language, concepts, organizations, and modes of action within the humanitarian sector with small-group work or simulations that enable students to imagine themselves facing hard choices in the field. Most students come to class with a sense of idealism; I want them to leave feeling more pragmatic about the realities of humanitarian politics. However, the risk is always that students may become cynical and jaded when presented with no-win scenarios time and again. It's important to temper that reality with cases of best practices and examples of things that have worked. I also leave time in class to help students process how the material affects them emotionally.

My assignments include regular online discussions, writing policy statements, an annotated bibliography, abstracts, and executive summaries.

12.5 Human Rights and Conflict

Daniel Chong
American University

COURSE DESCRIPTION

Upper-level undergraduate and graduate elective.

This course explores some of the links between international human rights, humanitarian practice, and violent conflict. It introduces students to many of the ethical and operational issues facing a range of state and non-state actors responding to today's conflicts. Although human rights advocates, humanitarian aid workers, and conflict resolution practitioners share the same fundamental goal of reducing human suffering, they tend to adopt different approaches to conflict that can come into mutual tension. As a result, scholars have traditionally treated these three fields as distinct, although they are increasingly recognizing the links between them.

This course is structured according to three stages of conflict. In the pre-conflict stage, human rights discourse and humanitarian practice can serve, incite, prevent, or delimit war. During armed conflict, human rights and humanitarian norms ostensibly protect civilians and noncombatants, but these efforts are often frustrated by problems of accountability, the challenges of terrorism, and the difficulties of meeting the needs of forced migrants. In the postconflict stage, human rights can become either an obstacle or a facilitator to a negotiated, lasting peace. In this context, we will examine the "peace versus justice" and "truth versus justice" dilemmas that are involved in designing peace agreements, truth commissions, courts and tribunals, and postconflict reconstruction programs.

REQUIRED TEXTS

Julie Mertus and Jeffrey Helsing, eds. *Human Rights and Conflict*. US Institute of Peace Press, 2006.

Mary Anderson. *Do No Harm: How Aid Can Support Peace—or War*. Lynne Rienner, 1999.

Seymour Hersh. *Chain of Command: The Road from 9/11 to Abu Ghraib*. HarperCollins, 2004.

Niklaus Steiner. *Problems of Protection: The UNHCR, Refugees, and Human Rights*. Routledge, 2003.

Christine Bell. *Peace Agreements and Human Rights*. Oxford University Press, 2005.

Priscilla Hayner. *Unspeakable Truths: Facing the Challenge of Truth Commissions*. Routledge, 2002.

COURSE SCHEDULE

Stage 1: Preconflict

Week 1: Introduction to the Links and Tensions Between Human Rights and Conflict Resolution

Ellen Lutz, Eileen Babbitt, and Hurst Hannum. "Human Rights and Conflict Resolution from the Practitioners' Perspectives." *Fletcher Forum of World Affairs* 27, no. 1 (2003). http://fletcher.tufts.edu/chrcr/pdf/Lutz4.pdf.

Mertus and Helsing, *Human Rights and Conflict:*
- Introduction, 3–20.
- "Understanding Human Rights Violations in Armed Conflict," by Ellen Lutz.
- "Human Rights: A Source of Conflict, State Making, and State Breaking," by Michael Lund.
- "The Human Rights Dimensions of War in Iraq: A Framework for Peace Studies," by Julie Mertus and Maia Carter Hallward.
- Human Rights Watch. "Genocide in Iraq: Introduction." 1993. http://hrw.org/reports/1993/iraqanfal/ANFALINT.htm.

Week 2: When Is Military Intervention Justified to Protect Human Rights?

Human Rights Watch. "War in Iraq: Not a Humanitarian Intervention." 2004. http://hrw.org/wr2k4/3.htm.

Nico Krisch. "Legality, Morality, and the Dilemma of Humanitarian Intervention After Kosovo." *European Journal of International Law* 13, no. 1 (2002).

International Commission on Intervention and State Sovereignty. *The Responsibility to Protect*. December 2001. http://www.iciss.ca/report2-en.asp.

Mertus and Helsing, *Human Rights and Conflict:*
- "Humanitarian Intervention After Kosovo," by Richard Falk.
- "Commentary," by Thomas Weiss.

Week 3: Human Rights and Humanitarian Nongovernmental Organizations (NGOs): Exacerbating or Alleviating Conflict?

Anderson, *Do No Harm,* chapters 1–6.

Mark Duffield. "NGOs and the Subcontracting of Humanitarian Relief." *Refugee Participation Network* 19 (May 1995). http://www.fmreview.org/rpn196.htm.

Sphere Project. "Humanitarian Charter" and "Common Standards." In *Sphere Handbook*. Oxford: Oxfam Publishing, 2004. http://www.sphereproject.org/content/view/24/84/lang,English/.

Stage 2: During Armed Conflict

Week 4: International Humanitarian Law: Protecting Civilians in Armed Conflict

Mertus and Helsing, *Human Rights and Conflict,* "Holding Military and Paramilitary Forces Accountable," by John Cerone.

Kenneth Watkin. "Controlling the Use of Force: A Role for Human Rights Norms in Contemporary Armed Conflict." *American Journal of International Law* 98, no. 1 (January 2004).

Human Rights Watch. "Fatal Strikes: Israel's Indiscriminate Attacks Against Civilians in Lebanon." August 2006. http://hrw.org/reports/2006/lebanon0806/.

Human Rights Watch. "BBC: Mock War Crimes Trial for Israel/Hezbollah." Listen to audio at http://hrw.org/audio/2006/english/israel_lebanon/roth_bbc.htm.

Week 5: Problems of Human Rights Accountability During Armed Conflict

Hersh, *Chain of Command,* excerpts from Part 1 (18–72).

Robin Rowland. "In Depth: Iraq: Abu Ghraib." CBC News Online, May 6, 2004. http://www.cbc.ca/news/background/iraq/abughraib.html.

P. W. Singer. "Private Military Contractors: Above Law, Above Decency." *Los Angeles Times,* May 2, 2004. http://www.commondreams.org/views04/0502-04.htm.

Human Rights Watch. "Q and A: Private Military Contractors and the Law." http://hrw.org/english/docs/2004/05/05/iraq8547.htm.

Center for Constitutional Rights. "CCR Files Lawsuit Against Private Contractors for Torture Conspiracy." June 2004. http://ccrjustice.org/newsroom/press-releases/ccr-files-lawsuit-against-private-contractors-torture conspiracy.

Week 6: Human Rights Implications of Efforts to Combat Terrorism

Mertus and Helsing, *Human Rights and Conflict:*

"Human Rights, Terrorism, and Efforts to Combat Terrorism," by Jordan Paust.

"Commentary," by David Stewart.

Human Rights Watch. "Briefing Paper on U.S. Military Commissions." June 23, 2006. http://www.hrw.org/backgrounder/usa/gitmo0606/.

Human Rights Watch. "US: Guantanamo Ruling Rejects Unfair Trials." June 29, 2006. http://hrw.org/english/docs/2006/06/29/usdom13663.htm.

Human Rights Watch. "Q and A: Military Commissions Act of 2006." October 2006. http://hrw.org/backgrounder/usa/qna1006/.

Week 7: The Challenges of Protecting the Rights of Forced Migrants During War

Mertus and Helsing, *Human Rights and Conflict,* "Promoting the Human Rights of Forced Migrants," by Susan Martin and Andrew Schoenholtz.

Steiner, *Problems of Protection,* chapters 1–4, 7.

National Public Radio. "Genital Mutilation Can Be Grounds for Asylum Status." Listen to audio at http://www.npr.org/templates/story/story.php?storyId=4531744.

Stage 3: Postconflict

Week 8: Are Human Rights an Obstacle to or Opportunity for Conflict Resolution?

Michelle Parlevliet. "Bridging the Divide: Exploring the Relationship Between Human Rights and Conflict Management." *Track Two* 11, no. 1 (March 2002).

Anonymous. "Human Rights in Peace Negotiations." *Human Rights Quarterly* 18, no. 2 (1996). http://muse.jhu.edu/journals/human_rights_quarterly/v018/18.2anonymous.html.

Mertus and Helsing, *Human Rights and Conflict:*

- "Human Rights, Peace Agreements, and Conflict Resolution: Negotiating Justice in Northern Ireland," by Christine Bell, 345–350 (excerpts).
- "Linking Human Rights and Conflict Transformation: A Peacebuilding Framework," by Lisa Schirch.
- "Bridging Conflict Transformation and Human Rights: Lessons from the Israeli-Palestinian Peace Process," by Mohammed Abu-Nimer and Edy Kaufman.

Week 9: Human Rights in Peace Agreements: The Search for Justice and Reconciliation

Bell, *Peace Agreements and Human Rights,* excerpts.

Week 10: Courts and Tribunals

Neil Kritz. "Coming to Terms with Atrocities: A Review of Accountability Mechanisms for Mass Violations of Human Rights." *Law and Contemporary Problems* 59 (Autumn 1996). http://www.law.duke.edu/journals/lcp/articles/lcp59dFall1996p127.htm.

Laura Dickinson. "The Promise of Hybrid Courts." *American Journal of International Law* 97, no. 2 (April 2003).

Mertus and Helsing, *Human Rights and Conflict:*
"Truth Versus Justice? Commissions and Courts," by Vasuki Nesiah.
"Commentary," by Richard Ashby Wilson.

Alana Erin Tiemessen. "After Arusha: Gacaca Justice in Post-Genocide Rwanda." *African Studies Quarterly* 8, no. 1 (2004). http://www.africa.ufl.edu/asq/v8/v8i1a4.htm.

Week 11: Truth Commissions
Hayner, *Unspeakable Truths,* chapters 1–4, 7–10, 13–15, epilogue.

Week 12: Human Rights in Postconflict Reconstruction
Anderson, *Do No Harm,* Part 2 (79–147).
Mertus and Helsing, *Human Rights and Conflict,* "Human Rights Education and Grassroots Peacebuilding," by Janet Lord and Nancy Flowers.
Steiner, *Problems of Protection,* chapter 11.
Hayner, *Unspeakable Truths,* chapter 11.
Michael O'Flaherty. "Sierra Leone's Peace Process: The Role of the Human Rights Community." *Human Rights Quarterly* 26, no. 1 (February 2004). http://muse.jhu.edu/journals/human_rights_quarterly/v026/26.1oflaherty.html.

Week 13: Is There a Right to Peace? Conclusions and Synthesis
Mertus and Helsing, *Human Rights and Conflict:*
"Peace as a Human Right: Toward an Integrated Understanding," by Abdul Aziz Said and Charles Lerche.
"Commentary," by Jack Donnelly.
"Toward a More Integrated Approach," 509–524.

TEACHING NOTES

Each week, students will play the role of a policy analyst involved in a different aspect of the relationship between human rights and conflict. Students will follow the human rights dimensions of various conflicts from their inception, through the outbreak of violence, to diplomatic negotiations, to the signing of peace agreements and attempts to build a just and lasting peace. An assignment will be provided each week as students, the analysts, are called upon to consider the various dimensions of human rights and conflict. For at least some of the weekly assignments, students will need to research outside sources (primarily on the Internet) for background information on their papers.

The majority of students' semester grades are based upon completing a 1,200-word written assignment each week. Students will post a weekly paper on a discussion board that will be accessible to other students and the professor. They are required to post their writing anytime *prior* to the class for which they are assigned. Late postings will be penalized except in extraordinary circumstances.

In addition to weekly papers, students should also use a discussion board to comment on the in-class discussions and lectures and to respond to the papers and posts from fellow students.

12.6 Human Rights

Maria J. Stephan
American University

COURSE DESCRIPTION

Upper-level undergraduate elective in international studies or peace and conflict resolution.

This course is designed for students of international studies and, in particular, those specializing in conflict studies, international law, international politics, and international development. The course examines human rights through multiple disciplinary perspectives and focuses on the role of state and nonstate actors as friends and foes of international human rights.

The course begins with an examination of the philosophical, historical, and political foundations of the international human rights movement, probing the ongoing debate over universality, culture, and human rights.

Second, we analyze, critique, and discuss international legal and institutional structures developed during the twentieth century to organize and legalize international human rights law. The course provides an overview of the United Nations and regional systems for human rights protection and promotion. We discuss the strengths and weaknesses of international legal standards as well as enforcement mechanisms.

Third, students become acquainted with the various roles of nonstate actors (nongovernmental organizations, transnational solidarity networks, and popular movements) in promoting and defending human rights. We examine successful and failed civilian-based struggles on behalf of civil and political rights and economic, social, and cultural rights.

Finally, the course challenges students to assume the role of human rights advocates as they examine US foreign policy choices, focusing in particular on the implications for human rights protection of the so-called war on terror.

The class is designed to be highly participatory and to encourage a diversity of opinion and expression of different viewpoints. To promote active learning, we use a series of in-class simulations, role plays, and other exercises.

REQUIRED TEXTS

Jack Donnelly. *Universal Human Rights: Theory and Practice*. Ithaca, NY: Cornell University Press, 2003.

Peter Ackerman and Jack DuVall. *A Force More Powerful: A Century of Nonviolent Conflict.* New York: Palgrave Macmillan, 2001.

Julie Mertus. *Bait and Switch: Human Rights and US Foreign Policy.* New York: Routledge, 2004.

Julie Mertus. *The United Nations and Human Rights.* New York: Routledge, and Taylor and Francis, 2005.

Daily Digest, newsletter of the International Center on Nonviolent Conflict. Access by joining a Listserv at ICNC@nonviolent-conflict.org.

Kurt Schock. *Unarmed Insurrections: People Power Movements in Nondemocracies.* Minneapolis: University of Minnesota Press, 2005.

Philip Aston and Ryan Goodman. *International Human Rights in Context,* 3rd ed., edited by Henry J. Steiner. New York: Oxford University Press, 2007.

COURSE SCHEDULE

Week 1: Foundations for Human Rights

The philosophical, historical, and political foundations for human rights and the international human rights movement; key international law concepts; thinking about human rights.

Universal Declaration of Human Rights. http://www.unhchr.ch/udhr/lang/eng.pdf.

Louis Henkin. "Human Rights: Ideology and Aspiration Reality and Prospect." In *Realizing Human Rights,* edited by Samantha Power. New York: St. Martin's Press, 2000, 3–38.

Donnelly, *Universal Human Rights,* chapters 1–3.

Michael Ignatieff. "Human Rights as Idolatry." In *Human Rights as Politics and Idolatry,* edited by Amy Gutmann. Princeton, NJ: Princeton University Press, 2001, 53–98.

Week 2: Development of an International Human Rights Regime

The development of a global human rights regime after World War II, theories of human rights in international relations, an overview of human rights, and US foreign policy.

Hans Peter Schmitz and Kathryn Sikkink, "International Relations Theory and Human Rights," chapter 1, available at http://www.polisci.umn.edu/courses/spring2001/4485/ir2.pdf.

Mertus, *Bait and Switch,* chapters 1, 2, 3, 5.

Donnelly, *Universal Human Rights,* chapter 9.

Week 3: Universalism Versus Cultural Relativism

Probe the universalism versus relativism debate: how can human rights advocates avoid being "cultural imperialists"?

Donnelly, *Universal Human Rights,* chapters 5–7.

Makau wa Mutua. "Savages, Victims, and Saviors: The Metaphor of Human Rights." *Harvard International Law Journal* 42, no. 1 (Winter 2001): 201–246.

Amartya Sen. "Human Rights and Asian Values." *New Republic,* July 14, 1997, 33–40.

Martha Nussbaum. "Women and Cultural Universals." In *Sex and Social Justice,* by Martha Nussbaum. New York: Oxford University Press, 1999, 29–54.

Abdullahi Ahmed An-Na'im. *Human Rights, Religion, and the Contingency of Universalist Projects.* Syracuse, NY: Maxwell School of Citizenship and Public Affairs, 2000, 1–32.

Charles Taylor. "Conditions of Unforced Consensus on Human Rights." In *The Politics of Human Rights,* edited by Obrad Savic. New York: Verso, 2002, 101–119.

Recommended reading:

Abdullahi Ahmed An-Na'im. "Human Rights in the Muslim World: Socio-Political Conditions and Scriptural Imperatives." *Harvard Human Rights Journal* 3, no. 13 (Spring 1990): 13–52.

Exercise: Divide students into two teams. Blue Team will argue this position: "The human rights movement is inherently Western, and its claim of universality is mistaken. The advocacy of human rights across cultural borders helps displace local cultures and is a form of neo-imperialism." Gray Team will argue this position: "Human rights are universally recognized, and certain cultural traditions and practices pose obstacles to the realization of these rights."

Week 4: Types of Rights: Civil and Political Rights and Economic, Social, and Cultural Rights

Examine both pillars of the International Bill of Human Rights and the substance of civil, political, economic, social, and cultural rights. Discuss the dichotomy between civil and political rights and economic, social, and cultural rights. Is there a hierarchy of rights, or are they indivisible and interdependent?

International Covenant on Civil and Political Rights, http://www.ohchr.org/english/law/ccpr.htm.

International Covenant on Economic, Social, and Cultural Rights, http://www.ohchr.org/english/law/cescr.htm.

Donnelly, *Universal Human Rights,* chapter 4.

1993 Vienna Conference on Human Rights (Final Declaration), http://www.ohchr.org/english/law/vienna.htm.

Kenneth Roth. "Defending Economic, Social, and Cultural Rights: Practical Issues Faced by an International Human Rights Organization." *Human Rights Quarterly* (February 2004): 63–73.

Thomas W. Pogge. "Eradicating Systemic Poverty: Brief for a Global Resource Dividend." In *World Poverty and Human Rights: Cosmopolitan Responsibilities and Reforms,* by Thomas W. Pogge. Cambridge: Polity Press, 2002, 1–26.

Recommended reading:

Aryeh Neier. "Social and Economic Rights: A Critique." *Human Rights Brief* (Winter 2006).

Thomas W. Pogge. "'Assisting' the Global Poor." In *The Ethics of Assistance: Morality and Distant Needy,* edited by Deen K. Chatterjee. Cambridge: Cambridge University Press, 2003, 1–21.

Exercise: Gray Team will defend this proposition: "Economic, social, and cultural rights are more like aspirations than human rights. It is a good thing that the United States has not signed the International Covenant on Economic, Social, and Cultural Rights (ICESCR)." Blue Team will defend this position: "Economic, social, and cultural rights are equal to civil and political rights in worth and validity. The United States should sign the ICESCR."

Week 5: Institutional Mechanisms for Protecting Human Rights: The UN Systems

This week we discuss the UN systems (treaty-based and non-treaty-based) for protecting human rights. Discuss the work and function of the UN Commission on Human Rights, treaty bodies and monitoring procedures, the UN High Commissioner for Human Rights, and other UN bodies and agencies.

Donnelly, *Universal Human Rights,* chapter 8.

Julie Mertus, *The United Nations and Human Rights,* chapters 2–5.

Browse the website of the UN High Commissioner for Human Rights (http://unhchr.ch), paying particular attention to www.unhchr.ch/html/menu6/2/OHCHR.pdf.

Browse the treaty body database and examine the core human rights treaties related to torture, gender discrimination, racial discrimination, and the rights of the child (www.unhchr.ch/tbs/doc.nsf).

Examine the compilation of general comments adopted by human rights treaty bodies (http://www.unhchr.ch/tbs/doc.nsf/0/ca12c3a4ea8d6c53c1256d500056e56f?Opendocument).

Recommended reading:

Andrew Clapham. "The UN High Commissioner for Human Rights: Achievements and Frustrations." *Columbia Human Rights Law Review* (2004).

Martha Davis and Roslyn Powell. "The International Convention on the Rights of the Child: A Catalyst for Innovative Child Care Policies." *Human Rights Quarterly* 25, no. 3 (August 2003): 689–719.

Week 6: Institutional Mechanisms for Protecting Human Rights: Regional Systems

Learn about regional systems for protecting human rights, including individual complaint mechanisms and regional enforcement measures.

African Human Rights System: United Nations, Department of Economic and Social Affairs, http://www.un.org/esa/socdev/enable/comp303.htm.

European Human Rights System: Human Rights Education Associates, http://www.hrea.org/index.php?base_id=143.

Inter-American Human Rights System: Human Rights Education Associates, http://www.hrea.org/index.php?base_id=150.

Week 7: Universal Jurisdiction and the International Criminal Court

Menno T. Kamminga. "Lessons Learned from the Exercise of Universal Jurisdiction in Respect of Gross Human Rights Offenses." *Human Rights Quarterly* 23 (2001): 940–974.

Week 8: Role of Nonstate Actors in the Enjoyment of Human Rights: Nongovernmental Organizations (NGOs) in Human Rights Monitoring and Enforcement

Mertus, *Bait and Switch,* chapter 4.

Margaret Keck and Kathryn Sikkink. "Human Rights Advocacy Networks in Latin America." In *Activists Without Borders: Advocacy Networks in International Politics,* by Margaret Keck and Kathryn Sikkink. Ithaca, NY: Cornell University Press, 1998.

Alston and Goodman, *International Human Rights in Context,* chapter 11 ("Civil Society, Human Rights NGOs, and Other Groups").

"New Tactics in Human Rights Project," Center for Victims of Torture, http://www.newtactics.org.

Browse websites of other human rights NGOs. This list, maintained by Duke University Libraries, is organized by region: http://docs.lib.duke.edu/igo/guides/ngo/db/rights.asp.

Recommended reading:

William Korey. *NGOs and the Universal Declaration of Human Rights.* New York: Palgrave Macmillan, 2001, introduction, chapters 7, 17.

Aryeh Neier. *Taking Liberties.* New York: Perseus Books, 2003, chapter 9, 10, and "Summing Up."

Week 9: Role of Nonstate Actors in the Enjoyment of Human Rights: An Overview of Nonviolent Conflict

Stephen Zunes. "Nonviolence and Human Rights." *PS: Political Science and Politics* 33, no. 2 (June 2000).

Gene Sharp. *There Are Realistic Alternatives.* Boston: Albert Einstein Institution, 2003, 1–16. www.aeinstein.org/organizations/org/TARA.pdf.

Peter Ackerman and Jack DuVall. "The Right to Rise Up: The Virtues of Civic Disruption. *Fletcher Forum on World Affairs* (Spring 2006).

Kurt Schock. "Nonviolent Action and Its Misconceptions: Insights for Social Scientists." *PS: Political Science and Politics* 36 (2003): 705–712.

View in class the segment on nonviolent struggle against the Pinochet regime in Chile in *A Force More Powerful,* directed by Steven York, DVD, 2000, 154 minutes.

Week 10: Role of Nonstate Actors in the Enjoyment of Human Rights: Nonviolent Struggles for Human Rights (Successful and Failed)

Ackerman and DuVall. *A Force More Powerful* (book), chapters 3, 7, 9, and 11.

Schock, *Unarmed Insurrections,* chapter 3.

Recommended reading:

Joshua Paulson. "Uprising and Repression in China." In *Waging Nonviolent Struggle: Twentieth-Century Practice and Twenty-First-Century Potential,* edited by Gene Sharp. Boston: Porter Sargent, 2005.

Stephen Zunes. "Unarmed Resistance in the Middle East and North Africa." In *Nonviolent Social Movements: A Geographical Perspective,* edited by Stephen Zunes, Lester R. Kurtz, and Sarah Beth Ashler. Oxford: Blackwell, 1999.

Week 11: Making Human Rights Norms Apply to Nonstate Actors

Office of the High Commissioner for Human Rights (OHCHR). "Human Rights, Poverty Reduction, and Sustainable Development: Health, Food, and Water." In *Human Rights in Development,* 2002. http://www.unhchr.ch/development/bp-summit.pdf.

Dana Clark. "The World Bank and Human Rights: The Need for Accountability." *Harvard Human Rights Journal* 15 (Spring 2002): 205.

Sanjeev Khagram. "Restructuring the Global Politics of Development: The Case of India's Narmada Valley Dams." In *Restructuring World Politics: Transnational Social Movements, Networks, and Norms,* edited by Sanjeev Khagram, James Riker, and Kathryn Sikkink. Minneapolis: University of Minnesota Press, 2002, 206–230.

Week 12: Genocide and Humanitarian Intervention

Debate military intervention (UN and regional alliances) for humanitarian purposes; discuss the growing norm of the "right to protect" and UN responses to genocide.

Donnelly, *Universal Human Rights,* chapters 10 and 14.

Mertus, *Bait and Switch,* chapter 3.

International Commission on Intervention and State Sovereignty. *The Responsibility to Protect.* http://www.iciss.ca/report-en.asp.

Gareth Evans. *Banishing the Rwanda Nightmare: The Responsibility to Protect.* Public Broadcasting Corporation, March 31, 2004. http://www.pbs.org/wgbh/pages/frontline/shows/ghosts/etc/protect.html.

William Schabas. "Preventing Genocide and Mass Killing: The Challenge for the UN." *Minority Rights Group International,* http://www.minorityrights.org/?lid=1070 (fee required).

Recommended reading:

Francis Bouchet-Saulnier. "Between Humanitarian Law and Principles." *MSF Activity Report,* Medecins sans Frontiers, 2000.

Week 13: Human Rights and Democracy

Donnelly, *Universal Human Rights,* chapter 11.

Thomas Carothers. "The Backlash Against Democracy Promotion." *Foreign Affairs* (March–April 2006).

Peter Ackerman and Michael J. Glennon. "Democracy Promotion, Interventionism, and Regime Change." *Annuaire Français de Relations Internationales* 7 (2007).

Julie Mertus. "The Law (?) of Regime Change." *Jurist,* February 20, 2003, http://jurist.law.pitt.edu/forum/forumnew98.php.

Recommended reading:

"How Freedom Is Won: From Civic Resistance to Durable Democracy." Freedom House Report, Summary, 2005.

Richard Lugar. "The Backlash Against Democracy Assistance." National Endowment for Democracy Report, June 8, 2006.

Activity: The Gray Team will defend this position: "Western (notably US) support for civil society and human rights groups in nondemocracies violates national sovereignty and is a form of neo-imperialism." Blue Team will defend this position: "Civic groups and human rights activists have a right to external assistance (technical support, educational materials, trainings) as long as they demonstrate a commitment to nonviolent activities."

Week 14: Human Rights and the Global Challenge of Terrorism

Hardy Merriman and Jack DuVall. "Dissolving Terrorism at Its Roots." In *Nonviolence: An Alternative for Countering Global Terror(ism)*. NOVA, 2007, 221–234.

Julie Mertus and Kathleen Clark. "Torturing the Law: The Justice Department's Legal Contortions on Interrogation." *Washington Post,* June 19, 2004, http://www.washingtonpost.com/wp-dyn/articles/A54025-2004Jun19.html.

Joseph E. Stiglitz. "Broken Promises." In *Globalization and Its Discontents,* by Joseph E. Stiglitz. New York: W.W. Norton, 2002, 23–52.

Thomas W. Pogge. "'Assisting' the Global Poor." In *The Ethics of Assistance: Morality and Distant Needy,* edited by Deen K. Chattergee. Cambridge: Cambridge University Press, 2003, 1–21.

Recommended reading:

Larry Nowels. *The Millennium Challenge Account: Congressional Consideration of a New Foreign Aid Initiative*. Congressional Research Service, 2003, 1–25.

TEACHING NOTES

I give students the option of playing the computer-based simulation game, *A Force More Powerful: The Game of Nonviolent Strategy,* which is the first videogame of its kind in which the player assumes the role of a strategist leading a nonviolent struggle against different rights-violating adversaries in nine scenarios (women's rights movement, self-determination struggle, movements against dictatorships, foreign occupations, etc.). Instructions for the game and the scenarios are online at www.afmpgame.com. Those who choose to play out one or more scenarios throughout the semester will be asked to describe their game-play experiences as they relate to course themes.

13
Multilateralism and Unilateralism

FOLLOWING THE COLLAPSE OF THE SOVIET UNION IN THE EARLY 1990s, many political theorists concluded that the world shifted from a bipolar to a unipolar structure. The events of September 11, 2001, however, and the ensuing "war on terrorism" called these assumptions into question. Some analysts suggest that concepts such as unipolarity, multipolarity, or even "tripolarity" with a focus on the United States, China, and Russia cannot adequately describe the contemporary world based on traditional definitions of power. They argue that in the wake of the failed US war in Iraq, coupled with the increasing importance of China and the European Union in the global marketplace, economic power plays a more influential and determinative role than does military power.

At the heart of these debates are traditional theoretical questions between, for example, realism, liberalism, and Marxism, as well as fundamental questions pertaining to identity and global priorities. Are concerns pertaining to international economic competition and the equitable allocation of global resources better answered from the perspective of global citizenship or as members of nation-states? Can the nations of the world better ensure human rights, reduce political violence, and create the basis for peaceful and just international relations by emphasizing the humanitarian and peacebuilding enterprises of the United Nations rather than the leadership of major powers or a world hegemon? Can the world foster an environmentally sustainable ecosystem with each nation-state singularly seeking to advance its national interest? Is it possible that the world may place imperialism and power politics, along with colonialism, in the dustbin of history and genuinely embrace the shared values of a global community?

G. John Ikenberry and Atul Kohli begin with a historical overview of the legacies of colonialism and imperialism before casting light on the foreign policies and current international activities of the United States. Stephen Zunes's seminar assesses US foreign policy within the context of major historical changes, such as the demise of the Soviet Union and the events of 9/11. Specific aspects of George W. Bush's National Security Strategy are weighed in light of the costs and consequences of unilateralism. The course devised by Andrew J. Loomis enables students to explore questions related to the character and effectiveness of US global leadership and the dynamics that lead both to resistance toward and acceptance of US authority. Robert C. Johansen examines, among other pertinent topics, the utility or inutility of war within the framework of international peace operations, multilateral diplomacy, international law, and modern international institutions. Students conclude their analysis by devising theories of a preferred world order. Michael T. Klare's course centers on what he refers to as the "big picture" of global resource competition, proceeding on the assumption that mounting international tensions over environmental decline and resource competition will lead to an increasingly unstable international order. In her course, Kelly Dietz examines the impact of militarization on the lives of US citizens and people in other countries, who are affected by the often obtrusive presence of the hundreds of US military bases around the world.

13.1 Empires and Imperialism

G. John Ikenberry and Atul Kohli
Princeton University

COURSE DESCRIPTION

Upper-level undergraduate and graduate seminar in international relations and international development.

Empires and imperialism are old subjects of enduring relevance. After years of oblivion, the terms have reentered mainstream political discourse in the United States. A number of scholars and public intellectuals have in recent publications described US foreign policies, especially toward the developing world, as constituting a type of imperialism. Of course, not everyone agrees. Yet others have suggested instead that the United States is not an imperialist power at all, and that the United States, as the world's preponderant power, needs to and must provide a global public good, namely, world order. In order to make sense of such disagreements, this course will systematically situate the US "informal empire" in a comparative and historical context. A major point of comparison will be colonial empires of the nineteenth and the early twentieth centuries, especially that of Great Britain, but also of Japan. With this as background, we will study how the US informal empire is similar to and how it differs from old colonial empires. While taking stock of the historical origins of US foreign policies in general, the focus will be on the US role in Europe, Asia, Latin America, and the Middle East since World War II.

The course is designed for researchers as well as for those with a serious policy interest in the subject. Moreover, the course ought to appeal to students of both international relations and developing countries. After situating the subject matter within the frame of competing theoretical perspectives (realism, liberalism, and Marxism) and providing a historical overview, we will devote some four weeks to a more detailed study of colonialism. Beyond overviews, specific topics will include British colonialism in India and Nigeria, Britain's informal empire, and Japanese colonialism in Korea. The second half of the course will focus on the global activities of the United States. Once again, beyond introducing students to competing interpretations and regional overviews, there will be an opportunity for them to focus more specifically on US modes of influence in one part of the world or another.

REQUIRED TEXTS

Stephen Howe. *Empire: A Very Short Introduction.* Oxford University Press, 2002.
Charles Maier. *Among Empires.* Harvard University Press, 2006.
Chalmers Johnson. *The Sorrows of Empire.* Metropolitan Books, 2004.
G. John Ikenberry. *After Victory.* Princeton University Press, 2001.
Niall Ferguson. *Colossus: The Price of America's Empire.* Penguin, 2004.
Tony Smith. *The Pattern of Imperialism.* Cambridge University Press, 1981. (Out of print but readily available from Amazon and other outlets.)
Stephen Kinzer. *Overthrow: America's Century of Regime Change.* Times Books, 2007.

Additional short readings appear in the course schedule.

COURSE SCHEDULE

Session 1: Introduction
Howe, *Empire: A Very Short Introduction.*

Session 2: Competing Perspectives on Imperialism
Thucydides, *The Peloponnesian War,* vii–ix; and (from Penguin edition), book 1, chapter 6 (the debate at Sparta); book 2, chapter 4 (Pericles' funeral ovation); and book 5, chapter 7 (the Melian debate).
Benjamin Cohen. *The Question of Imperialism.* Basic Books, 1973, 229–258.
John A. Hobson. *Imperialism.* Cosimo Classics, 2005, 71–93.
V. I. Lenin. *Imperialism: The Highest Stage of Capitalism.* Pluto Press, 1996, chapters 4–7.
Paul Baran. "On the Political Economy of Backwardness." *Manchester School of Economy and Social Studies* 20, no 1 (January 1952): 66–84.
Joseph Schumpeter. "The Sociology of Imperialism." In *Imperialism and Social Classes: Two Essays.* Ludwig von Mises Institute, 2007, chapter 5.
John Stuart Mill. *Essays on Equality, Law, and Education.* University of Toronto Press, 1984, 111–124.

Session 3: Historical Overview
Smith, *The Pattern of Imperialism.*

Session 4: British Colonialism (India and Nigeria)
The literature on these topics is vast, often written by historians. Aside from the two chapters by Atul Kohli, the rest of the readings assigned are by

historians. An attempt will be made in the seminar to compare and contrast early British colonialism (in India) with late British colonialism (in Nigeria) in terms of both shifting motivations and differing impacts.

H. V. Bowen, "British India, 1765–1813: The Metropolitan Context." In *The Oxford History of the British Empire* (hereafter *OHBE*), vol. 2, edited by P. J. Marshall. Oxford University Press, 2001, 530–551.

D. A. Washbrook, "India, 1818–1860: The Two Faces of Colonialism," *OHBE*, vol. 3, 395–421.

Robin J. Moore, "Imperial India, 1858–1914," *OHBE*, vol. 3, 422–446.

Toyin Falola and A. D. Roberts, "West Africa," *OHBE*, vol. 4, 515–529.

Atul Kohli. *State-Directed Development*. Cambridge University Press, 2004, chapters 6, 8.

Session 5: Britain's Informal Empire

John Gallagher and Ronald Robinson. "The Imperialism of Free Trade." *Economic History Review*, second series, vol. 6, no. 1 (1953).

D. C. M. Platt. "Further Objections to an "Imperialism of Free Trade, 1830–60." *Economic History Review*, second series, vol. 26, no. 1 (February 1973).

Andrew Porter, "Introduction," *OHBE*, vol. 3.

Martin Lynne, *OHBE*, vol. 3, 101–121.

Alan Knight, *OHBE*, vol. 3, 122–145.

Glen Balfour-Paul, "Britain's Informal Empire in the Middle East," *OHBE*, vol. 4, 490–514.

Session 6: Japanese Colonialism (in Korea)

Mark R. Peattie. "Introduction." In *The Japanese Colonial Empire, 1895–1945*, edited by Ramon H. Myers and Mark R. Peattie. Princeton University Press, 1987, 3–60.

Atul Kohli. "Where Do High Growth Political Economies Come From? The Japanese Lineage of Korea's Developmental State." *World Development* 22, no. 9 (1994): 1269–1293.

Stephan Haggard et al. "Japanese Colonialism and Korean Development: A Critique." *World Development* 25 (June 1997): 867–882; and Kohli's response, same issue, 883–888.

Bruce Cumings. "The Legacy of Japanese Colonialism in Korea." In *The Japanese Colonial Empire*, edited by Ramon Myers and Mark Peattie. Princeton University Press, 1987, chapter 13.

Session 7: America's Postwar Order in Comparative Perspective

Charles Maier. *Among Empires: American Ascendancy and Its Predecessors*. Harvard University Press, 2006.

G. John Ikenberry. "Liberal Hegemony or Empire? American Power in the Age of Unipolarity." In *American Power in the Twenty-First Century,* edited by David Held and Mathias Koenig-Archibugi. Polity Press, 2004, 83–113.

William Appleman Williams. *The Tragedy of American Diplomacy.* W.W. Norton, 1988, chapters 1, 2, and 6.

Session 8: America and the West: Liberal Hegemony and Empire by Invitation

Ikenberry, *After Victory,* chapters 1, 2, 3, 6, and 7.

Geir Lundestad. "Empire by Invitation." *Journal of Peace Research* 23 (September 1986): 263–277.

Session 9: America and East Asia: An Empire of Bases?

Johnson, *The Sorrows of Empire.*

Bruce Cumings. "Japan's Position in the World System." In *Postwar Japan as History,* edited by Andrew Gordon. University of California Press, Berkeley, 1993.

G. John Ikenberry. "America in East Asia: Power, Markets, and Grand Strategy." In *Beyond Bilateralism: The Emerging East Asian Regionalism,* edited by T. J. Pempel and Ellis Kraus. Stanford University Press, 2003.

Session 10: America and the Developing World: Regime Change

Kinzer, *Overthrow: America's Century of Regime Change from Hawaii to Iraq.*

Stephen Krasner. *Defending the National Interest: Raw Materials Investments, and US Foreign Policy.* Princeton University Press, 1978, chapter 2.

Session 11: Unipolarity and the Imperial Temptation

Ferguson, *Colossus: The Price of America's Empire.*

Alexander J. Motyl. "Is Everything Empire? Is Empire Everything?" *Comparative Politics* 38, no. 2 (2006): 229–249.

Session 12: Conclusion

No reading assigned.

13.2 US Foreign Policy in a Unipolar World

Stephen Zunes
University of San Francisco

COURSE DESCRIPTION

Upper-level undergraduate or lower-level graduate seminar for majors in political science, international studies, and peace and conflict studies.

This seminar critically examines US foreign policy in a unipolar world, analyzing the impact of the demise of the Soviet Union and the September 11, 2001, attacks on US foreign policy; the invasion of Iraq; concerns over the proliferation of weapons of mass destruction; the controversial National Security Strategy (or Bush doctrine); and the impact of such events on international law, the United Nations, and other international institutions.

The objectives of the course are for students to become better informed citizens during this unprecedented period of transformation regarding the US role in the world, to participate in engaged discussions on pressing foreign policy issues, and to be able to successfully complete an undergraduate thesis, which gives students the chance to explore in some depth a relevant topic of their choice.

REQUIRED TEXTS

Mark Gibney. *Five Uneasy Pieces: American Ethics in a Globalized World.* Rowman and Littlefield, 2005.

Nicholas Guyatt. *Another American Century? The United States and the World Since 9/11.* Zed Books, 2004.

Rashid Khalidi. *Resurrecting Empire: Western Footprints and America's Perilous Path in the Middle East.* Beacon Press, 2004.

Michael Klare. *Blood and Oil: The Dangers and Consequences of America's Growing Dependency on Petroleum.* Holt, 2005.

Robert Jay Lifton. *Superpower Syndrome: America's Apocalyptic Confrontation with the World.* Nation Books, 2003.

Brian Loveman, ed. *Strategy for Empire: US Regional Security Policy in the Post–Cold War Era.* SR Books, 2004.

John Newhouse. *Imperial America: The Bush Assault on the World Order.* Vintage Books, 2004.

Sibley Telhami. *The Stakes: America in the Middle East.* Westview Press, 2002.

COURSE SCHEDULE

Week 1: Introduction

Week 2: US Regional Security Policy: Mainstream Perspectives
Loveman, *Strategy for Empire*, introduction and chapters 1–8.

Week 3: US Regional Security Policy: Alternative Perspectives
Loveman, *Strategy for Empire*, chapters 9–15.

Week 4: Confronting Islamist Extremism
Lifton, *Superpower Syndrome*, entire.

Week 5: The United States and the Middle East, Part 1
Khalidi, *Resurrecting Empire*, entire.

Week 6: The United States and the Middle East, Part 2
Telhami, *The Stakes*, entire.

Week 7: The Bush Doctrine, Part 1
Newhouse, *Imperial America*, entire.

Week 8: The Bush Doctrine, Part 2
Guyatt, *Another American Century*, introduction and chapters 1–3.

Week 9: The Bush Doctrine, Part 3
Guyatt, *Another American Century*, chapters 4–5.

Week 10: The Impact of Oil
Klare, *Blood and Oil*, entire.

Week 11: Ethics in Foreign Relations
Gibney, *Five Uneasy Pieces*, entire.

Weeks 12–14: Student Presentations

TEACHING NOTES

The format of the seminar is largely one of discussion. I come prepared for a series of questions based on the readings, but I allow the discussion to evolve, as long as students stay on topic. The students are responsible for completing the readings by class time each week and are expected to participate fully. They must also keep a weekly journal of their reactions to the readings, which is to be turned in at the start of class each week or emailed prior to class time. I grade the journal entries with a check, check-plus, or check-minus system.

In addition, each student is required to write a senior thesis of at least fifteen pages, double-spaced. The last four classes of the semester consist of presentations by students of their research in progress.

Students are required to meet with me one-on-one at least twice during the semester. The first required meeting falls during the sixth week of the semester to discuss progress in the class. At that time I inform students of their midsemester grades, based on attendance and participation up to that point. The second meeting comes before or during the eighth week of class to discuss the topics of their term papers and research strategies.

13.3 International Perspectives on US Foreign Policy

Andrew J. Loomis
Georgetown University

COURSE DESCRIPTION

Intermediate- or upper-level undergraduate course in government or political science.

This course encourages students to inspect and evaluate international perspectives on the character of US foreign policy and the causes of international reactions they observe. The ability of the United States to achieve its policy goals often depends on a favorable response from its allies, yet allies sometimes resist US leadership. The central objective of this course is to develop greater understanding of the causes of both ally resistance to and ally acceptance of US authority. Is the best explanation provided by structural factors, such as power asymmetry, or by ideational or normative factors? Are international reactions to US policy primarily driven by policy elites or a culmination of mass public outcry? Under what conditions does international resistance to US policy have a consequential effect on US interests or world politics more generally?

The course explores answers to these questions and examines the distinction between power and authority, the nature and causes of international obstruction and acceptance of US policies, and the ultimate ability of the United States to operate in an environment with high levels of anti-American sentiment. The course devotes time to case studies that will enable students to apply their theoretical knowledge to near-historical and contemporary events, including the 1991 Gulf War, the wars in Bosnia and Kosovo, the 2003 Iraq War, and US response to international jihadism and the "war on terror."

REQUIRED TEXTS

G. John Ikenberry, ed. *America Unrivaled: The Future of the Balance of Power.* Ithaca, NY: Cornell University Press, 2002.

G. John Ikenberry, ed. *American Foreign Policy: Theoretical Essays,* 4th ed. New York: Longman, 2002.

G. John Ikenberry, ed. *American Foreign Policy: Theoretical Essays,* 5th ed. New York: Houghton Mifflin, 2005.

Peter Katzenstein and Robert Keohane, eds. *Anti-Americanisms in World Politics.* Ithaca, NY: Cornell University Press, 2007.

COURSE SCHEDULE

Unit 1: Theoretical Background

Session 1: Introduction to and Overview of International Relations Theory

Jack Snyder. "One World, Rival Theories." *Foreign Policy* (November–December 2004): 52–62.

Stephen G. Brooks and William C. Wohlforth. "International Relations Theory and the Case Against Unilateralism." *Perspectives on Politics* (September 2005).

Session 2: Contribution of IR Theory

G. John Ikenberry, *American Foreign Policy,* 67–89 ("Anarchic Orders and Balances of Power," by Kenneth Waltz).

David Baldwin. "Neorealism, Neoliberalism, and World Politics." In *Neorealism and Neoliberalism,* edited by David Baldwin. New York: Columbia University Press, 1993, 3–25.

Jeffrey Checkel. "The Constructivist Turn in International Relations Theory." *World Politics* 50, no. 2 (January 1998): 324–348.

Aaron Friedberg. "Compromise or Conflict? China, the United States, and Stability in Asia." *International Security* 30, no. 2 (Fall 2005): 7–45.

Unit 2: Conceptualizing International Leadership

Session 3: Rethinking US Leadership

Ikenberry, *America Unrivaled,* 181–210 ("Incomplete Hegemony and Security Order in the Asia-Pacific," by Michael Mastuanduno).

Charles Kupchan. "After Pax Americana: Benign Power, Regional Integration, and the Sources of a Stable Multipolarity." *International Security* 23, no. 2 (Fall 1998): 40–79.

Joseph Nye. *Bound to Lead: The Changing Nature of American Power.* New York: Basic Books, 1991, 25–48, 173–201.

G. John Ikenberry and Charles A. Kupchan. "Socialization and Hegemonic Power." *International Organization* 44, no. 3 (Summer 1990): 283–315.

Ian Hurd. "Legitimacy and Authority in International Politics." *International Organization* 53, no. 2 (Spring 1999): 379–408.

Session 4: Defying US Leadership

Ikenberry, *America Unrivaled,* 5th ed., 333–357 ("Structural Realism After the Cold War," by Kenneth Waltz).

Robert Pape. "Soft Balancing Against the United States." *International Security* 30, no. 1 (Summer 2005): 7–45, *or* T. V. Paul. "Soft Balancing in the Age of US Primacy." *International Security* 30, no. 1 (Summer 2005): 46–71.

G. John Ikenberry. "Strategic Reactions to American Preeminence." National Intelligence Council Report, 2003.

John G. Ruggie. "American Exceptionalism, Exemptionalism, and Global Governance." In *American Exceptionalism and Human Rights,* edited by Michael Ignatieff. Princeton, NJ: Princeton University Press, 2005, 304–338.

Peter Katzenstein and Robert Keohane. "Anti-Americanisms." *Policy Review* 139 (October–November 2006).

Thomas Carothers. "The Backlash Against Democracy Promotion." *Foreign Affairs* 85, no. 2 (March–April 2006): 55–68.

Peter Hakim. "Is Washington Losing Latin America?" *Foreign Affairs* 85, no. 1 (January–February 2006): 39–53.

Unit 3: Understanding Variation in Leadership Capacity

Session 5: A Realist Explanation and Power Politics

Ikenberry, *America Unrivaled,* 98–120 ("US Strategy in a Unipolar World," by William Wohlforth).

Christopher Layne. "The Unipolar Illusion Revisited." *International Security* 31, no. 2 (Fall 2006): 7–41.

Robert Art et al. "Correspondence: Striking the Balance." *International Security* 30, no. 3 (Winter 2005–2006): 177–196.

Ikenberry, *America Unrivaled,* 121–154 ("Keeping the World Off Balance: Self-Restraint and US Foreign Policy," by Stephen Walt).

Philip Gordon. "The End of the Bush Revolution." *Foreign Affairs* 85, no. 4 (July–August 2006): 75–86.

Session 6: The Neoliberal Explanation and Institutional Constraints

Robert Keohane. "Reciprocity in IR." *International Organization* 40, no. 1 (Winter 1986): 1–27.

Ikenberry, *America Unrivaled,* 213–238 ("Democracy, Institutions, and American Restraint," by Ikenberry).

Peter Beinart. "The Rehabilitation of the Cold-War Liberal." *New York Times Magazine,* April 30, 2006.

Ivo Daalder and James Goldgeier. "Global NATO." *Foreign Affairs* 85, no. 5 (September–October 2006): 105–113.

Ashton Carter. "America's New Strategic Partner?" *Foreign Affairs* 85, no. 4 (July–August 2006): 33–44.

Joseph S. Nye Jr. *Soft Power: The Means to Success in World Politics.* New York: Public Affairs, 2004, 1–32, 127–147.

Session 7: The Liberal Explanation and Domestic Politics

Ikenberry, *American Foreign Policy,* 5th ed., 333–357 ("Domestic Constraints on Regime Change in US Foreign Policy: The Need for Policy Legitimacy," by Alexander George).

Ikenberry, *American Foreign Policy,* 4th ed., 344–376 ("Public Opinion and Foreign Policy: Challenges to the Almond-Lippman Consensus," by Ole Holsti).

William Howell and Jon Pevehouse. "Presidents, Congress, and the Use of Force." *International Organization* 59 (Winter 2005): 209–232.

Daniel Yankelovich. "Poll Positions: What Americans Really Think About US Foreign Policy." *Foreign Affairs* 84, no. 5 (September–October 2005): 2–16.

Session 8: The Constructivist Explanation and the Role of Ideas

Ian Clark. *Legitimacy in International Society.* New York: Oxford University Press, 2005, 229–239.

Ikenberry, *America Unrivaled,* 239–259 ("Transnational Liberalism and American Primacy," by John Owen).

Judith Goldstein and Robert Keohane. "Ideas and Foreign Policy: An Analytic Framework." In *Ideas and Foreign Policy: Beliefs, Institutions, and Political Change,* edited by Judith Goldstein and Robert Keohane. Ithaca, NY: Cornell University Press, 1993, 3–30.

Session 9: A Synthesis of Explanations

J. Samuel Barkin. "Realist Constructivism." *International Studies Review* 5, no. 3 (Fall 2003): 325–342.

Gideon Rose. "Neoclassical Realism and Theories of Foreign Policy." *World Politics* 51, no. 1 (October 1998): 144–172.

Jeffrey Legro. *Rethinking the World: Great Power Strategies and International Order.* Ithaca, NY: Cornell University Press, 2005, 49–83, 161–187.

Session 10: Strategic Use of Norms

Robert Kagan. "America's Crisis of Legitimacy." *Foreign Affairs* 83, no. 2 (March–April 2004): 65–87.

Robert Tucker and David Hendrickson. "The Sources of American Legitimacy." *Foreign Affairs* 83, no. 6 (November–December 2004): 18–32.

Ian Hurd. "The Strategic Use of Liberal Internationalism: Libya and the UN Sanctions, 1992–2003." *International Organization* 59 (Summer 2005).

Stacie Goddard. "Uncommon Ground: Indivisible Territory and the Politics of Legitimacy." *International Organization* 50 (Winter 2006): 35–68.

Session 11: Legitimacy and the Time Dimension

Stephen Skowronek. *The Politics Presidents Make.* Cambridge, MA: Belknap Press, 1993, 17–32.

Rodney Bruce Hall. "Moral Authority as a Power Resource." *International Organization* 51, no. 4 (Autumn 1997): 591–622.

James Rosenau and Ole Holsti. "US Leadership in a Shrinking World: The Breakdown of Consensuses and the Emergence of Conflict Belief Systems." *World Politics* 35, no. 3 (April 1993): 368–392.

Session 12: Frameworks of US Grand Strategy

Robert Lieber. *The American Era.* Cambridge: Cambridge University Press, 2005, 11–37.

Stephen Walt. "Taming American Power." *Foreign Affairs* 84, no. 5 (September–October 2005): 105–120.

Ivo Daalder. *America Unbound.* Washington, DC: Brookings Institution Press, 2003, 1–16, 116–128.

Stanley Hoffmann, with Frédéric Bozo. *Gulliver Unbound.* Lanham, MD: Rowman and Littlefield, 2004, 67–80, 117–146.

Joseph Nye. *The Paradox of American Power.* Oxford: Oxford University Press, 2002, 1–40, 137–171.

TEACHING NOTES

This course works very well as a seminar since the course content lends itself to vigorous class discussion. A substantial portion of each class involves class discussion, which I actively facilitate in order to draw out the essential insights related to each day's objective.

In addition to completing the assigned readings, the students are required to stay current on contemporary international politics. I expect the students to read the front section of a major national newspaper each morning prior to class to enable them to participate effectively in class discussions and apply current examples in the paper, presentation, and exams. Throughout the course, the students are encouraged to apply their theoretical knowledge to current events as they unfold.

Student presentations simulate briefings from the national security adviser to the president on a specific set of policies that would reinforce US leadership. They first provide a brief overview of the strength of US leadership in a region or country of their choosing. The presentation is expected to include evidence from local sources of the opinions toward the United States. The students then present a set of prescriptions designed to reinforce US leadership, justifying their recommendations with the material covered in class.

Writing an analytic paper gives the students an opportunity to select a case or region of their choosing and evaluate the condition of US leadership and the causes of variation as they understand them by applying the various theoretical tools available. An underlying objective of the class is to encourage the students to reason as social scientists, evaluating the news with a critical eye and testing propositions by examining the evidence and developing metrics to enable them to test variation in US influence.

13.4 The Global Politics of Peacebuilding

Robert C. Johansen
University of Notre Dame

COURSE DESCRIPTION

Upper-level undergraduate course or graduate course for students in international relations and peace and conflict studies.

The purpose of this class is to develop critical thinking skills and a body of knowledge that will enable students (1) to analyze the origins of armed conflict, the denial of fundamental human rights, and the opportunities for building peace; and (2) to develop creative recommendations for addressing these problems and seizing these opportunities, with both short- and long-term initiatives for policy and structural change.

After two introductory sessions, we reflect on our own underlying beliefs, values, and assumptions and compare them to prevailing "realist" worldviews and to the perspectives of those engaged in peace research. We then examine human rights as a basis for developing strategies to build a more just and peaceful world society. Third, we examine current thinking on the utility or inutility of war and other forms of political violence for addressing threats to peace and human rights, followed by a fourth segment on the dynamics of peace operations and peacebuilding within the United Nations system. The final section explores concepts of positive human identity and the claims of some that inclusive identity, combined with nonviolent direct action, can enable effective strategic peacebuilding while maximizing respect for human life in the process.

Throughout our study, we review the strengths and weaknesses of the existing international system and address the former Secretary-General Kofi Annan's claim that "we are living through a crisis of the international system. [Recent events] force us to ask ourselves whether the institutions and methods we are accustomed to are really adequate." We explore the utility of multilateral diplomacy, international law, international institutions, and citizens' organizations for developing more peaceful and just international relationships. Students' diverse experiences are important resources in this exploration.

As you analyze your own and others' perspectives, please develop your own theory of a preferred world order. Try to identify beliefs, values, policies, and institutions for effective peacebuilding, both globally and locally. Consider the prospects for achieving (1) a global civilization made up of diverse cultures able to support fundamental human rights while celebrating differences among cultures, (2) a world at peace, with justice for everyone, and (3) forms of identity that undergird respect for all life. Other courses will add to your understanding of some aspects of these three topics, as well as facilitate your study of the prospects for (4) a global society built upon economic security and justice for all and (5) an ecosystem that is sustainable and congenial to human life and nature. Study of these five dimensions of a preferred system of world public order can provide a solid basis for future understanding and action.

COURSE SCHEDULE

Session 1: Approaches to International Relations, Peace Research, and Peacebuilding

Questions: What values and perspectives have shaped peace research, compared to the values and perspectives of traditional international relations? What utility does peace research have? How do peace researchers approach peacebuilding? What values and perspectives have shaped your approach to achieving a more just and peaceful world?

Peter Wallensteen. "The Origins of Peace Research." In *Peace Research: Achievements and Challenges,* edited by Peter Wallensteen. Boulder, CO: Westview, 1988, 7–29.

Patrick Hayden. *Cosmopolitan Global Politics.* Aldershot: Ashgate, 2005, 1–10.

Johan Galtung. "Twenty-Five Years of Peace Research: Ten Challenges and Some Responses." *Journal of Peace Research* 22 (1985): 141–158.

Session 2: Mind-sets

Questions: How do the mind-sets of policymakers and scholars shape our thinking about international relations and influence the likelihood of achieving a more just and peaceful world? What are the similarities and differences between political realists and peace researchers, between nationalists and cosmopolitans? How does each perspective influence people in becoming effective builders of peace and justice? What implicit values typically provide the foundation for making foreign policy decisions and conducting international relations? Do these vary significantly from state to state? How do you identify and prioritize the values that *you* prefer and want implemented in global society? How do three primary factors—human nature, the nature of a society and its state, and the nature of the international system—each contribute to or reduce political violence? Are differences in approaches to understanding violent conflict and peacebuilding related to psychological factors, "pedagogies," and concepts of interconnectedness? In what ways do insights from psychology and alternative worldviews, such as those drawn from Alice Miller or Johan Galtung, have relevance for understanding contemporary international conflict and peacebuilding?

Hayden, *Cosmopolitan Global Politics,* 11–36.
Glen Fisher. *The Mindsets Factor in Ethnic Conflict: A Cross-Cultural Agenda.* Yarmouth, ME: Intercultural Press, 1998, 10–16, 20–22, 27–36, 57–61.
Jack Levy. "Theories of Interstate and Intrastate War: A Levels-of-Analysis Approach." In *Turbulent Peace: The Challenges of Managing International Conflict,* edited by Chester A. Crocker, Fen Osler Hampson, and Pamela Aall. Washington, DC: US Institute of Peace Press, 2001, 3–27.
Alice Miller. "Poisonous Pedagogy." In *For Your Own Good,* by Alice Miller. New York: Farrar, Straus and Giroux, 1983, xiii–xvii, 3–17, 58–101.
Chris Hedges. *War Is a Force That Gives Us Meaning.* New York: Anchor, 2002, 1–17.

Browse the website of Transcend Peace University, where Johan Galtung is founding rector: http://www.transcend.org/tpu/.

Session 3: Alternative Visions of Peace, Human Rights, and Human Responsibilities
Questions: Am I my brother's and my sister's keeper? What duties do I have beyond the borders of my tribe? My nation? What worldviews support human rights or undermine compliance with them? How does the philosophical basis for humanitarian concern found in engaged Buddhism compare with Miller's psychoanalytic perspective and the approach of structural realists? What is the source of your understanding of whether you have duties beyond your tribe? Your nation? How do your views reflect, if at all, the dialectic noted in Paul Gordon Lauren? Of what relevance are visions of human rights to peacebuilding?

Thich Nhat-Hanh. *Being Peace.* Berkeley, CA: Parallax, 1987, 3–115.
Paul Gordon Lauren. *The Evolution of International Human Rights: Visions Seen.* Philadelphia: University of Pennsylvania Press, 2003, 1–102.

Session 4: Implementing Visions of Human Rights
Questions: What are international human rights? International human duties? Do human rights matter? Do rights exist if people are unaware of them and they are not respected? To what extent have human rights visions been transformed into realities?

Lauren, *The Evolution of International Human Rights: Visions Seen,* 103–304.
United Nations. Universal Declaration of Human Rights. 1948.

United Nations. International Covenant on Economic, Social, and Cultural Rights. 1966.

United Nations. International Covenant on Civil and Political Rights. 1966.

Session 5: Human Rights, Universality, and the Foundation of Cosmopolitan Global Politics

Questions: Are human rights universal? How can international human rights be more effectively implemented? Can human rights provide a useful framework for studying international relations, for making governmental policy, for reducing political violence, and for enhancing global justice?

Hayden, *Cosmopolitan Global Politics,* 37–38, 54–66.

David P. Forsythe. *Human Rights in International Relations.* Cambridge: Cambridge University Press, 2000, ix–xi, 3–86.

Shashi Tharoor. "Are Human Rights Universal?" *World Policy Journal* (Winter 2000): 1–6.

Thomas W. Pogge. "Human Rights and Human Responsibilities." In *Global Responsibilities: Who Must Deliver on Human Rights,* edited by Andrew Kuper. New York: Routledge, 2005, 3–35.

Browse the online version of *Human Rights Dialogue* at www.carnegie council.org.

Session 6: The United Nations, Regionalism, and Multilateralism

Questions: What are the UN's achievements and failures in implementing human rights? How do regional actors enhance or impede respect for human rights? What is their optimal relationship to global institutions? Do international human rights activities by the UN and regional organizations suggest incipient international protection of human rights? Global domination? Equitable inclusiveness? Empty rhetoric? What are the strengths and weaknesses of various strategies for implementing human rights?

Thomas G. Weiss, David P. Forsythe, and Roger A. Coate. *The United Nations and Changing World Politics.* Boulder, CO: Westview, 2004, 129–216.

Forsythe, *Human Rights in International Relations,* 121–185.

United Nations, Office of the High Commissioner for Human Rights. Convention on the Prevention and Punishment of the Crime of Genocide. 1951. http://www.unhchr.ch/html/menu3/b/p_genoci.htm.

United Nations, Office of the High Commissioner for Human Rights. Convention on the Elimination of All Forms of Discrimination Against Women. 1979. http://www.un.org/womenwatch/daw/cedaw/.

African Charter on Human and Peoples' Rights. 1986. http://www1.umn .edu/humanrts/instree/z1afchar.htm.

Session 7: Individual Accountability for Violations of Human Rights, the International Criminal Court, Nongovernmental Organizations, and the Politics of International Enforcement

Questions: Of what utility are international criminal courts and truth commissions? What positions do you and the governments located in your region of the world take on the preceding question? What are the optimal human rights roles for nongovernmental organizations and intergovernmental organizations in enforcing laws prohibiting genocide, crimes, against humanity, and war crimes?

Hayden, *Cosmopolitan Global Politics,* 95–97, 108–117.

Forsythe, *Human Rights in International Relations,* 89–119, 188–273.

Robert C. Johansen. "The Impact of US Policy Toward the International Criminal Court on the Prevention of Genocide, War Crimes, and Crimes Against Humanity." *Human Rights Quarterly* 28, no. 2 (2006): 301–331.

Browse the website of the International Coalition for the International Criminal Court, http://www.iccnow.org/.

Read about the International Criminal Court at http://www.hrw.org/ and http://www.amnesty.org/.

Session 8: National Security, Collective Security, Cosmopolitan Security, Human Security: What Does Each Contribute to Peacebuilding?

Questions: What are the theories of national security, collective security, cosmopolitan security, and human security? To what extent have collective security, peacekeeping, and enforcement been successfully practiced by the United Nations? How do emphases on national security, collective security, and human security contribute to peacebuilding? Is there a right to peace? If so, under what conditions is there a just war?

Hayden, *Cosmopolitan Global Politics,* 67–94.

Weiss, Forsythe, and Coate, *The United Nations and Changing World Politics,* 3–122.

Karen A. Mingst and Margaret P. Karns. *The United Nations in the Post–Cold War Era.* Boulder, CO: Westview, 2000, tables, 85, 89, 90.

Rudolph J. Rummel. *Death by Government.* New Brunswick, NJ: Transaction, 1994, 1–43.

Browse the resources of the Center for Human Security, http://www.humansecuritygateway.info/.

Session 9: New Wars, Terrorism, and Imperial Ambitions

Questions: What are "new wars"? How does unipclarity and the US National Security Strategy affect the prospects for addressing new wars, terrorism, and peacebuilding? What security concepts, policies, and value priorities are most useful for reducing collective violence? What are the most effective antidotes for terrorism?

Mary Kaldor. *New and Old Wars: Organized Violence in a Global Era,* 2nd ed. Stanford: Stanford University Press, 2007, introduction and chapter 6.

White House. *National Security Strategy of the United States of America.* 2006, 1–31. http://www.whitehouse.gov/nsc/nss.html.

G. John Ikenberry. "America's Imperial Ambition." *Foreign Affairs* 81 (September–October 2002): 44–60.

Richard Falk. *The Great Terror War.* New York: Olive Branch, 2003, xi–xxviii, 1–37.

Jeffrey Laurenti. "A Transformed Landscape: Terrorism and the UN After the Fall of the World Trade Center." In *Combating Terrorism: Does the UN Matter . . . and How?* edited by Jeffrey Laurenti. New York: United Nations Association of the United States of America, 2002, 19–31.

Angela Drakulich, ed. *A Global Agenda: Issues before the 60th General Assembly of the United Nations.* New York: United Nations Association of the United States of America, 2005, 10–11, 104–105.

Session 10: International Responses to Armed Conflict

Questions: How do various instruments of statecraft contribute to or impede peacebuilding and human security in an age of globalization? When is humanitarian intervention desirable? Feasible? How is constructive humanitarian intervention differentiated analytically from destructive forms of imperialism or international domination?

UN Declaration on the Right of Peoples to Peace. 1984. http://www.unhchr.ch/html/menu3/b/73.htm; also browse the right to peace, http://www.pdhre.org/rights/peace.html.

Crocker, Hampson, and Aall, *Turbulent Peace:*

Pages xv–xxix.

Jean-Marie Guehenno, "The Impact of Globalization on Strategy," 83–95.

Janice Gross Stein, "Image, Identity, and the Resolution of Violent Conflict," 189–205.

Chester A. Crocker, "Intervention: Toward Best Practices and a Holistic View," 229–247.

Stanley Hoffmann, "The Debate About Intervention," 273–282.

Recommended: Crocker, Hampson, and Aall, *Turbulent Peace,* articles by Mohammed Ayoob, Paul Collier, and Ted Robert Gurr, 127–188.

Hedges, *War Is a Force That Gives Us Meaning,* 19–121.

Session 11: New Wars, New Threats, but Old Responses?

Questions: How have UN peace operations contributed to peace, security, and human rights? What factors encourage effective war prevention roles for UN agencies and operations? For nongovernmental organizations (NGOs)?

Hedges, *War Is a Force That Gives Us Meaning,* 122–156.

Crocker, Hampson, and Aall, *Turbulent Peace:*
Pamela Aall, "What Do NGOs Bring to Peacemaking?" 365–381.
Rolf Ekeus, "New Challenges for the United Nations," 517–528.
Michael Doyle, "War Making and Peace Making: The United Nations Post–Cold War Record," 529–560.

Recommended: essays by Fen Hampson (387–406), Louis Kriesberg (407–426), and Saadia Touval and William Zartman (427–442).

Robert C. Johansen. "Proposal for a United Nations Emergency Peace Service." In *A United Nations Emergency Peace Service: To Prevent Genocide and Crimes Against Humanity,* edited by the World Federalist Movement, 21–41, http://www.globalactionpw.org/uneps/UNEmergencyPeaceService.pdf.

G. John Ikenberry. "The End of the Neo-Conservative Moment." In *Liberal Order and Imperial Ambition,* by G. John Ikenberry. London: Polity, 2006, 229–243.

Session 12: Current Peacebuilding Issues

Questions: How can peacebuilding strategies become more effective? What does sensitivity to women's human rights contribute to peacebuilding? What contributions can be made by arms control? By international law and institutions? What contributions can be made by civil society organizations?

Joseph A. Camilleri. "Major Structural Reform." In *Democratizing Global Governance,* edited by Esref Aksu and Joseph A. Camilleri. Hampshire, MA: Palgrave Macmillan, 2002, 255–270.

Crocker, Hampson, and Aall, *Turbulent Peace:*
Connie Peck, "The Role of Regional Organizations in Preventing and Resolving Conflict," 561–582.
William Schabas, "International Law and Response to Conflict," 603–618.
Michael Krepon, "Arms Control Treaties and Confidence-Building Measures as Management Tools," 619–636.
Mary B. Anderson, "Humanitarian NGOs in Conflict Intervention," 637–648.
Stephen John Stedman, "International Implementation of Peace Agreements in Civil Wars: Findings from a Study of Sixteen Cases," 719–750.

Richard Strickland and Nata Duvvury. "Gender Equity and Peacebuilding: From Rhetoric to Reality: Finding the Way." International Center for Research on Women, 1–31, http://www.icrw.org/docs/gender_peace_report_0303.pdf.

Robert C. Johansen. "Enforcing Norms and Normalizing Enforcement for Humane Governance." In *Principled World Politics: The Challenge of Normative International Relations,* edited by Paul Wapner and Edwin J. Ruiz. Lanham, MD: Rowman and Littlefield, 2000, 209–230.

Session 13: Democratic Worldviews and Peacebuilding

Questions: In what ways do democratic values and institutions contribute to peace? Under what conditions do citizen-based strategies relying on nonviolent direct action succeed in contributing to human rights, democracy, and peace? How do you define success? How are peace and human rights influenced by layered identities, incorporating family, clan, tribe, race, ethnicity, nation, religion, and the entire human species? If we take cultural pluralism seriously, to what extent are universal identities possible? Desirable?

Rudolph J. Rummel. *Power Kills: Democracy as a Method of Nonviolence.* New Brunswick, NJ: Transaction, 1997, 1–49.

Peter Ackerman and Christopher Kruegler. *Strategic Nonviolent Conflict.* Westport, CT: Praeger, 1994, xix–xxiv, 1–53.

Robert L. Holmes. "The Sleep of Reason Brings Forth Monsters." In *Nonviolence in Theory and Practice,* edited by Robert L. Holmes. Belmont, CA: Wadsworth, 1990, 132–140.

Gene Sharp. "Beyond Just War and Pacifism." In *Violence and Its Alternatives: An Interdisciplinary Reader,* edited by Manfred B. Steger and Nancy S. Lind. New York: St. Martin's Press, 1999, 317–333.

Martin Luther King Jr. "Excerpts from *Love, Law, and Civil Disobedience.*" In *Violence and Its Alternatives: An Interdisciplinary Reader,* edited by Manfred B. Steger and Nancy S. Lind. New York: St. Martin's Press, 1999, 302–307.

Mohandas K. Gandhi. "Excerpts from *The Essential Writings of Mahatma Gandhi.*" In *Violence and Its Alternatives: An Interdisciplinary Reader,* edited by Manfred B. Steger and Nancy S. Lind. New York: St. Martin's Press, 1999, 292–301.

Robert C. Johansen. "Radical Islam and Nonviolence: A Case Study of Religious Empowerment and Constraint Among Pashtuns." *Journal of Peace Research* 34, no. 1 (February 1997): 53–71.

Session 14: Realizing Peacebuilding Values

Questions: Of all the policy and structural changes recommended by *Global Action to Prevent War,* which are most promising? Why? What are the most serious structural impediments to realizing a just world peace and other values you prefer? What evidence seems most compelling in demonstrating that at least some of your most valued recommendations are politically feasible? What kind of religious or secular worldviews contribute most effectively to the prospects for a peaceful and just world? What significant international changes are likely within five years? What major changes are possible within your life expectancy?

Hedges, *War Is a Force That Gives Us Meaning,* 157–185.

Jonathan Dean et al., rapporteurs. *Global Action to Prevent War: A Coalition-Building Effort to Stop War, Genocide, and Internal Armed Conflict.* New York: Lawyers Committee on Nuclear Policy, 2003, 4–48.

Crocker, Hampson, and Aall, *Turbulent Peace,* 841–854 ("Civil Society and Reconciliation," by John Paul Lederach).

Peter Singer. *One World: The Ethics of Globalization.* New Haven, CT: Yale University Press, 2002, 1–13.

Hayden, *Cosmopolitan Global Politics,* 121–156.

TEACHING NOTES

Five questions guide students as they write essays for this seminar: (1) Imagine that you have been asked by the United Nations Secretary-General to prepare a brief report explaining the most promising ways of increasing compliance with international human rights. What would you recommend? Why? What are the strengths and weaknesses of various strategies for increasing international respect for human rights? (2) To what extent are international human rights a useful decisionmaking guide for national governments and intergovernmental organizations? To what extent should they be? (3) To what extent are international human rights recognized as universal? To what extent should they be so recognized? (4) Reflecting on authors and policymakers we have studied, to what extent do human rights shape your preferred system of world order? How can human rights discourse contribute effectively to your future work? (Note where you agree or disagree with relevant authors and policymakers.) (5) To what extent have states and intergovernmental organizations moved away from the traditional Westphalian system of international law and relations for the purpose of protecting internationally recognized human rights?

13.5 Global Resource Politics

Michael T. Klare
Hampshire College and University of Massachusetts

COURSE DESCRIPTION

Upper-level undergraduate course in peace and security studies, political science, and environmental politics.

This course is intended to provide students with a broad overview of international debates and disputes arising from global environmental decline and the competition over scarce and valuable resources. The course is predicated on the belief that environmental decline and resource competition—notably over such vital commodities as oil, water, farmland, timber, and minerals—will play an ever more central role in world affairs and, unless given greater attention by the global community, will prove a growing source of international friction and conflict. The course is further shaped by a belief that innovative new strategies are needed to solve resource disputes peacefully and to provide for the equitable allocation of the earth's natural bounty.

Competition for critical resources has, of course, figured in world affairs since the very dawn of "civilization." Throughout history, peoples and states have fought for control over vital waterways, fields, forests, and colonies. These struggles have, in fact, constituted much of what we think of as "history"—the rise and fall of powerful states, dynasties, and empires. Hence, resource conflict is nothing new. In the past, however, cities and states could compensate for excessive population growth and the overexploitation of their home territory by sending excess population elsewhere and by exploiting the resources of distant, "virgin" territories, such as the "New World" and Africa. But today, there are no more virgin continents waiting to be "discovered" and exploited in this fashion. Rather, we live in a time when the entire planet is being stripped of its assets at a maximum rate. And because the supplies of many critical materials are finite, we risk the total exhaustion of the planet's vital resources, including the climate.

From the fifteenth through the nineteenth centuries, it was understood by national elites among the major powers of Europe that international affairs were largely governed by the competitive—and often violent—pursuit of overseas colonies and the resources they provided. "Geopolitics" was the term widely used to describe this global competition, which culminated in World War I. But classical geopolitics was largely subordinated to ideological struggle during the final three-quarters of the twentieth century. Now, geopolitics is again defining much of the international landscape, as the major powers seek to enhance their control over (or access to) vital sources of critical materials. The emergence of China and India as economic powerhouses and the emergence of Russia as an "energy superpower" have given added momentum to this trend. This, in turn, has placed added pressure on the world's natural resource stocks and accelerated the process of global climate change.

Although the world community is becoming increasingly aware of such phenomena as global warming, "peak oil" (i.e., maximum sustainable world oil output), global fisheries depletion, and so forth, little is being done at the international level to address the dangers of resource depletion and scarcity. Most societies are accelerating rather than curbing their consumption of vital commodities. This means that the competitive struggle between major consuming nations is intensifying, and the risk of conflict over scarce or insufficient materials is growing. Various technological and behavioral solutions have been proposed to address these dangers, but not enough effort is being made to implement these initiatives. Much more thought must be given, then, to strategies for promoting international cooperation in the development and adoption of resource-saving methodologies.

In this course, we will discuss the historical role of resource competition in human affairs, drawing heavily on Jared Diamond's book *Collapse*, and consider how the current world situation both resembles and is different from the patterns of the past. We will also consider the resurgence of geopolitics as a force in international relations, looking in particular at the US-China-Russia triangular relationship. Class lectures and discussions will address the big picture of global resource competition, focusing in particular on energy and water; in addition, each student will become especially knowledgeable about one *particular* aspect of this topic and will write a research paper on it.

REQUIRED TEXTS

Jared Diamond. *Collapse: How Societies Choose to Fail or Succeed.* Viking, 2005.

Michael Klare. *Blood and Oil: The Danger and Consequences of America's Growing Dependence on Foreign Oil.* Holt, 2005.

Marq de Villiers. *Water: the Fate of Our Most Precious Resource.* Mariner Books, 2001.

James G. Speth and Peter M. Haas. *Global Environmental Governance.* Island Press, 2006.

COURSE SCHEDULE

Week 1

Session 1: Introduction to the Course

Session 2: The Global Predicament
Speth and Haas, *Global Environmental Governance,* chapter 2.
Diamond, *Collapse,* pages 1–15.

Week 2

Session 1: Is Easter Island an Apt Metaphor for "Spaceship Earth"?
Diamond, *Collapse,* chapter 2.

Session 2: The Historical Record of Resource Competition and Conflict
Diamond, *Collapse,* chapter 4.

Week 3

Session 1: The Historical Record of Resource Competition and Conflict (cont.)
Diamond, *Collapse,* chapters 5 and 8 (skim chapter 7 if you can).

Session 2: Successful Responses to Adversity
Diamond, *Collapse,* chapter 9.

Week 4

Session 1: Successful Responses to Adversity (cont.)
Diamond, *Collapse,* chapter 9.

Session 2: The Past as Present
Diamond, *Collapse,* chapters 10 and 11.

Week 5

Session 1: The Past as Present (cont.)
Diamond, *Collapse,* chapter 12.

Session 2: The Global Energy Dilemma
Klare, *Blood and Oil,* chapters 1 and 2.

Week 6

Session 1: The Global Energy Dilemma
Klare, *Blood and Oil,* chapter 3.

Session 2: Did the US Invade Iraq for Its Oil?
Klare, *Blood and Oil,* chapter 4.

Week 7

Session 1: Did the US Invade Iraq for Its Oil? (cont.)
Klare, *Blood and Oil,* chapter 4.

Session 2: The Global Struggle over Oil and Natural Gas
Klare, *Blood and Oil,* chapter 5.

Week 8

Session 1: The Global Struggle over Oil and Natural Gas (cont.)
Klare, *Blood and Oil,* chapter 6.

Session 2: Alternatives to Oil Conflict
Klare, *Blood and Oil,* chapter 7.

Week 9

Session 1: Is Water the Next Oil?
de Villiers, *Water,* chapters 1–3.

Session 2: Is Water the Next Oil? (cont.)
de Villiers, *Water,* chapters 4, 7, and 8.

Week 10

Session 1: Global Water Politics
de Villiers, *Water,* chapters 11–13.

Session 2: Global Water Politics (cont.)
de Villiers, *Water,* chapters 14–15.

Week 11

Session 1: Alternatives to Water Conflict
de Villiers, *Water,* chapter 16.

Session 2: Devising Global Solutions to Global Problems
Speth and Haas, *Global Environmental Governance,* chapter 3.

Week 12

Session 1: Devising Global Solutions to Global Problems (cont.)
Speth and Haas, *Global Environmental Governance,* chapters 4 and 5.

Session 2: Devising Global Solutions to Global Problems (cont.)
Speth and Haas, *Global Environmental Governance,* chapter 6.

Week 13

Session 1: Wrap Up, Last Class

Session 2: Term Papers Due

TEACHING NOTES

Students are expected to participate in class, come to class having read assignments, and read a daily newspaper or listen to National Public Radio.

Students are also required to complete a research project. In the fourth week of the semester, they turn in a one-page research proposal describing the topic of the project and the publications or websites they intend to consult. Since they are expected to draw on primary research materials (UN reports, government documents, specialized studies, etc.), they must choose a topic that is specific enough to acquire a command of the basic literature in the field without being overwhelmed by a mass of data. For example, they should choose "water disputes in the Nile River basin," not "water disputes in the Middle East." A list of suggested research topics follows.

Then, approximately halfway through the semester, they submit a ten-page (double-spaced) research paper on the origins and nature of the problem they have chosen to investigate. *This constitutes the first half of the final paper* and will be returned to them with considerable feedback, allowing them to make improvements before resubmitting for a final grade.

At the conclusion of the semester, students submit a twenty-page research paper on the topic of study. It will incorporate the revised text of the background paper submitted earlier, plus a new section focusing on efforts to solve the problem and proposals for further action. It should conclude with the student's suggestions for resolution of the problem. Each student should attach maps, tables, and charts as appropriate, along with a bibliography and footnotes or endnotes.

Possible term paper topics: These are suggestions only; students need not select a topic from this list, but should choose a topic of a similar nature:

1. Water conflict in the Nile River basin (or Jordan, Indus, Tigris/Euphrates, Ganges, Mekong, Colorado, Rio Grande, etc.).
2. Oil politics in the US-Venezuelan (or US-Iranian, US-Russian) relationship.
3. The role of oil in the current Iraqi insurgency.
4. The US role in guarding Colombian oil pipelines.
5. Energy-related territorial disputes in the Caspian Sea (or South China Sea).
6. The Japanese-Chinese struggle over natural gas in the East China Sea.
7. Russia's natural gas politics in Ukraine (Europe, the Baltic states, etc.).
8. Oil-related conflict in Sudan.
9. Ethnic unrest and oil production in Nigeria.
10. The resource dimensions of the Uighur revolt in Xinjiang, China.
11. The international politics of the Chad-Cameroon (or Baku-Ceyhan) pipeline.
12. The international politics of the proposed Iran-Pakistan-India gas pipeline.
13. China's energy needs and its geopolitical activism in Central Asia (or Iran).
14. China's pursuit of African (or Venezuelan) energy and its implications for the United States.
15. The international implications of Japan's growing reliance on nuclear energy.
16. The international implications of the 2006 US-India deal over nuclear energy.
17. Deforestation and timber conflict in Amazonia (or the Congo, Borneo, etc.).
18. Multinational mining and internal conflict in Indonesian Papua (or New Guinea).
19. The conflict over coltan mining in the Congo.
20. Land conflict in Zimbabwe (or Chiapas, Kenya, etc.).
21. Fisheries conflict in the North Atlantic (or other international fisheries).
22. The resource dimensions of native peoples' struggles in the United States, Canada, or Mexico (e.g., disputes over uranium mining on Native American reservations).

13.6 Militarization of Daily Life

Kelly Dietz
Ithaca College

COURSE DESCRIPTION

Introductory and midlevel undergraduate course. Adaptable for upper-level undergraduates.

How do fashion trends and Hollywood films reflect, shape, and distort our understanding and experience of militarization? Why do some people welcome military recruiters into their homes, schools, and neighborhoods, whereas others try to keep them out? We sometimes hear what war is like for communities caught in the cross fire, but what is life like for communities "hosting" military forces far from the front lines? How is our relationship to citizens of other countries shaped by the long-term presence of US military bases in their communities? If control over the military is the hallmark of a sovereign state, what are the implications of an increasingly powerful private military industry?

This course will address these and other questions in order to better understand our relationship to state power as individuals, as citizens, and as members of local and global communities. In theory, as citizens we recognize the government's legitimate control over the use of force. Yet, the greatest manifestation of this force—the military—is often "visible" to us only in times of war. The multiple ways the institution of the military and militarism shape the lives of individuals and, indeed, whole societies typically go unnoticed because the militarization of daily life is taken for granted.

The course takes a broad view of militarization as an everyday peace process. From fashion trends, family relations, and Hollywood films to recruitment in schools and the siting of military bases, we examine the ways in which people and communities become objects of militarization. We pay particular attention to how and why this is collectively embraced by some and resisted by others. Through readings, films, and your own experiences, we explore the processes and practices that give rise to and sustain militarization in our day-to-day lives. We look at a range of phenomena that reveal, challenge, or reframe the seemingly straightforward relationship between states and citizens and the ways in which we are all complicit in the militarization of daily life.

SUGGESTED TEXTS FOR UPPER-LEVEL STUDENTS

As currently designed, the course does not rely on a few key books but rather on a wide variety of books, journals, and films. To structure the course for upper-level undergraduate students, I suggest incorporating lengthier portions of one or more of the following texts.

Amilcar Antonio Barreto. *Vieques, the Navy, and Puerto Rican Politics.* Gainesville: University Press of Florida, 2002.

Cynthia Enloe. *Maneuvers: The International Politics of Militarizing Women's Lives.* Berkeley: University of California Press, 2000.

Catherine Lutz. "Introduction: Making War at Home." In *Homefront: A Military City and the American Twentieth Century,* by Catherine Lutz. New York: Beacon Press, 2002.

Laura McEnaney. *Civil Defense Begins at Home: Militarization Meets Everyday Life in the Fifties.* Princeton, NJ: Princeton University Press, 2000.

Katharine Moon. *Sex Among Allies.* New York: Columbia University Press, 1997.

Christopher Sandars. *America's Overseas Garrisons.* Oxford: Oxford University Press, 2000.

Peter Singer. *Corporate Warriors: The Rise of the Privatized Military Industry.* Ithaca, NY: Cornell University Press, 2003.

COURSE SCHEDULE

Part 1: The Militarization of Popular Culture

Week 1: Introduction: Militarization as a Process

Enloe, chapter 1.

Hector Saldana. "All Things Military Are Cool: War on Terrorism Spurs Big Shift in Pop Culture," *San Antonio Express-News,* December 16, 2001.

Week 2: Militainment and Military Chic: Locating Ourselves in the Production, Packaging, Branding, and Consumption of the American Military

Roger Stahl. "Have You Played the War on Terror?" *Critical Studies in Media Communication* 23, no. 2 (June 2006).

Michael Macedonia. "Games Soldiers Play." *IEEE Spectrum* 2002 (March).

William L. Hamilton. "Toymakers Study Troops, and Vice Versa." *New York Times,* March 30, 2003.

Week 3: Militainment: Images and Imaginations of War on the Home Front

Hollywood and the Pentagon, produced and directed by Maria Pia Mascaro and Jean-Marie Barrere, CAPA, DVD, 2003.

Tom Pollard. "The Hollywood War Machine." *New Political Science* 24, no. 1 (2002).

Karen Hall. "False Witness: Combat Entertainment and the Training of Citizens." In *The Image and the Witness*, edited by Frances Guerin and Roger Hallas. London: Wallflower Press, 2007.

Part 2: The Militarization of Social Institutions

Week 4: State, Citizen, and the (Un)Making of the "All Volunteer" Military, Part 1

Monroe Mann. *To Benning and Back: The Making of a Citizen Soldier*, vol. 1. Touchstone, 2002, chapters 1–4.

Charles Tilly. "War Making and State Making as Organized Crime." In *Bringing the State Back In*, edited by Peter Evans, Dietrich Rueschemeyer, and Theda Skocpol. Cambridge: Cambridge University Press, 1985.

David R. Segal. "Race, Gender and the United States Military." In *Recruiting for Uncle Sam: Citizenship and Military Manpower Policy*, by David R. Segal. Lawrence: University of Kansas Press, 1989. Read the introduction and an excerpt.

Population Reference Bureau. "America's Military Population." *Population Bulletin* 59, no. 4 (December 2004).

Week 5: State, Citizen and the (Un)Making of the "All Volunteer" Military, Part 2

Elliot Abrams and Andrew J. Bacevich. "Citizens and Soldiers: Citizenship. Culture, and Military Service." *Parameters* 31, no. 2 (Summer 2001).

Ilene Rose Feinman. "Feminist Antimilitarism/Feminist Egalitarian Militarism" and "The Soldier in the State." In *Citizenship Rites: Feminist Soldiers and Feminist Antimilitarists*, by Ilene Rose Feinman. New York: New York University Press, 2000.

US Citizenship and Immigration Services. 2004. *Military Naturalizations*. Department of Homeland Security Press Office, October 11.

"Green-Card Warriors: Military Service Eases Road to US Citizenship." *Tuscon Citizen*, December 4, 2004.

Edward Wong. "Swift Road for US Citizen Soldiers Already Fighting in Iraq." *New York Times*, August 9, 2005.

Week 6: Citizenship and the Military in Schools, Part 1

US Department of Education. "Armed Forces Recruiter Access to Students and Student Recruiting Information." Section 9528 of *No Child Left Behind Act of 2001*, www.ed.gov/policy/elsec/leg/esea02/pg112.html.

Stuart Tannock. "Is 'Opting Out' Really an Answer? Schools, Militarism, and the Counter-Recruitment Movement in Post–September 11 United States at War." *Social Justice* 32, no. 3 (2005). Can be purchased online.

Lesley Bartlett and Catherine Lutz. "Disciplining Social Difference: Some Cultural Politics of Military Training in Public High Schools." *Urban Review* 30, no. 2 (June 1998).

Week 7: Citizenship and the Military in Schools, Part 2

Invite guest speakers (on different days): a recruiter from a local US Army recruiting station and a counter-recruitment activist.

Christian Davenport. "The Mission." *Washington Post,* August 8, 2004.

Read US Army website and its page on benefits, http://www.goarmy.com/flindex.jsp and http://www.goarmy.com/benefits/index.jsp?hmref=tn.

Read selections from Friends of William Blake Society, "New Yorkers' Guide to Recruitment," www.counterrecruitmentguide.org.

Browse the website of Anti-Flag, a punk-rock band active in counter recruitment, http://www.militaryfreezone.org/.

Week 8: The Militarization of Family and Community

McEnaney, *Civil Defense Begins at Home* ("Introduction" and "Militarizing Domesticity, Domesticating War").

Lutz, *Homefront* ("Making War at Home" and "Many Reserve Armies").

Tara Copp. "US Bases Already Jockeying to Stay Off 2005 Base Closure List." *Scripps Howard News Service,* February 14, 2004.

Gregory Hooks and Chad Smith. "The Treadmill of Destruction: National Sacrifice Areas and Native Americans." *American Sociological Review* 69 (2004): 558–576.

Peter Eisler. "Pollution Cleanups Pits Pentagon Against Regulators." *USA Today,* October 14, 2004.

US Department of Defense. "Pentagon Is a Good Steward of the Environment: Response to *USA Today* Article." www.denix.osd.mil/denix/Public/News/OSD/Success/GoodSteward/GoodSteward.html. The article is a response to the one by Peter Eisler.

Week 9: Who Needs Citizens?
The Privatization of Military Service

Singer, *Corporate Warriors* ("An Era of Corporate Warriors?" and "Public Ends, Private Military Means?").

Nancy Updike. "I'm from the Private Sector and I'm Here to Help." In *This American Life,* radio documentary hosted by Ira Glass, Chicago Public Radio, June 4, 2004. http://www.thisamericanlife.org/Radio_Episode.aspx?sched=1031.

Week 10: The Military Industrial Complex

Why We Fight, directed by Eugene Jarecki, BBC Storeyville, DVD, 2005.

Dwight D. Eisenhower. "Farewell Address," January 17, 1961.

Ismael Hossein-Zadeh. "The Military-Industrial Giant." In *The Political Economy of US Militarism,* by Ismael Hossein-Zadeh. New York: Palgrave, 2006.

Read daily defense contracts of the Department of Defense, www.defense link.mil/Contracts/.

Nicholas Turse. "The Military-Academic Complex: Who's the Real National Champion?" TomDispatch.com, April 28, 2004. http://www.common dreams.org/views04/0428-08.htm.

Week 11: The Military-Industrial Complex in a Globalizing World

Singer, *Corporate Warriors* ("Market Dynamism and Global Security Disruptions").

John Feffer. "Globalization and Militarization." *Foreign Policy in Focus* 7, no. 1 (February 2002).

Renae Merle. "US Increasingly Looks Abroad for Competitive Defense Contracts." *Washington Post,* March 8, 2005.

Bryan Bender. "Major Arms Soar to Twice Pre-9/11 Cost." *Boston Globe,* August 19, 2006.

Part 3: US Military Bases Overseas

Week 12: Where Are We, and What Are We Doing There? (Or: Is the US an Empire?)

Read global map of US overseas bases, PDF file, http://respectsacredland .org/no-us-bases/.

White House. *The National Security Strategy of the United States of America,* 2006. Read excerpts. www.whitehouse.gov/nsc/nss/2006/nss2006.pdf.

Christopher Sandars, *America's Overseas Garrisons,* "Postwar Developments," in the introduction.

Chalmers Johnson. "Empire of Bases." In *Sorrows of Empire: Militarism, Secrecy and the End of the Republic,* by Chalmers Johnson. New York: Metropolitan Books, 2004.

Rachel Cornwell and Andrew Wells. "Deploying Insecurity?" *Peace Review* 11, no. 3 (1999).

Week 13: Beyond State Sovereignty: The Colonial Politics of Overseas Basing

Christopher Sandars. "The Colonial Dimension." In *America's Overseas Garrisons,* by Christopher Sandars. Oxford: Oxford University Press, 2000. Read excerpts.

Barreto, *Vieques, the Navy, and Puerto Rican Politics* ("Introduction").

Stealing a Nation, directed by John Pilger, Granada Television, DVD, 2004, 56 minutes.

Read US Navy website for its base on the island of Diego Garcia. www.dg.navy.mil/2006/html/.htm. Read "General Information" and "Island History."

Week 14: Overseas Bases and Local Livelihoods, Part 1: The Sex Industry

Cynthia Enloe. "Base Women." In *Bananas, Beaches and Bases: Making Feminist Sense of International Politics,* by Cynthia Enloe. Berkeley: University of California Press, 2001.

Moon, *Sex Among Allies* ("Preface" and "Partners in Prostitution").

Sarah Williams. "Hospitality—What Price? The US Navy at Subic Bay and the Women's Response." In *The Prostitution of Sexuality,* edited by Kathleen Barry. New York: New York University Press, 1995, 235.

Week 15: Overseas Bases and Local Livelihoods, Part 2: Boom and Bust

Gavin McCormack. "Tokyo's War with Its Peace Prefecture." *Japan Focus,* November 2006.

Development with Destruction, produced by Television for the Environment and Television Trust for the Enviroment, DVD, 2004, 23 minutes.

Julia Yonetani. "Playing Base Politics in a Global Strategic Theater." *Critical Asian Studies* 33, no. 1 (2001).

"International Grassroots Summit on Military Base Cleanup." *Foreign Policy in Focus,* Institute for Policy Studies, 2001, www.fpif.org/bascleanup/index.html. Read "Introduction" and "Country Reports."

TEACHING NOTES

This course introduces undergraduate students to the subject of militarization as a process related to, but distinct from, war and conflict. I find that this approach to militarization captures students' interest and provides them with a new lens through which to view social structures and institutions they typically take for granted (e.g., popular culture, education, citizenship, international relations).

The course is divided into three main parts. The first two parts focus on aspects of militarization within American society. Once students have a better understanding of how American society and their daily lives are militarized, the third part of the course explores how US foreign policy, and specifically the presence of US military bases overseas, militarizes the lives of others. I find that students are intrigued but perplexed by the idea that their *daily* lives are militarized. I deliberately begin with popular culture because it is both familiar and of great interest to most students. In order to help them understand the "taken-for-grantedness" of militarization, the first assignment asks students to visit a local shopping center or "big box" store to look for different examples of consumer products they think reflect the process of militarization. Students are required to take detailed "field notes" to prepare for class discussion and writing up their observations. I also have students keep a weekly "Militarization of Daily Life" journal in which they write about observations in their own daily lives or stories in the news that they think reflect the process of militarization. Each student presents something from his or her journal once during the semester. This successfully serves as a valuable source of material for our class discussions and students' other writing.

14

Conflict Transformation and Conflict Resolution

THE IDEA OF CONFLICT TRANSFORMATION HAS RISEN RAPIDLY TO prominence over the last fifteen to twenty years as an alternative or a complement to such concepts as conflict resolution, conflict reduction, or conflict management. Prominence does not mean, however, that "conflict transformation" has replaced other kinds of language, nor has prominence yielded a single, simple, or agreed definition. But conflict transformation does exhibit a few key characteristics of its own in the way it is employed, whether by an international array of nongovernmental organizations (NGOs) or by state actors. Students and practitioners of conflict transformation generally agree that conflict is not necessarily negative. Rather, it can be an opportunity for positive social change, one that expands the goal beyond ending, managing, reducing, or resolving conflict and develops a broad and forward-looking vision for change. The idea of conflict transformation has also gained some defining characteristics by virtue of having arisen alongside, and often in the context of, the intrastate conflicts characteristic of the period since the late 1980s. Conflict transformation practitioners are especially alert, then, to conflict as complex and many-faceted and to the role of identity issues (principally nationality, ethnicity, and religion) in both conflict and its transformation.

Of these seven syllabuses, four (Patrick G. Coy on reconciliation and transitional justice, Mohammed Abu-Nimer on postconflict reconciliation and justice, Craig Zelizer on peacebuilding, and Anthony Wanis–St. John on comparative peace processes) make explicit use of the language of transformation. Ironically, Howard Zehr (on restorative justice) and John Paul Lederach (on the call and character of the peacebuilder) do not speak directly of transformation, but both men have been prominently associated with developing and advocating conflict transformation. What they do in the courses described here is deeply rooted in that idea. The syllabus for "International Negotiation: Theories and Practices," taught by Cecilia

Albin, Jonathan Hall, Kristine Höglund, and Niklas Swanström, might seem most like a conventional international relations course, but their work repeatedly intersects with characteristic conflict transformation concerns and approaches. They "examine not only the official negotiation process, but also the important functions of prenegotiation, second-track diplomacy and postagreement negotiations," which takes them far beyond state actors in state-to-state negotiations. They are attentive to culture and ethnicity, and five of their six case studies involve complex and protracted intrastate, or contested-state, conflicts in which combinations of nationality, ethnicity, and religion play a prominent part.

14.1 Reconciliation Versus Revenge

Patrick G. Coy
Kent State University

COURSE DESCRIPTION

Upper-level undergraduate course in peace studies and conflict studies.

We are studying one of the fastest-growing, most relevant, and fascinating developments in the arena where human rights, conflict resolution, and political science intersect: "transitional justice" and the "politics of memory." That is one reason this course can easily be cross-listed with applied conflict management and political science. Another is that transitional justice and the politics of memory refer to those temporary civil, political, and legal processes that both civil society and governments establish to negotiate a pathway from widespread violence and tyranny to relative peace and democracy. That is where intense suffering and partial healing coalesce, where massive political repression gives way to modest social reconciliation, and where crippled political institutions are repaired so that justice and the rule of law may be partially restored. At least that is the theory, and the hope.

We critically examine apologies, forgiveness, reconciliation, truth commissions, amnesties, reparations, commemorations, and memorials, often with reference to how these mechanisms have been used in specific conflict transformation settings.

A two-page, double-spaced, typewritten and stapled response paper on required readings is due six times throughout the semester. At least one of the response papers must be from the *Mea Culpa* book listed below. In a couple of paragraphs, describe what you thought were the central arguments and most significant points made in the reading(s). The remainder, and majority, of the response paper should focus on your reactions to the reading(s), including your critical analysis of the material and your personal responses to the material. Proper grammar, spelling, and punctuation are expected. To help ensure productive class discussions of the assigned readings, response papers are due at class time on the day the reading is assigned and may not be handed in after that class. No electronic submissions are accepted. Please plan accordingly. If there are two readings assigned, respond to both of them. If there are three or more assigned, respond to the majority of them.

You will also write a research paper of fourteen to sixteen pages in length, excluding bibliography and notes. In the third week of class, you will turn in a one-page research paper description proposal. In week 5, a three-page project description (with sources) is due. In week 9, turn in a detailed four- to five-page outline, plus a full bibliography. A complete draft of the paper is due in week 12, and the final version of the paper is due in Week 15.

REQUIRED TEXTS

Martha Minow. *Between Vengeance and Forgiveness: Facing History After Genocide and Mass Violence*. Boston, MA: Beacon Press, 1998.

Nicholas Tavuchis. *Mea Culpa: A Sociology of Apology and Reconciliation*. Stanford, CA: Stanford University Press, 1991.

Charles Villa-Vicencio and Wilhelm Verwoerd, eds. *Looking Back, Reaching Forward*. London: Zed Books, 2000.

Nigel Bigger, ed. *Burying the Past: Making Peace and Doing Justice After Civil Conflict*. Washington, DC: Georgetown University Press, 2001.

Articles listed in the course schedule.

COURSE SCHEDULE

Week 1: Human Rights, Protracted Conflicts, and Transitional Justice

"International Declaration on Human Rights," http://www.un.org/Overview/rights.html. Print the declaration and read it multiple times. Note your reactions and observations. Bring those reactions and observations, along with the declaration, to class.

"United Nations International Covenant on Civil and Political Rights," http://www.hrweb.org/legal/cpr.html. Skim this document.

Peter Harris and Ben Reill, eds. *Democracy and Deep-Rooted Conflict: Options for Negotiators*. International Institute for Democracy and Electoral Assistance, 1998, http://www.idea.int/publications/democracy_and_deep_rooted_conflict/ebook_contents.htm. Read chapters 1 through 2.5.

Week 2: Promoting Human Rights and Nonviolent Transitions

Liam Mahony. "Peace Brigades International: Nonviolence in Action." In *Nonviolent Intervention Across Borders: A Recurrent Vision,* edited by Yeshua Moser-Puangsuwan and Thomas Weber. Honolulu: University of Hawaii Press, 2000, 133–147.

Patrick G. Coy. "Cooperative Accompaniment and Peace Brigades International in Sri Lanka." In *Transnational Social Movements and Global Politics: Solidarity Beyond the State,* edited by Jackie Smith, Charles Chatfield, and Ron Pagnucco. Syracuse, NY: Syracuse University Press, 1997, 81–100.

Patrick Coy. "Going Where We Otherwise Would Not Have Gone: Nonviolent Protective Accompaniment and Election Monitoring in Sri Lanka." *Fellowship* 61, nos. 9–10 (September–October 1995).

Browse the website of Peace Brigades International, http://www.peacebrigades.org/.

Week 3: Vengeance and Forgiveness

Minow, *Between Vengeance and Forgiveness,* foreword, introduction, and chapter 1.

Jean Bethke Elshtain. "Politics and Forgiveness." In *Burying the Past: Making Peace and Doing Justice After Civil Conflict,* edited by Nigel Biggar. Washington, DC: Georgetown University Press, 2001.

Week 4: The Nuremberg Trials and the International Criminal Tribunal for Rwanda

Minow, *Between Vengeance and Forgiveness,* chapters 2 and 3.

Gary Jonathan Bass. "Nuremberg." In *Stay the Hand of Vengeance: The Politics of War Crimes Tribunals,* by Gary Jonathan Bass. Princeton, NJ: Princeton University Press, 2000, 147–205.

Peter Uvin and Charles Mironko. "Western and Local Approaches to Justice in Rwanda." *Global Governance* 9 (2003): 219–231.

Week 5: The International Criminal Court and the United States

United Nations:

Overview document on the ICC, http://www.un.org/law/icc/general/overview.htm.

FAQ About the ICC, http://www.un.org/News/facts/iccfact.htm.

Human Rights Watch:

FAQ about the ICC, http://www.hrw.org/campaigns/icc/qna.htm.

"Myths and Facts About the ICC," http://www.hrw.org/campaigns/icc/facts.htm.

"Q & A About the ICC and the US," http://www.hrw.org/campaigns/icc/usqna.htm.

"US Hague Invasion Act Becomes Law," http://www.hrw.org/press/2002/08/aspa080302.htm.

"US Campaign for Permanent Immunity Fails," http://www.hrw.org/press/2002/07/icc071202.htm.

"US Should End Bully Tactics Against Court," http://hrw.org/press/2003/07/usa070103.htm. "Why the US Needs this Court," by Steve Crawshaw, http://www.hrw.org/editorials/2003/icc061503.htm.

US Department of State: "American Justice and the ICC," by John Bolton, http://www.state.gov/t/us/rm/25818.htm.

"Frequently Asked Questions About the U.S. Government's Policy Regarding the International Criminal Court (ICC)," http://www.state.gov/t/pm/rls/fs/23428.htm.

"FAQ About US Policy and the ICC," http://www.state.gov/p/9949.htm.

Lauren Comiteau. "In Dutch with America." *Chicago Tribune,* July 14, 2002, http://www.converge.org.nz/pma/cra0682.htm.

Kenneth Roth. "Resist Washington's Arm Twisting." *International Herald Tribune,* September 30, 2002, http://www.commondreams.org/views02/0930-02.htm.

Week 6: Comparative Perspectives on Truth Commissions

Minow, *Between Vengeance and Forgiveness,* 52–90.

Priscilla Hayner. "Five Illustrative Commissions" and "Sixteen Less Prominent Commissions." In *Unspeakable Truths: Facing the Challenge of the Truth Commission.* London: Routledge, 2001.

Week 7: Historical Truth Commissions in the United States for Race Crimes: Rosewood and Tulsa

K. Nunn, "Rosewood." In *When Sorry Isn't Enough,* edited by Roy Brooks. New York: New York University Press, 1999.

"Tulsa Panel Seeks Truth from 1921 Race Riot." *CNN,* August 3, 1999, http://www.cnn.com/US/9908/03/tulsa.riots.probe/.

Brent Staples. "Unearthing a Riot." *New York Times Magazine,* December 19, 1999, http://query.nytimes.com/gst/fullpage.html?res=9A04E5DD1E31F93AA25751C1A96F958260.

J. Yardley. "Panel Recommends Reparations in Long-Ignored Tulsa Race Riots." *New York Times,* February 5, 2000.

Renee Ruble. "Panel Recommends Reparations for Victims of 1921 Tulsa Race Riot." Associated Press, February 5, 2000, also available at http://www.commondreams.org/headlines/020500-01.htm.

Week 8: South Africa's Truth and Reconciliation Commission

Villa-Vicencio and Verwoerd, "Same Species, Different Animal: How South Africa Compares to Truth Commissions Worldwide," by Priscilla Hayner.

Villa-Vicencio and Verwoerd, "Getting on with Life: A Move Towards Reconciliation," by Charles Villa-Vicencio.

Biggar, "Restorative Justice in Social Context: The South African Truth and Reconciliation Commission," by Charles Villa-Vicencio.

Biggar, "National and Community Reconciliation: Competing Agendas in the South African Truth and Reconciliation Commission," by Hugo vad der Merwe.

View in class *Long Night's Journey into Day,* directed by Francis Reid and Deborah Hoffman, Iris Films, DVD, 2000.

Week 9: Amnesty and South Africa's Truth and Reconciliation Commission

Aryeh Neier. "The Trouble with Amnesty." In *War Crimes: Brutality, Genocide, Terror, and the Struggle for Justice,* by Aryeh Neier. New York: Times Books, 1998.

Villa-Vicencio and Verwoerd, "Justice Without Punishment: Guaranteeing Human Rights in Transitional Societies," by Paul Van Zyl.

Week 10: The Meanings of Apology and Third Parties and Apologies

Tavuchis, *Mea Culpa,* 1–68.

Week 11: The Multiple Modes of Apologies

Tavuchis, *Mea Culpa,* 68–124.

Week 12: Reparations for Japanese American Internment and Slavery in the United States

Minow, *Between Vengeance and Forgiveness,* 91–117.

Patrick Coy. "When People Lived in Horse Stalls." *Fellowship,* July–August 1988.

R. Brooks, ed. *When Sorry Isn't Enough.* New York: New York University Press, 1999:

Sandra Taylor, "The Internment of Americans of Japanese Ancestry."

"Report of the Commission on Wartime Relocation and Internment of Civilians."

Daniel Rogers, "Relocation, Redress, and the Report."

Leslie Hatamiya, "Institutions and Interests Groups."

T. Hall, "Defense of Congressional Resolution Apologizing for Slavery." *Congressional Record,* June 18, 1997.

J. Conyers, "The Commission to Study Reparations Proposals." *Congressional Record,* 1999.

"Clinton Opposes Slavery Apology." *US News and World Report,* April 6, 1998.

Ronald Slazberger and Mary Turck, eds. *Reparations for Slavery: A Reader.* Lanham, MD: Rowman and Littlefield, 2004:

David Horowitz, "The Latest Civil Rights Disaster: Ten Reasons Why Reparations are a Bad Idea—and Racist Too."

Ernest Allen, Jr. and Robert Chrisman, "Ten Reasons: A Response to David Horowitz."

Special guest speaker with personal experience of the internment and reparations process.

Week 13: Indigenous Claims and Reparations

Roy Brooks. *When Sorry Isn't Enough.* New York: New York University Press, 1999:

Lawrence Armand French, "Native American Reparations."

Turning Hawk and American Horse, "The Massacre at Wounded Knee."

Palaneapope, "How the Indians Are Victimized by Government Agents and Soldiers."

Naomi Mezey, "The Distribution of Wealth, Sovereignty, and Culture Through Indian Gaming."

R. Howard. "Why It's Time for Ottawa to Apologize." *Toronto Globe and Mail,* July 3, 1997.

E. Anderssen. "Natives Finally Get Ottawa's Apology." *Toronto Globe and Mail,* January 7, 1998.

Week 14: Facing History with Commemorations and Monuments, Including Kent State

Minow, *Between Vengeance and Forgiveness,* chapter 6.

Jutta Weldes and Mark Laffey. "US Foreign Policy, Public Memory and Autism: Representing September 11th and May 4th." *Cambridge Review of International* Affairs 17, no. 2 (July 2004).

Week 15: Class "Barometer" Exercise on Issues Raised in Course

TEACHING NOTES

This course is best taught as a seminar focused on in-depth discussions and small group work. Assignments, of course, vary, but as a seminar, the course requires considerable writing, including a research project and a take-home exam.

To direct students to more in-depth information on trasitional justice, see these important and useful websites:

- International Center for Transitional Justice, http://www.ictj.org/default.asp.
- U.S. Institute of Peace, Rule of Law Program, http://www.usip.org/rol.html.
- U.S. Institute of Peace, Truth Commissions, http://www.usip.org/library/tc/tc_coi.html.
- U.S. Institute of Peace, Trauma and Conflict Web Links, http://www.usip.org/library/topics/trauma.html.
- United Nations, International Law, http://www.un.org/law/index.html.
- South Africa's Truth and Reconciliation Commission, http://www.doj.gov.za/trc/index.html.
- Coalition for an International Criminal Court, http://www.iccnow.org/.

• War Crimes Research Portal, http://www.law.case.edu/war-crimes-research-portal/.

Much of the best information is *not* available online; much has been published in journals and books and is easily available in libraries. Here are three online bibliographies that will direct you to both online and paper resources:

• The Institute for Justice and Reconciliation (located in South Africa), http://www.ijr.org.za/research.html.

• The Transitional Justice Project in Berlin has published a useful bibliography by Gunnar Theissen on transitional justice, see http://userpage.fu-berlin.de/~theissen/biblio/.

• Catherine Morris's bibliography, http://www.peacemakers.ca/bibliography/bib26reconciliation.html.

14.2 Reconciliation and Justice in Postconflict Context

Mohammed Abu-Nimer
American University

COURSE DESCRIPTION

Upper-level undergraduate or graduate course in peace studies and conflict studies.

This course aims to expose students to the complexity and multidimensional aspects of the relationship between reconciliation and justice in a postconflict context. It also aims at developing a deeper understanding among students of the challenges involved in designing and applying a reconciliation project in a development context.

A number of political agreements have been negotiated in intractable conflict areas (South Africa, Northern Ireland, Israel-Palestine, Guatemala, Cambodia); however, both politicians and members of civil society organizations in these conflict areas struggle with ways to address the pressing need to reconcile historical animosity and the demand for justice. The fact that such efforts take place in a development context (countries in which economic, political, and social structure need to be rebuilt) does not make the task easier. The major questions this course will explore are:

• How does one go about resolving the tension between reconciliation and justice in a conflict situation?

• What roles do practices of forgiveness and healing play in reconciling political and social relationships in intergroup conflict?

• How does the need for economic development affect social peacebuilding (reconciliation)?

• What type of activities do development agencies and interveners use to address reconciliation? What models of intervention do they use?

The course will address the tension between the request for reconciliation, coexistence, and peace and the demand for justice. In the field of peace and conflict resolution, parties working for reconciliation often assume they must give up their demands for justice, or at least modify them in a way to accomplish the task of peace. Only recently have agreements been negotiated in deep-rooted conflicts such as Northern Ireland, Israel-Palestine, Guatemala, and South Africa, in which practitioners and policymakers began struggling with the need to restore local communities' relationships and reestablish harmony in cities and towns that were divided by the war.

Both development agencies and practitioners such as the Cooperative for Assistance and Relief Everywhere (CARE), Catholic Relief Services, Save the Children, and the United Nations High Commissioner for Refugees (UNCHR) find themselves facing the need to address issues related to social and psychological reconciliation, as well as classical development issues such as agriculture, small industries, and health. At the same time, peace workers in these areas begin dealing with questions such as this one: How can communities reconcile their relationships without addressing basic human needs of security, shelter, and food?

REQUIRED READING

Mohammed Abu-Nimer, ed. *Reconciliation, Justice, and Coexistence*. Lanham, MD: Rowman and Littlefield, 2001.

Alice Ackermann. "Reconciliation as a Peace-Building Process in Post War Europe: The Franco-German Case." *Peace and Change* 19, no. 3 (July 1994): 229–250.

Hizkias Assefa. *Peace and Reconciliation as a Paradigm*. Nairobi: ACIS Press, 1998.

Robert L. Rothstein. *After the Peace: Resistance and Reconciliation*. Boulder, CO: Lynne Rienner, 1999.

Colin Knox and Pádraic Quirk, eds. *Peace Building in Northern Ireland, Israel, and South Africa: Transition, Transformation, and Reconciliation*. New York: St. Martin's Press, 2000.

Nigel Biggar, ed. *Burying the Past: Making Peace and Doing Justice After Civil Conflict*. Washington, DC: Georgetown University Press, 2001.

Andrew Rigby. *Justice and Reconciliation After Violence*. Boulder, CO: Lynne Rienner, 2001.

RECOMMENDED READING

Ann Adelson. "Truth and Consequences." *Peace Magazine* (January–February 1999).

Ifi Amadiume and Abdullahi An-Na'im, eds. *The Politics of Memory: Truth, Healing and Social Justice*. London: Zed Books, 2000.

Harvey J. Langholtz, ed. *The Psychology of Peacekeeping*. Westport, CT: Praeger, 1998.

Pugh, Michael C., ed. *Regeneration of War-Torn Societies*. New York: St. Martin's Press, 2000.

COURSE SCHEDULE

Units 1–4: Reconciliation: Theoretical Foundations

Unit 1: Introductions, Syllabus Review, and Definitions: What is reconciliation?

Rigby, *Justice and Reconciliation After Violence,* chapter 1 ("Reconciliation and Forgiving the Past").

Unit 2: Reconciliation and Justice

Conditions for effective reconciliation, approaches and paradigms of reconciliation, and the cycle of reconciliation.

Abu-Nimer, *Reconciliation, Justice, and Coexistence:*
- Louis Kriesberg, "Changing Forms of Coexistence."
- Johan Galtung, "After Violence, Reconstruction, Reconciliation, and Resolution: Coping with Visible and Invisible Effects of War and Violence."
- Abu-Nimer et al., "The Long Road to Reconciliation."

Unit 3: After the Peace

Rothstein, *After the Peace: Resistance and Reconciliation:*
- Robert Rothstein, "After the Peace: Getting Past Maybe."
- Robert Rothstein, "Fragile Peace and Its Aftermath."
- Herbert Kelman, "Transforming the Relationship Between Former Enemies: A Social Psychological Analysis."

Recommended reading:
Hizkias Assefa. "The Meaning of Reconciliation." In *People Building Peace: 35 Inspiring Stories from Around the World,* edited by Pau Vantongeren et al. Utrecht: European Center for Conflict Prevention, 1999.

Unit 4: Sustainable Peace

Assefa, *Peace and Reconciliation as a Paradigm.*

Pugh, *Regeneration of War-Torn Societies:*
- John Cockell, "Conceptualizing Peacebuilding: Human Security and Sustainable Peace."

Rigby, *Justice and Reconciliation After Violence:*
- Chapter 2, "European Purges After World War II."

Units 5–10: The Reconciliation Process and the Quest for Justice: Some Challenging Dimensions

Week 5: Dealing with the Past

Biggar, *Burying the Past:*

Tuomas Forsberg, "The Philosophy and Practice of Dealing with the Past."
Martha Minow, "Innovating Responses to the Past."
Marie Smyth, "Putting the Past in Its Place: Issues of Victimhood and Reconciliation in Northern Ireland's Peace Process."
Terence McCaughey, "Northern Ireland: Burying the Hatchet, Not the Past."

Recommended reading:
Biggar, *Burying the Past:*
Stef Vandeginste, "Rwanda: Dealing with Genocide and Crimes Against Humanity in the Context of Armed Conflict and Failed Political Transition."

Abu-Nimer, *Reconciliation, Justice, and Coexistence:*
Amy Hubbard, "Understanding Majority and Minority Participation in Interracial and Interethnic Dialogue."

Unit 6: The Path to Justice
Retribution or restoration? In cases of genocide, can justice be served?

Abu-Nimer, *Reconciliation, Justice, and Coexistence:*
Joseph Montville, "Justice and the Burdens of History."

Biggar, *Burying the Past:*
Nigel Biggar, "Making Peace or Doing Justice: Must We Choose?"

Amadiume and An-Na'im, *The Politics of Memory:*
Nowrojee and Ralph, "Justice for Women Victims of Violence: Rwanda after the 1994 Genocide."

Rigby, *Justice and Reconciliation After Violence:*
Chapter 3, "Spain: Amnesty and Amnesia."

Recommended reading:
Pugh, *Regeneration of War-Torn Societies:*
Rama Mani, "The Rule of Law or the Rule of Might? Restoring Legal Justice in the Aftermath of Conflict."

Abu-Nimer, *Reconciliation, Justice, and Coexistence:*
Estrada-Hollenbeck, "The Attainment of Justice Through Restoration, Not Litigation."

Rigby, *Justice and Reconciliation After Violence:*
Chapter 4, "Truth and Justice as Far as Possible: The Latin America Experience."

Unit 7: The Psychology of Forgiveness

Biggar, *Burying the Past:*

Donald Shriver, "Where and When in Political Life Is Justice Served by Forgiveness?"

Jean Bethke Elshtain, "Politics and Forgiveness."

Abu-Nimer, *Reconciliation, Justice, and Coexistence:*

Joseph Montville, "Justice and the Burden of History."

Langholtz, *The Psychology of Peacekeeping:*

Tom Woodhouse, "Peacekeeping and the Psychology of Conflict Resolution."

Recommended reading:

Biggar, *Burying the Past:*

Brandon Hamber, "Does the Truth Heal? A Psychological Perspective on Political Strategies for Dealing with the Legacy of Political Violence."

Week 8: Political Agreements and Reconciliation

Reconciliation at macrosocial and macropolitical levels.

Abu-Nimer, *Reconciliation, Justice, and Coexistence:*

J. Lewis Rasmussen, "Negotiating Revolution: Toward Integrating Relationship Building and Reconciliation into Official Peace Negotiations."

Erin McCandless, "The Case of Land in Zimbabwe: Cause of Conflict, Foundation for Sustainable Peace."

Wendy Lambourne, "Justice and Reconciliation: Post Conflict Peacebuilding in Cambodia and Rwanda."

Langholtz, *The Psychology of Peacekeeping:*

Eileen Borris and Paul Diehl, "Forgiveness, Reconciliation, and the Contribution of International Peacekeeping."

Recommended reading:

Langholtz, *The Psychology of Peacekeeping.*

Fabrizio Pagani, "The Peace Process at its Culmination: The Reconciliation Election."

Gonzales Posse, "Post Conflict Peacebuilding and Making Efforts Count: Reconstruction, Elections, and Beyond."

Week 9: Cultural and Traditional Approaches to Reconciliation

Is there a generic cultural model for reconciliation? What are the different roles of justice in the reconciliation process?

Susan Collin Marks. "Ubuntu, The Spirit of Africa: Example for the World." In *Watching the Wind: Conflict Resolution During South Africa's Transition to Democracy,* by Susan Collin Marks. United States Institute of Peace Press, 2000.

Abu-Nimer, *Reconciliation, Justice, and Coexistence:*
Lisa Schirch, "Ritual Reconciliation: Transforming Identity/Reframing Conflict."
Hizkias Assefa, "Coexistence and Reconciliation in Northern Region of Ghana."

Week 10: Religious and Spiritual Approaches to Reconciliation: Forgiveness in Different Religions

Abu-Nimer, *Reconciliation, Justice, and Coexistence:*
Marc Gopin, "Forgiveness as an Element of Conflict Resolution in Religious Cultures: Walking the Tightrope of Reconciliation and Justice."

Rothstein, *After the Peace: Resistance and Reconciliation:*
Donald W. Shriver, "The Long Road to Reconciliation: Some Moral Stepping-Stones."

Recommended reading:
Redmond Fitzmaurice. "Other Religions and Reconciliation." In *Reconciliation in Religion and Society,* edited by Michael Hurley. Dufour Editions, 1994.

Units 11–13: Applied Examples of Reconciliation Projects in a Development Context: A Comparative Perspective

Unit 11: Reconciliation in Northern Ireland: The Post–Good Friday Agreement

Knox and Quirk, *Peace Building in Northern Ireland, Israel, and South Africa:*
Chapter 1, "The Comparative Context for Peace Building."
Chapter 2, "Northern Ireland: Macro Political Development."
Chapter 5, "Northern Ireland: Micro Grassroots Activities."

Rothstein, *After the Peace: Resistance and Reconciliation:*
Duncan Morrow, "Seeking Peace Amid the Memories of War: Learning from the Peace Process in Northern Ireland."

Recommended reading:
Abu-Nimer, *Reconciliation, Justice, and Coexistence:*
Mari Fitzduff, "The Challenge to History: Justice, Coexistence, and Reconciliation Work in Northern Ireland."

Rothstein, *After the Peace:*
Paul Arthur, "The Anglo-Irish Peace Process: Obstacles to Reconciliation."

Unit 12: Reconciliation in Israel-Palestine: Post-Oslo Reality

Rothstein, *After the Peace:*

Khalil Shakaki, "Internal Consequences of Unstable Peace: Psychological and Political Responses of the Palestinians."

Moshe Ma'oz, "The Oslo Agreements: Towards Arab-Jewish Reconciliation."

Knox and Quirk, *Peace Building in Northern Ireland, Israel, and South Africa:*

Chapter 4, "Israeli/Palestine: Macro Political Development."

Chapter 5, "Israeli/Palestine: Micro Grassroots Activities."

Rigby, *Justice and Reconciliation After Violence:*

Chapter 7, "Palestine: Collaboration and Its Consequences—A Worst-Case Scenario?"

Recommended reading:

Abu-Nimer, *Reconciliation, Justice, and Coexistence:*

Colin Knox and Pádraic Quirk, "Education for Coexistence in Israel: Potential and Challenges."

Unit 13: Reconciliation in South Africa: Post-TRC Challenges

Knox and Quirk, *Peace Building in Northern Ireland, Israel, and South Africa:*

Chapter 6, "South Africa: Macro Political Development."

Chapter 7, "South Africa: Micro Grassroots Activities."

Biggar, *Burying the Past:*

Villa-Vicencio, "Restorative Justice in Social Context: The South African Truth and Reconciliation Commission."

Abu-Nimer, *Reconciliation, Justice, and Coexistence:*

Hugo van der Merwe, "Reconciliation and Justice in South Africa: Lessons from the TRC's."

Knox and Quirk, *Peace Building in Northern Ireland, Israel, and South Africa:*

Chapter 8, "Conclusion Towards Peace Building."

Recommended reading:

Amadiume and An-Na'im, *The Politics of Memory:*

Mahmoud Mamdani, "The Truth According to TRC."

Rigby, *Justice and Reconciliation After Violence:*

Chapter 6, "South Africa: Amnesty in Return for Truth."

Unit 14: Conclusions

Presentations of research papers and findings.

Abu-Nimer, *Reconciliation, Justice, and Coexistence:*
Barry Hart, "Refugee Return in Bosnia and Hertzegovina: Coexistence Before Reconciliation."

Alice Akermann. "Reconciliation as Peacebuilding Process in Postwar Europe: The Franco-German Case." *Peace and Change* 19, no. 3 (1994).

Rigby, *Justice and Reconciliation After Violence:*
Chapter 9, "Toward a Culture of Reconciliation."

TEACHING NOTES

To help students study and prepare to take an active role in class, I ask for ten reading summaries of whole units in the semester. Each summary is two pages (single-spaced), highlighting interesting points, comparing articles, and expressing an informed opinion. In other words, the summary is an exercise in critiquing what they have read.

I require that each student participate in a Reconciliation Project. In pairs, students are expected to select a reconciliation project in a domestic or international context and contextualize that project in the theoretical framework of reconciliation.

Students are also expected to conduct a research paper using primary or secondary sources. The paper's topic can be on any case study or question that deals with reconciliation and justice in a postconflict or postagreement society.

14.3 Restorative Justice: The Promise, the Challenge

Howard Zehr
Eastern Mennonite University

COURSE DESCRIPTION

Upper-level undergraduate course or graduate course in peace and conflict studies.

This course will provide a critical introduction to the fundamental principles and practices of restorative justice. The course explores the needs and roles of key stakeholders (victims, offenders, communities, justice systems), outlines the basic principles and values of restorative justice, and introduces some of the primary models of practice. It also identifies challenges to restorative justice—the dangers, the pitfalls—as well as possible strategies to help prevent restorative justice from failing to live up to its promise.

As a case study, the course is organized around the issue of crime within a Western legal context. However, attention is given to applications and lessons from other contexts. Of particular interest is the contribution of traditional or indigenous approaches to justice, as well as their applications in postconflict situations.

This course is intended to provide critical awareness of the prevailing practice and philosophy of justice, including the experiences and needs of victims, offenders, and communities; restorative justice principles and practices; possible "new" applications; and potential problems and pitfalls in the field.

REQUIRED TEXTS

Howard Zehr. *Changing Lenses: A New Focus for Crime and Justice.* Herald Press, 2005.

Howard Zehr. *The Little Book of Restorative Justice.* Good Books, 2002.

Rupert Ross. *Returning to the Teachings: Exploring Aboriginal Justice.* Penguin, 1996.

David Cayley. *The Expanding Prison: The Crisis in Crime and Punishment and the Search for Alternatives.* House of Anansi, 1998.

Gerry Johnstone. *Restorative Justice: Ideas, Practices, Debates.* Willan Publishing, 2001.

Alan MacRae and Howard Zehr. *The Little Book of Family Group Conferencing: New Zealand Style.* Good Books, 2004.

Howard Zehr. *Transcending: Reflections of Crime Victims*. Good Books, 2001.

RECOMMENDED TEXTS

Lorraine Stutzman Amstutz and Judy Mullet. *The Little Book of Restorative Discipline for Schools*. Good Books, 2005.

Barb Toews. *The Little Book of Restorative Justice for People in Prison*. Good Books, 2006.

Kay Pranis. *The Little Book of Circle Processes*. Good Books, 2005.

Chris Marshall. *The Little Book of Biblical Justice*. Good Books, 2005.

Martha Minow. *Between Vengeance and Forgiveness*. Beacon Press, 1999.

Michael Hadley, ed. *The Spiritual Roots of Restorative Justice*. State University of New York Press, 2001.

Daniel Van Ness and Karen Heetderks Strong. *Restoring Justice*, 3rd ed. Anderson Publishing, 2006.

CLASS SCHEDULE

Session 1: Orientation to the Class and Issues

Session 2: What Does Justice Require for Victims?
Zehr, *Changing Lenses*, 11–32.
Zehr, *Transcending: Reflections of Crime Victims*. Read selectively.

Johnstone, *Restorative Justice*, 62–85. Johnstone will be used intensely toward the end of the course, but because he adds to the understanding of restorative justice, it is helpful to read as scheduled here.

Session 3: What Does Justice Require for/from Offenders?
Zehr, *Changing Lenses*, 33–59.
Cayley, *The Expanding Prison*, 1–121.
Johnstone, *Restorative Justice*, 87–134. Recommended.

Ross, *Returning to the Teachings*, chapter 6. Ross brings a very important perspective to this issue. This text is not assigned until later, but you may want to read ahead.

Session 4: What Does Justice Require for/from Communities? . . . and Offenders? (cont.)
Zehr, *Changing Lenses*, 63–94.
Cayley, *The Expanding Prison*, 123–164.

Zehr, *Doing Life: Reflections of Men and Women Serving Life Sentences*, Good Books, 1996. Recommended that you read selectively in *Doing Life*.

Session 5: What Does Justice Require?
Criminal Justice and Restorative Justice (Principles)

Zehr, Changing Lenses, 177–229.

Ross, Returning to the Teachings, 52–130 (preferably also 1–51).

Zehr, *The Little Book of Restorative Justice,* all. You may read this *after* this class, as a review.

John Braithwaite. "Restorative Justice and a Better Future." In *Restorative Justice Reader,* edited by Gerry Johnstone. Willan Publishing, 2003. Recommended.

Session 6: Restorative Justice and Victim-Offender Conferencing

Zehr, *Changing Lenses,* 158–174.

Cayley, *The Expanding Prison,* 167–237.

Session 7: Family Group Conferences

Zehr, *Changing Lenses,* 256–262.

MacRae and Zehr, *The Little Book of Family Group Conferencing,* all.

Session 8: Circle Processes

Ross, *Returning to the Teachings,* 1–51.

Cayley, *The Expanding Prison,* 239–294.

MacRae and Zehr, *The Little Book of Family Group Conferencing,* all (if not read for previous week).

Pranis, *The Little Book of Circle Processes.* Recommended.

Session 9: Indigenous and Religious Traditions

Zehr, *Changing Lenses,* 97–125. Also recommend 126–157.

Johnstone, *Restorative Justice,* 36–60. Also recommend 172–174.

Ross, *Returning to the Teachings,* 131–274. Review earlier sections as well.

Hadley, *Spiritual Roots of Restorative Justice,* essays on various religious traditions.

Session 10: Restorative Justice in Severe Violence, and Other Applications

Cayley, The Expanding Prison, 295–365.

Session 11: Restorative Justice and Large-Scale Wrongdoing

Browse the websites about truth commissions: www.truthcommission.org and http://www.doj.gov.za/trc/.

Minow, *Between Vengeance and Forgiveness.* Recommended.

Session 12: Work Group Reports

Session 13: Work Group Reports

Session 14: Critical Issues in Restorative Justice

Johnstone, *Restorative Justice,* 1–171. Parts of this have been assigned or recommended earlier.

Zehr, *Changing Lenses,* 232–236.

Session 15: Wrap-up

TEACHING NOTES

In addition to exams, assignments in this course include (1) an explanation assignment, (2) working groups, (3) and four options for a writing project.

Explanation assignment. Find someone who is not in this class and does not have a background in restorative justice. Describe restorative justice in your own words and solicit their feedback and questions. In a brief paper (two to four pages), summarize this experience, their reactions, and what, if anything, you learned about restorative justice and/or how to present it.

Working groups. During the course, each student will be part of a small group that will work together on an issue as it relates to restorative justice. Toward the end of the semester, the groups will present the results of their work to the class. Also, in a brief paper, each member (individually) should describe and reflect on the group process. Note that the paper is not a summary of the group's conclusions or report, but rather comments on the process. Also note that this project could be the basis for a course paper.

Writing project. Students choose one of four options for writing a standard academic paper, including notes and bibliography. The paper may build on the research in the working group. It is also possible for several people to collaborate on this paper.

Project Option 1: Restorative justice "audit." Evaluate an actual justice or justice-related program from a restorative framework. Briefly describe the program or approach and then assess ways it does and does not measure up to a restorative justice "yardstick." Suggest ways it does and does not point in a restorative direction and how it could become, or be part of, a more restorative approach.

Students are not expected to do a study of how well the program is doing in actual fact, although if information about that is available, it is of course relevant. Rather, they should look at how the program is conceived and designed and then do an "audit" in which they measure it against restorative justice principles. To do this project, they will need to develop, adopt, or adapt a restorative justice "yardstick," that is, a set of principles or criteria against which they will assess the program or approach.

Examples of possible topics include a school or church disciplinary procedure, a postconflict justice approach such as a truth commission, a specific restorative justice program, a traditional criminal justice program, their own tradition, or a specific case.

Project Option 2: Design a restorative process for a specific application or case. Students will pick a situation or case of harm or wrongdoing about which they can find sufficient information. They will assess the needs, resources, and context and then design a restorative process that is as *specific and realistic* as possible. (Susan Sharpe, *Restorative Justice*, may be helpful.)

Project Option 3: Evaluate uses of the term "restorative justice." In the last few years, the concept of restorative justice has become very popular in various countries and many arenas beyond criminal justice circles. To what extent is this use consistent with restorative justice philosophy? For this project, students conduct a form of literature review, locating and then evaluating the use of this term. To evaluate the use of the term, they will need to develop, adopt, or adapt a restorative justice "yardstick" of their own.

Papers should provide an overview of how the term is being used and then evaluate these uses according to the restorative justice criteria students have adopted or developed. In addition to the bibliographies provided for the course, they should use the Internet and other sources.

Project Option 4: A topic of the student's choice. To best fit students' program needs, they may wish to write papers exploring a topic of their choice within the restorative justice field. Students who choose this option should discuss their topic with the instructor before proceeding.

14.4 International Negotiation: Theories and Practices

Cecilia Albin, Jonathan Hall,
Kristine Höglund, and Niklas Swanström
Uppsala University

COURSE DESCRIPTION

Upper-level undergraduate or graduate-level course in peace and conflict studies, political science, and business.

International negotiation has become the most widely used means of conflict management, rulemaking, and decisionmaking in international affairs. It concerns not only tangible matters, such as diplomatic relations, wars, and material resources, but also identity issues, symbols, rules and norms, and regime and relationship building for cooperative ventures, governance, and conflict prevention. I. William Zartman's classic text on negotiation, *The 50 Percent Solution,* pointed out some twenty years ago: "Ours is an age of negotiation. The fixed positions and solid values of the past seem to be giving way, and new rules, roles, and relations have to be worked out. . . . From bipolarity to polycentrism, from colonialism to independence, from nuclear stalemate to disarmament, . . . the transition in each case requires negotiation."

Negotiations of international significance are today conducted not only between individual states, but also within and beyond them. At the same time, negotiation practice itself is undergoing much change because of changing patterns of conflict and intervention, new urgent issues on the global agenda, new actors, and new emerging norms.

This course provides an overview of negotiation theories and practices of international importance—bilateral, regional, and multilateral. The emphasis is on different approaches to understanding what drives negotiation process and explains the outcome. Why do some negotiations succeed, while others keep failing? We will examine not only the official negotiation process, but also the important functions of prenegotiation, second-track diplomacy, and postagreement negotiations concerned with implementation and compliance. Among the themes covered in the course are the roles of power, leadership, ethics, information technology, and nongovernmental organizations (NGOs). Case studies and examples from different issue areas are used to learn more generally about contemporary international negotiation—its features and many faces, its limitations and possibilities for greater effectiveness.

COURSE SCHEDULE

Part 1: Overview of Basic Concepts and Actors

Session 1: Introduction: International Negotiation in Theory and Practice

I. William Zartman. "Common Elements in the Analysis of the Negotiation Process." In *Negotiation Theory and Practice,* edited by William Breslin and Jeffrey Rubin. Harvard Program on Negotiation, 1991, 147–159.

See the website of Beyond Intractability for descriptions of "integrative" negotiation (problem-solving, cooperative) and "distributive" bargaining (competitive): http://www.beyondintractability.org/essay/interest-based_bargaining/; and http://www.beyondintractability.org/essay/distributive_bargaining/.

Daniel Druckman. "Negotiating in the International Context." In *Peacemaking in International Conflict,* edited by I. William Zartman and Lewis Rasmussen. US Institute of Peace Press, 1997, chapter 3.

Victor Kremenyuk. "The Emerging System of International Negotiation." In *International Negotiation: Analysis, Approaches, Issues,* 2nd ed., edited by Victor Kremenyuk. Jossey-Bass, 2002, chapter 2.

Christer Jönsson. "Bargaining, Negotiation and Diplomacy." In *Handbook of International Relations,* edited by Walter Carlsnaes, Thomas Risse, and Beth A. Simmons. Sage, 2005, 212–234.

Session 2: Who Negotiates? New Players in the Old Game

Tom Farer. "New Players in the Old Game: The De Facto Expansion of Standing to Participate in Global Security Negotiations." *American Behavior Scientist* 38, no. 6 (May 1995): 842–866.

Cecilia Albin. "The Global Security Challenge to Negotiation." *American Behavior Scientist* 38, no. 6 (May 1995): 921–948.

Cecilia Albin. "Can NGOs Enhance the Effectiveness of International Negotiation?" *International Negotiation* 4, no. 3 (1999): 371–387.

Jeffrey Rubin. "The Actors in Negotiation." In *International Negotiation: Analysis, Approaches, Issues,* 2nd ed., edited by Victor Kremenyuk. Jossey-Bass, 2002, chapter 7.

Robert Putnam. "Diplomacy and Domestic Politics: The Logic of Two-Level Games." *International Organization* 41 (1988): 427–460.

Natalie Florea et al. "Negotiating from Mars to Venus: Gender in Simulated International Negotiations." *Simulation and Gaming* 34, no. 2 (June 2003): 226–248, http://sag.sagepub.com/cgi/content/abstract/34/2/226.

Session 3: Obstacles to Negotiation and Negotiation Phases: Prenegotiation and Problem-Solving, Bargaining, and Postagreement Negotiations

Brad Spangler. "Distributive Bargaining." Beyond Intractability, June 2003, http://www.beyondintractability.org/essay/distributive_bargaining.

L. Ross. "Barriers to Conflict Resolution." *Negotiation Journal* 7, no. 4 (October 1991): 389–404.

I. William Zartman. "Timing of Peace Initiatives: Hurting Stalemate and Ripe Moments." *Global Review of Ethnopolitics* 1, no. 1 (2001).

I. William Zartman. "Prenegotiation: Phases and Functions." In *Getting to the Table*, edited by J. Gross Stein. Johns Hopkins University Press, 1989, 237–253.

Christer Jönsson and Jonas Tallberg. "Compliance and Post-Agreement Bargaining." *European Journal of International Relations* 4 (1998): 371–408.

R. Avenhaus. "Game Theory." In *International Negotiation: Analysis, Approaches, Issues*, edited by Viktor Kremenyuk. Jossey-Bass, 2002, chapter 13.

Search the Internet for information on game theory's "Game of Chicken."

Part 2: The Process and Context of Negotiation

Session 4: What Drives the Negotiation Process? Power, Interests, and Ethics

David Lax and James Sebenius. "Interests: The Measure of Negotiation." In *Negotiation Theory and Practice*, edited by W. Breslin and Jeffrey Rubin. Harvard Program on Negotiation, 1991, 161–180.

I. William Zartman and Jeffrey Rubin. "The Study of Power and the Practice of Negotiation." In *Power and Negotiation*, edited by I. William Zartman and Jeffrey Rubin. University of Michigan Press, 2000, chapter 1.

Cecilia Albin. "Justice, Fairness, and Negotiation." In *International Negotiation: Actors, Structure/Process, Values*, edited by P. Berton, H. Kimura, and I. William Zartman. St. Martin's Press, 1999, chapter 9.

Cecilia Albin. "Negotiating International Cooperation: Global Public Goods and Fairness." *Review of International Studies* 29, no. 3 (July 2003): 370–381.

David Lax and James Sebenius. "The Power of Alternatives or the Limits to Negotiation." In *Negotiation Theory and Practice*, edited by W. Breslin and J. Rubin. Harvard Program on Negotiation, 1991, 94–113.

Session 5: The Role of Culture (Professional and Ethnic/National)

J. W. Salacuse. "Ten Ways That Culture Affects Negotiating Style." *Negotiation Journal* (July 1998): 221–240.

Walter Weight. "Cultural Issues in Mediation: Individualist and Collectivist Paradigms." Association of Attorney-Mediators, 1998, http://www.attorney-mediators.org/wright.html.

I. William Zartman. "A Skeptic's View." In *Culture and Negotiation*, edited by G. O. Faure and J. Z. Rubin. Sage, 1993, 17–21.

Gunnar Sjöstedt, ed. *Professsional Cultures in International Negotiation: Bridge or Rift?* Lexington Books, 2003, chapters 1 and 9.

Session 6: Negotiating Intractable Conflicts: Ethnic and Internal Disputes

Chester A. Crocker, Fen Osler Hampson, and Pamela Aall. "Introduction: Mapping the Nettle Field." In *Grasping the Nettle: Analyzing Cases of Intractable Conflict*, edited by Chester A. Crocker, Fen Osler Hampson, and Pamela Aall. US Institute of Peace Press, 2005.

Donald Rothchild. "Ethnic Bargaining and the Management of Intense Conflict." *International Negotiation: A Journal of Theory and Practice* 2, no. 1 (1997).

I. William Zartman. "Negotiations and Prenegotiations in Ethnic Conflict: The Beginning, the Middle, and the Ends." In *Conflict and Peacemaking in Multiethnic Societies*, edited by Joseph V. Monteville. Lexington Books, 1991, 514–533.

Session 7: Negotiation in the Age of Information and Technology

Margarita Studemeister. "The Impact of Information and Communications Technologies on International Conflict Management." *Bulletin of the American Society for Information Science* (February–March 1998).

Gordon S. Smith. "Reinventing Diplomacy: A Virtual Necessity." Virtual Diplomacy Report (VDS 6), US Institute of Peace, February 25, 1999, http://www.usip.org/virtualdiplomacy/publications/reports/gsmithISA99.html.

James Rosenau. "States, Sovereignty, and Diplomacy in the Information Age." Virtual Diplomacy Report (VDS 5), US Institute of Peace, February 25, 1999, http://www.usip.org/virtualdiplomacy/publications/reports/jrosenauISA99.html.

Willemijn Tuinstra, Leen Hordjik, and Markus Amann. "Using Computer Models in International Negotiations." *Environment* (November 1999).

Session 8: Third-Party Mediation and Negotiation: Types and Roles

J. Bercovitch. *Studies in International Mediation.* Palgrave Macmillan, 2002, introduction and conclusion.

Marieke Kleiboer. "Understanding Success and Failure of International Mediation." *Journal of Conflict Resolution* 40, no. 2 (1996).

Saadia Touval and I. William Zartman. "International Mediation in the Post–Cold War Era." In *Turbulent Peace,* edited by Chester Crocker, Fen Osler Hampson, and Pamela Aall. US Institute of Peace Press, 2001, 427–443.

Session 9: The Role of Violence: Negotiation in the Midst of Violence

John Darby, ed. *The Effects of Violence on Peace Processes.* US Institute of Peace Press, 2001, 1–14, 38–75, 96–100, 116–126.

Richard Hayes, Stacey Kaminski, and Steven Beres. "Negotiating the Non-Negotiable: Dealing with Absolutist Terrorists." *International Negotiation* 8, no. 3 (2003).

Niklas Swanström and Emma Björnehed. "Conflict Resolution of Terrorist Conflicts in Southeast Asia." *Terrorism and Political Violence* 16, no. 2 (Summer 2004).

I. William Zartman. "Negotiating with Terrorists." *International Negotiation* 8, no. 3 (2003).

Part 3: Explaining Specific Cases of Negotiation

Session 10: Northern Ireland

John Darby. "Profile: Northern Ireland." *The Effects of Violence on Peace Processes.* US Institute of Peace Press, 2001.

John de Chastelain. "The Good Friday Agreement in Northern Ireland." In *Herding Cats,* edited by Chester Crocker, Fen Osler Hampson, and Pamela Aall. US Institute of Peace Press, 435–368.

James K. Sebenius and Daniel F. Curran. "'To Hell with the Future, Let's Get on with the Past': George Mitchell in Northern Ireland." Harvard Business Online (9-801-393), 2001.

"Striking a Balance: The Northern Ireland Peace Process." *Accord: An International Review of Peace Initiatives* 8 (1999, 2003), www.c-r.org/our-work/accord/northern-ireland.index.php.

Session 11: South Africa

Timothy D. Sisk. "Profile: South Africa." In *The Effects of Violence on Peace Processes,* edited by John Darby. US Institute of Peace Press, 2001.

I. William Zartman. "Negotiating the South African Conflict." In *Elusive Peace: Negotiating an End to Civil War,* edited by I. William Zartman. Brookings Institution, 1995.

Allister Sparks. *Tomorrow Is Another Country: The Inside Story of South Africa's Road to Change.* University of Chicago Press, 1996.

Session 12: Sri Lanka

K. M. De Silva. "Profile: Sri Lanka." In *The Effect of Violence on Peace Processes,* edited by John Darby. US Institute of Peace Press, 2001.

Jayadeva Uyangoda. "Negotiation for Conflict Resolution: Lessons from Sri Lanka's Past Experience." In *Conflict, Conflict Resolution, and Peace Building: An Introduction to Theories and Practices,* edited by Jayadeva Uyangoda. University of Colombo, 2005.

Robert I. Rothberg, ed. *Creating Peace in Sri Lanka: Civil War and Reconciliation.* Brookings Institution Press, 1999.

Session 13: The Middle East: Israel-Palestine and Jerusalem

John Wallach. "The Israeli-Palestinian Conflict." In *The Effects of Violence on Peace Processes,* edited by John Darby. US Institute of Peace Press, 2001.

Cecilia Albin. "Securing the Peace of Jerusalem: On the Politics of Unifying and Dividing." *Review of International Studies* 23, no. 2 (1997): 117–142.

Charles Smith. *Palestine and the Arab-Israeli Conflict,* 4th ed. Bedford/St. Martin's Press, 2001, chapters 10–12.

S. Telhami. "Camp David II: Assumptions and Consequences." *Current History* (January 2001).

Session 14: The Global Environment: The Law of the Sea Negotiations

"The United Nations Convention on the Law of the Sea: A Historical Perspective." United Nations Division for Ocean Affairs and the Law of the Sea, http://www.un.org/Depts/los/convention_agreements/convention_historical_perspective.htm#Third%20Conference.

James Sebenius. *Negotiating the Law of the Sea.* Harvard University Press, 1984, chapters 1–2.

Read overviews, reports, and documents, at the website of the United Nations Division for Ocean Affairs and the Law of the Sea, http://www.un.org/Depts/los/convention_agreements.

Session 15: Negotiation Day: From Truce to Peace in Guatemala

Simulation with role plays from the Program on Negotiation at Harvard Law School.

"Negotiating Rights: The Guatemalan Peace Process." *Accord: An International Review of Peace Initiatives* 2 (1997), www.c-r.org/our-work/accord/guatemala/index.php.

Dinorah Azpuru. "Peace and Democratization in Guatemala: Two Parallel Processes." In *Comparative Peace Processes in Latin America,* edited by Cynthia Arnson. Woodrow Wilson Center Press, 1999, 97–125.

Susanne Jonas. *Of Centaurs and Doves: Guatemala's Peace Process.* Westview, 2000.

"Guatemala: From Truce to Peace" (Teachers' Package). Consensus Building Institute: Program on Negotiation at Harvard Law School. Order at http://www.pon.org/catalog/product_info.php?products_id=243.

TEACHING NOTES

This course is taught through lectures, seminars, and exercises and is designed to give students: (1) an introduction to key questions and concepts in the study of international negotiations; (2) an understanding of how different factors and contexts can influence the negotiation process and its outcome; (3) an overview of actual cases of international negotiations concerning peace and security (broadly defined), and the ability to analyze such cases independently using theories or concepts commonly applied in the field; and (4) a limited, hands-on feel for the complexity of conducting international negotiations, using role plays.

Among many excellent resources for this course is the website of Beyond Intractability. It provides explanations of key terms, concepts, and elements in the study of international negotiation. If the subject matter is new to you, you may find it useful as a dictionary, particularly in the beginning of the course when covering basic terms and issues. Another good Internet resource is the website of the Conflict Research Consortium at http://conflict.colorado.edu.

14.5 Peacebuilding

Craig Zelizer
Georgetown University

COURSE DESCRIPTION

Intermediate- or upper-level course for majors in political science, peace and conflict studies, and international relations.

Since the publication of *An Agenda for Peace* in 1992 by UN Secretary General Boutros Boutros-Ghali, peacebuilding has become increasingly a central area of focus within the field of conflict resolution. This course provides an overview of the theory and practice of peacebuilding and explores how the concept has evolved over the past decade. Given that peacebuilding activities increasingly are integrated into other sectors, including development, business, and human rights, this course also explores cross-disciplinary approaches to peacebuilding. Current challenges in the field, such as a lack of coordination among multiple interveners, ethics, power relations between northern and southern nongovernmental organizations (NGOs), and how to measure impact, will also be highlighted.

By taking this course, students will be better prepared to undertake research, practice peacebuilding, and enter policy careers within conflict resolution and related fields. The course will cover theory and real world cases, helping to contextualize many key concepts covered in the course.

REQUIRED TEXTS

Mary Anderson. *Do No Harm: How Aid Can Support Peace—or War.* Lynne Rienner, 1999.

Johan Galtung, Carl Jacobsen, and Kai Frithjof Brand-Jacobsen. *Searching for Peace: The Road to Transcend.* Pluto Press, 2002.

Paulette Goudge. *The Whiteness of Power: Racism in Third World Development and Aid.* Lawrence and Wishart, 2003.

Ho Wan Jeong. *Peacebuilding in Postconflict Societies: Strategy and Process.* Lynne Rienner, 2005.

Roland Paris. *At War's End: Building Peace After Civil Conflict.* Cambridge University Press, 2004.

Luc Reychler and Thania Paffenholz. *Peacebuilding: A Field Guide.* Lynne Rienner, 2001.

Paul van Tongeren, Malin Brenk, Marte Hellema, and Juliette Verhoeven, eds. *People Building Peace II: Successful Stories of Civil Society.* Lynne Rienner, 2005.

Occasional readings assigned in the course schedule.

COURSE SCHEDULE

Week 1: Introduction

Overview of class. Expectations. What peacebuilding is; related terminology.

Week 2: Historical Overview

Mapping the field. Theoretical underpinnings.

Galtung, Jacobsen, and Brand-Jacobsen, *Searching for Peace,* preface, chapters I.1, I.2.
Paris, *At War's End,* introduction, chapters 1, 2, and 9.

Week 3: Key Actors and Processes in Peacebuilding

A who's who of the peacebuilding industry. Third-party roles and motivations. Overview of processes.

Galtung, Jacobsen, and Brand-Jacobsen, *Searching for Peace,* chapters 1.2, 1.7, and 2.1.
Jeong, *Peacebuilding in Postconflict Societies,* chapter 1.
Reychler and Paffenholz, *Peacebuilding: A Field Guide,* chapters 1.1, 1.2, 2.1, 2.2, 6.1, 6.2, and 7.1.
Van Tongeren et al., *People Building Peace II,* chapters 1 and 3.
Ronald Fisher. "Methods of Third-Party Intervention." In *Berghof Handbook for Conflict Transformation,* edited by Martina Fischer, Hans J. Geissman, and Beatrix Schmelzlé. Center for Constructive Conflict Management, 2005, http://www.berghof-handbook.net/articles/fisher_hb.pdf.

Browse the background notes at the United Nations Political and Peacebuilding Missions page of the United Nations website, http://www.un.org/peace/ppbm.pdf.

Week 4: Assessment and Program Design

Strategies and tools for assessment. Program design. Strategic peacebuilding.

Galtung, Jacobsen, and Kai Frithjof Brand-Jacobsen, *Searching for Peace,* 200–208, 237–243, 281–283.
Jeong, *Peacebuilding in Postconflict Societies,* chapter 2.
Reychler and Paffenholz, *Peacebuilding: A Field Guide,* chapters 6.1 and 6.2.
Van Tongeren et al., *People Building Peace II,* chapter 2.
Dan Smith. *Towards a Strategic Framework for Peacebuilding: Getting Their Act Together.* Overview Report of the Joint Utstein Study of Peacebuilding. Ministry of Foreign Affairs, Norway, 2004, http://www.regjeringen.no/upload/kilde/ud/rap/2000/0265/ddd/pdfv/210673-rapp104.pdf.

Hugh Miall. "Conflict Transformation: A Multi-Dimensional Task." In *Berghof Handbook for Conflict Transformation,* Research Center for Constructive Conflict Management, 2004, http://www.berghof-handbook.net/uploads/download/miall_handbook.pdf.

"Manual for Conflict Analysis." Swedish International Development Co-operation Agency, 2006, http://www.sida.se/shared/jsp/download.jsp?f=SIDA4334en_Web.pdf&a=3351.

Week 5: Development and Conflict

The relationship between peacebuilding and development. The goal to "Do no harm." Conflict sensitivity in practice.

Anderson, *Do No Harm,* chapters 1–8 and 12.

Reychler and Paffenholz, *Peacebuilding: A Field Guide,* chapter 9.1.

Van Tongeren et al., *People Building Peace II,* chapters 16.

"Conflict-Sensitive Approaches to Development, Humanitarian Assistance, and Peacebuilding," chapter 1. Conflict Sensitivity, 2004, http://www.conflictsensitivity.org/resource_pack/chapter_1__265.pdf.

Maria Lange and Mick Quinn. "Conflict, Humanitarian Assistance, and Peacebuilding: Meeting the Challenges." International Alert, 2003, http://www.international-alert.org/publications/getdata.php?doctype=Pdf&id=57.

Week 6: Economics and Peacebuilding

Economics, war, and peace. The role of international financial institutions. Potential contributions of the private sector.

Galtung, Jacobsen, and Brand-Jacobsen, *Searching for Peace,* 198–199.

Van Tongeren et al., *People Building Peace II,* chapters 13, especially 13.2 and 13.3.

Paris, *At War's End,* chapter 7.

Jessica Banfield, Virginia Haufler, and Damian Lilly. "Transnational Corporations in Conflict-Prone Zones: Public Policy Responses and a Framework for Action." International Alert, 2003, http://www.international-alert.org/publications/getdata.php?doctype=Pdf&id=55.

James K. Boyce. "Aid Conditionality as a Tool for Peacebuilding: Opportunities and Constraints." *Development and Change* 33, no. 5 (2002): 1025–1049.

Paul Collier. "Economic Causes of Civil War and Their Implications for Policy." World Bank, 2000, http://siteresources.worldbank.org/DEC/Resources/econonmic_causes_of_civilwar.pdf.

Neil Cooper. "Picking Out the Pieces of the Liberal Peaces: Representations of Conflict Economies and the Implications for Policy." *Security Dialogue* 36, no. 4 (2005): 463–478.

Heiko Nitzschke and Kaysie Studdard. "The Legacies of War Economies: Challenges and Options for Peacemaking and Peacebuilding." *International Peacekeeping* 12, no. 2 (2005): 222–239.

"Livelihoods and Conflict: A Toolkit for Intervention." US Agency for International Development, 2005, http://www.usaid.gov/our_work/cross-cutting_programs/conflict/publications/docs/CMM_Livelihoods_and_Conflict_Dec_2005.pdf.

Week 7: Disarmament, Demobilization, and Reintegration; Security Sector Reform; and Peacebuilding

Galtung, Jacobsen, and Brand-Jacobsen, *Searching for Peace,* chapter 1.6 and pages 288–290.

Ho-Wan Jeong, *Peacebuilding in Postconflict Societies,* chapter 3.

Reychler and Paffenholz, *Peacebuilding: A Field Guide,* chapters 13.1, 13.4, and 13.7.

Van Tongeren et al., *People Building Peace II,* chapters 22, especially 22.1 and 22.2.

Michael Brzoska. "Introduction: Criteria for Evaluating Post-Conflict Reconstruction and Security Sector Reform in Peace Support Operations." *International Peacekeeping* 13, no. 1 (2006): 1–13.

Clem McCartney. "Engaging Armed Groups in Peace Processes: Reflections for Practice and Policy from Colombia and the Philippines." Conciliation Resources, 2006, http://www.c-r.org/our-work/accord/comparative-learning/documents/CR_Engaging_armed_groups2006.pdf.

Robert Muggah. "No Magic Bullet: A Critical Perspective on Disarmament, Demobilization, and Reintegration (DDR) and Weapons Reduction in Post-Conflict Contexts." *Round Table* 94, no. 379 (2005): 239–252.

Week 8: Political Processes and Peacebuilding

Democratization. The rule of law. Human rights.

Jeong, *Peacebuilding in Postconflict Societies,* chapter 4.

Paris, *At War's End,* chapters 5, 6, and 10.

Reychler and Paffenholz, *Peacebuilding: A Field Guide,* chapter 8.2.

Development Assistance Committee. "Issues Brief: Democratisation and Violent Conflict." Organization for Economic Development and Cooperation, 2005, http://www.oecd.org/dataoecd/40/47/35033677.pdf.

Richard Youngs. "Democratic Institution-Building and Conflict Resolution: Emerging EU Approaches." *International Peacekeeping* 11, no. 3 (2004): 526–543.

Week 9: Reconciliation, Justice, and Peacebuilding

Reconciliation versus justice. Trauma healing. Truth commissions.

Galtung, Jacobsen, and Brand-Jacobsen, *Searching for Peace,* 256–257.
Jeong, *Peacebuilding in Postconflict Societies,* chapter 6.
Reychler and Paffenholz, *Peacebuilding: A Field Guide,* chapters 12.2, 12.3, and 12.4.
Van Tongeren et al., *People Building Peace II,* chapters 18.2 and 23, especially 23.2, and 23.4.
David Bloom, Teresa Barnes, and Luc Huyse. "Reconciliation After Violent Conflict: A Handbook." International Institute for Democracy and Electoral Assistance (IDEA), 2003, http://www.idea.int/publications/reconciliation/index.cfm.
Development Assistance Committee. "Issues Brief: Reconciliation." Organization for Economic Cooperation and Development, 2005, http://www.oecd.org/dataoecd/13/28/35034360.pdf.

Week 10: Gender and Peacebuilding

Adopting a gender lens. The role of women in peacebuilding. Case study.

Reychler and Paffenholz, *Peacebuilding: A Field Guide,* chapter 4.2.
Van Tongeren et al., *People Building Peace II,* chapter 7, especially 7.3 and 7.5.
Cordula Reimann. "Roles of Women and Men in Violent Conflicts." Swisspeace Foundation Info information sheet, January 2004, http://www.swisspeace.ch/typo3/fileadmin/user_upload/pdf/KOFF/InfoSheet/InfoSheet1_RolesOf.pdf.
Jasmine Whitbread. "Mainstreaming Gender in Conflict Reduction: From Challenge to Opportunity." *Gender and Development* 12, no. 3 (2004): 41–49.
Elaine Zuckerman and Marcia Greenberg. "The Gender Dimensions of Post-Conflict Reconstruction: An Analytical Framework for Policymakers in Sweetman." In *Gender, Peacebuilding, and Reconstruction,* edtied by Caroline Sweetman. Oxfam UK, 2004.

Week 11: Ethics, Power, and Peacebuilding

North-South relations. Ethics.

Goudge, *The Whiteness of Power,* entire book.
Alejandro Bendana. "From Peacebuilding to State Building: One Step Forward and Two Steps Back?" *Development* 48, no. 3 (2005): 5–15.
Nicolas de Torrenté. "Humanitarianism Sacrificed Integration's False Promise." *Ethics and International Affairs* 18, no. 2 (2004): 3–12.
Hannah Reich. "Local Ownership in Conflict Transformation Projects: Partnership, Participation, or Patronage?" Occasional Paper, Berghof Research Center for Constructive Conflict Management, Germany, 2006, http://www.berghof-center.org/std_page.php?LANG=e&id=173&parent=11.

Week 12: Group Presentations

Week 13: Group Presentations

Week 14: Current Challenges in Peacebuilding
Issues of coordination. Measuring impact. Terrorism and conflict.

Galtung, Jacobsen, and Brand-Jacobsen, *Searching for Peace,* chapter 1.3.
Jeong, *Peacebuilding in Postconflict Societies,* chapter 7.
Paris, *At War's End,* chapter 11 and conclusion.
Van Tongeren et al., *People Building Peace II,* chapter 5.
Neclâ Tschirgi. "Post-Conflict Peacebuilding Revisited: Achievements, Limitations, and Challenges." International Peace Academy, 2004, http://www.ipacademy.org/PDF_Reports/POST_CONFLICT_PEACEBUILDING.pdf.
Richard V. Wagner. "Terrorism: A Peace Psychological Analysis." *Journal of Social Issues* 62, no. 1 (2006): 155–171.
"Civil Society and Peacebuilding: Potential, Limitation and Critical Factors." Draft Report 36445-GLB, World Bank, 2006, http://www.civicus.org/new/media/ESW_Civil_Society_and_Peacebuilding_Final_Draft.pdf.

TEACHING NOTES

This course is designed to be an interactive seminar that combines lectures, short videos, discussions, small group exercises, and simulations. For most classes, a forty-five-minute lecture is followed by discussions and questions. The remainder of each class usually consists of an interactive exercise (such as asking students to design and/or critique one aspect of peacebuilding), a short film on peacebuilding practices, and occasionally guest speakers with particular expertise. Students are also responsible for presenting short interactive presentations from the readings. The presentations could range from identifying key questions to designing a short simulation to presenting a case study on the theme of the week.

I divide the class into several groups early in the semester for group projects. Each group selects a conflict region (region, country, part of a country, etc.) of the world and conducts a brief conflict analysis of this region. Based on the analysis, groups will be responsible for developing a peacebuilding strategy for the region that includes the type of peacebuilding activities needed, actors who are responsible for these activities, and a projection of the intended and possible unintended outcomes of the approach. If possible, groups are encouraged to conduct interviews with individuals representing communities involved in the conflict and/or individuals involved with peacebuilding work to strengthen their understanding of their conflict.

I also assign individual papers in which students pretend to have been hired by a leading international agency to help develop an organizational policy on the agency's approach to the theory and practice of peacebuilding. Students prepare a policy paper defining their own approach to peacebuilding. The paper should also address some of the most significant challenges related to peacebuilding, such as ethics, power, how to measure impact, conflict sensitivity, and explore different perspectives on each of those issues.

14.6 Comparative Peace Processes

Anthony Wanis–St. John
American University

COURSE DESCRIPTION

Graduate elective in international relations or peace and conflict studies. Adaptable for undergraduates.

This course seeks to increase our learning about the optimal negotiation of peace processes. To do so, we examine peace process negotiations that have failed, those that seem to be succeeding, and those whose outcome remains unclear. To do so, we must understand negotiation and bargaining, including how to conceptualize an optimal negotiation. Also of critical importance, we must distinguish peace process negotiations from other peacemaking activities and other kinds of negotiations in the international sphere. Peace processes are negotiations that are typically far more complex than any other kind of international negotiation. First of all, the primary goal of outside interveners (mediators) and sometimes, of the conflict parties, involves the ambitious transformation of violent, militarized conflict and the transition to "normal" politics.

The record of negotiation success is not a hopeful one. Peace process negotiations are daunting, and yet success is critical to avoid reverting to violence and all it brings in its wake. Knowledge about peace negotiations, in terms of analytical concepts, issues, and dynamics, is therefore critical for scholars and practitioners who are interested in sustained peace. Peace processes involve bargaining between the principal conflict parties and among their own factions and constituencies, and sometimes involve outside interveners who want to mediate among the parties. Thus, a course on peace processes benefits from knowledge of both international negotiation directly between the parties and international mediation by third parties. Although classic approaches to peace processes tend to either emphasize the internal and external political contexts to explain success or failure or test the theories of international relations related to the termination of war, this course looks inside peace processes, analyzing them as complex negotiations that should lead—ideally—to the end of armed conflict and continue into implementation and the reconstruction of peaceful social and political relations. Their complexity includes aspects such as multiple armed groups, splinter factions, entrenched conflict dynamics, multiple political and economic grievances, multiple intervenors, the salience of issues of religious and ethnic identity, and the numerous social-psychological obstacles to negotiated solutions.

In this course, we will analyze cases of peace negotiations in depth and explore the analytical variables that affect negotiations, including who was included and excluded from the negotiation table, which issues were addressed or left unaddressed, which problems were resolved or deferred, the choice of negotiation process used, and numerous others.

REQUIRED TEXTS

Chester A. Crocker, Fen Osler Hampson, and Pamela R. Aall. *Taming Intractable Conflict*. US Institute of Peace Press, 2004.

John Darby and Roger MacGinty, eds. *Contemporary Peacemaking: Conflict Violence and Peace Processes*. Palgrave Macmillan, 2003.

Accord: An International Review of Peace Initiatives (online). Conciliation Resources. http://www.c-r.org/accord/index.php.

Daniel Druckman. "Negotiating in the International Context." In *Peacemaking in International Conflict,* edited by I. William Zartman and Lewis Rasmussen. US Institute of Peace Press, 1997.

Jacob Bercovitch. "Mediation in International Conflict: An Overview of Theory, a Review of Practice." In *Peacemaking in International Conflict,* edited by I. William Zartman and Lewis Rasmussen. US Institute of Peace Press, 1997.

Saadia Touval and I. William Zartman. "International Mediation in the Post–Cold War World." In *Turbulent Peace: The Challenges of Managing International Conflict,* edited by Chester A. Crocker, Fen Osler Hampson, and Pamela R. Aall. US Institute of Peace Press, 2001.

COURSE SCHEDULE

Week 1: Introduction

Week 2: Negotiating Peace, Piece by Piece: Aspects, Dynamics, and Patterns of Peace Processes

John Paul Lederach. *The Moral Imagination*. New York: Oxford University Press, 2005, chapter 5 ("On Peace Accords").

John Darby and Roger MacGinty, eds. *The Management of Peace Processes*. St. Martin's Press, 2000, introduction and conclusion.

Lotta Harbom, Stina Hogbladh, and Peter Wallensteen. "Armed Conflict and Peace Agreements." *Journal of Peace Research* 43, no. 5 (2006): 617–631.

Week 3: Interstate Processes: Egypt and Israel, Ecuador and Peru, Ethiopia and Eritrea

William Quandt. *Peace Process: American Diplomacy and the Arab-Israeli Conflict Since 1967*. Brookings Institution, 1993, 255–331, 560–565.

Crocker, Hampson, and Aall, *Taming Intractable Conflict*, chapters 1, 5–9.

David Scott Palmer. "Overcoming the Weight of History: 'Getting to Yes' in the Peru-Ecuador Border Dispute." *Diplomacy and Statecraft* 12, no. 2 (June 2001): 29–47.

Darby and MacGinty, *Contemporary Peacemaking*, introduction and chapter 2.

John Prendergast. "US Leadership in Solving African Conflict: The Case of Ethiopia-Eritrea." *USIP Special Report*, no. 74 (September 7, 2001), http://www.usip.org/pubs/specialreports/sr74.html.

Week 4: Sectarian Strife: Northern Ireland, Lebanon, and Cyprus

Accord 8 (1999), http://www.c-r.org/our-work/accord/northern-ireland/contents.php.

Stephen Farry. "Northern Ireland: Prospects for Progress in 2006?" *USIP Special Report* 173 (September 2006), http://www.usip.org/pubs/specialreports/sr173.html.

Ron Fisher. "Cyprus: The Failure of Mediation and the Escalation of an Identity-Based Conflict to an Adversarial Impasse." *Journal of Peace Research* 38, no. 3 (2001): 307–326.

Hassan Krayem. "The Lebanese Civil War and the Taif Agreement." In *Conflict Resolution in the Arab World: Selected Essays*, edited by Paul Salem. American University of Beirut, 1997.

Augustus Richard Norton. "Lebanon After Ta'if: Is the Civil War Over?" *Middle East Journal* 45, no. 3 (Summer 1991): 457–473.

Week 5: Ethnic and Internal Wars: Armenia and Azerbaijan

Accord 17 (2005), http://www.c-r.org/our-work/accord/nagorny-karabakh/index.php.

Darby and MacGinty, *Contemporary Peacemaking*, chapters 5–11.

Week 6: Georgia and Abkhazia

Accord 7 (1999), http://www.c-r.org/our-work/accord/georgia-abkhazia/index.php.

"Peace Agreement Drafter's Handbook." Online publication of the Public International Law and Policy Group, 2006, http://www.publicinternationallaw.org/areas/peacebuilding/peacehandbook/index.html.

Week 7: Sierra Leone and Democratic Republic of Congo

Accord 9 (2000), http://www.c-r.org/our-work/accord/sierra-leone/index.php.

Patricia Daley. "Challenges to Peace: Conflict Resolution in the Great Lakes Region of Africa." *Third World Quarterly* 27, no. 2 (2006): 303–319.

William Lacy Swing. "War, Peace and International Engagement in the Congo." May 2006, United Nations Organization Mission in the Democratic Republic of the Congo, http://www.monuc.org/downloads/wswing_usip_en.pdf.

Week 8: Uganda

Accord 11 (2002), http://www.c-r.org/our-work/accord/northern-uganda/index.php.

Week 9: Burundi and Rwanda

Mohammed Maundi, I. William Zartman, Gilbert Khadiagala, and Kwaku Nuamah. *Getting In: Mediators' Entry into the Settlement of Africa's Conflicts*. US Institute of Peace Press, 2006, chapter 3 ("Burundi").

International Crisis Group. "Burundi's Peace Process: The Road from Arusha." ICG Burundi Report no. 2 (July 20, 1998), http://www.crisisgroup.org/library/documents/report_archive/A400219_20071998.pdf.

International Crisis Group. "Burundi After Six Months of Transition: Continuing the War or Winning Peace?" Africa Report no. 46 (May 24, 2002), http://www.crisisgroup.org/library/documents/report_archive/A400667_24052002.pdf.

Bruce D. Jones. *Peacemaking in Rwanda: The Dynamics of Failure*. Lynne Rienner, 2001, chapters 3 and 4.

Week 10: Nepal

International Crisis Group. "Nepal: From People Power to Peace." ICG Asia Report no. 115 (May 10, 2006), http://www.crisisgroup.org/home/index.cfm?id=4099&l=1.

Week 11: Sudan

Accord 18 (2006). "Accord Sudan Project." http://www.c-r.org/our-work/accord/sudan/index.php.

Hugo Slim. "Dithering Over Darfur: A Preliminary Review of the International Response." *International Affairs* 80, no. 5 (October 2004): 811–828.

Shadrack Wanjala Nasang'o and Godwin Rapando Murunga. "Lack of Consensus on Constitutive Fundamentals: Roots of the Sudanese Civil War and Prospects for Settlement." *African and Asian Studies* 4, nos. 1–2 (2005): 51–82.

Lydia Polgreen. "US Governor Brokers Truce for Darfur." *New York Times*, January 11, 2007.

Week 12: Palestine-Israel

Anthony Wanis–St. John. "Back Channel Negotiation: International Bargaining in the Shadows." *Negotiation Journal* 22, no. 2 (April 2006): 119–144.

Week 13: The Philippines, Indonesia, and Sri Lanka

Accord 6 (1999), http://www.c-r.org/our-work/accord/philippines-mindanao/contents.php.

Accord 4 (1998), http://www.c-r.org/our-work/accord/sri-lanka/index.php.

Bruce Matthews. "In Pursuit of an Interim Administration in Sri Lanka's North and East: Opportunity or Peace Trap?" *Round Table* 93, no. 373 (January 2004): 75–94.

John Stephen Moolakkattu. "Peace Facilitation by Small States: Norway in Sri Lanka." *Cooperation and Conflict* 40, no. 4 (2005): 385–402.

Week 14: Prospects for Negotiating Peace: Iraq, Kosovo, and Afghanistan

Darby and MacGinty, *Contemporary Peacemaking,* chapters 20–21 and conclusion.

TEACHING NOTES

In my experience, this seminar worked best for advanced graduate students and midcareer diplomatic and military professionals from national agencies and international organizations, but it is adaptable for other groups.

There are several structural components of the course, each of which maximizes the opportunity to learn about the challenges inherent in the negotiation of peace.

Readings and seminar discussions. These have been carefully selected from vast literatures on negotiation and on peace, with an eye toward global coverage, regional distribution, and thematic content.

Peace process negotiation simulation. The course is organized around a major peace process negotiation simulation that evolves and unfolds across the entire semester. This is not simply a role play, but an opportunity to strategize, react to dynamics, learn from experiences and mistakes, anticipate moves, and plan. Plans for simulations, some of which I created, are available at the US Institute of Peace (USIP) website and can be conducted during a regular semester course schedule. USIP makes its simulations available for free at http://www.usip.org/class/simulations/.

Student research. Students write a medium-length research paper totaling forty pages and discussing at least one major thematic aspect of peace negotiations across several peace processes or analyzing several critical thematic aspects of an in-depth single peace process case study. Those papers are due at the end of the course. Each paper will be the result of intense teamwork and will be the collective, original product of a small group of four students.

Guests and visits. If possible, invite a professional peace process negotiator to meet with the class by phone, videoconference, or onsite visit.

14.7 The Vocation of Peacebuilding

John Paul Lederach
University of Notre Dame

COURSE DESCRIPTION

Upper-level undergraduate course.

Our narrative. Our lives are stories unfolding. We live by them and into them. So what story will we tell; what story will unfold in this "place" we call "class," this intersection of time and space we share a few hours each week for four months? The word "school" comes from the Latin and Greek *scola,* which was originally connected to leisure, time off from work, a time apart. In this sense school represented a time and space to come into touch with being more fully human, to develop an appreciation for the intriguingly complex world around us, an understanding of place and our direction in life uncluttered by the demands and pace of day-to-day work that afforded little time to reflect on these deeper matters. We have long lost this sense of school.

In this course, I propose we attempt to unravel a different narrative. Let us dare to pursue a time apart, a time to listen to other parts of who we are as humans in a life journey. Let us unfold other aspects of our being mostly untouched by the purely intellectual journey. These aspects include space for letting our imaginations loose, the nurturing of character and soul, the courage to be vulnerable, the ability to listen to our lives and find deeper, authentic voice.

But what, you may ask, do such pursuits and spaces have to do with peacebuilding? At its core, peacebuilding poses deep questions. How do we face threat without retreat or aggression? How do we accompany those who have suffered far more than we will ever know in our lives? How do we sustain a life of hope in the face of despair? How do we build compassion when surrounded by hatred and bitterness? How do we find evidence of God in our enemy? How do we promote the unexpected sparks of imagination that break cycles of violence?

The pathway to open these questions, not answer them, lies in large part with nurturing vocation—the capacity to touch and follow Voice and find our place in the world. Doing so requires character and compassion, imagination and a sense of self, and the ability to listen and sustain vision and place. Vocation builds from humility, a life of learning, and a commitment to seeking Truth. These same qualities underpin the essence of imaginative peacebuilding.

Can we teach qualities of "being" such as these? No. But we can create opportunities wherein they can be sought, touched though fleetingly, and perhaps learned.

What then is our narrative for this place we call class? I propose we create a space to explore a mostly uncharted geography on the modern university campus: to experiment with how we find our voice, build a life of meaning, and forge a commitment to nurture life-giving relationships and societies. In short, we will do strange things in different ways that open up a space to listen to our lives, dreams, journeys, and voices—in hopes that we sustain our pursuit of and commitment to building peace in a broken world.

Our horizons. Instead of course goals, I propose we envision horizons. Horizons embody a paradox. Permanent and ever changing, they lie before us each morning and night. Always within sight, they excite our senses and guide our pathways but are never reached. This course proposes such a spatial view of learning, development, and exploration of life disciplines in relationship to vocation and peacebuilding. I propose several horizons worthy of the pathways that seek them:

1. To listen to yourself, your life;
2. To pursue a sense of character and voice;
3. To experiment with a variety of disciplines and approaches that excite the imagination and artfully engage the too-busy, overly noisy, and deeply conflicted world that surrounds our lives; and
4. To explore a life of meaning committed to seeking and practicing peace.

Four qualities of human character accompany these pathways:

5. The discipline to listen to your own life
6. The gift of vulnerability
7. The willingness to experiment and explore your Voice
8. The abiding commitment to respect your own and others' journeys

Our activities and your responsibilities. We will:

1. Take class walks, or walking talks.
2. Create periods of silence for private journal reflection during part of each class period (please come with journals and hand writing utensils).
3. Receive brief input (mostly from the professor), leaving open spaces for discussion and exchange.
4. Provide a series of short exercises to provoke reflection and imagination about life and vocation (come prepared to experiment).

For your work during the semester, you will develop a vocational portfolio. Portfolios are often used by disciplines in the arts to demonstrate accomplishment, approach, and style. Portfolios are less common in the social sciences. However, we will adapt this approach for our purposes. Your vocational portfolio will include original work in these areas, to be determined by you without qualification from the professor as to length (with the exception of the haiku autobiography).

1. A haiku autobiography.
2. Photography of other people in the class/topics of choice.
3. A self-produced chapbook of poetry or short essay/story/photos/artwork.
4. A hand-bound gathering of preferred journal entries and class exercises.
5. A letter of vocational gratitude.
6. A Wittgensteinian essay on the topic of "Let My Life Speak."

Your portfolio will be available for a public sharing during one class period, at which time you will also make a five-minute presentation of one of your items as a gift to the class.

Finally, as a class we will produce a chapbook that includes photos of each class member and their haiku autobiography. Everyone will be responsible for providing photos of one other person and submitting their autobiography. Several volunteers will be needed to complete the chapbook by semester's end.

COURSE TEXTS

This course builds from and around my recent text, *The Moral Imagination*. Other texts will explore themes that might seem tangential to our course initially. They are not. They are penned words, journeys, and wisdom from people who carved unique pathways toward the horizon we seek, a life of meaning, purpose, and integrity, a vocation in its deepest sense. These texts can be read in a single setting and can be probed for wisdom across a thousand readings. Although there is no exact time or concrete order in which you should read these books, the calendar suggests the themes we will explore and the texts you may wish to enter and deepen as we proceed.

Matsuo Basho. *The Narrow Road to Oku*. New York: Kodansha, 1996.
Julia Cameron. *The Artist's Way*. New York: Penguin Putnam, 1992.
John Paul Lederach. *The Moral Imagination*. New York: Oxford University Press, 2005.
Mark Nepo. *Surviving Has Made Me Crazy*. Boston: CavanKerry Press, 2007.
Parker Palmer. *Let Your Life Speak*. San Francisco: Jossey-Bass, 2000.
Rainer Maria Rilke. *Letters to a Young Poet*. New York: Modern Library, 2001.
Henry David Thoreau. *Walking*. San Francisco: HarperCollins, 1994.
Margaret Wheately. *Turning to One Another*. San Francisco: Barrett-Koehler, 2002.

Howard Zehr. *The Little Book of Contemplative Photography.* Intercourse, PA: Good Books, 2005.

Van Morrison. *Poetic Champions Compose* (compact disc). Polygram Records, 1994.

Occasional readings listed in the course schedule.

OUR CALENDAR

Week 1: The Social Construction of a Meaningful Class

Week 2: Four Stories—How Did She or He Do That?
Lederach, *The Moral Imagination,* chapters 1–3.
Cameron, *The Artist's Way,* xxi–24.

Exploration: Begin a journal you will keep throughout the semester.

Week 3: Creative Essence
Basho, *The Narrow Road to Oku,* all.
Lederach, *The Moral Imagination,* chapters 4–7.
Zehr, *The Little Book of Contemplative Photography,* all.

Week 4: Voice and Vulnerability
Rilke, *Letters to a Young Poet,* all.
Palmer, *Let Your Life Speak,* all.

Week 5: Place and Humility
Lederach, *The Moral Imagination,* chapters 8–10.
Thoreau, *Walking,* all.

Week 6: Serendipity
Lederach, *The Moral Imagination,* chapter 11.
Wheatley, *Turning to One Another,* all.

Week 7: Time
Lederach, *The Moral Imagination,* chapter 12.

Week 8: Sound
Lederach, *The Moral Imagination,* chapter 13.
Listen to Van Morrison, *Poetic Champions Compose,* all.

Week 9: Poetry Workshop Retreat
Nepo, *Surviving Has Made Me Crazy,* all.

Week 10: Meaningfulness

Lederach, *The Moral Imagination,* chapter 14–Epilogue.

Week 11: Gifts and Portfolios

Presentations of gifts and portfolios.

Week 12: The Sending

15
Globalization and Human Security

WHEN PEACE AND SECURITY STUDIES WERE STARTING TO EMERGE as an academic field in the initial decades after World War II, and when peace was defined more commonly as "the absence of war," it was traditional for peace advocates to argue that there were tight and essential connections between peace and prosperity (Quincy Wright, Karl Deutsch, David Mitrany) and between world peace and international trade (Kenneth Boulding). As peace studies has been heir to the work of the 1980s World Order Models Project and as the academic field has moved beyond its initial Eurocentrism, scholars and practitioners have resonated to the conceptions that positive peace must, in addition to the absence of war, include social justice, economic well-being, and ecological balance. In the era after the Cold War and after the attacks of September 11, 2001, and with the establishment of the World Trade Organization (WTO), scholars and practitioners of peace studies have become more skeptical of global economic relationships and have been more likely to assume that, "in terms of social justice and fairness of trade, everything is wrong with globalization" (Hamid Rafizadeh). The syllabuses in this chapter of the curriculum guide touch on themes of globalization spanning the curriculum from political science to economics to environmental studies and business ethics. David A. Welch sketches the broad contours of the "ontology" of security. His course includes readings from those who argue for the broad integration of concerns about environment, culture, politics, society, and economy with national security. The Brazilian (Maria Guadalupe Moog Rodrigues), Canadian (Lowell Ewert), Iranian (Hamid Rafizadeh), and American (Stephen Zunes) contributors to this chapter examine definitions of development, the tensions between human rights and traditional economic policy, the characteristics of economic justice, and the differences between economic theory and globalization in practice. Pedagogically, these professors engage in case studies (Rafizadeh) and in experiential learning such as writing letters to practitioners and chief executive officers (Ewert), while acknowledging that the primary goal of the courses is to raise questions and that "the lack of solutions is unnerving to students" (Rodrigues).

15.1 Security Ontology: Referents, Values, Threats

David A. Welch
University of Toronto

COURSE DESCRIPTION

Upper-level undergraduate seminar for students of peace and conflict studies, political science, and security studies.

This is a seminar on the ontology of security. Security is a contested concept, and in this course we ask what it is and how best to pursue it. What do we mean by security? What are we trying to protect? From what? Why? How do we do it? We begin by considering the concept of security in the abstract and proceed to explore various specific conceptions. Along the way we encounter both traditional and nontraditional approaches to security.

COURSE SCHEDULE

Week 1: Course Introduction

Week 2: Security and Securitization

Jessica T. Mathews. "Redefining Security." *Foreign Affairs* 68, no. 2 (1989): 162–177.

Barry Smith. "John Searle: From Speech Acts to Social Reality." In *John Searle,* edited by Barry Smith. Cambridge University Press, 2003, 1–33, http://ontology.buffalo.edu/smith/articles/SearleIntro.pdf.

Ken Booth. "Security and Emancipation." *Review of International Studies* 17, no. 4 (October 1991): 313–326.

Barry Buzan, Ole Waever, and Jaap de Wilde. *Security: A New Framework for Analysis*. Lynne Rienner, 1998, 21–47.

Daniel Deudney. "The Case Against Linking Environmental Degradation and National Security." *Millennium* 19, no. 3 (1990): 461–476.

Week 3: What Is Worth Securing, and Why?

M. Bernstein. "Intrinsic Value." *Philosophical Studies: An International Journal for Philosophy in the Analytic Tradition* 102, no. 3 (2001): 329–343.

Ruth Cigman. "Death, Misfortune, and Species Inequality." *Philosophy and Public Affairs* 10, no. 1 (1981): 47–64.

Steven F. Sapontzis. "What's More Important?" *Essays in Philosophy* 5, no. 2 (2004), http://www.humboldt.edu/~essays/sapontzis.html.

Wendy Lynne Lee. "The Aesthetic Appreciation of Nature, Scientific Objectivity, and the Standpoint of the Subjugated: Anthropocentrism Reimagined." *Ethics Place and Environment* 8, no. 2 (2005): 235–250.

J. Stan Rowe. "Ethical Ecosphere." Ecocentrism. http://www.ecospherics.net/pages/RoEthicalEcosp.html. Reproduced with minor changes from *Home Place: Essays in Ecology.* NeWest Press, 1990, 139–143.

Week 4: Ecospheric Security I: Referents and Values

James E. Lovelock. "Hands Up for the Gaia Hypothesis." *Nature* 344 (March 8, 1990): 100–102.

Axel Kleidon. "Beyond Gaia: Thermodynamics of Life and Earth System Functioning." *Climatic Change* 66, no. 3 (2004): 271–319.

James W. Kirchner. "The Gaia Hypothesis: Conjectures and Refutations." *Climatic Change* 58, nos. 1–2 (2003): 21–45.

Arne Naess. "The Deep Ecological Movement: Some Philosophical Aspects." In *Deep Ecology for the Twenty-First Century,* edited by George Sessions. Shambhala, 1995, 64–84.

Jerry A. Stark. "Postmodern Environmentalism: A Critique of Deep Ecology." In *Ecological Resistance Movements,* edited by Bron Raymond Taylor. State University of New York Press, 1997, 259–281.

Week 5: Ecospheric Security II: Threats

Daniel Gilbert. "If Only Gay Sex Caused Global Warming: Why We're More Scared of Gay Marriage and Terrorism Than a Much Deadlier Threat." *Los Angeles Times,* July 2, 2006.

David M. Wilkinson. "Catastrophes on Daisyworld." *Trends in Ecology and Evolution* 18, no. 6 (2003): 266–268.

James Hansen et al. "Earth's Energy Imbalance: Confirmation and Implications." *Science* 308 (2005): 1431–1435.

Peter Jacques. "The Rearguard of Modernity: Environmental Skepticism as a Struggle of Citizenship." *Global Environmental Issues* 6, no. 1 (2006): 76–101.

Stephene Dovers and John W. Handmer. "Ignorance, the Precautionary Principle, and Sustainability." *Ambio* 24, no. 2 (March 1995): 92–97.

L. Hunter Lovins and Amory B. Lovins. "Pathways to Sustainability: Natural Capitalism Offers Our Best Hope for Achieving a Sustainable Future." *Forum for Applied Research and Public Policy* 15, no. 4 (Winter 2000): 13–22.

Peter W. Huber. *Hard Green: Saving the Environment from the Environmentalists: A Conservative Manifesto.* Basic Books, 1999, xi–xxi, 101–117.

Week 6: State Security I: Referents and Values

Michael Walzer. "The Moral Standing of States: A Response to Four Critics." *Philosophy and Public Affairs* 9, no. 2 (1980): 209–229.

Martha C. Nussbaum, ed. *For the Love of Country?* Beacon Press, 2002, ix–29, 72–77, 85–90 (essays by Nussbaum, Appiah, Himmelfarb, and Pinsky).

Daniel B. Klein. "The People's Romance: Why People Love the Government (as Much as They Do)." *Independent Review* 10, no. 1 (2005): 5–37.

David Rodin. *War and Self-Defense*. Clarendon Press, 2002, 141–162.

Charles Tilly. "War Making and State Making as Organized Crime." In *Bringing the State Back In,* edited by Peter B. Evans. Cambridge University Press, 1985, 169–191.

Week 7: State Security II: Threats

White House. *National Security Strategy of the United States of America*. 2002. http://www.whitehouse.gov/nsc/nss.pdf.

White House. *National Security Strategy of the United States of America*. 2006. http://www.whitehouse.gov/nsc/nss/2006/nss2006.pdf.

Nuclear Posture Review. January 8, 2002, excerpts, http://www.globalsecurity.org/wmd/library/policy/dod/npr.htm.

"Is Major War Obsolete? An Exchange." *Survival* 41, no. 2 (Summer 1999): 139–152.

Brock F. Tessman. "Critical Periods and Regime Type: Integrating Power Cycle Theory with the Democratic Peace Hypothesis." *International Interactions* 31, no. 3 (2005): 223–249.

Kenneth N. Waltz. "More May Be Better." In *The Spread of Nuclear Weapons: A Debate,* edited by Scott D. Sagan and Kenneth Waltz. W.W. Norton, 1995, chapter 1.

James G. Blight and David A. Welch. "Risking 'the Destruction of Nations': Lessons of the Cuban Missile Crisis for New and Aspiring Nuclear States." *Security Studies* 4, no. 4 (Summer 1995): 811–850.

Walter Enders and Todd Sandler. "Is Transnational Terrorism Becoming More Threatening?" *Journal of Conflict Resolution* 44, no. 3 (2000): 307–332.

Walter Enders and Todd Sandler. "After 9/11: Is It All Different Now?" *Journal of Conflict Resolution* 49, no. 2 (2005): 259–277.

Week 8: Societal Security I: Referents and Values

Karen Frecker. *Beyond GDP: Enabling Democracy with Better Measures of Social Well-Being*. Kiessling Paper no. 1. Trudeau Centre for Peace and Conflict Studies, 2005.

C. S. Holling. "Understanding the Complexity of Economic, Ecological, and Social Systems." *Ecosystems* 4, no. 5 (2001): 390–405.

Paul Starobin. "Rethinking Capitalism." *National Journal,* January 18, 1997, 106–109.

Rajni Bakshi. "Gross National Happiness." AlterNet, 25 January 2005, http://www.alternet.org/envirohealth/21083/.

Week 9: Societal Security II: Threats

John M. Shandra, Bruce London, and John B. Williamson. "Environmental Degradation, Environmental Sustainability, and Overurbanization in the Developing World." *Sociological Perspectives* 46, no. 3 (2003): 309–329.

Suzana Sawyer and Arun Agrawal. "Environmental Orientalisms." *Cultural Critique* 45 (2000): 71–108.

"Social Cohesion and Demographic Challenges," "Europe Is Running Low on Children," and "Turning the Age Pyramid on Its Head." *RTD Info* 49 (May 2006): 4–7, 11–13.

R. W. Bentley. "Global Oil and Gas Depletion." *Energy Policy* 30, no. 3 (2002): 189–205.

Colin Campbell and Jean Laherrère. "The End of Cheap Oil." *Scientific American* 278, no. 3 (1998): 78–83.

David Goodstein. "The Future" and "Energy Myths and a Brief History of Energy." In *Out of Gas: The End of the Age of Oil,* by David Goodstein. Norton, 2004, chapters 1–2.

"ITER Takes Its First Steps." *RTD Info* 49 (May 2006): 18–21.

Week 10: Cultural Security I: Referents and Values

Johan Galtung. "On the Social Costs of Modernization: Social Disintegration, Atomie/Anomie and Social Development." United Nations Research Institute for Social Development Discussion Paper, May 1995.

Will Kymlicka. "Culturally Responsive Policies." Background Paper for Human Development Report Office, HDR2004. United Nations Development Programme, 2004–2005.

Jose A. Del Pilar and Jocelynda O. Udasco. "Deculturation: Its Lack of Validity." *Cultural Diversity and Ethnic Minority Psychology* 10, no. 2 (2004): 169–176.

Week 11: Cultural Security II: Threats

Robert van Krieken. "Rethinking Cultural Genocide: Aboriginal Child Removal and Settler-Colonial State Formation." *Oceania* 75, no. 2 (2004): 125–151.

Barry Sautman. "Tibet: Myths and Realities." *Current History* 100, no. 647 (2001): 278–283.

C. J. W.-L. Wee. "Capitalism and Ethnicity: Creating 'Local' Culture in Singapore." *Inter-Asia Cultural Studies* 1, no. 1 (2000): 129–143.

Steven Leonard Jacobs. "Language Death and Revival After Cultural Destruction: Reflections on a Little Discussed Aspect of Genocide." *Journal of Genocide Research* 7, no. 3 (2005): 423–430.

Bron Taylor. "Earthen Spirituality or Cultural Genocide? Radical Environmentalism's Appropriation of Native American Spirituality." *Religion* 27, no. 2 (1997): 183–216.

Week 12: Human Security I: Referents and Values

"New Dimensions of Human Security." In *Human Development Report 1994*. United Nations Development Program, 1994, http://hdr.undp.org/en/reports/global/hdr1994/.

Foreign Affairs and International Trade Canada. "Human Security Program." Government of Canada, http://www.humansecurity.gc.ca/psh-en.asp#sec.

John Daudelin and Fen Osler Hampson. *Human Security and Development Policy.* Ottawa: CIDA Policy Branch Strategic Planning Division, 1999.

Roland Paris. "Human Security: Paradigm Shift or Hot Air?" In *New Global Dangers: Changing Dimensions of International Security,* edited by Michael Brown et al. MIT Press, 2004, 249–264.

Week 13: Human Security II: Threats

Andrew Price-Smith and John Daley. "Downward Spiral: HIV/AIDS, State Capacity, and Political Conflict in Zimbabwe." *Peaceworks* 53 (July 2004). ww.usip.org/pubs/peaceworks/pwks53.html.

Patrick Moore. "Murder and Hypocrisy." *Advocate* 31 (January 2006): 36–37.

J. Ann Tickner. "Feminist Perspectives on 9/11." *International Studies Perspectives* 3, no. 4 (2002): 333–350.

Mary Lynne Gasaway Hill. "Re-Shaping Our Words, Re-Shaping Our World: Crimes Against Humanity and Other Signs of the Times." *Social Science Journal* 39, no. 4 (2002): 539–557.

Richard Maclure and Myriam Denov. "'I Didn't Want to Die So I Joined Them': Structuration and the Process of Becoming Boy Soldiers in Sierra Leone." *Terrorism and Political Violence* 18, no. 1 (2006): 119–135.

15.2 Global Economic Justice

Stephen Zunes
University of San Francisco

COURSE DESCRIPTION

Upper-level undergraduate course for majors in political science, international studies, or sociology.

Why is there hunger when there is a surplus of food in the world? Why is there such enormous wealth amid such poverty? Why do expanding national economies often fail to improve the quality of life for most people? Has economic liberalization and the spread of multinational corporations been an asset or a hindrance to global development? What is the impact of inequality on the environment, the role of women, and the risk of war? Is US foreign economic policy helping or hurting development efforts? What are the causes and implications of increasing inequality in industrialized countries? Can we continue our high-consumption lifestyle and still make possible sustainable development and environmental quality? These are some of the questions we will examine as we look at the politics, economics, and ethics of the rapidly changing global political economy.

This course offers a critical inquiry into the politics, economics, and ethical questions regarding inequality, poverty, population growth, the environment, energy consumption, and related issues, with special attention given to relations between countries of the North (industrialized countries) and the South (the "Third World").

No background or prior classes in politics or economics is necessary.

REQUIRED TEXTS

John Cavanagh and Jerry Mander, eds. *Alternatives to Economic Globalization,* 2nd ed. Berrett-Koehler Publishers, 2004.

John D. Clark. *Worlds Apart: Civil Society and the Battle for Ethical Globalization.* Kumarian Press, 2003.

Chuck Collins and Felice Yeskel. *Economic Apartheid in America: A Primer on Economic Inequality and Insecurity.* New Press, 2005.

John DeGraaf, David Wann, and Thomas Naylor. *Affluenza: The All-Consuming Epidemic,* 2nd ed. Berrett-Koehler Publishers, 2005.

Charles Dunkley. *Free Trade: Myth, Reality, and Alternatives.* Zed Books, 2004.

Wayne Ellwood, *The No-Nonsense Guide to Globalization.* Verso Books, 2001.

Si Kahn and Elizabeth Minnich. *The Fox in the Henhouse: How Privatization Threatens Democracy*. Berrett-Koehler Publishers, 2005.

Barbara Thomas-Slayter. *Southern Exposure: International Development and Global South in the Twenty-First Century*. Kumarian Press, 2003.

COURSE SCHEDULE

Part 1: Introduction to the Contemporary International Political Economy

Week 1: Globalization and its institutions.
Week 2: Debt, corporate power, and global finance.
Week 3: The impact of globalization.
Week 4: Free trade and its critics.

Part 2: The International Political Economy and the Global South

Week 5: The making of the global south.
Week 6: Food and population.
Week 7: The environmental consequences of globalization.

Part 3: The US Political Economy

Week 8: The causes and impact of privatization.
Week 9: Economic stratification in the United States.
Week 10: The causes of and solutions to inequality.
Week 11: The symptoms and causes of "affluenza."
Week 12: Alternatives to consumerism.

Part 4: Critiques of Corporate Globalization and Proposed Alternatives

Week 13: Alternative visions and popular challenges.
Week 14: The commons and subsidiarity.
Week 15: Global institutions and alternatives to them.

TEACHING NOTES

Each student is required to complete a final research project on any approved topic relevant to the course, which is due on the last day of class. It can take the form of a research paper of approximately twelve pages or some other original research project of comparable effort, such as a detailed report on the process of getting a particular commodity from source to market. (The report could also be a video, audio recording, or other medium.) Students must schedule a time to meet with the professor to discuss the topics and media of their final projects by the end of the tenth week of class.

15.3 Global Economy and Organizations

Hamid Rafizadeh
Bluffton University

COURSE DESCRIPTION

Upper-level undergraduate or graduate course in business administration, economics, political science, or management.

This course provides the student with an understanding of the increased interdependence of national economies, the spread of common political and economic ideologies, and the issues of fairness, economic justice, and the use of force. Students use economic concepts and actual examples to identify the effects of increased globalization on individual organizations and countries. Upon completion of the course, the student will:

- Have a foundational understanding of important structural principles that direct national and global economic and political behavior.
- Understand the basics of distribution of the economic gains of globalization and international trade as a vehicle of its implementation.
- Develop a holistic understanding of the economic, political, and social problems associated with globalization.
- Learn about the structure and function of global organizations that define and influence patterns of international trade and globalization, such as the World Trade Organization (WTO) and the International Monetary Fund (IMF).
- Understand regional economic agreements, such as US economic ties with Mexico in the context of the North American Free Trade Agreement (NAFTA).
- Develop an integrated view of the role of government in international trade and the political implications of globalization.

REQUIRED TEXTS

The following textbooks are selected for their contrasts. *International Economics* offers a mainstream view of globalization and sees only a few shortcomings with globalization. To the contrary, *Real World Globalization* provides specific examples to claim that, in terms of social justice and fairness of trade, everything is wrong with globalization. The course will also use videos from the Inside the Global Economy series, produced by the Educational Film Center of Annenberg/CPB and available by download from the Internet at www.learner.org. Though somewhat dated, these videos provide biased confirmation of the necessity of globalization and, as such, create an excellent environment for discussion of the dynamics and features of globalization based on material learned from the textbooks.

Amy Offner, Alejandro Reuss, and Chris Sturr, eds. *Real World Globalization,* 8th ed. Dollars and Sense, 2004. The 9th edition of *Real World Globalization* is also available but contains several different articles. Readings in this syllabus come from the 8th edition.

Robert J. Carbaugh. *International Economics,* 11th ed. South-Western College Publishing, 2007.

COURSE SCHEDULE

Unit 1: The Historical Foundations of Economic Systems

Unit 2: International Economy and Globalization

Carbaugh, *International Economics,* chapter 1.

Offner, Reuss, and Sturr, *Real World Globalization,* "A Short History of Neoliberalism," by Susan George; and "Environmental Justice in South Africa," by Heidi Vogt.

View *Trade: An Introduction,* from the Inside the Global Economy series at www.learner.org.

Unit 3: Comparative Advantage: One View of Trade

Carbaugh, *International Economics,* chapter 2.

Offner, Reuss, and Sturr, *Real World Globalization,* "The Gospel of Free Trade: The New Evangelists," by Arthur Macewan.

View *Labor and Capital,* from the Inside the Global Economy series, at www.learner.org.

Unit 4: Sources of Comparative Advantage

Carbaugh, *International Economics,* chapter 3.

Offner, Reuss, and Sturr, *Real World Globalization,* "Fair Trade and Farm Subsidies," by Gawain Kripke.

View *Multinational Corporations,* from the Inside the Global Economy series, at www.learner.org.

Unit 5: Overview and Alternative Views of Comparative Advantage

Offner, Reuss, and Sturr, *Real World Globalization,* "The Middle Way," by Charles Sackrey and Geoffrey Schneider.

Unit 6: Tariffs

Carbaugh, *International Economics,* chapter 4.

Offner, Reuss, and Sturr, *Real World Globalization,* "The IMF and World Bank's Cosmetic Makeover," by Sarah Anderson.

View *Protectionism Versus Free Trade,* from the Inside the Global Economy series, at www.learner.org, especially the case study on French agricultural subsidies.

Unit 7: Nontariff Barriers

Carbaugh, *International Economics,* chapter 5.

Offner, Reuss, and Sturr, *Real World Globalization,* "Genetic Engineering and the Privatization of Seeds," by Anuradha Mittal and Peter Rosset.

View *Protectionism Versus Free Trade,* from the Inside the Global Economy series, at www. learner.org, especially the case study on export restraints on Japanese cars.

Unit 8: Trade Regulations and Industrial Policy

Carbaugh, *International Economics,* chapter 6.

Offner, Reuss, and Sturr, *Real World Globalization,* "The Business of War in the Democratic Republic of Congo," by Dena Montegue and Frida Berrigan.

Unit 9: Trade Policies for Developing Nations

Carbaugh, *International Economics,* chapter 7.

Offner, Reuss, and Sturr, *Real World Globalization,* "Korea's Neoliberal Restructuring," by James Crotty and Kang-Kook Lee.

View *Developing Countries,* from the Inside the Global Economy series, at www.learner.org.

Unit 10: Another Look at Trade Policies for Developing Nations

Offner, Reuss, and Sturr, *Real World Globalization,* "Is It Oil?" by Arthur Macewan, and "Factory Takeovers in Argentina," by Andrés Gaudin.

Unit 11: Regional Trading Arrangements

Carbaugh, *International Economics,* chapter 8.

Offner, Reuss, and Sturr, *Real World Globalization,* "The Real Winners: A Rogue's Gallery of War Profiteers," by Todd Tavares.

View *Trade Liberalization and Regional Trade Blocs,* from the Inside the Global Economy series, at www.learner.org.

Unit 12: Multinational Enterprises

Carbaugh, *International Economics,* chapters 9 and 10.

Offner, Reuss, and Sturr, *Real World Globalization,* "US Banks and the Dirty Money Empire," by James Petras; and "Wages for Housework," by Lena Graber and John Miller.

Unit 13: Foreign Exchange

Carbaugh, *International Economics,* chapter 11.

Offner, Reuss, and Sturr, *Real World Globalization,* "Economic Debacle in Argentina," by Arthur Macewan.

Unit 14: Project Presentations

TEACHING NOTES

In general, globalization is not a well-defined concept, though in its most basic form it is the global exchange of goods and services. It is assumed that such exchanges will be fair and just and take place in an environment of decreasing exchange barriers. Yet, in practice, globalization can be unfair and at times deploys new barriers. The topics in this course seek to provide a portfolio of examples for the student. Certain facts about globalization are clear: economic resources are scarce and unequally distributed among nations as each seeks to position itself better in the world competition for resources. The assignments in this course are designed to study the challenges of the global economy in order to develop a better understanding of the global economic environment. The starting points are the principles, dynamics, and structure of the world economy from a simple and foundational view. Examples of how the global economic system has actually worked complement these points. This approach results in a better understanding of international monetary and financial systems and the global institutions that direct the world's financial structure.

I assign students two types of analysis. In the first, a student, or a group of no more than three students, will examine case studies, discuss written assignments, and develop analyses of specific situations to share with the class. Individuals or small groups may study the same case and pool their findings, or they may each explore a different case. The other analytic exercise is a course project. Early in the course, each student submits a brief proposal for an individual project. The proposal will be based on the recognition that knowledge of international trade and investment learned in class is applicable to many situations, ranging from improving a nation's balance of trade to resolving world hunger. The main purpose of the project is to provide the student with an opportunity to manage a certain aspect of earth's economy to improve it. The student will identify and choose an aspect of the global economy that needs improvement. The focus of improvement could be protectionism, a rationale for trade, coordination of national economic policies, the operational focus of multinational corporations, the political positioning of nations, poor and rich differentials, labor and capital migration, institutional integration and control, conflicts manifesting as war and terrorism, or any other aspect of the world economy of interest to the student. The project requires an implementation plan that, when executed, would improve the global economy.

15.4 Politics of Development

Maria Guadalupe Moog Rodrigues
College of the Holy Cross

COURSE DESCRIPTION

Intermediate undergraduate elective for general education students or majors in political science, peace and conflict studies, and environmental studies.

The purpose of this course is to challenge, both theoretically and ethically, students' ideas about development and sustainable development. What does "development" mean? Who benefits from it? What strategies have been used in its pursuit? How sustainable, and environmentally sustainable, have they been? What conflicts—economic, political, religious, ethnic, and environmental—has the process of development triggered? What kind of developmental path(s) should the international community and individual nations pursue in the twenty-first century?

Part 1 of the course surveys the many definitions of development, including the most recent notions of "sustainable development" and "environmentally sustainable development." The course fosters discussion about the strengths and weaknesses of theories that attempt to explain underdevelopment. Part 2 surveys the main agents of development—the state, national and international businesses ("the market"), and multilateral agencies—and the development strategies they have fostered. Part 3 encourages an assessment of both the positive and negative aspects of such development strategies, with a particular focus on how they have contributed to the emergence or intensification of economic, social, environmental, and political conflicts. Finally, in Part 4, the course evaluates some of the "solutions" to development challenges that have been proposed and/or implemented in recent decades throughout the world, and assesses the extent to which they provide alternatives to the current development paradigm. Discussions, readings, and assignments in each of these four sessions will be guided by overarching ethical questions.

REQUIRED TEXTS

Maria Rodrigues. *Global Environmentalism and Local Politics.* State University of New York Press, 2004.

Howard Handelman. *The Challenge of Third World Development,* 4th ed. Prentice Hall, 2003.

Jan Scholte. *Globalization: A Critical Introduction.* St. Martin's Press, 2000.

Samuel Huntington. *Political Order in Changing Societies.* Yale University Press, 1968.

John T. Rourke, ed. *Taking Sides: Clashing Views on Controversial Issues in World Politics,* 11th ed. Dushkin, 2003. This series contains valuable materials, but they are updated annually. The instructor will decide whether the current year is appropriate for the course.

Susan George and Fabrizio Sabelli. *Faith and Credit: The World Bank's Secular Empire.* Westview, 1994.

COURSE SCHEDULE

Part 1: Introduction to Development: Concept and Theories

Ethical questions: Are Western values superior to non-Western values? Is development a matter of choice? If so, whose choice is it?

Week 1: What Is Development?

Handelman, *The Challenges of Third World Development,* pages 1–13.

Bill Emmot and Vandana Shiva. "Is Development Good for the Third World?" In *Annual Editions: Developing World, 2001–2002,* edited by Robert J. Griffiths. Dushkin, 2001.

J. A. Castro. "Environment and Development: The Case of Developing Countries." In *Green Planet Blues,* edited by Ken Conca and Geoffrey Dabelko. Westview, 2004.

Stephen Chilton. "Five Fundamental Theoretical Challenges in Conceptualizing Political Development." In *Defining Political Development,* GSIS Monograph Series in World Affairs. Lynne Rienner, 1987.

Week 2: Explanations for Development and Underdevelopment

The Causes of Underdevelopment: Climate and Culture?:

Paul Harrison. *Inside the Third World.* Penguin, 1993, chapters 1 and 2.

A. Inkeles and D. Smith. "Becoming Modern." In *Development and Underdevelopment,* edited by Mitchell Selingson and John Passe-Smith. Lynne Rienner, 1998.

A. Portes. "On the Sociology of National Development: Theories and Issues." In *Development and Underdevelopment,* edited by Mitchell Selingson and John Passe-Smith. Lynne Rienner, 1998.

The Causes of Underdevelopment: A Matter of Time?:

Huntington, *Political Order in Changing Societies,* chapter 1.

W. W. Rostow. "The Five Stages of Growth." In *Development and Underdevelopment,* edited by Mitchell Selingson and John Passe-Smith. Lynne Rienner, 2003.

Scholte, *Globalization,* chapters 3 and 5.

Week 3: The Causes of Underdevelopment: Global Capitalism?

T. Santos. "The Structure of Dependence." In *Development and Underdevelopment,* edited by Mitchell Selingson and John Passe-Smith. Lynne Rienner, 2003.

I. Wallerstein. "The Present State of the Debate on World Inequality." In *Development and Underdevelopment,* edited by Mitchell Selingson and John Passe-Smith. Lynne Rienner, 1998.

Part 2: Pursuing Development and Breeding Conflict (Actors and Strategies)

Ethical questions: Development by whom? For whom?

Week 4: The State as Entrepreneur and "Mediator" of Social Conflict

The Socialist Avenue:

Huntington, *Political Order in Changing Societies,* chapter 5.

Handleman, *The Challenge of Third World Development,* chapters 6 and 10.

E. S. Simpson. "China." In *The Developing World,* by E. S. Simpson. John Wiley and Sons, 1994, or any other case study of China's socialist/collectivist path to development.

The Capitalist Avenue:

Huntington, *Political Order in Changing Societies,* chapter 4.

E. S. Simpson: "South Korea" and "Brazil." In *The Developing World,* by E. S. Simpson. John Wiley and Sons, 1994, or any other case studies of South Korea's and Brazil's paths to development, similar in the level of state intervention but different in their relations with international markets.

Week 5: Multilateral Organizations

The Bretton Woods System—the United Nations:

"A Decade to Eradicate Poverty: United Nations Development Programme. *Social Education* (October 1997). http://members.ncss.org/se/6106/610602.html.

J. Dunlop et al. "Women Redrawing the Map: The World After the Beijing and Cairo Conferences." In *Perspectives: Comparative Politics,* edited by Eve Sandberg. Coursewise, 1999.

Dallaire, Romeo. *Shake Hands with the Devil.* Avalon, 2003. Read the conclusion.

Browse the United Nations website, www.un.org.

The Bretton Woods System—The World Bank, the IMF and the WTO:

George and Sabelli, *Faith and Credit,* "Introduction and Basics."
Devesh Kapur. "The IMF: A Cure or a Curse?" In *Annual Editions: Developing World, 2000–2001.*
"World Trade: Fifty Years On." *The Economist.* In *Annual Editions: World Politics, 1999–2000.*

Browse the World Bank website, www.worldbank.org.

Week 6: Criticism of the Bretton Woods System

Handleman, *The Challenge of Third World Development,* chapter 10 (269–277).
Rourke, *Taking Sides,* "An Interview with Joseph Stiglitz."
George and Sabelli, *Faith and Credit,* chapters 3 and 4 (read them in this order).
"Reforming the United Nations." In *Annual Editions: World Politics,* 1999–2000.
Jackie Smith and Timothy Patrick Moran. "WTO 101: Myths About the World Trade Organization." In *Annual Editions: Developing World, 2001–2002.*

Week 7: The Market and Multinational Corporations

George and Sabelli, *Faith and Credit,* chapter 5.
Jagdish Bhagwati, "The Case for Free Trade"; and Herman Daly, "The Perils of Free Trade." In *Scientific American* (November 1993).
Rourke, *Taking Sides,* issue 6, "Will China Become an Asian Superpower," 88–103.
Nancy Bord. "Multinational Corporations: Saviors or Villains?" In *Annual Editions: Developing World, 1999–2000.*

Case studies:
Bronwen Manby. "Shell in Nigeria: Corporate Social Responsibility and the Ogoni Crisis." Case study for the Carnegie Council on Ethics and International Affairs, 2000, available at the Georgetown University Institute for the Study of Diplomacy, www.guisd.org.
Olsen and Princen. "Hazardous Waste Trade North and South: The Case of Italy and Koko, Nigeria." Case study for the Carnegie Council on Ethics and International Affairs, 1994.

Part 3: The Impact of Development

Ethical question: Development at what cost?

Week 8: On Politics and the State

Handleman, *The Challenge of Third World Development,* chapter 4.
John Bowen. "Ethnic Conflict: Challenging the Myths." In *Annual Editions: Developing World, 2000–2001.*

Marina Ottaway. "Post-Imperial Africa at War." In *Annual Editions: Developing World, 2000–2001.*

Individual class presentations: Ethnic conflict and nationalism (e.g., the Soviet Union, Yugoslavia, Rwanda).

Week 9: On Women and Marginalized Populations and on Social Structures

Handleman, *The Challenge of Third World Development,* chapters 5 and 7.
Beatrice Newberry. "Laboring Under Illusions." In *Annual Editions: Developing World, 2001–2002.*
David Price. *Before the Bulldozer.* Seven Locks Press, 1990, chapter 1.
Scholte, *Globalization,* chapter 10.

Individual class presentations: The struggles for women's rights (and the backlash they may generate) and the consequences of migration for urban centers (shantytowns, violence) would be interesting additions to the theoretical materials in this session.

Week 10: On the Environment

Maria Rodrigues. "Privatization and Socioenvironmental Conditions in Brazil's Amazonia: Political Challenges to Neoliberal Principles." *Journal of Environment and Development* 12, no. 2 (2003).
Dilip D'Souza. *Narmada Dammed: An Inquiry into the Politics of Development.* Penguin, 2002, chapter 2.

Individual class presentations.

Part 4: Social and Institutional Responses to Development Challenges

Ethical questions: What are the limits of protest initiatives? Are there moral justifications for the use of violence? Should development be limited in pace and scope? If so, who should determine such limits?

Week 11: Institutional Responses I: Reforming the Bretton Woods System

Jonathan Fox. "Introduction: Framing the Inspection Panel." In *Demanding Accountability: Civil Society Claims and the World Bank Inspection Panel,* edited by Dana Clark, Jonathan Fox, and Kay Treakle. Rowman and Littlefield, 2003.
Rourke, *Taking Sides,* issue 16, "Should the United Nations Be Given Stronger Peacekeeping Capabilities?"

Browse the World Bank website for evidence of how the World Bank has changed (new priorities, new practices, new development strategies, new partnerships). Also, find the websites of organizations campaigning to reform the WTO (publiccitizen.org, Global Action, International Forum on Globalization, the Association for the Taxation of Financial Transactions for the Aid of Citizens (ATTAC), the Third World Network, World Social Forum, etc). Who are they? What do they propose?

Group or individual class presentations: Assess the reforms of the Bretton Woods institutions.

Week 11: Institutional Responses II: The Democratic State

Scholte, *Globalization,* chapter 11.

G. Munck. "Past Successes, Present Challenges: Latin American Politics at the Crossroads." *Annual Editions: Developing World, 2003–2004.*

H. Wiarda. "Problems of Democracy in Developing Countries." In *Political Development in Emerging Nations.* Wadsworth, 2003.

D. Kotz. "Capitalist Collapse: How Russia Can Recover." In *Annual Editions: World Politics, 1999–2000.*

Group or individual class presentations: The quality of democracy in a neoliberal context (possible case studies are Russia, Poland, and Nicaragua).

Week 12: Responses by Civil Society Actors

Transnational Advocacy Networks (TANs):

Rodrigues, *Global Environmentalism and Local Politics,* pages 1–9 and the chapters on India (the Narmada Campaign) or Ecuador (the campaign against oil exploitation in Ecuador).

Rourke, *Taking Sides,* issue 11, "Are Patents on HIV/AIDS Drugs Unfair to Poor Countries?"

Community-Based Development and Grassroots Initiatives:

David Bornstein. *The Price of a Dream: The Story of the Grameen Bank.* University of Chicago Press, 1997, part 3 ("The Organization").

Individual class presentations: Suggested cases are indigenous rights campaigns in Latin America and the rubber-tappers' movement in Brazil's Amazon forest.

Week 13: Corporate Social Responsibility

Michael Clancy. "Sweating the Swoosh: Nike, the Globalization of Sneakers and the Question of Sweatshop Labor." Pew Case Studies in International Affairs, 2000, available at the Georgetown University Institute for the Study of Diplomacy, www.guisd.org.

Jennifer Nash and John Ehrenfeld. "Code Green." *Environment* 38, no. 1 (January/February 1996): 16–20, 36–45.

Robin Broad, ed. *Global Backlash.* Rowman and Littlefield, 2002, chapter 4 ("Challenging Corporate Conduct").

Individual class presentations: The corporate response to critics.

Week 14: Radical Religious and Political Movements

Benjamin Barber. "Jihad vs. McWorld." *Atlantic Monthly,* March 1992.

K. Dunn. "Killing for Christ? The Lord's Resistance Army of Uganda." *Current History* 103, no. 673 (May 2004).

S. Huntington. "A Debate on Cultural Conflicts." In *Annual Editions: Comparative Politics, 1999–2000.*

Week 15: Conclusion: Toward People-Centered Development?

Scholte, *Globalization,* chapter 12.

Jeffrey Sachs et al. "Ending Africa's Poverty Trap." Brookings Institution Papers on Economic Activity no. 1, 2004.

C. Alger. "Grassroots Perspectives on Global Policies for Development." *Journal of Peace Research* 27, no. 2 (1990).

TEACHING NOTES

This course is not meant to provide answers, which often unnerves students. It raises all sorts of questions: theoretical ("What is the most effective explanation for development and underdevelopment?"), ethical ("Development by whom? For whom?"), and empirical ("Is institutional reform an answer to development problems?" and "What type of development do you want?"). It is also meant to raise awareness about the complexity of development issues, from the multiple agents of development to the interdependence of problems and limits of solutions. I often refer to the course as a puzzle: though students have to work hard to understand where each piece fits, they will only see the "big picture" of the "politics of development" after the course is over. To consolidate knowledge of the pieces of the puzzle, I am partial to exams and quizzes. Class discussions and class presentations, as well as a term paper exploring a specific problem of development (in a single country or region of a country), provide opportunities for students to reflect more profoundly about the complexities of development and be creative about potential solutions.

15.5 Human Rights in the Marketplace

Lowell Ewert
Conrad Grebel University College

COURSE DESCRIPTION

Intermediate undergraduate course for peace studies majors or upper-level general education students.

"Human Rights in the Marketplace" is an exploration of the tension between the values of human security and human rights on the one hand and traditional economic policy on the other. The impact of this dynamic relationship on the well-being of individuals, as well as on corporations and international economic institutions to promote peace and just development, will also be analyzed.

In practical terms, the focus of the class will be to examine how business has been, and can be, a positive partner for promoting peace and justice in areas in which it is engaged, with the people it employs, and with those who make up its primary market. This approach will not be naively taken, as this course will acknowledge the very significant negative impact some business and certain multinational corporate practices have had on the poor. However, rather than dwelling on the negative, this course will attempt to emphasize the positive stories of hope that have emerged in recent years, which illustrate how the business community has embraced the idea of promoting social justice, human rights, or the well-being of the communities in which it operates as part of its business plan.

REQUIRED TEXTS

Substantial use is made of Internet materials, corporate social responsibility reports, and human rights reports available online. Web addresses are noted in the course schedule under the appropriate unit. They can also be found by searching organizational websites.

George Lodge and Craig Wilson. *A Corporate Solution to Global Poverty: How Multinationals Can Help the Poor and Invigorate Their Own Legitimacy.* Princeton University Press, 2006.

Paul Gordon Lauren. "Proclaiming a Vision: The Universal Declaration of Human Rights." In *The Evolution of International Human Rights: Visions Seen,* by Paul Gordon Lauren. University of Pennsylvania Press, 2003.

Peter R. Baehr. "Universalism Versus Cultural Relativism." In *Human Rights: Universality in Practice,* by Peter R. Baehr. Palgrave Macmillan, 2002.
Jack Donnelly. "Human Rights and 'Asian Values.'" In *Universal Human Rights in Theory and Practice,* by Jack Donnelly, 2nd ed. Cornell University Press, 2003.
Gavin Fridell. "Fair Trade Coffee in Canada." In *Fair Trade Coffee: The Prospects and Pitfalls of Market-Driven Social Justice,* by Gavin Fridell. University of Toronto Press, 2007.
Andreas Wenger and Daniel Mockli. "Corporate Conflict Prevention: Paths to Engagement." In *Conflict Prevention: The Untapped Potential of the Business Sector,* by Andreas Wenger and Daniel Mockli. Lynne Rienner, 2003.

Note: Substantial use is made of Internet materials, corporate social responsibility reports, and human rights reports available online. Web addresses are noted in the course schedule under the appropriate unit. They can also be found by searching organizational websites.

COURSE SCHEDULE

Introduction

Unit 1: Review of Student Awareness,
Knowledge of Topic, Biases, and Experiences

No reading assignment.

International Law

Unit 2: Introduction to Human Rights Law:
The Foundation for New Expectations

Lodge and Wilson, *A Corporate Solution to Global Poverty,* acknowledgments, abbreviations, prologue.

Search the Internet for the following titles; read and bring copies of the following to class:

"The Universal Declaration of Human Rights" (all thirty articles).
"International Covenant on Economic, Social, and Cultural Rights" (preamble through article 25).
"International Covenant on Civil and Political Rights" (preamble through article 27).
Lauren, "Proclaiming a Vision."

Unit 3: Human Rights:
Is It Cultural Imperialism or Universally Applicable?

Lodge and Wilson, *A Corporate Solution to Global Poverty,* chapter 1.
Baehr, "Universalism Versus Cultural Relativism."

Donnelly, "Human Rights and 'Asian Values.'"

Application of International Standards Affecting Business

Unit 4: Overview of Various Regulatory Mechanisms That Build on Human Rights Principles

The United Nations Global Compact, Business Leaders' Initiative on Human Rights, Sullivan principles, norms of transnational corporations, and Equator Principles.

Lodge and Wilson, *A Corporate Solution to Global Poverty,* chapters 2 and 4.

Visit the website of United Nations Global Compact, www.globalcompact.org. From the home page, go to "About the GC" and read all items shown in the left column, except "Contact Us," "Internships," "Job Opportunities," and "GC Foundation."

Also, at the website of United Nations Global Compact, go to "How to Participate." Click on "Business Participation" and read all items.

Unit 5: Measuring Corporate Social Compliance

Lodge and Wilson, *A Corporate Solution to Global Poverty,* chapter 3.

At the Global Reporting Initiative website (www.globalreporting.org), click "learn more" at the quick link to G3 Guidelines tab. Then go to the G3 Guidelines (pdf). Read pages 3–6 and 30–44.

Unit 6: Conflict Commodities

Lodge and Wilson, *A Corporate Solution to Global Poverty,* chapter 6.

"There Are No Clean Diamonds: What You Need to Know About Canadian Diamonds." *Mining Watch Canada,* December 6, 2006, http://www.miningwatch.ca/index.php?/Africa/No_Clean_Diamonds.

Diamond Facts (website of the World Diamond Council). Read the information under the tabs labeled "Home," "The Facts," and "Conflict Diamonds" ("What Are Conflict Diamonds?" "Background," and "Eliminating Conflict Diamonds"). http://www.diamondfacts.org/conflict/index.html.

CASE STUDIES

Unit 7: Case Study of a Partnership Between a Business and a Nongovernmental Organization

Lodge and Wilson, *A Corporate Solution to Global Poverty,* chapter 5.

"Responsibility Report 2006." Website of Barrick Company, a gold-mining corporation. http://www.barrick.com/CorporateResponsibility/Reporting/EHSSReports/default.aspx.

Unit 8: Case Study of Nike

Lodge and Wilson, *A Corporate Solution to Global Poverty,* chapter 5.

"Innovate for a Better World." Nike fiscal year 2005–2006 corporate responsibility report. Nike corporate website. Read pages 1–30. http://www.nike.com/nikebiz/nikeresponsibility/pdfs/bw/Nike_FY05_06_CR_Report_BW.pdf.

Unit 9: Case Study of Fair Trade

Fridell, "Fair Trade Coffee in Canada."

Asha Handicrafts, website of the Asha Handicrafts Association. Read all the information under "Message from the CEO," "News and Events," "Asha Handicrafts-Fair Trade," "Our Products," "Community Products," "Meet Our Artisans," and "Wholesale." http://www.ashahandicrafts.org.

"Principles of Fair Trade" and "Learning Centre, Ten Thousand Villages Canada," website of Ten Thousand Villages fair trade company, http://www.tenthousandvillages.ca. Articles are found under the "Fair Trade" tab.

International Fair Trade Association (IFTA), "Standards for Fair Trade Organizations," www.ifat.org.

Unit 10: Case Study: Jobs for Children, Blessing or Curse?

"The End of Child Labour: Within Reach." Available at the website of the International Labour Organization. http://www.ilo.org/ipecinfo/product/viewProduct.do;?productId=2419. Read the preface through page 22.

Synthesis

Unit 11: Developing a Summary Statement on Human Rights and Business

Lodge and Wilson, *A Corporate Solution to Global Poverty,* chapter 7.

Wenger and Mockli, "Corporate Conflict Prevention."

Unit 12: Summarize, Tie Things Together, and Determine Next Steps for Class Members

No reading assignment.

TEACHING NOTES

I incorporate a significant number of guests into the class by long-distance speakerphone. These diverse international perspectives, including Africans who are cynical about what they perceive to be the imperialistic tendencies of human rights advocates, business leaders from North America or fair trade groups, and working children in the Middle East who demand the right to work, allow students to hear firsthand the voice of those affected by the movement to apply human rights to business decisions.

I also require that students draft a memo to a chief executive officer of a business that has not endorsed the UN Global Compact, making the case for why it would be in the best interests of the business to join it, and suggesting a sample letter of application to the compact. I encourage students to study a business with which they can actually interact by meeting staff in person to discuss ideas. They must then present a final report.

The biggest challenge at times appears to be the difficulty of setting aside prejudices and biases in order to actually listen to the diverse array of voices attempting to encourage economic institutions to become more sensitive to human rights. There has been a sea change over the past five to ten years in how corporations view human rights. This change should be recognized, while still acknowledging the long journey that remains.

16

Religion, Conflict, and Peace

SINCE THE PREVIOUS EDITION OF THIS CURRICULUM GUIDE, THEMES of religion, conflict, and peace have risen sharply to the forefront of popular and scholarly awareness. Much of that new consciousness, often a response to religiously rooted acts of terrorism and violence, has been understandably fearful of the power of religion for evil. The scholars writing syllabuses for this section work from a different and more complex perspective, however. Although they do not dismiss religion's mixed legacy or underestimate its damaging possibilities, they give greater attention in these syllabuses to the resources for peace offered by religious faith, communities, traditions, and institutions. Within that general interpretive framework, the four syllabuses in this section represent two complementary approaches. Matthew Bailey-Dick writes specifically on Christian approaches to peacemaking in a course by the same name. Marc Gopin spans numerous religions and contexts in "World Religions, Violence, and Conflict Resolution." S. Ayse Kadayifci-Orellana presents a Muslim perspective in "Islamic Peace Paradigms," then closes the chaper with a broad survey of religious contributions to peace in "Religion and Peacebuilding." Both the wide and focused approaches represented in this chapter are necessary for sound scholarship and good practice.

16.1 Christian Approaches to Peacemaking

Matthew Bailey-Dick
Conrad Grebel University College

COURSE DESCRIPTION

Introductory and intermediate course for liberal arts majors and students in peace studies and religious studies.

The purpose of this course is threefold: (1) to familiarize ourselves with a wide variety of strategies, methods, and actions undertaken by Christian peacemakers; (2) to uncover and analyze the biblical, theological, and historical foundations for the actions of Christian peacemakers; and (3) to create opportunities for each of us to be personally affected and motivated by the people and movements we study.

This course can be seen as a companion to other peace studies and religious studies courses. It is unique, however, in the way it brings together several themes—history, theology, social movement theory, spirituality—and encourages students to see how these various fields can complement each other. An additional distinction of this course arises from the fact that although its subject is the peacemaking activity emerging from a particular religious tradition (i.e., Christianity), the basic pedagogical assumption is that anyone can learn from the successes, failures, and imaginative work of that tradition, especially when they are set alongside the parallel experiences of other faith-based or secular peace movements.

In addition to offering an interesting academic challenge, this course can also be seen as a resource for life beyond the academy; at a time when conflict and violence threaten our planet in so many ways, this kind of course is profoundly relevant. How, then, will we weave the course materials (the study of peacemaking strategies, spiritualities, individuals, and movements) into our everyday lives?

The following questions will guide the study of each Christian peacemaking approach:

1. What is this approach's definition of "peace" and "peacemaking"?
2. How does this approach fit into the broader trajectory of Christian peacemaking?
3. What are the biblical and theological roots of this approach?
4. What sustains and nourishes those involved in this approach?
5. In what ways does this approach run parallel to peacemaking and social change efforts beyond the Christian community?
6. Does this approach inspire or motivate you? Why or why not?

REQUIRED TEXTS

Tricia Gates Brown, ed. *Getting in the Way: Stories from Christian Peacemaker Teams,* Waterloo, ON: Herald Press, 2005.
Holy Bible (hard copy or electronic version).

Readings listed in the course schedule.

COURSE SCHEDULE

Unit 1: Introducing and Gazing

1. Gaze at the whole landscape of peacemaking in general and Christian approaches in particular.
2. Consider overall conceptual frameworks; identifying basic definitions and key questions.

Daniel Smith-Christopher. "Political Atheism and Radical Faith: The Challenge of Christian Nonviolence in the Third Millenium." In *Subverting Hatred: The Challenge of Nonviolence in Religious Traditions,* edited by Daniel Smith-Christopher. Maryknoll: Orbis, 1998.
Ron Pagnucco. "A Comparison of the Political Behavior of Faith-based and Secular Peace Groups." In *Disruptive Religion: The Force of Faith in Social Movement Activism,* edited by Christian Smith. New York: Routledge, 1996.

Unit 2: Collaborating and Constructing

1. Making peace by developing partnerships with other peace groups, government and nongovernmental bodies, and others.
2. Missional theology, the concept of "shalom," and building a culture of peace.

Dafne Plou. "Boston." In *Peace in Troubled Cities: Creative Models of Building Community Amidst Violence,* by Dafne Plou. Geneva: WCC Publications, 1998.
Alan Kreider, Eleanor Kreider, and Paulus Widjaja. "Does Peace Work?" and "Peace Inside the Church." In *A Culture of Peace: God's Vision for the Church,* by Alan Kreider, Eleanor Kreider, and Paulus Widjaja. Intercourse, PA: Good Books, 2005.
Alix Lozano. "Being a Peace Church in the Colombian Context." In *Seeking Cultures of Peace: A Peace Church Conversation,* edited by Fernando Ens, Scott Holland, and Ann K. Riggs. Scottdale: Herald Press, 2004.

Unit 3: Disobeying and Disarming

1. Calling for disarmament and refusing to participate in warfare (both direct combat and military taxation).

2. Guest speaker on disarmament (from national disarmament advocacy organization).

Lisa Schirch and Daryl Byler. "Effective and Faithful Security Strategies." In *At Peace and Unafraid: Public Order, Security, and the Wisdom of the Cross,* edited by Duane Friesen and Gerald Schlabach. Waterloo: Herald Press, 2005.

Duane K. Friesen. "In Search of Security: A Theology and Ethic of Peace and Public Order." In *At Peace and Unafraid: Public Order, Security, and the Wisdom of the Cross,* edited by Duane Friesen and Gerald Schlabach. Waterloo: Herald Press, 2005.

Unit 4: Mediating and Transforming

1. The theory and practice of mediation and conflict resolution.

2. The theological basis for Christians acting as catalysts for conflict transformation.

Carolyn Schrock-Shenk. "Introducing Conflict and Conflict Transformation." In *Making Peace with Conflict: Practical Skills for Conflict Transformation,* edited by Carolyn Schrock-Shenk and Lawrence Ressler. Waterloo: Herald Press, 1999.

John D. Brewer. "Northern Ireland: Peacemaking Among Protestants and Catholics." In *Artisans of Peace: Grassroots Peacemaking Among Christian Communities,* edited by Mary Ann Cejka and Thomas Bamat. Maryknoll: Orbis Books, 2003.

Unit 5: Dismantling and Retooling

1. Dismantling the structures of violence and war.

2. Overcoming racism, sexism, and militarism.

3. Guest speaker on antiracism (experienced facilitator of antiracism training).

Iris de León-Hartshorn, Tobin Miller Shearer, and Regina Shands Stoltzfus. "Preface." In *Set Free: A Journey Toward Solidarity Against Racism,* edited by Iris de León-Hartshorn, Tobin Miller Shearer, and Regina Shands Stoltzfus. Waterloo: Herald Press, 2001.

Regina Shands Stoltzfus. "Naming the Problem" and "The Decision to Be Whole." In *Set Free: A Journey Toward Solidarity Against Racism,* edited by Iris de León-Hartshorn, Tobin Miller Shearer, and Regina Shands Stoltzfus. Waterloo: Herald Press, 2001.

Unit 6: Advocating and Challenging

1. God's call to work for economic justice—Isaiah 58 as a "peacemaker's manifesto."

2. Local, national, and international efforts to overcome poverty.

Jane Orion Smith. "Wrestling with the Peace Testimony: In Spirit and in Truth." In *Friends' Peace Witness in a Time of Crisis,* edited by Nancy Irving, Vicki Hain Poorman, and Margaret Fraser. Philadelphia: Friends World Committee for Consultation, 2005.

Joyce Hollyday. "Justice: To Undo the Thongs of the Yoke" and "Compassion: To Share Your Bread with the Hungry." In *Then Shall Your Light Rise: Spiritual Formation and Social Witness,* by Joyce Hollyday. Nashville: Upper Room Books, 1997.

Unit 7: Loving and Overcoming

1. Readings about Christians exploring the theory and practice of nonviolence.
2. Jesus' "third way" of responding to violence with creative, nonviolent disobedience.
3. Guest speaker on love of one's enemy (Christian peace activist).

Leonard Desroches. "Cross and Ploughshare or Cross and Sword? A Brief History of the Public Witness." In *Love of Enemy: The Cross and the Sword Trial,* by Leonard Desroches. Ottawa: Dunamis, 2002.

Ron Mock. "Loving Without Giving In: Christians, Terror, and Tyranny." In *Loving Without Giving In: Christian Responses to Terrorism and Tyranny,* by Ron Mock. Waterloo: Herald Press, 2004.

John Dear. "Daniel Berrigan, Apostle of Peace: An Introduction (of Sorts)." In *Apostle of Peace: Essays in Honor of Daniel Berrigan,* edited by John Dear. Maryknoll: Orbis, 1996.

Unit 8: Remembering and Redeeming

1. Peacemaking as a journey of truth telling, reconciliation, and memory-work.
2. Ecumenical dialogue and redeeming the fractured and fracturing Christian community.

Desmond Tutu. "Without Forgiveness There Really Is No Future." In *No Future Without Forgiveness,* by Desmond Tutu. New York: Doubleday, 1999.

Ian Linden. "The Church and Genocide: Lessons from the Rwandan Tragedy." In *The Reconciliation of Peoples: Challenge to the Churches,* edited by Gregory Baum and Harold Wells. Maryknoll: Orbis Books, 1997.

Stanley McKay and Janet Silman. "A First Nations Movement in a Canadian Church." In *The Reconciliation of Peoples: Challenge to the Churches,* edited by Gregory Baum and Harold Wells. Maryknoll: Orbis Books, 1997.

Unit 9: Singing and Praying

1. Naming the power of prayer and song in Christian peacemaking.

2. Practicing the discipline of social exorcism (i.e., exorcising the demons of violence and warfare).

George D. McClain. "Spiritual Struggle with the Powers" and "Exorcising the Social Demons." In *Claiming All Things for God: Prayer, Discernment, and Ritual for Social Change,* by George D. McClain. Nashville: Abingdon Press, 1998.

Henri Nouwen. "Resistance as Prayer." In *Peacework: Prayer, Resistance, and Community,* by Henri Nouwen. Maryknoll: Orbis Books, 2005.

Paul Westermeyer. "Hymnody and Justice." In *Let Justice Sing: Hymnody and Justice,* by Paul Westermeyer. Collegeville: Liturgical Press, 1998.

Unit 10: Sheltering and Accompanying

1. Christians involved in transnational solidarity and nonviolent accompaniment.

2. Guest speaker on the refugee sanctuary movement (activist from an urban refugee support center).

Kathryn Anderson. "The Christian Task Force on Central America in British Columbia" and "Creating Relationships: The 'Spirit' of Solidarity." In *Weaving Relationships: Canada-Guatemala Solidarity,* by Kathryn Anderson. Waterloo: Wilfrid Laurier University, 2003.

Unit 11: Eating and Counter-recruiting

1. Eating the way Jesus lived: The food system as an arena for peacemaking.

2. From food to military service: Comparing food system justice and the parallel counter-recruitment strategies of those resisting military recruitment.

Michael Schut. "Food as Sacramental." In *Food and Faith: Justice, Joy, and Daily Bread,* edited by Michael Schut. Denver: Living the Good News, 2002.

Elizabeth Johnson. "God's Beloved Creation." In *Food and Faith: Justice, Joy, and Daily Bread,* edited by Michael Schut. Denver: Living the Good News, 2002.

Unit 12: Educating and Encouraging

1. Peace education inside and outside the church: What is it ideally, and how well are Christians doing it?

2. Having (Christian) faith in the future: Where do people find hope in today's world?

Jim Wallis. "Change the Wind." In *Faith Works: How Faith-Based Organizations Are Changing Lives, Neighborhoods, and America,* by Jim Wallis. Berkeley: Page Mill Press, 2001.

Mitri Raheb. "The Light of Right, Not the Power of Might" and "Building Walls or Planting Olive Trees?" In *Bethlehem Besieged: Stories of Hope in Times of Trouble*, by Mitri Raheb. Minneapolis: Fortress Press, 2004.

TEACHING NOTES

The course can include guest speakers, videos, and role plays in addition to regular discussions, readings, and lectures. The intent is to strike a balance between, on the one hand, looking for overarching principles and, on the other hand, examining the details of individual peacemakers' lives, the intricacies of certain peace theologies, or the trivial facts of specific nonviolent campaigns.

In addition to several conventional assignments (a book review of *Getting in the Way* as well as a research project on a topic of the student's choosing), the course is also designed to include a practicum component called a "praxis report" in which students have the opportunity to complement what they learn by getting involved in some kind of peacemaking activity outside class (e.g., volunteering with a local peace agency, participating in an on-campus justice group, initiating a peace rally, etc.) and then submitting reflections on that experience based on concepts and insights gained in the classroom. All assignments are intended to be occasions for testing out and/or reflecting on various critical concepts relating to Christian peacemaking.

The course readings offer a variety of perspectives; to supplement them, the instructor can deliberately add alternative, corroborating, and competing sources (from both within and beyond the Christian tradition). One final pedagogical note: it is important to regularly interrogate the course materials, asking whether there is something uniquely Christian about certain peacemaking approaches. Why or why not? Do Christians choose to make use of peace and social change strategies that have actually originated in other places? If so, why does this matter?

16.2 World Religions, Violence, and Conflict Resolution

Marc Gopin
George Mason University

COURSE DESCRIPTION

Upper-level undergraduate or lower-level graduate seminar in religion and conflict transformation.

This course is designed to analyze the roles world religions play in conflict, war, peacemaking, and conflict resolution. Every religion has a broad range of cultural resources and values that have formed the basis for personal and communal values that prevent or successfully manage conflict. War, violence, and repression, however, have been justified at one time or another by important representatives of every major religion. Understanding each religion's values, worldview, and, especially, the hermeneutics through which the religion changes and evolves, are the keys to discovering conflict resolution methodologies that may be effective in violent contexts, whether domestic or global, in which religion is playing some role.

Analyzing the role of religion in these phenomena is particularly challenging because human beings come to be engaged in war or peacemaking out of a host of complex motivating factors, only one of which may be their religious beliefs and practices. Furthermore, religious language is often used as a mask by political leaders and perpetrators of violence to hide other motivating factors that may be less noble or persuasive to their cause.

Key questions to keep in mind as we explore these issues include the following: What are the warrants for making war and making peace in a given religious tradition? Are they at odds with each other, or do they complement each other? Do they emanate historically from competing visions within the same religion? How do these varying traditions affect current practice and belief? What is the role of change and evolution in the religion's practices and beliefs, and how does change occur? How would you attempt to untangle multiple motivations for war or peace among religious people? Is religious motivation a mask for economic, ethnic, or psychological needs? Always? Sometimes? For political leaders but not for followers? What would you do in a given region of the world where religion played a major role in violence? Would you attempt to secularize the public, redirect the religious motivations, or repress the violent representatives of religion?

Would you attempt to employ a variety of conflict resolution strategies? If so, which ones—problem-solving workshops, mediation strategies, or psychodynamic approaches to interpersonal reconciliation? What is religious violence? Is it a more authentic or less authentic expression of a religion? How do you go about answering this question—by taking a poll of co-religionists, studying the primary sources of that tradition, or imposing a value that you and many others are convinced is universal, for example, that killing of innocents by terror, for whatever reason, cannot be sanctioned by a decent religion? Can you know what a religion has truly meant to its adherents if you only speak to or study male representatives of that faith? Is self-described religious peacemaking that advocates for and relates to only one side to be considered peacemaking or conflict resolution, or is it something else? These are but a fraction of the questions that are raised by our subject matter. Some questions will be addressed in class. Other questions I would like you to ponder as you prepare innovative research.

REQUIRED TEXTS

Marc Gopin. *Holy War, Holy Peace: How Religion Can Bring Peace to the Middle East*. Oxford University Press, 2002.

Marc Gopin. *Between Eden and Armageddon: The Future of World Religions, Violence, and Peacemaking*. Oxford University Press, 2002.

R. Scott Appleby. *The Ambivalence of the Sacred: Religion, Violence, and Reconciliation*. Rowman and Littlefield, 1999. http://www.ics.si.edu/subsites/ccpdc/pubs/apple/toc.htm.

Douglas Johnston, ed. *Faith-Based Diplomacy: Trumping Realpolitik*. Oxford University Press, 2003.

Douglas Johnston and Cynthia Sampson, eds. 1995. *Religion: The Missing Dimension of Statecraft*. Oxford University Press, 1995.

Mohammed Abu-Nimer. *Nonviolence and Peace Building in Islam: Theory and Practice*. University Press of Florida, 2003.

RECOMMENDED BOOKS

Henry Thompson. *World Religions in War and Peace*. McFarland, 1988. Out of print.

Christopher S. Queen and Sallie B. King. *Engaged Buddhism: Buddhist Liberation Movements in Asia*. State University of New York Press, 1996.

Abdul Aziz Said, Nathan C. Funk, and S. Ayse Kadayifci-Orellana, eds. *Peace and Conflict Resolution in Islam: Precept and Practice*. University Press of America, 2001.

David Smock, ed. *Interfaith Dialogue and Peacebuilding*. US Institute of Peace Press, 2002.

REQUIRED EXCERPTS FROM BOOKS OR ARTICLES

Hans Gadamer. *Truth and Method,* translated and revised by Joel Weinsheimer and Donald Marshall. Crossroads, 1989, 300–307.

C. R. Mitchell. "Psychological Dimensions of Conflict." In *The Structure of International Conflict* by C. R. Mitchell. St. Martin's Press, 1981, 71–98.

Mary Ann Stenger. "Gadamer's Hermeneutics as a Model for Cross-Cultural Understanding and Truth in Religion." In *Religious Pluralism and Truth: Essays on Cross-Cultural Philosophy of Religion,* edited by Thomas Dean. State University of New York Press, 1995, 151–168.

Joseph V. Montville. "Psychoanalytic Enlightenment and the Greening of Diplomacy." In *The Psychodynamics of International Relationships,* vol. 2, edited by Vamik D. Volkan, Joseph V. Montville, and Demetrios A. Julius. Lexington Books, 1991, 177–192.

Vamik D. Volkan. "Psychological Processes in Unofficial Diplomacy Meetings." In *The Psychodynamics of International Relationships,* vol. 2, edited by Vamik Volkan, Joseph V. Montville, and Demetrios A. Julius. Lexington Books, 1991, 207–222.

Dennis J. D. Sandole. "Paradigm, Theories, and Metaphors in Conflict and Conflict Resolution: Coherence or Confusion?" In *Conflict Resolution Theory and Practice,* edited by Dennis Sandole. Manchester University Press, 1993, 3–24.

COURSE SCHEDULE

Unit 1: Theory

Session 1: Religion and Conflict Resolution: Mapping a New Field

Gopin, *Between Eden and Armageddon,* 3–86, 199–228.
Appleby, *Ambivalence of the Sacred,* 1–56.
Johnston, *Faith-Based Diplomacy,* 231–258.

Session 2: The Psychological and Social Foundations of Conflict

Montville, "Psychoanalytic Enlightenment," all.
Volkan, "Psychological Processes," all.
Sandole, "Paradigm, Theories, and Metaphors," all.

Session 3: Hermeneutics, Religion, and the Psychosocial Dynamics of Religious Conflict and Violence

Gadamer, *Truth and Method,* all.
Mitchell, "Psychological Dimensions of Conflict," all.

Stenger, "Gadamer's Hermeneutics," all.
Appleby, *Ambivalence of the Sacred,* 57–120.

Unit 2: Applications

Session 4: Peacebuilding in Islam I
Abu-Nimer, *Nonviolence and Peace Building in Islam,* introduction, chapter 1 ("The Study of Islam, Nonviolence, and Peace"), and chapter 2 ("Islamic Principles of Nonviolence and Peacebuilding: A Framework").

Session 5: Peacebuilding in Islam II
Abu-Nimer, *Nonviolence and Peace Building in Islam,* chapter 3 ("Peacebuilding and Nonviolence in a Sociocultural Context: Traditional Arab-Muslim Mechanisms for Dispute Resolution"), chapter 4 ("Nonviolent Peace-Building Initiatives in Arab-Muslim Communities: Myths and Obstacles in a Training Framework"), and conclusion.

Session 6: Christian Peacemaking: Introduction, France/Germany, East Germany
Appleby, *Ambivalence of the Sacred,* 121–308.
Gopin, *Between Eden and Armageddon,* 139–166.
Johnston, *Religion,* 37–63, 119–152.

Session 7: Christian Peacemaking: Bosnia, Nicaragua, Nigeria, South Africa, Zimbabwe, and the Philippines
Johnston, *Religion,* 64–118, 177–257, 153–176.
Johnston, *Faith-Based Diplomacy,* 124–177.

Session 8: The Arab-Israeli Conflict: Religious, Secular, and Intermonotheistic Conflict
Gopin, *Between Eden and Armageddon,* 115–138.
Gopin, *Holy War,* 3–102.
Johnston, *Faith-Based Diplomacy,* 91–123.

Session 9: The Arab-Israeli Conflict: Abrahamic Pathways Toward Relationship Transformation
Gopin, *Holy War,* 103–143, 160–228.
Gopin, *Between Eden and Armageddon,* 167–198.

Session 10: Kashmir: Hindu and Islamic Possibilities
Johnston, *Faith-Based Diplomacy,* 33–75.
Johnston, *Faith-Based Diplomacy,* 76–90 (Buddhist liberation movements).

Session 11: Islam and Peacemaking from a Sunni Normative Perspective: Applications to Sudan
Johnston, *Faith-Based Diplomacy,* 178–230.

Session 12: The Question of Interfaith Dialogue
Gopin, *Holy War,* 144–159.

16.3 Islamic Peace Paradigms

S. Ayse Kadayifci-Orellana
American University

COURSE DESCRIPTION

Upper-level undergraduate and lower-level graduate course for students in peace and conflict studies, religion, Islamic studies, and Middle Eastern studies.

The ideal of peace is deeply embedded in the religious vision of Islam, but ideas for achieving peace have differed among adherents. This course explores the interpretive foundations, history, and practice of peace within the context of major Islamic paradigms—tradition, reformism (*islah*), renewalism (*tajdid*), and Sufism (*tasawwuf*)—and compares and contrasts them with the peace paradigms developed in the West. The origins, value structure, and methodology of each paradigm are examined in light of the challenges facing contemporary Islamic societies. We will employ the approach developed by the pioneer of this area of inquiry, Professor Abdul Aziz Said, and examine the following paradigms:

1. Peace Through Coercive Power: Realist/Power Politics.
2. Peace Through the Power of Law: World Order and Institutions.
3. Peace Through Willpower: Nonviolence and Movements for Social Change.
4. Peace Through the Power of Communication: Conflict Resolution.
5. Peace Through the Power of Love: Transformation, Person, and Community.

By the end of the course, the student should have a clear understanding of the following: (1) the salient concepts and theoretical approaches to the study of Islamic peace paradigms; (2) the proponents of the most general, systemic, and philosophical Islamic approaches to peace and conflict resolution; and (3) the roles of Muslim individuals, governmental, and non-governmental agencies in conflict resolution.

REQUIRED TEXTS

Charles Kurzman, ed. *Liberal Islam: A Sourcebook.* Oxford University Press, 1998.

Abdul Aziz Said, Nathan Funk, and S. Ayse Kadayifci-Orellana. *Peace and Conflict Resolution in Islam: Peace and Practice.* University Press of America, 2001.

Ralph H. Salmi, Cesar Adib Majul, and George K. Tanham. *Islam and Conflict Resolution: Theories and Practices.* University Press of America, 1998.

Ihkwan al Safa. *Animals' Law Suit Against Humanity.* Translated by Rabbi Anson Laytner. Fons Vitae, 2005.

RECOMMENDED TEXTS

Abdul Aziz Said and Meena Sharify-Funk, eds. *Cultural Diversity in Islam.* University Press of America, 2003.

Abdul Aziz Said, Meena Sharify-Funk, and Mohammed Abu-Nimer. *Contemporary Islam: Dynamic, Not Static.* Routledge, 2006, 129–212.

Shafiq Muhammad and Mohammed Abu-Nimer. *Interfaith Dialogue: A Guide for Muslims.* International Institute for Islamic Thought, 2007.

Abdul Karim Bangura. *Islamic Peace Paradigms.* Kendall/Hunt, 2005.

COURSE SCHEDULE

Week 1: Introduction

Presentation of the course overview, discussion of students' backgrounds and interests, preliminary perspectives on Islamic peace paradigms, and assignment of collaborative presentations.

Week 2: What Is Islam? Where Is Islam? Why a Paradigmatic Approach?

Ahmet Karamustafa. "Islam: A Civilizational Project in Progress." In *Progressive Muslims: On Justice, Gender, and Pluralism,* edited by Omid Safi. Oneworld Publications, 2003.

Said, Funk, and Kadayifci-Orellana. *Peace and Conflict Resolution in Islam,* introduction.

David Smock. "Ijtihad: Reinterpreting Islamic Principles for the Twenty-First Century," Special Report 125, US Institute of Peace, August 2004, www.usip.org.

Ahmad S. Dallal. "Ummah." In *The Oxford Encyclopedia of the Modern Islamic World,* edited by John L. Esposito. Oxford University Press, 1995.

Kurzman, *Liberal Islam,* chapter 4.

Recommended reading:

Karen Armstrong. *Muhammad: A Biography of the Prophet.* Harper San Francisco, 1992.

Ali Mazrui. "Islamic and Western Values." *Foreign Affairs* 76, no. 5: 118–132.

Unit 1: Peace Through Coercive Power: Realist/Power Politics

Week 3: The Development of Islamic Perspectives on Security and Social Order

Majid Khadduri. "The Islamic Theory of International Relations and Its Contemporary Relevance." In *War and Peace in the Law of Islam*, by Majid Khadduri. Johns Hopkins University Press, 1955.

Abdul Aziz Said, Nathan Funk, and S. Ayse Kadayifci-Orellana, eds. *Peace and Conflict Resolution in Islam*, chapters 2, 3, and 6.

S. Ayse Kadayifci-Orellana. *Standing on an Isthmus: Islamic Narratives of War and Peace in Palestinian Territories*. Lexington Books, 2007, introduction and chapter 4.

Recommended reading:

Majid Khadduri. "The Role of Military in the Middle East." *American Political Science Review* 47, no. 2 (1953): 511–524.

Ibn Khaldun. *An Arab Philosophy of History: Selections from the Prolegomena of "Ibn Khaldun of Tunnis" (1332–1406)*, translated and arranged by Charles Issawi. Darwin Press, 1987.

"Globalization and Civil Society in the Muslim World," an online panel discussion sponsored by the Library of Congress, November 14, 2001, http://www.loc.gov/locvideo/mslm/mslmcvl/. Six participants explore the dimensions of civil society in the Muslim world from a variety of perspectives.

Week 4: Islamic Extremism and Fundamentalism in the Age of Globalization

Said and Sharify-Funk, *Cultural Diversity in Islam*, chapters 8–9.

Mahmoud Suaed. "Islamic Unity and Political Change: Interview with Shaykh Muhammad Hussayn Fadlallah." *Journal of Palestine Studies* 25, no. 1 (Autumn 1995): 61–75.

Hilal Khashan. "The New World Order and The Tempo of Militant Islam." *British Journal of Middle Eastern Studies* 24, no. 1 (May 1997): 5–24.

Richard T. Antoun. *Understanding Fundamentalism*. Altamira Press, 2001, 1–35 (introduction).

Kurzman, *Liberal Islam*, chapter 22.

Recommended reading:

Abdulaziz Sachedina. "The Creation of a Just Social Order in Islam." *In State, Politics, and Islam*, edited by Mumtaz Ahman. American Trust Publishers, 1986.

Unit 2: Peace Through the Power of Law: World Order and Institutions

Week 5: Islamic Law of Nations: Siyar and International Institutions

Salmi, Majul, and Tanham, *Islam and Conflict Resolution,* 1–63.

Noor Mohammad. "The Doctrine of Jihad: An Introduction." *Journal of Law and Religion* 3, no. 2 (1985): 381–397.

Kurzman, *Liberal Islam,* chapters 16–19.

Recommended reading:

Mustapha K. Pasha and A. I. Samatar. "The Resurgence of Islam." In *Globalization: Critical Reflections,* edited by James H. Mittleman. Lynne Rienner, 1997.

Organization of the Islamic Conference, http://www.oic-oci.org/.

Week 6: Islamic Cosmopolitanism in the Contemporary Muslim Intellectual Context

Said, Funk, and Kadayifci-Orellana, *Peace and Conflict Resolution in Islam,* chapters 1 and 5.

Kurzman, *Liberal Islam,* chapters 1, 2, 3, 6, 7, 10, and 21.

Recommended reading:

Asad Abu Khalil. "Islam." In *The Oxford Encyclopedia of the Modern Islamic World,* edited by John L. Esposito. Oxford University Press, 1995.

Fazlur Rahman. *Revival and Reform in Islam.* Oneworld Publications, 1999.

Abdeslam M. Maghraoui. "American Foreign Policy and Islamic Renewal." US Institute of Peace, http://www.usip.org/pubs/specialreports/sr164.html.

David Smock. "Ijtihad: Reinterpreting Islamic Principles for the Twenty-first Century." US Institute of Peace, http://www.usip.org/pubs/specialreports/sr125.html.

Week 7: Islamic Reform and Renewal: Reconciling Change and Islamic Precepts

John Esposito, ed. *Voices of Resurgent Islam.* Oxford University Press, 1983.

Kurzman, *Liberal Islam,* chapters 23–24 and 27–30.

Ameer Ali. "Islamic Revivalism in Harmony and Conflict: The Experience in Sri Lanka and Malaysia." *Asian Survey* 24, no. 3 (March 1984): 296–131.

Sohail Hashmi. "Is There an Islamic Ethics of Humanitarian Intervention?" *Ethics and International Affairs* 7 (1993): 55–73.

Recommended reading:

Ann Elizabeth Mayer. *Islam and Human Rights: Tradition and Politics,* 3rd ed. Westview, 1999.

Abdullahi An-Na'im. *Toward an Islamic Reformation: Civil Liberties, Human Rights, and International Law.* Syracuse University Press, 1990.

M. A. Muqtedar Khan, ed. "Islamic Democratic Discourse: Theory, Debates and Philosophical Perspectives." www.ijtihad.org/book3.htm.

Islamic Human Rights Commission, http://www.ihrc.org/. 'Allamah Abu al-'A'la Mawdudi. "Islam and Human Rights." Witness-Pioneer, http://www.witness-pioneer.org/vil/Books/M_hri/.

David Smock. "Islam and Democracy." US Institute of Peace, http://www.usip.org/pubs/specialreports/sr93.html.

"The Doha Declaration." No Peace Without Justice, http://www.npwj.org/modules.php?name=News&file=print&sid=1715.

Center for the Study of Islam and Democracy, www.islam-democracy.org.

Week 8: Women and Islam

Kurzman, *Liberal Islam,* part 3.

Islah Jad. "Between Religion and Secularism: Islamist Women of Hamas." In *On Shifting Ground: Muslim Women in the Global Era,* edited by Fereshteh Nouraie-Simone. Feminist Press, 2005.

Meena Sharify-Funk. "Women and the Dynamics of Transnational Networks." In *On Shifting Ground: Muslim Women in the Global Era,* edited by Fereshteh Nouraie-Simone. Feminist Press, 2005.

M. Elaine Combs-Schilling. "Sacred Refuge: The Power of a Muslim Female Saint." *Fellowship* 60, nos. 5–6 (May–June 1994).

W. Flagg Miller. "Public Words and Body Politics: Reflections on the Strategies of Women Poets in Rural Yemen." *Journal of Women's History* 14, no. 1 (Spring 2002): 94–122.

Unit 3: Peace Through Willpower:
Nonviolence and Movements for Social Change

Week 9: Defining Nonviolence and the Application of Islamic Principles in Nonviolent Social Movements

Bangura, *Islamic Peace Paradigms,* chapter 4.

Said and Sharify-Funk, *Cultural Diversity in Islam,* chapters 10 and 11.

Said, Sharify-Funk, and Abu-Nimer, *Islam: Dynamic, Not Static,* pages 129–212.

Recommended reading:

Paige Glenn, Chaiwat Satha Anand, and Sarah Gilliatt, eds. *Islam and Nonviolence.* University of Hawaii Press, 1993.

Mohammed Abu-Nimer. *Nonviolence and Peacebuilding in Islam: Theory and Practice.* University of South Florida Press, 2003.

S. Ayse Kadayifci-Orellana. "Islamic Tradition of Nonviolence: A Hermeneutic Approach." In *Identity, Morality, and Threat: Towards a Theory of Identity-based Conflict,* edited by Daniel Rothbart and Karina Korostelina. Lexington Books, 2007.

Glenn Paige, Chaiwat Satha-Anand, and Sara Gilliat. "Islam and Nonviolence." Center for Global Nonviolence, 1986, http://www.globalnonviolence.org/islam.htm.

Meir Amor. "Nonviolence in the Middle East: A Talk with Mubarak Awad." *Peace Magazine* 16, no. 4 (October–December 2000), http://www.peacemagazine.org/archive/v16n4p13.htm.

LibForAll website, http://www.libforall.org/.

Week 10: Nonviolent Case Studies in the Islamic Tradition

Said, Funk, and Kadayifci-Orellana, *Peace and Conflict Resolution in Islam,* chapters 4, 10, 11, and 14.

Robert C. Johansen. "Radical Islam and Nonviolence: A Case Study of Religious Empowerment and Constraint Among Pashtuns." *Journal of Peace Research* 34, no. 1 (1997): 53–71.

Recommended reading:

E. Easwaran. *A Man to Match His Mountains: Badshah Khan, Nonviolent Soldier of Islam.* Nilgiri Press, 1984.

Farid Esack. *Qur'an, Liberation, and Pluralism.* Oneworld Publications, 1997.

Unit 4: Peace Through the Power of Communication: Conflict Resolution

Week 11: Western and Islamic Approaches to Conflict Resolution

Paul Salem, ed. *Conflict Resolution in the Arab World: Selected Essays.* Beirut: American University of Beirut, 1997, preface, chapters 1 and 2.

Salmi, Majul, and Tanham, *Islam and Conflict Resolution,* remainder of book.

Said, Funk, and Kadayifci-Orellana, *Peace and Conflict Resolution in Islam,* chapters 7–9.

Recommended reading:

Shafiq and Abu-Nimer, *Interfaith Dialogue: A Guide for Muslims.*

Aliyana Traison. "Peace in the Middle East: One Gathering at a Time." *Haaretz,* http://www.haaretz.com/hasen/pages/ShArtUnd.jhtml?itemNo=603974&contrassID=2&subContrassID=1&sbSubContrassID=0&listSrc=Y.

Week 12: Islamic Conflict Resolution in Practice

Al-Safa, *Animals' Law Suit Against Humanity.*

Gideon Weigert. "A Note on Hudna: Peacemaking in Islam." In *War and Society in the Eastern Mediterranean, 7th-15th Centuries,* edited by Yaacov Lev. Brill Academic Publishers, 1996.

Chaiwat Satha-Anand. "Core Values for Peacemaking in Islam: The Prophet's Practice as Paradigm." *Building Peace in the Middle East: Challenges for States and Civil Society,* edited by Elise Boulding. Lynne Rienner, 1994.

George E. Irani. "Islamic Mediation Techniques for Middle East Conflicts." *Middle East Review of International Affairs* 3, no. 2 (June 1999), http://meria.idc.ac.il/journal/1999/issue2/jv3n2a1.html.

Unit 5: Peace Through the Power of Love: Transformation, Person, and Community

Week 13: Islamic Understandings of Consciousness and Its Cultivation

Said and Sharify-Funk, *Cultural Diversity in Islam,* introduction.

Seyyed Hossein Nasr. *Sufism and the Integration of Man: Sufi Essays.* State University of New York Press, Albany, 1972.

Said, Funk, and Kadayifci-Orellana. *Peace and Conflict Resolution in Islam,* chapters 13–15.

Recommended reading:

Gnosis: A Journal of the Western Inner Traditions 30 (Winter 1994), special issue on Sufism.

Marshall Hodgson. *The Expansion of Islam in the Middle Periods.* Venture of Islam Series, vol. 2. University of Chicago Press, 1977, book 3, chapter 4 ("The Sufism of the Tariqah Orders").

Frederick M. Denny. "Islam and Ecology: A Bestowed Trust Inviting Balanced Stewardship." *Earth Ethics: Evolving Values for an Earth Community* 10, no. 1 (Fall 1998): 10–11.

Mohammad Reza Rikhtehgaran. "Sufi Paradigm of Peace-Making." Indira Gandhi National Centre for the Arts, 1999, http://ignca.nic.in/cd_09018.htm.

Yoginder Sikand. "Peace in Kashmir: Engaging Creatively with Religion." Countercurrents, July 20, 2006, http://www.countercurrents.org/kashmir-sikand200706.htm.

Week 14: A Sufi Perspective on the Pursuit of Unity

Said, Funk, and Kadayifci-Orellana, *Peace and Conflict Resolution in Islam,* "Peace in the Sufi Tradition: Ecology of the Spirit."

Abdul Aziz Said. "Tawhid: The Sufi Tradition of unity," *Creation* 4, no. 4 (September–October 1988): 24–25, 39.

Julia Day Howell. "Sufism and Islamic Revival in Indonesia." *Journal of Asian Studies* 60, no. 3 (May 2001): 701–729.

Nizar Hamzeh and R. Hrair Dekmejian. "A Sufi Response to Political Islamism: Al-Ahbash of Lebanon." *International Journal of Middle East Studies* 28 (1996): 217–229. http://ddc.aub.edu.lb/projects/pspa/al-ahbash.html.

Camille Adams Helminski. "Women and Sufism." *Gnosis* 30 (Winter 1994). Available at the website of the Threshold Society, http://www.sufism.org/society/articles/women.html.

International Association of Sufism, http://www.ias.org/aboutias.html.

TEACHING NOTES

This is an interactive course in which students are expected to engage with the ideas and thoughts presented in the class assignments, by the professor, and by other students. Teaching resources also include visual materials relevant to class themes, such as PowerPoint lectures, documentaries, and films. Guest speakers, carefully chosen from among the practitioners and scholars in the field, also enrich the learning experience of the students. The philosophy of teaching followed is "collaborative learning," in which students engage in active learning by critically analyzing the readings and ideas of others, including the professor's, in the light of historical and current events, and participating in class assignments on which they collaborate with other students. To that end, students are *required* to partner with other students to make a collaborative presentation (one presentation of thirty to thirty-five minutes by two to three students). These presentations should have clear learning objectives that are elaborated in a brief paper (three to five pages). In these presentations creativity is strongly encouraged. At the end of the course students are also required to submit their own in-depth research of a case study. They are encouraged to conduct interviews to gain a better understanding of the course material, themes, and perspectives in light of contemporary developments.

16.4 Religion and Peacebuilding

S. Ayse Kadayifci-Orellana
American University

COURSE DESCRIPTION

Upper-level undergraduate and graduate course for students in peace and conflict resolution, political science, religious studies, and cross-cultural communication.

This course explores the role of religious traditions in peacebuilding. As individuals and communities struggle with the meaning of socioeconomic and political changes in a rapidly globalizing world, societies are turning to cultural and religious traditions to address contemporary problems. With the rise of religiously motivated violence around the world over the last few decades, especially since the events of September 11, 2001, religion has been perceived as a source of conflict and violence. Under the pressure of rapid social, political, and economic changes, it has become easier to manipulate and abuse religion to incite hatred and justify communal violence in disadvantaged societies. However, religious traditions also embody ideas of peace, human dignity, and social harmony, and religious actors have been and are still making significant contributions to peacebuilding and conflict resolution.

In this course we examine the role religion plays in both contexts and how it ultimately influences peacebuilding. We explore, from a comparative perspective, how religious traditions are used to justify violence and extremism or to promote peaceful coexistence, tolerance, and justice. The course also looks at different religious perspectives on key issues relating to peacebuilding, including, but not limited to, economic and environmental justice and human rights. It also explores the benefits of and challenges to interfaith dialogue and the role of religious advocacy groups in peacebuilding. This course also addresses the following questions: What are the critical factors that contribute to the rise of religious fundamentalism and extremism? How can religion, as an integral part of our cultures, be a resource for peaceful coexistence, peacemaking, and the establishment of just and sustainable relations between different communities, as well as tool to protect our environment?

By the end of the course, students should be able to (1) critically evaluate the role religion plays in peacebuilding, (2) critically analyze the changing role of religious traditions in the global arena, and (3) present coherent and empirically informed accounts of the use and abuse of religion in international conflicts and peacebuilding.

REQUIRED TEXTS

R. Scott Appleby. *The Ambivalence of the Sacred: Religion, Violence, and Reconciliation*. Rowman and Littlefield, 2000.

Mark Juergensmeyer. *Terror in the Mind of God*. University of California Press, Berkeley, 2000.

Douglas Johnston and Cynthia Sampson. *Religion: The Missing Dimension of Statecraft*. Oxford University Press, 1994.

Daniel Smith-Christopher, ed. *Subverting Hatred: The Challenge of Nonviolence in Religious Traditions*. Boston Research Center for the Twenty-First Century, 1998.

David Smock. *Religious Perspectives on War: Christian, Muslim, and Jewish Attitudes Toward Force After the Gulf War*. US Institute of Peace Press, 1992.

David Smock. *Interfaith Dialogue and Peacebuilding*. US Institute of Peace Press, 2002.

Joanna Macy. *Dharma and Development: Religion as Resource in the Sarvodaya Self-Help Movement*. Kumarian Press, 1983.

RECOMMENDED TEXTS

Marc Gopin. *Between Eden and Armageddon: The Future of World Religions, Violence, and Peacemaking*. Oxford University Press, 2002.

Lisa Schirch. *Ritual and Symbol in Peacebuilding*. Kumarian Press, 2005.

Paul F. Knitter and Chandra Muzaffer, eds. *Subverting Greed: Religious Perspectives on the Global Economy*. Orbis Books, 2002.

Leroy Rouner, ed. *Human Rights and the World's Religions*. University of Notre Dame Press, 1988.

COURSE SCHEDULE

Week 1: Introduction to the Course

Week 2: Peacebuilding and Challenge of Religion

Johnston and Sampson, *Religion: The Missing Dimension of Statecraft*, chapters 1–3.

S. Ayse Kadayifci-Orellana. "Hermeneutics of Truth: Religion and Violence Reconsidered." In *Identity, Morality and Threat*, edited by Daniel Rothbart and Karina Korostelinat. Lexington Books, 2007.

Appleby, *The Ambivalence of the Sacred*, introduction and chapters 1–3.

Marc Gopin. "Religion, Violence and Conflict Resolution," *Peace and Change* 22, no. 21 (January 1997).

Recommended reading:

Especially for students who do not have a background in the fields of conflict resolution, conflict transformation, and peacebuilding.

I. William Zartman and J. Lewis Rasmussen, eds. *Peacemaking in International Conflict: Methods and Techniques*. US Institute of Peace Press, 2005, 2007.

John Paul Lederach. *The Little Book of Conflict Transformation*. Good Books, 2003.

Sandra Cheldelin, Daniel Druckman, and Larissa Fast. *Conflict: From Analysis to Intervention*. Continuum, 2003.

Week 3: Religion as a Source of Conflict

Smock, *Religious Perspectives on War.*

Hubert G. Locke. "Religion and the Rwandan Genocide: Some Preliminary Considerations." In *Genocide in Rwanda: Complicity of the Churches?* edited by Carol Rittner, John K. Roth, and Wendy Whitworth. Paragon House, 2004.

Juergensmeyer, *Terror in the Mind of God,* 1–116.

Recommended reading:

Matthias Bjørnlund, Eric Markusen, Peter Steenberg, and Rafiki Ubaldo. "The Christian Churches and the Construction of a Genocidal Mentality." In *Genocide in Rwanda: Complicity of the Churches?* edited by Carol Rittner, John K. Roth, and Wendy Whitworth. Paragon House, 2004.

Douglas Johnston and Jonathan Eastvold. "Religion in the Bosnian Conflict." In *Religion and Peacebuilding,* edited by Harold G. Coward and Gordon S. Smith. State University of New York Press, 2004. Available online at the website of the International Center for Religion and Diplomacy, http://www.icrd.org/docs/Bosnia.html.

Week 4: The Use and Abuse of Religion and Religious Fundamentalism

Richard T. Antoun. *Understanding Fundamentalism.* Altamira Press, 2001, 1–35.

Juergensmeyer, *Terror in the Mind of God,* 119–242.

Thomas Carr. "Apartheid and Hermeneutics: Biblical Interpretations." In *Religious Fundamentalism in Developing Countries,* edited by Santosh C. Saha and Thomas K. Carr. Greenwood Press, 2001, 49–66.

Recommended reading:

Martin Marty and Scott Appleby, eds. *Fundamentalisms and the State: Remaking Polities, Economies, and Militance.* University of Chicago Press, 1993, conclusion.

Jacob Abadi. "Religious Zionism and Israel Politics: Gush Emunim Revisited." In *Religious Fundamentalism in Developing Countries,* edited by Santosh C. Saha and Thomas K. Carr. Greenwood Press, 2001, 67–90.

Week 5: Religion as a Source of Peace and Peacemaking

Johnston and Sampson, *Religion: The Missing Dimension of Statecraft,* chapters 4, 5, and 7.

Appleby, *The Ambivalence of the Sacred,* chapters 4–6.

David R. Smock, ed. "Religious Contributions to Peacemaking: When Religion Brings Peace, Not War." *Peaceworks* 55 (January 2006), http://www.usip.org/pubs/peaceworks/pwks55.html.

Recommended reading:

Gopin, *Between Eden and Armageddon.*

S. Ayse Kadayifci-Orellana. *Standing on an Isthmus: Islamic Narratives of War and Peace in Palestinian Territories.* Lexington Books, 2007, introduction and chapter 4.

Week 6: Faith-Based Organizations and Peacebuilding

Cynthia Sampson. "Religion and Peace Building." In *Peacemaking in International Conflict: Methods and Techniques,* edited by I. William Zartman and J. Lewis Rasmussen. US Institute of Peace Press, 1997.

US Institute of Peace. "Can Faith-Based NGOs Advance Interfaith Reconciliation? The Case of Bosnia and Herzegovina." March 2003.

Tsjeard Bouta, S. Ayse Kadayifci-Orellana, and Mohammed Abu-Nimer. "Faith-Based Peace-Building: Mapping and Analysis of Christian, Muslim, and Multi-Faith Actors." CRU Occasional Paper, Clingendael Institute, The Hague, November 2005. Available at the website of the Netherlands Institute of International Relations, http:www.clingendael.nl.

Johnston and Sampson, *Religion: The Missing Dimension of Statecraft,* chapters 6, 8, and 10.

Recommended reading:

Andrea Bartoli. "Mediating Peace in Mozambique: The Role of the Community of Sant'Egidio." In *Herding Cats: Multiparty Mediation in a Complex World,* edited by Chester Crocker et al. US Institute of Peace Press, 1999, chapter 11.

Schirch, *Ritual and Symbol in Peacebuilding.*

Jeff Haynes. "Transnational Religious Actors and International Politics." *Third World Quarterly* 22, no. 2 (2001): 143–158.

George Irani and Nathan C. Funk. "Rituals of Reconciliation: Arab-Islamic Perspectives." *Arab Studies Quaterly* 20, no. 4 (Fall 1997): 53–73.

Week 7: Nonviolence and Religion

Daniel Smith-Christopher, ed. *Subverting Hatred: The Challenge of Nonviolence in Religious Traditions.* Boston Research Center for the Twenty-First Century, 1998.

S. Ayse Kadayifci-Orellana. "Religion, Violence, and the Islamic Tradition of Nonviolence." *Turkish Yearbook of International Relations* 34 (2003).

Todd Whitmore. "The Reception to Catholic Approaches to Peace and War in the United States." *Modern Catholic Social Teaching,* edited by Ken Himes. Georgetown University Press, 2004.

Recommended reading:

Robert C. Johansen. "Radical Islam and Nonviolence: A Case Study of Religious Empowerment and Constraint Among Pashtuns." *Journal of Peace Research* 34, no. 1 (1997): 53–71.

Dolores Leckey, ed. *Just War, Lasting Peace: What Christian Traditions Can Teach Us.* Orbis Press, 2006.

Week 8: Environment, Economic Justice, and Religion

David Nicholls. "God and the Market." In *God and Government in an Age of Reason.* Routledge, 1995, 13–42.

Thomas Weber. "Gandhi, Deep Ecology, Peace Research, and Buddhist Economics." *Journal of Peace Research* 36, no. 3 (1999).

Joanna Macy. *Dharma and Development: Religion as Resource in the Sarvodaya Self-Help Movement.* Kumarian Press, 1983.

Recommended reading:

Gustavo Gutierrez. *A Theology of Liberation: History, Politics and Salvation.* New York: Orbis Books, 1971, chapters 1–3, 6–7, 9, and 11.

His All-Holiness Bartolomeus, Professor Rabbi Arthur Hertzber, and Fazlun Khalid. "Religion and Nature: The Abrahamic Faiths' Concept of Creation." In *Spirit of the Environment: Religion, Value, and Environmental Concern,* edited by David E. Cooper and Joy A. Palmer. Routledge, 1996.

Knitter and Muzaffer, *Subverting Greed.*

Norman K. Gottwald. "Values and Economic Structures." In *Religion and Economic Justice,* edited by Michael Zweig. Temple University Press, 1991, 53–77.

Arthur Waskow. *Torah of the Earth,* vols. 1 and 2. Jewish Lights Publishing, 2000.

Week 9: Democratization, Human Rights, and Religious Pluralism

Appleby, *The Ambivalence of the Sacred,* chapter 7.

Rouner, *Human Rights and the World's Religions.*

Steven Hood. "Rights Hunting in Non-Western Traditions." In *Negotiating Culture and Human Rights,* edited by Lynda S. Bell, Andrew J. Nathan, and Ilan Peleg. Columbia University Press, 2001, 96–122.

David Little. "Human Rights, East and West." US Institute of Peace, http://www.usip.org/research/rehr/eastwest.html.

Recommended reading:

Amina Wadud-Muhsin. *Qur'an and Woman.* Kuala Lumpur, Malaysia: Penerbit Fajar Bakti Sdn. Bhd, 1992.

Peter Juvilet. "Introduction: Ambiguities of the Divine." In *Religion and Human Rights: Competing Claims,* edited by Garrie Gustafson and Peter Juvilet. M.E. Sharp, 1999.

David Little. "The Universality of Human Rights." US Institute of Peace, http://www.usip.org/research/rehr/universality.html.

Pamela S. Nadell. *Women Who Would Be Rabbis.* Beacon Press, 1999.

Week 10: Interfaith Dialogue

Smock, *Interfaith Dialogue and Peacebuilding.*

US Institute of Peace. "What Works? Evaluating Interfaith Dialogue Programs." Special Report no. 123 (July 2004), www.usip.org.

Mohammed Abu-Nimer. "Conflict Resolution, Culture, and Religion: Toward a Training Model of Interreligious Peacebuilding." *Peace Research* 38, no. 6 (2001): 685–704.

Appleby, *The Ambivalence of the Sacred,* chapter 8.

Johnston and Sampson, *Religion: The Missing Dimension of Statecraft,* chapters 11, 13, and 15.

Recommended reading:

Venerable Havanpola Ratanasara. "The Importance of Interfaith Dialogue: A Buddhist Perspective." Lecture given at the Intermonastic Dialogue, Gethsemani Monastery, Louisville, Kentucky, July 1996, http://www.urbandharma.org/bcdialog/bcd2/interfaith.html.

Editorial Committee of the Parliament of the World's Religions. "Declaration Toward a Global Ethic." Global Ethic Foundation, http://www.weltethos.org/dat_eng/index3_e.htm.

Shafiq Muhammad and Mohammed Abu-Nimer. *Interfaith Dialogue: A Guide for Muslims.* International Institute for Islamic Thought, 2007.

Week 11: Simulation Exercise

Students will simulate a conflict where religion has been used and abused to justify violence. A conflict will be chosen during the second week of class based on the interests of the students.

Week 12: Conclusion and Summary

Week 13: Student Presentations

Week 14: Student Presentations

Week 15: Student Presentations

TEACHING NOTES

This is an interactive course in which students are expected to engage with the ideas and thoughts presented in the class assignments, by the professor, and by other students. Teaching resources also include visual materials relevant to class themes, such as PowerPoint lectures, documentaries, and films. Guest speakers, carefully chosen from among practitioners and scholars in the field, also enrich the learning experience of students. The course is based on a philosophy of teaching called "collaborative learning," in which students engage in active learning by critically analyzing the readings and ideas of others, including the professor, in light of historical and current events.

Students are also expected to participate in class assignments in which they collaborate with other students. Along those lines, students are required to partner with other students to make a presentation (one presentation of thirty to thirty-five minutes by two to three students). These presentations should have clear learning objectives that are elaborated in a brief paper (three to five pages). In these presentations, creativity is strongly encouraged.

This course also involves a simulation of a conflict in which religion has been used and abused to continue a culture of peace. The instructor will distribute a scenario and specific roles to each student. This exercise gives students the opportunity to apply the course materials and themes in a simulated environment, experience a conflict from within, and develop empathy. The simulated conflict that will be chosen during the second week of the course should be based on student interests. Also, at the end of the course, groups of students are required to present an in-depth research of a case study, in which they are encouraged to conduct interviews to gain a better understanding of the course material, themes, and perspectives in the light of contemporary developments.

17
Cultures of Peace

THE UNITED NATIONS LED THE WAY IN PROMOTING THE IDEA OF A "culture of peace." The UN Educational, Scientific, and Cultural Organization (UNESCO) coined the phrase in 1989, establishing a Culture of Peace Program in 1992. Over the course of the 1990s, the United Nations as a whole took up the theme, issuing a Declaration on a Culture of Peace and pronouncing 2000 the International Year for the Culture of Peace. The years 2001–2010 were subsequently established as the International Decade for a Culture of Peace and Non-Violence for the Children of the World. Although users of the phrase "culture of peace" may be unaware of its strong connection to the United Nations, they generally and consistently use the term to advocate for some combination of tolerance, education for peace, democracy, freedom of information, disarmament, human rights, sustainable development, and gender equality.

In the first two syllabuses offered here, Marlene Epp and Abbie Jenks explore the history of peace movements, especially in North America but with substantial attention directed further afield as well. In "Arts and Peacebuilding," Craig Zelizer investigates how art forms from both high and popular culture can nurture peace and illuminate the study of peace. Daniel Chong analyzes the mass media as powerful, double-edged swords, sometimes championing and sometimes undermining human rights. In their roles as teachers of teachers, Sue L. T. McGregor is especially concerned that peace education be done by means of a peace pedagogy deeply congruent with the ideas and practices being taught, and Tony Jenkins and Janet Gerson help their students consider the range of ways in which they can teach children how to address conflict nonviolently.

17.1 A History of Peace Movements

Marlene Epp
Conrad Grebel University College

COURSE DESCRIPTION

Lower-level undergraduate course for liberal arts students or majors in peace and conflict studies.

How did people in the past attempt to make peace in a world of war and conflict? This course is an introductory survey of individuals and groups who have created popular movements for peace globally and locally throughout history. The scope will be international, with a particular focus on nineteenth- and twentieth-century movements. The choice of peace movements will allow for a contrast in comparison of ideology, strategy, and impact.

Required texts appear in the course schedule.

COURSE SCHEDULE

Week 1: Introduction: Characteristics of Peace Movements

Elise Boulding. "Peace Movements and Their Organizational Forms: The Seedbed of Peace Cultures." In *Cultures of Peace: The Hidden Side of History,* by Elise Boulding. Syracuse, NY: Syracuse University Press, 2000.

Richard Deats. "The Global Spread of Active Nonviolence." In *An Anthology of Nonviolence: Historical and Contemporary Voices,* edited by Krishna Mallick and Doris Hunter. Westport, CT: Greenwood Press, 2002.

Week 2: Early Peace Movements and Ideas: Ancient Greece, Historical Peace Churches, Henry David Thoreau, and Leo Tolstoy

Peter Brock. "Tolstoy's Idea of Nonviolence." In *Freedom from War: Nonsectarian Pacifism, 1814–1914,* by Peter Brock. Toronto: University of Toronto Press, 1991.

Peter Brock. "The Peace Sects of Upper Canada and the Military Question." In *Against the Draft: Essays on Conscientious Objection from the Radical Reformation to the Second World War,* by Peter Brock. Toronto: University of Toronto Press, 2006.

Week 3: World War I Women Peace Activists

Anne Marie Pois. "'Practical' and Absolute Pacifism in the Early Years of the US Women's International League for Peace and Freedom." In

Challenge to Mars: Essays on Pacifism from 1918 to 1945, edited by Peter Brock and Thomas P. Socknat. University of Toronto Press, 1999.

Barbara Roberts. "Women Against War, 1914–1918." In *Up and Doing: Canadian Women and Peace*, edited by Janice Williamson and Deborah Gorham. Toronto: Women's Press, 1989.

Week 4: World War II Conscientious Objectors

Thomas P. Socknat. "Conscientious Objection in Canada." In *Challenge to Mars: Essays on Pacifism from 1918 to 1945*, edited by Peter Brock and Thomas P. Socknat. Toronto: University of Toronto Press, 1999.

Peter Brock. "Conscientious Objectors in Nazi Germany." In *Challenge to Mars: Essays on Pacifism from 1918 to 1945*, edited by Peter Brock and Thomas P. Socknat. University of Toronto Press, 1999.

Week 5: Mahatma Gandhi and Noncooperation

Peter Ackerman and Jack DuVall. "India: Movement for Self-Rule." In *A Force More Powerful: A Century of Nonviolent Conflict*, by Peter Ackerman and Jack DuVall. New York: St. Martin's Press, 2000.

Week 6: The US Civil Rights Movement

James C. Juhnke and Carol M. Hunter. "The Civil Rights Movement: Participatory Democracy and Nonviolence in Action." In *The Missing Peace: The Search for Nonviolent Alternatives in United States History*, by James C. Juhnke and Carol M. Hunter. Kitchener, ON: Pandora Press, 2001.

Week 7: Resistance Movements as Peace Movements: World War II Denmark and Chile in the 1970s

Peter Ackerman and Jack DuVall. "Denmark, the Netherlands, the Rosenstrasse: Resisting the Nazis." In *A Force More Powerful: A Century of Nonviolent Conflict*, by Peter Ackerman and Jack DuVall. New York: St. Martin's Press, 2000.

Peter Ackerman and Jack DuVall. "Argentina and Chile: Resisting Repression." In *A Force More Powerful: A Century of Nonviolent Conflict*, by Peter Ackerman and Jack DuVall. New York: St. Martin's Press, 2000.

Week 8: The Anti–Vietnam War Movement and Contemporary Conscientious Objectors

Tom Wells. "The Anti–Vietnam War Movement in the United States." In *The Vietnam War*, edited by Peter Lowe. New York: St. Martin's Press, 1998.

Week 9: The Anti-Nuclear Movement

Lawrence S. Wittner. "The Transnational Movement Against Nuclear Weapons, 1945–1986: A Preliminary Survey." In *Peace Movements and*

Political Cultures, edited by Charles Chatfield and Peter van den Dungen. Knoxville: University of Tennessee Press, 1986.

Lawrence S. Wittner. "The Power of Protest." *Bulletin of the Atomic Scientists* 60, no. 4 (July–August 2004): 20–26.

Gwyn Kirk. "Our Greenham Common: Feminism and Nonviolence." In *Rocking the Ship of State: Toward a Feminist Peace Politics,* edited by Adrienne Harris and Ynestra King. Boulder: Westview, 1989.

Week 10: Buddhist Peace Movements

Metta Spencer. "Buddhist Peacemakers." *Peace Magazine,* April–June 2004, 11.

Christopher S. Queen. "Introduction." In *Engaged Buddhism: Buddhist Liberation Movements in Asia,* edited by Christopher S. Queen and Sallie B. King. Albany: State University of New York Press, 1996.

Week 11: The Nobel Peace Prize and Its Winners

Øyvind Tønnesson. "Lists and Categories of Nobel Peace Prize Laureates" and "Trends in Nobel Peace Prizes in the Twentieth Century." *Peace and Change* 26, no. 4 (October 2001): 428–442.

Week 12: Contemporary Peace Movements: A Department of Peace, Women in Black, and Christian Peacemaker Teams

TEACHING NOTES

Classes combine lectures, small-group discussion, films, and guest peace activists. Defining a peace movement is one of the problems of the course. Creating an open classroom for both pacifists and nonpacifists is an ongoing challenge. In my course, assignments include the options of essay writing (on a historic peace movement or event), group projects (designing a peace movement), or service learning projects (contributing to local community peace organizations).

17.2 Peacemaking in Practice: Seminar in Nonviolence and Social Action

Abbie Jenks
Greenfield Community College

COURSE DESCRIPTION

Intermediate-level undergraduate course for peace and justice studies majors and elective course for the liberal arts. Designed for the community college setting, but usable in any undergraduate college.

This course offers an exploration of the concepts of nonviolence and how individuals have used them as a strategy for social change, both past and present. Students study the history of nonviolent movements and actions, the women and men who promote nonviolence, and the cultural conditions under which social change occurs. Students complete a service learning project in the form of a placement or action in the wider peace community.

REQUIRED TEXTS

Ira Chernus. *American Nonviolence: The History of An Idea.* Orbis Books, 2004.

David Cortright. *Gandhi and Beyond: Nonviolence for an Age of Terrorism.* Paradigm Publishers, 2006.

SUGGESTED TEXTS

Rachel M. MacNair, ed. *Working for Peace: A Handbook of Practical Psychological and Other Tools.* Impact Publishers, 2006.

Kim Bobo, Jackie Kendall, and Steve Max, eds. *Organizing for Social Change: Midwest Academy Manual for Activists.* Seven Locks Press, 2001.

COURSE SCHEDULE

Week 1: Course Introduction, Requirements and Expectations, Overview of Topic

Session 1: Course Introduction

Session 2: Anabaptists and Quakers

Chernus, *American Nonviolence,* introduction and chapters 1–2.

Week 2: Abolition

Session 1

Invite a local representative of a grassroots group that advocates for nonviolence to speak about its nonviolent methods, how they use them, and what they accomplish.

Session 2: William Lloyd Garrison and Abolitionists

Chernus, *American Nonviolence,* chapter 3.

Week 3: Thoreau and Anarchists

Session 1: Henry David Thoreau

Chernus, *American Nonviolence,* chapter 4.

Session 2: The Anarchists

Chernus, *American Nonviolence,* chapter 5.

Week 4: World War I

Session 1: World War I

Chernus, *American Nonviolence,* chapter 6.

Observation assignment due.

Week 5: Gandhi and Niebuhr

Session 1: Mohandas K. Gandhi

Chernus, *American Nonviolence,* chapter 7.

Session 2: Reinhold Niebuhr

Chernus, *American Nonviolence,* chapter 8.

Week 6: Religious Pacifism

Session 1: A. J. Muste

Chernus, *American Nonviolence,* chapter 9.

Session 2: Dorothy Day and the Catholic Worker Movement

Chernus, *American Nonviolence,* chapter 10.

Week 7: The Civil Rights Movement

Session 1: Martin Luther King Jr.

Chernus, *American Nonviolence,* chapter 11.

Interview assignment due.

Session 2
View before class *An Act of Conscience,* directed by Robbit Leppzer, 90 minutes, 1997.

Week 8: The Antiwar Movement

Session 1: Barbara Deming
Chernus, *American Nonviolence,* chapter 12.

Session 2: Thich Nhat Hanh
Chernus, *American Nonviolence,* chapter 13 and conclusion.

Week 9: Gandhi and Beyond

Session 1: Grasping Gandhi
Cortright, *Gandhi and Beyond,* 1–36.

Session 2: Gandhi USA
Cortright, *Gandhi and Beyond,* 36–52.

Week 10: Martin Luther King Jr.

Session 1: King, an American Gandhi
Cortright, *Gandhi and Beyond,* 53–72.

Session 2: Gandhi in the Fields
Cortright, *Gandhi and Beyond,* 73–96.

Week 11: Dorothy Day

Session 1: A Mission of Love
Cortright, *Gandhi and Beyond,* 97–110.

Session 2: The Power of Nonviolence
Cortright, *Gandhi and Beyond,* 111–136.

Week 12: Learning Lessons

Session 1: Learning Lessons
Cortright, *Gandhi and Beyond,* 137–162.

Personal Theory of Social Change paper due.

Session 2: Gender Matters
Cortright, *Gandhi and Beyond,* 163–190.

Week 13: Principles of Action

Session 1: Principles of Action
Cortright, *Gandhi and Beyond,* 191–222.

Session 2
Visiting speaker (a local peace activist).

Week 14: Next Steps

Session 1: Time for Creating Next Steps to develop a deep and lasting change. . . . Imagine!

Session 2: Review

TEACHING NOTES

My assignments require that students experiment with concepts by putting them into action. They must engage in activities such as service learning projects, interviews with experienced activists, and grassroots organizing meetings. And, more importantly, they must write about their own theory of social change.

Service learning project. Students volunteer with local or national agencies that are working nearby, such as social service agencies, political advocacy groups, legal aid organizations, and educational support agencies. Each week, they reflect on their experience in a journal, asking themselves, How am I doing with this project? What came up for me this week? What do I need to do to take care of myself? How does this relate to the course material? What excitement or concerns do I have about any of the aspects of the project?

Interview assignment. In this assignment, students identify a person who has been or is active in peace movements or in developing or implementing peace education programs. They arrange to conduct a thirty- to sixty-minute structured interview, focusing on the person's experiences in their work and how they conceptualize peace and the role of nonviolence. They write a three- to five-page paper about the interview using the following guidelines: Describe how and why you selected the interviewee. Describe the person's background, work, and other relevant information. Describe the person's conception of peace and the role of nonviolence. Discuss any insights you gained and the implications for your own life and work. Use class readings to clarify and illustrate your points.

Observation assignment. Students attend and/or participate in a meeting, educational program, march/rally, or other event related to peace movements or peace education. After the experience, they write a two- to three-page paper addressing these areas or questions: Why did you select this event? How did you relate it to your understanding of peace movements or peace education? Describe what you observed or how you participated and how it related to the course material. What thoughts and feelings did you have?

Personal theory of social change. The idea behind this paper is to help students maintain their involvement in an ongoing struggle for social change. Research shows that doing so is aided by developing one's own personal theory. A personal theory does not remain static, of course, and will develop over time, influenced by your personal experiences. For the purposes of this three- to five-page paper, students should talk about their view of the following: the nature of human beings, the nature and sources of power, the nature and sources of truth and authority, the causes of social problems, the role of individuals and institutions in social change, and the role of the use of nonviolence and violence.

For this assignment, students should use resources to support their arguments and positions, compiled from readings from this course and others, personal experiences, and personal interviews. This class is an overview of many views of peace and provides many ideas, concepts, and issues to illustrate students' thinking.

17.3 Arts and Peacebuilding

Craig Zelizer
Georgetown University

COURSE DESCRIPTION

Upper-level course for majors in political science, peace and conflict studies, theater, and the arts.

Around the globe, numerous individuals, groups, and organizations are using arts-based processes to support peacebuilding efforts in severely conflicted societies. Arts processes such as theater, music, and film can be an especially effective means to bring together identity groups who are in conflict to share common cultural experiences and engage in cooperative creative projects. The power of various art forms to affect individuals emotionally, psychologically, and spiritually, via the creative process, can help foster change within and between conflicted groups. However, the arts are not necessarily a panacea for addressing conflicts; at times they are the means for legitimating cultures of violence in conflict regions.

The course will cover both theory and real world cases in an effort to contextualize many key concepts. In addition, students will receive practical exposure to several arts-based processes through exercises, guest speakers, and research projects. By taking this course, students will develop an understanding of how professionals and organizations are incorporating innovative, arts-based peacebuilding processes in diverse settings that can help inform their future work.

REQUIRED TEXTS

Augusto Boal. *Theater of the Oppressed.* Theatre Communications Group, 1985.

Debra Kalmanowitz and Bobby Lloyd, eds. *Art Therapy and Political Violence: With Art, Without Illusion.* Routledge, 2005.

Michelle LeBaron. *Bridging Troubled Waters: Conflict Resolution from the Heart.* Jossey-Bass, 2002.

John Paul Lederach. *The Moral Imagination.* Oxford University Press, 2005.

Lisa Schirch. *Ritual and Symbol in Peacebuilding.* Kumarian, 2005.

Philip Taylor. *Applied Theatre: Creating Transformative Encounters in the Community.* Heinemann Drama, 2003.

Craig Zelizer. "The Role of Artistic Processes in Peacebuilding in Bosnia-Herzegovina." Ph.D. diss., George Mason University, 2004.

Occasional readings assigned in the course schedule.

COURSE SCHEDULE

Week 1: Introduction
Overview of course. Expectations. Review of arts-based processes.

Week 2: The Art of Community and the Community of Arts
Key theories and models.

Andrea Assaf, Pam Korza, and Barbara Schaffer-Bacon. "Inroads: The Intersection of Art and Civic Dialogue." Community Arts Network, 2002, http://www.communityarts.net/.
William Cleveland. "Mapping the Field: Arts-based Community Development." Community Arts Network, 2002, http://www.communityarts.net/.
Jan Cohen-Cruz. "An Introduction to Community Art and Activism." Community Arts Network, 2002, http://www.communityarts.net/.
Office of Juvenile Justice and Delinquency Prevention. "Arts and Performances for Prevention." *Youth in Action Bulletin,* January 2000, Department of Justice, Office of Justice Programs. Washington, DC.
James Thompson. "Why Social Theatre?" *Drama Review* 48, no. 3 (2004): 12–16.
Craig Zelizer, "The Role of Artistic Processes in Peacebuilding in Bosnia-Herzegovina," 9–27.

Week 3: Peacebuilding and Identity Conflicts
Structural versus identity sources of conflict. General approaches to peacebuilding (a multitrack model).

LeBaron, *Bridging Troubled Waters,* chapter 1.
Schirch, *Ritual and Symbol in Peacebuilding,* chapter 3.
Benjamin J. Broome. "Building Shared Meaning: Implications of a Relational Approach to Empathy for Teaching Intercultural Communication." *Communication Education* 40, no. 3 (1991): 235–250.
Marc Howard Ross. "Cultural Strategies of Ethnic Conflict Mitigation." Paper presented at the annual meeting of the International Studies Association, Montreal, Quebec, Canada, 2004.
Craig Zelizer, "The Role of Artistic Processes in Peacebuilding in Bosnia-Herzegovina."

Week 4: Art in War and Art in Peace
Art, relationship building, and community. Existential needs for meaning. Overview of processes.

Kalmanowitz and Lloyd, *Art Therapy and Political Violence,* introduction and chapter 1.
LeBaron, *Bridging Troubled Waters,* chapters 3, 4, and 5.
Schirch, *Ritual and Symbol in Peacebuilding,* chapter 1.
C. Cohen. "Creative Approaches to Reconciliation." In *The Psychology of Resolving Global Conflicts: From War to Peace,* edited by Mari Fitzduff and Christopher E. Stout. Praeger, 2005. http://www.brandeis.edu/programs/Slifka/about/Creative%20Approaches.pdf.
Mary Marsh and Helen Gould. *Routemapping and Cultural Development.* London: Creative Exchange, 2003. http://www.creativexchange.org/node/657.
Craig Zelizer. "The Role of Artistic Processes in Peacebuilding in Bosnia-Herzegovina." *Peace and Conflict Studies* 10, no. 2 (2003): 62–75.
Craig Zelizer. "The Role of Artistic Processes in Peacebuilding in Bosnia-Herzegovina," 107–149.

Week 5: Ritual and Reconciliation
The importance of ritual. Creativity and rationality.

LeBaron, *Bridging Troubled Waters,* chapters 6 and 8.
Schirch, *Ritual and Symbol in Peacemaking,* chapters 4–9.

Week 6: Arts and Trauma Healing
Art, trauma, and conflict. The therapy of art therapy.

Kalmanowitz and Lloyd, *Art Therapy and Political Violence,* chapters 2, 4, 6, 9, and 11.
Laura Edmonson. "Marketing Trauma and the Theatre of War in Northern Uganda." *Theatre Journal* 57, no. 3 (2005): 451–474.

Week 7: Performing for Peace
Theater for peacebuilding. Theater for development.

Boal, *Theater of the Oppressed,* entire.
Taylor, *Applied Theatre,* chapters 1–2.
David Grant. "Playing the Wild Card: A Survey of Community Drama and Smaller Scale Theater from a Community Relations Perspective." Belfast, Northern Ireland, 1993, Community Relations Council, http://www.gppac.net/documents/pbp/7/3_n_irel.htm.

Week 8: Performing for Peace (cont.)
Review of key processes. Skills overview.

Taylor, *Applied Theatre,* chapter 3.
C. Reardon. "Democracy on Stage." *Ford Foundation Report,* 2001.
G. Schininà. "Here We Are: Social Theatre and Some Open Questions About Its Developments." *Drama Review* 48, no. 3 (2004): 17–31.

Lena Slachmuijlder. "Participatory Theatre for Conflict Transformation." Proposal submitted to Ashoka Changemakers Competition, 2006, http://www.changemakers.net/cm/journal/peace/displaypeace.cfm?ID=226.

James Thompson. "Digging Up Stories: An Archaeology of Theatre in War." *Drama Review* 48, no. 3 (2004): 150–164.

Week 9: Narratives of Peace and Conflict

Dueling narratives and conflict. Integrative storytelling.

LeBaron, *Bridging Troubled Waters,* chapter 7.

Dietrich Fischer. "Short Stories with Meaning." Transcend, September 14, 2003, http://www.transcend.org.

D. Grazar. "In the Telling." *Jerusalem Post,* December 16, 2006, http://www.jerusalemstories.org/.

Jessica Senehi. "Constructive Storytelling: A Peace Process." *Peace and Conflict Studies* 9, no. 2 (2002): 41–63.

Week 10: Music for Peace

Tools and techniques. Examples.

Roy Arbuckle. "How I Came to This Music." *World on the Street: The Global Music Challenge,* British Broadcasting Corporation, radio interview, http://www.bbc.co.uk/radio3/world/onyourstreet/msroya1.shtml.

Gerald L. Philipps. "Can There Be 'Music for Peace'?" *International Journal of World Peace* 21, no. 2 (2004): 63–74.

Lena Slachmuijlder. "The Rhythm of Reconciliation: A Reflection on Drumming as a Contribution to Reconciliation Processes in Burundi and South Africa." A working paper of Recasting Reconciliation Through Culture and the Arts, 2005, http://www.brandeis.edu/programs/Slifka/vrc/papers/lena/Slachmuijlder.pdf.

Week 11: Cinema of War and Peace

Film to be determined.

Ronit Avni. "Mobilizing Hope: Beyond the Shame-Based Model in the Israeli-Palestinian Conflict." *American Anthropologist* 108, no. 1 (2006): 205–215.

Carrie Menkel-Meadow. "Legal Negotiation in Popular Culture: What Are We Bargaining For?" In *Law and Popular Culture,* edited by Michael Freeman. Oxford University Press, 2005, 583–605.

Week 12: Evaluation of Arts-Based Programming

Tools for analysis. The proof is in the process. The ethics of practice and power relations.

Taylor, *Applied Theatre,* chapters 4–5.

Emery Brusset and Ralf Otto. "Nashe Maalo: Design, Implementation, and Outcomes—Social Transformation Through the Media." Evaluation done for Search for Common Ground, 2004, http://www.sfcg.org/sfcg/evaluations/nash2004.pdf.

William Cleveland. *Making Exact Change: How US Arts-Based Programs Have Made a Significant and Sustained Impact on Their Communities: A Report from the Community Arts Network.* Art in the Public Interest, 2005, http://www.communityarts.net/readingroom/archive/mec/index.php.

Mark Stern and Susan Seifert. "Culture Builds Community: Evaluation Summary Report." University of Pennsylvania School of Social Work, 2002, http://www.sp2.upenn.edu/SIAP/wholerep.pdf.

Week 13: Project Presentations

Week 14: Integrating and Planning Arts-based Programs in Peacebuilding

Review of semester and outstanding questions. Tools and resources for planning arts-based programs.

Lebaron, *Bridging Troubled Waters,* chapter 9.

Marian Liebmann. *Art Therapy for Groups.* Brunner-Routledge, 2004, chapter 16.

Schirch, *Ritual and Symbol in Peacebuilding,* chapter 10.

Judd Hardy. "Mother Africa Laughs: The Rwandan Folk Tale Project." Community Arts Network, 2006, http://www.communityarts.net/readingroom/archivefiles/2006/12/mother_africa_l.php.

Craig Zelizer. "The Role of Artistic Processes in Peacebuilding in Bosnia-Herzegovina," chapter 7.

TEACHING NOTES

One of the most important components of class is the assignments, which encourage students to meet and interact with professionals working in the field by attending events and conducting interviews. In addition, students are also responsible for developing their own arts-based group projects and presenting them to the group.

Informational interview. To better understand the opportunities and challenges of scholars and practitioners working on arts and peacebuilding, each student will conduct an informational interview with at least one practitioner or scholar working at the intersection of arts and peacebuilding.

Reflection on an arts event. Over the course of the semester, students will attend at least one arts-based event that involves some aspect of arts and conflict, such as a community theater performance with an audience discussion, film on a conflict topic or a region in conflict, visual arts exhibit connected to conflict, and so on. Students will write a short reflection paper or review (four to six pages) about the event, connecting it to some of the relevant theories and concepts from class.

Arts-based project. Students, individually or in small groups, will create their own arts-based projects that explore an aspect of arts and peacebuilding. Students choose a medium (narrative, film, visual art, music, etc.) and produce a work that explores some aspect of arts and peacebuilding. For example, students interested in refugees and conflict might do a short film in which they interview students and community members about their perspectives. A student with an interest in literary approaches could create a short story, poetry, or a short theater piece.

Paper on arts and peacebuilding. Students write seven- to ten-page papers in which they define for themselves the relationship between arts and peacebuilding. In the paper, students should integrate material from the class, highlight the key opportunities and challenges related to conducting arts and peacebuilding activities, and discuss the theories and models that are most useful.

17.4 Human Rights and the Media

Daniel Chong
American University

COURSE DESCRIPTION

Upper-level undergraduate elective for students of communication, journalism, political science, and peace and justice studies.

This course examines how various means of mass communication—movies, television, radio, music, the Internet, and others—affect the realization of human rights. Through the close study of documentary films and other audiovisual material, students will be introduced to the concept of human rights and debates about their implementation, such as the effect of US foreign policy on human rights, the role of the United Nations, the use of war to protect or threaten human rights, and the changing nature of human rights activism. Students will also examine how representatives of the media can help (deliberately or unwittingly) to build a human rights culture, expose human rights violations, become victims of human rights abuses, or facilitate those very violations. The course will feature in-class guest speakers, role plays, and other individual and group activities.

The course is designed to help students think creatively and critically about human rights in the context of global issues and to hone their writing and communication skills. In addition, after having taken this course, students should be able to:

- Understand key concepts of human rights;
- Think critically about the role of the media in human rights promotion and human rights violations;
- Identify threats and challenges facing journalists, filmmakers, and other media professionals; and
- Discuss current topics on human rights with greater understanding and skill.

REQUIRED TEXTS

June Carolyn Erlick. *Disappeared: A Journalist Silenced.* Seal Press, 2004.

Sam Gregory et al., eds. *Video for Change: A How-to Guide on Using Video in Advocacy and Activism.* Pluto Press, 2005.

Susan Moeller. *Compassion Fatigue: How the Media Sell Disease, Famine, War, and Death.* Routledge, 1999.

Susan Carruthers. *The Media at War.* St. Martin's Press, 2000.

Mark Thompson and Monroe Price. *Forging Peace.* Indiana University Press, 2002.

Readings assigned in the course schedule.

COURSE SCHEDULE

Week 1: Introduction

Film: *Good Night and Good Luck.* Co-written, directed by, and starring George Clooney, 2005, 93 minutes. Drama about the 1950s battle between CBS reporter Edward R. Murrow and Senator Joseph McCarthy over McCarthy's anticommunist tactics.

Week 2: Introduction to Human Rights

The Universal Declaration of Human Rights.

Nancy Flowers, *Human Rights Here and Now.* Human Rights USA, 1998, part 1.

"Three Challenges for the Human Rights Movement: Darfur, Abu Ghraib, and the Role of the United Nations." Lecture by Kenneth Roth. Listen to the audio lecture at the Carnegie Council website, http://www.cceia.org/resources/audio/data/000003.

Questions to consider when reading: What are human rights? How does the international human rights system work, and what are the various ways in which human rights are enforced? What are the actions someone can take when they believe their rights have been violated? What is the role of US foreign policy, the United Nations, and military intervention in human rights enforcement?

Week 3: The Link Between Human Rights and the Media

Cees J. Hamelink. "Introduction: Human Rights and the Media." In *The Ethics of Cyberspace,* by Cees J. Hamelink. Sage, 2000, chapter 3.

Paul Martin Lester and Susan Dente Ross, eds. *Images That Injure.* Praeger, 2003, introduction and chapters 3–4.

Susan Carruthers. *The Media at War,* conclusion.

Browse the Project Censored website for a view of how media biases affect, distort, or ignore human rights issues, www.projectcensored.org.

Watch the five-minute video clip with L. Brent Bozell, author of *Weapons of Mass Distortion,* for a different view of media biases, http://www.mediaresearch.org/books/wmd.asp.

Questions to consider: In what situations can media organizations either promote or threaten human rights? In your opinion, are certain media outlets "biased" and others "unbiased"? If so, how does this affect the protection of specific human rights, and what are the media's responsibilities for reporting human rights issues?

Week 4: Using the Media to Incite Genocide and War

Susan Carruthers. *The Media at War,* introduction.

Alison Des Forges. "Silencing the Voices of Hate in Rwanda." In *Forging Peace,* edited by Monroe Price and Mark Thompson. Indiana University Press, 2002.

Alexander Nikolaev and Ernest Hakanen, eds. *Leading to the 2003 Iraq War.* Palgrave, 2006, introduction, chapters 1, 3, and 8.

"A Question of Human Rights." *Le Monde Diplomatique,* web edition, October 2002. http://mondediplo.com/2002/10/03rights.

Ken Roth. "War in Iraq: Not a Humanitarian Intervention." Human Rights Watch, *World Report 2004,* http://hrw.org/wr2k4/3.htm#_Toc58744952.

Dominic Evans. "Britain Blames Saddam for Human Rights Abuses." Global Policy Forum, online, December 2, 2002, www.globalpolicy.org/security/issues/iraq/2002/1202hr.htm.

Questions to consider: How are the media used, both deliberately and unwittingly, to incite violence, crimes against humanity, and war? How was the US war in Iraq both justified and opposed on human rights grounds? In your opinion, has the war in Iraq protected or violated human rights?

Week 5: How the Media Affect Humanitarian Intervention

"'The CNN Effect': How Twenty-Four-Hour News Coverage Affects Governmental Decisions and Public Opinion." Brookings Institution online, January 2, 2002, www.brookings.edu/events/2002/0123media_journalism.aspx.

Warren P. Stroebel. "Assessing the Gap." *Late-Breaking Foreign Policy.* US Institute of Peace Press, 1997.

Moeller, *Compassion Fatigue,* chapters 1, 3, and 5.

Mark Thompson and Monroe Price. *Forging Peace,* introduction.

Questions to consider: What role do the news media play in encouraging or limiting humanitarian interventions? What specific role do visual images, satellite communications, cable news formats, and other media trends play? Does sensationalizing suffering induce "compassion fatigue"? What kinds of interventions are legitimate when the media are being used to incite human rights violations?

Week 6: Film: *Amandla*

A. G. Basoli. "Redefining Human Rights: The Human Rights Watch International Film Festival." Cineaste, 2002.

Browse the Internet to read any short history of apartheid in South Africa.

By email, send the instructor the lyrics of a song that deals with a human rights issue. Include a one-page explanation of the song and an analysis of how the song inspires, angers, or encourages you to think about human rights.

View in class *Amandla: A Revolution in Four-Part Harmony,* directed by Lee Hirsch, 2002, 108 minutes.

Week 7: Film: *The Agronomist*

Anup Shah. "Haiti and Human Rights." Global Issues, www.globalissues.org.
Anna Mance, Quinn Smith, and Rebecca Yagerman. "Haiti Human Rights Investigation." University of Miami School of Law, 2006.
Erlick, *Disappeared: A Journalist Silenced,* 2004.

View in class *The Agronomist,* directed by Jonathan Demme, 2003, 90 minutes.

Week 8: Film: *Maquilopolis*

View in class *Maquilopolis,* directed by Vicky Funari and Sergio de la Torre, 2006, 68 minutes.

Week 9: Film: *China Blue*

Lucy Ash. "Inside China's Sweatshops." BBC News online, July 2002.
Radley Balko. "Labor: Sweatshops and Globalization." A World Connected, www.aworldconnected.org.

View in class *China Blue,* directed by Micha Peled, 2005, 86 minutes.

Week 10: Promoting Human Rights Through Video

Gregory et al., *Video for Change,* selected chapters.

Browse www.witness.org to learn how this organization promotes grassroots filmmaking for human rights.

Questions to consider: How has the wide dissemination of video technology affected activists' ability to witness human rights violations? What kinds of filmmaking and storytelling strategies are effective? What are the best ways to target a specific audience or reach a mass audience?

Week 11: Promoting Human Rights Through the Internet and Communication Technologies

Read, watch, and listen to audio commentaries, podcasts, photo essays, and videos from Human Rights Watch website, www.hrw.org.

Browse the One Campaign's website, www.one.org.

Questions to consider: What is the potential for each of these forms of media to reach different audiences? How are human rights issues portrayed differently in each format? Are some rights easier to portray through these technologies than others? What strategies and messages are most effective?

Week 12: Promoting Human Rights Through Other Creative Communication Strategies

Allan Madrid. "Gaming the Poor." MSNBC/Newsweek online, July 11, 2006, http://www.emscharf.com/latestupdates/latestupdates_2006/latestupdates_2006_article_afmp04.htm.

Shira Golding. "Games for Change: Serious Fun." MediaRights website, July 21, 2006, www.mediarights.org. Follow the links in this article to learn about or play some of these games: Darfur Is Dying, Water Alert!, A Force More Powerful, Community Organizing Toolkit, or Peacemaker.

"Bono Backing Venezuela-Invasion Video Game." Venezuela Solidarity Network on the Autonomy and Solidarity website, http://oat.tao.ca/node/view/486.

Optional: Download and play other video games, e.g., America's Army or Food Force.

Questions to consider: How do video games differ from other forms of media in their impact, their target audience, and their depiction of human rights issues? Are some games more effective in inspiring human rights activism than others?

Week 13: Presentation of Class Projects and Research Papers

Second half of class: Film or exercise.

Week 14: Presentation of Class Projects and Research Papers

Second half of class: Course wrap-up.

TEACHING NOTES

Grades for this course are based upon a midterm exam, final exam, short response papers, and a research paper or project. The short response papers are brief responses to any four sets of weekly readings of their choice. Students are expected to respond critically to the readings. The research paper or project is the most substantial part of students' grades in the course. Students can work individually or in groups of up to three people. The precise topic or project is the students' choice, but they must meet with the professor first to get approval. Students have two options:

Write a traditional research paper. Write an original, well-researched, scholarly paper analyzing some aspect of the link between human rights and the media. For example, students could analyze a particular human rights organization's media strategy, or analyze how a TV program's ideological biases affect how it covers human rights issues.

Design a human rights media campaign. Create a short film, music video, website, podcast, school curriculum, game, or other public campaign designed to direct attention to a human rights issue students are concerned about.

17.5 Peace and Social Practice: Pedagogy and Practice

Sue L. T. McGregor
Mount Saint Vincent University

COURSE DESCRIPTION AND OBJECTIVES

Master's-level course for teachers.

As peace educator Ian Harris notes, peace education assumes people are naturally inclined toward living in peace and is about teaching (1) children and others how to *be peaceful;* (2) teaching strategies to build a desire for peace, including a respect for the role of conflict in daily life; and (3) how to build a culture of peace, a culture of nonviolence (that is, teaching how to resolve conflict constructively). Peace education brings together multiple traditions of pedagogy, theories of education, and international initiatives for the advancement of human development through learning. Peace education has both a consciousness-raising component (one's desire to live in peace) and a teaching component (how to achieve peace).

Pedagogy. Pedagogy is the act of imparting knowledge to someone and is made up of two things: (1) what counts as knowledge; and (2) what is the most effective way to get this knowledge across to, or solicit it from, the "learner." James Banks, multicultural education expert, claims that knowledge can come from (1) people and culture as lived each day; (2) popular culture and the media—mainstream and alternative; (3) mainstream academics (in the Western research paradigm); (4) transformative academics (this approach challenges the mainstream academic tradition); or (5) knowledge found in books and curriculum guides. One's pedagogical approach is a key determinant of human relationships in the educational process. It is the medium of communication between teacher and learner and the aspect of teaching that *most* affects what learners receive from their teachers and vice versa. Also, some pedagogical approaches challenge, reveal, or expose the status quo, whereas others reinforce, conceal, or obscure the status quo, that being the current context that perpetuates violence, oppression, exclusion, injustice, and so on.

Peace pedagogy. Peace education brings together multiple traditions of pedagogy. Learners should leave the course with a closer appreciation of their own professional understanding of a peace education pedagogy. To that end, each learner will be expected to participate fully in class seminars on each of the building blocks of the course and be prepared to lead discussions and share comparative analyses. This engagement with other learners and course material should lead the student to a deep understanding of how various scholars (including the student) understand what a peaceful classroom "looks like." The word "look" means more than just outward appearances: it includes peace education processes and philosophies (values, attitudes, goals, and principles) that create that peaceful look you see when you peek into a peaceful classroom.

REQUIRED TEXTS

Ian Harris and M. L. Morrison. *Peace Education*, 2nd ed. Jefferson, NC: McFarlane, 2003.

Occasional articles from the Internet listed in the course schedule.

COURSE SCHEDULE

Unit 1: The Big Picture: Challenges to Peace Education in the Current World Paradigm

Session 1: Globalization and Neoliberalism

Sue McGregor and N. E. Chesworth. "Positioning Human Spirituality in Home Economics." *Journal of the Home Economics Institute of Australia* 12, no. 3 (2005): 27–44 (article no. 3 at http://www.consultmcgregor.com).

Sue McGregor. "A Concept Paper on Human Security, the Human Family and Human Potential." Unpublished manuscript, December 2000 (article no. 4 at http://www.consultmcgregor.com).

Economic and Social Council. "2001 Report on the World Social Situation." United Nations, 2001, 1–19.

"Preparing for a Future of Peace and Development." Research Issues in Peace and Development Education, http://www.prasena.com/public/peace/9.htm.

Robin Burns. "Globalization and the Possibility of Transformative Educational Practices." University of Tromsø, Higher Education for Peace Conference, 2000, http://www.peace2.uit.no/hefp/contributions/papers/Burns_Robin_11E_1.pdf.

Session 2: Current State of the School System in the Context of Globalization and Neoliberalism

Michael Apple. "Rhetorical Reforms: Markets, Standards, and Inequality." *Current Issues in Comparative Education Journal*, 1999.

Kai-Ming Cheng. "Education and Market." *Current Issues in Comparative Education Journal*, 1999, http://www.tc.columbia.edu/cice/Archives/1.2/12cheng.pdf.

Peter W. Cooksen. "Privatization and Educational Equity." *Current Issues in Comparative Education* (1999), http://www.tc.columbia.edu/cice/Archives/1.2/12cookson.pdf.

Bob Stewart. "Modelling Education in a Culture of Peace." Canadian Centers for Peace, 2003, pages 1–4, http://www.peace.ca/modellingpeaceeducation.htm.

Gerald J. Biesecker-Mast. "Peace Pedagogy and the Practice of Persuasion." Bluffton University, http://www.bluffton.edu/~mastg/PEACE%20WORKS%20.htm.

Session 3: Challenge to Peace Education (in Current School Systems)

Jackie Kirk. "Education and Peacebuilding: Changing Beliefs and Attitudes." Canadian Bureau for International Education Research, Millennium Series No. 5, November 2002. Contact info@cbie.ca for a copy of this newsletter, or order at http://www.cbie.ca/english/media_research1_e.htm.

Harris and Morrison, *Peace Education,* chapters 5, 8, and 9.

B. K. Passi. "Three Challenges to Peace Education." 2003, http://www.prasena.com/public/peace/9.htm.

Session 4: How Schools Need to Change: A New Paradigm for Peace

Harris and Morrison, *Peace Education,* chapter 11.

Cynthia Duada. "Henry Giroux: What Is Role of Schools?" Website of Rage and Hope (click on Role of Schools page), 1999, http://www.perfectfit.org/CT/giroux1.html.

Svi Shapiro. "Peace or Hate? Education for a New Millennium." *Tikkun Magazine* 15, no. 1 (2000): 59–61.

Vachel Miller and Alessandra Ramos. "Transformative Teacher Education for a Culture of Peace." Unpublished paper, University of Massachusetts, Amherst, April 1999, http://www.eric.ed.gov/ERICDocs/data/ericdocs2sql/content_storage_01/0000019b/80/15/f0/35.pdf.

Unit 2: Peace Education as a Philosophy

Session 5: Different Conceptualizations of Peace over Time, Religions, Famous People, and Through the Peace Movement

David P. Barash and Charles P. Webel. *Peace and Conflict Studies.* San Francisco: Sage, 2002, chapter 2.

Session 6: What Is Peace, and What Are the Six Strategies of Peace (One Being Peace Education)?

Harris and Morrison, *Peace Education,* chapter 1.

David Hicks. "Which Way to Peace?" from "Understanding the Field." In *Education for Peace,* edited by David Hicks. Peace Pledge Union, 1988, http://www.ppu.org.uk/learn/peaceed/pe_which.html.

Leo Sandy and Ray Perkins Jr. "The Nature of Peace and Its Implications for Peace Education." *Online Journal of Peace and Conflict Resolution* 4, no. 2 (2002): 1–8, http://www.trinstitute.org/ojpcr/4_2natp.pdf.

Session 7: What Is Peace Education (Goals, Values, Attitudes, Principles)?

Harris and Morrison, *Peace Education,* chapter 1.

Sue McGregor. "Leadership for the Human Family: Reflective Human Action for a Culture of Peace," Part 1. Kappa Omicron Nu monograph series, 2001, http://www.kon.org/leadership/peace.html.

Toh Swee Hin. "Education for Sustainable Development and the Weaving of a Culture of Peace." 2006. http://www.unescobkk.org/fileadmin/user_upload/esd/documents/workshops/kanchanburi/toh_culture_of_peace.pdf.

David Hicks. "The Nature of Peace Education" from "Understanding the Field." In *Education for Peace,* edited by David Hicks. Peace Pledge Union, 1988, http://www.ppu.org.uk/learn/peaceed/pe_which1.html.

UNESCO (United Nations Educational, Scientific, and Cultural Organization). "Education for Peace, Human Rights and Democracy." 1995, pages 7–14, http://www.unesco.org/education/nfsunesco/pdf/REV_74_E.PDF.

UNICEF (United Nations Children's Fund). "Peace Education in UNICEF." 1999. Read the table of contents and pages 22–24 at http://www.unicef.org/girlseducation/files/PeaceEducation.pdf.

Brian Hoepper. "Peace Education in Queensland as a Key Learning Area." Queensland School Curriculum Council University, 2002, pages 1–22, http://www.qsa.qld.edu.au/downloads/publications/research_qscc_sose_peace_02.doc. Includes instructions on creating a peaceful classroom and practicing peace.

Session 8: Fields Related to Peace Education

For example, global education, international development, human rights, humane education, gender equity, multiculturalism, environmental, social justice, citizenship, health education, media literacy, and indigenous education.

Harris and Morrison, *Peace Education,* chapter 3.

Susan Fountain. "Peace Education." working paper, Education Section, UNICEF, June 1999, Section 2, http://www.unicef.org/girlseducation/files/PeaceEducation.pdf.

Unit 3: Peace Education as a Knowledge Base

Session 9: Collection of General Concerns Forming a Conceptual Base for Peace Education

For example, violence, conflict, justice, rights, war and defense, security, nonviolence, and responsibilities.

Harris and Morrison, *Peace Education,* chapter 6.

United Nations Cyber Schoolbus website. Browse the five units listed at the left of the opening page, http://www0.un.org/cyberschoolbus/peace/frame3.htm.

Peace Seed Connection, online publication of the American Montessori Society, http://www.amshq.org/peaceseedconnection/index.htm.

Unit 4: Peace Education as a Process

Session 10: Five Types of Knowledge and Their Effects on Peace Pedagogy

James Banks. "The Canon Debate, Knowledge Construction, and Multicultural Education." *Educational Researcher* 22, no. 5 (1993): 4–14.

Session 11: Seven News Types of Knowledge Related to Peace

Edgar Morin. "Seven Complex Lessons in Education for the Future." UNESCO, 1999, http://unesdoc.unesco.org/images/0011/001177/117740eo.pdf.

"New Curriculum: Seven New Kinds of Knowledge." A summary of Edgar Morin, 2003. See http://www.prasena.com/public/peace/9.htm.

Session 12: Pedagogical Approaches Relevant to Peace Education

Pedagogical approaches include contextual learning, transformative learning, critical science pedagogy, and critical and creative thinking.

Harris and Morrison, *Peace Education,* chapters 4 and 10.

Sue McGregor. "Transformative Learning: We Teach Who We Are." *Kappa Omicron Nu Forum* 14, no. 2 (2004), http://www.kon.org/archives/forum/14-2/forum14-2_article4.html.

Sue McGregor. "Critical Science Approach: A Primer." *Kappa Omicron Nu Forum* 15, no. 1 (2003), http://www.kon.org/cfp/critical_science_primer.pdf.

Cynthia Duda. "Henry Giroux: What Is Critical Pedagogy?" Rage and Hope, University of Texas course: Systems of Human Inquiry, taught by Dr. James Scheurich, 1999, http://www.perfectfit.org/CT/giroux1.html.

Leonisa Ardizzone. "Towards Global Understanding: The Transformative Role of Peace Education." *Current Issues in Contemporary Education,* 2001, http://www.tc.columbia.edu/cice/Archives/4.1/41ardizonne.pdf.

David Hicks. "Educational Ideologies." "Understanding the Field." In *Educating for Peace*. Peace Pledge Union, http://www.ppu.org.uk/learn/peaceed/pe_which.html.

"Constructivist Model for Learning." North Central Educational Research Laboratory, http://www.ncrel.org/sdrs/areas/issues/content/cntareas/science/sc5model.htm.

"Democratic Classrooms." New Horizons for Learning, 2006 (collection of articles on democratic classrooms), http://www.newhorizons.org/strategies/democratic/front_democratic.

Session 13: Peace Education Curriculum and Course Design Issues

Harris and Morrison, *Peace Education*, chapter 5.

David Hicks. "Looking at Peace Education." Peace Pledge Union, http://www.ppu.org.uk/learn/peaceed/pe_ednetcurriculum.html. Read section titled "Toward a Peace Education Curriculum."

Session 14: Peace-Teaching Strategies Stemming from Pedagogies Used to Create a Peaceful Classroom

Harris and Morrison, *Peace Education*, chapters 4, 5, 7, and 10.

Ministers of Education. "Education for Peace, Human Rights, and Democracy." November 1995, UNESCO, http://www.unesco.org/education/nfsunesco/pdf/REV_74_E.PDF. Read pages 7–14.

"Teacher as Learner: Theory and Pedagogy." United Nations Cyber Schoolbus website, http://www0.un.org/cyberschoolbus/peace/frame.htm.

Brian Hoepper. "Peace Education and Years 1–10: Studies of Society and Environment, Key Learning Area." Queensland School Curriculum Council, 2002, www.qsa.qld.edu.au/downloads/publications/research_qscc_sose_peace_02.doc. Relevant material is in section 6.1 and 6.2.

TEACHING NOTES

I assign groups of students to lead a one-hour class seminar on one of five topics: (1) peace education as empowerment for social change, (2) moral development, (3) controversial dimensions of peace education, (4) overcoming the culture of war, (5) five pedagogical approaches for peace education that surpass all other applications. They will find material for the presentations in chapters 4, 7, 8, 9, and 10 of the textbook. Credit is based on the presentation and students' preparatory notes.

Additional ideas for assignments include compiling a glossary of terms (400-word entries), and class dialogue based on terms in the glossaries (students prepare a short paper of 500–750 words completing the following sentence: "When applying [glossary term] in the classroom, I would . . ."). Glossary terms might include transformative learning, critical pedagogy, reflective pedagogy, progressive education, contextual learning, critical thinking, creative thinking, collaborative learning, cooperative learning, the constructivist approach and constructivism, the participatory approach, a global perspective, an emancipatory approach, a democratic classroom, the dialogical approach, the empowerment approach, and being a political change agent (the participatory domain of learning). The full list of terms is available from Sue McGregor.

17.6 Peace and Conflict Resolution: A Holistic Approach

Tony Jenkins and Janet Gerson
Teachers College, Columbia University

COURSE DESCRIPTION

Upper-level course for pre-professional teachers and students of education.

In light of the proliferation of violent conflicts, which range from global terrorism to school-based violence, there is a need for inquiry into how education can contribute to reducing violence, defined as "avoidable and preventable harm." Theorists generally agree that manifestations of violence are interrelated and these relationships should be examined in order to understand and address the culture of violence in today's world (e.g., Betty Reardon, Kumar Rupesinghe, Sue McGregor and Marcial Rubio, Johan Galtung). Peace education is premised on the assumption that human beings have agency and capacities to construct cultures of peace as delineated in the United Nations Declaration and Resolution on a Decade for a Culture of Peace and Nonviolence for the Children of the World (UNESCO). Of central importance is the problematic of how to separate violence from conflict.

How is conflict understood? Conflict is often assumed to be both violent and inevitable. While maintaining that conflict *is* an inherent part of life, this inquiry will challenge the assumption that conflict is necessarily violent. The Seville Statement on Violence supports this challenge. Scholars refute the contention that making war (organized political violence) is genetic or biological. Social psychologist Susan Opotow points out that humans have capacities to make war, and yet, because warfare has changed so drastically over time, culture must be central to war's perpetuation. Education plays a role in this continuity of violence because culture is created and sustained through the values, beliefs, knowledge, and practices that are taught to and by persons and sustained through generations.

The overall goal of this course is to gain a comprehensive view of ways in which educators can teach students to address conflict without violence. Within this broad perspective, three general (and nonexclusive) approaches to conflict have been chosen for deeper analysis: (1) conflict resolution, (2) conflict management, and (3) conflict escalation for social change, also known as nonviolent strategic action.

The first approach, "conflict resolution," is generally regarded as a problem-solving approach frequently used in schools and in face-to-face and interpersonal relations. Conflict analysis, interpersonal conflict resolution, constructive controversy, and popular theater techniques will be presented. The second, "conflict management," will be viewed from a global perspective. Global systems and constitutional justice will be explored by using the World Order Models Project and by reading legal theorists. Forgiveness and reconciliation will be considered through the Indonesian case of Baku Bae and work with children in Northern Ireland. The third category, "conflict escalation for social change," or "nonviolent strategic action," is based on assumptions that injustice is embedded in social stability (the status quo). Strategies of nonviolent protest, noncooperation, and nonviolent intervention are used to precipitate social change. All these approaches will be considered in light of the core problematic of peace education—how to nurture the capacities in individuals to prevent, minimize, and ultimately eliminate violence.

Education is a primary institution for the perpetuation of culture. On the one hand, it can provide preparation for violence and war. Critical analysis of formal and informal public and private educational practices has identified teaching practices that prepare students for participation in the culture of violence. On the other hand, educators have the opportunity to educate for practices that prepare students for peaceful coexistence and well-being. Teachers can model, present, and facilitate conflict approaches that contribute to peaceful conflict outcomes. The United Nations Declaration and Resolution on a Decade for a Culture of Peace and Nonviolence for the Children of the World offers a vision for constructive conflict education and action within a comprehensive framework and vision for a culture of peace. For human society to survive and flourish, teaching the necessity of renouncing and the responsibility to renounce violence and war as acceptable responses to conflict is central. Education can also offer humane, inclusive, and thoughtful conflict response possibilities.

REQUIRED TEXT

Betty A. Reardon and Alicia Cabezudo. *Learning to Abolish War: Teaching Toward a Culture of Peace*. New York: Hague Appeal for Peace, 2002. Book 1 (rationale and conceptual framework), Book 2 (sample lessons), Book 3 (additional resources). Available online at http://www.haguepeace.org/index.php?action=resources.

COURSE SCHEDULE

Unit 1: A Holistic Framework for Understanding Conflict, Violence, and Peace

Key concepts covered in this unit are problematic, violence, direct violence, indirect violence, structural violence, a culture of violence, and types of conflict; peace, a culture of peace, personal peace, political peace, ecological peace, interconnectedness, interdependence, circles of community, worldview, social roles, and participation; conflict web, conflict as frame, crisis and opportunity, stabilization, destabilization, phases of conflict, and ripeness; conflict processes, i.e., problem solving, conflict management, institutional (formal) mechanisms, social (informal) mechanisms, transformation, strategies for change, nonviolent intervention, resolution, reconciliation, reconstruction, and healing.

Relevant reading:

"Seville Statement Against Violence." UNESCO, 1989, http://www.unesco.org/human_rights/hrfv.htm.

"United Nations Declaration and Resolution on a Decade for a Culture of Peace and Nonviolence for Children of the World." UNESCO, 1999, http://www.unesco.org/cpp/uk/declarations/200.htm.

"The Hague Agenda for Peace and Justice in the 21st Century." 1999. http://www.haguepeace.org/index.php?action=resources.

Abelardo Brenes. *Building a Culture of Peace in Our Community; Summary of Didactic Modules*. San Jose, Costa Rica: University for Peace, 2002.

Adam Curle. "Ending the Culture of Violence." *WYSE International Newsletter,* 2002, www.wyse-ngo.org.

Reardon and Cabezudo, *Learning to Abolish War.* Read Book 1 with special attention to Strand 3 ("Prevention, Resolution, and Transformation of Violent Conflict"). See Chart 6 ("Conflict Prevention, Resolution, and Transformation Educational Goals"), 61.

Unit 2: Conflict Analysis, Resolution, and Prevention

Key concepts and terms: cooperation, competition, dual concern model, win-win, compromise, respect, valuing, inclusion, exclusion, conflict frame, rewriting the story, and role plays; conflict strategies, avoidance, face-to-face conflict resolution, negotiation, outside-party conflict resolution, mediation, adjudication, litigation, force, and waging war; conflict analysis, issues, disputants, Positional clash, underlying needs and interests, reframe, brainstorming, developing solutions, agreements, ritual sharing, climate, emotions, behaviors, culture and conflict, and worldview.

Relevant reading:

Maya Uzelac. *Za Svemire: Peaceful Conflict Resolution Workshops for Primary and Secondary Schools.* Zagreb, Croatia: Mali Korak, 2001, 20–24.

Susan Coleman, Ellen Raider, and Janet Gerson. "Teaching Conflict Resolution Skills in a Workshop." In *The Handbook of Conflict Resolution,* edited by Morton Deutsch and Peter T. Coleman. San Francisco: Jossey-Bass, 2000, 499–521.

David W. Johnson, Roger T. Johnson, and Dean Tjosvold. "Constructive Controversy: The Value of Intellectual Opposition." In *The Handbook of*

Conflict Resolution, edited by Morton Deutsch and Peter T. Coleman. San Francisco: Jossey-Bass, 2000, 65–85.

Hossain B. Danesh and Roshan Danesh. "Has Conflict Resolution Grown Up? Toward a Developmental Model of Decision Making and Conflict Resolution." *International Journal of Peace Studies* 7, no. 1 (Spring 2002): 59–76.

Unit 3: Global Systems and Constitutional Justice; Forgiveness and Reconciliation

Key concepts and terms: dialogue, debate, constructive controversy, transivity, participation, and dynamization transformation; civil society, rule of law, human rights, justice, global citizenship, international law, humanitarian law, and peaceful institutional procedures.

Relevant reading:

Reardon and Cabezudo, *Learning to Abolish War: Teaching Toward a Culture of Peace.* Read Book 1 with special attention to Strand 2 ("International Humanitarian and Human Rights Law and Institutions"), 31–35. See Chart 5 ("Goals for Human Rights Education: Developmental Sequence for Core Concepts and Content"), 58.

Augusto Boal. *Legislative Theater,* translated by Adrian Jackson. London: Routledge, 1998, 19–23.

Ichsan Malik. *Baku Bae: The Community-Based Movement for Reconciliation in Mauku.* Jakarta, Indonesia: TIFA, 2003.

Unit 4: Escalating Conflict for Social Change: Nonviolent Strategic Action

Key concepts and terms: nonviolent protest and persuasion; social, political, and economic nonviolent actions; nonviolent intervention; strategies, tactics, and preparation: action, inaction, passivity, compromise negotiation, dissolution of power, extraconstitutional actions, acts of omission, acts of commission, and symbolic actions.

Relevant reading:

Gene Sharp. *Nonviolence in Theory and Practice,* edited by Robert L. Holmes. Belmont, CA: Wadsworth, 1990: "Nonviolent Action: An Active Technique of Struggle," 147–150. "The Technique of Non-Violent Action," 151–152.

Martin Luther King Jr. "Letter from a Birmingham Jail." In *Nonviolence in Theory and Practice,* edited by Robert L. Holmes. Belmont, CA: Wadsworth, 1990, 68–77.

War Resistors League. "100 Ways You Can Help Stop Violence." In *Celebrating the Decade for a Culture of Peace and Nonviolence: A Resource Manual.* Nyack, NY: Fellowship of Reconciliation USA, 2001, http://www.nonviolence.org.

TEACHING NOTES

These ten questions help students identify core concepts in the readings and prepare them for discussion in class.

1. What are the authors' assumptions and assertions about conflict? About peace?
2. How can conflict be viewed in relation to peace?
3. How is violence defined and what examples are used?
4. What is a holistic approach, and how can it be applied to understanding a culture of violence?
5. What values and purposes of a culture of peace would guide approaches to conflict?
6. What are conflict processes, and how are they related to a holistic perspective?
7. What are the purposes and limits of conflict resolution?
8. What actors are involved in formulating and enacting various conflict approaches? Who and what benefits from each approach? Who and what are excluded?
9. What are social and institutional mechanisms for addressing and managing conflict?
10. What is nonviolent action, and how does it differ in purpose and method from conflict resolution and conflict management as processes that are nonviolent? What processes support the transformative potential of conflicts, and why is transformation important to a culture of peace?

18
Cultural Dynamics

BESIDES COMPETING ECONOMIC INTERESTS OR POLITICAL INTERESTS, numerous other pressures bear on the state of human security. Religion, for one, is treated in a section of its own because of its centrality to worldwide conflict in the early twenty-first century, but dynamics such as race, gender, age, ethnicity, nationalism, mal-development, and access to natural resources are also important pressures at work in conflict. Left to their competing claims, these dynamics will erode the peace, but put to good use as tools of negotiation, they play a role in transforming conflict to positive peace.

Zheng Wang offers a course to help students better understand how culture and identity, and other ideational factors, influence state behaviors and international relations. Marc Howard Ross explores the interaction of ethnicity and political power, focusing largely on U.S. history to see how ethnicity is defined; who defines it; who is assigned to particular ethnic groups; and what that means in terms of politics, economics, culture, and human rights. Veteran peace educators Betty A. Reardon and Tony Jenkins deal with the intersection and interrelationship of gender and peace and the consequences of gender inequality for the achievement of peace. Susan Shepler analyzes age, particularly youth and childhood, as a dynamic of conflict and peace. She examines the experiences of young people caught up in war, its effect on them, and their efforts to engage in peacebuilding. And Arthur Blaser broaches the much undertreated issue of people with disabilities in politics and society, shifting the definition of disability from a medical one to a sociopolitical one that reclaims important abilities and the contributions of disabled citizens.

18.1 The Politics of Cultural and Ethnic Pluralism

Zheng Wang
Seton Hall University

COURSE DESCRIPTION

Upper-level seminar for majors in political science, international relations, and conflict studies.

The striking proliferation of deadly conflicts between ethnic and other so-called identity groups after the end of the Cold War has become a major concern of international security. This course examines the issues of cultural diversity through a focus on the concepts of ethnicity, national identity, and nationalism. It explores the causes, consequences, and management of ethnic conflict and nationalism. This course aims to help students to understand better how culture and identity, and other ideational factors, influence state behaviors and international relations. Students will form case study groups, each choosing a case of cultural and/or ethnic conflict to analyze, using frameworks and literature reviewed in the course, as well as additional literature.

In this age of globalization, the fundamental objective of international relations education is to empower students to understand other countries' or cultures' frames of reference or worldviews, and by doing so, to groom future leaders who will promote greater tolerance and cooperation among people and among different cultures. Through this course, students should (1) become familiar with the theoretical insights from several scholarly disciplines, including political science, sociology, anthropology, and conflict resolution, regarding the causes and management of nationalism and ethnic conflict; (2) develop an ability to integrate different fields of study into the analysis of a complex social phenomenon; and (3) improve critical thinking skills and develop a tolerance for the diversity, differences, and complexities of our world.

REQUIRED TEXTS

Benedict Anderson. *Imagined Communities: Reflections on the Origin and Spread of Nationalism*. London: Verso, 1991.

Vamik Volkan. *Bloodlines: From Ethnic Pride to Ethnic Terrorism*. New York: Farrar, Straus and Giroux, 1997.

James G. Kellas. *The Politics of Nationalism and Ethnicity.* New York: St. Martin's Press, 1998.

SUPPLEMENTAL READING

Stuart J. Kaufman. *Modern Hatred: The Symbolic Politics of Ethnic War.* Ithaca, NY: Cornell University Press, 2001.

COURSE SCHEDULE

Unit 1: Introduction:
The Politics of Cultural and Ethnic Pluralism
Kellas, *The Politics of Nationalism and Ethnicity,* introduction and chapter 1.

Unit 2: Globalization and Ethnic Revival
Samuel P. Huntington. "The Clash of Civilizations." *Foreign Affairs* 72, no. 3 (February 1993): 22–49.
Volkan, *Bloodlines,* preface.

Unit 3: Culture, Identity, and International Conflict
Kellas, *The Politics of Nationalism and Ethnicity,* chapter 10.
Volkan, *Bloodlines,* chapters 1, 2, and afterword.

Unit 4: Sources of Identity I: Primordialism
Volkan, *Bloodlines,* chapters 3–4.
Kellas, *The Politics of Nationalism and Ethnicity,* chapter 3.

Unit 5: Sources of Identity II: Constructivism
Anderson, *Imagined Communities,* chapters 1–3.

Unit 6: Sources of Identity III: Instrumentalism
Kaufman, *Modern Hatred,* chapters 1–2.
Anderson, *Imagined Communities,* chapter 5.

Unit 7: Social Identity Theory
Henri Tajfel and John C. Turner. "The Social Identity Theory of Inter-group Behavior." In *Psychology of Intergroup Relations,* edited by Stephen Worchel and William G. Austin. Chicago: Nelson-Hall, 1986, 7–24.
Volkan, *Bloodlines,* chapters 5–6.

Unit 8: Nationalism, Patriotism, and Racism
Kellas, *The Politics of Nationalism and Ethnicity,* chapter 2.
Anderson, *Imagined Communities,* chapters 6, 7, and 8.

Unit 9: Cultural Diversity and Intercultural Dialogue

Johan Galtung. "Rethinking Conflict: The Cultural Approach." Strasbourg: Council of Europe. Cultural Policy and Action Department, 2002, http://www.coe.int/t/dg4/cultureheritage/Completed/Dialogue/pub2002galtung_en.asp.

Kellas, *The Politics of Nationalism and Ethnicity,* chapter 11.

Unit 10: Historical Memory and Ethnic Conflict

Minxin Pei. "The Paradoxes of American Nationalism." *Foreign Policy* (May–June 2003): 30–37.

Jerzy Jedlicki. "Historical Memory as a Source of Conflicts in Eastern Europe." *Communist and Post-Communist Studies* 32 (September 1999): 225–232.

Anderson, *Imagined Communities,* chapter 9.

Unit 11: Case Study: September 11 and Anti-Americanism (I)

Michael H. Hunt. "In the Wake of September 11: The Clash of What?" *Journal of American History* 89, no. 2 (September 2002).

Anderson, *Imagined Communities,* chapters 10–11.

Unit 12: Case Study: September 11 and Anti-Americanism (II)

Barry Rubin. "The Real Roots of Arab Anti-Americanism." *Foreign Affairs* 81, no. 6 (November-December 2002).

Edward Schatz. "Islamism and Anti-Americanism in Central Asia." *Current History* 101, no. 657 (October 2002).

Unit 13: Group Presentations and Discussion I

Small groups for case studies (four or five people per group) will be formed in the first session. The class will be asked to choose from a number of cases of contemporary cultural and/or ethnic conflict representing a range of analyses. At the end of the term, each group will write a paper and make a presentation providing an overview and synthesized analysis of the group's case.

Unit 14: Group Presentations and Discussion II

TEACHING NOTES

In an age of globalization, international relations education should aim to help students develop a tolerance for the diversity, differences, complexities, and ambiguities of our world. A curriculum therefore must challenge students to observe and explain phenomena. I believe that teaching toward this objective produces within students an awareness of the validity of competing and even contradictory points of view, a willingness to acknowledge the possible limits of knowledge, and sensitivity to the complexities of difficult situations. When I designed this course, I tried to combine theoretical analysis with empirical case studies. At the same time, within any student body, enormous diversity exists. Educators should help students welcome this diversity and be ready and open to learn from each other.

18.2 The Politics of Ethnic and Racial Groups

Marc Howard Ross
Bryn Mawr College

COURSE DESCRIPTION

Upper-level undergraduate course for students of political science and peace and conflict studies.

The purpose of this course is to consider the politics of ethnicity and race, focusing particularly on the United States, although the questions we raise during the semester are certainly relevant to other multiracial and multiethnic societies. The central focus comes out of the apparent contradiction in the American experience associated with the narrative of the melting pot and assimilation of people from many different lands into "one nation," and the reality throughout US history that there were people always considered unassimilatable. Although the definition of who these people are has changed, the most enduring cleavage has been that of race. There have been questions as well about the extent to which the United States is, or should be, a multicultural, multiethnic, or multiracial society, and what it is that all citizens must share. Is it language, religion, core values, a set of political institutions, a common identity? How are people from different ethnic and racial backgrounds able to acknowledge their differences and effectively communicate with each other?

The first part of the semester explores the concepts of ethnicity and race and how they have changed in popular and scholarly usage over time. We will also identify some conceptual tools to understand this change. A central goal of the course is to recognize the contextual nature of American identities and to consider the contradictions between the apparent "objective" indicators of group identity and their subjective, socially constructed nature. In many ways this is especially well illustrated through examination of the apparently simple question, Who is white? As Matthew Jacobson argues, answers to this question are anything but straightforward: whiteness is a category whose boundaries have been renegotiated by nearly every generation.

Considering the dynamics of group definition and redefinition is a first step toward understanding the political consequences of these dynamics. Who defines group boundaries and privileges, and how is this done? These issues encourage us to consider who gains and who loses from alternative frameworks and how ideas about belonging and citizenship interact with specific questions about politics, such as apology and reconciliation, political campaigns and advertising, affirmative action, and symbolic inclusion.

The course seeks to provide an interplay between specific cases and general questions about ethnicity, race, and conflict in multicultural societies. Each student is encouraged to explore these links (and the problem of establishing them) in class discussions and papers. The problems the readings raise are important and complicated ones; the active engagement of each student through careful reading, writing, and dialogue is important in making this experience successful. At times, it is reasonable to be puzzled about how the different pieces come together and how to make sense of American race and ethnicity, uncertain about how to locate one's own experiences in the theories and cases that are explored, and unclear about what is expected. The best solution is not to suppress these reactions but to raise them with each other and in class.

REQUIRED TEXTS

Clara Rodriguez. *Changing Race: Latinos, the Census, and the History of Ethnicity in the United States*. New York University Press, 2000.

Matthew Jacobson. *Whiteness of a Different Color.* Harvard University Press, 1999.

Yen Le Espiritu. *Asian-American Panethnicity: Bridging Institutions and Identities*. Temple University Press, 1992.

Joseph Tilden Rhee. *Race Pride and American Identity.* Harvard University Press, 1997.

COURSE SCHEDULE

Week 1: Introduction: Considering Ethnicity and Race
No assigned readings.

Week 2: Ethnicity and Race as Social and Political Categories
Milton Esman. *Ethnic Politics*. Cornell, 1994, chapter 1 (pages 1–25).

Donald Horowitz. "A Family Resemblance." *Ethnic Groups in Conflict*. University of California Press, 1985, chapter 2 (pages 55–92).

Milton Gordon. "Assimilation in America: Theory and Reality." *Daedalus* (1961): 263–285.

Herbert Gans. "Symbolic Ethnicity: The Future of Ethnic Groups and Cultures in America." *Ethnic and Racial Studies* 2 (1979): 1–20.

Week 3: The Census and Category Definition
Rodriguez, *Changing Race*, all.

Week 4: The Political History of Whiteness

Jacobson, *Whiteness of a Different Color,* introduction and chapters 1–3 (pages 1–136).

Week 5: Manufacturing Whiteness

Jacobson, *Whiteness of a Different Color,* chapters 6–8 and Epilogue (pages 201–282).

Week 6: Constructing Asian American Identity

Espiritu. *Asian-American Panethnicity,* all.

Week 7: Blackness as a Social and Political Category

Joseph Hraba. *American Ethnicity,* 2nd ed. F. E. Peacock, 1994, chapters 10–11 (pages 347–419).

Nicholas Leman. *The Promised Land.* Vintage, 1992, 1–58.

Week 8: Framing Race in American Politics I

Donald R. Kinder and Lynn M. Sanders. *Divided by Color: Racial Politics and Democratic Ideals.* University of Chicago Press, 1996, chapters 1–2 (pages 3–34).

Week 9: Framing Race in American Politics II

Tali Mendelberg. *The Race Card: Campaign Strategy, Implicit Messages, and the Norm of Equality.* Princeton University Press, 2001, chapters 1 and 4 (pages 1–27 and 111–116).

Week 10: The Politics of Race and Affirmative Action

William G. Bowen and Derek Bok. *The Shape of the River: Long-Term Consequences of Considering Race on College and University Admissions.* Princeton University Press, 1999, chapters 1–2, 9–10 (pages 1–52 and 256–290).

Paula R. Skedsvold and Tammy L. Mann, eds. "The Affirmative Action Debate: What's Fair in Policy and Programs." *Journal of Social Issues* (1996). Read the articles by Skedsvold and Mann, Oportow, and Plous.

Week 11: Racial Inclusion and Exclusion in the Symbolic Landscape

Kirk Savage. *Standing Soldiers and Kneeling Slaves.* Princeton University Press, 1997, chapter 1 (pages 3–20).

Gary B. Nash. "For Whom the Liberty Bell Tolls: From Controversy to Collaboration." Independence Hall Association, January 25, 2003, http://www.ushistory.org/presidentshouse/controversy/nash.htm.

Week 12: Community from Within

Rhee. *Race Pride and American Identity,* all.

Weeks 13–14: Presentations of Student Research Projects

TEACHING NOTES

This is not a lecture class, although at times relevant material will be presented. Rather, classes are discussion-based, so students are expected to complete the assigned readings *before* each session. There is a good deal of reading and writing required for this course, and students are expected to read and to have thought about the material and to be ready to engage in class discussion. Most discussions will develop from issues raised in each week's readings, but all sessions try to make connections between that session's readings and material considered in other weeks and between the theory and specific cases.

Students are asked to write six comments on the readings, one page in length and posted on a discussion board. Each person may choose which weeks to post comments, but a student must not skip more than two weeks at any point. The comments should incorporate reactions to the readings and can also include issues that were raised in prior classes and readings. These comments are intended to help students clarify their own thinking and to raise issues that help structure the class discussion. I sometimes suggest possible topics for these postings, but students should feel free to write about issues that seem most important to them. In addition, I require two formal papers, one that will be due at the end of week 8 and a term paper due at the end of the exam period.

18.3 Gender and the War System: An Inquiry into Equality and Security

Betty A. Reardon and Tony Jenkins
Teachers College, Columbia University

COURSE DESCRIPTION

Upper-level undergraduate or graduate course in gender studies, security studies, or peace and conflict studies.

This course explores the intersections and interrelationships of gender and peace and the consequences of gender inequality to the achievement of peace. Situated in the broader context of violence as the core problem of peace education, it will consider the foundations of the field of feminist perspectives on peace and war. To complement this theme, we will also discuss more recent developments in the field contributed by masculinities studies. From the inclusive perspective provided by these two areas of scholarship, the course will then address the initiatives and activities undertaken to move toward forms of gender equality intended to serve the cause of peace. Movements arising from the traditional exclusion of women from the international politics of peacemaking and their effects on the current politics of peace will be included within this theme.

Much of the analysis will derive from a diagnosis of the traditional mind-sets and practices of patriarchy that continue to affect most societies. The ways in which patriarchal concepts of the roles of men and women and the way in which characteristics of masculinity and femininity affect and are affected by modes of conflict and security systems will be central to the consideration of possibilities for peace and gender equality.

COURSE SCHEDULE

Session 1: Feminist Perspectives on Peace and War: Foundations of the Field

Introduction: class participants and instructors; issues, methods of inquiry, basic assumptions, and core arguments in the field of gender and peace.

Tony Jenkins and Betty Reardon. "Gender and Peace: Towards a Gender Inclusive, Holistic Perspective." In *Handbook of Peace and Conflict Studies,* edited by Charles Webel and Johan Galtung. Routledge, 2007, 209–231.

R. W. Connell. "The Question of Gender." In *Gender,* by R. W. Connell. Polity, 2002, 1–11.

Betty Reardon. *Education for a Culture of Peace in a Gender Perspective.* UNESCO, 2003, read sections 1 and 5 (17–34, 111–128).

View excerpts from *The Long Walk Home,* directed by Richard Pearce, DVD, 1990, 97 minutes.

Session 2: The Patriarchy Paradigm: A Conceptual Framework for the Study of Gender and Peace
Identify indicators of gender differentials within the patriarchy paradigm.

Gerda Lerner. "The Creation of Patriarchy." In *The Creation of Patriarchy,* by Gerda Lerner. Oxford University Press, 1987.

Elvira Vasquez and Concha Moreno. "Relations Between Women: Toward an Alternative Policy Through Radical Changes in Patriarchy." In *Women for Peace,* edited by Staša Zajovi. Belgrade: Women in Black, 2005, 73–76.

People's Movement for Human Rights Education (PDHRE). "Transforming the Patriarchal Order to a Human Rights System: Toward Economic and Social Justice for All." http://www.pdhre.org/patriarchy.html.

Session 3: Feminist Critiques of Security Policy and Analysis
The limits of masculine "objectivity."

Anne Tickner. "Man, the State, and War: Gendered Perspectives on National Security." *Gender in International Relations.* Columbia University Press, 1992, 27–66.

Betty Reardon. "Toward Human Security: A Gender Approach to Demilitarization." *Women in Asia,* 2004.

Hanne-Margret Birckenbach. "Balancing Co-operation and Critique: Preliminary Considerations for a Feminist View of the Agenda for Peace." In *Towards a Women's Agenda for a Culture of Peace,* edited by I. Breines, D. Gierycz, and Betty Reardon. UNESCO, 1999, 113–126.

Session 4: Sexism and Militarism
Exploring connections between women's status and the institution of war.

Cynthia Enloe. "Base Women." In *Bananas, Beaches, and Bases,* by Cynthia Enloe. University of California Press, 1990, 65–92.

Betty Reardon. "Core Concepts, Basic Assumptions, and Fundamental Values." In *Sexism and the War System,* by Betty Reardon. Syracuse University Press, 1996, 10–36.

Session 5: Violence Against Women as Social Control and Military Strategy
Rape and sexual slavery.

Mohammed Boabaid. "Masculinity and Gender Violence in Yemen." In *Islamic Masculinities,* edited by Lahoucine Ouzgane. Zed Books, 2006, 161–183.

George Hicks. *The Comfort Women: Japan's Brutal Regime of Enforced Prostitution in the Second World War.* W.W. Norton, 2006, introduction (11–23) and chapter 1 (27–44).

Vesna Kesiç. "Establishing Rape as a War Crime." In *Transforming a Rape Culture,* edited by Emilie Buchwald, Pamela Fletcher, and Martha Roth. Milkweed Editions, 2005, 269–288.

View during class: *Calling the Ghosts,* directed by Mandy Jacobson and Karmen Jelincic, DVD, 1996, 63 minutes, depicting rape as a strategy of war in Bosnia.

Session 6: Masculinities and Militarism

Male identity formation and war.

Mark Gerzon. "War: Virility and Violence." *A Choice of Heroes.* Houghton Mifflin, 1982, 46–58.

Achim Rohde. "Opportunities for Masculinity and Love: Cultural Production in Ba'thist Iraq During the 1980s." In *Islamic Masculinities,* edited by Lahoucine Ouzgane. London: Zed Books, 2006, 184–201.

View excerpts during class: *The Great Santini,* directed by Lewis John Carlino, DVD, 1979, 115 minutes.

Session 7: Masculinities and Politics

Ayse Gul Altinay. "Becoming a Man, Becoming a Citizen." *The Myth of the Military-Nation: Militarism, Gender, and Education in Turkey.* Palgrave Macmillan, 2005, 61–86.

Robert W. Connell. "Arms and the Man: Using the New Research on Masculinity to Understand Violence and Promote Peace in the Contemporary World." In *Male Roles, Masculinities, and Violence: A Culture of Peace Perspective,* edited by Ingeborg Breines, Robert Connell, and Ingrid Eide. Paris: UNESCO, 2000, 21–33.

Session 8: Masculine National Identities, Armaments, and Gender Violence

Fears of disempowerment feeding violent conflict.

Prem Vijayan. "Nationalism, Masculinity, and the Development State: Exploring Hindu Masculinities." In *Masculinities Matter!* edited by Frances Cleaver. Zed Books, 2002, 28–56.

Kirti Singh. "Obstacles to Women's Rights in India." In *Human Rights of Women,* edited by Rebecca J. Cook. University of Pennsylvania Press, 1994, 373–396.

View Part 1 of *Father, Son, and Holy War,* directed by Anand Patwardhan, DVD, 1994, 120 minutes, http://www.frif.com/cat97/f-j/father__.html.

View selections from *The Final Solution,* directed by Rakesh Sharma, DVD, 2003, 218 minutes (gender and communal/sectarian violence).

Session 9: Men's Antiviolence Initiatives
Counteracting men's violence against women; antiwar activities.

Michael Kaufman, "Working with Men and Boys to Challenge Sexism and End Men's Violence." UN Educational, Scientific, and Cultural Organization, 2000, 213–222.
Michael Kimmel, "Reducing Men's Violence: The Personal Meets the Political," UNESCO, 2000, 239–247.

View excerpts from *The Handmaid's Tale,* directed by Volker Schlöndorff, DVD, 1990, 109 minutes (learning from dystopias).

Session 10: Human Rights International Law: Legal Approaches to Peace and Justice
Maria Elena Valenzuela. "Gender, Democracy, and Peace: The Role of Women's Movements Mobilization in Latin America." In *Towards a Women's Agenda for a Culture of Peace,* edited by Ingeborg Breines, Dorata Gierycz, and Betty Reardon. Paris: UNESCO, 1999, 157–164.
Cynthia Cockburn. "Challenging the Line: Women's Activism." In *The Line: Women, Partition, and the Gender Order in Cyprus,* by Cynthia Cockburn. London: Zed Books, 2004, 143–168.

Session 11: Civil Society and People's Tribunals
Citizens' action for change.

International conventions, declarations, and resolutions:
- Convention on the Elimination of All Forms of Discrimination Against Women (CEDAW), http://www.un.org/womenwatch/daw/cedaw/.
- UN Declaration on the Elimination of Violence Against Women, http://www.unhchr.ch/huridocda/huridoca.nsf/(Symbol)/A.RES.48.104.En.
- Beijing Declaration and Platform for Action, http://www.un.org/womenwatch/daw/beijing/platform/declar.htm.
- Statute of the International Criminal Court, http://www.un.org/icc/final.htm.
- Security Council Resolution 1325, http://www.un.org/events/res_1325e.pdf.

Hilary Charlesworth, "What Are 'Women's International Human Rights'?" In *Human Rights of Women: National and International Perspectives,* edited by Rebecca J. Cook. University of Pennsylvania Press, 1994, 58–84.

Mona Rishmawi, "The Developing Approaches of the International Commission of Jurists to Women's Human Rights," 340–348.

View *Breaking the History of Silence: The Women's International War Crimes Tribunal on Japan's Military Sexual Slavery,* VHS, 2001, http://www.jca.apc.org/video-juku/haag-eng.html.

Session 12: Simulation of a People's Tribunal on Military Gender Violence

Prepare in teams for roles on the simulated tribunal. Share research for evidence. Using *Breaking the History of Silence* as a model, students will conduct a general tribunal on military-based gender violence. The perpetrators can be chosen from among any active military leaders.

18.4 Youth and Conflict

Susan Shepler
American University

COURSE DESCRIPTION

Undergraduate course for majors in sociology, social work, political science, conflict studies, and peace and justice studies.

This course will examine the relationship between youth and conflict. We will start with an exploration of varying definitions of youth as a biological, cultural, and political category. We will discuss youth and children both as victims of conflict and as perpetrators of violence. Other topics include youth and nation, the effect of conflict on educational systems, the special concerns of girls, the efforts of international child protection agencies and nongovernmental organizations (NGOs), children's testimonies of violence, and youth-sponsored peacebuilding activities internationally.

This is an interdisciplinary endeavor. We will move around the world and back and forth across levels of analysis. Our task is to simultaneously try to understand the experiences of young people caught up in war, the literature on youth and conflict, and to carry out a multidisciplinary critique of that literature. Throughout, our task will be to uncover the taken-for granted assumptions and subsequent political effects within this field.

REQUIRED TEXTS

Jo Boyden and Joanna de Berry, eds. *Children and Youth on the Front Line: Ethnography, Armed Conflict, and Displacement*. Studies in Forced Migration. Berghahn Books, 2004.

David Rosen. *Armies of the Young: Child Soldiers in War and Terrorism*. Rutgers University Press, 2005.

Readings listed in the course schedule.

COURSE SCHEDULE

Week 1: Introduction

Search the Internet for information on youth and conflict in Nepal and West Africa.

What are the assumptions regarding youth/childhood and war/conflict?

Week 2: The International Humanitarian Discourse on Youth and Conflict

"Convention on the Rights of the Child." United Nations Office of the High Commissioner for Human Rights, November 20, 1989, http://www.unhchr.ch/html/menu3/b/k2crc.htm.

Graça Machel. "Impact of Amed Conflict on Children." UNICEF, 1996, http://www.unicef.org/graca/.

Olara Otunno. "Report to the Security Council on Children and Armed Conflict." United Nations Security Council, 2003.

Jenny Kuper. "Children in Armed Conflicts: The Law and Its Uses." *Development* 43, no. 1 (2000): 32–39.

Week 3: Critical Youth Theory

What is a child? A youth? This section addresses the literature on childhood studies.

Allison James and Alan Prout, eds. *Constructing and Reconstructing Childhood.* Falmer Press, 1997, chapters 1, 2, and 9.

Deborah Durham. "Youth and the Social Imagination in Africa." *Anthropological Quarterly* 73, no. 3 (2000): 113–120.

Week 4: Youth and Politics

Sometimes youth participating in violence are seen as dupes of their elders; other times their participation is lauded. Can children have political views?

Rosen, *Armies of the Young,* chapters 1–2.

Afua Twum-Danso. "The Political Child." In *Invisible Stakeholders: Children and War in Africa,* edited by A. McIntyre. Institute for Security Studies, 2005.

Christine Liddell, Jennifer Kemp, and Molly Moema. "The Young Lions: African Children and Youth in Political Struggle." In *The Psychological Effect of War and Violence on Children,* edited by Lewis Leavitt and Nathan Fox. Lawrence Erlbaum Associates, 1993.

Boyden and Berry, *Children and Youth on the Front Lines,* chapter 9.

Week 5: Youth and Conflict— Causal Connections?

The youth bulge in population, youth and unemployment, youth and education, youth and HIV/AIDS.

United Nations Development Programme. *Youth and Violent Conflict: Society and Development in Crisis?* 2006, http://www.undp.org/cpr/whats_new/UNDP_Youth_PN.pdf. Read chapter 2.

Henrik Urdal. *The Devil in the Demographics: The Effect of Youth Bulges on Domestic Armed Conflict, 1950–2000*. Social Development Papers: Conflict Prevention and Reconstruction Paper no. 14. World Bank, 2004. http://www-wds.worldbank.org/servlet/WDSContentServer/WDSP/IB/2004/07/28/000012009_20040728162225/Rendered/PDF/29740.pdf.

D. C. O'Brien. "A Lost Generation?" In *Postcolonial Identities in Africa*, edited by Richard Werbner and Terence Ranger. Zed Books, 1996, 55–74.

Eg Ali El-Kenz. "Youth and Violence." In *Africa Now: People, Policies, and Institutions*, by Stephen Ellis. The Hague, Ministry of Foreign Affairs, in association with James Currey, 1996.

Week 6: Child Soldiers

What are child soldiers? How do they move into and out of participation in armed conflict? What about children and disarmament, demobilization, and reintegration (DDR)?

Browse reports on the website of the Coalition to Stop the Use of Child Soldiers, http://www.child-soldiers.org/home.

E. Delap. *No Place Like Home?* Save the Children, 2004.

Julia Dickson-Gomez. "Growing Up in Guerrilla Camps: The Long-Term Impact of Being a Child Soldier in El Salvador's Civil War." *Ethos* 30, no. 4 (2002): 327–356.

Mats Utas. "Building a Future?" In *No Peace, No War: An Anthropology of Contemporary Armed Conflicts*, edited by Paul Richards. Ohio University Press, 2005.

Week 7: Youth, Trauma, and Healing

How do we understand the effects, especially the psychological effects, of armed conflict on children and youth?

Peter S. Jensen and Jon Shaw. "Children as Victims of War." *Journal of the American Academy of Child and Adolescent Psychiatry* 32, no. 4 (1993): 697–708.

Naomi Richman. "Annotation: Children in Situations of Political Violence." *Child Psychology and Psychiatry* 34, no. 8 (1993): 1286–1302.

Sara Gibbs. "Post-War Social Reconstruction in Mozambique." *Disasters* 18, no. 3 (1994): 268–276.

Michael Wessells and C. Monteiro. "Healing Wounds of War in Angola." In *Addressing Childhood Adversity*, edited by David Donald, Andrew Dawes, and Johann Louw. David Philip Publishers, 2000, 176–201.

Paul M. Kline and Erin Mone. "Coping with War." *Child and Adolescent Social Work Journal* 20, no. 5 (2003): 321–333.

Atle Dyregrov, et al. "Is the Culture Always Right?" *Traumatology* 8, no. 3 (2002): 135–145.

Week 8: A Gender Analysis

Why are girls and young women so frequently left out of discussions of youth and conflict? What can we say about their specific experiences?

Susan McKay and Dyan Mazurana. *Where Are the Girls?* Rights and Democracy, 2004, chapters 1–2.

Boyden and Berry, *Children and Youth on the Front Line,* chapters 3, 4, and 6.

Asmita Naik. "Protecting Children from the Protectors." *Forced Migration Review* 15 (2002): 16–19.

Week 9: Other Effects of War on Children: War Orphans, Separated Children

What about children and young people who are not direct participants in armed conflict, but who are nonetheless affected by it?

Boyden and Berry, *Children and Youth on the Front Line,* chapter 1.

Carolyn Nordstrom. *Shadows of War.* University of California Press, 2004, chapter 13.

Jessaca Leinaweaver. "Peru's War Orphans, 1983–2003." Rutgers Center for Historical Analysis Spring Conference, 2005.

Week 10: Children in the Symbolic Mode

What are the political uses of the rhetoric of childhood?

Susan D. Moeller. "A Hierarchy of Innocence." *Press/Politics* 7, no. 1 (2002): 36–56.

Shraf Zahedi. "Ideology of Martyrdom and Martyr's Children of the Iran-Iraq War." Rutgers Center for Historical Analysis Spring Conference on "Children and War," 2005.

Week 11: Critiques of Children's Rights

Rosen, *Armies of the Young,* chapter 5.

Vanessa Pupavac. "Misanthropy Without Borders: The International Children's Rights Regime." *Disasters* 25, no. 2 (2001): 95–112.

Susan Shepler. "The Rites of the Child: Global Discourses of Youth and Reintegrating Child Soldiers in Sierra Leone." *Journal of Human Rights* 4, no. 2 (2005).

Week 12: Research Methods and Ethics in Youth and Conflict, Children's Voices

Boyden and Berry, *Children and Youth on the Front Line,* chapter 12 ("Anthropology Under Fire," by Jo Boyden).

Jane Lowicki. "Beyond Consultation: In Support of More Meaningful Adolescent Participation." *Forced Migration Review* 15 (2002): 33–35.

Gillian Mann and David Tolfree. *Children's Participation in Research: Reflections from the Care and Protection of Separated Children in Emergencies Project.* Save the Children, Sweden, 2003.

Week 13: Current Trends in Programming for Children Affected by War

Jason Hart. *Children's Participation in Humanitarian Action: Learning from Zones of Armed Conflict.* Oxford University Refugee Studies Centre, 2004.

Jack Goldstone et al. *Youth and Conflict: A Toolkit for Intervention.* US Agency for International Development (USAID), 2004, http://www.usaid.gov/our_work/cross-cutting_programs/conflict/publications/docs/CMM_Youth_and_Conflict_Toolkit_April_2005.pdf.

18.5 People with Disabilities in Politics and Society

Arthur Blaser
Chapman University

COURSE DESCRIPTION

Intermediate-level undergraduate course in the liberal arts, political science, sociology, peace studies, and disability studies.

This course explores the participation of people with disabilities (PWD) in politics and society. We consider differences (1) over time; (2) between countries and cultures; and (3) between conventional and unconventional strategies for political, social, and economic participation. We examine similarities to and differences from representations of other historically disadvantaged groups and social movements, including the women's movement, gay and lesbian rights movements, and ethnic movements. The role and implications of charity will also be explored. A final theme is the relationships between disability issues and issues of war and peace.

The shift from medical to sociopolitical approaches for understanding disability issues is central to this course. We also consider what is meant by terms such as moral, charity, deficit, vocational rehabilitation, administrative/programmatic, social welfare, independent living, minority group, civil rights, human rights, and cultural approaches to disability issues.

REQUIRED TEXTS

Mary Johnson, ed. *Disability Awareness: Do It Right!* Louisville: Advocado Press, 2006.

Mary Johnson and Barrett Shaw, eds. *To Ride the Public's Buses: The Fight That Built a Movement*. Louisville: Advocado Press, 2001.

Ruth O'Brien, ed. *Voices from the Edge: Narratives About the Americans with Disabilities Act*. New York: Oxford University Press, 2004.

Joseph Shapiro. *No Pity: People with Disabilities Forging a New Civil Rights Movement*. New York: Times Books, 1994.

American Association of People with Disabilities (AAPD). Justice for All, www.jfanow.org. Course participants will subscribe to the free weekly email from AAPD.

British Broadcasting Corporation. *Ouch!* Web-based newsletter on disability news. Course participants will subscribe to the free electronic newsletter, http://www.bbc.co.uk/ouch/newsletter/.

Articles assigned in the course schedule.

RECOMMENDED TEXTS

Doris Zames Fleischer and Frieda Zames. *The Disability Rights Movement: From Charity to Confrontation.* Philadelphia: Temple University Press, 2001.

Jacqueline Vaughn Switzer. *Disabled Rights: American Disability Policy and the Fight for Equality.* Washington, DC: Georgetown University Press, 2003.

COURSE SCHEDULE

Unit 1: Concepts in Transition

Peace (positive and negative), violence (structural and direct), disability, disablement, and ableism.

Johnson, *Disability Awareness,* introduction.

O'Brien, *Voices from the Edge,* part 1.

Johan Galtung. "Twenty Five Years of Peace Research: Ten Challenges and Responses." *Journal of Peace Research* 22 (1985): 141–158.

Michael Oliver. *The Politics of Disablement.* Palgrave Macmillan, 1997, 1–11.

Ju Gosling. Helping the Handicapped (website), http://sinnlos.st/help/index.html. Depicts charity, medical, administrative, and social models of disability.

School of Industrial and Labor Relations (ILR) at Cornell University. Disability Statistics, www.disabilitystatistics.org (featuring US statistical information).

The Unusual Suspects: How Society and People with Disabilities Regard Each Other, hosted by Tom Shakespeare, BBC, video, 2002, 30 minutes.

Unit 2: Disability and Diversity

Johnson, *Disability Awareness,* chapters 1–5.

O'Brien, *Voices from the Edge,* preface, introduction.

Greg Smith. "Brother in the Wheelchair." *Essence,* July 2001, 162.

Kathi Wolfe. "Get Proud by Practicing Gay: The ADA's Anniversary Is Independence Day for 'Queer Crips.'" *Washington Blade,* July 20, 2007, www.washingtonblade.com/2007/7-20/view/columns/10925.cfm.

Beth Hall. Who's News? personal weblog, http://spj.org/blog/blogs/diversity/.

My Country: The Civil Rights Movements That Created the Americans with Disabilities Act, hosted by James DePriest, DVD, 1996, 60 minutes.

Dane E. Vion. *Loud, Proud, and Passionate.* Mobility International USA video, Sky's the Limit Productions, 2002. Provides perspectives on women with disabilities.

Unit 3: "Tiny Tims" and "Supercrips"; the Independent Living Movement

Johnson, *Disability Awareness,* appendixes A and D.
Shapiro, *No Pity*, chapters 1, 2, 4.

Browse the website *Ouch!* www.bbc.co.uk/ouch/.

Disability Rights and Independent Living Movement, University of California, Berkeley. http://bancroft.berkeley.edu/collections/drilm/. Includes audio and video excerpts.
Irene M. Ward. *A Little History Worth Knowing*. DVD, 1998, 22 minutes.

Unit 4: Independent Living, Institutionalization, and People First

Shapiro, *No Pity,* chapters 5, 6, and 8.
National Council on Independent Living, www.ncil.org.
Institute for Independent Living, www.independentliving.org. The international organization is based in Sweden.
Beth Hall. Who's News? http://spj.org/blog/blogs/diversity/.
People in Motion, produced by Bill Einreinhofer and Ruth Anne Goldfarb, Public Broadcasting System, DVD, 1995. Excerpt with Ed Roberts ("father of independent living").
Unforgotten: Twenty-Five Years After Willowbrook, directed by Jack Fisher, VHS, 1996. Story of the exposé of a large New York institution and its aftermath.

Unit 5: The Disability Rights Movement, Disability Culture, and the Right/Duty to Die

Shapiro, *No Pity,* chapters 8–10, epilogue, and postscript.
Paul Longmore. "The Second Phase: From Disability Rights to Disability Culture." *Disability Rag and ReSource,* September–October 1995, www.independentliving.org/docs3/longm95.html.
Mike Ervin. "Clip 'n Save Advance Medical Directive." Not Dead Yet, www.notdeadyet.org/docs/ervinhumor.html. Chicago-area disability rights organization opposed to assisted suicide.

View DVDs depicting disability culture: *Vital Signs: Crip Culture Talks Back,* directed by David T. Mitchell and Sharon Snyder, DVD, 1997, 48 minutes, or *Tools for Change: Disability Identity and Culture,* directed by Jerry Smith, produced by Advocating Change Together, 2000, 22 minutes.

Unit 6: Deafness and Deafness; Wheelchairs in Global Perspective

Shapiro, *No Pity,* chapters 3 and 7.
iBot Mobility System, www.independencenow.com/ibot/index.html.
Whirlwind Wheelchair International, www.whirlwindwheelchair.org/index.htm.

Sound and Fury, directed by Josh Eronson, DVD, 2000. Film depicting contending perspectives on cochlear implants.

Unit 7: Days in the Life, Disability Awareness Activities, and the Disability Media

Johnson, *Disability Awareness,* part 2, appendices B, C, E, and F.

Ragged Edge Magazine Online, www.raggededgemagazine.com. Source of numerous opinion articles by Mary Johnson and others.

Mouth: Voice of the Disability Nation, newsletter from Free Hand Press. Several issues are published online at www.mouthmag.com.

On a Roll, produced and directed by Joanne Caputo, Independent Television Service, DVD, 2004 ("the disability experience in America," with Greg Smith).

Unit 8: Employment and Disability

O'Brien, *Voices from the Edge,* part 2.

Equal Employment Opportunity Commission. Disability Discrimination. www.eeoc.gov/types/ada.html.

US Department of Justice. *Americans with Disabilities Act.* www.ada.gov.

When Billy Broke His Head, directed by Billy Golfus and David Simpson, Fanlight Productions, DVD, 1994, 57 minutes. Sundance Film Festival award-winning video covering many disability rights issues.

Unit 9: Public Services (Including Parks, Courthouses, Public Schools), Personal Assistance Services, and the Olmstead Mandate

O'Brien, *Voices from the Edge,* part 3.

United States Department of Health and Human Services, Office for Civil Rights. www.hhs.gov/ocr/mis.htm. Read about implementation of the Olmstead Mandate.

Bazelon Center for Mental Health Law. www.bazelon.org/issues/disability rights/incourt/olmstead/index.htm.

If I Can't Do It, directed by Walter Brock, *Point of View* series, Public Broadcasting System, DVD, 1998, 54 minutes.

Unit 10: Public Accommodations (Malls, Restaurants, Universities)

O'Brien, *Voices from the Edge,* part 4.

John Hockenberry. "Yes You Can." *Parade* online, July 24, 2005, www.parade.com/articles/editions/2005/edition_07-24-2005/featured_0.

Disabled in Action, www.disabledinaction.org/. New York City civil rights organization.

Concrete Change, www.concretechange.org. Website of the Statewide Independent Living Council of Georgia, providing information on universal design in housing.

People in Motion, produced by Bill Einreinhofer and Ruth Anne Goldfarb, Public Broadcasting System, DVD, 1995.

Unit 11: Civil Disobedience, ADAPT, and Disability Studies

Johnson and Shaw, *To Ride the Public's Buses,* foreword, chapters 1–3.

Browse the website of ADAPT, www.adapt.org.

Society for Disability Studies, http://www.disstudies.org/.

The Power of 504, produced by the 504 Anniversary and Commemoration Committee, video, 1977, 18 minutes. Features the 1977 disability rights protests for implementation of the 1973 Rehabilitation Act.

Unit 12: ADAPT and Attendant Programs Today, Public Interest Law, Social Change, and Political Change

Johnson and Shaw, *To Ride the Public's Buses,* chapters 4–8.

Disability Rights Advocates, www.dralegal.org. A Bay Area public interest law firm.

Disability Rights Legal Center, Loyola University Law School, Los Angeles, www.disabilityrightslegalcenter.org/.

National Public Radio. Audio files on institutionalization and community-based alternatives, with Joseph Shapiro. Search for "Joseph Shapiro" at www.npr.org.

Unit 13: Activism and the Future

Johnson and Shaw, *To Ride the Public's Buses,* chapter 9 and epilogue.

Ann Hubbard. "A Military-Civilian Coalition for Disability Rights." *Mississippi Law Journal* 75 (Spring 2006): 975–1006.

United Nations Convention on the Rights of Persons with Disabilities. Enable (website). See "Latest News" at www.un.org/disabilities/convention/index.shtml.

Landmine Survivors Network, www.landminesurvivors.org/.

Turtles Can Fly, directed by Bahman Ghobadi, co-production of Iran and Iraq, DVD, 2004.

TEACHING NOTES

Some of the course materials will need to be adapted to the classroom setting. Johnson's *Disability Awareness,* for example, is designed as a "how-to guide . . . for a successful awareness day." The course is an opportunity for an "awareness semester," and some, but not all, of the exercises can be adapted to the classroom setting. This course lends itself well to involvement, finding out information in the community, and making use of the abundant resources in the community, in the disability media, and on the World Wide Web. Discussion of current controversies (such as legislative debates on the

Community Choice Act and Americans with Disabilities Restoration Act), placed in historic context, is vital. Class members will have viewed disability issues through a medical/deficit "lens" for many years and may have some resistance to looking at disability issues as ones of social and political justice. Multiple print, audio, and visual media are therefore useful in countering this resistance.

Each class member will post at least twice to the electronic discussion board. I also assign a paper on an individual or group mentioned in one of our texts. Students must use at least one source that is not a website or one of our texts and indicate how and why assessments of the individual or group's contributions vary. They must also prepare a website analysis and give a five-minute oral report with a two-page handout (one page should be from the website).

The final project is a seven-page double-spaced paper. They must consult and cite at least five references in addition to the required texts. One source must be www.raggededgemagazine.com, www.mouthmag.com, or www.newmobility.com. Nonprint sources (for instance, interviews) are encouraged. Excessive reliance on web sources is discouraged.

19
Skills in Conflict Resolution

THE COURSES REPRESENTED BY THESE FIVE SYLLABUSES VARY SIGnificantly in the amount of attention they give to theory; in their characteristic mix of the language of conflict transformation, mediation, resolution, management, and negotiation; and in the arenas of application, whether small-scale or large, local or international. What they share most clearly is a commitment to developing appropriate and necessary skills for third-party involvement in a range of conflict settings. Undergirding the emphasis on skills is a shared assumption that third-party conflict engagers often have little by way of formal authority and power and so will flourish or fail according to their capacity to keep disputants engaged, which in turn is based on the quality of the third party's skills.

Mohammed Abu-Nimer focuses on conceptions and practices of dialogue, which in recent decades has come to the fore as a means of positive intervention in a variety of conflict settings. The far-reaching work of mediation is represented here by Zheng Wang's emphasis on using mediation to address international, and therefore typically cross-cultural, conflicts, whereas Carolyn Schrock-Shenk emphasizes mediating small-scale and interpersonal conflicts. Nathan C. Funk works with the broad and basic concept of negotiation, taking in everything from applications in daily life to cross-cultural and multiparty situations. Framing his work in terms of alternative dispute resolution, Isaac Noam Ebner begins with negotiation and then moves on to arbitration, facilitation, and mediation.

19.1 Dialogue: Approaches and Applications

Mohammed Abu-Nimer
American University

COURSE DESCRIPTION

Upper-level undergraduate or lower-level graduate course.

Since the late 1970s, dialogue has occupied a central stage in the theoretical and practical development of the fields of conflict resolution and peace studies. Dialogue is being constantly proposed as a framework of intervention and a set of instruments and skills to address complex conflicts on community, national, international, and global levels.

This course aims to capture the major developments in the study and practice of dialogue, both on the academic and practical levels. It focuses on theoretical models of dialogue in interethnic, interreligious, intercultural, interorganizational, and other forms of identity-based conflicts. A set of theories and models rooted in an interdisciplinary perspective (sociology, social psychology, and anthropology) constitute the main theoretical framework for this course. The course covers studies related to principles of intergroup relations, cultural factors, elements of identity formation and transformation, and models of decisionmaking.

The course explores the necessary skills to conduct dialogue in conflict settings, such as basic conflict assessment, communication skills, designs, and evaluation of dialogue processes. In addition, it examines conditions and criteria for effective dialogue frameworks based on actual examination of various case studies of interethnic and interfaith dialogue, such as those derived from US interracial and interethnic relations, in addition to cases from Sri Lanka, the Philippines, and other regions.

The course has four major objectives:

• To examine the multiplicity of methodologies (theoretical and applied models) that have evolved in the field of identity-based dialogue;

• To highlight the potential constructive role that various dialogue frameworks can play in reducing violence and building a culture of peace;

• To empower participants by acknowledging their experience with dialogue and by learning new, hands-on skills and designs of dialogue;

• To practice various settings of identity-based dialogue to heighten participants' awareness of their own attitudes and views on controversial subjects.

Some of the major questions to be addressed include the following: How can dialogue be linked to policy change? What are the conditions for effective dialogue? What are the major necessary pre-dialogue activities?

REQUIRED TEXTS

Harold Saunders. *A Public Peace Process: Sustained Dialogue to Transform Racial and Ethnic Conflicts*. New York: St. Martin's Press, 1999.

David Schoem and Sylvia Hurtado, eds. *Intergroup Dialogue: Deliberative Democracy in School, College, Community, and Workplace*. Ann Arbor: University of Michigan Press, 2001.

David Smock. *Interfaith Dialogue*. Washington, D.C.: US Institute of Peace, 2002.

David Bohm. *On Dialogue*. London: Routledge, 1996.

William Isaacs. *Dialogue: The Art of Thinking Together*. New York: Currency, 1999.

Milton Bennett. "Towards Ethnorelativism: A Developmental Model of Intercultural Sensitivity." In *Education for the Intercultural Experience*, edited by Michael Paige. Yarmouth, ME: Intercultural Press, 1993, 22–71.

RECOMMENDED READING

Mohammed Abu-Nimer. *Dialogue, Conflict Resolution, and Change: Arab-Jewish Encounters in Israel*. Albany: State University of New York Press, 1999.

Rupert Brown. *Prejudice: Its Social Psychology*. London: Blackwell, 1995.

Janet E. Helmes. *Black and White Racial Identity: Theory, Research, and Practice*. Westport, CT: Greenwood Press, 1990.

Miles Hewstone and Rupert Brown, eds. *Contact and Conflict in Intergroup Encounters*. Oxford: Basil Blackwell, 1986.

Linda Ellinor and Glenna Gerard. *Dialogue: Rediscovering the Transforming Power of Conversation*. New York: John Wiley and Sons, 1998.

COURSE SCHEDULE

Unit 1: Introductions and Definitions

Discuss norms of the group—cultural and personal. Look at definitions of conflict transformation, including terminology and basic principles. See also the definitions of peacebuilding and dialogue, the principles of peacebuilding as a field, and the principles of dialogue.

Bohm, *On Dialogue*, foreword.

Unit 2: Nature of Identity-Based Conflicts: Theoretical Principles and Approaches

What theoretical assumptions and principles underlie the dialogue processes? Why does dialogue work? What is your own experience with intergroup dialogue? Share personal stories about cultural, ethnic, or religious dialogue and identify common patterns and principles.

Schoem and Hurtado, *Intergroup Dialogue,* chapter 1 ("Intergroup Dialogue Democracy at Work in Theory").
Isaacs, *Dialogue: The Art of Thinking Together,* part 1 ("What Is Dialogue?").
Bohm, *On Dialogue,* "On Communication" and "The Nature of Collective Thoughts," chapters 1 and 2.

Recommended reading:
Schoem and Hurtado, *Intergroup Dialogue,* chapter 4.
Hewstone and Brown, *Contact and Conflict in Intergroup Encounters,* chapters 1–3.

Unit 3: The Foundations of Dialogue: From the Self Out; Building the Inner

Bohm, *On Dialogue,* chapters 2, 3, and 4.

Recommended reading:
Hewstone and Brown, *Contact and Conflict in Intergroup Encounters,* chapters 4–6.

Unit 4: Basic Foundational Skills for Dialogue Process

What are the basic foundational skills for the dialogue process, and how are they acquired?

Bohm, *On Dialogue,* chapters 5, 6, and 7.
Isaacs, *Dialogue: The Art of Thinking Together,* parts 2 and 3.

Recommended reading:
Schoem and Hurtado, *Intergroup Dialogue,* chapter 15.
Helmes, *Black and White Racial Identity,* chapters 1–3.

Unit 5: The Complexity of Intergroup Dialogue

Looks at how to engage in a dialogue process. Examine the core paradox in a dialogue framework: content/process and individual/group. Review the history of the field of dialogue: Who are the first "dialoguers"?

Isaacs, *Dialogue: The Art of Thinking Together,* chapters 3 and 4.
Schoem and Hurtado, *Intergroup Dialogue,* chapters 16, 3, and 6.

Recommended reading:
Helms, *Black and White Racial Identity,* chapters 4–6.

Unit 6: Dialogue Framework

Continue exploring the core paradox in dialogue framework: process and content. Study personal and institutional change through dialogue. Ask how dialogue and conflict resolution bring about change through dialogue. Look at attitudes, behaviors, and situations. Begin preparing case studies of dialogue and change.

Schoem and Hurtado, *Intergroup Dialogue*, chapters 17 and 7.

Recommended reading:
Schoem and Hurtado, *Intergroup Dialogue*, chapter 5.
Helms, *Black and White Racial Identity*, chapters 9–11.

Unit 7: Dialogue Framework: Talk Versus Action

Schoem and Hurtado, *Intergroup Dialogue*, chapters 19, 10, and 11.

Recommended reading:
Schoem and Hurtado, *Intergroup Dialogue*, chapter 8.
Helms, *Black and White Racial Identity*, chapters 12–14.

Units 8–12: Intensive Dialogue Sessions on Culture, Faith, and Race

The five units that follow are especially effective as an intensive experience organized over two and a half days or five three–hour sessions. They may also be used in regularly scheduled class periods.

Unit 8: Dialogue: A Framework for Political Peace Process Dialogue

Examine the unique features of a dialogue process in a public peace process and look at case studies from different ethnic conflict areas.

Saunders, *A Public Peace Process*, chapters 1–3.
Schoem and Hurtado, *Intergroup Dialogue*, chapter 20.

Unit 9: A Framework for Political Peace Process Dialogue

Saunders, *Public Peace Process*, chapters 4–6.
Isaacs, *Dialogue: The Art of Thinking Together*, part 5.

Unit 10: Intercultural Dialogue Process and Outcomes

Ask how cultural differences affect dialogue processes. What aspects of cultural identity are expressed in the dialogue process? What are the desired outcomes of an intercultural dialogue process?

Bennett. "Towards Ethnorelativism."
Schoem and Hurtado, *Intergroup Dialogue*, chapter 12.

Recommended reading:
Helms, *Black and White Racial Identity,* chapters 4–5.

Unit 11: Interfaith Dialogue: Achieving the Miracles!
Interfaith dialogue: Is it unique? Look at the principles and processes of interfaith dialogue. Look at case studies of effective interfaith dialogue.

Smock, *Interfaith Dialogue,* chapters 1–4.

Unit 12: Interfaith Dialogue: Interethnic and International
Smock, *Interfaith Dialogue,* chapters 5–8 and Conclusion.

Unit 13: Evaluation and Impact of Dialogue Processes
Review and evaluate the principles of effective dialogue, the indicators of successful dialogue and its impact and your own indicators of success for your dialogue project. Can dialoguers have different criteria for success? Evaluate course.

"Evaluating Interfaith Peacebuilding Program." Special Report, US Institute of Peace, 2004, www.usip.org.
Schoem and Hurtado, *Intergroup Dialogue,* chapters 21 and 2.

TEACHING NOTES

The success of this course depends on each student taking an active role in class discussions and presentations. I also expect each student to have an email account in order to subscribe to at least two networks that provide information on current dialogue programs in any conflict region.

Two types of assignments are designed to help students discipline themselves in reading and preparing for class. The first is a requirement of ten reading summaries. Students are expected to hand in a two-page, single-spaced summary of the weekly readings for at least ten reading sessions. Instead of describing what is in each article, I ask them to highlight points they find interesting in the readings, compare articles, and express their opinion—in other words, evaluate what they read.

The second assignment is a group project. Working in pairs, they identify a dialogue project in a town or outside community from a list of potential organizations that I distribute. They must contact the organizers of the project and ask permission to observe and/or participate for research purposes. A minimal commitment of five to six meetings is required. The purpose of the assignment is to help them learn about a specific model of dialogue used by an actual organization, evaluate its criteria of success, and observe examples of effective dialogue and linkages to theoretical framework of dialogue. Then each student completes a separate research paper using primary and secondary sources. These requirements may change depending on whether the course is an undergraduate or graduate offering.

19.2 International Mediation

Zheng Wang
Seton Hall University

COURSE DESCRIPTION

Upper-level undergraduate course in international relations, conflict, and peace studies.

This course will focus on the analytical, methodological, and practical tools of conflict mediation and resolution, with an emphasis on conflict prevention, management, and resolution. We will examine (1) the causes and sources of international conflict, (2) the dynamics of third-party intervention, and (3) mediation skills. The course will include a blend of lectures, class discussions, individual and group exercises, and mediation role plays in class.

The objectives of this course are (1) to introduce and explore the role of international mediation in the current international system in preventing, managing, or resolving conflicts; (2) to understand the strategies and tactics that have been adopted in previous mediation efforts in order to assess their usefulness in the future; and (3) to help students think systematically and analytically about international conflict.

REQUIRED TEXTS

Christopher W. Moore. *The Mediation Process: Practical Strategies for Resolving Conflict.* San Francisco: Jossey-Bass, 1996.

David W. Augsburger. *Conflict Mediation Across Cultures: Pathways and Patterns.* Louisville: Westminster/John Knox Press, 1992.

Jacob Bercovitch, ed. *Resolving International Conflicts: The Theory and Practice of Mediation.* Boulder, CO: Lynne Rienner, 1996.

SUPPLEMENTAL TEXT

Sandra Cheldelin, Daniel Druckman, and Larissa Fast, eds. *Conflict: From Analysis to Intervention.* London: Continuum, 2008.

COURSE SCHEDULE

Unit 1: Introduction to the Field of Mediation and Conflict Resolution
Moore, *The Mediation Process*, chapters 1–2.

Unit 2: International Conflict: Sources

Cheldelin, Druckman, and Fast, *Conflict,* chapter 4 ("Sources," by Richard E. Rubenstein).

Augsburger, *Conflict Mediation Across Cultures,* introduction and chapters 1 and 5.

Unit 3: International Conflict: Dynamics and Structure

Augsburger, *Conflict Mediation Across Cultures,* introduction and chapters 2 and 8.

Cheldelin, Druckman, and Fast, *Conflict,* chapter 14 ("Mediation and Arbitration," by Sandra Cheldelin).

Unit 4: Intervening in Conflict and the Development of Mediation

Bercovitch, *Resolving International Conflict,* foreword, introduction, and chapter 1.

Augsburger, *Conflict Mediation Across Cultures,* chapter 7.

Unit 5: Mediation: Strategies, Techniques, and Processes I

Moore, *The Mediation Process,* chapters 3–6.

Unit 6: Mediation: Strategies, Techniques, and Processes II

Moore, *The Mediation Process,* chapters 10–14.

Unit 7: Mediation Simulation Exercise: Little Versus Jenks

Role simulation developed by the Program of Negotiation (PON), Harvard Law School, http://www.pon.org/catalog/product_info.php?products_id=56.

Unit 8: Mediation Case Study: The Oslo Accord

Dean G. Pruitt. "The Tactics of Third-Party Intervention." *Orbis: A Journal of World Affairs* 44 (2000): 245–254.

Jan Egeland, "The Oslo Accord: Multiparty Facilitation Through the Norwegian Channel." In *Herding Cats: Multiparty Mediation in a Complex World,* edited by Chester A. Crocker et al. Washington, DC: US Institute of Peace Press, 1999.

View *The 50 Years War: Israel and the Arabs,* PBS Home Video, 2000, 300 minutes.

Unit 9: The Mediators

Bercovitch, *Resolving International Conflict,* chapter 2, 4, and 10.

Unit 10: Conflict Mediation Across Cultures

Augsburger, *Conflict Mediation Across Cultures,* chapters 3–6.

Bercovitch, *Resolving International Conflict,* chapter 5.

Unit 11: Case Study: Sri Lanka Conflicts and the Mediation Efforts

Bercovitch, *Resolving International Conflict,* chapter 7.

In class preparation for Sri Lanka peace process simulation exercise.

Unit 12: Mediation Simulation Exercises: Sri Lanka Peace Process (I)

The Public International Law and Policy Group (PILPG), http://www.publicinternationallaw.org/areas/peacebuilding/simulations/index.html.

Unit 13: Mediation Simulation Exercises: Sri Lanka Peace Process (II)

The Public International Law and Policy Group (PILPG), http://www.publicinternationallaw.org/areas/peacebuilding/simulations/index.html.

Unit 14: Conditions for Successful Mediations in Intractable Conflicts

Marieke Kleiboer. "Understanding Success and Failure of International Mediation." *Journal of Conflict Resolution* 40, no. 2 (1996).

Bercovitch, *Resolving International Conflict,* chapter 6.

Unit 15: Peacebuilding, Conflict Transformation, and Reconciliation

Augsburger, *Conflict Mediation Across Cultures,* chapter 9.

Cheldelin, Druckman, and Fast, *Conflict,* chapter 19 ("Peace-building," by Ho-Won Jeong).

TEACHING NOTES

Among the challenges that today's conflict resolution teachers confront, three stand out for me as the most significant: (1) How do I teach a generic conflict resolution process and address the role of culture, emotion, and identity? (2) Are students able to transfer practice in the classroom to practice in other settings? and (3) Since mediation/conflict resolution is a practice, how do I evaluate my own effectiveness as a teacher? And how do I evaluate students' performance in a negotiation simulation? In my mediation class, I use five or six mediation role-play simulations in each semester. Simulations help students connect theory and practice. To increase simulation effectiveness, I also designed an evaluation process. First, students submit a strategy paper on how they plan to produce the best negotiated settlement for their delegation. Second, students are asked after the simulation to fill out an evaluation form to assess their own performance and also other groups' strengths and weaknesses. The forms consist of six different categories for grading, including pre-negotiation, teamwork, role play, critical thinking, problem solving, and oral presentation. After reviewing the returned evaluation forms, I prepare a more detailed evaluation report to each team. Critical feedback is helpful to both students and instructors.

19.3 Mediation: Process, Skills, and Theory

Carolyn Schrock-Shenk
Goshen College

COURSE DESCRIPTION

Intermediate or upper-level undergraduate course for majors in peace and conflict studies.

Most societies have some form of third-party conflict transformation process. This course will focus on mediation and the third-party role of the mediator. It will take a brief look at the historical roots of mediation, the various streams of its more current manifestation in North America, its theoretical basis, the arenas or situations in which mediation is appropriate and indicated and those in which it is not, the cultural implications of mediation, and some of the ethical dilemmas mediators face.

This is largely a skills course; much class time will be spent learning the process of mediation and the skills needed to be a mediator, whether in its formal sense or informally as a life skill. It is experiential in nature, in that it will elicit and build upon students' experience of conflict and will use various experiential learning tools to develop these practical mediation skills. A previous understanding of conflict, conflict transformation, and communication skills and principles is helpful.

OBJECTIVES OF THE COURSE

1. To demonstrate a basic understanding of conflict and its transformation, the vocabulary, and definitions in the field;
2. To understand the history of mediation and to examine the principles, strategies, and underlying values of the current streams of mediation;
3. To develop skills in interpersonal mediation (including assessment, communication, negotiation, and facilitation) through observation, discussion, role plays, and other exercises;
4. To locate mediation within the gamut of conflict transformation strategies and third-party roles, understanding the arenas or situations in which mediation is appropriate and indicated and those in which it is not;
5. To identify intrapersonal, interpersonal, and systemic/structural components of various conflicts;
6. To consider the implications of culture on mediation as well as various potential ethical dilemmas for mediators; and

7. To understand the philosophical underpinnings of restorative justice and the Victim-Offender Reconciliation Program (VORP) as a primary application of restorative justice.

REQUIRED TEXTS

Robert A. Baruch Bush and Joseph P. Folger. *The Promise of Mediation*, 2nd ed. Jossey-Bass, 2004.

Roger Fisher and William Ury. *Getting to Yes: Negotiating Agreement Without Giving In*. Penguin, 1991.

Carolyn Schrock-Shenk, ed. *Mediation and Facilitation Training Manual: Foundations for Constructive Conflict Transformation*, 4th ed. Mennonite Conciliation Service, 2000.

Howard Zehr. *The Little Book of Restorative Justice*. Good Books, 2002.

Occasional readings assigned in the course schedule.

OVERVIEW OF GRADED LEARNING ACTIVITIES

Activity A: Attendance and participation. This is critical, given the interactive and skills-oriented nature of the course.

Activity B: Exploring types of mediation. Students are assigned the job of researching one of the many types of mediation, drawing from at least four sources (including an interview with a mediator) and creating a handout for the class.

Activity C: Book review. Students choose a book that focuses on one of the many types of mediation that interests them and write a review responding to a set of questions.

Activity D: Group research/presentation projects. In groups of four, students investigate a research question or controversial issue in the field. They begin with a proposal for their research and end with a class presentation.

Activity E: Two exams.

Activity F: One-hour mediation-related practicum (required for majors). Students who enroll for this fourth credit hour must undertake twenty to thirty hours of a mediation-related practicum that helps cement the principles, skills, and processes learned in class by applying them outside class. A practicum consists of shadowing a mediator or engaging with a conflict transformation program, developing a project that applies mediation and conflict transformation skills, a log of practicum activity, and a synthesis paper.

OVERVIEW OF COURSE SCHEDULE

Session 1: Introduction to the Course and Each Other.

Session 2: Class Covenant, Personal Conflict Styles, and Conflict and Faith.

Session 3: Conflict and Conflict Transformation Overview and Review.

Session 4: Communication in Mediation: Listening and Speaking Skills.

Session 5: Principled Negotiation.

Session 6: Third-Party Roles and Mediation: Overview, History, Values.

Session 7: Getting People to the Table, the Context, and Co-Mediation.

Session 8: Mediation Process Overview; Mediation Video or Demonstration.

Session 9: Stages I, II, and III Overview.

Session 10: Role Play I with Debriefing.

Session 11: Stage IV Overview; Role Play 2.

Session 12: Role Play 2 Debriefing; Stage V Overview.

Session 13: Working with Emotions and Healing Strategies.

Sessions 14–15: Transformative Mediation Principles and Practice.

Session 16: Cultural Implications and Power Imbalances.

Session 17: Role Play 3.

Session 18: Role Play 3 Debriefing, Caucusing, Impasse, and Listening Revisited.

Session 19: Role Play 4.

Session 20: Role Play 4 Debriefing, Ethical Challenges, and Mediation Follow-Up.

Sessions 21–23: Presentations.

Session 24: Restorative Justice and Victim-Offender Reconciliation Programs.

Session 25: Peer Mediation and Violence Prevention.

TEACHING NOTES

A primary emphasis of the course is learning the skills and process of mediation, which is achieved in large part through exercises and role playing. Role plays can be obtained from one of the role play books in the field or by writing or eliciting situations appropriate to the context. A pattern that has worked well with this course outline is: Role play 1: Conflict that is simple and familiar, such as roommate conflict about noise; Role play 2: Conflict that includes the complexities of values or theological differences; Role play 3: Conflict involving a significant power imbalance; and Role play 4: Conflict involving two distinctly different cultural groups. Role plays are done in groups of four with a co-mediator model and are held in separate breakout rooms. Groups stay the same for role play 1 and 2 (switching roles) and then form different groupings for role play 3 and 4. Careful debriefing is critical to ensuring that students learn from the role plays.

19.4 Negotiation: Theories and Practices

Nathan C. Funk
Conrad Grebel University College

COURSE DESCRIPTION

Intermediate undergraduate course for general education students and peace studies majors.

Negotiation has often been described as the most basic and fundamental form of dispute resolution. In the home and the workplace as well as in community affairs and international relations, efforts to negotiate and renegotiate conflicting positions, interests, and values are a necessity of daily life. Beginning with our own experiences, this course provides an opportunity to explore different ways of understanding and engaging in the negotiation process. Attention will be given not only to the theories behind various practices but also to the challenge of developing better skills for analyzing disputes, managing human interdependence, and improving relationships through the maximization of shared interests and values.

COURSE OBJECTIVES

- To increase theoretical as well as experiential knowledge of negotiation processes and dynamics.
- To encourage analytical reflection on the negotiation processes in which students are involved as well as on negotiations that affect the quality of public life (including international and intercultural relations).
- To enhance awareness of preferred as well as habitual negotiating style(s).
- To provide a basis for recognizing, evaluating, and responding to different negotiation strategies and tactics.
- To stimulate reflection on similarities and differences between "micro-" and "macro-" level negotiation processes.
- To encourage experimentation with negotiation methods that can be used to advance high-priority interests and values while protecting or improving relationships.
- To support the formulation of strategies for improving personal negotiation skills and resolving public conflict.

REQUIRED TEXTS

Brad McRae. *Negotiating and Influencing Skills: The Art of Creating and Claiming Value*. Thousand Oaks, CA: Sage, 1998.

Reading assignments listed in the course schedule.

RECOMMENDED TEXT

Roy J. Lewicki, Bruce Barry, and David M. Saunders, and John Minton. *Essentials of Negotiation,* 3rd ed. Toronto: McGraw-Hill, 2004.

COURSE SCHEDULE

Week 1: Meeting One Another, Defining Our Purpose

Week 2: Negotiation as a Daily Practice

McRae, *Negotiating and Influencing Skills,* introduction, chapters 1 and 2.
Lewicki et al., *Negotiation,* pages 26–31 ("The Significance of Human Conflict," by Kenneth D. Benne) and pages 430–434 ("Universal Computer Company").

Further reading:
Lewicki et al., chapter 1 ("The Nature of Negotiation").
Dudley Weeks. *The Eight Essential Steps of Conflict Resolution.* Los Angeles: Tarcher, 1994.

Week 3: Negotiation Styles

McRae, *Negotiating and Influencing Skills,* chapter 3 ("Assessing Your Current Negotiating Style").
Roger Fisher and William Ury. "Don't Bargain over Positions." In *Getting to Yes: Negotiating Agreement Without Giving In,* by Roger Fisher and William Ury. New York: Penguin, 1991, 3–14.
Dean G. Pruitt and Peter J. Carnevale. "The Dual Concern Model and the Determinants of Problem Solving." In *Negotiation in Social Conflict,* by Dean G. Pruitt and Peter J. Carnevale. Pacific Grove, CA: Brooks/Cole Publishing, 1993, 104–118.

Further reading:
Lewicki et al., chapter 2 ("Negotiation: Strategizing, Framing and Planning").

Week 4: Negotiation Strategies and Tactics

McRae, *Negotiating and Influencing Skills,* chapter 4 ("Principles and Techniques for Creating and Claiming Value").
Lewicki et al., *Negotiation,* pages 111–113 ("Attack by Question," by Jacques Lalanne) and pages 472–476 ("Personal Bargaining Inventory").

Further reading:

Lewicki et al., *Negotiation,* chapter 3 ("Strategy and Tactics of Distributive Bargaining") and chapter 4 ("Strategy and Tactics of Integrative Negotiation").

Brad McRae. *The Seven Strategies of Master Negotiators: Featuring Real-Life Insights from Canada's Top Negotiators.* Toronto: McGraw-Hill, 2002.

Week 5: Difficult Situations and Personality Conflicts

McRae, *Negotiating and Influencing Skills,* chapter 5 ("Dealing with Difficult People and Difficult Situations").

William Ury. "Conclusion: Turning Adversaries into Partners." In *Getting Past No: Negotiating Your Way from Confrontation to Cooperation.* New York: Bantam Books, 1993, 159–171.

Further reading:

James L. Greenstone and Sharon C. Leviton. *Elements of Crisis Intervention: Crises and How to Respond to Them.* Forest Grove, CA: Brooks/Cole Publishing, 2002.

Lewicki et al., *Negotiation,* chapter 9 ("Managing Difficult Negotiations: Individual Approaches").

Randall G. Rogan, Mitchell R. Hammer, and Clinton R. Van Zandt, eds. *Dynamic Processes of Crisis Negotiation: Theory, Research, and Practice.* Westport, CT: Praeger, 1997.

Douglas Stone, Bruce Patton, and Sheila Heen. *Difficult Conversations: How to Discuss What Matters Most.* New York: Penguin Books, 1999.

Week 6: Approaches to Skill Development

McRae, *Negotiating and Influencing Skills,* chapter 6 ("Developing Higher-Order Skills") and chapter 8 ("Conclusion").

Frederick J. Lanceley. "Active Listening." In *On-Scene Guide for Crisis Negotiators,* 2nd ed. New York: CRC Press, 2003, 21–30.

Further reading:

Robert S. Adler, Benson Rosen, and Elliot M. Silverstein. "Emotions in Negotiation: How to Manage Fear and Anger." *Negotiation Journal* 14, no. 2 (April 1998): 161–179.

Lewicki et al., *Negotiation,* chapter 5 ("Perception, Cognition, and Communication"), chapter 6 ("Finding and Using Negotiation Leverage"), and pages 302–304 ("Squeak Up! My Turn," by Gerald Nachman).

Week 7: Test no. 1.

Week 8: Peace Negotiations

Roger Fisher, Elizabeth Kopelman, and Andrea Kupfer Schneider. "Focus on Their Choice." *Beyond Machiavelli: Tools for Coping with Conflict.* Cambridge, MA: Harvard University Press, 1994, 42–66.

J. Lewis Rasmussen. "Negotiating a Revolution: Toward Integrating Relationship Building and Reconciliation into Official Peace Negotiations." In *Reconciliation, Justice, and Coexistence: Theory and Practice,* edited by Mohammed Abu-Nimer. New York: Lexington Books, 2001, 101–127.

Further reading:

Fred Charles Ikle. "The Role of Emotions in International Negotiations." In *International Negotiation: Actors, Structure/Process, Values,* edited by Peter Berton, Hiroshi Kimura, and I. William Zartman. New York: St. Martin's Press, 1999, 335–350.

Bertram I. Spector. "Negotiating with Villains." In *International Negotiation: Actors, Structure/Process, Values,* edited by Peter Berton, Hiroshi Kimura, and I. William Zartman. New York: St. Martin's Press, 1999, 309–334.

Janet Gross Stein. *Getting to the Table.* Baltimore: Johns Hopkins University Press, 1989.

Week 9: Intercultural Negotiation

Guy Olivier Faure. "International Negotiation: The Cultural Dimension." In *International Negotiation: Analysis, Approaches, Issues,* edited by Victor A. Kremenyuk. San Francisco: Jossey-Bass, 2002, 392–415.

Glen Fisher. "Fourth Consideration: Coping with Cross-Cultural Noise." In *International Negotiation: A Cross-Cultural Perspective,* by Glen Fisher. Chicago: Intercultural Press, 1980, 53–57.

Further reading:

Raymond Cohen. *Negotiating Across Cultures: International Communication in an Interdependent World,* rev. ed. Washington, DC: US Institute of Peace Press, 1997.

Jayne Seminare Docherty. *Learning Lessons from Waco: When the Parties Bring Their Gods to the Negotiation Table.* Syracuse: Syracuse University Press, 2001.

Lewicki et al., *Negotiation,* chapter 8 ("Global Negotiation").

Week 10: Complex and Multiparty Negotiations

Ralph A. Johnson. "Organizing Constituents for Representative Bargaining." In *Negotiation Basics: Concepts, Skills, and Exercises.* Newbury Park: Sage, 1993, 105–119.

Lewicki et al., *Essentials of Negotiation,* pages 426–429 ("Twin Lakes Mining Company").

Further reading:

E. Franklin Dukes. *Resolving Public Conflict: Transforming Community and Governance.* Manchester University Press, 1996.

Fen Osler Hampson, with Michael Hart. *Multilateral Negotiations: Lessons from Arms Control, Trade, and the Environment.* Baltimore: Johns Hopkins University Press, 1999.

Week 11: Ethics and Relationships

McRae, *Negotiating and Influencing Skills,* chapter 7 ("The Power of Commitment").

Lewicki et al., *Negotiation,* pages 332–339 ("Trust and Gullibility," by Julian B. Rotter).

Phyllis Beck Kritek. "Way of Being Number Two: Be a Truth Teller." In *Negotiating at an Uneven Table: Developing Moral Courage in Resolving Our Conflicts.* San Francisco: Jossey-Bass, 2002, 216–228.

Further reading:

Lewicki et al., *Essentials of Negotiation,* chapter 7 ("Ethics in Negotiation").

I. William Zartman. "Justice in Negotiation." In *International Negotiation: Actors, Structure/Process, Values,* edited by Peter Berton, Hiroshi Kimura, and I. William Zartman. New York: St. Martin's Press, 1999, 291–307.

Week 12: Test no. 2

Week 13: Group Presentations

Week 14: Group Presentations

TEACHING NOTES

Because this class is directly concerned with practices that are meaningful at an individual level, it presents many opportunities for blending conceptual and experiential learning. To create a dynamically effective classroom, instructors can creatively blend theory and practice by supplementing lectures with weekly simulations and with efforts to elicit the tacit knowledge and life experiences of students. Journal assignments can also facilitate integration of theory with practice, while encouraging reflection on readings, films, and classroom activities. Some instructors may even find it rewarding to offer students the option of "renegotiating" the relative weight given to assignments in the syllabus. Interested learners can present the instructor with a proposed "Learning Contract" early in the term, proposing alterations to the relative weight given to participation, tests, journals, group projects, and other assignments.

Simulations and role plays of varying length and complexity provide vital "points of reference" for the learning process. Simple scenarios (some involving full class participation and others "modeled" so that most students are observing) can reinforce course concepts while requiring very little preparation and class time. More complex scenarios have their own distinct value and provide rich experiences that can inform debriefing and discussion sessions throughout the term. Whenever complex scenarios are used, however, care should be taken to provide ample class time for students to enter into their roles. Students playing the same parts in different simulation groups should be allowed to discuss their roles and strategies confidentially before beginning an exercise. It is helpful to provide general background information about a complex simulation to all students before class begins (online learning environments can be quite useful in this regard), but "warm-up time" remains necessary to ensure adequate preparation.

Debriefing for simulations and role plays should be managed in a way that helps students connect the simulation to major course themes, while also making space for them to share their own unique experiences and personal responses to the scenario. To provide scope for student creativity and encourage reflection about the applications of the course material, instructors may wish to design a final group project in which students research ongoing negotiations over social, international, or public policy issues in order to develop a presentation, paper, and/or simulation to share with the larger class. Team evaluation forms can be provided to each working group member to ensure a measure of accountability and reward exceptional contributions, but the instructor may nonetheless wish to remind students that managing responsibilities for this group project is likely to require application of negotiation skills they are learning in class.

19.5 Dispute Resolution

Isaac Noam Ebner
Sabanci University

COURSE DESCRIPTION

Upper-level undergraduate course suitable for general education students or majors in conflict resolution, peace studies, law, and management.

This course explores methods for resolving disputes other than by formal adjudication. It aims to provide participants with an understanding of the way human interactions—on the individual, group, and international levels—have the potential for agreement and disagreement, cooperation and conflict. This understanding does not remain abstract: the course focuses on skill building in communication and conflict management. First, students will learn to improve their own negotiation skills, allowing them to act consciously and skillfully in tough situations. They will also grow aware of the many obstacles to any negotiation reaching a successful outcome and of the potential for any negotiation to deteriorate into conflict. The second part of the course introduces a range of third-party interventions aimed at resolving conflict, including arbitration, mediation, and facilitation. The third part of the course emphasizes mediation in its various forms alongside other collaborative decisionmaking processes. Mediation is a process in which a third party, lacking decision-imposing power (as opposed, for example, to a court or a binding arbitrator), uses his negotiation expertise, his creativity, and his relationship with the parties to aid them in reaching agreement and transforming their relationship. By understanding how the mediation process is designed and managed, students will be able to bring their improved negotiation skills to bear in assisting others with negotiating and resolving conflicts peacefully.

REQUIRED TEXTS

Most of the readings recommended in the course units refer to these three books. Courses emphasizing arbitration practices are advised to assign reading from country- or context-specific sources.

Roger Fisher and William Ury. *Getting to Yes,* 2nd ed. New York: Penguin Books, 1991.

Christopher Moore. *The Mediation Process,* 3rd ed. San Francisco: Jossey-Bass, 2003.

Leigh Thompson. *The Mind and Heart of the Negotiator,* 3rd ed. Upper Saddle River, NJ: Prentice Hall, 2004.

COURSE SCHEDULE

Unit 1: Course Introduction and Overview

1. Introduce the teacher and the course.
2. Review ground rules.
3. Group forming: I recommend beginning with one or two interactive activities to familiarize students with the dynamic nature of the course and with each other. Any activity in which students mingle, introduce themselves to one another, and exchange information is fine. The dynamics can be debriefed as a lead-in to negotiation.
4. Review the course format, sessions, and schedule.
5. Introduce alternative dispute resolution (ADR) processes; familiarize students with such terms as mediation, arbitration, and facilitation. Stress that the second half of the course will focus on mediation, which you might loosely introduce as "facilitated negotiation" or "assisted negotiation." This provides the rationale for opening the course with a focus on negotiation.
6. Go over the levels of ADR: interpersonal, intergroup and international. This section should stress the level of ADR the course will focus on (depending on the course's context, academic framework, etc.), and describe how this focus will manifest (e.g., reading material, choice of simulations, etc.).

Unit 2: Introduction to Negotiation

Thompson, *The Mind and Heart of the Negotiator,* chapter 1.

1. Negotiation definition and basics. Ask students how they would define negotiation. You will get a variety of suggestions, and you can stress similarities and differences. Either continue working with these or offer definitions from the literature.
2. Discuss some of the common elements or characteristics you expect to encounter in negotiation (e.g., time, power, pressure, communication) and then lead into an introduction of a comprehensive model.
3. Introduction to the "Elements of Negotiation" model. Choose a model, breaking negotiation down into distinct elements. Fisher, Ury, and Patton stress four elements; Harvard's Program on Negotiation (PON) syllabus emphasizes seven; and I employ my own ten-element model. Choose whichever you deem most suitable for class and introduce it at this stage so that participants understand they will be following a roadmap, and to set the stage for repeated mention of the model.

Unit 3: Prisoners' Dilemma Simulation-Game

Thompson, *The Mind and Heart of the Negotiator,* chapter 11.

Recommended simulations: Fisher's "Oil Pricing" (available through Harvard's Program on Negotiation's Clearinghouse, www.pon.org), my own "The Pasta Wars" (in *Simulation and Gaming,* http://intl-sag.sagepub.com/), or the popular "XY Game" (variations of which can be found through an online search).

Debriefing points:

1. Trust, communication, and relationship in negotiation, and the relationship between those variables.
2. Cooperation and competition.
3. The negotiator's dilemma. Describe, with examples, the basic dilemma at the heart of any negotiation: the conflict between the understanding that one can use negotiation to create value, and the desire, or instinct, to ignore that and focus on claiming value immediately.
4. The prisoners' dilemma.

Unit 4: Cooperative and Competitive Elements of Negotiation

Dean Pruitt and Sung Hee Kim, *Social Conflict: Escalation, Stalemate, and Resolution,* 3rd ed. New York: McGraw-Hill, 2004, chapter 3.

1. Negotiation strategies. Based on the previous simulation, or a different interactive experience, point out different types of strategies negotiators adopt, such as cooperation, competition, avoidance, yielding, and compromising.
2. Integrative and distributive elements of negotiation. Demonstrate how all negotiation processes employ integrative elements (in which parties work together to enlarge the pie and create value) and distributive elements (in which parties work against each other, each hoping to grab a larger slice of the pie for themselves).

Unit 5: The Hidden Level of Negotiation

Daniel Goleman. *Emotional Intelligence.* New York: Bantam, 1995, chapter 2.

1. Emotions, instincts, and mutual reactions in negotiation. The purpose of this section is to explore the positive and negative effects of emotion in negotiation and to expose the irrational level at which we so often negotiate.
2. The effect of partisan perceptions on negotiation. Any activity is suitable here that is designed to show how people can view the same "facts" or "objective reality" yet form different opinions of what they saw or infer something different from it. Tie this into the previous discussion on emotions, explaining the mutual effect between our perception of reality and our emotional state.

Unit 6: Interests and Positions

Fisher and Ury, *Getting to Yes,* chapters 1, 3.

1. Positional bargaining and interest-based negotiation. To illustrate the differences between these two approaches to negotiation, choose a simulation in which the parties need to choose between information sharing, joint thinking, and cooperation on the one hand and information hoarding, arm twisting, linear bargaining, and competition on the other. The well-known "Ugli Orange" simulation (authorship unknown) is often used for this purpose, since the scenario places parties in a situation in which information sharing is key to both of them achieving what they need.
2. Debrief the elements of positional bargaining and the elements of interest-based negotiation encountered by the parties in the negotiation.
3. Debrief the communication dynamics encountered in the negotiation.

Unit 7: Communication Skills in Negotiation and Dispute Resolution

Through interactive exercises, movie clips, and brief demonstrations, introduce students to such important communication tools as active listening, summarizing/reflecting, use of questions, and reframing.

Unit 8: Negotiation Collapse and Its Remedies

Moore, *The Mediation Process,* chapter 1.

1. Summary: Students summarize what they have learned about negotiation.
2. Summary: Causes of negotiation collapse. Depending on class experiences and discussions, the list of causes might include scarce resources, win-lose outlooks, extreme competition, poor communication, emotional effects, or personal and personality effects. Stress that ADR processes are possible remedies for broken-down negotiation processes.
3. The Spectrum of dispute resolution processes. Map out the variety of processes. Stress the difference between situations in which parties attempt to work things out on their own (i.e., negotiation or armed conflict) and situations in which parties enlist a third party to help them (i.e., adjudication, arbitration, and mediation). Additionally, stress the varying role of the third party: decisionmaking (in adjudication and arbitration) as opposed to assisting and facilitating (in mediation).

Unit 9: Arbitration

Depending on the course's focus, arbitration can be taught briefly or at length. If arbitration is not a major focus of the course, skip ahead to the alternate unit 9. If the course is designed to focus on ADR in general, giving equal weight to each process, or to focus on arbitration in particular, one or several lessons can be dedicated to the process, stressing: (1) arbitration's aims and advantages; (2) common uses of arbitration (employment agreements, labor relations); (3) commercial international arbitration; (4) public international arbitration (arbitration between feuding countries); (5) the arbitration agreement; and (6) arbitration rules and procedures (focusing on those particularly relevant to the course's context).

Recommended: Conduct a simulation of an arbitration procedure, using a simple case based on the rules and procedures stressed in class. You can find cases through the resources listed in the Teaching Notes at the end of this syllabus. Or use a simulation students have already used as a negotiation simulation. Break the class down into groups of three students, two of whom are assigned roles as parties and one of whom is designated the arbitrator. Through oral instructions, tweak the background story a bit to explain how an arbitrator became involved in the scenario.

Unit 9 (Alternate): Arbitration and Mediation
Moore, *The Mediation Process,* chapter 1.

If the course focuses on mediation rather than arbitration, teach about arbitration, both in order to fill out the ADR spectrum and to make it clear what mediation is *not*. Use any of the points in the previous unit as you deem necessary. Stress the difference between imposed decisionmaking and party-based agreement.

Use a simulation in order to stress this last point. For a simple case, split the class into groups of three: two parties to a dispute and one neutral third party. Without informing participants beforehand, conduct two rounds of the simulation. In the first round, instruct the neutrals that they are arbitrators: They must design and conduct an arbitration process, at the end of which they *must* give a written verdict or decision. In the second round (consider rotating neutrals to a new pair of parties), instruct neutrals to act as mediators. As they have not yet learned how to conduct a mediation process, assign them one simple rule: You may do *anything* you see fit *except* impose a decision.

Debriefing points:

1. Which process did neutrals find to be more comfortable?
2. Which process did parties feel more comfortable in?
3. What specific actions did the neutral take while acting as mediator? Answers will usually include listening, asking questions, suggesting solutions, setting ground rules, and managing communication. This will serve as an entry point to the art of mediation.

Unit 10: Introduction to Mediation
Moore, *The Mediation Process,* chapter 1.

1. The underlying premises of mediation: it is voluntary; it respects parties' autonomy; it is not paternalistic; it does not provide verdicts.

2. Provide a mediation process model or map. Many frameworks for mediation exist. For example, Moore, in chapter 2 of *The Mediation Process,* suggests a twelve-step framework. I employ my own ten-step model, and others can be found in the literature or on the Internet. Choose a model that seems suitable to the course's context and use it to provide participants with a "road map" for step-by-step conduct of the process. At this stage, provide a brief overview of the process' stages, which will all be explored in detail in later units.

Unit 11: The Early Stages of Mediation

Moore, *The Mediation Process,* chapters 3, 5, and 8.

1. Preparation for mediation. Discuss the various preparations that need to be completed before the mediation process actually begins. They might include initial contact with the parties, initial information intake, meeting logistics, and room setup.

2. Have mediators introduce themselves. Participants will explore these stages of mediation by writing their own introductory speech, setting up a room for mediation, and presenting their introduction to classmates who are simulating disputing parties.

3. Dispute presentation: Describe the process through which mediators invite and encourage parties to present their side of the story.

4. Obtaining additional information: Stress how mediators employ yet another communication tool, such as asking questions or conducting private meetings with each party in order to solicit information that parties did not choose to share in their original presentations.

5. Mediation simulation: Use an exercise to practice the first stages of the mediation process. Preferably it should be a simple case with straightforward information, to allow students to practice the mechanics of the first stages. A good simulation for this purpose might be I. Noam Ebner and Yael Efron, "The Silence of the Dogs," in *The 2006 ASTD Training and Performance Sourcebook,* edited by Mel Silberman and Patricia Philips (ASTD Press, 2006), and available under "Publications" at http://people.sabanciuniv.edu/~ebner. Through oral instructions, tweak the background story a bit, in order to explain how a mediator became involved in the scenario.

Unit 12: Midprocess Stages of Mediation

Moore, *The Mediation Process,* chapters 9 and 10.

1. Mediator formation of a shared story: the shared story serves as a joint, agreed-upon framework for the dispute.

2. Agenda forming. Framing the issues that need to be discussed and agreed on and the order in which they will be discussed.

3. Mediation simulation. Dedicate sufficient time for participants to reach and practice the shared story and agenda stages of mediation.

Unit 13: Advanced Stages of the Mediation Process
Moore, *The Mediation Process,* chapter 13.

1. Identifying interests.
2. Generating and evaluating options.
3. Reaching final agreement.

Unit 14: Full-Length Mediation Simulation
Aimed at allowing participants to get a full picture of what a mediation process looks like, start to finish.

Unit 15: The Legal Aspects and Legislative Framework of Mediation
This unit is context specific and should be taught according to the course's focus, purpose, and locale.

1. Legislation regarding mediation.
2. Mediator qualifications.
3. Court-referred and court-annexed mediation.
4. The legal status of mediation agreements.
5. Mediation and the court process.
6. Mediating with attorneys participating.

Unit 16: Mediator Methods and Styles
Moore, *The Mediation Process,* 368–377.

1. The mediation forum. Joint sessions, separate sessions (caucusing), and mediator sessions.

2. Solo mediation and co-mediation. The advantages and disadvantages of both modes.

Unit 17: Issues in Mediation
This unit can be used to air questions participants will have raised at different points during the course. Relevant mediator codes of conduct (such as those accepted by the American Bar Association as well as the Association for Conflict Resolution, or country-specific codes) can be reviewed and applied. Use of vignettes or minisimulations can bring a philosophical discussion of ethics down to earth.

1. Neutrality, impartiality, and objectivity.
2. Mediator professional and ethical issues.

Unit 18: Transformative and Problem-Solving Approaches to Mediation

Joseph P. Folger and Robert A. Baruch Bush. *The Promise of Mediation: Responding to Conflict Through Empowerment and Recognition,* 2nd ed. San Francisco: Jossey-Bass, 2004, chapters 1 and 2.

Unit 19: Course Summary and Looking Forward

1. Professional tracks in ADR.
2. Academic programs focusing on ADR.
3. Final assignment.
4. Course summary.

TEACHING NOTES

This course is designed to prepare students for practical application of the knowledge and skills they acquire in class. The nature of class activities is therefore experiential rather than the classic read-and-discuss format. Accordingly, this syllabus is presented more in the shape of a teaching guide than as a list of topics and reading material.

While preparing to use this syllabus, teachers should consider incorporating other experiential activities they are familiar with. Another valuable teaching method highly suitable for this course is to view and analyze movie clips.

The units in this syllabus can be reshaped to form the basis for other courses (such as courses focusing only on negotiation or only on mediation). Some units, while recommended, are not absolutely vital for some courses on alternative dispute resolution (e.g., units 14, 15, 18, and 19). Others can be shifted to earlier or later parts of the course (e.g., units 7, 15, 16, and 17).

Taking the time framework of your course into account, the more you can incorporate simulation games, the better. Any simulations used should follow these general guidelines:

- Be subject-suitable to the course's context, or to that of the students. (For example, management students might benefit from a simulation centering on a dispute between two sales representatives. They would also benefit from a simulation in which two students who share a dormitory room need to negotiate shared living arrangements.)
- Have clear instructions.
- Entail as little setup time as possible.
- Be designed to target the specific learning objectives of the unit or units with which they are used.

Teachers using this syllabus can design their own simulations, tailoring them to the specific aims and context of their course. For some excellent resources on designing simulations, see Cathy Stein Greenblat, *Designing*

Games and Simulations: An Illustrated Handbook (Newbury Park, CA: Sage, 1988); and Ken Jones, *Designing Your Own Simulation* (London: Routledge, 1985). Simulations can also be found on the Internet. Some of my own published simulations can be accessed through my homepage at http://people.sabanciuniv.edu/~ebner/. A variety of simulations focusing on campus-based mediation can be found at www.campus-adr.org. A collection of simulations focusing on international conflict is available at the US Institute for Peace website (http://www.usip.org/class/simulations/). Simulations of large-scale conflicts focusing on public governance and collaborative problem solving can be found at the website of the Program on Analysis and Resolution of Conflict (PARC) at Syracuse University (www.maxwell.syr.edu/parc/eparc).

One can purchase ready-to-use simulations from the following sources: the Program on Negotiation at Harvard Law School, available through www.pon.org; the Dispute Resolution Research Center at Northwestern's Kellogg School of Management, http://www.kellogg.northwestern.edu/drrc/teaching_materials.htm; and The Center for Dispute Resolution at Willamette University School of Law, at http://www.willamette.edu/wucl/cdr/simbank/login.cgi.

20

Peace Studies in Disciplinary Perspective

BECAUSE THE ISSUES OF HUMAN SECURITY AND CONFLICT ARE MULTI-faceted, many undergraduate programs in peace studies take an interdisciplinary approach, drawing on the faculty and resources of various departments. Nearly all disciplines, even the hard sciences and professional programs in business and accounting, have contributions to make to the study of peace, justice, and human security. The possibility of unthinkable nuclear Armageddon helped spawn peace studies in the late 1940s, and physicists such as Albert Einstein and J. Robert Oppenheimer of the Manhattan Project were among the first to speak out for arms control and alternatives to war. Likewise, globalization has drawn economists, bankers, and policymakers into the global discussion of peace issues such as human rights, sustainable development, justice, and environmental security. Add these approaches to the more traditional efforts of the social sciences and the humanities, and no part of higher education is left out of the search for human security.

Eight syllabuses in this collection explore peace studies from a variety of fields. Two course plans come from anthropology. Robert A. Rubinstein examines the cultural roots of conflict and the contributions of language and culture to the resolution of conflict. Marc Howard Ross looks particularly at ethnic conflict through the lenses of culture and identity. Martha Starr examines the economic dimensions of violence and peace, acknowledging the interaction of economic and noneconomic factors, such as religion and identity, in both violence and conflict resolution. Sociologist Michelle Gawerc probes the conditions under which social conflicts tend to become violent and how they can be resolved nonviolently, addressing perennial questions about society, conflict, and human and social behavior. Historian Perry Bush studies the phenomenon of war in a democracy by looking at US combat experience alongside US opposition to war in the Civil War, two world wars, and the Vietnam War. Rachel M. MacNair enters the discussion through psychology, asking basic questions about why people behave violently or peacefully and what skills they need to achieve peace. The final two courses address issues of environmental security. Philosopher Steven S. Naragon asks how to fairly distribute the resources (and burdens) of the world, assuming that the human community is a moral one. He challenges students to answer the questions, "What is my proper relation to other humans?" and "What is my relationship with the rest of nature?" Finally, Jeremy Youde's course takes students to the intersection of politics and disease, demonstrating the impact of disease on states and governance, focusing on both history and current research.

20.1 Anthropology: Culture and Conflict

Robert A. Rubinstein
Syracuse University

COURSE DESCRIPTION

Upper-level undergraduate or graduate course in anthropology, international relations, or peace studies.

The enterprises of international relations and conflict management are conditioned by cultural issues. They are of two kinds: the general background that is formed by cultural activities and phenomena that are specifically cultural. Both of these levels of culture are becoming more important in international relations. This course offers a basic and systematic survey of a variety of domains of world affairs in which culture is of particular importance. Special attention is paid to the roots of conflict and to the way in which language and culture can contribute to the management of conflicts and the resolution of disputes.

REQUIRED TEXTS

William O. Beeman. *The "Great Satan" vs. the "Mad Mullahs": How the United States and Iran Demonize Each Other.* Westport, CT: Greenwood Press, 2005.

John Collins and Ross Glover, eds. *Collateral Language: A User's Guide to America's New War.* New York: New York University Press, 2002.

Alison Dundes Rentein. *The Cultural Defense.* New York: Oxford University Press, 2004.

David I. Kertzer. *Ritual, Politics, and Power.* New Haven, CT: Yale University Press, 1988.

Douglas Johnston and Cynthia Sampson. *Religion: The Missing Dimension of Statecraft.* New York: Oxford University Press, 1994.

Sandra D. Lane. *Why Are Our Babies Dying? Pregnancy, Birth, and Death in America.* Boulder, CO: Paradigm, 2008.

Vijayendra Rao and Michael Walton, eds. *Culture and Public Action.* Stanford: Stanford University Press, 2004.

Beth Roy. *Some Trouble with Cows: Making Sense of Social Conflict.* Berkeley: University of California Press, 1994.

Robert A. Rubinstein. *Peacekeeping Under Fire: Culture and Intervention.* Boulder, CO: Paradigm, 2008.

Robert B. Edgerton. *Sick Societies: Challenging the Myth of Primitive Harmony.* New York: Free Press, 1992.

Occasional articles listed in the course schedule.

COURSE SCHEDULE

Week 1: Course Introduction
Structure of the class.

Inventory of professional skills incorporated in the class.

Outline of the area of study.

Selection of topics covered.

Week 2: Political Symbolism and Authority 1
Political authority is rooted in part, an important part, in the manipulation of political symbols. Being familiar with the cultural logic of political symbols helps to figure out the sources and prospects of particular claims for political authority. In addition, these symbols provide the meanings that inform political systems of diverse forms.

Kertzer, *Ritual, Politics, and Power,* chapters 1–6.
Robert A. Rubinstein. "Cultural Analysis and International Security." *Alternatives* 13 (1988): 529–542.

Week 3: Political Symbolism and Authority 2
Barry O'Neill. *Honor, Symbols, and War.* University of Michigan Press, 1999, 3–62 ("Symbolism: An Introduction," "Message Symbols in Practice," "Message Symbols in Theory," "Focal Symbols").
Stephen C. Pepper. "Root Metaphors." *World Hypotheses: A Study in Evidence.* University of California Press, 1942, 84–114.
Marco Verweij, Andrew Oros, and Dominique Jacquin-Berdal. "Culture in World Politics." In *Culture in World Politics,* edited by Marco Verweij, Andrew Oros, and Dominique Jacquin-Berdal. St. Martin's Press, 1998, 1–10.
G. Lakoff and M. Johnson. "Conceptual Metaphor in Everyday Life." *Journal of Philosophy* 77 (1980): 463–486.

Week 4: Moral, Normative, and Religious Dimensions of Social life
Moral, normative, and religious factors frequently provide the motivation for and background upon which claims are advanced in international settings. Understanding the operation of such variables becomes critical in developing and evaluating policy.

Mary Catherine Bateson. "Compromise and the Rhetoric of Good and Evil." In *The Social Dynamics of Peace and Conflict,* by Robert A. Rubinstein and M. L. Foster. Kendall Hunt, 1997, 35–45.

A. Hinton. "A Head for an Eye: Revenge in the Cambodian Genocide." *American Ethnologist* 25 (1998): 352–377.

Johnston and Sampson, *Religion: The Missing Dimension of Statecraft,* pages 8–19 ("The Missing Dimension," by E. Luttawk) and pages 20–35 ("Religion and International Affairs," by B. Rubin).

Week 5: Politics, Identity, Language, and Ethnicity

One of the toughest areas of international relations revolves around language and education policies. Language is deeply rooted in culture, and understanding the effects of particular policy initiatives depends on understanding their cultural implications.

Collins and Glover, *Collateral Language,* introduction, pages 39–51 ("Civilization versus Barbarism," by M. Llorente), and pages 94–107 ("Fundamentalism," by L. Renold).

Ted Robert Gurr. "Minorities, Nationalist, and Ethnopolitical Conflict." In *Managing Global Chaos: Sources of and Responses to International Conflict,* edited by Chester Crocker, Fen Osler Hampson, and Pamela Aall. US Institute of Peace Press, 1996, 52–78.

J. G. Stein. "Image, Identity, and Conflict Resolution." In *Managing Global Chaos: Sources of and Responses to International Conflict,* edited by Chester Crocker, Fen Osler Hampson, and Pamela Aall. US Institute of Peace Press, 1996, 93–111.

Kenneth McRae. "Canada: Reflections on Two Conflicts." In *Conflict and Peacemaking in Multiethnic Societies,* edited by Joseph V. Montville. Lexington Books, 1990, 197–218.

Week 6: Politics, Identity, Language, and Ethnicity

Beeman, *The "Great Satan" vs. the "Mad Mullah's,"* chapters 1–6 (pages 1–90).

Week 7: Identity: Local and Global Dimensions

Increasingly, international relations deals with issues of competing identities that are rooted in cultural conceptions of history. Sometimes these identities lead to competition among groups, which in turn may lead to conflict.

Manuel Castells. *The Power of Identity: Economy, Society and Culture.* Blackwell, 1997, chapter 1 ("Communal Heavens: Identity and Meaning in a Network Society").

Rao and Walton, *Culture and Public Action,* pages 328–358 ("The Mayan Movement and National Culture in Guatemala," by S. Davis).

Week 8: Human Rights

Although the Universal Declaration of Human Rights is said to be universal, there is increasing debate about it. In this debate cultural defenses are often invoked. The tension between universalism and relativism is debated against specific cultural backdrops. It is increasingly important to understand the dynamics of this debate on many issues, including gender issues, education, health, and the flow of refugees.

Martin Chanock. "'Culture' and Human Rights." In *Beyond Rights Talk and Culture Talk: Comparative Essays on the Politics of Rights and Culture,* edited by Mahmood Mamdani. St. Martin's Press, 2000, 15–36.

Dundes Rentein, *The Cultural Defense,* pages 10–19 ("Why Culture Matters for Justice"), 185–210 ("The Cultural Defense in Theory and Practice"), and 211–219 ("The Right to Culture"). Choose one topic in the case studies.

Edgerton, *Sick Societies,* pages 16–45 ("From Relativism to Evaluation").

Week 9: Culture and Gender Issues

Gender roles and conflicts about what is "gender appropriate" are increasingly part of the discourse and content of international affairs.

Edgerton, *Sick Societies,* pages 75–104 ("Women and Children First: From Inequality to Exploitation").

Gunhild Hoogensen and Svein Vigeland Rottem. "Gender Identity and the Subject of Security." *Security Dialogue* 35 (2004): 155–171.

M. C. Inhorn. "Global Infertility and the Globalization of New Reproductive Technologies: Illustrations from Egypt." *Social Science and Medicine* 56 (2003): 1835–1851.

Sandra D. Lane and Robert A. Rubinstein. "Judging the Other: Responding to Traditional Female Genital Surgeries." *Hastings Center Report* 26, no. 3 (1996): 31–40.

Robert A. Rubinstein and Sandra D. Lane. "Population, Identity, and Political Violence." *Social Justice: Anthropology, Peace, and Human Rights* 3 (2002): 139–152.

Week 10: Health and Development

A wide variety of nonstate actors play a role in international relations today. International organizations, nongovernmental organizations (NGOs), militaries, and other organizations interact and bring to the table distinct organizational cultures. Sometimes these cultures clash and make joint work difficult.

Rao and Walton, *Culture and Public Action,* pages 59–84 ("The Capacity to Aspire: Culture and the Terms of Recognition," by A. Appadurai), pages

138–162 ("Cultural Goods Are Good for More Than Their Economic Value," by A. Klamer), and pages 307–327 ("Relief and an Understanding of Local Knowledge: The Case of Southern Sudan," by S. Harragin).

James Trostle. *Epidemiology and Culture*. Cambridge University Press, 2005, pages 74–95 ("Cultural Issues in Measurement Bias") and 150–167 ("Perceiving and Representing Risk").

Week 11: Organizational Culture

Economic, technological, and health development are all met by peoples who organize themselves in diverse ways. How they engage development, what it means, and the ties it creates are all embedded in their cultural understandings. Being able to describe and analyze culture can mean the difference between success and futility in development efforts.

L. Pulliam. "Achieving Social Competence in the Navy Community." In *The Social Dynamics of Peace and Conflict*, edited by Robert A. Rubinstein and Mary Lecron Foster. Kendall Hunt, 1997, 91–106.

Majken Schultz. *On Studying Organizational Cultures: Diagnosing and Understanding*. Walter de Gruyter, 1995, chapter 1 ("Culture in Organization Theory").

Donna Winslow. *The Canadian Airborne Regiment in Somalia: A Socio-Cultural Inquiry*. Canadian Government Publishing, 1997, chapter 6 ("The Airborne in Somalia").

Week 12: Conflict Management, Dispute Resolution, and Intervention

Although international regimes create structures within which disputes can be settled, the way in which different groups (states and nonstates) respond to and participate in these regimes is conditioned by their indigenous mechanisms for conflict management. In addition, the details of how different cultural groups negotiate—what their expectations are about good conflict management—vary.

Rao and Walton, *Culture and Public Action*, pages 210–233 ("Participatory Development: Where Culture Creeps In," by Anita Abraham and Jean-Philippe Platteau).

J. Chopra and T. Hohe. "Participatory Intervention." *Global Governance* 10, no. 3 (2004): 289–305.

T. Duffey. "Cultural Issues in Contemporary Peacekeeping." *International Peacekeeping* 7, no. 1 (2000): 142–168.

Robert A. Rubinstein. "Intervention and Culture: An Anthropological Approach to Peace Operations." *Security Dialogue* 36, no. 4 (2005): 527–544.

T. Hohe. "Totem Polls: Indigenous Concepts of 'Free and Fair' Elections in East Timor." *International Peacekeeping* 9, no. 4 (Winter 2002): 69–88.

Week 13: Case Study—
A Hindu-Muslim Riot in a Bangladeshi Village
Roy, *Some Trouble with Cows.*

Week 14: Case Study—Peacekeeping
Rubinstein, *Peacekeeping Under Fire: Culture and Intervention.*

Week 15: Case Study—Structural Violence in the United States
Lane, *Why Are Our Babies Dying? Pregnancy, Birth, and Death in America.*

TEACHING NOTES

I try to make this class highly interactive. Students are required to read materials and share comments on the readings with their colleagues one day before the class meets. If the class is large enough, I divide it into two groups. One group submits comments on the readings to a web-based class site two days prior to class. The second group submits reactions the day before class. The groups alternate roles each week. This enhances the amount and quality of discussion in class.

To link a systematic understanding of cultural processes to contemporary problems, issues, and conflicts in world affairs, students monitor contemporary news and analyzes developments from a cultural perspective. They may focus on a particular geographic area or on a specific topic in world affairs. They should be prepared to discuss in class what they have read and prepare a brief paper summarizing their observations.

Each student in the class prepares a paper examining a contemporary issue, problem, or conflict. The papers use a problem-based method, in that students will address an actual issue that is a source of conflict or policy dilemma and will highlight and explain the role of culture in the chosen issue.

20.2 Anthropology: Culture and Ethnic Conflict Management

Marc Howard Ross
Bryn Mawr College

COURSE DESCRIPTION

Upper-level undergraduate course in political studies and peace and conflict studies.

Many observers see intransigent ethnic conflicts as the greatest contemporary threat to peace. Although some of these conflicts, such as in Sri Lanka or Northern Ireland, are long-term disputes, others develop an unexpected intensity in a very short time. Clearly there is widespread interest in understanding the origin, escalation, and peaceful settlement of ethnic conflicts. A number of frameworks exist for the examination of ethnic conflict, but the one developed here emphasizes the role of culture and identity in these conflicts. It focuses on the power of symbolic phenomena such as the language of street signs in Montreal and Bratislava, Orange Order marches in Northern Ireland, and religious sites and imagery in Jerusalem. Underlying this emphasis is the central hypothesis that identity and threats to identity embedded in cultural practices are at the core of many ethnic conflicts. This hypothesis says that successful conflict resolution must consider cultural, as well as political, dynamics if it is to be successful. However, this does not mean that cultural differences cause conflict directly; rather it is the uses to which these differences are put that matter politically. For example, there are many societies with significant cultural differences and low conflict, as well as those with small differences in which intergroup conflict is high. To examine the role of culture in ethnic conflict, this course raises general questions about the importance of symbolic and ritual processes in the definition of the concrete interests and the culturally rooted interpretations that drive ethnic conflicts. Through case studies, the course develops an analysis of how culture offers constraints *and* opportunities to governments and leaders to move ethnic conflicts from contention to cooperation.

The goal of this course is to analyze approaches to culture (and symbolic and ritual action) to understand both the escalation and de-escalation of ethnic conflict. Some weeks the readings and class discussions emphasize theoretical questions, such as the nature of ethnic identity and culture, whereas other weeks we consider the role of culture in specific long-term ethnic conflicts.

However, the semester-long focus is to develop connections between theory and specific cases. The readings and discussions introduce a number of relevant cases from many parts of the world; if students have an interest in other cases that are not covered in the course, they are encouraged to bring these cases into the discussions and to do their term paper on any case in which culture plays a core role in an identity conflict.

REQUIRED TEXTS

Edward Linenthal. *Preserving Memory: The Struggle to Create America's Holocaust Museum.* Columbia University Press, 2001.

Neil Jarman. *Material Culture: Parades and Visual Displays in Northern Ireland.* Berg, 1997.

Sanford Levinson. *Written in Stone: Public Monuments in Changing Societies.* Duke University Press, 1998.

COURSE SCHEDULE

Week 1: Introduction: Why and How Do Groups Fight About Culture?

Consider the role of culture in ethnic conflict. What is culture, and why does cultural expression become the focal point of bitter disputes? Why does one group care what language others speak? How do others celebrate a holiday? What are another group's religious practices? Cultural conflicts are particularly intense because culture represents deeper identity issues, and threatened identities provoke fear and threat for groups and individuals. This means that culture and cultural differences don't cause conflicts, people do; so how do people use culture when they fight with each other? Rudolph and Rudolph provide a dramatic example from India.

Suzanne Hoeber Rudolph and Lloyd I. Rudolph. "Modern Hate: How Ancient Animosities Get Invented." *New Republic,* March 22, 1993, 24–29.

Eric Hobsbawm. "The Nation as Invented Tradition." In *Nationalism,* edited by John Hutchinson and Anthony D. Smith. Oxford University Press, 1994, 76–83.

In-class screening of *The QuébeCanada Complex,* produced and directed by Peter Wintonick and Patricia Tassinai, Necesssary Illusions Productions with CBC Newsworld, DVD, 1998, 45 minutes.

Week 2: The Intersection of Culture, Identity, and Ethnic Conflict

If identity is at the core of bitter ethnic conflicts, it is important to clearly identify the meaning of ethnicity and the nature of ethnicity as a social identity. Donald Horowitz offers a wide-ranging discussion to help you understand the nature of ethnicity. Anthony Smith connects ethnic identity, beliefs about descent, and the idea of the nation. Vamik Volkan's discussion of Serbian identity and their defeat at the Battle of Kosovo in 1389 illustrates Smith's points and demonstrates the psychocultural dimensions of ethnic identity and its power in political conflict. Marc Howard Ross's article spells out the dynamics of identity in ethnic conflict. It emphasizes the concepts of psychocultural narratives and dramas. Narratives offer an explanation for events and serve as reflectors, exacerbaters, and causes of conflict, shaping how people understand and respond to it.

Marc Howard Ross. "The Political Psychology of Competing Narratives: September 11 and Beyond." In *Understanding September 11,* edited by Craig Calhoun, Paul Price, and Ashley Timmer. New York: New Press, 2003, 303–320.

Donald L. Horowitz. "The Primordialists." In *Ethnonationalism in the Modern World: Walker Connor and the Study of Nationalism,* edited by Danielle Conversi. Routledge, 2003, 72–82.

Vamik Volkan. "Ancient Fuel for a Modern Inferno: Time Collapse in Bosnia-Herzegovina." In *Bloodlines,* by Vamik Volkan. Farrar, Straus and Giroux, 1997, 50–80.

Anthony D. Smith. "National Identity and Myths of Ethnic Descent." In *Myths and Memories of the Nation,* by Anthony D. Smith. Oxford University Press, 1999, 57–95.

Week 3: Monuments, Memorials, and Memory

Public monuments and permanent buildings are powerful efforts to place social and political markers on a physical landscape. They assert a connection between the past, present, and future, making claims about sacrifice, identity, and ownership. The monuments we see upon a visit to a new city or country are not the only ones of relevance, however. Archaeological records provide objects that link people across time and space and enhance a group's political claims. Consider, however, why, from a psychocultural perspective, the past matters so much and can become such a powerful basis for ethnic claims and conflicts in the present.

Required reading:
Levinson, *Written in Stone,* all.

Weeks 4–5: Museums and the Politics of Public Memory

Week 4: Who Controls a Narrative, and How Do They Control It?

Once a museum is built, the narratives it recounts seem "natural." However, as Edward Linenthal's account makes clear, museums are social and cultural constructions, and the important decisions they make about such questions as displays and texts accompanying them, implicitly and explicitly, offer clear accounts of inclusion and exclusion. In this study of the Holocaust Museum in Washington, D.C., Linenthal describes the politics of memorial sites such as Gettysburg, Little Bighorn, and Oklahoma City. The theme running through his works is the existence of multiple narratives associated with all memorials and the ways in which museums privilege certain group claims and narratives over others.

Linenthal, *Preserving Memory,* all.

Week 5: Museums and Monuments in the New South Africa

What happens when a racialized society such as South Africa is transformed into a democratic "rainbow nation"? What is to be done with the old regime's memorials, museums, and street names? In the former Soviet Union the answer was clear: they were removed. In South Africa a different decision was made: these articles discuss the transformation of older Afrikaner sites and the construction of newer postapartheid ones. Can the old and the new successfully coexist and contribute to a democratic South Africa?

Ciraj Rassool. "Community Museums, Memory Politics, and Social Transformation: Histories, Possibilities, and Limits." In *Museum Frictions: Public Cultures/Global Transformations,* edited by Ivan Karp et al. Duke University Press, 2006, 286–321.

Charmaine McEachern. "Working with Memory: The District Six Museum in the New South Africa." *Social Analysis* 42 (1998): 48–72.

Annie E. Coombes. "Translating the Past: Apartheid Monuments in Post-Apartheid South Africa." In *Hybridity and Its Discontents: Politics, Science, and Culture,* edited by Avtar Brah and Annie E. Coombes. Routledge, 2000, 173–197.

Sabine Marschall. "Gestures of Compensation: Post-Apartheid Monuments and Memorials." *Transformation: Critical Perspectives on Southern Africa* 55 (2004): 78–95.

Week 6: Symbolic Conflicts over Parades and Festivals in the British Isles

Neil Jarman provides an excellent description of the contentious nature of parades and other visual displays in Northern Ireland. Why is it that parades are so conflict-laden there? How are parades an expression of the long-term conflict in the region? What does Jarman mean by the "performance of memory"? How do groups stake claims to territory, assert political dominance, and articulate their identity through symbolic and ritual actions such as parades, murals, and the recovery of a dying language? Abner Cohen's chapters come from his larger study of the Notting Hill carnival in London and its evolution over a twenty-year period. Consider how the carnival helps West Indians articulate their identity in Britain, which is related to an argument he has made for a long time that cultural organization is a mechanism to achieve political goals in many contexts. Consider the wider relevance of Cohen's argument, especially with regard to the politics of music and art.

Abner Cohen, *Masquerade Politics*. University of California Press, 1993, chapters 6–7 (79–105).

Jarman, *Material Culture: Parades and Visual Display in Northern Ireland*, all.

Week 7: Clothing and Bodily Displays of Identity: Islamic Headscarves in France

For more than fifteen years, France has experienced a series of psychocultural dramas over the issue of schoolgirls wearing Islamic headscarves. In 2003 the country made it illegal for students to wear conspicuous religious signs in school. What is at stake? Why is this country with no apparent dress code so preoccupied with a simple religious sign? The issue has engaged two competing narratives: the French narrative and the Muslim narrative, both of which have core identities at stake. Sarah V. Wayland, in comparing Canada and France, outlines a striking contrast between two different ways to manage multicultural expressions.

Marc Howard Ross. "Dressed to Express: Islamic Headscarves in French Schools." *Cultural Contestation in Ethnic Conflict*. Cambridge University Press, 191–223.

Sarah V. Wayland. "Religious Expressions in Public Schools: Kirpans in Canada, Hijab in France." *Ethnic and Racial Studies* 20 (1997): 545–561.

Week 8: Language, Identity, and Conflict in Catalonia

A focal point of conflict in Catalonia, as in Quebe , is the status and use of a regional language to maintain its identity and existence in the absence of statehood. In both cases the outcome is very similar, though the two have very different historical paths. The articles by Michael Keating and David Laitin provide important details about Catalan-Spanish relations, and John Hargreaves and Manual Garcia Ferrando offer a striking case of cultural contestation around identity issues that never turned violent. In the end the conflict produced a decent outcome for all parties. Language is sometimes an explosive issue. Think, for instance, about the debate in the United States about bilingual education and "English Only" policies. Why is the politics of language so emotionally charged?

Michael Keating. "Catalonia." In *Nations Against the State: The New Politics in Quebec, Catalonia, and Scotland*, by Michael Keating. Macmillan, 1996, 115–162.

David Laitin. "Linguistic Revival: Politics and Culture in Catalonia." *Comparative Studies in Society and History* 31 (1989): 297–317.

John Hargreaves and Manual Garcia Ferrando. "Public Opinion, National Integration, and National Identity in Spain: The Case of the Barcelona Olympic Games." *Nations and Nationalism* 3 (1997): 65–87.

Weeks 9–10: Sacred Spaces and Ethnic Conflict

Many see Jerusalem, particularly its holy sites, as the epicenter of the Israeli-Palestinian conflict. This set of readings introduces the concept of sacred places, asking how the narratives surrounding them are central to group identity, examining why conflicts around these spaces are so intense, and considering what each side does in making its case. In Jerusalem, this takes us to issues of history, archaeology, and politics and leaves us with the puzzling question of when, if ever, groups can either develop more inclusive narratives or develop arrangements for sharing sacred places.

Nadia Abu El-Haj. "Translating Truths: Nationalism, the Practice of Archaeology, and the Remaking of Past and Present in Contemporary Jerusalem." *American Ethnologist* 25 (1998): 168–188.

Roger Friedland and Richard D. Hecht. "The Politics of Sacred Place: Jerusalem's Temple Mount/*al-haram al-sharif*." In *Sacred Places and Profane Spaces,* edited by Jamie Scott and Paul Simpson-Housley. Greenwood Press, 1991, 21–61.

Neil Asher Silberman. "Structuring the Past: Israelis, Palestinians, and the Symbolic Authority of Archaeological Monuments." In *The Archaeology of Israel: Constructing the Past, Interpreting the Present,* Journal for the Study of the Old Testament, Supplemental Series 237, edited by Neil Asher Silberman and David Small (1997): 62–81.

Al-Quds University. "Jerusalem History." http://www.alquds.edu/gen_info/index.php?page=jerusalem_history.

Temple Mount Controversy, articles from *Ha'aretz* (newspaper), May–September 2000.

Week 11: Religious Sites and Ethnic Conflict in South Asia

Roger Friedland and Richard Hecht point to many parallels between Jerusalem and Ayodhya, where ethnoreligious conflict is as bitter as it is anywhere in the world. In India and Sri Lanka, religiously based violence is a regular occurrence. In India the destruction of the Mosque at Ayodhya and the rise of the Bharatiya Janata Party (BJP) are associated with an effort to transform what was ostensibly a secular state into a Hindu one, with consequences for Muslims. Sovereignty (whatever that means) is what each group says they want. On what basis might competing claims be decided? Or is this the wrong question? Is there a need for a redefinition of the issue and the development of a solution in which the core of each side's claims are recognized? Can holy sites be shared, and if so, what would be required for that to occur?

David Ludden, ed. *Contesting the Nation: Religion, Community, and the Politics of Democracy in India*. University of Pennsylvania Press, 1996, excerpts.

Peter van der Veer. *Religious Nationalism: Hindus and Muslims in India*. University of California Press, 1994, ix–24.

Roger Friedland and Richard Hecht. "The Bodies of Nations: A Comparative Study of Religious Violence in Jerusalem and Ayodhya." *History of Religions* 38 (1998): 101–149.

Week 12: Race and America's Symbolic Landscape

Groucho Marx reportedly asked Sigmund Freud, "When is a cigar just a good smoke?" The same sort of question can be asked about flags and monuments and archaeological findings. Do they always carry deep symbolic meaning, or are they ever just a piece of cloth, stone, or metal? Consider how these objects evoke the powerful feelings around the issues of race and slavery in the United States and how these disputes are part of much deeper conflicts in American society.

Carolyn Marvin and David W. Ingle. "Dismemberment and Reconstruction: The Domain of the Popular and Its Flag." In *Blood Sacrifice and the Nation: Totem Rituals and the American Flag*, by Carolyn Marvin and David W. Ingle. Cambridge University Press, 1999, 215–247.

Marc Howard Ross. "Flags, Heroes, and Statues: Inclusive Versus Exclusive Identity Markers in the American South," unpublished manuscript.

Brian Black and Bryn Varley. "Contesting the Sacred: Preservation and Meaning on Richmond's Monument Avenue." In *Monuments to the Lost Cause: Women, Art, and the Landscapes of Southern Memory*, edited by Cynthia Mills and Pamela H. Simpson. University of Tennessee Press, 2003, 234–250.

Gary B. Nash. "For Whom Will the Liberty Bell Toll: From Controversy to Collaboration." Independence Hall Association, http://www.ushistory.org/presidentshouse/controversy/nash.htm.

Weeks 13–14: Synthesis, Conclusions, and Discussion of Student Projects

TEACHING NOTES

There is a good deal of reading assigned in this course and an expectation that students will participate in discussions designed to explore ideas in the readings and react to them, linking theory to the cases authors present. I also require that students write two or three short papers and a term paper. Coauthored term papers are encouraged but not required. In addition, students prepare biweekly ungraded (but required) comments in response to the readings or any other issues relevant to the course's questions. These comments are to be a paragraph to a page in length, are to be handed in at the beginning of each class, and are used to help structure the discussion for that day.

20.3 Economics: Economics of Violence and Peace

Martha Starr
American University

COURSE DESCRIPTION

Upper-level undergraduate or graduate-level course in economics, peace, justice, and conflict studies.

This course examines the economic dimensions of violence and peace. In general, the study of economics concerns material aspects of human livelihoods, including the production and consumption of goods and services, employment, incomes, wealth, spending and revenues, and trade. In particular, this course covers arms production and trade; the economics of terrorism; the economic causes of civil wars, including economic grievances, resources, environmental problems, and poverty; and the economic consequences of war and the economic dimensions of conflict prevention and resolution, as well as postconflict reconstruction. The course emphasizes the interaction between economic and noneconomic factors, including identity and religion and culture, in explaining the causes of violence and their resolution.

REQUIRED TEXTS

Karen Ballentine and Heiko Nitzschke, eds. *Profiting from Peace: Managing the Resource Dimensions*. Lynne Rienner, 2005.

Paul Collier et al. *Breaking the Conflict Trap: Civil War and Development Policy*. World Bank Publications, 2003.

Paul Collier and Nicolas Sambanis, eds. *Understanding Civil War: Evidence and Analysis,* Vol. 1. World Bank Publications, 2005.

Paul Collier and Nicolas Sambanis, eds. *Understanding Civil War: Evidence and Analysis,* Vol. 2. World Bank Publications, 2005.

COURSE SCHEDULE

Session 1: Overview:
The Economic Dimensions of War and Peace

Macartan Humphreys. "Economics and Violent Conflict." Harvard University, 2002, http://www.preventconflict.org/portal/economics/Essay.pdf.

Session 2: Capitalism and Conflict—
Production and Sale of the Means of Deadly Force

T. Hunt Tooley. "Merchants of Death Revisited: Armaments, Bankers, and the First World War." *Journal of Libertarian Studies* 19, no. 1 (Winter 2005).

Mark Phythian. "The Illicit Arms Trade: Cold War and Post–Cold War." *Crime, Law, and Social Change* 33, nos. 1–2 (2000).

Owen Greene. "Examining International Responses to Illicit Arms Trafficking." *Crime, Law, and Social Change* 33, nos. 1–2 (2000).

Bob French. "The Business of Land-Mine Clearing." *EPS Journal* 1, no. 2 (2006): 54–56.

Session 3: The Economics of Terrorism

Alan Krueger and Jitka Maleckova. "Education, Poverty, and Terrorism: Is There a Causal Connection?" *Journal of Economic Perspectives* 17, no. 4 (Fall 2003): 119–144.

David Gold. "The Economics of Terrorism." New School University, 2004, at the website of Columbia International Affairs Online, http://www.ciaonet.org/casestudy/god01/.

Donato Masciandaro. "Combating Black Money: Money Laundering and Terrorism Finance, International Cooperation, and the G8 Role." University of Bocconi, 2004, at the website of the Social Science Research Network, http://papers.ssrn.com/sol3/papers.cfm?abstract_id=561183.

Session 4: Economics and Civil War:
Causes and Consequences

Issues:

Collier, *Breaking the Conflict Trap*.

Macartan Humphreys. "Economics and Violent Conflict." Harvard University, 2002, http://www.preventconflict.org/portal/economics/Essay.pdf. Revisit the article.

Martha Starr. "Growth and Conflict in the Developing World: Neo-liberal Narratives and Social-Economy Alternatives." *Review of Social Economy* 64, no. 2 (June): 205–224.

Ballentine and Nitzschke, *Profiting from Peace*, pages 123–152 ("Combating Organized Crime in Armed Conflict," by Phil Williams and John T. Picarelli) and pages 153–184 ("Protecting Livelihoods in Violent Economies," by Stephen Jackson).

Michael Ross. "What Do We Know About Natural Resources and Civil War?" *Journal of Peace Research* 41 (2004): 337–356.

Macartan Humphreys and Jeremy Weinstein. "What the Fighters Say: A Survey of Ex-Combatants in Sierra Leone." Center on Globalization and Sustainable Development, working paper no. 20, 2004, website of the

Earth Institute at Columbia University, http://www.earthinstitute.columbia.edu/cgsd.

Case studies:
Collier, *Understanding Civil War*:
vol. 2, 259–298 ("Civil Wars in the Caucasus").
vol. 2, 59–85 ("The Lebanese Civil War").
vol. 2, 191–227 ("Bosnia's Civil War").
vol. 1, 193–219 ("Sudan's Civil War").
vol. 2, 119–159 ("Conflict, Violence, and Crime in Colombia").
vol. 1, 247–302 ("Senegal and Mali").
vol. 2, 231–257 ("Greed and Grievance Diverted").
vol. 1, 89–121 ("Theory Versus Reality").

Session 5: Economics and Peacemaking, Peacekeeping, and Peacebuilding

General reading:
Lloyd Dumas. "An Economic Approach to Peacemaking and Peacekeeping." *EPS Journal* 1, no. 2 (2006): 7–12.
Ballentine and Nitzschke, *Profiting from Peace*, 447–484.
Michael Doyle and Nicholas Sambanis. "International Peacebuilding: A Theoretical and Quantitative Analysis." *American Political Science Review* (December 2000): 779–802.
Macartan Humphreys and Jeremy Weinstein. "Disentangling the Determinants of Successful Demobilization and Reintegration." Center for Global Development, working paper no. 69, http://www.cgdev.org/content/publications/detail/4155.

The role of resource flows:
Ballentine and Nitzschke, *Profiting from Peace*, pages 25–44 ("Natural Resources and Armed Conflict," by Macartan Humphreys), pages 47–68 ("What Lessons from the Kimberley Process Certification Scheme?" by Ian Smillie), pages 69–94 ("Tracking Conflict Commodities and Financing," by Jonathan Winer), and pages 337–394 ("Improving Sanctions Through Legal Means," by Pierre Kopp).
David Gold. "The Attempt to Regulate Conflict Diamonds." *EPS Journal* 1, no. 1 (2006): 49–52.

Waging war against war via corporate social responsibility:
Ballentine and Nitzschke, *Profiting from Peace*, pages 185–206 ("Assessing Company Behavior in Conflict Environments," by Luc Zandvliet), pages 207–233 ("Private Financial Actors and Corporate Responsibility in Conflict Zones," by Mark Mansley), and pages 317–343 ("Regulating Business in Conflict Zones: Challenges and Options," by Leiv Lunde and Mark Taylor).

John Tepper Marlin. "The 'No Dirty Gold' Campaign." *EPS Journal* 1, no. 2 (2006): 58–64.

Session 6: Economics and the War in Iraq

Bassam Yousif. "Economic Aspects of Peacekeeping in Iraq." *EPS Journal* 1, no. 2 (2006): 24–30.

Linda Bilmes and Joseph Stiglitz. "The Economic Costs of the Iraq War." National Bureau of Economic Research, working paper no. 12054. Website of the Columbia Business School, http://www2.gsb.columbia.edu/faculty/jstiglitz/download/2006_Cost_of_War_in_Iraq_NBER.pdf.

Scott Wallsten and Katrina Kosec. "The Economic Costs of the War in Iraq." AEI-Brookings Joint Center, working paper no. 05-19, September 2005, http://www.aei-brookings.org/publications/abstract.php?pid=988.

20.4 Sociology: Social Conflict

Michelle Gawerc
Boston College

COURSE DESCRIPTION

Intermediate-level course in sociology for nonsociology majors in a general education curriculum, peace studies, or conflict studies. Minimum enrollment for simulation: fifteen; maximum: fifty.

The end of the Cold War has not put an end to either war or violent conflicts within society. Some old conflicts that were dormant have now flared up. Problems of large-scale, violent conflicts unfortunately remain central in the modern world. The probability of nuclear proliferation and the possible use of chemical weapons make such conflicts even scarier. The purpose of this course is to increase students' understanding of the conditions under which social conflicts tend to become violent and how they can be resolved nonviolently.

Since this is a core sociology course, we address some of the perennial questions that concern sociologists about society, conflict, and human and social behavior. More specifically, we consider rebellion, conflict and conflict resolution, socialization and culture, war, genocide and the breakdown of social order, and finally, the possibilities for peace and justice. In this course, we explore issues of causality (human nature or social creation); the characteristic of societies with and without war; the tension between peace and justice; and finally, questions concerning the potential for human agency within larger social structures. Throughout this broader exploration, we keep an eye on the following questions: Why is there so much destructive conflict? How can it be transformed to more constructive conflict? What is needed for building more peaceful and just societies, taking into account both structures and relationships?

In this course, we also incorporate culturally diverse perspectives that bring new and critical insight into these perennial topics of rebellion, conflict, war, genocide, and peace. These voices and perspectives are vital for the study of social conflict and often serve to bring issues of oppression, justice, discrimination, and prejudice to the forefront.

Finally, we will bring a historical perspective to the course, looking at where we have come from, where we are now, and where we may be going. Society is not static; change is inevitable. So the question is not whether there will be change, but what kind of change there will be and where we will be in relation to it. It is my intention that this course help you to recognize the moral significance of your life, both for you and society, and encourage you to create a life philosophy that integrates your values, commitments, and the type of change you would like to see in this world.

The format of the class sessions is unusual, with very few lectures. It is discussion-based and involves experiential learning and active learning/participative methods. A highlight around which much of the course is built is a SIMSOC weekend, a simulation game created by William A. Gamson. SIMSOC will be held outside normal class hours but will count for time spent in class.

In most regular class sessions, students are divided into learning groups of five to seven people to carry out exercises we discuss later.

REQUIRED TEXTS

Roger Fisher and William Ury. *Getting to Yes: Negotiating Agreement Without Giving In,* 2nd ed. New York: Penguin, 1991.

William A. Gamson. *SIMSOC (Simulated Society): Participant's Manual,* 5th ed. New York: Free Press, 2000.

Dan Smith. *The Penguin Atlas of War and Peace,* 4th ed. New York: Penguin, 2003.

Francesca M. Cancian and James William Gibson, eds. *Making War/Making Peace: The Social Foundation of Violent Conflicts.* Belmont, CA: Wadsworth Publishing, 1990.

Additional readings as listed in the course outline.

COURSE OUTLINE

Unit 1: Rebellion (two weeks/six class hours)
Focus on the dynamics of conflict. Case study: Berkeley in the 1960s.

William A. Gamson and Andre Modigliani. *Conceptions of Social Life: A Text Reader for Social Psychology.* Little, Brown, 1973, 496–545. Read "Why Do People Rebel?" including introduction and excerpts by Eric Hoffer, William Kornhauser, James C. Davies, and Charles Tilly.

Gamson, *SIMSOC: Participant's Manual:*
"Social Protest and Social Change," 75.
Saul D. Alinsky, "The Process of Power," 75–78.
William A. Gamson, Bruce Fireman, and Steve Rytina, "The Theory and Practice of Rebellion," 78–80.
Robert A. Dahl, "Legitimacy and Authority," 80.

View *Berkeley in the Sixties,* directed by Mark Kitchell, VHS 1990, DVD 2002, 117 minutes.

Unit 2: Conflict and Conflict Resolution (three weeks/nine class hours)
Focus on theories of conflict, the SIMSOC game, the positive value of conflict, game theoretical models, framing conflicts, and conflict resolution and transformation.

Read prior to playing SIMSOC Gamson, *SIMSOC: Participant's Manual:* "Rules," 3–32.
William A. Gamson, "On the Use of Simulation Games," 41.
Clark C. Abt, "The Reunion of Action and Thought," 41–43.
John R. Raser, "What and Why Is a Simulation?" 43–48.

Play SIMSOC.

Readings for postgame class sessions:
William A. Gamson. "SIMSOC in Action: The Theoretical Model." In *SIMSOC: Coordinator's Manual*. Distribute in class after game is completed.
Máire A. Dugan. "Power." In *Beyond Intractability,* edited by Guy Burgess and Heidi Burgess. Boulder: Conflict Research Consortium, University of Colorado, June 2003.
Otomar Bartos and Paul Wehr. "Understanding Conflict." In *Using Conflict Theory,* by Otomar Bartos and Paul Wehr. Cambridge: Cambridge University Press, 2002, 12–28.

Gamson, *SIMSOC: Participant's Manual:*
"Social Conflict," 83.
Lewis Coser, "The Functions of Conflict," 83–84.
Robert A. Dahl, "Conflict: A Paradigm," 85–87.

Fisher and Ury, *Getting to Yes,* all.
John Paul Lederach and Michelle Maiese. "Conflict Transformation." In *Beyond Intractability,* edited by Guy Burgess and Heidi Burgess. Boulder: Conflict Research Consortium, University of Colorado, 2003.

Unit 3: Socialization and Culture (one week/three class hours)
Francesca M. Cancian. "A Conversation on War, Peace, and Gender." In *Making War, Making Peace: The Social Foundation of Violent Conflicts,* edited by Francesca M. Cancian and James William Gibson. Belmont, CA: Wadsworth Publishing, 1990, 64–67.
Elise Boulding. "History at Sword's Point? The War-Nurtured Identity of Western Civilization." *Cultures of Peace,* by Elise Boulding. Syracuse University Press, 2000, 13–28.

View before class *Tough Guise,* produced and directed by Sut Jhally, DVD, 1999, 82 minutes.

Unit 4: War and Peace

Four weeks/twelve class hours.

Positive and negative peace, characteristics of societies without war, war and democracy, international conflict management, the World Court, and peacekeeping.

Smith. *The Penguin Atlas of War and Peace,* read chapters 1–3; skim chapters 4–8; read chapter 9.

Cancian and Gibson, *Making War, Making Peace,* 1–10.

David Fabbro. "Equality in Peaceful Societies," in *Making War, Making Peace,* 127–142.

Margaret Mead. "Warfare Is Only an Invention—Not a Biological Necessity." In *War and Peace in an Age of Terrorism: A Reader,* edited by William Evan Pearson. Allyn and Bacon, 2006, 218–221.

Michael Renner. "Security Redefined." *State of the World 2005.* Worldwatch Institute, 2005, 3–19.

Michelle Gawerc. "Peace-building: Theoretical and Concrete Perspectives." *Peace and Change* 31, no. 4 (2006): 435–478.

Hilary French, Gary Gardner, and Erik Assadourian. "Laying the Foundations for Peace." *State of the World 2005,* by Hilary French, Gary Gardner, and Erik Assadourian. Worldwatch Institute, 2005, 160–166.

Unit 5: Genocide

One week/three class hours.

Defining genocide and making important distinctions; preventing it. Case study: Darfur, and the tension between peace and justice.

Helen Fein. "Genocide: A Sociological Perspective." In *Genocide: An Anthropological Reader,* edited by Alexander Laban Hinton. Blackwell, 2002, 74–90.

Helen Fein. "Lessons from the Past: Preventing Genocide." *Facing History and Ourselves* (online campus), 2004, http://www.facinghistory.org/campus/reslib.nsf/online+campus?openform.

Kofi Annan. "Genocide Is Threat to Peace Requiring Strong, United Action, Secretary-General Tells Stockholm International Forum." United Nations Press Release SG/SM/9126, January 26, 2004, http://www.unis.unvienna.org/unis/pressrels/2004/sgsm9126.html.

Eric Reeves. "A Darfur 'Crash Course.'" *New Republic,* July 18–22, 2005.

View *Translating Genocide,* directed by Kirsten Dirkson, Ross Martin, and Stephen K. Friedman, MTV special, 2005.

Unit 6: Possibilities for Peace
After Genocide, War, and Other Atrocities
One week/three class hours.

Justice, truth, forgiveness, reconciliation, and coexistence. Case study: South Africa after apartheid.

Eric Brahm. "Peacebuilding and Reconciliation Stage." In *Beyond Intractability,* edited by Guy Burgess and Heidi Burgess. Conflict Research Consortium, University of Colorado, October 2003.

Pamela Harris, ed. *Long Night's Journey into Day: Facilitation Guide:*
Priscilla Hayner, "The Truth and Reconciliation Commission."
David Anthony, "A Comparative History of South Africa and the United States" and "The Rise and Fall of Apartheid: A Timeline."
Martha Minow, "Vengeance, Retribution, and Forgiveness."
Pumla Gobodo-Madikezela, "On Trauma and Forgiveness."
Lynn Walker Huntley, "Conflict Resolution."

View *Long Night's Journey into Day,* directed by Mary Burton and Frances Reid, DVD, 2001, 94 minutes.

Unit 7: Peace Politics
One week/three class hours.

Common security, an alternative vision of international relations, and the role of peace movements.

Pam Solo, Ted Sasson, and Rob Leavitt. "Outlining the Future: Principles of Common Security." In *Making War, Making Peace,* edited by Francesca M. Cancian and James W. Gibson. Wadsworth Publishing, 1990, 280–281.

Paul Joseph. "Peace Movements Make a Difference." In *Peace Politics,* by Paul Joseph. Temple University Press, 1993, 140–181.

TEACHING NOTES

The course explores works in the fields of sociology, conflict resolution, and peace studies that draw on comparative, historical, and case study methods. Students mainly read qualitative material, but readings also contain quantitative data relating to social conflict and war. Students will also take an in-depth and critical look at issues of framing for understanding conflict and the ways in which individual conflicts are represented in mass media.

The course is very participatory. Each student is assigned to a group of five to seven people with whom he or she works regularly during the term, completing a series of exercises. These groups are intended to be as diverse as possible. Students run these groups themselves as the instructor floats back and forth among them, adding comments where it seems helpful. Most sessions involve reports back from the group to the class as a whole, so each group must elect a spokesperson for each session. They must also elect a recorder. The recorder fills out one or more simple forms to record the result of the group's discussion. Finally, the small group chooses a discussion leader to move the group forward to complete its task in the time allotted. The group can decide whether to rotate these positions or to let the same people serve each time. The learning group activities (which come with instructor notes) are available at the Movement/Media Research Action website, http://www.mrap.info/.

20.5 History: War and Peace in American History

Perry Bush
Bluffton University

COURSE DESCRIPTION

Intermediate or upper-level undergraduate seminar in history or peace studies.

This course explores what it has meant to make war and peace in US history. War has profoundly shaped the history of the United States, registering both a deep impact on larger society and also on the people who have been called upon to engage in it. So, too, though in ways perhaps not as easily discernible, have peace movements shaped the course of this nation's history. We will carefully sift through the different effects of war on its participants and on those who opposed it, and discuss together how to evaluate these people and the larger developments that emanated from their actions.

War and peace in US history is an awfully broad topic, and thus we will have to narrow our range of focus. We will look at the last four major conflicts in the United States: the Civil War, World Wars I and II, and then the Cold War culminating in the engagement in Vietnam, focusing our primary attention on the *effects,* rather than the *causes,* of the conflicts. In particular, we will examine three interrelated themes. First, the course will look carefully at the experience of combat, how it both changed and remained the same through this time period. Second, it devotes some energy to exploring the larger results of this combat on a democratic society, a matter that leads to a whole host of very important questions. (For instance, it considers the larger question of whether total war is compatible with the aims and practices of a democracy). Third and finally, this course will look at the various peace movements arising in opposition to these conflicts and evaluate their tactics, reasoning, and relative success.

Students are responsible for presenting material in class and writing questions for the whole class to consider.

REQUIRED TEXTS

Phillip Caputo. *Rumor of War.* New York: Ballantine Books, 1977.

Paul Fussell. *Wartime: Understanding and Behavior in the Second World War.* New York: Oxford University Press, 1989.

David Kennedy. *Over Here: The First World War and American Society.* New York: Oxford University Press, 1980.

Gerald Linderman. *Embattled Courage: The Experience of Combat in the American Civil War.* New York: Free Press, 1987.

Lawrence Wittner. *Rebels Against War: The American Peace Movement, 1933–1983*. Philadelphia: Temple University Press, 1984.

COURSE SCHEDULE

Unit 1: The Civil War

Two to three weeks.

Oral presentations: Civil War as total war and Civil War peace movement.

Linderman, *Embattled Courage*.

Russell Weigley. "A Strategy of Annihilation: U.S. Grant and the Union." In *The American Way of War,* edited by Russell Weigley. New York: Macmillan, 1973, 129–152.

Charles DeBenedetti. "The Humanitarian Reform, 1815–1865." In *The Peace Reform in American History,* by Charles DeBenedetti. Bloomington: Indiana University Press, 1980, 32–58.

The Civil War, directed by Ken Burns, PBS home video, 1997. The piece on Fredericksburg in episode 4 illustrates Linderman's argument about the horrendous casualty rates resulting from Civil War battle tactics and technology.

Unit 2: Progressives Go to War: World War I

Two to three weeks.

Oral presentations: Combat in World War I and the impact of World War I on US civil liberties.

Kennedy, *Over Here*, 3–92, 144–295.

John Keegan. "The Somme, 1 July, 1916." In *The Face of Battle*, by John Keegan. London: Penguin, 1976, 207–219, 229–258.

James Juhnke. "The Great War." In *Vision, Doctrine, War: Mennonite Identity and Organization in America, 1890–1930,* by James Juhnke. Scottdale, PA: Herald Press, 1989, 208–242.

Unit 3: World War II: Combat

One to two weeks.

Oral presentation: World War II as total war.

Fussell, *Wartime*, 3–29, 35–78, 79–95, 251–297.

Ronald Schaffer. "The Bombing of Germany: Transition to Douhetian Warfare." In *Wings of Judgment: American Bombing in World War II,* by Ronald Schaffer. New York: Oxford University Press, 1985, 80–106.

Unit 4: World War II and a Democratic Society
One week.

Oral presentation: Polling data on popular attitudes in the United States during World War II.

Fussell, *Wartime,* 115–199.
Richard Steele. "American Popular Opinion and the War Against Germany: The Issue of a Negotiated Peace, 1942." *Journal of American History* 45 (December 1978): 704–732.

Unit 5: World War II: Opposing the "Good War"
One to two weeks.

Oral presentation: The case against Christian pacifism.

Wittner, *Rebels Against War,* 1–150.
Reinhold Niebuhr. "Why the Christian Church Is Not Pacifist." In *Christianity and Power Politics,* edited by Reinhold Niebuhr. New York: Charles Scribner's Sons, 1940, 1–32.
The Good War and Those Who Refused to Fight It, Paradigm Productions, Bullfrog Films, DVD, 2000.

Unit 6: Combat in Vietnam
Two to three weeks.

Oral presentation: The view that more bombing would have won the Vietnam War.

Caputo, *Rumor of War.*
Alan Gropman. "Lost Opportunities: The Air War in Vietnam, 1961–1973." In *The American War in Vietnam: Lessons, Legacies, and Implications for Future Conflicts,* edited by Lawrence Grinter and Peter Dunn. New York: Greenwood Press, 1987, 49–67.

Unit 7: The Vietnam Antiwar Movement
Two to three weeks.

Oral presentations: Pacifism as a response to the war in Vietnam and radicalism as a response to the war in Vietnam.

Wittner, *Rebels Against War,* 240–306.

Guenter Lewy. "The Moral Crisis of American Pacifism." *This World* 20 (1988): 3–25.

Maurice Isserman and Michael Kazin. "The Failure and Success of the New Radicalism." In *The Rise and Fall of the New Deal Order, 1930–1980*, edited by Steve Fraser and Gary Gerstle. Princeton: Princeton University Press, 1989, 212–242.

The War at Home, directed by Glenn Silber and Barry Brown, First Run Films, video, 1979.

Berkeley in the Sixties, directed by Mark Kitchell, First Run Films, VHS, 1990.

TEACHING NOTES

The number of articles assigned for oral presentations throughout the semester is based on the number of students in the course. Each student takes his or her turn making one fifteen- to twenty-minute presentation of an article in class, both summarizing the piece and underscoring its connection to the larger course material. This syllabus is predicated on an enrollment of ten students. I require that each student schedule a meeting with me ahead of time in which we thoroughly dissect the argument in the article until I am satisfied the student is capable of teaching its major points to the class. I usually manage to maneuver the class to make sure better students receive tougher articles to teach (like the Niebuhr, Lewy, Steele, and Weigley pieces). If I see a student struggling, I do my best to assist him or her lay out the piece to the class, and often follow with a brief summary of the piece myself to ensure the class has grasped the major points of the argument. In this manner, these pieces become part of our shared conversation about the course material. We return to them over and over.

Although the class is punctuated by lectures on key points, both by me and by students, one of its key features is the regular use of student discussion questions. I require each student to send to me by email, by a prescribed deadline (four to six hours before class), two or three discussion questions on the assigned reading. I keep a record of these discussion questions as hard data upon which I can root the substantial portion of a grade assigned to class participation. Before class, I group the questions by topic and then in class project them for all of us to read. I regularly integrate them into my lectures or else orient the entire class session around them. Although I always come with my own questions and lecture points, I find that students have often anticipated my questions or else pose additional thoughtful questions about the course material that haven't occurred to me. I have come to rely on these questions, and as I tell the class, I am to a great degree surrendering agency over the course to them. Usually I find the more I rely on students and give the class over to them, the better they respond; they come to own the course, a project for which all of us are jointly responsible rather than a show put on by the professor.

Finally, in addition to a written, final (essay) exam, regular class participation, a term paper, and an oral presentation on an article, the other major assignment of the course is the student's summary of an oral interview with a military or peace movement veteran that the student conducts over the course of the semester. Even though students are often eager to arrange these on their own—often with family members—I help students identify such people in the community (relying on my own private list of local people I know will agree to participate in the project). I also work with students to obtain approval from the university's Institutional Review Board to complete the interview, lecturing briefly on oral interviewing dos and don'ts.

When students interview military veterans, I encourage them to ask questions such as, What induced you to join the military? What factors played on your decision? Where did your service take you? What memories stand out most clearly in your mind about this experience? Overall, in retrospect, was your experience a positive or negative one for you, and why? What did you, or the larger effort, accomplish? When students interview peace movement veterans, I encourage them to explore questions such as, What induced you to become active in the peace movement in the manner that you did? What kinds of activities and causes did you engage in and espouse? Why? What kind of sacrifices did you or your fellow activists engage in? What particular memories of your activism stand out most clearly in your mind? Overall, in retrospect, was your experience a positive or negative one for you? What did you, or the larger effort, accomplish? Overall such interviews prove profoundly meaningful for students and also help to translate the course material from an abstract, theoretical plane into real life.

20.6 Psychology: Introduction to Peace Psychology

Rachel M. MacNair
Institute for Integrated Social Analysis

COURSE DESCRIPTION

Introductory or intermediate-level undergraduate course in psychology or peace studies with adaptations for upper levels.

The human mind, individual behavior, and behavior in groups provide the basic building blocks to explain why violence happens, how nonviolence works, and how peace can be built. The first half of this course deals with the psychological knowledge behind peace: the psychological causes and consequences of violence; the psychological causes and consequences of nonviolence; the problem-solving orientation in which conflict resolution is used when parties are willing to talk, or nonviolent struggle when they are not; and public policy and personal lifestyles, including art. The second half of the course focuses on the psychology of activism: how to improve effectiveness individually, how to be more persuasive as a group, and how to avoid the well-known psychological pitfalls of activism. Students should gain an overview of both knowledge and skills: what we know about why people behave violently or peacefully and what research remains to be done on this, and skills on how to effectively decrease violence of various kinds and increase peaceful behavior.

REQUIRED TEXTS

Rachel M. MacNair. *The Psychology of Peace: An Introduction.* Westport, CT: Praeger, 2003.

Rachel M. MacNair, ed. *Working for Peace: A Handbook of Practical Psychology and Other Tools.* San Luis Obispo, CA: Impact Publishers, 2006.

Articles listed in the course schedule.

Additional readings for upper-level students are in brackets.

COURSE SCHEDULE

Week 1: The Psychological Causes of Violence
MacNair, *The Psychology of Peace: An Introduction,* chapter 1.

Albert Bandura, Claudio Barbaranelli, Gian Vihorio Caprara, and Concetta Pastorelli. "Mechanisms of Moral Disengagement in the Exercise of Moral Agency." *Journal of Personality and Social Psychology* 71 (1996): 364–374.

William Brennan. *Dehumanizing the Vulnerable: When Word Games Take Lives*. Chicago: Loyola University Press, 1995, chapter 1 [upper-level students read the entire book].

View the slide show "Stanford Prison Experiment" at www.prisonexp.org in class.

Week 2: The Psychological Effects of Violence

MacNair, *The Psychology of Peace: An Introduction,* chapter 2.

Read examples from Shakespeare and other literature online at www.rachelmacnair.com/lit.

[Rachel MacNair, *Perpetration-Induced Traumatic Stress: The Psychological Consequences of Killing*. Westport, CT: Praeger, 2002, chapters 1, 2, 3, 6, and 12.]

Week 3: The Psychological Causes of Nonviolence

MacNair, *The Psychology of Peace: An Introduction,* chapter 3.

Note: The jigsaw technique discussed in chapter 3 is described in more detail at http://www.jigsaw.org.

Week 4: The Psychological Effects of Nonviolence

MacNair, *The Psychology of Peace: An Introduction,* chapter 4.

Use the jigsaw technique again, but with different groups: the impact of nonviolence on attackers, the impact on observers, direct effects on participants, humor, optimism, and burnout. Groups report to the whole group at the end of the session.

Week 5: Conflict Resolution

MacNair, *The Psychology of Peace: An Introduction,* chapter 5.

Use the jigsaw technique again with groups on differing cultures, diplomacy, postwar reconciliation, and restorative justice. Groups will report to the whole group at the end of the session.

Week 6: Nonviolent Struggle

MacNair, *The Psychology of Peace: An Introduction,* chapter 6.

Kate Cohen-Posey. *How to Handle Bullies, Teasers, and Other Meanies.* Highland City, FL: Rainbow Books, 1995. This children's book is a quick read and optional for the course.

Option: Read teacher-selected or student-selected sections of A. Ruth Fry's *Victories Without Violence: True Stories of Ordinary People Coming Through Dangerous Situations Without Using Physical Force.* Santa Fe: Ocean Tree Books, 1986.

Before class, students play A Force More Powerful: A Game of Nonviolent Strategy, available at http://www.aforcemorepowerful.org/game/index.php. They will play the game as homework and debrief the experience in class.

Week 7: Public Policy

MacNair, *The Psychology of Peace: An Introduction,* chapter 7.

L. G. Conway, P. Suedfeld, and P. E. Tetlock. "Integrative Complexity and Political Decisions That Lead to War or Peace." In *Peace, Conflict, and Violence: Peace Psychology for the Twenty-First Century,* edited by Daniel J. Christie, Richard V. Wagner, and Deborah DuNann Winter. Upper Saddle River, NJ: Prentice-Hall, 2001, 66–75.

Week 8: Private Lifestyles and Art

MacNair, *The Psychology of Peace: An Introduction,* chapter 8.

"Fostering Sustainable Behavior: An Introduction to Community-Based Social Marketing," the website of MacKenzie-Mohr and Associates at http://www.cbsm.com. Users must register to enter site.

Browse the website of the Center for Nonviolent Communication, http://www.cnvc.org/.

Week 9: Activists Improving Themselves Personally

MacNair, *Working for Peace,* chapters 2, 3, 6, and 7.

Week 10: Getting Groups Organized

MacNair, *Working for Peace,* chapters 11–14.

Week 11: Transforming Conflict into Creativity

MacNair, *Working for Peace,* chapters 17–21.

Week 12: Getting the Message Out

MacNair, *Working for Peace,* chapters 24, 25, 27, and 28.

Week 13: Changing Attitudes with Peaceful Persuasion

MacNair, *Working for Peace,* chapters 29, 30, 31, 33, and 34.

Week 14

Set aside time to discuss the special interests of students who have delved more deeply into a specific topic.

TEACHING NOTES

This course uses the outlines of the two assigned textbooks, one right after the other, and supplements them with pertinent additional readings. Any instructor can easily add or substitute relevant material found in these or other texts. The proposed reading assignments are suggestions rather than requirements in all cases. I have also divided this course into one section or chapter per week, but experience shows that the very first topic, the psychology of why people are violent, requires more time than other topics due to the novelty of the ideas many students find there.

The following assignments have also worked well for me in engaging students in class discussion.

• Bring in an example of any of the psychological concepts from current news (or classics), and we will discuss the applications in class.

• Select an issue about which you feel strongly. Write a two- to three-page paper arguing your position. Then write a two- to three-page paper arguing the opposite position. A passing grade depends on the instructor not being able to tell which is your actual position, showing you understand the opponents' views well enough to express them.

• A midterm exam: Find five examples of the psychological concepts we've been discussing in class in the book *An Inquiry into War* by Jonathan Dymond (1824), available online at http//www.qhpress.org/texts/dymond/index.html. This is a take-home exam; group work is encouraged, though each person will turn in his or her own work.

• Pick any topic, real or imagined, and design a one-page leaflet using the principles described in chapter 25 of *Working for Peace*. It can include educating on an issue, explaining an organization and its needs, or advertising an event.

• Bring in a short written example of an attempt at persuasion done well and another attempt done poorly, according to the principles discussed in *Working for Peace*, and explain why one was done well and the other done poorly.

20.7 Environmental Studies: Environmental Philosophy

Steven S. Naragon
Manchester College

COURSE OVERVIEW

Upper-level undergraduate course for majors in philosophy, environmental studies, political science, and peace studies.

This course explores a number of competing traditions that answer the question, How should we distribute benefits (e.g., land, clean air and water, food, healthcare, iPods) and burdens (e.g., polluting factories, incinerators, toxic dump sites) among all those who enjoy moral standing? This exploration involves two fundamental questions: What determines this distribution? and What determines moral standing? Almost every issue in environmental philosophy turns on these questions of distributive justice and the breadth and width of our moral community. The schedule of discussion and readings offers a closer account of the specific topics.

The objective of this course is that—through reading, study, and conversation—students will increase their knowledge of factual information regarding environmental matters and that they will fine-tune their understanding of relevant moral principles and their application. More specific goals include the following: (1) Become aware of the implications of environmental problems and investigate various likely causes of these problems; (2) Gain facility in distinguishing empirical claims from moral claims; (3) Search for a moral theory that offers adequate protection to the nonhuman world; (4) Develop skills for critically evaluating arguments and beliefs; and (5) Have the opportunity to reflect on two basic questions confronting each of us: What is my proper relationship to other humans? What is my proper relationship with the rest of nature?

REQUIRED TEXT

All readings are found in Louis P. Pojman and Paul Pojman. *Environmental Ethics: Readings in Theory and Application,* 5th ed. Thomson/Wadsworth, 2008. The number indicates the chapter's position in the book.

COURSE SCHEDULE

Unit 1: Population and Consumption

Session 1

John Locke, *Second Treatise on Civil Government,* chapter 5, www.constitution.org/jl/2ndtreat.htm.

Session 2

Garrett Hardin, "The Tragedy of the Commons," no. 45.

Session 3

Bill McKibben, "A Special Moment in History," no. 44; and Louis Pojman, "The Challenge of the Future," no. 77.

Unit 2: Food Ethics

Session 4

Garrett Hardin, "Lifeboat Ethics," no. 49; William W. Murdoch and Allan Oaten, "Population and Food: A Critique of Lifeboat Ethics," no. 50.

Session 5

Tristram Coffin, "The World Food Supply," no. 54; and Michael Allen Fox, "Vegetarianism and Treading Lightly on the Earth," no. 55.

Unit 3: Animal Rights

Session 6

Immanuel Kant, "Rational Beings Alone Have Moral Worth," no. 7; and Holly Wilson, "The Green Kant," no. 8.

Session 7

Peter Singer, "A Utilitarian Defense of Animal Liberation," no. 9.

Session 8

Tom Regan, "The Radical Egalitarian Case for Animal Rights," no. 10; and Mary Ann Warren, "A Critique of Regan's Animal Rights Theory," no. 11.

Unit 4: Species and Biodiversity

Session 9

Donella Meadows, "Biodiversity," no. 30; and Lilly-Marlene Russow, "Why Do Species Matter?" no. 31.

Session 10

Martin Krieger, "What's Wrong with Plastic Trees?" no. 32; and Robert Elliot, "Faking Nature," no. 33.

Unit 5: Constructing an Environmental Ethic

Session 11

Holmes Rolston, "Naturalizing Values," no. 13.

Session 12

Albert Schweitzer, "Reverence for Life," no. 16; and Kenneth Goodpaster, "On Being Morally Considerable," no. 18.

Session 13

Aldo Leopold, "Ecocentrism: The Land Ethic," no. 19; and J. Baird Callicott, "The Conceptual Foundations of the Land Ethic," no. 20.

Session 14

Arne Naess, "The Shallow and the Deep, Long-Range Ecological Movement," no. 24; and Arne Naess, "Ecosophy T: Deep Versus Shallow Ecology," no. 25.

Session 15

Murray Bookchin, "Social Ecology Versus Deep Ecology," no. 28.

Session 16

James Sterba, "Environmental Justice," no. 29.

Unit 6: Religious Perspectives

Session 17

Genesis 1–3, no. 1; Lynn White, "The Historical Roots of Our Ecological Crisis," no. 2; Lewis Moncrief, "The Cultural Basis of Our Environmental Crisis," no. 3; and Patrick Dobel, "The Judeo-Christian Stewardship Attitude to Nature," no. 4.

Session 18

O. P. Dwivedi, "Satyagraha for Conservation," no. 35; Lily de Silva, "The Buddhist Attitude Towards Nature," no. 36; Mawil Y. Izzi Deen, "Islamic Environmental Ethics, Law, and Society," no 37.

Unit 7: Economics and the Environment

Session 19

William Baxter, "People or Penguins," no. 58; and David Schmidtz, "On the Value and Limits of Cost-Benefit Analysis," no. 69.

Session 20

Herman Daly, "Consumption," no. 67; and Mark Sagoff, "At the Shrine of Our Lady of Fatima, or Why Political Questions Are Not All Economic," no. 68.

Unit 8: Environmental Justice

Session 21

Robert Bullard, "Overcoming Racism in Environmental Decision Making," no. 70; and Peter Wenz, "Just Garbage," no 72.

Session 22

Maria Mies, "Deceiving the Third World," no. 73; Ramachandra Guha, "Radical Environmentalism and Wilderness Preservation," no. 39.

Unit 9: Sustainable Societies

Session 23

Todd Saunders, "Ecology and Community Design," no. 78; and Louis Pojman, "Pedaling Power," no. 79.

Session 24

Michael Martin, "Ecosabotage and Civil Disobedience," no. 80; and Dave Foreman, "Strategic Monkeywrenching," no. 81.

Session 25

Lester Brown, Christopher Flavin, and Sandra Postel, "A Vision of a Sustainable World," no. 82.

TEACHING NOTES

Students take a brief quiz each day on the topic for the day. These exercises keep me informed of their comprehension of the material and motivate them to read the material when it is due. The quizzes will consist of three to four objective questions (multiple choice or true/false) or a short essay question.

I also divide the class into small research groups of three or four people each. Groups research and write one five-page essay for the group. They must turn in a draft and a revision of the essay. The essay must focus on a consumer good and the environmental and social effects of its manufacture, distribution, and consumption. In preparing the essays, groups will also need to develop a one-page "summary sheet" for other members of the class and make it available to them by email or website. Finally, each group presents its research as a brief video clip, which should be posted on a file-sharing website such as YouTube; this is an opportunity to share their research findings with the rest of the class, and anyone else in the world with an Internet hook-up. The summary sheets should be clear and concise, with all factual claims carefully documented and a concise bibliography included. The video should be accurate, informative, cinematically gripping, and no longer than fifteen minutes. Borrowed sounds, images, and footage must be credited and appropriate to the project.

20.8 Environmental Studies: Disease, Death, and World Politics

Jeremy Youde
Grinnell College

COURSE DESCRIPTION

Intermediate or upper-level undergraduate course for students in environmental studies, general education, political science, and public health.

Thucydides' descriptions of the Peloponnesian War tells in detail how the spread of a plague throughout Athens sapped its war-fighting capabilities. Bubonic plague wiped out up to one-third of Europe's population in the fourteenth century, which had the unintended consequence of laying the foundation for the end of feudalism. Hernán Cortés defeated a vastly superior Aztec army in the sixteenth century by unwittingly bringing smallpox to Mexico. Over 40 million people around the world are infected with HIV, three-quarters of whom live in sub-Saharan Africa. An outbreak of mad cow disease in Canada caused the United States to ban beef imports from Canada, costing that country's beef industry billions of dollars. The outbreak of SARS in Hong Kong and Toronto in 2003 cost the tourism industries of both cities billions in lost revenue.

These are just a few instances that demonstrate how politics and disease intersect; however, political science has devoted little attention to how diseases influence politics and vice versa. Do diseases in fact have any political, economic, military, or social influence on states or how states relate to one another? Does disease fit into political science, or is it better studied by other fields like public health? If diseases do matter, then how can we understand their importance? This course introduces students to these issues from both historical and contemporary perspectives. We examine the debates over the appropriateness of including health and disease within a political science framework, look at the role of disease in history, and examine the most current research on the impact of disease on states and governance.

REQUIRED TEXTS

Chris Beyrer. *War in the Blood: Sex, Politics, and AIDS in Southeast Asia*. London: Zed Books, 1998.

Jennifer Brower and Peter Chalk. *The Global Threat of New and Reemerging Infectious Diseases*. Santa Monica, CA: Rand, 2003, http://www.rand.org/pubs/monograph_reports/MR1602/.

Paul Farmer. *Infections and Inequalities: The Modern Plagues*. Berkeley: University of California Press, 1999.

Andrew T. Price-Smith. *The Health of Nations: Infectious Disease, Environmental Change, and Their Effects on National Security and Development*. Cambridge, MA: MIT Press, 2002.

ADDITIONAL READINGS/SUGGESTED TEXTS

Rx for Survival: A Global Health Challenge. WGBH Boston Public Television, six-part video series, 2005. http://www.pbs.org/wgbh/rxforsurvival/.

National Intelligence Council. "The Global Infectious Disease Threat and Its Implications for the United States." 1999. http://www.fas.org/irp/threat/nie99-17d.htm.

Peter Baldwin. *Disease and Democracy*. Berkeley: University of California Press, 2005.

State of Denial, produced and directed by Elaine Epstein, Public Broadcasting Corporation (Point of View), DVD, 2003. http://www.pbs.org/pov/pov2003/stateofdenial/.

COURSE SCHEDULE

Unit 1: The Nature of the Debate—Is Disease Political?

Focus on whether disease can/should fit into a national security or political framework; discuss how disease is conceptualized within politics and political debates.

Laurie Garrett. "The Return of Infectious Disease." *Foreign Affairs* 75 (January–February 1996): 66–79.

Catherine Boone and Jake Batsell. "Politics and AIDS in Africa: Research Agendas in Political Science and International Relations." *Africa Today* 48 (2001): 3–33.

Price-Smith, *The Health of Nations*, introduction.

Unit 2: Disease and History

Provides an overview (from Peloponnesian War to influenza epidemic of 1918) of the role of disease in history and how epidemics led to changes in political institutions and actors.

William McNeil, *Plagues and Peoples*. Anchor, 1976, chapter 5.

Sylvia Noble Tesh, *Hidden Arguments*. Rutgers University Press, 1988, chapters 1–2.

Maynard W. Swanson. "The Sanitation Syndrome: Bubonic Plague and Urban Native Policy in the Cape Colony, 1900–1909." *Journal of African History* 18 (1977): 387–410.

Alfred Crosby. *America's Forgotten Pandemic*. Cambridge University Press, 1989, chapter 10.

Unit 3: Empirical Evidence
Evaluate preliminary statistical and empirical evidence that shows the direct and indirect effects of disease epidemics on economic and political development; question what evidence is used and how.

Price-Smith, *The Health of Nations*, chapters 1–5 and conclusion.

Unit 4: Disease and National Security
Examine the arguments for incorporating disease into a national security paradigm; illustrate the costs and benefits of such an integration.

Brower and Chalk, *The Global Threat of New and Reemerging Infectious Diseases*, chapters 1–2 and 4–6.

Unit 5: Disease and Social Inequalities
Call attention to inequities in health care systems, the provision of health care, and the social construction of risk groups.

Farmer, *Infections and Inequalities*, chapters 2–10.
Beyrer, *War in the Blood*, chapter 9.

Unit 6: Disease and Economics
Calculate the monetary costs to national governments imposed by epidemics.

John Luke Gallup and Jeffrey D. Sachs. "The Economic Burden of Malaria." *American Journal of Tropical Medicine and Hygiene* 64 (2001): 85–96.

Richard Fredland. "AIDS and Development: An Inverse Correlation?" *Journal of Modern African Studies* 36 (1998): 547–568.

Jeffrey D. Lewis. "Assessing the Demographic and Economic Impact of HIV/AIDS." In *AIDS and South Africa: The Social Expression of a Pandemic,* edited by Kyle Kauffman and David Lindauer. Palgrave Macmillan, 2004.

Nana Poku. "Confronting AIDS with Debt: Africa's Silent Crisis." In *The Political Economy of AIDS in Africa,* edited by Nana Poku and Alan Whiteside. Ashgate Publishing, 2004.

Global Health Watch, website, part E (E1–E4), http://www.ghwatch.org/2005_report_contents.php.

Unit 7: Disease and the Political System
Note how different states have responded (or failed to respond) to epidemics; compare national responses; question the effect of disease on democratic practices.

Anthony Butler. "The Negative and Positive Impacts of HIV/AIDS on Democracy in South Africa." *Journal of Contemporary African Studies* 23 (2005): 3–26.

Teresa Reitan. "Too Sick to Vote? Public Health and Voter Turnout in Russia During the 1990s." *Communist and Post-Communist Studies* 36 (2003): 49–68.

Tim Allen and Suzette Heald. "HIV/AIDS Policy in Africa: What Has Worked in Uganda and What Has Failed in Botswana?" *Journal of International Development* 16 (2004): 1141–1154.

Yanzhong Huang. "The Politics of China's SARS Crisis." *Harvard Asia Quarterly* (Autumn 2003): 9–16.

Unit 8: AIDS

Focus in-depth on the effects of AIDS on politics, economics, social inequalities, and security; query what the international community can learn from AIDS and apply to future disease outbreaks.

Beyrer, *War in the Blood,* chapters 1–8, 11, and 17–22.

Unit 9: New Threats on the Horizon?

Take the measure of potential new threats like avian flu; evaluate how states can prepare for disease outbreaks without inducing panic.

Laurie Garrett. "The Next Pandemic?" *Foreign Affairs* 84 (July–August 2005): 3–23.

Michael T. Osterholm. "Preparing for the Next Pandemic." *Foreign Affairs* 84 (July–August 2005): 24–37.

Homeland Security Council. *National Strategy for Pandemic Influenza*. 2005, http://www.whitehouse.gov/homeland/nspi.pdf.

TEACHING NOTES

This class does not require an in-depth knowledge of biology, but it can be helpful to have at least a rudimentary understanding of how various diseases are transmitted, what their symptoms are, and how they are treated.

Films are helpful for driving home the realities of disease and how they continue to affect life around the world. Both *Rx for Survival* and *State of Denial* do an effective job of illustrating this. Students may not have had previous exposure to health care systems outside the United States (or areas of the United States with less access to health care). The films add a visual component to the readings, and both provide opportunities for people from around the world to address how disease has affected their own lives.

I find that students are very interested in learning how to solve these problems. I provide time in every class period to allow brainstorming. Students often come up with very creative methods to address these problems.

The Contributors

Mohammed Abu-Nimer is professor in the School of International Service, American University, and director of the university's Peacebuilding and Development Institute. He has conducted research on conflict resolution and dialogue for peace among Palestinians and Jews in Israel, the application of conflict resolution models in Muslim communities, interreligious conflict resolution training, and interfaith dialogue. He is the cofounder and coeditor of the *Journal of Peacebuilding and Development*.

Cecilia Albin teaches in the Department of Peace and Conflict Research at Uppsala University in Sweden.

Matthew Bailey-Dick teaches Christian approaches to peacemaking and the history of peace movements at Conrad Grebel University College. In addition to teaching, he has worked as a pastor, a peace and justice animator for a Mennonite Church (Canada) project, and a "Countering Militarism Advocate" for Mennonite Central Committee Ontario.

Richard K. Betts is Arnold Saltzman Professor of War and Peace Studies at the School of International and Public Affairs, Columbia University. Betts is a specialist on national security policy and military strategy. He was a senior fellow and research associate at the Brookings Institution in Washington, D.C., from 1976 to 1990 and has taught at Harvard University and the Johns Hopkins University's Nitze School of Advanced International Studies. He is the author of *Military Readiness; Soldiers, Statesmen, and Cold War Crises*, 2nd ed.; *Nuclear Blackmail and Nuclear Balance;* and *Surprise Attack*.

Arthur Blaser is professor of political science at Chapman University in California. He is the author of "Taking Disability Rights Seriously" in *New Political Science*, "People with Disabilities (PWDs) and Genocide: The

Case of Rwanda" in *Disability Studies Quarterly*, and "How to Advance Justice Without Really Trying: An Analysis of Non-governmental Tribunals" in *Human Rights Quarterly*.

Thomas E. Boudreau is assistant professor of political science at the Maxwell School, Syracuse University, and author of the forthcoming *The Law of Nations: Global Governance in a Violent World*.

Katy Gray Brown is assistant professor of philosophy and peace studies at Manchester College. With David Boersema, she coedited *Spiritual and Political Dimensions of Nonviolence and Peace*.

Kenneth L. Brown is emeritus professor of philosophy at Manchester College and former director of peace studies. Brown wrote "Was the 'Good War' a Just War?" in Jim Junke's book *Nonviolent America*. He was awarded the Life Time Achievement Award from the Peace and Justice Studies Association in 2005.

Perry Bush is professor of history at Bluffton University in Bluffton, Ohio. He is the author of *Two Kingdoms, Two Loyalties: Mennonite Pacifism in Modern America*, as well as numerous articles.

R. Charli Carpenter is assistant professor of international affairs at the University of Pittsburgh's Graduate School of Public and International Affairs. Her research and teaching interests include international norms and identities, gender and violence, transnational advocacy networks, war crimes, comparative genocide studies, children and armed conflict, and humanitarian action. She is the author of "Innocent Women and Children: Gender, Norms, and the Protection of Civilians" and is currently writing a book about the former Yugoslavia.

Daniel Chong teaches at the School of International Service, American University. His graduate research focused on the causes of war, nonviolent social activism, and the US defense budget. His current interests turn on economic and social rights, extreme global poverty, the construction and framing of rights, social justice NGOs, and conflict and development.

Patrick G. Coy is the director of the Center for Applied Conflict Management and associate professor of political science at Kent State University. He is editor of the annual research series, *Research in Social Movements, Conflicts, and Change*.

Kelly Dietz is assistant professor in the Politics Department at Ithaca College. She teaches courses in militarization and the politics of security relations, with a special focus on East Asia. Her current research focuses on the colonial dimensions of foreign military basing.

Isaac Noam Ebner directs Tachlit Mediation and Negotiation Training in Jerusalem. He holds the position of visiting professor at both Sabanci University in Istanbul, Turkey, and at the United Nation's University for Peace in Costa Rica. Noam practices and teaches negotiation and conflict management and specializes in negotiation and mediation processes conducted online.

Robert Elias teaches in the Department of Politics at the University of San Francisco (USF) and is founder of the USF Legal Studies and the Peace and Justice Studies programs. He is the author of *Victims of the System,* and coeditor of *Rethinking Peace* (Lynne Rienner) and *The Peace Resource Book,* and editor of *Peace Review.*

Morten G. Ender is associate professor of sociology in the Department of Behavioral Sciences and Leadership at the US Military Academy at West Point.

Marlene Epp is associate professor of history and peace and conflict studies at Conrad Grebel University College, University of Waterloo, in Ontario, Canada. She is author of *Women Without Men: Mennonite Refugees of the Second World War,* and chief editor, with Franca Iacovetta and Frances Swyripa, of *Sisters or Strangers? Immigrant, Ethnic, and Racialized Women in Canadian History.*

Lowell Ewert is director of peace and conflict studies, Conrad Grebel University College, University of Waterloo, in Ontario, Canada. He is the author of "Rights-Based Approaches to International Development" in *Challenges and Paths to Global Justice,* edited by H. Richard Firman.

Nathan C. Funk is assistant professor of peace and conflict studies at the University of Waterloo's Conrad Grebel University College. His writings on international conflict resolution and the role of cultural and religious factors in peacemaking include two coedited volumes, *Peace and Conflict Resolution in Islam* and *Ameen Rihani: Bridging East and West.* He is coauthor of the forthcoming book, *Islam and Peacemaking in the Middle East.*

Barry Gan is associate professor of philosophy and director of the Center for Nonviolence at St. Bonaventure University. He is the editor of *The Acorn: Journal of the Gandhi-King Society* and coeditor of *Peace and Change,* journal of the Peace History Society and the Peace and Justice Studies Association.

Michelle Gawerc is a Ph.D. candidate and presidential fellow in the Department of Sociology at Boston College. In 2006, she was awarded the Graduate Student Fellow Award of the Peace, War, and Social Conflict Section of the American Sociological Association. In October 2006 she published an article titled "Peace-building: Theoretical and Concrete Perspectives," in *Peace and Change*.

Janet Gerson is codirector with Tony Jenkins of the Peace Education Center at Teachers College, Columbia University.

Marc Gopin is James H. Laue Professor of World Religions, Diplomacy, and Conflict Resolution at George Mason University and directs the Center for World Religions, Diplomacy, and Conflict Resolution. He is author of *Holy War, Holy Peace: How Religion Can Bring Peace to the Middle East*.

Jonathan Hall teaches in the Department of Peace and Conflict Research at Uppsala University in Sweden.

Kristine Höglund teaches in the Department of Peace and Conflict Research at Uppsala University in Sweden.

G. John Ikenberry is Albert G. Milbank Professor of Politics and International Affairs at Princeton University in the Department of Politics and the Woodrow Wilson School of Public and International Affairs. He is the author of *After Victory: Institutions, Strategic Restraint, and the Rebuilding of Order After Major Wars*.

Tony Jenkins is codirector with Janet Gerson of the Peace Education Center at Teachers College, Columbia University.

Abbie Jenks is professor of peace and social justice studies, psychology, and human services, and program coordinator of the Human Service Program at Greenfield Community College.

Robert C. Johansen is senior fellow and professor of political science at the Kroc Institute for International Peace Studies at the University of Notre Dame, specializing in issues of international ethics and global governance, the United Nations and the maintenance of peace and security, and peace and world order studies.

Richard Johnson is emeritus professor of German and peace studies at Indiana University–Purdue University Ft. Wayne, where he founded the

Women's Studies Program and the Peace and Conflict Studies Program. He is the author of *Ich schreibe mir die Seele frei: Wege zue Harmonisierung des ganzen Gehirns* ("I Write My Soul Free: Harmonizing the Whole Brain"), and editor of *Gandhi's Experiments with Truth: Essential Writings by and About Mahatma Gandhi*.

S. Ayse Kadayifci-Orellana is assistant professor of international peace and conflict resolution and associate director of the Salam Institute for Peace and Justice at the School of International Service, American University. He is the author of *Standing on an Isthmus: Islamic Approaches to War and Peace in Palestine*.

Michael T. Klare is Five College Professor of Peace and World Security Studies at Hampshire College, University of Massachusetts, and author of *Blood and Oil: The Danger and Consequences of America's Growing Dependence on Foreign Oil*.

Atul Kohli is the David K. E. Bruce Professor of International Affairs and professor of politics and international affairs at Princeton University.

George Lakey taught Nonviolent Responses to Terrorism as the Lang Visiting Professor at Swarthmore College. He is the head of Training for Change, an organization known for its leadership in creating and teaching strategies for nonviolent social change.

John Paul Lederach is professor of international peacebuilding at the Joan B. Kroc Institute for International Peace Studies, University of Notre Dame, and the author of *The Moral Imagination*.

Daniel Lieberfeld is assistant professor in the Center for Social and Public Policy at Duquesne University. He is the author of *Talking with the Enemy;* articles on conflict and negotiation in the *American Behavioral Scientist* and other journals; and film criticism in the *American Scholar, Film Quarterly,* and the *Journal of Popular Film and Television*.

Uli Linke is associate professor of anthropology and women's and gender studies at Rochester Institute of Technology.

Andrew J. Loomis is a Ph.D. candidate in the Department of Government at Georgetown University and the author of "Legitimacy Norms as Change Agents: Examining the Role of the Public Voice," in *Legality and Legitimacy in International Order,* edited by Richard Falk and Vesselin Popovski.

George A. Lopez is Reverend Theodore M. Hesburgh, C.S.C., Professor of Peace Studies at the Joan B. Kroc Institute for International Peace Studies, University of Notre Dame. An expert on state violence and coercion, ethics and the use of force, and counter terrorism, he has served as an adviser to the UN Security Council, the European Union, governments, foundations, and organizations on issues of human rights, international affairs, and peace research.

Rachel M. MacNair is director of the Institute for Integrated Social Analysis and author of *The Psychology of Peace* and *Working for Peace: A Handbook of Practical Psychology and Other Tools*.

Sue L. T. McGregor is professor and director of graduate education for the Faculty of Education at Mount Saint Vincent University in Halifax, Nova Scotia. She is the author of "Mater or Steward Degree Designations: Implications for a Culture of Peace" in *Culture of Peace Online Journal* and "Consumer Scholarship and Transdisciplinarity" in the *International Journal of Consumer Studies*.

Steven S. Naragon is professor of philosophy at Manchester College, editor and translator (with Karl Ameriks) of Immanuel Kant's *Lectures on Metaphysics*, and creator of a website called Kant in the Classroom that focuses on Kant's lecturing activity and student lecture notes.

Hamid Rafizadeh is associate professor of business at Bluffton University and a native of Iran, where he served for a time as vice president of Atomic Energy Organization of Iran.

Betty A. Reardon is founding director emeritus of the Peace Education Center at Teachers College, Columbia University.

Gloria Rhodes is assistant professor of sociology and conflict studies at Eastern Mennonite University (EMU). She is the department coordinator for the justice, peace, and conflict studies undergraduate program at EMU and former codirector of the Summer Peacebuilding Institute.

Richard Robyn is assistant professor of political science at Kent State University and director of Kent State's Washington Program in National Issues. He is editor and author of *The Changing Face of European Identity*.

Maria Guadalupe Moog Rodrigues is associate professor of political science at the College of the Holy Cross in Worcester, Massachusetts. Her areas of interest are environmental politics and Latin American politics.

Rodrigues is the author of *Global Environmentalism and Local Politics: Transnational Advocacy Networks in Brazil, Ecuador, and India.*

Marc Howard Ross is the William Rand Kenan Jr. Professor of Political Science at Bryn Mawr College and author of *Cultural Contestation in Ethnic Conflict.*

Robert A. Rubinstein is professor of anthropology and international relations at the Maxwell School of Citizenship and Public Affairs, Syracuse University. He is author of *Peacekeeping Under Fire: Culture and Intervention* and coeditor with Mary Lecron Foster of *The Social Dynamics of Peace and Conflict: Culture in International Security.*

Carolyn Schrock-Shenk is associate professor of peace, justice, and conflict studies at Goshen College and editor of *Mediation and Facilitation Training Manual: Foundations for Constructive Conflict Transformation.*

Susan Shepler is assistant professor of international peace and conflict resolution in the School of International Service at American University. She has studied the reintegration of former child soldiers in Sierra Leone and has worked most recently on issues of children displaced by war in West Africa.

Danielle Taana Smith is assistant professor of sociology at Rochester Institute of Technology.

Michael W. Smith is associate professor of sociology at Saint Anselm College and the author of "The Denial of Asylum: Is There Organizational Justice Under the Department of Homeland Security" in *The International Journal of Diversity in Organizations, Communities and Nations.* He also practices immigration, civil rights, and criminal defense law in Massachusetts.

Martha Starr is professor of economics at American University with interests in social economics, economics of war and peace, and economic development. She is coeditor of *Review of Social Economy.*

Maria J. Stephan is director of educational initiatives for the International Center on Nonviolent Conflict (ICNC) and adjunct professor at the Edmond A. Walsh School of Foreign Service, Georgetown University.

Joanna Swanger is assistant professor of peace and global studies and director of the PAGS program at Earlham College. She is author, with Howard Richards, of *The Dilemmas of Social Democracies: Overcoming Obstacles to a More Just World.*

Niklas Swanström teaches in the Department of Peace and Conflict Research at Uppsala University in Sweden.

Zheng Wang is assistant professor in the John C. Whitehead School of Diplomacy and International Relations at Seton Hall University.

Anthony Wanis–St. John is assistant professor of international peace and conflict resolution at the School of International Service, American University. He is a practitioner with extensive experience mediating disputes within partnerships, corporations, and government agencies as well as between unions and management. Wanis–St. John consults with the World Bank on international alternative dispute resolution programs throughout Latin America and consults on peacebuilding projects in the Middle East and elsewhere.

David A. Welch is professor of political science at the University of Toronto. His special interest is the interface between empirical and normative issues in global politics. He is the author of *Painful Choices: A Theory of Foreign Policy Change*.

Barbara J. Wien is a peace activist and educator, serving as adjunct professor at Columbia University, Georgetown University, and Catholic University on alternatives to war and violence, community organizing for peace, and introduction to peace studies. She was editor of the fourth edition of *Peace and World Order Studies: A Curriculum Guide*, a predecessor to this volume, and served as director of Peace Brigades International USA from 2003 to 2008.

Jeremy Youde is assistant professor of political science at Grinnell College. He has published articles in *International Relations, Electoral Studies, Whitehead Journal of International Relations and Diplomacy, PS*, and *Africa Today*. His book, *AIDS, South Africa, and the Politics of Knowledge* was published by Ashgate as part of their Global Health series in 2007.

Howard Zehr is professor of restorative justice at Eastern Mennonite University and faculty for the Graduate Center for Justice and Peacebuilding. He is author of *The Little Book of Restorative Justice*.

Craig Zelizer is visiting assistant professor in the Department of Government at Georgetown University. His areas of expertise include programs for youth from violent conflict regions, civil society development and capacity building in transitional societies, program evaluation and design, conflict sensitivity and mainstreaming across development sectors, the connection between trauma and conflict, the role of the private sector in peacebuilding, and the arts and peacebuilding.

Stephen Zunes is professor of politics at the University of San Francisco, where he chairs the peace and conflict tract in the international studies major. He is the author of *Tinderbox: U.S. Middle East Policy and the Roots of Terrorism*.

About the Book

FULLY REVISED TO REFLECT THE REALITIES OF THE POST–SEPTEMBER 11 world, this acclaimed curricular reference provides a comprehensive review of the field of peace, justice, and security studies. Seven introductory essays systematically cover the state of the discipline today, surveying current intellectual and pedagogical themes. These are followed by seventy classroom-tested syllabuses organized by topics and including course descriptions, schedules, bibliographies, and notes on successful teaching practices. In keeping with the multifaceted nature of the subject, multiple perspectives, among them political science, philosophy, religious studies, sociology, and anthropology, are fully represented in this indispensable resource.

Timothy A. McElwee is Plowshares Associate Professor of Peace Studies and director of the Peace Studies Institute at Manchester College. **B. Welling Hall** is professor of politics and international studies and Plowshares Professor of Peace Studies at Earlham College. **Joseph Liechty** is associate professor of peace, justice, and conflict studies at Goshen College. **Julie Garber** is editor of Plowshares publications for Earlham, Goshen, and Manchester Colleges.